NATO ASI Series

Advanced Science Institutes Series

A series presenting the results of activities sponsored by the NATO Science Committee, which aims at the dissemination of advanced scientific and technological knowledge, with a view to strengthening links between scientific communities.

The Series is published by an international board of publishers in conjunction with the NATO Scientific Affairs Division.

A	Life Sciences	Plenum Publishing Corporation
B	Physics	London and New York
C	Mathematical and Physical Sciences	Kluwer Academic Publishers
D	Behavioural and Social Sciences	Dordrecht, Boston and London
E	Applied Sciences	
F	Computer and Systems Sciences	Springer-Verlag
G	Ecological Sciences	Berlin Heidelberg New York Barcelona
H	Cell Biology	Budapest Hong Kong London Milan
I	Global Environmental Change	Paris Santa Clara Singapore Tokyo

Partnership Sub-Series

1.	Disarmament Technologies	Kluwer Academic Publishers
2.	Environment	Springer-Verlag / Kluwer Academic Publishers
3.	High Technology	Kluwer Academic Publishers
4.	Science and Technology Policy	Kluwer Academic Publishers
5.	Computer Networking	Kluwer Academic Publishers

The Partnership Sub-Series incorporates activities undertaken in collaboration with NATO's Cooperation Partners, the countries of the CIS and Central and Eastern Europe, in Priority Areas of concern to those countries.

NATO-PCO Database

The electronic index to the NATO ASI Series provides full bibliographical references (with keywords and/or abstracts) to about 50 000 contributions from international scientists published in all sections of the NATO ASI Series. Access to the NATO-PCO Database is possible via the CD-ROM "NATO Science & Technology Disk" with user-friendly retrieval software in English, French and German (© WTV GmbH and DATAWARE Technologies Inc. 1992).

The CD-ROM can be ordered through any member of the Board of Publishers or through NATO-PCO, B-3090 Overijse, Belgium.

Series F: Computer and Systems Sciences, Vol. 163

Springer
Berlin
Heidelberg
New York
Barcelona
Budapest
Hong Kong
London
Milan
Paris
Singapore
Tokyo

Face Recognition

From Theory to Applications

Edited by

Harry Wechsler

Department of Computer Science
George Mason University
Fairfax, VA 22030, USA

P. Jonathon Phillips

NIST, Building 225, Room A216
Gaithersburg, MD 20899, USA

Vicki Bruce

Department of Psychology
University of Stirling
Stirling, Scotland FK9 4LA, UK

Françoise Fogelman Soulié

Atos Ingénierie Integration
1 Avenue Newton, BP 207
F-92142 Clamart Cedex, France

Thomas S. Huang

Beckman Institute for Advanced Science and Technology
University of Illinois at Urbana-Champaign
405 N. Mathews Avenue
Urbana, IL 61801, USA

Springer

Published in cooperation with NATO Scientific Affairs Division

Proceedings of the NATO Advanced Study Institute on
Face Recognition: From Theory to Applications,
held in Stirling, Scotland, UK, June 23–July 4, 1997

Library of Congress Cataloging-in-Publication Data

Face recognition : from theory to applications / edited by Harry
Wechsler ... [et al.].
        p.   cm. -- (NATO ASI series. Series F, Computer and systems
sciences ; vol. 163)
    "Published in cooperation with NATO Scientific Affairs Division."
    "Proceedings of the NATO Advanced Study Institute on Future
Recognition: From Theory to Applications, held in Stirling,
scotland, UK, June 23-July 4, 1997"--T.p. verso.
    Includes bibliographical references.
    ISBN 3-540-64410-5 (hardcover : alk. paper)
    1. Human face recognition (Computer science)   I. Wechsler, Harry,
1948-   . II. North Atlantic Treaty Organization. Scientific
Affairs Division.   III. NATO Advanced Study Institute on Future
Recognition: From Theory to Applications (1997 : Stirling, Scotland)
IV. Series: NATO ASI series.   Series F, Computer and systems
sciences ; no. 163.
TA1650.F33   1998
006.3'7--dc21   98-25070
                                                                CIP

ACM Subject Classification (1998): I.5, I.4, I.2

ISBN 3-540-64410-5 Springer-Verlag Berlin Heidelberg New York

© Springer-Verlag Berlin Heidelberg 1998
Printed in Germany

Typesetting: Camera-ready by authors
Printed on acid-free paper
SPIN: 10676374   45/3142 – 5 4 3 2 1 0

Preface

The NATO Advanced Study Institute (ASI) on Face Recognition : From Theory to Applications took place in Stirling, Scotland, UK, from June 23 through July 4, 1997. The meeting brought together 95 participants (including 18 invited lecturers) from 22 countries. The lecturers are leading researchers from academia, government, and industry from all over the world. The lecturers presented an encompassing view of face recognition, and identified trends for future developments and the means for implementing robust face recognition systems. The scientific programme consisted of invited lectures, three panels, and (oral and poster) presentations from students attending the ASI. As a result of lively interactions between the participants, the following topics emerged as major themes of the meeting: (i) human processing of face recognition and its relevance to forensic systems, (ii) face coding, (iii) connectionist methods and support vector machines (SVM), (iv) hybrid methods for face recognition, and (v) predictive learning and performance evaluation. The goals of the panels were to provide links among the lectures and to emphasis the themes of the meeting. The topics of the panels were: (i) How the human visual system processes faces, (ii) Issues in applying face recognition: data bases, evaluation and systems, and (iii) Classification issues involved in face recognition. The presentations made by students gave them an opportunity to receive feedback from the invited lecturers and suggestions for future work.

Face recognition, a complex and difficult problem, is important for surveillance and security, telecommunications and digital libraries, human-computer intelligent interactions, and medicine. The solutions presented were synergetic efforts from fields such as signal and image processing, pattern recognition, machine learning, neural networks and evolutionary computation, psychophysics of human perception and neurosciences, and system engineering. Many of the face recognition methods presented implement some variation on either the principal component analysis (PCA) approach (also known as the eigenfaces) or the dynamic link architectures (DLA). In DLA, elastic graph matching is attempted between locally derived forensic landmark grids, possibly encoded using Gabor wavelets. PCA methods encode second order statistics of the face and can be enhanced using spatiotemporal constraints encoded as manifold trajectories corresponding to the views obtained as the face rotates in the three-dimensional space. Further enhancements on basic face recognition methods considered were active vision, modular forensic systems, and multimodal systems; for example, fusing video and audio for verification and surveillance.

To provide a broad overview of face recognition, lectures were presented on psychophysics and neuroscience. Example of topics in the area were: Does color information help face detection, and do sequential classifiers perform better than flat classifiers on face recognition ? Another concept discussed was consensus networks for handling the inherent variability of the image formation process and the uncertainty involved in modeling the overall face recognition system. Also, the discussion emphasized the increasing role video processing will play in face recognition. Video is of interest because the additional frames of facial imagery and the resulting motion information can contribute to increased confidence in face recognition.

A new topic in face recognition is the synergy between predictive learning and performance evaluation. One has to develop the means both to assess performance on given data sets and to make predictions about future performance on unseen data sets. Statistical learning theory provides the means to estimate the guaranteed risk for testing on future facial imagery. This risk is formulated in terms of the empirical risk calculated during training and the complexity of the classification model underlying the face recognition system. Performance thus depends on both the complexity of the classifier and the relative size and quality of the training versus test data sets. It also became clear that one has to develop standard data bases of face images, such as FERET, in order to assess and compare among competing face recognition systems. Decision theory and receiver operating characteristics (ROC) provide the tools needed to eventually quantify the level of performance displayed by specific face recognition systems.

The feedback from the participants regarding the contents of the scientific programme and the social contacts made during this meeting was very positive. The NATO ASI was made possible through the efforts of the organizing committee: Harry Wechsler (USA), Jonathon Phillips (USA), Vicki Bruce (UK), Françoise Fogelman Soulié (France) and Thomas Huang (USA). We are grateful for the financial support provided by the North Atlantic Treaty Organization, Scientific Affairs Division, and for additional financial support provided by the Beckman Institute, USA, and the PITO, Home Office, UK. Finally, special thanks are due to Jeffrey Huang from George Mason University who spent endless hours on organization of the ASI and provided invaluable assistance in editing this volume, and to Steve Langton and Elaine Stewart from the University of Stirling, UK, who provided much help and assistance with the local arrangements.

July 1998   Harry Wechsler (Director)
                                   P. Jonathon Phillips (Co-Director)
                                   Vicki Bruce (Organizing Committee)
                                   Françoise Fogelman Soulié (Organizing Committee)
                                   Thomas Huang (Organizing Committee)

Contents

Part II : Participant Presentations
(participant's name printed in bold face)

Part I

Lectures

Neural and Psychophysical Analysis of Object and Face Recognition

Irving Biederman and Peter Kalocsai

Department of Psychology and Computer Science
University of Southern California
Los Angeles, California 90089, U.S.A.
{ib, kalocsai}@selforg.usc.edu

Abstract. A number of behavioral phenomena distinguish the recognition of faces and objects, even when members of the set of objects are highly similar. Because faces have the same parts in approximately the same relations, individuation of faces typically requires specification of the metric variation in a holistic and integral representation of the facial surface. The direct mapping of a hypercolumn-like pattern of activation onto a representation layer that preserves relative spatial filter values in a 2D coordinate space, as proposed by C. von der Malsburg and his associates (Lades et al., 1993; Wiskott, et al., 1997), may account for many of the phenomena associated with face recognition. An additional refinement, in which each column of filters (termed "a jet") is centered on a particular facial feature (or fiducial point), allows selectivity of the input into the holistic representation to avoid incorporation of occluding or nearby surfaces. The initial hypercolumn representation also characterizes the first stage of object perception, but the image variation for objects at a given location in a 2D coordinate space may be too great to yield sufficient predictability directly from the output of spatial kernels. Consequently, objects can be represented by a structural description specifying qualitative (typically, nonaccidental) characterizations of an object's parts, the attributes of the parts, and the relations among the parts, largely based on orientation and depth discontinuities (e.g., Hummel & Biederman, 1992). A series of experiments on the name priming or physical matching of complementary images (in the Fourier domain) of objects and faces (See Kalocsai & Biederman, this volume) documents that whereas face recognition is strongly dependent on the original spatial filter values, object recognition evidences strong invariance to these values, even when distinguishing among objects that are as similar as faces.

Keywords. Face recognition, object recognition

Acknowledgements. This research was supported by ARO NVESD grant DAAH04-94-G-0065. This paper is excerpted, with minor modifications, from Biederman and Kalocsai (1997).

1 Introduction

We propose a theoretical account of the neural, perceptual, and cognitive differences that are apparent in the individuation of faces and the entry- and subordinate-level classification of objects. After a general theoretical overview, we review some of the behavioral and neural phenomena by which face and object recognition can be contrasted and then present a neurocomputational account of these differences, with particular attention to the perceptual representation of faces. Last, original experiments testing a key assumption of this account are described.

2 A Theoretical Overview of Face and Object Recognition

The basic theoretical differences that we will propose are diagrammed in Figure 1. The object model follows that of Hummel and Biederman (1992) and only a brief overview will be presented here. Specification of the edges at an object's orientation and depth discontinuities in terms of nonaccidental properties (NAPs) is employed to activate units that represent simple, viewpoint invariant parts (or *geons*), such a bricks, cones, and wedges. Other units specify a geon's attributes, such as the geon's approximate orientation (e.g., HORIZONTAL) and aspect ratio, and still other units specify the relative relations of pairs of geons to each other, such as TOP-OF, LARGER-THAN, END-TO-MIDDLE-CONNECTED. The

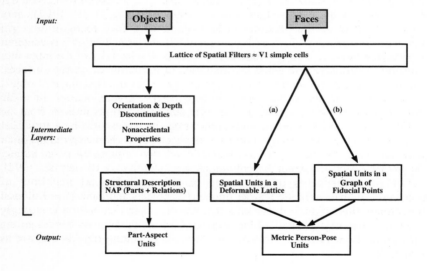

Figure 1. Relations between presumed models of object and face recognition. Both start with a lattice of columns of spatial filters characteristic of V1 hypercolumns. The object pathway is modeled after Biederman(1987) and Hummel and Biederman (1992) and computes a geon structural description (GSA) which represents the parts and their relations in a view of an object. Both face pathways retain aspects of the original spatial filter activation patterns. In the (a) pathway, modeled after Lades et al. (1993), the default position of the columns (termed "jets") of filters is a lattice similar to that of the input layer but which can be deformed to provide a best match to a probe image. In the (b) pathway, modeled after Wiskott, Fellous, Krüger, & von der Malsburg (1997), the jets are centered on a particular facial feature, termed a fiducial point.

separate units associated with a given geon, its attributes, and its relations, are bound (though correlated firing) to a unit termed a geon feature assembly, GFA. A unit representing a geon structural description, *GSD*, specifying the geons and their relations in a given view of the object can then self-organize to the activity from a small set of GFAs.

Differences in GFAs are usually sufficient to distinguish entry level classes and most subordinate level distinctions that people can make quickly and accurately in their everyday lives. Sometimes the GSDs required for subordinate level distinctions are available at a large scale, as in distinguishing a square from a round table. Sometimes they are at a small scale, as when we use a logo to determine the manufacturer of a car.

Although there are some person individuation tasks that can be accomplished by the information specified by a GSD ("Steve is the guy wearing glasses"), generally we will focus on cases where such easy information as a distinctive GSD or texture field ("Steve is the guy with freckles") is insufficient. We will argue that the information required for general purpose face recognition is holistic, surface-based, and metric, rather than parts-based, discontinuous, and nonaccidental (or qualitative), as it is with objects. A representation that preserves the relative scale of the original spatial filter values in a coordinate space that normalizes scale and position may allow specification of the metric variation in that region for determining the surface properties of a face. The coordinate system is preserved because the location of facial characteristics are highly predictable from a given pose of a face. For objects they are not. (What is in the upper, right hand part of an object?) Relative (cycles/face) rather than absolute (cycles/degree) allows invariance over size changes of the face.

We consider two recent proposals by C. von der Malsburg and his associates for face representation. The first, labeled (a) in figure 1, is described by Lades et al. (1993). This system maps columns (or "jets") of V1-like spatial filter activation values to images of faces or objects. The jets are arranged in a hypercolumn-like lattice where they are stored. This stored lattice serves as a representation layer and is then matched against probe faces or objects by correlating the filter values of the original lattice against a new lattice that has been allowed to deform to achieve its own best match. The second model, labeled (b), proposed by Wiskott et al. (1997), positions each of the jets not on the vertices of a rectangular lattice but to assigned "fiducial points" on a face, such as the left corner of the mouth. These face models will be considered in more detail in a later section.

3 Distinguishing Face and Object Recognition: Empirical Results

One problem with an effort to distinguish face and object recognition is that there are a large number of tasks that can be loosely described as "recognition." This problem will be examined in more detail below but for the present purposes we will consider the identification of an image of a face to the criterion of individuation and that of an object with its assignment to its basic level or common subordinate level class.

Table 1 lists seven behavioral differences between face and object recognition. These will be considered in turn with respect to the different properties that should be captured by a particular representation.

	FACES	OBJECTS
Configural Effects?	YES	NO
Basis of Expertise?	Holistic Representation	Feature Discovery
Differences Verbalizable?	NO	YES
SENSITIVE TO:		
Contrast Polarity?	YES	NO
Illumination Dir?	YES	NO
Metric Variation?	YES	SLIGHTLY
Rotation in Depth?	YES	NO, within part aspects ($\approx$60°)
Rotation in the Plane?	YES	SLIGHTLY

Table 1. Some Differences in the recognition of Faces and Objects

1. *Configural Effects.* Tanaka and Farah (1993) trained their subjects to recognize a set of Identikit faces, each with a different eyes, nose, and mouth. In testing, they presented pairs of images that differed in the shape of a single face part, the eyes, nose, or mouth (Figure 2). In one condition, only a pair of face parts was shown, for example, two slightly different noses. In the other, the stimuli were part of a context of a whole face, one with one of the noses the other with the other nose. The subjects did not know which face part might differ when they viewed a complete face. Remarkably, the context of the face facilitated detection of the difference. The facilitation from the presence of the context was not found for non-face objects, such as a house, or when the faces were inverted.

2. *Expertise.* Good face recognizers use the whole face, although with unfamiliar faces, the overall external shape and hairline receive extremely high weight (Young, Hay, McWeeny, Flude, & Ellis, 1985). When asked to describe a picture of a person's face, these individuals will often refer to a famous person, perhaps with some modification in the descriptions (Cesa, 1994). Poor recognizers tend to pick a single feature or small set of distinctive features. As people age, face recognition performance declines. This decline is marked by a qualitative shift in the representation such that older people, like poor face recognizers in general, search for distinctive features. Prosopagnosics often report a distinctive feature strategy as well (Davidoff, 1988).

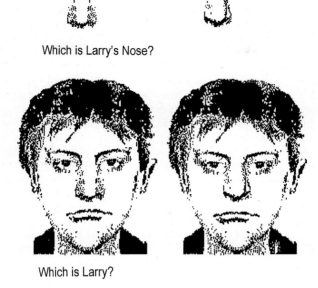

Which is Larry's Nose?

Which is Larry?

Figure 2. Sample stimuli from Tanaka & Farah's (1993) single feature and whole face conditions. In the single feature condition, subject's where presented with, for example, the upper pair of noses and were to judge, "Which is Larry's nose?" In the whole face condition, the subjects were presented with a pair of faces whose members were identical except the they differed in a single feature, the one shown in the feature condition, and they had to judge, "Which is Larry?" Used with permission.

In contrast to the holistic processing of faces, expertise in the identification of an object from a highly similar set of objects is most often a process of discovery or instruction as to the location and nature of small differences that reliably distinguish the classes (Gibson, 1947; Biederman & Shiffrar, 1988). If such features are not present then performance is often slow and error prone (Biederman & Subramaniam, 1997). Gibson (1947) described the consequences of attempting to teach aircraft identification during World War II by "total form" versus distinctive features of the parts:

"Two principle observations made by the instructors who took part in the experiment are of some bearing on the question of the two methods under consideration. The impression was obtained by all three of the instructors, at about the time the course was two-thirds completed, that the group taught by emphasis on total form was definitely 'slipping' in comparison with the other group. The second observation was that a single question was insistently and repeatedly asked by the cadets in the group taught by emphasis on total form. This question was 'How can I distinguish between this plane and the one which resembles it closely (e.g., the C-46 and the C-47)?" (Gibson, 1947, p. 120.)

Whether still more extensive training on non-face stimuli can lead to face-like processing is an open issue. Gauthier and Tarr (In press) provided extensive training to some of their subjects, Termed "experts," in distinguishing among a family of "greebles," a set of stimuli composed of three rounded parts--a base, body, and head--one on top of the other with protrusions that are readily labeled penis, nose, and ears. These rounded, bilaterally symmetrical creatures, closely resemble humanoid characters, such as the Yoda (in Return of the Jedi). Despite Gauthier and Tarr's conclusions that they were able to mimic certain aspects of face processing with their training, none of the expected face results were obtained. Some were clearly inconsistent with face-like processing. For example, the identification of the parts (Is this Pimo's quiff?) was unaffected by inversion or scrambling of the greebles. Closer analysis of the stimuli suggest that the invariance to 2D orientation and the lack of a configural effects might have been a consequence of geon differences among the parts, rather than the metric variation in smooth surfaces required for face processing. Another shortcoming of the greebles as stimuli for the study of face perception is their resemblance to people. The parts that were tested are readily identified as ears, nose, and penis, so even if only metric variation in the surfaces of the parts had been varied, it would be unclear whether the stimuli engaged face or body processing because of their physical resemblance to people to because of the training.

3. *Differences Verbalizable*? People find it exceedingly difficult to express verbally the differences between two similar faces. This fact is well known to the chagrin of police investigators interviewing witnesses. When asked to describe an object, however, people readily name its parts and provide a characterization of the shape of these parts in terms of NAPs (Tversky & Hemenway, 1984; Biederman, 1987). Within highly similar shape classes, such as Western U. S. male Quail, people will spontaneously employ local shape features that closely correspond to those specified--verbally--by the bird guides (Biederman, 1997). Gibson (1947) concluded that the problem of training aircraft spotters was best solved by informing them as to the nonaccidental differences in the shapes of parts. It was a simple matter for Gibson to construct an outline--in words--providing this information.

4. *Sensitivity to contrast polarity and illumination direction*? Whereas people have great difficulty in identifying a face from a photographic negative or when illuminated from below (Johnston, Hill, & Carmen, 1992), there is little, if any, effect of reversing the polarity of contrast of a picture of an object (Subramaniam & Biederman, 1997). Viewing an object at one polarity provides essentially the same information as to the structure of the object as does the other polarity. A major reason for this difference between faces and objects is that, as noted previously, object recognition is largely based on distinguishable parts based on differences in NAPs of edges marking orientation and depth discontinuities. The position of these edges and their nonaccidental values (e.g., straight or curved) are unaffected by contrast reversal. Individuating faces typically requires metric differences that may be specified in terms of the convexities and concavities that characterize a facial structure. A change in contrast polarity would reverse the interpretation of the luminance and shadow gradients that are employed to

9

determine the convexity or concavity of a smooth surface. A similar explanation may account for some of the increased difficulty in identifying faces when they are illuminated from below as this would violate the strong assumption that illumination is from above.

5. *Metric variation*? Metric properties are those such as aspect ratio or degree of curvature that vary with the orientation of the object in depth. Such properties are to be contrasted with NAPs, such as whether an edge is straight or curved, which are only rarely affected by slight changes in viewpoint of an object. Other NAPs are the vertices that are formed by coterminating lines and whether pairs of edges are approximately parallel or not, given edges that are not greatly · extended in depth.

Before looking at figure 3 (from Cooper & Wojan, 1996), please cover the left and center columns. In looking at the right column, the reader can assess for himself or herself how modest variation in the metrics of a face can result in marked interference in the recognition of that face (see also Hosie, Ellis, & Haig, 1988). In these images of celebrities, the eyes have been raised. A similar variation in the length (and, hence, aspect ratio) of an object part, as illustrated in figure 4, has little or no effect in the assignment of objects to classes. As long as the relative relations, such as LARGER-THEN or ABOVE, between parts are not changed by altering a part's length, the effects of the variation appear to be confined to that part, rather than affecting the object as a whole. Unlike what occurs with the holistic effects with faces, there is little effect of the variation on a metric attribute of a part in the recognition of objects. Biederman and Cooper (1993) presented two images of simple, two-part objects (illustrated in Figure 4) sequentially. Subjects had to judge whether the two objects had the same name. When the objects differed in the aspect ratio of a part, RTs and error rates were only slightly elevated compared to when the images were identical A change in a NAP produced a much larger interfering effect on the matching.

6. *Rotation in depth.* If objects differ in NAPs, then little or no cost is apparent when they are rotated in depth, as long as the same surfaces are in view (Biederman & Gerhardstein, 1993). In contrast, when the differences are in metric properties, such as aspect ratio or degree of curvature, then marked rotation costs are observed (e.g., Edelman, 1995). The robustness of the detection of nonaccidental differences under depth rotation is not simply a function of greater discriminability of NAPs compared to metric properties. Biederman and Bar (1995) equated the detectability of metric and nonaccidental part differences in a sequential same-different matching task with novel objects. Presenting the objects at different orientations in depth had no effect on the detectability of nonaccidental differences. When easy nonaccidental cues are eliminated, such as glasses, facial hair, and the hairline, even modest rotations of faces, from 20° left to 40° right, as illustrated in figure 7 (middle row), can result in marked increases in RTs and error rates in their matching (Kalocsai, Biederman, & Cooper, 1994).

7. *Rotation in the plane.* Recognizing an upside-down face is extremely difficult relative to identifying an upside-down object, such as a chair (e.g., Yin, 1969; Johnston, et al., 1992; Jolicoeur, 1985). According to the Hummel and

No Eyes Moved   One Eye Moved   Two Eyes Moved

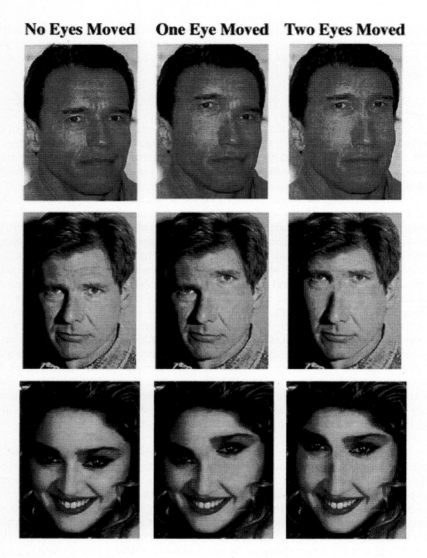

Figure 3. Sample stimuli from Cooper and Wojan (1996). Subjects were much worse at identifying the celebrities in the third column, where both eyes were raised, compared to those in the second column where only one eye was raised, despite the greater difficulty in judging the later as a face. Copyright Eric E. Cooper. Used with permission.

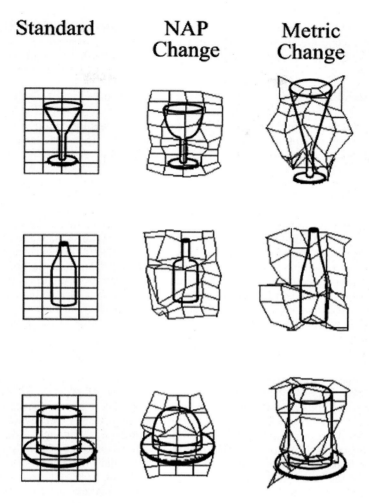

Figure 4. Sample object stimuli from Cooper and Biederman (1993). Given the standard object on the left, a NAP of only a single part was changed in the objects in the middle column (NAP condition) and that same part was lengthened in the Metric condition illustrated by the objects in the third column. The magnitude of the Metric changes were slightly larger than the NAP changes, according to the Lades et al. (1993) model. Whereas the difference between Metric and Standard images were more readily detected when performing a simultaneous physical identity matching task (Are the objects identical?) , in a sequential object matching task (Do the objects have the same name?), a change in a NAP resulted in far more disruption than a change in a metric property.

Biederman (1992) network, turning an object upside down would leave most of the units coding the structural description intact, affecting only the relations TOP-OF and BELOW. Consequently, only a small effect for objects would be expected.

Some of the large effect of inversion with face photos lies in the misinterpretation of luminance gradients where the light source is typically assumed to be coming from above. But when the light source is controlled, there still remains a large cost to viewing a face upside-down (Johnston, et al., 1992; Enns & Shore, 1997).

3.2 Neural Differences Between Faces and Objects

There are several neural differences distinguishing the representation of faces and objects. Only a brief summary will be presented here. (See Grüsser & Landis, 1991, for a comprehensive treatment of this general area.)

1. *Selective impairment: Prosopagnosia and object agnosias.* Prosopagnosia, the inability to recognize familiar faces but with a normal or near normal capacity for object recognition, is a well documented phenomenon, generally associated with lesions to the right, inferior mesial hemispheric (Grüsser & Landis, 1991), although some (e.g., Damasio, Damasio, Van Hoesen, 1985) have argued that the lesions must be bilateral. Farah (1990) theorized that the underlying continuum in visual recognition extended from holistic processing, which would be required for faces, to the capacity to represent multiple shapes (or parts), which would be typified by the integration of letters into words in reading. She surmised that right inferior occipital-temporal lesions affected holistic processing whereas bilateral lesions to the inferior temporal-occipital region (including the fusiform) resulted in a condition (ventral simultagnosia) in which the patient could not simultaneously process multiple parts of an object or letters of a word (alexia). (Other authors, e.g., Behrmann & Shallice, 1995, have also argued that alexia is associated with lesions to the left hemisphere.) Object recognition, according to Farah, employs both types of processing so object agnosia should be accompanied by either prosopagnosia or alexia. Several recent cases, however, have described individuals manifesting strong object agnosias who are neither prosopagnosic nor alexic (Rumiati, Humphreys, Riddoch, & Bateman, 1994; Moscovitch, Winocur, & Behrmann, 1997). We interpret these findings as evidence that object recognition does not generally entail holistic processing and that the integration of letters into a word in reading may not necessarily be engaging the same mechanisms or representations that mediate face recognition.

2. *Imaging studies.* Recent fMRI studies in humans give clear evidence for object and shape specific regions in the occipital cortex. Tootell, Dale, Sereno, & Malach (1996) have documented an area just anterior to V4v and partly overlapping with regions of the fusiform, termed Lateral Occipital (LO), that gives vigorous responses to interpretable faces and objects even when they are unfamiliar, such as an abstract sculpture, but not to these stimuli when they have been rendered into textures as, for example, digitized blocks characteristic of the "Lincoln" illusion or in gratings, texture patterns, or highly jumbled object images. In contrast to LO, V4 does not show this specificity to objects as compared to textures. LO is thus sensitive to shapes--faces or objects--that have an interpretable structure rather than being characterizable as a texture pattern. More anterior regions in the ventral pathway such as IT are sensitive to the familiarity of the objects, as described in the next section. That LO's responsivity

is unaffected by familiarity suggests that it may be a region where shape descriptions--even novel ones--are created. A number of fMRI and PET studies have demonstrated that the processing of faces and objects activate different loci in or near LO. These areas are generally consistent with the results of the lesion work, showing greater posterior right hemisphere activity, particularly in the fusiform gyrus, for face processing and greater left hemisphere activity for object processing (Kanwisher, Chun, & McDermott, 1996; Sergent, Ohta, Macdonald, & Zuck. 1994; Sergent, Ohta, & Macdonald; 1994). The two Sergent et al. PET studies are noteworthy in showing virtually identical loci for the differential activity of judging whether a face was that of an actor. The control task was one of judging whether the orientation of a gratings was horizontal or vertical.

3. *Single unit recording.* It is well established that individual IT cells can be found that are differentially tuned either to faces or to complex object features, but not both (e.g., Bayliss, Rolls, & Leonard, 1987; Kobatake & Tanaka, 1994; Young & Yamane, 1992). However, as recently argued by Biederman, Gerhardstein, Cooper, & Nelson (1997), it is likely that these IT cells are not involved in the initial perceptual description of an image--which they suggest is accomplished by LO or in the area immediate anterior to it--but, instead, in coding episodic memories *following* perception. Because these experiences include contribution of the dorsal system in which position, size, and orientation of the stimulus is specified, it is not surprising to find cells that are tuned to the specific orientations and characteristics of the trained stimuli (e.g., Logothetis, Pauls, Bülthoff, & Poggio, 1994). That IT may not be involved in the perceptual recognition of a face or object is suggested by the requirement of an interval between stimulus presentation and testing in order to show any deficits in object processing of macaques who have undergone bilateral ablation of IT (Desimone & Ungerleider, 1989). However, the differential tuning of IT cells to faces and complex object features indicates that these two classes of stimuli are distinguished neurally. A given IT face cell does not fire in all-or-none fashion to a given face but participates in a population code to that face by which the firing of the cell is modulated by the specific characteristics of the face (Young & Yamane, 1992; Rolls, 1992). Young and Yamane showed that the code for macaques looking at pictures of men could be summarized by two dimensions, one coding the width of the face and one the distance of the pupil of the eye to the hairline. Somewhat remarkably, as noted earlier, these same two dimensions characterize human performance with unfamiliar faces. Recently, Scalaidhe, Wilson and Goldman-Rakic (1997) showed that the isolation of face and object processing extended to the prefrontal cortex where they found cells in the macaque that were tuned exclusively to faces and were quite unresponsive to objects, scrambled faces, or objects of interest such as food.

4. *Universal Classes of Facial Attributes.* All cultures appear to processes faces in highly similar ways. Faces are not only processed for identity, but for the information they provide about emotion, age, sex, direction of gaze, and attractiveness. Different areas mediate at least some of these attributes. Cells tuned to differences in emotional expression and direction of gaze are found in the superior temporal sulcus in the macaque, an area different from the IT locus of the

units that contribute to a population code that can distinguish identity. Prosopagnosics can often readily judge these other attributes, e.g., sex, age, etc., as we have recently witnessed in our laboratory. To the extent that these areas are segregated from those for object recognition, we have additional evidence supporting the face-object distinction. However, it is not clear to what extent, if any, these classes contribute to face individuation.

4   A Theory of Perceptual Recognition of Faces

A biologically inspired face recognition system developed by Christoph von der Malsburg and his associates (Lades, et al., 1993; Wiskott, et al., 1997) suggests a theoretical perspective from which many of the phenomena associated with face perception described in the previous section might be understood. The fundamental representation element is a column of multiscale, multiorientation spatial (Gabor) kernels with local receptive fields centered on a particular point in the image. Each column of filters is termed a "Gabor jet" and each jet is presumed to model aspects of the wavelet-type of filtering performed by a V1 hypercolumn. We will first consider the initial version of the model (Lades et al, 1993), which will be referred to as the lattice version. This model can be applied to the recognition of faces and objects so it has the potential to serve as a device for the scaling of both kinds of stimuli. A more recent version (Wiskott et al., 1997) , the "fiducial point" model, incorporates general face knowledge. We will ignore preprocessing stages by which a probe image is translated and scaled to achieve a normalized position and size. Overall illumination levels and contrast are similarly normalized.

As illustrated in figure 5, Lades et al. (1993) posited a two-layer network. The input layer is a rectangular lattice of Gabor jets. The pattern of activation of the 80 kernels (5 scales X 8 orientations X 2 phases, sine and cosine) in each of the jets is mapped onto a representation layer, identical to the input layer, that simply stores the pattern of activation over the kernels from a given image. An arbitrary large number of facial images can be stored in this way to form a gallery. Matching of a new image against those in the gallery is performed by allowing the jets (in either the probe or a gallery image) to independently diffuse (gradually change their positions) to determine their own best fit, as illustrated by the arrows on the jets in the input layer. The diffusion typically results in distortion of the rectangular lattice, as illustrated in Figures 6 and 7. The similarity of two images is taken to be the sum correlation in corresponding jets of the magnitudes of activation values of the 80 corresponding kernels. The correlation (range 0 to 1) for each pair of jets is the cosine of the angular difference between the vectors of the kernels in a 80 dimensional space. (If the values are identical, the angular difference will be 0 deg and the cosine will be 1. A 90 deg [orthogonal] difference in angles will be 0.00.) The correlations over the jets are summed to get a total similarity score. Figure 7 illustrates distortion of the lattice as a person changes expression, orientation, and both expression and orientation. Typically, the greater the deformation of the lattice, the lower the similarity of the match.

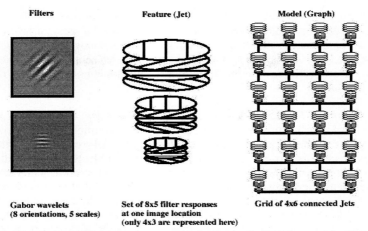

Filters

Feature (Jet)

Model (Graph)

Gabor wavelets
(8 orientations, 5 scales)

Set of 8x5 filter responses
at one image location
(only 4x3 are represented here)

Grid of 4x6 connected Jets

Figure 5. Illustration of the input layer to the Lades et al. (1993) network. The basic kernels are Gabor filters at different scales and orientations, two of which are shown on the left. The center figure illustrates the composition of a jet, with the larger disks representing lower spatial frequencies. The number of jets, scales, and orientation can be varied.

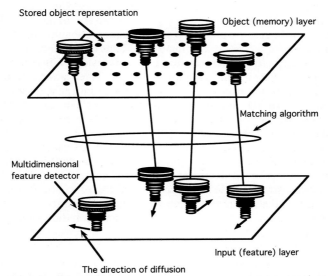

Stored object representation

Object (memory) layer

Matching algorithm

Multidimensional
feature detector

Input (feature) layer

The direction of diffusion

Figure 6. Schematic representation of the Lades et al. (1993) two-layer spatial filter model. The model first convolves each input image with a set of Gabor kernels at five scales and eight orientations and sine and cosine kernels arranged in a 5 x 9 lattice. These values can be varied. The set of kernels at each node in the lattice is termed a "Gabor jet". The activation values of the kernels in each jet along with their positions are stored for each of the images to form a "gallery". The figure shows the diameters of the receptive fields to be much smaller than actual size in that the largest kernels had receptive fields that were almost as large as the whole face.

Given a test image against a number of stored images, the most similar image, if it exceeds some threshold value, is taken to be the recognition choice.[1]

As noted earlier, the model does a good job at recognizing faces. Given modest changes in pose and expression, recognition accuracy can exceed 90 percent. How well does the model reflect the phenomena associated with faces listed in Table 1?

1. *Rotation Effects.* We will first consider the model's handling of rotation effects, particularly rotation in depth, as that is an extremely common source of image variation and we have assessed its effects under well controlled conditions.

Kalocsai, Biederman, & Cooper (1994) had subjects judge whether two sequentially presented faces were of the same or different person. The faces could be at different orientations in depth and/or with a different expression, as shown in Figure 7. Easy cues, such as facial hair, clothing and the hairline (all stimulus models wore a white bathing cap) were eliminated. A change in the depth orientation of the two poses, such as that shown in the middle row of figure 7, increased RTs and error rates for 'same' trials. The magnitude of this cost was strongly and linearly correlated with the lattice model's similarity values for the pair of pictures, .-90 for RTs and -.82 for error rates. That is, the more dissimilar the two figures according the model, the longer the RTs and error rates for judging them to be the same person. We can consider the effects of depth rotation as a yardstick for determining the model's adequacy for handling other effects.

Turning a face upside down would greatly reduce its similarity to that of the original image. Although it would be a simple matter, computationally, to rotate the coordinate space of the jets to eliminate the effects of planar rotation, the large cost to human recognition performance from inversion suggests that such a transformation is not available to human vision. Given a yardstick of depth rotation, it is an open question whether the same similarity function would also account for the cost of 2D inversion or other variables. That is, would a 60 deg rotation in depth (around the y-axis) result in as much cost as a 60 deg rotation in the plane? What would human subjects evidence?

Given that we have a scaling device (viz., the Lades et al. model), the analysis that could be undertaken to compare rotation in depth to rotation in the plane can be illustrated by Kalocsai et al.'s (1994) comparison of the effects of differences in depth orientation to the effects of differences in expression. Kalocsai et al. (1994) showed that when the degree of image dissimilarity of two images of the same person produced by differences in depth orientation (holding expression

---

[1]In terms of a current psychological theory of face recognition, the two-layer network would be an alternative to Bruce's "Face Recognition Units (or FRUs). Whereas FRUs are pose independent (Burton, 1994), the Lades et al. (1993) network has only modest capabilities to generalize over large rotations in depth, insofar as it starts with the facial image itself and the image is altered by even modest variations in pose, lighting direction, etc. It would be by associating different person-pose units (the output of the Lades et al. model) to the same Person Identification Node, or *PIN*, (Bruce, 1988) that the same semantic information about a person could be activated independent of the pose.

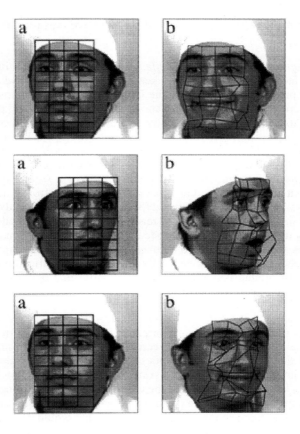

Figure 7. Sample images from the Kalocsai, Biederman, and Cooper (1994) experiment with the Lades et al. (1993) lattice deformations superimposed over different pairs of images of the same person. The positioning of the lattice over an original image is shown in the left hand column (a) and the deformed lattice is shown in the right column (b). Top, middle, and bottom rows show changes in expression, orientation (60°), and both expression and orientation, respectfully. The similarities as determined by the Lades et al. (1993) model correlated highly with performance in matching a pair of images when there were at different orientations and expressions (Kalocsai et al., 1994).

constant) and expression differences (holding depth orientation constant) were equated, the increase in RTs and error rates in responding "same" were three times greater when the dissimilarity was produced by expression differences than when produced by depth rotation. They modeled this effect by assuming that a classifier for expression, which was also highly correlated with Gabor similarity, would signal a mismatch to a decision stage [same vs. different person?] between two face images that differed in expression, even though the images were of the same person. That mismatch signal resulted in the increased cost for faces differing in expression.

2. *Configural and verbalization effects.* Contrast variation within any small region of the face would affect all those kernels whose receptive fields included that region. The pattern of activation of the kernels implicitly contains a holistic or configural representation in that the shape of all facial features and their positions with respect to each other are implicitly coded by the activation of the kernels. Indeed, the representation if run with sufficient jets would be equivalent to a picture of a face and so it does not distinguish contrast variation arising from the shape of facial features from contrast variation arising from translation of those features. It would be impossible to move a region or a feature or to change a feature without affecting the coding of a number of kernels from a number of jets. The representation thus becomes integral (Shepard, 1964) or nonanalytical (Garner, 1966) in that it is not decomposed into readily perceivable independent attributes. This spatially distributed population code of activation values of many kernels of varying scales and orientations in a number of different jets thus captures many of the characteristics of what is generally meant by "holistic representations." Consistent with human performance, this spatially distributed code would be extraordinarily difficult to verbalize.

3. *Lighting, and Contrast Reversal Effects.* Although the model's normalization routines allows its performance to be invariant to overall lighting and contrast levels, a change in the direction of lighting would result in a cost in similarity for the lattice model. It is not clear whether changing the light source vertically, from top to bottom, would result in a greater reduction in similarity, than a right to left change, nor would the cost of contrast reversal necessary be as severe as that evidenced in human performance when compared to, say, rotation in depth. There is nothing in the model, at present, that would identify regions on the surface as convex or concave.

4. *Metric sensitivity.* Metric variation such as that performed by Cooper and Wojan (1996) in raising the eyes in the forehead would alter the pattern of activation values in the lattice. Although the distortion of the lattice might be sufficient to account for the effects on recognition performance of such an operation, it is not obvious how lattice distortion would handle the much smaller effect of moving only one eye. In this case, the relation between the eyes would be disrupted, although one half of the lattice would, most likely, not be affected. We will return to this problem when we consider the incorporation of fiducial points.

Another result that is not obviously derived from the lattice model is the extraordinary difficulty in recognizing the components of a face where the upper half is of one famous person and the lower half another, with the upper and lower halves smoothly aligned to constitute a single face (Young, Hellawell, & Hay, 1987). When the upper and lower halves are offset it is much easier to identify the component individuals.

A third result is that we experience little distortion of other regions when a face is partially occluded as, for example, when a person holds his chin with his hand. The hand is not seen as part of the face but instead is regarded as another object, with the occluded regions contributing little, if anything, to the perception of the face.

5. *Direct tests of filter-based matching in face but not object recognition.* A series of experiments on the name priming or physical matching of complementary images (in the Fourier domain) of objects and faces (See Kalocsai & Biederman, this volume) documents that whereas face recognition is strongly dependent on the original spatial filter values, object recognition evidences strong invariance to these values, even when distinguishing among objects that are as similar as faces.

5 Beyond a lattice of spatial features: Fiducial points

We now consider the fiducial point version of the face recognition system so that we can appreciate the potential gains in making facial features explicit by centering designated jets onto salient feature points. We will also consider two other possible extensions of the model: The explicit use of spatial distances and normative coding by which a face is represented in terms of its deviations from a population norm.

In the fiducial point model (Wiskott, Fellous, Krüger, & von der Malsburg, 1997), the jets are not initially arranged in a rectangular lattice but, instead, each jet is centered on a particular landmark feature of the face, termed a *fiducial point,* such as the corner of the right eye. This step has been implemented and was achieved by centering each of 45 jets (by hand) on a particular fiducial feature, e.g., the outside corner of the right eye, for a "learning set "of 70 faces, which differed in age, sex, expression, depth orientation, etc. Figure 8 shows some of the fiducial points on a face at different orientations and expressions. The 70 jets for each of the 45 points are stored as a "bunch graph." When a new face is presented to the system, not the mean *but the closest fitting* of the 70 jets for each feature is taken as a basis for refining the position by undergoing local diffusion.   For example, if the right eye in the probe image is blinking, then a best match might be an eye that is blinking, rather than the mean.   A jet on the center of the chin might come from another face. Once a sufficiently large set of faces are included in the bunch graphs (≈ 50), it is possible to automatically add new fiducial points. After the matching jet from the bunch graph finds its optimal position, the actual pattern of activation for a jet at that fiducial point is taken to be one of the jets representing that particular face.

The fiducial points, in addition to potentially allowing better resolution in matching, can readily be employed to reject inappropriate image information, such as would occur if the face were partially occluded by a hand. When none of the jets for a given fiducial point in the bunch graph can match their feature to some confidence level in a circumscribed region (constrained in part, by the neighboring jets), that jet is simply not employed in the matching phase. In this way partial occlusion can be made to exact a much smaller cost on recognition than it would if the occluder were incorporated into the representation of a face. Although not implemented, it may be possible to suppress the activity from parts of the receptive fields of jets that lie outside of the bounding contours of the face so they

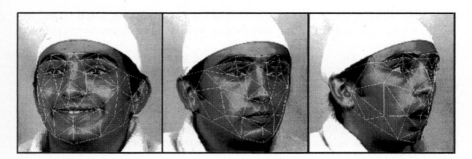

Figure 8. Illustration of the mapping of jets onto fiducial points (the vertices of the triangles) on three images of the same person at different orientations and expressions.

do not contribute to the representation as well. Young et al.'s (1987) finding that offsetting the upper and lower halves of a composite face resulted in much better performance in recognizing the component individuals might be handled by a similar application of a fiducial point model. In this case the fiducial points in the upper and lower halves of the face were not in their expected locations so there activation pattern would not be included in matching one half of the face to the other half. It is possible, of course, that beyond the offset of the fiducial points, the matched cusps provide strong evidence of separate parts and this evidence could also enter into the easier retrieval of the offset face.

It will be recalled that in the Cooper and Wojan (1996) experiment, better recognition was obtained for faces in which one eye was raised, rather than both of them, despite the former stimuli looking less like a face. If the expected locations of the fiducial points for the eye on the opposite side of the head differed for the left and right halves of the face, then each face half might not have been integrated the fiducial points of the eye in the opposite half. Consequently, the original half could vote for the correct face, without incorporation of the distorted region.

In summery, in addition to greater accuracy in recognizing faces over a wider range of conditions, the great value in employment of a fiducial point representation is that it allows selective attention to be exercised over a holistic representation of the face.

5.1 The use of topological relations

A second modification of the filter model would be the incorporation of the *distances* between the jets. This could be done either with the original lattice or with the fiducial points. Figures 7 and 8 show both arrangements with the nodes of the lattice (upper) connected to its nearest nodes and the fiducial points (lower) connected to their nearest fiducial points to form a set of triangles. A change in the image of a face produced by changes in orientation and expression, as in figures 7 and 8, results in distortion of the lattice or the triangles. A potentially important representational problem is whether the distances among the jets (or the distortions of these distances) should be incorporated into the representation or whether the jet similarities are sufficient to account for the accuracy of the model's performance in modeling human face recognition. Many issues remain about the possible inclusion of an explicit measure of distance (e.g., the sum of the squares of the differences in corresponding distances) as a component of similarity in the matching phase. The fiducial point model has a strong potential for serving as a research platform for addressing these and a number of the other issues in face recognition, such as norm based coding.

5.2 Norm Based Coding?

In the current versions of the model, the match of a probe face to a face stored in the gallery is only a function of the similarity between the two. An alternative basis for matching could be to include not only the similarity of the two faces but their distances from the norms of a population of faces. There are several effects that would suggest some role of such norm based coding in face recognition. Caricatures can be created by enhancing deviations (e.g., by 50%) of points on a particular face from the population values (see Rhodes & Tremewan, 1994, for a recent review). Moreover, for famous faces the recognition accuracy of such caricatures does not suffer in comparison to--and can sometimes be found to exceed-- the recognition accuracy of the original face (Rhodes & Tremewan, 1994). Carey (1992) and Rhodes (1994) tested whether the caricature gains its advantage in recognition (or resists a loss) because of the increased "distinctiveness" of the distortions in face space. They showed that "lateral" caricatures, in which the distortions were made in a direction orthogonal to the direction of the deviation of a point, were recognized less well than 50% characters, which were recognized as well as the original, and even less well than *anticaricatures*, faces where the distortion was reduced by 50% towards the norm. Thus, it is not merely *any* distortion that produces an advantage, but only those that enhance the deviations from the norm.

The fiducial point model of Wiskott et al. (1997) would seem to be particularly well designed to incorporate norm-based coding. Whether the perception of caricatures differs from that of non caricatured faces can be assessed with such a representation. A caricature matched against its original image will have a lower similarity value with the standard matching routines in the Wiskott at al. system. But it would be a simple matter to include deviations of both the jet locations and the kernel activation values from a normed face. One can also ask whether the advantage of the caricature is one of deviations from the norm or deviations from near neighbors? In general these two measures will covary. An explicit model also offers the possibility of more detailed tests of how caricatures function. When performed over a set of faces, would it be possible to predict which faces would enjoy a caricature advantage and which not? Should greater weight in matching be given to kernels in proportion to their departure from their normed activation value? This last question raises a possible issue with respect to caricatures. People typically realize that they are looking at a caricature and not the original face. Is it possible that caricature perception alters the way in which faces are coded or matched? Specifically, do models that predict the distinctiveness of uncaricatured faces also serve to predict the distinctiveness of caricatured faces?

6 Conclusion

A number of differences are apparent in the behavioral and neural phenomena associated with the recognition of faces and objects. Readily recognizable objects can typically be represented in terms of a geon structural description which specifies an arrangement of viewpoint invariant parts based on a nonaccidental characterization of edges at orientation and depth discontinuities. The parts and relations are determined in intermediate layers between the early array of spatially distributed filters and the object itself and they confer a degree of independence between the initial wavelet components and the representation. The units in a structural description of an object allow ready verbalization. The nonaccidental characterization of discontinuities endows the representation with considerable robustness over variations in viewpoint, lighting, and contrast variables. Last, object experts discover mapping of small nonaccidental features. Individuation of faces, by contrast, requires specification of the fine metric variation in a holistic representation of a facial surface. This can be achieved by storing the pattern of activation over a set of spatially distributed filters. Such a representation will evidence many of the phenomena associated with faces such as holistic effects, nonverbalizability, and great susceptibility to metric variations of the face surface, as well as to image variables such as rotation in depth or the plane, contrast reversal, and direction of lighting. Face experts represent the whole face. A series of experiments demonstrated that the recognition or matching of objects is largely independent of the particular spatial filter components in the image whereas the recognition or matching of a face is closely tied to these initial filter values.

References

Baylis, G. C., Rolls, E. T., and Leonard, C. M. (1987). Functional subdivisions of the temporal lobe neocortex. *Journal of Neuroscience*, 7, 330-342.

Behrmann, M., Winocur, G., & Moscovitch, M. (1992). Dissociation between mental imagery and object recognition in a brain-damaged patient. *Nature*, 359, 636-637.

Behrmann, M., & Shallice, T. (1995). Pure alexia: A nonspatial visual disorder affecting letter activation. *Cognitive Neuropsychology*, 12, 409-454.

Biederman, I. (1987). Recognition-by-components: A theory of human image understanding. *Psychological Review, 94*, 115-147.

Biederman, I. (1995). Visual object recognition. In S. F. Kosslyn and D. N. Osherson (Eds.). *An Invitation to Cognitive Science*, 2nd edition, *Volume 2., Visual Cognition*. MIT Press. Chapter 4, pp. 121-165.

Biederman, I., & Bar, M. (1995). One-Shot Viewpoint Invariance with Nonsense Objects. Paper presented at the Annual Meeting of the Psychonomic Society, 1995, Los Angeles, November.

Biederman, I. & Cooper, E. E. (1991). Priming contour-deleted images: Evidence for intermediate representations in visual object recognition. *Cognitive Psychology, 23*, 393-419.

Biederman, I., & Cooper, E. E. (1992). Size invariance in visual object priming. *Journal of Experimental Psychology: Human Perception and Performance*, 18, 121-133.

Biederman, I., & Gerhardstein, P. C. (1995). Viewpoint-dependent mechanisms in visual object recognition: Reply to Tarr and Bülthoff (1995). *Journal of Experimental Psychology: Human Perception and Performance*, 21, 1506-1514.

Biederman, I. & Gerhardstein, P. C. (1993). Recognizing depth-rotated objects: Evidence and conditions for three-dimensional viewpoint invariance. *Journal of Experimental Psychology-Human Perception and Performance*, 19(6), 1162-1182.

Biederman, I., Gerhardstein, P.C. , Cooper, E. E., & Nelson, C. A. (1997). High Level Object Recognition Without an Anterior Inferior Temporal Cortex. *Neuropsychologia*, 35, 271-287.

Biederman, I., & Kalocsai, P. (1997). Neurocomputational bases of object and face recognition. *Philosophical Transactions of the Royal Society of London B*, 352, 1203-1219.

Biederman, I., & Subramaniam, S. (1997). Predicting the shape similarity of objects without distinguishing viewpoint invariant properties (VIPs) or parts. *Investigative Ophthalmology & Visual Science*, 38, 998.

Biederman, I., Subramaniam, S., Kalocsai, P, and Bar, M. (1998). Viewpoint-invariant information in subordinate-level object classification. In D. Gopher & A. Koriat (Eds.) *Attention and Performance XVII. Cognitive Regulation of Performance: Interaction of Theory and Application*. Cambridge, MA: MIT Press.

Bruce, V. (1988). *Recognizing Faces*. Hove and London, UK: Erlbaum.

Bruce, V., & Humphreys, G. W. (1994). Recognizing objects and faces. Visual Cognition, 1, 141-180.

Cesa, I. L. (1994). Of attractive librarians and lop-sided faces: Development and testing of a training procedure for improving the accuracy of eyewitnesses. Unpublished Doctoral Dissertation, Department of Psychology, Univ. of Southern California.

Cooper, E. E., & Biederman, I. (1993). Metric versus viewpoint-invariant shape differences in visual object recognition. *Investigative Ophthalmology & Visual Science*, 34, 1080.

Cooper, E. E., & Wojan, T. J. (1996). Differences in the coding of spatial relations in faces and objects. *Investigative Ophthalmology & Visual Science*, 37, 177.

Damasio, A. R., Damasio, H., & Van Hoesen, G. E. (1982). Prosopagnosia: Anatomic basis and behavioral mechanisms. *Neuropsychologia*, 2, 237-246.

Davidoff, J. B. (1988). Prosopagnosia: A disorder of rapid spatial integration. In G. Denes, C. Semenza, & P. Bisiachi (Eds/), *Perspectives on Cognitive Neuropsychology*, (pp. 297-309). Hillsdale, NJ: Erlbaum.

Desimone, R., & Ungerleider, L. G. (1989). Neural mechanisms of visual processing in monkeys. (Chapter 14, Pp. 267-299). In F. Boller & J. Grafman (Eds.) Handbook of neuropsychology, Vol. 2. Amsterdam: Elsevier.

Edelman, S. (1995). Representation of similarity in 3D object discrimination. *Neural Computation*, 7, 407-422.

Enns, J. T., & Shore, D. I. (1997). Separate influences of orientation and lighting in the inverted-face effect. *Perception & Psychophysics*, 59, 23-31.

Farah, M. J. (1990). *Visual Agnosia: Disorders of Object Recognition and What They Tell Us About Normal Vision.* Cambridge, MA: MIT Press.

Farah, M. J. (1995). Dissociable systems for visual recognition: A cognitive neuropsychology approach. In S. F. Kosslyn and D. N. Osherson (Eds.). *An Invitation to Cognitive Science*, 2nd edition, *Volume 2., Visual Cognition.* MIT Press. Chapter 3, pp. 101-119.

Fiser, J., Biederman, I., & Cooper, E. E. (1997). To what extent can matching algorithms based on direct outputs of spatial filters account for human shape recognition? *Spatial Vision*, 10, 237-271.

Garner, W. R. (1966). To perceive is to know. American Psychologists, 1966, 31, 11-19.

Gauthier, I., & Tarr, M. J. (1977). Becoming a "Greeble" expert: Exploring mechanisms for face recognition. *Spatial Vision*, in press.

Grüsser, O.-J., & Landis, T. (1991). *Visual Agnosias and Other Disturbances of Visual Perception and Cognition.* Boca Raton: CRC.

Hosie, J. A., Ellis, H. D., & Haig, N. D. (1988). The effect of feature displacement on the perception of well-know faces. *Perception*, 17, 461-474.

Hummel, J. E., & Biederman, I. (1992). Dynamic binding in a neural network for shape recognition. *Psychological Review*, 99, 480-517.

Johnston, A., Hill, H., & Carman, N. (1992). Recognizing faces: effects of lighting direction, inversion, and brightness reversal. *Perception*, 21, 365-375.

Jolicoeur, P. (1985). The time to name disoriented natural objects. *Memory & Cognition*, 13, 289-303.

Kanwisher, N., Chun, M., M., & McDermott, J. (1996). fMRI in individual subjects reveals loci in extrastriate cortex differentially sensitive to faces and objects. *Investigative Ophthalmology & Visual Science*, 37, 193.

Kalocsai, P., Biederman, I., & Cooper, E. E. (1994). To what extent can the recognition of unfamiliar faces be accounted for by a representation of the direct output of simple cells. *Investigative Ophthalmology & Visual Science*, 35, 1626.

Kobatake, E., & Tanaka, K. (1994). Neuronal selectivities to complex object features in the ventral visual pathway of the macaque cerebral cortex. *Journal of Neurophysiology*, 71, 856-867.

Lades, M., Vortbrüggen, J. C., Buhmann, J., Lange, J., von der Malsburg, C., Würtz, R. P., & Konen, W. (1993). Distortion Invariant Object Recognition in the Dynamic Link Architecture. *IEEE Transactions on Computers, 42*, 300-311.

Logothetis, N. K., Pauls, J., Bülthoff, H. H., & Poggio, T. (1994). View-dependent object recognition by monkeys. *Current Biology*, 4, 401-414.

Moscovitch, M., Winocur, G., Behrmann, M. What is special about face recognition? Nineteen experiments on a person with visual object agnosia and dyslexia but normal face recognition. *Journal of Cognitive Neuroscience*, 9, 555-604.

Rolls, E. T. (1992). Neurophysiological mechanisms underlying face processing within and beyond the temporal cortical visual areas. *Philosophical Transactions of the Royal Society of London B, 335,* 11-21.

Rhodes, G., & Tremewan, T. (1994). Understanding face recognition: Caricature effects, inversion, and the homogeneity problem. *Visual Cognition*, 1, 275-311.

Rumiati, R., I., Humphreys, G. W., Riddoch, M., J., & Bateman, A. Visual object agnosia without prosopagnosia or alexia: Evidence for hierarchical theories of visual object recognition. *Visual Cognition*, 1, 181-225.

Scalaidhe, P. Ó., Wilson, A. W., Goldman-Rakic, P. S. (1997). Areal segregation of face-processing neunrons in preferontal cortex. *Science*, 278, 1135-1138.

Schiller, P. H. (1995). Effect of lesions in visual cortical area V4 on the recognition of transformed objects. *Nature*, 376, 342-344.

Sergent, J., Ohta, S., & MacDonald, B. (1992). Functional neuroanatomy of face and object processing: A PET study. *Brain*, 115, 15-29.

Sergent, J., Ohta, S., MacDonald, B., & Zuck, E. (1994). Segregated processing of facial identity and emotion in the human brain: A PET study. *Visual Cognition*, 1, 349-369.

Shepard, R. N. (1964). Attention and the metric structure of the stimulus space. *Journal of Mathematical Psychology*, 1964, 1, 54-87.

Shepard, R. N., & Cermak, G. W. (1973). Perceptual-cognitive explorations of a toroidal set of free-from stimuli. *Cognitive Psychology*, 4, 351-377.

Subramaniam, S. & Biederman, I. (1997). Does contrast reversal affect object identification. *Investigative Ophthalmology & Visual Science*, 38, 998.

Tanaka, J. W., & Farah, M. J. (1993). Parts and wholes in face recognition. *The Quarterly Journal of Experimental Psychology*, 46A, 225-245.

Tootell, R. B. H., Dale, A. M., Sereno, M. I., Malach, R. (1996). New images from human visual cortex. *Trends in Neural Science*, 19, 481-489.

Tversky, B., & Hemenway, K. (1984). Objects, parts, and categories. *Journal of Experimental Psychology: General*, 113, 169-193.

Wiskott, L., Fellous, J-M., Krüger, N., & von der Malsburg, C. (1997). Face recognition by elastic bunch graph matching. *PAMI*, in press.

Yin, R. K. (1969). Looking at upside down faces. *Journal of Experimental Psychology*, 81, 141-145.

Young, A. W., Hay, D. C., McWeeny, K. H., Flude, B. M., & Ellis, A. W. (1985). Matching familiar and unfamiliar faces on internal and external features. *Perception*, 14, 737-746.

Young, A. W., Hellawell, D., & Hay, D. C. (1987). Configural information in face perception. *Perception*, 16, 747-759.

Young, M. P., & Yamane, S. (1992). Sparse population coding of faces in the inferotemporal cortex. *Science*, 256, 1327-1331.

Multi-Modal Person Authentication

J.Bigün[1], B. Duc[2], F. Smeraldi[1], S. Fischer[2], and A. Makarov[1]

[1] EPFL Microprocessor and Interface Laboratory CH-1015 Lausanne
[2] EPFL Signal Processing Laboratory CH-1015 Lausanne

Abstract. This paper deals with the elements of a multi-modal person authentication systems. Test procedures for evaluating machine experts as well as machine supervisors based on leave-one-out principle are described. Two independent machine experts on person authentication are presented along with their individual performances. These experts consisted of a face (Gabor features) and a speaker (LPC features) authentication algorithm trained on the M2VTS multi-media database. The expert opinions are combined yielding far better performances by using a trained supervisor based on Bayesian statistics than individual modalities aggregated by averaging.

1 Introduction

Person authentication has been gathering considerable interest due to the easy access to computers and communication technologies. Recently, the audio and video based authentication techniques have been jointly used [5] in an attempt to find dependable solutions for the challenging problem of person authentication. The need for multi-modality is motivated by the fact that the speech and image based mono-modal authentication technologies are starting to reach a performance saturation.

With the increase of computation performance, authentication using multi-modalities, in particular vision and sound, is becoming more realistic. A fundamental reason for multi-modality is the inherent limitations of the information in a single modality. Biological systems tend to solve the problem by using multiple cues. It is more difficult to find people who resemble each other pictorially *and* vocally than for example to find people who resemble each other only pictorially. Consequently, the multi-modal authentication is helped by this low prior-probability. We investigate two modalities to be used in person authentication.

However, using multi-modal techniques require an automatic mechanism, a *machine supervisor*, for conciliating (sometimes contradictory) machine "opinions" to a single and more reliable opinion. It also requires test procedures for evaluation of algorithms constituting the machine experts and the machine supervisor which delivers a joint opinion by calibrating and aggregating the expert opinions, [1]. The supervisor algorithm used here is based on [2] which was originally developed for human experts assessing the risks for rare events such as catastrophes. This is motivated in that erroneously rejecting a client of a system or accepting an impostor can be assumed to be a rare event for a machine expert, as they are designed to reduce the risk of these events.

Here we describe the elements of multi-modal person authentication by using speech and face sensors which are not perceived as intrusive by their users. The works of [8,12,19] share conceptually similar interests with this paper.

2   System Model and Definitions

2.1   Identification versus Authentication

Person authentication and *person identification* are of primary interest for a number of security applications. Both will be briefly summarised as there is an important distinction, which has practical consequences, between the two.

In *authentication* applications, the clients are known to the system whereas the impostors can potentially be the world population. In such applications the scenario is cooperative, that is the users provide their pretended identities which are known to the system. In case the candidate provides an unknown identity, he will be rejected without further check. Authentication is the focus of the concepts developed in this work, although many of these are also useful for person identification.

In *identification* applications, the scenario is non-cooperative and therefore there is no identity claim. The situation is very much like that of a database query. The candidate is compared to the entire database, and the correct identity should be among the best matches. This is the simplest form of identification which is also called *closed-universe identification.* In the more elaborate versions of the identification, the candidate may or may not belong to the database. In the case of the latter, the system should detect this and reject the query in order to reduce the identification error. This is called *open-universe identification.* The rejection process in open-universe identification systems is an implicit authentication step.

2.2   Supervisor and Experts

We have a system consisting of one supervisor and m experts. The supervisor does not interfere with the computational processes of the experts. It only asks the experts their opinions about the claims of a candidate. Below is a list of the major notations we use throughout the paper, see also Figure 1. Other notations only important for a module are described in place.

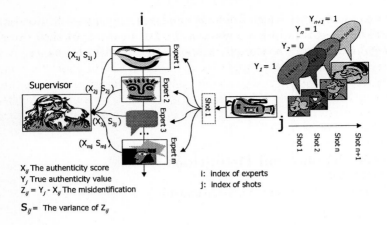

Fig. 1. The system model of multi-modal person authentication.

A take: A data package (e.g. speech+image) of a candidate, without identity claim

A shot: A data package of a candidate with an identity claim

i, j: Indices of the experts, $i \in 1 \cdots m$, and of the shots, $j \in 1 \cdots n, n+1$.

K, L: The number of persons and takes in a database

X_{ij}:   Authenticity score delivered by expert i on shot j's being a take of the claimed client

s_{ij} The variance of X_{ij} as estimated by expert i. The experts are allowed to provide a quality of the score which is modelled to be inversely proportional to s_{ij}.

Y_j The true authenticity score of shot j's being that of a client.

Z_{ij} The error score of an expert $Z_{ij} = Y_j - X_{ij}$

T: Hard decision threshold (accept or reject)

Single variable indices, e.g. s_j, P_j, Z_j represent aggregated (supervisor) variables instead of expert variables. In the context of supervisor design, we assume that the shots $1 \cdots n$ are new shots of the clients, i.e. the experts have trained on other shots of the corresponding clients. Shot $n + 1$ is the shot of a candidate which neither the experts nor the supervisor have trained on. Therefore shot $n + 1$ can be considered to belong to a future instant, or an instant when the system is in full use. During supervisor training, we also assume that the training phase of the experts is already achieved.

3 Evaluation

3.1 Methodology

The machine opinions are pairs of (X_{ij}, s_{ij}). They are originally in form of distances to the reference model. But for comparison purposes these are mapped to the $]0, 1]$ interval by the experts themselves. The a priori threshold for separating acceptance and rejection is assumed to be 0.5. By varying it in the $]0, 1]$ interval, one can influence two types of error rates: for example, if the threshold increases, the *false acceptance* (FA) rate decreases, but the *false rejection* (FR) rate increases. Several ways of displaying the behaviour of the error rates are possible. Receiver Operating Characteristics (ROC) curves show the false acceptance versus the false rejection. The threshold value is an implicit parameter of the curve. The terminology is taken from radar technology where the problem is to detect a target. When comparing two such curves, the one closest to the axes corresponds to the best method. However, the sensitivity of a point on the ROC curve with respect to the threshold is not possible to view as the threshold is implicit. This is sometimes desirable since threshold explicit curves reveal how easy it is to find the best operational threshold. By varying the threshold, one can reach a point where the FA and FR rates take the same value. This value, called Equal Error Rate (EER), provides a way to characterise a method with a single number, allowing a quick comparison.

Normally, by using a threshold T, the inequality $X_{i,j} > T$ can be turned to a decision of *accept* when fulfilled, or to a decision of *reject* otherwise. We rewrite this inequality by subtracting it from y_j yielding $Z_{i,j} < y_j - T$. The inequality yields an acceptance decision when it is fulfilled, rejection otherwise. Therefore an acceptance is a false acceptance when the inequality is fulfilled for $y_j = T_f = 0$. Likewise a rejection decision represents a false rejection when the inequality is *not* fulfilled for $y_j = T_t = 1$:

$$\text{False Acceptance} \Leftrightarrow Z_{i,j} < T_f - T = -T \tag{1}$$

$$\text{False Rejection} \Leftrightarrow Z_{i,j} \geq T_t - T = 1 - T \tag{2}$$

Consequently, the integral of the frequency function of Z taken over the semi-axes defined by (1) and (2) represent the FA and FR functions. To be more precise

$$FA(T) = \int_{z<T_f-T} f(z)/C\,dz = F(T_f - T) \qquad (3)$$

$$FR(T) = \int_{z \geq T_t-T} f(z)/C\,dz = 1 - F(T_t - T) \qquad (4)$$

where $f(z)$ is the frequency of Z, and C is a normalisation constant so that F, the integral of f, is a distribution function i.e. $F(\infty) = 1$.

This conclusion is interesting since f can be estimated via the histogram of Z in practice. As both histogram and summation (integral) routines are widely available in computer environments, the implementations of $FA(T)$ and $FR(T)$ computations are particularly simple, as compared to a straightforward approach, in which T's must be varied. This approach is also the one adopted here. FA, FR and the Total Error TE, which is FA + FR, are functions of the same threshold. The FA and FR discussion is valid for both experts and supervisors.

3.2 Test Protocols for Experts and Supervisors

Authentication algorithms need to be compared. For this reason databases which represent realistic situations should play a central role in evaluating verification technologies. The M2VTS database, [21], is a digital multi-media person database which, to the extent limited by storage requirements, takes into account the demands of current speech and image based authentication technologies. This database contains speech and video data of speaking persons and images representing head rotations of each person. Due to storage requirements, the speech is restricted to utterances of the digits 0..9. The database is made up from $K = 37$ different people and provides $L = 4$ takes for each person. The takes were recorded at one week intervals or when drastic face changes occurred in the meantime. During each take, people have been asked to count from '0' to '9' in their native languages (most of the people are French speaking).

For evaluation experiments, a database should ideally be split into three subsets: a *training set*, which is used for designing the system, an *evaluation set*, which is used for determining thresholds and which should consist of data independent from the training set, and a *test set* for estimating the performance of the system, i.e. the system is completely determined and works in the authentication mode. The error rates are estimated on the test set. Here, as few persons are available due to the nature of the multi-modal authentication, we prefer not to consider an evaluation set, and use a priori chosen thresholds for a functioning system.

Several methods have been described in the literature in order to maximise the use of the information in a database during a test [16]. However, it appears that only variants of bootstrap sampling are relevant for applications such as authentication. The details of our *Expert Protocol*, which has similarities with the Jack knife sampling and uses the leave-one-out principle, is given below.

The experiments have been conducted by leaving out both one person (all her takes) and one take (all persons). Alternatively, each person is labelled as an impostor, while the $K - 1$ (i.e. 36) others are considered as *clients*. For each combination, $L - 1$ (i.e 3) takes of the $K - 1$ clients build the training set and the L'th take (i.e. 4'th) series is used as evaluation set in the following way: each client tries to access under the correct identity, and the impostor tries to access under the identities of the $K - 1$ clients. This makes $K - 1$ authentic tests and $K - 1$ impostor tests. The procedure is repeated L times, by considering each take as the test series alternatively. In total, the client and impostor verification amount each to $K \times L \times (K - 1)$, which evaluates to 5328 shots for the M2VTS database. Testing impostor access with persons belonging to the training set has not been used, as it is considered too easy to discriminate between persons present in the training set, even if the data themselves are not present in the training set. The Expert Protocol is summarised in Figure 2. All experts are supposed to give their opinions on a particular shot, according to the Expert Protocol. Therefore for a given expert such an opinion description can be unambiguously represented by a tuple

$$(\text{ET\_LABEL}, \text{C\_ID}, Y_j, X_{i,j}, P_{i,j}) \tag{5}$$

where ET_LABEL and C_ID represent the unique identities of the expert training set and the claimed identity (of a client). For simplicity we use the combination of the left-out person identity and the left out take in order to obtain the ET_LABEL. For example the tuple $(\text{BP\_04}, \text{CC}, 0, 0.4, 0.8)$ represents an impostor (since $Y_j = 0$, this is an impostor claim and ET_LABEL=BP_04 reveals that the actual identity of the person is BP) trial which obtained the score of 0.4, and the quality of the score 0.8.

Such opinions and ground truths are used to estimate the two main performance characteristics of the authentication, namely the FA rate and the FR rate of an expert. However, assuming that the experts deliver their opinions according to the Expert Protocol, we need another test procedure for evaluating the performance of the multi-modal system. We call this protocol, the *Supervisor Protocol* as it is slightly different than the Expert Protocol, even though it embraces the same principle.

The Supervisor Protocol uses the opinions and the ground truth delivered by the Expert Protocol for each expert, as given by (5), yielding 2×5328 such tuples for the M2VTS database. This leaves out all opinions related to the identity of a single person. That is, tuples with ET_LABEL or C_ID (whichever contains the identity of the person to be left out) are left out. The left-out opinions are used to test the supervisor, while the inliers are used to train the supervisor. Consequently the supervisor training set, ST_LABEL, can be represented by using the left out identity.

To fix the ideas let the left out person be ST_LABEL=BP. As a result of the procedure, there are $4 \times L \times (K - 1) = 576$ opinions in the test set which leaves $2 \times K \times L \times (K - 1) - 4 \times L \times (K - 1) = 10080$ opinions for the training set by leaving out all BP related opinions from the Expert Protocols. By rotating the left out person one can obtain $K = 37$ training and test sets yielding $4 \times K \times L \times (K-1)$ expert opinion descriptions represented by tuples:

$$(\text{ST\_LABEL}, \text{C\_ID}, Y_j, X_j, P_j) \qquad (6)$$

in which the supervisor and the expert training sets have no, or reasonable dependencies. These can be aggregated by taking their means in order to compute FA and FR curves for a supervisor. A complementary way of testing two supervisor performances independent of the experts relies on simulating expert opinions, see [3].

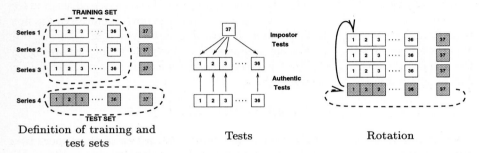

Definition of training and test sets	Tests	Rotation

Fig. 2. Expert Protocol. The database is divided into a training set of $L - 1 = 3$ takes of $K - 1 = 36$ persons and a test set consisting of all K persons. Each configuration brings a total of $K - 1$ authentic accesses, and $K - 1$ impostor accesses.

4 Face Expert

Attributed graphs describe objects on sparse locations, by attaching to each node a feature vector that contains information on the local neighbourhood of the node location. Here, we use the modulus of complex Gabor responses as features, from filters with 6 orientations and 3 resolutions. For a discussion on their usefulness for image analysis applications, see [6,10].

4.1 Elastic Graph Matching

Each face is represented by a set of feature vectors positioned on nodes of a coarse, rectangular grid placed on the image. Comparing two face images is accomplished by matching and adapting a grid taken from one image to the features of the other image [20].

Elastic Graph Matching (EGM) consists in locating an attributed graph on the image that is as close as possible to the reference graph. The distance between two graphs is evaluated by a distance function, that considers both the feature vectors of each node and the deformation information attached to the edges.

We consider distance measures where the contribution from nodes and edges are independent, more precisely:

$$d(\Gamma, R) = \sum_{i=1}^{N_n} d_n(\Gamma_{n_i}, R_{n_i}) + \lambda \sum_{j=1}^{N_e} d_e(\Gamma_{e_j}, R_{e_j}), \qquad (7)$$

where Γ_{n_i} and R_{n_i} represent the Gabor feature vectors at the ith node of the test and reference grids respectively. The edge vector of the test and reference grid are represented by Γ_{e_j} and R_{e_j}. N_n, N_e are the number of nodes and edges, respectively. λ is a weighting factor which characterises the stiffness of the graph. A *plastic* graph which opposes no reaction to deformation corresponds to $\lambda = 0$, while a totally rigid graph corresponds to the limit case $\lambda = \infty$.

The matching procedure consists of two consecutive steps [20]. The first step is used for obtaining an approximate match, with a rigid grid, which is equivalent to setting a high value of λ. Starting from this initial guess, the grid is deformed in order to minimise (7).

4.2   Coarse-to-Fine Matching

The computation of a feature vector for a node at a given location requires a filtering operation for each feature. If Gabor filters are used with 6 orientations and 3 resolutions, 18 filtering operations are required. As this can be computationally demanding, we suggest the use of coarse to fine matching when doing the rigid Gabor response matching.

For a graph matching, the filter responses may be needed only on a reduced subset of points in the image. Depending on the number of points visited, it may become computationally less expensive to compute the Gabor responses only at required points by convolution in the spatial domain.

We consider a multi-resolution description of the image. First, the lowest resolution image is considered for matching. As a consequence, the objective function is smoothed, and the matching may be undertaken on a sub-sampled lattice. This property is intimately related to the fundamental sampling theorem: as the objective function has been low-pass filtered, it may be sampled at a coarser step without loss of information. Figure 3 shows that the low-resolution image provides a smooth objective function, while the high frequency information generates a forest of local minima. However, the minima are more precisely localised when the high frequencies are incorporated. Consecutive refinements are obtained by incorporating higher resolution information and by searching on a finer grid around the current estimate.

Coarse-to-fine strategies may get trapped in local minima [15]. A remedy to this weakness consists in the elaboration of mixed fine-to-coarse and coarse-to-fine strategies. However, if only one head is present and occupies a significant part of the image, we noticed that this problem does not occur.

In practice, a Gaussian pyramid is built [9]. In a pyramidal implementation, the size of images depends on the resolution. The pyramid is built recursively, by

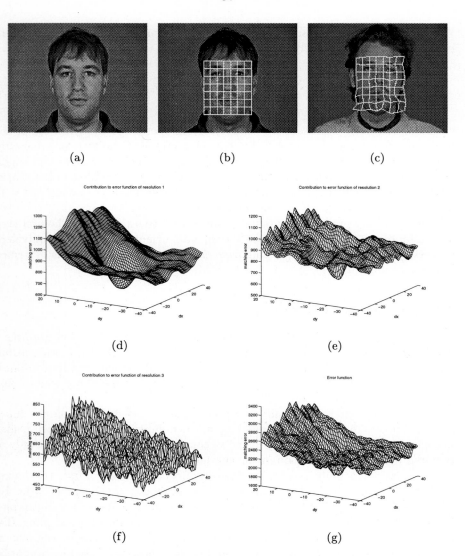

(a)   (b)   (c)

(d)   (e)

(f)   (g)

Fig. 3. Objective function for the rigid translation of the graph on the search window. Gabor responses on three resolutions are used. Here, the contribution of each resolution is shown separately. (a) original image from which the reference graph is taken. (b) reference graph superimposed on the reference image. (c) matched graph superimposed on the test image. (d) objective function with only the lowest resolution. (e) objective function with only the medium resolution. (f) objective function with only the highest resolution. (g) total objective function. While low resolution provide smooth, convex objective functions, high resolution responses provide sharper minima, and are used for refinement.

building a new, lower-resolution level from the previous one by low-pass filtering and sub-sampling with a factor two, so that the size of the image is divided by two at each iteration. The low-pass filtering was achieved with separable Gaussian filters. With the pyramidal implementation, the lattice spacing in *pixels* is kept constant through all levels: a displacement of 1 pixel at level n of the pyramid corresponds to a displacement of 2^n pixels in the level 0 of the pyramid, which is the original image.

The definition of filters is simplified by defining a set of filters for a single resolution and a complete set of orientations. These filters are applied to each level of the pyramid, to obtain a complete set of resolutions. A significant reduction of the amount of computations is obtained for low frequency responses, compared to filtering the original image, as bandpass filters selecting low frequencies have a large support.

4.3   Dimensionality Reduction and Local Discriminants

The first step of the authentication consists in matching the image with the prototype grid of the claimed class (in the following, each person in the database is considered as a *class* of the classification problem). This prototype is taken as the mean of the feature vectors provided by all images of the considered person in the training set. It is expected that if the claimed identity is correct, the feature vector will be close to the prototype of the class; in case of an impostor, the matching will perform poorly. Unfortunately, early experiments showed that the *Residual Matching Error* (RME), i.e. $d(G, R)$ after matching with $\lambda = 0$, is not sufficient to discriminate between an impostor and the authentic person, see Section 4.4. This is partly due to the presence of noise in the measurement, but also due to the fact that not all nodes are discriminative. Indeed, the feature space considered here is very large: for an 8 by 8 grid comprising 18 Gabor responses at each node, a total of $N_G = 1152$ features is obtained.

Reducing the dimensionality is an efficient way to reduce the influence of noise [11,4]. From a training set consisting of several frontal views of each person, one establishes subspaces which maximise the dispersion of all classes while minimising the dispersion within the classes.

However, the number of training samples is small compared to the number of features. Also, the features on two graph nodes may be considered as independent. Therefore, it is reasonable to address dimensionality reduction independently at each node of the graph. If features are considered locally, the number of training samples is larger than the dimension of the feature space, which allows to apply feature reduction methods.

Local Discriminants Suppose that the dimensionality of the considered feature space is small compared to the number of training elements in each of the c considered classes. One would like to establish a decision criterion for the acceptance or rejection of the candidate. This criterion should be "small" if the candidate is the right person, and "large" in case of an impostor. Obviously, this decision has to be made on the difference between the prototype of the claimed class and the measured feature vector. The components of this difference do not bear the same significance, as some may be more relevant than others for the given class. Therefore, we propose the following discriminant criterion:

$$d_k(r) = \left(\sum_{i=1}^{N_g} v_{k_i}(r_i - \mu_{k_i}) \right)^2 = \left(v_k^t(r - \mu_k) \right)^2 \qquad (8)$$

for class $k, k = 1...c$, where r_i are the components of the measurement vector r, N_g is the dimension of the local feature space. Here, the local spaces are chosen as the sets of all orientations for a given resolution at a given node, so that $N_g = 6$. μ_k is a mean of vectors r averaged over a set that will be precised in (9). The unknown coefficient vector v_k's are determined on the training set by minimising the ratio:

$$
\begin{aligned}
D_k &= \frac{\sum_{r \in S_k} d_k(r)}{\sum_{r \in (S-S_k)} d_k(r)} \\
&= \frac{\sum_{r \in S_k} v_k^t(r - \mu_k)(r - \mu_k)^t v_k}{\sum_{r \in (S-S_k)} v_k^t(r - \mu_k)(r - \mu_k)^t v_k} \\
&= \frac{v_k^t W v_k}{v_k^t B v_k},
\end{aligned}
\qquad (9)
$$

where S_k is the set of training vectors belonging to class k, S is the whole training set, so that $(S - S_k)$ is the set of all impostors for class k. Here, μ_k is the mean on S_k. By this, we are back to a two-class classification problem, where the classes are S_k and $(S - S_k)$. This formulation leads to a generalised eigenvalue problem: $W v_k = \lambda B v_k$, and v_k is given by the eigenvector corresponding to the smallest generalised eigenvalue. This is very similar to Fisher's discriminant ratio [11].

All local responses have to be combined in order to provide a unique, global dissimilarity measure for the considered face. Here, we build the global response by simply adding the contributions from the local discriminants. This discriminant measure will be abbreviated as LD.

Separation Parameters It is necessary to choose a threshold for defining acceptance/rejection intervals in the domain of possible responses from training data. Here we assume that the system will provide a soft decision between $[0, \infty[$, therefore a mapping between the original response interval and the interval $]0, 1]$ is needed.

A natural invertible mapping from $[0, \infty[$ to $]0, 1]$ is provided by the hyperbolic tangent function. For our purpose, the soft score $S \in]0, 1]$ should be 1 for an identity claim acceptation, and 0 for an identity claim rejection, whereas the global discriminant value tends to 0 for a perfect matching and to infinity for a maximum mismatch. We suggest the mapping:

$$S(x) = \tanh\left(\frac{\log(3)}{2x}t\right) \tag{10}$$

where t is an empirically chosen constant. Since by definition $S(t) = 0.5$, t will be called the *Separation Parameter* (SP), as it acts like a decision point on x between acceptance and rejection intervals. In the case of a soft decision the SP acts as a parameter selecting the mapping function. In the case of a hard decision SP is simply the threshold. We have chosen it as the minimal distance measure among the training impostors.

4.4 Experiments with Face Authentication

Local Feature Reduction for Authentication In order to motivate the process of dimensionality reduction, we first want to show that the Euclidean distance between features, i.e. the residual matching error $d(G, R)$ with $\lambda = 0$, is not sufficient for a reliable decision. Figure 4 shows as an example distances of training and test samples with person 15 used as reference. It turns out that the distance to the reference view is clearly not sufficient to detect impostors.

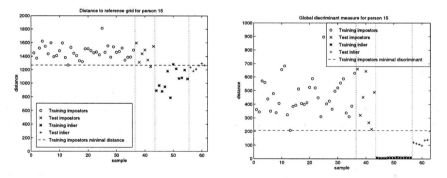

Fig. 4. Plot of distances for person (or class) 15. The distance of the grids of different kind of images, namely impostors in the training and the test set, members of the class in the training and test set, are shown. If one uses the minimal distance on the training impostors as a threshold for the decision, some members of the class in the training and test set are misclassified if the residual matching error is used (Left), whereas all members of the class are correctly classified with the local discriminants (Right).

A representation of discriminant values for the same person is also shown in the same figure. Now the discrimination of impostors is much more powerful. One can notice that there seems to be some over-training, as the discrimination measure is almost zero for all members of the considered class in the training set, and significantly larger for images of the same class in the test set, while

38

remaining smaller than the threshold. This is due to the small number of training samples for each person in the database.

At that point, the discriminant values in the $[0, \infty[$ interval are normalised to the $[0, 1]$ interval, so that they can be combined with or compared to other verification modalities like speech [13]. As an illustration of the usefulness of the discriminant measure over all classes, we show the ROC for the residual matching error (RME) and the local discriminants (LD) in Figure 5. Such curves reflect the performance of a given solution averaged on *all* classes. The points on the ROC were obtained by scaling the minimum threshold displayed in Figure 4 with a varying factor. Clearly, the LD outperforms the RME everywhere. At the threshold value 0.5, the false alarm rate is 6.8% and the false acceptance rate is 3.6%.

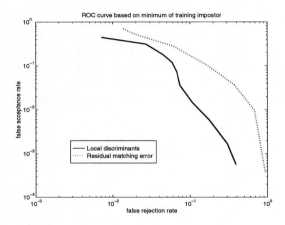

Fig. 5. Experimental ROC curve for the residual matching error and the local discriminants in a log-log scale. Results were obtained with $\lambda = 2$.

Figure 6 shows the LD measures for a particular person, revealing which nodes have little relevance for discrimination. The LD approach provides an automatic way of suppressing the nodes which do not contribute to authentication.

Evaluation of Elasticity Significance In order to assess the effectiveness of grid elasticity, we compare an elastic and a non-elastic graph matching procedure. The non-elastic graph matching is obtained by skipping the second step of the matching procedure described in Section 4.1, which is equivalent to choosing a very large λ in (7). A completely "plastic" grid is obtained with $\lambda = 0$: as the second term vanishes, each grid node is free to move in the image. By running the simulations according to the expert protocol of Section 3.2 with several values of λ, it is possible to assess the usefulness of the elastic step, and also to

Fig. 6. LD measures at each node, for three resolutions. The lowest resolution is shown left, the highest resolution is shown right.

study the tolerance of the discriminant approach with respect to the rigidity of the grid. To the best of our knowledge no such quantitative analysis of λ has been documented before. For preventing any convergence problems at low values of λ, the number of iterations on the elastic matching was limited to 100.

Figure 7 shows the total error rate defined by TE=FA+FR, for the rigid matching and the elastic graph matching, for both types of discriminant measures. Clearly, the presence of the local discrimination has a larger influence on the results than the elastic deformation.

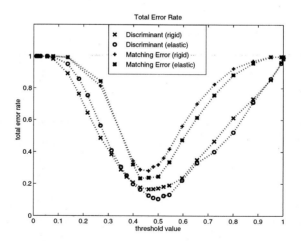

Fig. 7. Total error rates according to the threshold for the rigid matching and the elastic graph matching, with $\lambda = 2$.

Results at the 0.5 threshold are shown for several values of λ in Table 1. The *Equal Error Rate* (EER), defined as the point where FA = FR, is also shown. There is a transition from elastic to rigid matching. The local discrimination is able to provide almost constant results for λ between 0.5 and 3.0. For larger values of λ, the performance degrades. The elastic graph matching improved the rigid graph matching, which can be observed by inspecting Figure 7. Table 1 shows that the EER is improved from 14% down to 11%. However, combining the rigid graph matching with local discriminants is better than elastic graph matching. Not surprisingly, combining the elastic deformation with local discrimination yielded the best results.

λ	FR	FA	EER
∞	29.7	2.1	14.4
10.0	26.3	2.2	12.0
5.0	25	2.3	11.9
4.0	22.9	2.5	12.1
3.0	22.9	2.4	12.3
2.0	22.3	2.2	11.8
1.0	21.6	2.3	11.2
0.5	21.6	2.0	10.8
0.0	24.3	1.6	11.6

λ	FR	FA	EER
∞	13.3	3.7	8.5
10.0	11.1	3.6	7.3
5.0	10.7	3.5	8.4
4.0	11.3	3.6	9.2
3.0	6.9	3.6	6.5
2.0	6.8	3.6	6.1
1.0	7.1	3.9	5.4
0.5	6.8	4.3	6.2
0.0	9.4	4.0	6.0

Table 1. Error rates at the 0.5 threshold and Equal Error Rates. (a) with residual matching error as dissimilarity measure, (b) with local discriminants. The rigid case corresponds to a very large λ, denoted here by $\lambda = \infty$. The equal error rates are obtained by interpolation.

As a conclusion, it has been shown that a small degree of elasticity provides an improvement of the performance. The behaviour remains constant over a certain range of λ, but from a certain rigidity on, the performance degrades.

4.5 Eye Detection by Saccadic Search for Normalisation

It is known that, if face images are normalised, the authentication performance of the matching system is improved. Normalising the ocular positions is such a procedure which can be implemented in an active vision based face authentication. Here we suggest to detect the eye positions of a person by using the Gabor responses dynamically. We use a rigid graph composed of nodes on concentric circles obtained by log polar mapping as in Figure 8. As the procedure is not person specific it can also be used in identification applications. The performance may be of course improved if person specific eye models are used. However, the face expert we described above functioned without eye normalisation on the M2VTS database. The eye normalisation technique suggested below is not intended for a database in which the person is already in the central part of the image and has approximately the correct size, but rather a dynamic environment where the camera is active in order to get the best takes of a face.

Saccadic Search At the beginning of the search, the retinal sampling grid is placed at a random position on the image and the corresponding set of Gabor features at grid nodes, represented by the set $\mathcal{G}_0$, is extracted. Each vector in $\mathcal{G}_0$, after division by its Euclidean norm, is subsequently matched against a reference vector $\mathbf{e}_{av}$. In order to construct the latter, the average Gabor responses from the centre of the right and left eye of six persons are computed. These two standard vector responses are then geometrically averaged component-wise so that $\mathbf{e}_{av}$ captures the features which are common to the right and the left eye. The point of the grid for which the Euclidean distance from $\mathbf{e}_{av}$ is minimal is selected as the target for the next saccade. The search is terminated when saccades become short, here shorter than 1/6 of the sampling grid's outer radius. If no saccade target whose distance from $\mathbf{e}_{av}$ is reasonably low can be found (which can be the case if the search starting point happens to fall in a blank region of the image), the search is restarted from a random position.

The Eye Model The a priori knowledge about the appearance of the left and right eyes of the generic person is respectively encoded into a left eye model and a right eye model. The models are constructed from the sets $\mathcal{L} = \bigcup_p \Gamma_p$ and $\mathcal{R} = \bigcup_q \Gamma_q$ of Gabor features obtained by placing the retinal sampling grid on either of the eyes (Figure 8) and computing the Gabor responses Γ_p at each of its points.

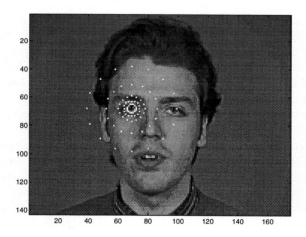

Fig. 8. The retinal sampling grid placed on a person's right eye for model creation.

The features in $\mathcal{L}$ and $\mathcal{R}$ are then rearranged in a collection of matrices $\mathsf{M} = \{\mathsf{M}_{r\omega}\}_{r\omega}$ so that each one of the $\mathsf{M}_{r\omega}$ contains the responses for a fixed Gabor frequency radius ω and a given spatial circle with radius r of the sampling grid. The rows and columns of each $\mathsf{M}_{r\omega}$ therefore correspond to the variation of the angular coordinates in the spatial and frequency domains. Matrices $\mathsf{M}_{r\omega}$ are then normalised separately with respect to the norm defined by $|\mathsf{M}_{r\omega}| = \sqrt{\mathrm{Trace}(\mathsf{M}_{r\omega}^t \mathsf{M}_{r\omega})}$, which is equivalent to the Euclidean norm if $\mathsf{M}_{r\omega}$

is interpreted as a vector. All Gabor features from a single frequency channel ω belong to the same matrix $\mathsf{M}_{r\omega}$. Since each frequency channel is characterised by a specific bandwidth which is common to all the orientations, normalisation takes care of the variation of filter bandwidths across the frequency channels. Also, by grouping together all the points of the sampling grid circle of radius r in a single $\mathsf{M}_{r\omega}$ and then normalising, one makes sure that illumination changes are compensated for.

The eye model for the left eye, L, is computed by combining the collections of matrices M^i obtained by placing the grid manually on the left eye of six persons according to the relation

$$\mathsf{L} = \{\mathsf{L}_{r\omega}\}_{r\omega} = \left\{ \frac{\sum_i \mathsf{M}^i_{r\omega}}{|\sum_i \mathsf{M}^i_{r\omega}|} \right\}_{r\omega}$$

The same procedure is applied to obtain the eye model for the right eye.

Matching of the retinal grid samples I extracted from an image with the model is performed (e.g. in the case of a left eye) by minimising the value of the function $d(\mathsf{I}, \mathsf{L}) = \sum_{r\omega} |\mathsf{I}_{r\omega} - \mathsf{L}_{r\omega}|$.

Refining the Search After the saccadic phase of the search has converged to the target pattern, the Gabor responses in the points currently "viewed" by the grid are compared with both the left and the right eye models described in the preceding section. According to the model which obtains the best result, the candidate eye is assumed to be a left or a right eye. The appropriate model is then selected and the exact position of the local minimum is determined. If the resulting displacement is larger than a few pixels the saccadic search is restarted from a random position.

Experiments have shown that the saccadic search may detect some erroneous local minima (e.g. the corners of the mouth, ear-rings or details in the hair). In order to discriminate such fake targets, the difference is computed between the candidate's distance from the attributed eye model and its distance from the alternate model. The ratio of this difference to the minimum distance, which we call the *asymmetry*, measures the amount to which the chirality of the detected feature contributes to the match. In our experiments, the asymmetry always turned out to be grater than 0.1 for correct matches, while it generally dropped of one or two orders of magnitude in the case of spurious identifications. The errors thus detected are treated by restarting the search from a random position.

Looking for the Other Eye After localisation of one eye, the system performs a saccade in the presumed direction of the other eye. Normal saccadic search is then performed until an eye is found. Due to scale differences between images, the initial saccade may not turn out to be long enough to prevent the system from finding again the same eye. In this case, further attempts are performed with an increasing starting distance from the known eye until the other eye is found. In case the search refinement detects a low asymmetry target, search is restarted with a random offset. If this condition persists for several attempts, it is assumed that the position of the first eye has been incorrectly assigned and eye detection is restarted from scratch. Although the assumption that faces are presented in an upright orientation is used to speed up the detection of the second eye, no strict constraint is imposed on its position relative to the first. Therefore, detection remains robust also in the case of subjects having their head tilted to one side.

Experimental Results The algorithm has been tested using a Gabor decomposition rosette consisting of six texture orientation sectors and five frequency magnitude octaves, ranging from $\frac{\pi}{16}$ to π. The retinal sampling grid employed had 5 rings and 16 rays, with the ring radii being distributed between $\rho_{\min} = 3$ and $\rho_{\max} = 30$ pixels.

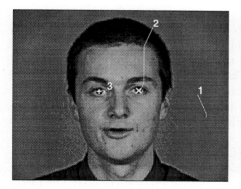 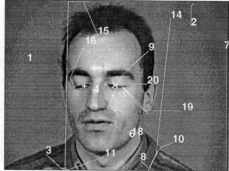

Fig. 9. The + and × signs denote the best match with the right and left eye models respectively. Numbers identify successive starting points for saccades. Eye detection for the left picture required 51 fixations. Note how saccadic search 1 was considered uninteresting and therefore discarded. A random restart (2) then lead to detection of the left eye, after which saccadic search resumed (3) near the location of the right eye. In the case of the right picture, information from the outline of the orbit allows eye detection even if the person's eyes are shut. During this trial the centre of the sampling grid explored 99 pixels and 14 targets were rejected after comparison with the eye models.

Our test set consists of forty takes of twenty persons from the M2VTS database. The image resolution is 143×175 pixels. Differences between the takes of the same persons consist in tan changes, haircut, makeup, eyelid position, head position (heads are often slightly rotated) and slight scale changes. Several persons in the database wear eyeglasses.

Single takes from six persons were used to extract the left and the right eye models. Repeated testing was then performed on the whole set without any mismatch being found. Information obtained from the outline of the orbit allows correct detection of the features even when the subject's eyes are closed (Figure 9). In our trials we found the median of the number of fixation points to be 49 for the detection of both eyes, that is to say that the centre of the retinal sampling grid explores 0.2% of the image pixels. The number of fixations is considerably increased (typically 100) for subjects wearing glasses with strong reflections or having their eyes shut. This is mainly due to the fact that since the algorithm knows nothing about facial features other than the eyes, no alternative cues can be used to infer their spatial position when their visibility is low. Nevertheless, detection is always correctly accomplished at the end. However, the results are indicative. The performance of the method should be tested using an active camera setup in the future.

5 Speech Expert

5.1 Feature Extraction

One of the earliest applications of speech features as biometrics is forensics. The physical and behavioural phenomena which help making the speech so personal include, the characteristics of the vocal tract, the shape of the oral cavity, the nerve signals, and muscle dynamics. The interplay and the exact role of the different elements influencing the characteristics of the speech is too complex to be identified through the resulting one dimensional signal, the voice. However, many personal characteristics are possible to capture in the local power spectra of this signal.

The Linear Prediction Coefficients, (LPC) as derived from the Cepstrum information, is the local spectral information which is most frequently utilised in speech processing in general and speaker authentication in particular. The LPCs, their first and second order time derivative approximations (first and second deltas) are commonly used together as a feature vector describing the characteristics of speech, in typically 10 ms of partly overlapping time intervals, [22,17].

5.2 Text Dependent Speaker Authentication

The techniques described here define the second processing step of a speech expert. As our speech expert, an implementation of the work in [18], uses the fusion of decisions coming from three matching algorithms to deliver a final opinion, we present these below. The final combined graded opinion which is obtained by weighting the individual decisions with the distance to the decision threshold (used in decision making of each method) for each client. The LPCs are used as feature vectors in all three methods. The ROC curves of the speech expert alone is given by Figure 10.

Dynamic Time Warping This is a template matching technique which has many similarities with our face authenticator technique in that the reference feature vector sequence is warped (geometrically distorted) towards the test

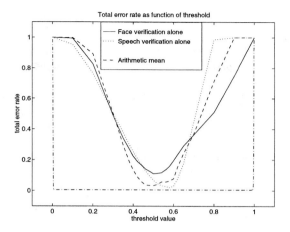

Fig. 10. The total error rates of speech modality as compared to face modality.

sequence and a scalar product is performed between the two. The time warping attempts to align the test and the reference speech features in that the changing speed with which the speech is uttered, is normalised and the feature vectors are possible to compare with each other after the warping, [24].

Sphericity The reference LPC sequence x_k defines the covariance matrix

$$X = \frac{1}{M} \sum_{i=1}^{M} x_i x_i^t \tag{11}$$

where M is the total number of the local analysis intervals. Similarly the test LPC sequence covariance matrix, Y is obtained. If the dimension of the X is $m \times m$ the sphericity measure is defined as

$$\mu(X, Y) = \log \frac{m^{-1} \operatorname{trace}(Y X^{-1})}{m(\operatorname{trace}(XY^{-1}))^{-1}} \tag{12}$$

The larger the sphericity measure between two vectors is, the more likely it is that they represent two different speakers [7].

Hidden Markov Models, HMM HMMs have been used to model the time series. A major use of HMMs is to build models of sub-parts of speech, such as phonemes, or words, see [22] for a tutorial. Here we used text dependent speaker authentication by using the digits {0..9}. One way of exploiting HMMs in speaker verification consists in creating one set of models for the client and one (small) set of models for all impostors (world model), [23]. The two sets of models contain the HMM models of the digits, as uttered by a client and as uttered by the world. A decision is made by computing

$$\arg \max_{\omega \in \{\text{CL, IM}\}} \{P(\omega|O)\} \tag{13}$$

where O is the observed speech (feature vector), and CL and IM represent client and impostor respectively, by using Bayes rule $P(\omega|O) \propto P(O|\omega)$. The latter distribution, $P(O|\omega)$ is modelled by replacing ω with M, a Markov model of the uttered word (by a client or an impostor) ass $P(O|\omega) \propto P(O|M)$. This is in turn modelled as a Markov chain with unknown states (the number of states are known), unknown transition probabilities between the states, and a model of the symbol probability distribution for each state. Computable estimations of $P(O|M)$ are obtained through training which uses the well established Viterbi algorithm and the Baum-Welch re-estimation for doing so. The parameters of the world model is speaker independent. In our case the client set consisted of the speech takes of the M2VTS data-base, [14], whereas the world model was computed by a separate database consisting of 300 occurrences of each digit (uttered by 500 persons), [18]. Furthermore, the number of states of the digits were determined by allocating each phoneme one state, and the model of the symbol probabilities was assumed to consist of one Gaussian per state. All digits had a left-right structure as state transition model.

6   Opinion Fusion by Supervisor

A more extensive presentation of the mathematical background of the model we used can be found in Bigün [3,2].

Basics of the Supervisor Algorithm We perform the following steps

1. (Supervisor Training) Estimate the bias parameters of each expert, i.e. $\{M_i, V_i, \alpha_i\}$, according to (14)

$$M_i = \frac{\sum_{j=1}^{n} \frac{z_{ij}}{\sigma_{ij}^2}}{\sum_{j=1}^{n} \frac{1}{\sigma_{ij}^2}} \quad \text{and} \quad V_i = \frac{1}{\sum_j^n \frac{1}{\sigma_{ij}^2}} \tag{14}$$

by using a training set i.e. x_{ij}, y_j, and p_{ij} with j up to n. The bias parameters will be computed for each expert by using all available persons in the training set. σ_{ij}^2 are computed according to (15), (16).

$$\bar{\sigma}_{ij}^2 = \frac{\alpha_i}{p_{ij}^2} = \frac{(G_i - D_i)}{n-3} \cdot \frac{1}{p_{ij}^2} \tag{15}$$

$$G_i = \sum_{j=1}^{n} \left(\frac{z_{ij}^2}{s_{ij}} \right) \quad \text{and} \quad D_i = \left(\sum_{j=1}^{n} \left(\frac{z_{ij}}{s_{ij}} \right) \right)^2 \left(\sum_{j=1}^{n} \left(\frac{1}{s_{ij}} \right) \right)^{-1} \tag{16}$$

2. (Authentication Phase) At this step, the supervisor is operational, meaning that the time instant is always $n + 1$ and that the supervisor has access to expert opinions $x_{i,n+1}$, and $p_{i,n+1}$, but not access to the true authentication scores, y_{n+1}. The expert opinions are normalised yielding M', and V' according to (17).

$$M_i' = x_{i,n+1} + M_i \quad \text{and} \quad V_i' = V_i + \sigma^2_{i,n+1}. \tag{17}$$

M'' and/or V'' are computed according to (18) (and are ready to be thresholded to yield a definite decision).

$$M'' = \frac{\sum_{i=1}^{m} \frac{M_i'}{V_i'}}{\sum_{i=1}^{m} \frac{1}{V_i'}} \quad \text{and} \quad V'' = \sum_{i=1}^{m} \frac{1}{V_i'} \tag{18}$$

$\sigma^2_{i,n+1}$'s are computed according to (15).

Score Transformation

Depending on the algorithms they use, the scores of the experts, X_{ij}, may or may not be dimensionless (scaled) or in the correct range i.e. $[-\infty, \infty]$. The prime "$'$" on X and Y variables represent these variables before transformation. For our purposes, the transformation

$$X_{ij} = \log \frac{X_{ij}'}{1 - X_{ij}'} \tag{19}$$

which is also known as the "odds of X_{ij}'", will be used to map the scores in $[0, 1]$ to $[-\infty, \infty]$.

Fusion Experiments In Table 2 we present the minimum total error rates of the speech and the face modalities individually, the Bayesian supervisor, and the plain mean of the scores of the face and speech experts, as an alternative supervisor. The test followed the Supervisor Test Protocol described earlier. The FA and FR curves of the Bayesian Supervisor are much smaller than those corresponding to the Mean Supervisor, Figure 11. Furthermore, the minimum total error rate for the Bayesian supervisor is **0.006** , which should be compared to that of the Mean Supervisor, **0.015** . However, in both cases there is a significant improvement as compared to individual modalities, Table 2. While the standard threshold yields the lowest TE for the Bayesian supervisor, this figure is increases to 0.0165 for the Mean Supervisor.

These and other experiments indicate that the Bayesian supervisor is more successful in decision making due its capability of symmetrising the score error densities.

TE_1	TE_2	TE_{bs}	TE_{ms}
0.056	0.035	0.006	0.015

Table 2. Minimum total error rates of machine supervisor opinions based on face and speech signals. TE_1 and TE_2 are expert minimum total error rates of face and speech respectively.

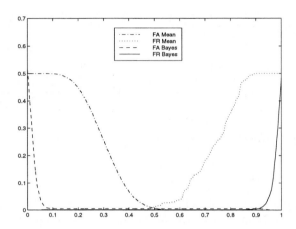

Fig. 11. False Acceptance and False Rejection curves for Mean and Bayesian supervisor tested on 1 speech and 1 image expert.

7   Conclusions

We have presented a framework for multi-modal person authentication, this included test procedures using a bootstraping technique, modelling the experts and the supervisor as opinion providers rather than hard decision makers. We implemented a face expert based on Gabor decomposition, a speech expert using LPCs, and a supervisor based Bayesian statistics and evaluated the individual experts as well as the supervisor on real data.

We demonstrated that a multi-modal system is capable of improving decisions in the context of person authentication significantly, by decreasing the total error rate as much as 600 % (reaching the rate of 0.006 on a rotational test procedure) as compared to the best modality.

In addition to the the general framework, our contribution has been in i) improving the Elastic Graph Matching approach by Local Discriminants, ii) quantifying the contribution of the elastic part of the matching as compared to the rigid graph matching, iii) proposing log-polar based eye detection by saccadic movements for image normalisations for a dynamic camera, and iv) proposing the Bayesian Supervisor in order to improve the multi-modal decision making.

Acknowledgements

This work has been supported by the European projects IT-VIRSBS and ACTS-M2VTS. We thank Gilbert Maitre, IDIAP, Switzerland, for his help with speech experiments.

References

1. J. M. Bernardo and M. F. A. Smith. *Bayesian Theory*. Wiley and Son, Chichester, 1994.
2. E. S. Bigün. Risk analysis of catastrophes using experts' judgements: An empirical study on risk analysis of major civil aircraft accidents in Europe. *European J. Operational research*, 87:599–612, 1995.
3. E. S. Bigun, J. Bigun, B. Duc, and S. Fischer. Expert conciliation for multi modal person authentication systems by bayesian statistics. In J. Bigun, G. Chollet, and G. Borgefors, editors, *Audio and Video based Person Authentication - AVBPA97*, pages 311–318. Springer, 1997.
4. J. Bigün. Unsupervised feature reduction in image segmentation by local transforms. *Pattern Recognition Letters*, 14:573–583, 1993.
5. J. Bigun, G. Chollet, and G. Borgefors; Eds. *Proceedings of the first international conference on Audio and Video based Person Authentication - AVBPA97*, volume LNCS-1206. Springer, 1997.
6. J. Bigun and J. M. H. du Buf. N-folded symmetries by complex moments in Gabor space. *IEEE-PAMI*, 16(1):80–87, 1994.
7. F. Bimbot and L. Mathan. Second order statistical measures for text independent speaker identification. In *ESCA*, pages 51–54, 1994.
8. R. Brunelli and D. Falavigna. Person identification using multiple cues. *IEEE Transactions on Pattern Analysis and Machine Intelligence*, 17(10):955–966, October 1995.
9. P. J. Burt. Fast filter transforms for image processing. *Computer Graphics and Image Processing*, 16:20–51, 1981.
10. J. G. Daugman. Complete discrete 2-d Gabor transforms by neural networks for image analysis and compression. *IEEE Transactions on Acoustics, Speech, and Signal Processing*, 36(7):1169–1179, July 1988.
11. P.A. Devijver and J. Kittler. *Pattern Recognition: a Statistical Approach*. Prentice-Hall International, London, 1982.
12. U. Dieckmann, P. Plankensteiner, R. Schamburger, B. Froeba, and S. Meller. SESAM: A biometric person identification system using sensor fusion. In J. Bigun, G. Chollet, and G. Borgefors, editors, *Audio and Video based Person Authentication - AVBPA97*, volume LNCS-1206, pages 301–310. IAPR, Springer, 1997.
13. B. Duc, G. Maître, S. Fischer, and J. Bigün. Person authentication by fusing face and speech information. In J. Bigün, G. Chollet, and G. Borgefors, editors, *First International Conference on Audio- and Video-based Biometric Person Authentication (AVBPA '97)*, volume 1206 of *LNCS*, pages 311–318, Crans-Montana, Switzerland, March 12-14 1997. Springer.
14. B. Duc, G. Maître, S. Fischer, and J. Bigun. Person authentication by fusing face and speech information. In J. Bigun, G. Chollet, and G. Borgefors, editors, *Audio and Video based Person Authentication - AVBPA97*, volume LNCS-1206, pages 311–318. IAPR, Springer, 1997.

15. F. Dufaux and F. Moscheni. Motion estimation techniques for digital TV: A review and a new contribution. *IEEE Proceedings*, 83(6):858–876, June 1995.

16. B. Efron and R. J. Tibshirani. *An introduction to the Bootstrap*. Chapman & Hall, New York, 1993.

17. S. Furui. Cepstral analysis technique for automatic speaker verification. *IEEE Trans. Acoust. Speech, Signal Processing*, 29(2):254–272, 1981.

18. D. Genoud, F. Bimbot, G. Gravier, and G. Chollet. Combining methods to improve speaker verification decision. In *Proceedings of The Fourth International Conference on Spoken Language Processing*, Philadelphia, October 3-6 1996. ICSLP.

19. P. Jourlin, J. Luettin, D. Genoud, and H. Wassner. Acoustic-labial speaker verification. In J. Bigun, G. Chollet, and G. Borgefors, editors, *Audio and Video based Person Authentication - AVBPA97*, volume LNCS-1206, pages 319–326. IAPR, Springer, 1997.

20. M. Lades, J. Buhmann J. C. Vorbrüggen, J. Lange, C. v.d. Malsburg, R. P. Würtz, and W. Konen. Distortion invariant object recognition in the dynamic link architecture. *IEEE Transactions on Computers*, 42(3):300–311, March 1993.

21. S. Pigeon and L. Vandendorpe. The M2VTS multi modal face database (release 1.0). In J. Bigun, G. Chollet, and G. Borgefors, editors, *Audio and Video based Person Authentication - AVBPA97*, pages 403–409. Springer, 1997.

22. L. R. Rabiner. A tutorial on hidden markov models and selected applications in speech recogniton. *Proceedings of the IEEE*, 77(2):257–286, 1989.

23. A. E. Rosenberg, C. H. Lee, and S. Gokon. Connected word talker verification using whole word hidden Markov model. In *ICASSP*, pages 381–384, 1991.

24. H. Sakoe and Chiba. Dynamic programing algorithm optimization for spoken word recognition. *IEEE Trans. Acoust. Speech, Signal Processing*, 26(1):43–49, 1978.

Human Face Perception and Identification

Vicki Bruce[1], Peter J.B. Hancock[1] and A. Mike Burton[2]

[1] Department of Psychology, University of Stirling, Stirling, Scotland, FK9 4LA.
[2] Department of Psychology, University of Glasgow, Glasgow, G12 8QB.

Abstract. This chapter reviews factors which affect the perception and recognition of faces by humans, in order to describe those characteristics that must be exhibited by any computational or engineering system which claims psychological or neurobiological plausibility. Effects of photographic negation and the difficulty of recognising line-drawings suggest that the representations mediating human face recognition are based upon image-features rather than on more abstract derived measurements of face features. However, to understand which image-based coding scheme has most psychological plausibility requires that different models are compared against human similarity ratings and memory performance data using the same face images. Some recent investigations of pixel-based PCA and wavelet-based graph-matching models are briefly discussed.

Keywords. Face perception, psychology, neuropsychology, negation and inversion of faces, effects of movement on face recognition, viewpoint specificity, configuration, Principal Components Analysis, Interactive Activation and Competition

1 Introduction

Engineers and computer scientists may develop face processing systems for a number of reasons. Sometimes a particular tool is needed for a specific application - e.g. a gaze- or eye-blink monitoring device. There is no necessary link between the development of such systems and an understanding of how humans perceive gaze. At other times, however, engineers may be trying to solve a difficult image-processing problem which the human brain appears to solve effortlessly, and here it can be instructive to consider natural image-processing mechanisms - and their limitations. Things may be claimed of human vision which are not true - for example humans are not good at recognising faces in novel viewpoints after viewing a single different viewpoint. Moreover, there is a tendency to view any computer model of face recognition, particularly if it incorporates neurone-like units, as a plausible model of the human face recognition system. Such models may be good at the jobs for which they were designed, but to be good candidate theories of human face processing they must be tested against relevant psychophysical data. In this chapter we will review psychological evidence about how humans perceive, encode and identify faces, and consider what constraints this evidence places upon computational models of face processing which claim psychological (or biological) plausibility.

2 Neuropsychological observations

Neuropsychological observations, together with psychological experiments, suggest that the human brain processes faces via a number of functionally independent information processing channels. There is very strong evidence that facial expressions and identities are analysed by distinct processing routes, and reasonably strong evidence for a separation in processes used to match unfamiliar faces from those involved in identifying familiar ones. For example, Young et al (1993) examined face processing abilities in a number of patients with focal brain injuries compared with uninjured controls. The different abilities tested were recognising familiar faces, matching unfamiliar faces and recognising expressions. Each of these abilities was tested by two different tasks, and Young et al concluded that a patient had a deficit in a particular ability only if they were statistically inferior to controls on both the tests of this ability. Using this stringent criterion, Young et al were able to identify different individual patients with discrete deficits. For example, one patient was poor at both tests of familiar face recognition, but normal on all tests of unfamiliar face matching and face expression processing. A second patient was poor at both tests of unfamiliar face matching but normal at familiar face identification and at face expression processing. Several patients were poor at expressions but normal at recognising and matching familiar and unfamiliar faces. These data indicate *double dissociations* between different face processing abilities. When one patient or group of patients is found to be normal at one task but impaired at another, and another patient shows the opposite pattern, this gives strong evidence for functional separation of the two abilities. These neuropsychological observations have also been supported by neuro-imaging results (Sergent et al, 1994) and by analysis of the functional specialisation of single cells in the macaque temporal lobe. Of those cells responsive to faces, some show additional specialisation for particular identities and others show specialisation for emotional expressions, but these different types of cells are found in distinct areas (for reviews see Gross, 1992; Heywood & Cowey, 1992; Perrett et al, 1992; Rolls, 1992).

As well as functional specialisation within the mature brain, there is also developmental evidence that humans may be born with some predisposition to respond to face-like patterns. Goren, Sarty and Wu (1975) and more recently Johnson et al (1991) found that new-born babies will follow a face-like pattern with head and eye movements further than they track control patterns with similar visual characteristics to faces.

Such observations have led people to suggest that faces are "special" objects in the visual world of the human. However, demonstrations of functional specialisation do not necessarily indicate that the processes of face recognition differ fundamentally from those used to recognise other kinds of object. After all, there is strong evidence for functional specialisation of visual word recognition in humans, with brain damage often resulting in different types of acquired dyslexia (e.g. see Coltheart et al, 1980; Patterson et al, 1985), but it would be absurd to suggest that printed words have a special neurological status over and above that which derives from their sheer importance in the life of every educated individual.

Neuropsychological investigations therefore indicate clearly that the brain seems to parcel out the tasks of interpreting faces in different ways to functionally distinct neurological pathways. This makes sense when different face processing tasks make differing representational demands. The representational demands of processing identities and expressions are readily separable. Identity processing requires that different expressive postures of a face are ignored, so that a person's face can be recognised whatever their expression. In contrast, emotional expressions need to be identifiable independent of the particular individual mouths or brows which enter into these expressions. However, the neuropsychological distinction between unfamiliar and familiar face processing is much more surprising and is instructive, suggesting that we must be careful about which experimental tasks that are used to draw conclusions about the representational processes of face recognition. Tasks of unfamiliar face matching or memory will not necessarily inform us about more durable face representations (see Bruce & Young, 1986, for further discussion).

3 Representations for face recognition: Importance of image-features

Representations for face recognition appear to be based upon the encoding of relatively low-level image features. The evidence for this includes the dramatic effects of transforming faces into photographic negative; the poor recognition of simple line-drawings of faces unless these include some information about areas of relative light and dark; and the effects of changes in lighting on matching faces for identity. It seems that relative lightness and darkness of areas of the face are important for accessing human face representations. Recent studies have attempted to tease out the relative importance of information about pigmentation (light vs dark hair or skin) and shading.

3.1. Effects of photographic negation

It has long been observed informally that photographic negatives of faces are difficult to recognise, and Galper (1970) produced an early published study of this effect. However, relatively little work has explored why it is so difficult to recognise negated images of faces. After all, a negative image contains the same range of brightnesses, and (plausibly) the same information about edges or other important features defined by luminance gradients. Thus the sizes, shapes and arrangements of face features such as the eyes and the nose should be reasonably easy to retrieve from negatives.

The effects of negation are dramatic. Bruce and Langton (1994) asked students to attempt identification of a set of celebrity faces from a list of supplied names, and presented the faces either upright positive, upright negative or inverted positive and negative. In this study effects of negation reduced identification rates by 40%, exceeding those of inversion, which reduced identification rates by 25% (see Section 4.1). The combined effects of the two manipulations were approximately additive, reducing identification performance from 95% in the upright, positive condition to a mere 25% in the inverted, negated condition. This additivity of effects suggests that each of these manipulations may impair a different aspect of face representation.

Phillips (1972) showed that the detrimental effects of negation do not depend on there being a gradation of grey-scales in the original image. When faces were reduced to black-on-white "lith" (thresholded) images, effects of negation were still profound. This line of research was pursued by Hayes and colleagues (Hayes et al, 1986; Hayes, 1988), who showed that black-on-white images of faces *could* be immune from negation, but only if these images were produced as a result of high pass spatial filtering. Thus the recognition of an outline black-on-white drawing of a face is not impaired by negation, but a black-on-white thresholded image of a face is badly affected. This result is itself important in indicating that reversing polarity *per se* does not create the problem, it is the reversal of polarity specifically of the relatively low spatial frequency information within faces that is problematic.

So, negative images of faces are difficult to recognise, and these difficulties result from the alteration of the relative brightnesses within the lower, but not the higher, spatial frequency components of face images. Other evidence also suggests that face recognition depends rather more on relatively low than relatively high spatial frequencies (e.g. see Costen et al, 1996, for one recent study). Effects of negation suggest that representations for face recognition in some way preserve or rely upon the preservation of relative brightness levels in the original image, but in a rather crude way as preserved in thresholded images.

3.2. Line-drawings and face recognition

The classification of most visual objects into basic categories such as "dog" vs "cat" or "car" vs "truck" can be performed as well with line-drawings as with full grey-scale or coloured images. It is only when discriminations must be made between objects with very similar overall shapes that other information about surface colour or texture appears useful (see Bruce and Humphreys, 1994). In contrast, face recognition is poor when only simple line drawings are available. Davies, Ellis and Shepherd (1978) showed that the spatial layout of face features depicted by line drawings was not very informative for face recognition. When careful tracings were made of the facial features of a number of famous faces, performance dropped from 90% correct identification in the original images to only 47% with the detailed line drawings. It may be because of the poverty of representation afforded by a simple line drawing that caricature can exert such noticeable effects on identification (Rhodes, Brennan and Carey, 1987). As images of faces become more veridical, the effects of caricaturing are much more subtle and difficult to detect (e.g. Benson & Perrett, 1991).

Pearson and Robinson (1985) experimented with different kinds of line-drawing of faces in their search for ways of compressing full images of moving faces and hands for transmission of deaf sign-language over limited bandwidth phone lines. They found that the addition of a threshold component to blacken in dark areas from the original gave line drawings of faces a better aesthetic appeal. We (Bruce et al, 1992) were able to show that this use of thresholding did indeed enhance these representations for person identification. We compared computer-drawn faces within which just the edges of features were sketched (using the Pearson and Robinson "valledge" detector), with those which just showed areas of light and dark (via thresholding), and these two conditions were each compared with the "full cartoon" condition where the two operations of valledge and threshold were combined. Edges alone gave the worst recognition performance, followed by threshold alone. Full cartoons were recognised almost as well as the original photographs of the celebrities. Thus compression of a grey-scale to a one-bit-per-pixel image can yield remarkably recognisable representations, provided the right "bits" are there.

While compressing a photographic image into a one-bit-per pixel drawing yields an image which is highly recognisable, human face recognition also seems to be sensitive to manipulations of the precise format of the image itself. Bruce et al (1994) showed that repetition priming - the savings in recognition speed found following an earlier presentation of the item - was much reduced when a photographic image was followed by a line-drawn cartoon, or vice-versa, compared with standard repetition priming conditions where format is maintained between the first and second presentation.

3.3. Effects of lighting change on face recognition

Johnston, Hill and Carmen (1992) explored whether difficulties with negative images of faces, and inverted images of faces, arose because each of these manipulations reverses the apparent direction of lighting, rendering a top-lit image of a face apparently lit from below. They were able to demonstrate that bottom lighting does indeed make it harder to identify familiar faces, and that effects of inversion and of negation are somewhat moderated if lighting direction is reversed. So, a bottom-lit picture of a familiar face does not suffer as much when it is inverted or negated as does one which is lit from above.

Hill and Bruce (1996) demonstrated the importance of top-lighting for face recognition using a different task of matching surface images of faces for identity (Fig. 1 shows an example of a surface image). On each trial in their studies, two faces were shown and the task was to decide whether they showed the same or different identities. Faces were shown for as long as it took participants to respond, so there was plenty of opportunity for careful scrutiny of each pair of images. The two displayed faces could show the same or different viewpoints, and the same or different directions of lighting. Hill and Bruce showed that matching of two images, even when these showed identical viewpoints, was made much more difficult when lighting directions differed. Moreover, matching across viewpoint was very much more successful when lighting was from above rather than from below. Similar effects were shown when photographs of real faces rather than surface images were used in these experiments. Again, these studies point out the importance of brightness values for face representation and recognition.

3.4. Hue, lightness and negation

Bruce and Langton (1994) investigated whether problems with photographic negatives arose because these inverted luminance values of shaded regions, hence disrupting normal shape-from-shading processes, or whether it was the inversion of luminance in pigmented regions such as hair and eyebrows which created the problem. In a negative image, a dark-haired person with light skin becomes a dark-skinned person with light hair, and this might effectively disguise identity. To examine this, Bruce and Langton investigated identification rates of 3D surface images of faces displayed by projecting a lighting model on to a faceted model of the 3D co-ordinates of a face surface obtained by laser-scanning (cf. Bruce et al, 1991; Hill, Schyns & Akamatsu, 1997, and several contributions to this volume). These images are interesting to use here, since they have no pigmented surface areas, and the contribution of 2D and 3D shape to recognition can be explored in isolation. Negating images of faces displayed in this way had no statistically significant effect on identification of the surface images, suggesting that the contribution of 3D shape-from-shading, which should have been disrupted when these surface images were negated, was relatively minor.

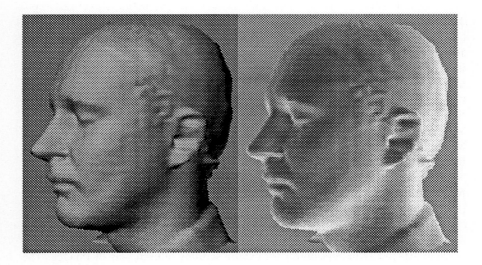

Fig. 1. Example of 3D surface image in positive and negative.

However, although Bruce and Langton argued that it was the effects of negation on pigmented areas that mediated identification performance deficits, it is clearly not pigmentation *per se* which matters. Kemp et al (1996) demonstrated this very convincingly by separating out hue from luminance in negative images. They were able to produce images of faces within which either hue values or lightness values or both were independently negated. Identification of familiar faces was impaired only when lightness was negated, but was unaffected by hue negation. Interestingly, however, recognition memory for pictures of faces was affected by both forms of negation, suggesting that pictorial memories, but not the representations which allow recognition of familiar faces, are sensitive to variations in colour. However, in recent unpublished studies in Stirling, where participants are asked simply to indicate which face from a small array matches a target displayed simultaneously, we have found that matching unfamiliar faces is relatively unaffected by whether the target or array faces are in shown in colour or grey-scale, or by whether the target is shown in colour and the array in grey-scale and vice-versa. In our studies, target and array faces are drawn from different media (video vs photographs) which show subtle variations in recorded colour and brightness. Our studies along with those of Kemp et al suggest that, unless colours match perfectly, even picture memory is relatively insensitive to hue.

Kemp and colleagues concluded that it is the disruptive effects of negation on shape-from-shading processes which are most important in reducing identification of such images, but we believe these conclusions may be premature. Clearly the effects arise from luminance and not hue, but it could still be that it is the luminance of the pigmented regions rather than shading patterns that matters.

There is possibly a third reason why negative images are so hard to recognise, and this is because of the effects of negation on eyes. Negative images make pupils light and sclera dark, and this could disrupt face processing in various ways if, for example, the eyes are an important key to alignment of face images. However, negative images of faces are difficult to process even when the eyes are shown closed (Bruce et al, 1993), so this cannot be the major reason why negative images pose such problems.

3.5. Movement and face recognition

The human face is highly mobile, and both rigid (head-nodding or shaking) and non-rigid (expressive) movements convey information which is important for interpersonal communication. However, the question of the role played by rigid and non-rigid motion in the recognition of faces has been researched rather little. Knight and Johnston (1997) have recently published an intriguing study which shows that famous faces made difficult to recognise by negation are easier to recognise when shown in moving sequences than still photographs. We (Lander, Christie and Bruce, submitted) have extended this observation to show that movement helps the recognition of familiar faces shown in a range of different types of degradation - whether negated, inverted or shown in threshold (black on white) images only.

One reason   why a moving image might preferentially access stored representations of faces is that it contains additional information about a range of different viewpoints and expressions in the multiple frames present in any moving sequence. However, Lander et al (submitted) have shown rather convincingly that there is a benefit for movement even if the information content is equated in the moving and static comparison conditions, suggesting that it may genuinely be an effect of the dynamic characteristics of moving images which helps to access representations of face identities.

This benefit of movement seems to arise when face identities are probed, but does not necessarily mean that movement will help in the building up of face representations. Our own research using unfamiliar faces (Christie and Bruce, 1998) suggests no additional benefit for viewing animated rather than static sequences when the task is to recognise previously unfamiliar faces. In these studies, participants were tested for recognition memory of a small number of target faces. Target faces were studied either in short, animated sequences of a small number of frames cycling through expressive or rigid head movements (e.g. frame 12345, 12345, etc.) , or each of the same frames was studied for the same total amount of time, but not animated (e.g. frame 11111, 44444, etc.). Under these conditions, there was no significant advantage of the animated condition for recognising faces later tested in the same or different views from those studied. This contrasts with data reported by Hill et al (1997) who showed that animating sequences of viewpoints of surface images of heads (see Fig. 1, left image) did enhance immediate recognition memory performance. The discrepancy may arise because structure-from-motion may be more important for surface images lacking pigmented features, than for images of real heads whose pigmented features may form an important component of their representation.

It is possible that explorations using a richer repertoire of movements in such face learning studies would yield clearer benefits of movement at study, but for now our conclusion is that movement does not provide information useful for building representations, but can help to access them. While this seems somewhat paradoxical, one possibility is that prolonged acquaintance with familiar faces results in the storage of characteristic gestures of these faces alongside static image-based representations. It may be that professional impersonators are able to do their job by mimicking such characteristic movements to provide a cue for identification even though other aspects of their faces do not match those of the celebrities that they are impersonating. Another possibility is that a dynamic test image provides movement trajectories which allow access to more deviant static view-based exemplars than can be contacted with static test images. Current work in our laboratory is investigating whether or not the advantages of moving test images depend upon the preservation of precise temporal information.

4. Configural processing of faces

Another difference between the recognition of faces and of other objects (at least at basic level, see Bruce & Humphreys, 1994) is that face processing also appears to involve "configural" or "holistic" processing more than (most) other object classes. The strongest evidence comes from studies of the face inversion effect, and in this part of the chapter we review a number of recent studies of the inversion effect and consider what these have, and have not, revealed about the representation of faces by humans.

4.1. Face inversion effect

Most things get harder to recognise when they are turned upside down, but Yin (1969) first demonstrated that faces get disproportionately difficult to recognise compared with other "mono-oriented" objects. He compared recognition of upright and inverted faces, houses, and human figures in motion, and found that the faces were best recognised when upright but suffered more through inversion than other classes of item. This basic effect has been replicated and extended by numerous other workers (see review by Valentine, 1988). Recent work suggests that faces suffer through inversion because of the specific disruption of the processing of information about the configuration of the face.

4.2. Evidence for configural processing of faces

One elegant demonstration of the effect of inversion on face processing was Young et al's (1987) use of the face composite effect. They showed that when the upper and lower halves of different faces were aligned, the individual identities of the two halves were extremely difficult to perceive. The half-faces were much more readily identified when each was presented separately, or when the two halves of the composite were off-set so that the face outline of the composite was disrupted. However this aligned composite effect was only observed when the composites were shown upright. The identities of the half faces were much easier to see when the composites were inverted. This effect can be explained if the individual features of each individual half face can be more readily perceived in the inverted composite because the overall configuration is harder to see. Presented upright, the configural relationships between the features from the two halves of the composite can not be ignored.

Bartlett and Searcy (1993) made innovative use of Thompson's (1980) "Thatcher illusion". In the Thatcher illusion, eyes and mouth of an expressing face are excised and inverted (Thompson used Margaret Thatcher's face to illustrate the effect, but any expressive face can be used). The result looks grotesque in an upright face, as can be seen in the right hand side of Fig. 2. When shown inverted, however, the face looks fairly normal in appearance, and the violation of the internal features is not readily noticed. This is seen clearly in the left hand image of Fig. 2, where a naive reader may assume that the image shows a normal picture of Thatcher upside-down. In fact this is the same image as that shown at the left, as can be readily confirmed by inverting the page. One explanation of this effect is that the spatial relationships between the different features are less evident in the inverted face, and so the lack of correspondence between the orientation of the eyes and the mouth and that of the other features such as the nose cannot be seen.

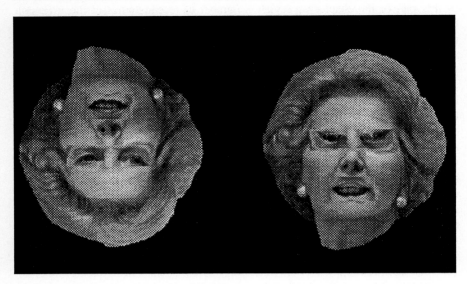

Fig. 2. The Thatcher Illusion (after Thompson, 1980)

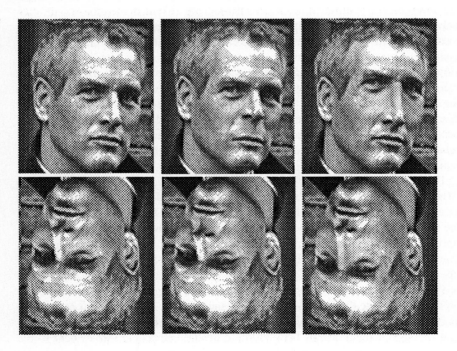

Fig. 3. Changes to configuration are much more visible in upright faces.

Bartlett and Searcy (1993; Searcy & Bartlett, 1996) used rated grotesqueness as their dependent measure in experiments where effects of "Thatcherising" faces, and other kinds of manipulation made to face features, were compared. For Thatcherised faces, and for faces whose grotesqueness was produced by moving features apart or nearer together (see Fig.3), grotesqueness was virtually eliminated when the face was inverted. However, when faces were made grotesque by making changes to local features such as making vampire teeth, orientation made little difference to the impression created by the face.

4.3. What is meant by "configural"?

The demonstrations described above clearly indicate that faces are not stored simply as discrete lists of independent features, but it is not very clear what is meant by the term "configuration". A number of possibilities have been explored in the literature. The clearest distinction is between configuration meaning the encoding of explicit spatial relationships between face features, and configuration meaning holistic processing without decomposition into face features at all. The former position was most clearly articulated by Diamond and Carey (1986) who argued that faces are distinguished one from another on the basis of second-order spatial relationships between their features. All faces share the same first order arrangement of eyes above nose above mouth, but second-order variations in this arrangement specify the differences between individual faces. If face recognition encodes the spatial arrangement of face features explicitly, then we see that Fig. 3 would produce three different specifications of the distance between eyes, nose and mouth. Only one of these matches the stored description of Paul Newman's face, and hence the manipulated versions are harder to recognise than the original on the left. In contrast, the holistic processing account (e.g. see Tanaka and Farah, 1993) suggests that face patterns are not decomposed into discrete features at all, and that effects of configuration arise because changing spatial relationships (as in Fig. 3) distorts the whole face pattern.

It can be extremely difficult to distinguish these two interpretations of the term "configuration" empirically, particularly since most manipulations that can be made to faces confound the spatial relationships between face features with the holistic patterns shown by these arrangements of features, and each of these types of information is usually also confounded with local feature information. Thus, for example, if a face is shown with a stretched nose, as in the right hand panel of Fig. 3, this changes spatial relationships (the distance between nose and mouth, etc.) and the whole face pattern, and it also changes the specification of a local face feature too, since the new nose is a different type of nose to the original. Nonetheless, in recent collaborative work between Fribourg and Stirling (Leder & Bruce, 1997a, 1997b), we have made some progress at exploring these issues and have provided firm evidence for the inversion effect arising as a result of the specific disruption of the processing of spatial relationships in inverted faces. Helmut Leder summarises some of these recent findings in his contribution to this volume.

5. Representation of faces in memory

5.1. View specificity

Much work in visual object recognition (e.g. Biederman, 1987) has been cast within a theoretical framework introduced by Marr (1982, Marr & Nishihara, 1978), in which different views of objects are analysed in a way which allows access of (largely) viewpoint-invariant descriptions. Recently, however, there has been some debate about whether object recognition is viewpoint-invariant or not (Tarr & Bulthoff, 1995). In face recognition it seems clear that memory is highly viewpoint-dependent. Bruce (1982), for example, showed that recognition memory for faces drops dramatically if viewpoint and/or expression is changed between study and test, even though the set of items shown had clearly visible extraneous features such as distinctive hairstyles and visible clothing that might have acted to aid viewpoint-invariance. Hill et al (1997) showed that generalisation even from one profile viewpoint to another was poor, though generalisation from one 3/4 view to the other was very good. Current unpublished findings in our laboratory show that simultaneous face matching suffers significantly even when the two viewpoints to be matched differ by only 30 degrees. Such findings suggest that human face representations are either viewpoint-specific, or based around a number of discrete canonical views.

Of course views of faces vary not just as a result of rigid head rotations but also through non-rigid expressive and other changes. Bruce and Young (1986) proposed that face representations were viewpoint-dependent but expression-independent. One idea would be that, at each of a number of discrete views, there is a stored representation of the prototype or "average" of that face over a number of different expressions (see Bruce, 1994, and Cabeza et al, 1998 for some experimental evidence for this suggestion).

5.2. Distinctiveness and caricature

Faces are represented in human memory in a way which gives rise to face distinctiveness effects. Unfamiliar faces which are rated as being distinctive in appearance are better-remembered than those rated as more typical (e.g. Light et al, 1979). More distinctive faces give rise to higher hit rates, and more typical faces give rise to higher false positive rates. Highly familiar (famous) faces also give rise to distinctiveness effects, with distinctive items identified more quickly than typical ones (e.g. Valentine & Bruce, 1986). So, for example, Bill Clinton's face, which is fairly typical in appearance would be recognised more slowly than Ronald Reagan's, which is rather more unusual in appearance. However, if the task requires that people decide whether each item is a face or a non-face (non-faces show face features rearranged, so that mouth is above nose, for example) then the advantage is found for the more typical items (Valentine & Bruce, 1986). Valentine (1991) describes how these different patterns might be explained by appealing to a "space" of face representations within which typical items are clustered more closely together. It has proved rather difficult to get beyond such a descriptive framework and to understand the representational basis of such distinctiveness effects, but recent work described in section 6 has shown how such effects can be attributed to physical features of face images (see also Bruce et al, 1994).

The distinctiveness of faces can be enhanced by caricaturing them. Both automatic and artist's caricatures exaggerate the way that an individual face deviates from the norm or average face. Line-drawings of famous faces, which are extremely difficult to recognise unless enhanced with areas of dark and light, can become effective representations when caricatured (Rhodes et al, 1987). There are even some slight advantages found for caricaturing photographs of faces (Benson & Perrett, 1991), thus it is possible to produce a distorted (caricatured) photograph of someone which is seen as being a better likeness of them than their actual face. Rhodes (1997) provides an interesting review of caricatures and the possible bases of such effects.

To be a good candidate model for human face perception and memory, a computer model should naturally generate these distinctiveness effects which are a feature of human memory. Moreover, when evaluating computer models against human performance, ideally a computer system should find the same faces, or images of faces, distinctive, as do humans.

6. Models of face representation

The review above has suggested that to have any psychological plausibility, a computational model of face recognition should build representations on the basis of relatively low-level image features, so that, like people, the systems would suffer when faces were negated or when lighting conditions were altered from those previously associated with this face. Moreover, any computer system claiming that its methods have psychological plausibility should naturally give rise to effects of distinctiveness and similarity which closely resemble those seen by humans.

6.1. Principal Components Analysis

One method of coding faces which has attracted interest from psychologists (e.g. Abdi et al, 1995; O'Toole et al, 1991, 1994; Hancock et al, 1995, 1996, 1998) as well as from computer scientists (Sirovich & Kirby, 1987; Turk & Pentland, 1991) involves the analysis of patterns of correlation between the pixel intensities (though other inputs could be used) of a large number of individual faces, and extracting the Principal Components of this variation. A number of other papers in this volume describe this method and its application, so we will not elaborate here. Briefly, the PCA approach suggests that individual faces may be represented as the weighted sum of a set of "eigenfaces", with the lower-order eigenfaces capturing major dimensions of variation between the set of faces used to establish the components. For example, masculinity/femininity may emerge as a key property of a lower-order eigenface when the coded set contains both male and female faces (Abdi et al, 1995). Higher-order components capture more idiosyncratic variations.

Using this representation, O'Toole and her colleagues have found strong correlations between human discrimination of faces in recognition memory tasks (as measured by d') and the discrimination of the same set of faces coded by PCA. Moreover, they (O'Toole et al, 1991, 1994) have demonstrated that this approach naturally gives rise to the "cross-race" effect, where participants from one racial group (e.g. Caucasian Americans) find it harder to recognise faces from a different racial group (e.g. Japanese) and vice versa. They have shown that when the faces in the group used to extract the components (eigenfaces) are mostly of one racial type, then the coding system developed does not do a good job of coding faces from another racial group whose visual characteristics are rather different.

However, one problem with the PCA approach is that it makes sense only if the different faces to be coded are carefully aligned (see Craw, this volume). If faces are all aligned to a common shape, then the PCA of their texture components can be analysed separately from that of the shape vector needed to restore their original shapes. Hancock, Burton and Bruce (1996) showed that separating out shape and texture vectors in this way somewhat improved the correlations between human and computer recognition of the faces. Of more interest was the additional observation that the shape-free faces (texture vectors) gave a particularly good account of faces to which false positive errors were made. Most of this correlation came from just the first component, suggesting that PCA might usefully capture something of the way we respond to faces.

6.2. Comparisons with other models

While the PCA approach yields some interesting correlations with human face memory, the analysis of image features at the level of pixels lacks some basic neuropsychological plausibility. It is of course perfectly possible to extend the PCA approach to the analysis of image features extracted at different spatial scales by Gabor or other filtering operations, and Hancock, Burton & Bruce, (1995) described an initial exploration. This revealed that coarse spatial scales carry information about distinctiveness, while fine spatial scales correlate with false positive scores. The distinctiveness result is readily explicable in terms of hair and gross shape information, both of which will survive coarse scale filtration. Wild hair or a particularly strange shaped face will be regarded as distinctive. Why fine scale information should correlate with false positive scores is less easily explained, and further work is needed to pursue this rather curious result.

It is also important to explore whether other systems based upon the analysis of low-level image features could explain human performance as well, or even better, than PCA. In recent work in our lab, we (Hancock, Bruce and Burton, 1998) have compared how well PCA (based on analysis of image pixels) compares with the wavelet-based graph-matching system developed at Bochum and USC by Von der Malsburg and colleagues (see Malsburg, this volume, for details). Note that it is not a comparison of equals: the PCA system is entirely descriptive, simply recoding the input, while the graph-matching system explicitly codes relationships between its low-level image descriptors.

We tested our human participants for the ability to recognise both the same image of a target and a different one. Recognising the same image permits picture, rather than face recognition. Both computer systems showed significant correlations with human memory scores when the latter were doing the picture matching task, but only the graph-matching system correlated with the human face matching scores obtained when pictures differed between study and test. The systems were equally good at predicting human distinctiveness ratings. We interpret this as evidence that the PCA system is more image-based, capturing aspects of a picture that may make it distinctive and therefore easy to recognise, while the graph-matching system provides a better account of face recognition.

We also asked participants to perform similarity judgements on the faces, with and without hair. Both computer systems gave low but significant correlations with human similarity ratings. However when hair was absent, the PCA system showed much lower correlations while the graph-matching system was almost unaffected. The graph-matching system is designed to concentrate on the inner facial features, while the PCA system weights the whole image equally.

On both counts, the graph-matching system gives a better account of face processing, while the PCA system is doing something more like image analysis. However, other work in progress at Stirling is indicating just how bad people actually are at face recognition if the images differ in quality. PCA may therefore give rather a good account of human abilities at unfamiliar face recognition, which seems to be dominated by pictorial details, while the graph-matching system is closer to our abilities at recognising familiar faces, which relies more on inner features and less on external ones such as hair and spectacles.

6.3. Drawbacks of these approaches

Although our initial comparisons between these image-processing models and human representation of faces yield interesting and promising findings, there remain some problems in accepting that either of the candidate approaches that we have explored captures enough of human performance. Examples of discrepancies between the approaches are numerous. For example, it is not clear that the graph-matching model readily accounts for the phenomenal difficulty experienced by humans viewing negative images, while the PCA systems, on the other hand, could not easily explain how any negative faces at all could be recognised. Second, while certain transformations such as changes in lighting will both humans and these computer models, other kinds of changes, such as local highlights on a face, are easy for human vision to ignore but can have dramatic effects on the computer model (Von der Malsburg, personal communication). One example from our own laboratory is described in Hancock et al (1998). We could not understand why one of our face images was repeatedly missed by the PCA implementation until we discovered that this image had been unwittingly mirror-reversed. This was virtually unnoticeable to the human eye, but, presumably because of the reversal in some rather subtle brightness gradient across the pixels, had a fatal effect on the pixel-sensitive PCA model.

Further problems are that - while each of the candidate image-processing models in some sense processes the face "holistically" - it is not clear that either of them allow the explicit representation of the spatial relationships between face features that seem to play such an important role in human face representation (see Leder, and Bruce, this volume). Moreover, while each of the models we have tested produces reasonable correlations with human judgements of distinctiveness and similarity, the numerical size of these correlations is not great. It is possible that human face representations use multiple descriptions, derived and stored at different spatial scales, and perhaps using different kinds of representational primitives. There is a good deal of further work to be done before we will be satisfied that we have an adequate account of the details of human face representation.

6.4. From perception to cognition

All the above work helps to constrain a model of the "front" end of the human face recognition system. In our laboratories at Stirling and Glasgow we have been modelling this front end with a Principal Components Analysis (PCA) of face images, in which "shape-free" images (after morphing to a common face shape) and shape components (the deviation from the common face shape) are separated. However, human face recognition usually involves more than a decision that a face is familiar or unfamiliar - we are able to retrieve knowledge of a person's identity, occupation and so forth for those faces that we recognise. These later stages of person identification have been modelled successfully in recent years using a simple interactive activation (IAC) architecture (Burton et al, 1990, 1991; Burton & Bruce, 1992, 1993; Bruce et al, 1992; Burton 1994). In our recent work we have developed a complete model of face recognition by combining a PCA-based front end with the IAC back end (Burton et al, submitted). This complete model will allow us to explore effects which emerge from this interface of perception (visually-based effects) with cognition (memory-based effects), and which cannot be fully understood by a focus on perception alone.

References

Abdi, H., Valentin, D., Edelman, B. & O'Toole, A.J. (1995). More about the difference between men and women: evidence from linear neural network and principal component approach. *Perception, 24,* 539-562.

Bartlett, J.C. & Searcy, J. (1993). Inversion and configuration of faces. *Cognitive Psychology, 25,* 281-316.

Benson, P.J. & Perrett, D.I. (1991). Perception and recognition of photographic quality facial caricatures: implications for the recognition of natural images. *European Journal of Cognitive Psychology, 3*, 105-135.

Biederman, I (1987). Recognition by components: a theory of human image understanding. *Psychological Review, 94*, 115-147.

Bruce, V. (1982). Changing faces: Visual and non-visual coding processes in face recognition. *British Journal of Psychology, 73*, 105-116.

Bruce, V. (1994). Stability from variation: the case of face recognition. *Quarterly Journal of Experimental Psychology, 47A*, 5-28.

Bruce, V., Burton, A.M. & Craw, I. (1992) Modelling face recognition. *Philosophical Transactions of the Royal Society, B335*, 121-128.

Bruce, V, Burton, A.M., Carson, D., Hanna, E. & Mason, O. (1994). Repetition priming of face recognition. *Attention and Performance XV, 15*, 179-201.

Bruce, V., Burton, A.M. & Dench, N. (1994). What's distinctive about a distinctive face? *Quarterly Journal of Experimental Psychology, 47A*, 119-142.

Bruce, V., Burton, A.M., Hanna, E., Healey, P., Mason, O., Coombes, A., Fright, R. & Linney, A. (1993). Sex discrimination: how do we tell the difference between male and female faces? *Perception, 22*, 131-152.

Bruce, V., Hanna, E., Dench, N., Healy, P., & Burton, A.M. (1992). The importance of "mass" in line drawings of faces. *Applied Cognitive Psychology, 6*, 619-628.

Bruce, V., Healey, P., Burton, M., Doyle, T., Coombes, A. & Linney, A. (1991). Recognising facial surfaces. *Perception, 20*, 755-769.

Bruce, V. & Humphreys, G.W. (1994). Recognising objects and faces. *Visual Cognition, 1*, 141-180.

Bruce, V. & Langton, S (1994). The use of pigmentation and shading information in recognising the sex and identities of faces. *Perception, 23*, 803-822.

Bruce, V., Valentine, T. & Baddeley, A.D. (1987). The basis of the 3/4 view advantage in face recognition. *Applied Cognitive Psychology, 1*, 109-120.

Bruce, V. & Young, A.W. (1986). Understanding face recognition. *British Journal of Psychology, 77*, 305-327.

Burton, A.M., Bruce, V. & Hancock, P.J.B. (1998). From pixels to people: a model of familiar face recognition. Manuscript submitted for publication.

Burton, A.M., Bruce, V. & Johnston, R.A. (1990) Understanding face recognition with an interactive activation model. *British Journal of Psychology, 81,* 361-380.

Burton, A. M., Young, A.W., Bruce, V., Johnston, R.A. & Ellis, A.W. (1991) Understanding covert recognition. *Cognition, 39,* 129-166.

Burton, A. M. & BRUCE, V. (1992). I recognise your face but I can't remember your name. A simple explanation? *British Journal of Psychology, 83,* 45-60.

Burton, A.M. & BRUCE, V. (1993) Naming faces and naming names. *Memory, 1,* 457-480.

Burton, A.M. (1994). Learning new faces in an interactive activation and competition model. *Visual Cognition, 1,* 313-348.

Cabeza, R., Bruce, V., Kato, T. & Oda, M. (1998). The prototype effect in face recognition: Extension and limits. Manuscript under revision for *Memory & Cognition.*

Christie, F. & Bruce, V. (1997). The role of movement in the recognition of unfamiliar faces. *Memory & Cognition, in press.*

Coltheart, M., Patterson, K.E. & Marshall, J.C. (1980). *Deep Dyslexia.* London: Routledge, Kegan & Paul.

Costen, N.P., Parker, D.M. & Craw, I. (1996). Effects of high-pass and low-pass spatial filtering on face identification. *Perception & Psychophysics, 58,* 602-612.

Davies, G.M., Ellis, H.M. & Shepherd, J.W. (1978). Face recognition accuracy as a function of mode of representation. *Journal of Applied Psychology, 63,* 180-187.

Diamond, R. & Carey, S. (1986). Why faces are and are not special: an effect of expertise. *Journal of Experimental Psychology: General,* 115, 107-117.

Galper, R.E. (1970). Recognition of faces in photographic negative. *Psychonomic Science, 19,* 207-208.

Gross, C.G. (1992) Representation of visual stimuli in inferior temporal cortex, *Philosophical Transactions of the Royal Society of London, B335,* 3-10.

Goren, C.C., Sarty, M. & Wu, P.Y.K. (1975). Visual following and pattern discrimination of face-like stimuli by newborn infants. *Pediatrics, 56,* 544-549.

Hancock, P.J.B., Burton, A.M. & Bruce, V. (1995). Preprocessing images of faces: correlations with human perceptions of distinctiveness and familiarity. *Proceedings of the IEE Fifth International Conference on Image Processing and its Applications*. London: IEE.

Hancock, P.J.B., Burton, A.M. & Bruce, V. (1996). Face processing: human perception and principal components analysis. *Memory & Cognition, 24*, 26-40.

Hancock, P.J., Bruce, V. & Burton, A.M. (1998). A comparison of two computer-based face identification systems with human perceptions of faces. *Vision Research, in press.*

Hayes, A. (1988). Identification of two-tone images: some implications for high- and low-spatial frequency processes in human vision. *Perception, 17*, 429-436.

Hayes, T., Morrone, M.C. & Burr, D.C. (1986). Recognition of positive and negative bandpass-filtered images. *Perception, 15*, 365-375.

Heywood, C.A. & Cowey, A. (1992). The role of the 'face-cell' area in the discrimination and recognition of faces by monkeys. *Philosophical Transactions of the Royal Society of London, B335*, 31-38.

Hill, H. & Bruce, V. (1996). Effects of lighting on matching facial surfaces. *Journal of Experimental Psychology: Human Perception and Performance, 22*, 986-1004.

Hill, H., Schyns, P.G. & Akamatsu, S (1997) Information and viewpoint dependence in face recognition, *Cognition, 62*, 201-222.

Johnson, M.H., Dziurawiec, S., Ellis, H.D. & Morton, J. (1991). Newborns preferential tracking of faces and its subsequent decline. *Cognition, 40*, 1-19.

Johnston, A, Hill, H. & Carman, N. (1992). Recognising faces: effects of lighting direction, inversion and brightness reversal. *Perception, 21*, 365-375.

Kemp, R., Pike, G., White, P. & Musselman, A. (1996). Perception and recognition of normal and negative faces - the role of shape from shading and pigmentation cues. *Perception, 25*, 37-52.

Knight, B. and Johnston, A. (1997). The role of movement in face recognition. *Visual Cognition, 4*, 265-274.

Lander, K., Christie, F., & Bruce, V. (1997) The role of dynamic information in the recognition of famous faces. Manuscript submitted for publication.

Leder, H. & Bruce, V. (1997a). Local and relational aspects of face distinctiveness. *Quarterly Journal of Experimental Psychology, in press.*

Leder, H. & Bruce, V. (1997b). When inverted faces are recognised. Manuscript submitted for publication.

Light, L.L., Kayra-Stuart, F., & Hollander, S. (1979). Recognition memory for typical and unusual faces. *Journal of Experimental Psychology: Human Learning and Memory, 5*, 212-228.

Marr, D. (1982). *Vision: A computational investigation into the human representation and processing of visual information.* San Francisco: Freeman.

Marr, D. & Nishihara, H.K. (1978). Representation and recognition of the spatial organisation of three-dimensional shapes. *Proceedings of the Royal Society of London, B200*, 269-294.

O'Toole, A.J., Abdi, H., Deffenbacher, K.A., Valentin, D. & Bartlett, J.C. (1991). Simulating the "other-race effect" as a problem in perceptual learning. *Connection Science, 3*, 163-178.

O'Toole, A.J., Deffenbacher, K.A., Valentin, D. & Abdi, H. (1994). Structural aspects of face recognition and the other-race effect. *Memory & Cognition, 22*, 208-224.

Patterson, K.E., Marshall, J.C. & Coltheart, M. (1985). *Surface dyslexia: Neuropsychological and cognitive studies of phonological reading.* London: Lawrence Erlbaum Associates Ltd.

Pearson, D.E. & Robinson, J.A. (1985). Visual communication at very low data rates. *Proceedings of the IEEE, 73*, 795-811.

Perrett, D.I., Hietanen, J.K., Oram, M.W. & Benson, P.J. (1992). Organisation and functions of cells responsive to faces in the temporal cortex. *Philosophical Transactions of the Royal Society of London, B335*, 23-30.

Phillips, R.J. (1972). Why are faces hard to recognise in photographic negative? *Perception & Psychophysics, 12*, 425-426.

Rhodes, G. (1997). *Superportraits: Caricatures and Recognition.* Hove: Psychology Press.

Rhodes, G., Brennan, S. & Carey, S. (1987). Recognition and ratings of caricatures: Implications for mental representation of faces. *Cognitive Psychology, 19*, 473-497.

Rolls, E.T. (1992). Neurophysiological mechanisms underlying face processing within and beyond the temporal cortical visual areas. *Philosophical Transactions of the Royal Society of London, B335,* 11-21.

Searcy, J.H. & Bartlett, J.C. (1996). Inversion and processing of component and spatial-relational information in faces. *Journal of Experimental Psychology: Human Perception and Performance, 22,* 904-915,

Sergent, J., Ohta, S., MacDonald, B. & Zuck, E. (1994). Segregated processing of facial identity and emotion in the human brain: A PET study. *Visual Cognition, 1,* 349-369.

Sirovich, L. & Kirby, M. (1987). Low dimensional procedure for the characterisation of human faces. *Journal of the Optical Society of America, 4,* 519-524.

Tanaka, J. W. & Farah, M.J. (1993) Parts and wholes in face recognition. *Quarterly Journal of Experimental Psychology, 46A,* 161-204.

Tarr, M.J. & Bulthoff, H.H. (1995). Is human object recognition better described by geon structural descriptions or by multiple views- comment on Biederman and Gerhardstein (1993). *Journal of Experimental Psychology: Human Perception & Performance, 21,* 1494-1505.

Thompson, P (1980). Margaret Thatcher - A new illusion. *Perception, 9,* 483-4.

Turk, M. & Pentland, A. (1991). Eigenfaces for recognition. *Journal of Cognitive Neuroscience, 3,* 71-86.

Valentine, T. (1988). Upside-down faces: a review of the effect of inversion upon face recognition. *British Journal of Psychology, 79,* 471-491.

Valentine, T (1991) A unified account of the effects of distinctiveness, inversion and race in face recognition. *Quarterly Journal of Experimental Psychology, 43A,* 161-204.

Valentine, T. & Bruce, V. (1986) The effect of distinctiveness in recognising and classifying faces. *Perception, 15,* 525-535.

Yin, R.K. (1969) Looking at upside-down faces. *Journal of Experimental Psychology, 81,* 141-151.

Young, A.W., Hellawell, D.J. & Hay, D.C. (1987). Configurational information in face perception. *Perception, 16*, 747-759.

Young, A.W., Newcombe, F., De Haan, E.H.F., Small, M. & Hay, D.C. (1993). Face perception after brain injury. *Brain, 116*, 941-959.

Discriminant Analysis of Principal Components for Face Recognition

Wenyi Zhao[1], Arvindh Krishnaswamy[2], Rama Chellappa[1]
Daniel L. Swets[3], John Weng[4]

[1]Center for Automation Research, University of Maryland
College Park, MD 20742-3275, USA
Email:{ *wyzhao, rama*}*@cfar.umd.edu*
[2]Electrical Engineering Dept, Stanford University
Stanford, CA 94305, USA
[3]Computer Science Department, Augustana College
Sioux Falls, SD 57197, USA
[4]Computer Science Dept, Michigan State University
East Lansing, MI 48824-1027, USA

Abstract. In this paper we describe a face recognition method based on PCA (Principal Component Analysis) and LDA (Linear Discriminant Analysis). The method consists of two steps: first we project the face image from the original vector space to a face subspace via PCA, second we use LDA to obtain a linear classifier. The basic idea of combining PCA and LDA is to improve the generalization capability of LDA when only few samples per class are available. Using FERET dataset we demonstrate a significant improvement when principal components rather than original images are fed to the LDA classifier. The hybrid classifier using PCA and LDA provides a useful framework for other image recognition tasks as well.

1 Introduction

The problem of automatic face recognition is a composite task that involves detection and location of faces in a cluttered background, normalization, recognition and verification. Depending on the nature of the application, e.g. sizes of training and testing database, clutter and variability of the background, noise, occlusion, and finally speed requirements, some of the subtasks could be very challenging. Assuming that segmentation and normalization haven been done, we focus on the subtask of person recognition and verification and demonstrate the performance using a testing database of about 3800 images.

There have been many methods proposed for face recognition. And one of the key components of any methods is facial feature extraction. Facial feature could be a gray-scale image, a low-dimensional abstract feature vector, and it could be either global or local. There are two major approaches to facial feature extraction for recognition, holistic template matching based systems and geometrical local feature based schemes [1]. The algorithm we present belongs to the first category.

2 LDA of Principal Components face recognition system

2.1 PCA and LDA

Principal Component Analysis is a standard technique used to approximate the original data with lower dimensional feature vectors [2]. The basic approach is to compute the eigenvectors of the covariance matrix, and approximate the original data by a linear combination of the leading eigenvectors. The mean square error (MSE) in reconstruction is equal to the sum of the remaining eigenvalues. The feature vector here is the PCA projection coefficients. PCA is appropriate when the samples are from one class or group(super-class). In real implementation, there are two ways to compute the eigenvalues and eigenvectors: SVD decomposition and regular eigen-computation. For efficient way to compute or update the SVD, please refer to [4, 3]. In many cases, even though the matrix is a full-rank matrix, the large condition number will create a numerical problem. One way around this is to compute the eigenvalues and eigenvectors for $C + \kappa I$ instead of C, where κ is a positive number. This is based on the following lemma:

Lemma 1 *Matrices C and $C + \kappa I$ have same eigenvectors but different eigenvalues with the relationship: $\lambda_{C+\kappa I} = \lambda + \kappa$ as long as $\lambda + \kappa$ is not equal to zero.*

On the other hand, LDA produces an optimal linear discriminant function $\mathbf{f}(\mathbf{x}) = W^T \mathbf{x}$ which maps the input into the classification space in which the class identification of this sample is decided based on some metric such as Euclidean distance [17, 12, 13]. A typical LDA implementation is carried out via scatter matrices analysis [2]. We compute the within and between-class scatter matrices as follows:

$$S_w = \frac{1}{M} \sum_{i=1}^{M} Pr(C_i) \Sigma_i \tag{1}$$

$$S_b = \frac{1}{M} \sum_{i=1}^{M} Pr(C_i)(\mathbf{m}_i - \mathbf{m})(\mathbf{m}_i - \mathbf{m})^T \tag{2}$$

Here S_w is the *Within-class Scatter Matrix* showing the average scatter Σ_i of the sample vectors $\mathbf{x}$ of different class C_i around their respective mean $\mathbf{m_i}$:

$$\Sigma_i = E[(\mathbf{x} - \mathbf{m}_i)(\mathbf{x} - \mathbf{m}_i)^T | C = C_i] \tag{3}$$

Similarly S_b is the *Between-class Scatter Matrix*, representing the scatter of the conditional mean vectors $\mathbf{m}_i$'s around the overall mean vector $\mathbf{m}$.

Various measures are available for quantifying the discriminatory power [2], the commonly used one being,

$$J(W) = \frac{\| W^T S w W \|}{\| W^T S b W \|}. \tag{4}$$

Here W is the optimal discrimination projection and can be obtained via solving the generalized eigenvalue problem [10]:

$$S_b W = \lambda S_w W \tag{5}$$

The distance measure used in the matching could be a simple Euclidean, or a weighted Euclidean distance. It has been suggested that the weighted Euclidean distance will give better classification than the simple Euclidean distance [8], where the weights are the normalized versions of the eigenvalues defined in (5). But it turns out that this weighted measure is sensitive to whether the corresponding persons have been seen during the training stage or not. To account for this, we devised a simple scheme to detect whether the person in the testing image has been trained or not and then use either a weighted Euclidean distance or a simple Euclidean distance respectively.

2.2 LDA of Principal Components

Both PCA and LDA have been used for face recognition [5, 6, 7, 8, 15, 16, 11]. With PCA, the input face images usually needed to be warped to a standard face because of the large within-class variance [6, 7]. This preprocessing stage reduces the within-class variance dramatically, thus improving the recognition rate.

We first built a simple system based on pure LDA [8], but the performance was not satisfactory on a large dataset of persons not present in the training set. The idea of combining PCA and LDA has been previously explored by Weng *et al* [15].

Although the pure LDA algorithm does not have any problem discriminating the trained samples, we have observed that it does not perform very well for the following three cases:

1. when the testing samples are from persons not in the training set

2. when markedly different samples of trained classes are presented

3. samples with different background are presented

Basically this is a generalization problem since the pure LDA based system is very much tuned to the specific training set, which has the same number of classes as persons, with 2 or 4 samples per class!

Combining PCA and LDA, we obtain a linear projection which maps the input image $\mathbf{x}$ first into the face-subspace $\mathbf{y}$, and then into the classification space $\mathbf{z}$:

$$\mathbf{y} = \Phi^T \mathbf{x} \tag{6}$$

$$\mathbf{z} = W_y^T \mathbf{y} \tag{7}$$

$$\mathbf{z} = W_x^T \mathbf{x} \tag{8}$$

where Φ is the PCA transform, W_y is the best linear discriminating transform on PCA feature space, and W_x is the composite linear projection from the original image space to the classification space. After this composite linear projection, recognition is performed in the classification space based on some distance measure criterion.

3   Experiments

To process the face images, we manually locate the eyes and then perform geometric normalization with the eye locations fixed and perform intensity normalization, histogram equalization or zero mean unit variance. The normalized image size is chosen to be 48×42 since similar performance has been observed with the image size 96×84 in our experiments.

To obtain the principal components, we used 1038 FERET images from 444 classes (These images are so-called *training* set which was distributed to participants prior to the FERET test, the *gallery* set and the *probe* set were either constructed by ourselves for our own experiments or distributed during the test for the FERET test). Then we retained eigenvectors corresponding to the top 300 eigenvalues, based on the observation that the higher order eigenvectors do not look like a face (figures 3, 4). A wrong choice of this number will result in bad performance. We have tested the algorithm that performs LDA on principal components using the first 15 eigenvectors and 1000 eigenvectors on both USC dataset and Stirling dataset. Both choices produced lower scores while the latter choice did better than the pure LDA algorithm. Since an *orthonormal linear* projection can be viewed as projection onto a set of bases, we can visualize these bases. Three different sets of bases from three different linear projections are shown here: (1) pure LDA projection W (figure 1), (2) pure PCA projection Φ (figure 3), and (3) PCA + LDA projection W_x (figure 2). All these bases are computed using the FERET *training* set, the PCA + LDA bases being based on the first 300 PCA bases.

3.1   Our experiments

All the experiments conducted here are similar to the FERET test: we have a gallery set and a probe set. In the prototyping stage, the weights that characterize the projections of images in the gallery set are computed. In the testing stage, the weights that characterize the projections of images in the probe set are calculated. Using these weights and the nearest-neighbor criterion, for each image in the probe set a rank ordering of all the images in the gallery set is produced. The cumulative match score in figure 6 is computed the same way as in FERET test [9].

3.1.1   Comparison of LDA and LDA of Principal Components

To test our system (figure 5), we constructed a gallery set which contains 738 images, with 721 from the FERET training set and 17 from the USC dataset [18].

The probe set has 115 images with 78 images in the training set, 18 images from the FERET data set but not trained, and 19 images from the USC dataset.

For the 78 trained images, both system works perfectly even though most of these images do no appear in the gallery set. But for the other 18 and 19 images from the FERET and USC datasets, the performance between these two methods is quite different.

Figure 6 shows the performance comparison between pure LDA with different intensity preprocessing and LDA of principal components with histogram equalization preprocessing.

3.1.2 Sensitivity test of LDA of Principal Components

In addition to the above experiments, we also conducted a sensitivity test. We took one original face image, and then electronically modified the image by creating occlusions, applying Gaussian blur, randomizing the pixel location, and adding artificial background. Figure 7 shows the various electronically-modified face images which have been correctly identified.

3.2 FERET test

Although we are not one of the participants in the FERET program, we agreed to take the FERET test in September 1996 to test the efficacy of the pure LDA approach. The gallery and probe datasets had 3323 and 3816 images respectively. Thus for each image in the probe set we produced a set of 3323 ordered images from the gallery set. The detailed description of the FERET test can be found at [9]. In March 1997, we re-took the FERET test to test the effect of different intensity preprocessing for LDA and also to test the improvement due to LDA of Principal Components. Figure 8 shows a significant improvement of LDA of principal components approach over LDA in every category [1]. More recently, some preliminary results show that our system's performance for the task of *person verification* is very competitive.

3.3 Faces and Other Objects Combined

In order to test the performance when objects include more than faces, we experimented with image database that include human faces as well as other natural objects. The face part used in this combination test was organized by individual; each individual had a pool of images from which to draw training and test data sets. Each individual had at least two images for training with a change of expression. The images of 38 individuals (182 images) came from the Michigan State University Pattern Recognition and Image Processing laboratory. Images of individuals in this set were taken under uncontrolled conditions, over several days, and

---

[1] Even though the zero-mean-unit-variance preprocessing showed better results for pure LDA approach than histogram-equalization on the experiment reported in figure 6, the FERET test showed inferior performance. The plots here are only for the histogram-equalization preprocessing case.

No. of training images	1316 from 526 classes
No. of test images	298 from 298 classes
No. nodes in the tree	2388
No. of explored paths	10
Top one	95.0%
Top 10	99.0%

Table 1: Summary of experiment for faces and other objects.

under different lighting conditions. 303 classes (654 images) came from the FERET database. All of these classes had at least two images of an individual taken under controlled lighting, with a change of expression. 24 of these classes had additional images taken of the subjects on a different day with very poor contrast. Sixteen classes (144 images) came from the MIT Media lab under identical lighting conditions (ambient laboratory light). Twenty-nine classes (174 images) came from the Weizmann Institute, and are images with three very controlled lighting conditions for each of two different expressions. The nonface objects includes a wide range of scenes, ranging from street signs to aerial photographs. A small sample of images from the classes learned is given in Figure 9. The views differ in expression, viewing angle, lighting, etc.

Most classes in the database were represented by two images, and 19% of the classes had three or more images, up to twelve for some objects (e.g., fire hydrant). Each image consisted of a well-framed object of interest. The different images from each class were taken either in a different setting or from a different angle; where possible a change in the lighting arrangement was used to provide variation in the training images.

Following training, the PCA+LDA method was tested using a test set completely disjoint from the training set of images. In this version, the tree index method explained in [14] was also used. At each node of the tree, a new projection matrix is computed based the training samples belonging to the node. Each projection matrix represents PCA projection followed by LDA projection. The subspace created by the projection matrix is used to determine the further partition of the sample space, one child node is assigned with the samples falling into the region represented by the child node. Such recursive partition is carried on for every node until the samples assigned to the node belong to a single class. In order words, the PCA+LDA projection is applied recursively to smaller and smaller sets of samples, and thus better separating classes while the number of classes become small deep down the tree. The data that show the improvement of recognition rate and the speed gain due to this recursive PCA+LDA tree partition can be found in [14]. A summary of the results using this tree-based PCA+LDA system is shown in Table 1.

In the experiments further conducted, we trained the system using training samples artificially generated from the original training samples to vary in (a) 30% of size, (b) positional shift of 20% of size and 20% of size; (c) 3D face orientation by about 45 degrees and testing with 22.5 degrees. Training and test data sizes are similar to that in Table 1. The top 1 and top 10 correct recognition rates were, respectively, (a) 93.3% and 98.9%, (b) 93.1% and 96.6%, (c) 78.9% and 89.4%.

4 Conclusions

We have presented in this paper a face recognition system which combines PCA and LDA. Performance improvement of this method over pure LDA based method is demonstrated through our own experiments and FERET test. We believe that by combining PCA and LDA, using PCA to construct a task-specific subspace and then applying LDA on that subspace, other image recognition systems such as fingerprint, optical character recognition can be improved.

Acknowledgments

We would like to thank Saad Sirohey for participating in the FERET test, and Hyeonjoon Moon for providing us the FERET test plots. Zhao and Chellappa are supported by the ONR MURI contract N00014-95-1-0521, under ARPA order C635. Weng's work was supported by NSF Grant No. IRI 9410741 and ONR grant No. N00014-95-1-0637.

References

[1] R. Chellappa, C.L. Wilson and S. Sirohey, "Human and Machine Recognition of Faces, A Survey," *Proc. of the IEEE*, Vol. 83, pp. 705-740, 1995.

[2] K. Fukunaga, *Statistical Pattern Recognition*, New York: Academic Press, 1989.

[3] M. Gu, S.C. Eisenstat, "A stable and Fast Algorithm for Updating the singular Value Decomposition," Research Report YALE DCR/RR-966, 1994, Yale University, New Haven, CT.

[4] S. Chandrasekaran, B.S. Manjunath, Y.F. Wang, J. Winkeler, and H. Zhang, "An Eigensapce update algorithm for image analysis,", to appear in the journal *Graphical Model and Image Processing*, 1997.

[5] M. Turk and A. Pentland, "Eigenfaces for Recognition," *Journal of Cognitive Neuroscience*, Vol. 3, pp. 72-86, 1991.

[6] B. Moghaddam and A. Pentland, "Probabilistic Visual Learning for Object Detection," in *Proc. International Conference on Computer Vision*, Boston, MA, 1995, pp. 786-793.

[7] N. Costen, I. Craw, T. Kato, G. Robertson and S. Akamatsu, "Manifold Caricatures: on the Psychological Consistency of Computer Face Recognition," in

Proc. Second International Conference on Automatic Face and Gesture Recognition, Killington, Vermont, 1996, pp. 4-9.

[8] K. Etemad and R. Chellappa, "Discriminant Analysis for Recognition of Human Face Images," *Journal of Optical Society of America A*, pp. 1724-1733, Aug. 1997.

[9] P.J. Philips, H. Moon, P. Rauss, and S.A. Rizvi, "The FERET Evaluation Methodology for Face-Recognition Algorithms," in *Proc. of Computer Vision and Pattern Recognition*, Puerto Rico, 1997, pp. 137-143.

[10] S.S. Wilks, *Mathematical Statistics,* New York: Wiley, 1963.

[11] P.N. Belhumeur, J.P. Hespanha, and D.J. Kriegman, "Eigenfaces vs. fisherfaces: Recognition using class specific linear projection," in *Proc. European Conf. on Computer Vision*, April 1996.

[12] R.A. Fisher, "The statistical utilization of multiple measurements," *Annals of Eugenics*, 8:376–386, 1938.

[13] A.K. Jain and R.C. Dubes, *Algorithms for Clustering Data*, Prentice-Hall, New Jersey, 1988.

[14] D.Swets and J.Weng, "Discriminant analysis and eigenspace partition tree for face and object recognition from views," in *Proc. Int'l Conference on Automatic Face- and Gesture-Recognition*, pages 192–197, Killington, Vermont, Oct. 14-16 1996.

[15] J.Weng, "On comprehensive visual learning," in *Proc. NSF/ARPA Workshop on Performance vs. Methodology in Computer Vision*, pages 152–166, Seattle, WA, June 1994.

[16] D.L. Swets and J. Weng, "Using Discriminant Eigenfeatures for Image Retrieval," *IEEE trans. on PAMI*, Vol. 18, pp. 831-836, Aug. 1996.

[17] J.H. Wilkinson, *The Algebraic Eigenvalue Problem*, Oxford University Press, New York, NY, 1965.

[18] B.S. Manjunath, R. Chellappa and C.V.D. Malsburg, "A Feature Based Approach to Face Recognition," in *Proc. of Computer Vision and Pattern Recognition*, Urbana Champaign, Illinois, 1992, pp. 373-378.

Figure 1: The first five pure LDA bases

Figure 2: The first five PCA + LDA bases

The average face and first four eigenfaces

Eigenfaces 15, 100, 200, 250, 300

Figure 3: Useful eigenfaces

Eigenfaces 400, 450, 1000, 2000

Figure 4: Suspicious eigenfaces: statistically insignificant.

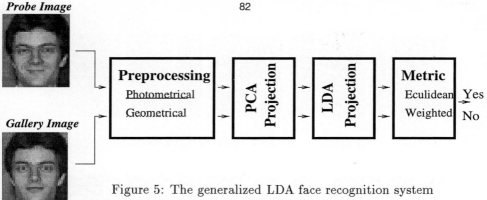

Figure 5: The generalized LDA face recognition system

(a)

(b)

Figure 6: (a) Performance comparison on the 19 images from USC dataset, (b) Performance comparison on the 18 images from FERET dataset but not included in the training set. Legends used in figure: HIST is the abbreviation for HIS-Togram equalization preprocessing, while ZMUV is for Zero Mean Unit Variance preprocessing.

Original image

Figure 7:
Electronically-modified images which have been correctly identified.

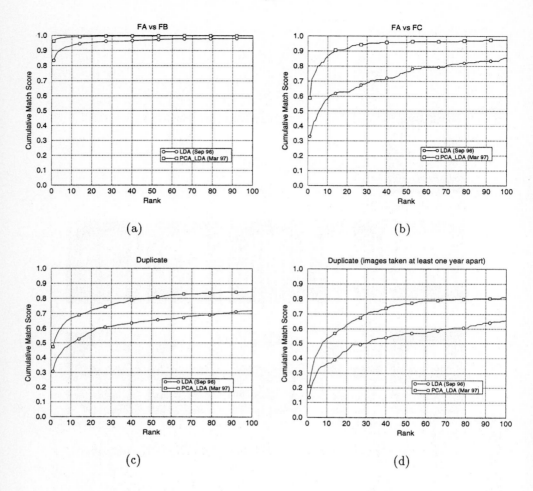

Figure 8: FERET test results from September 96 and March 97: (a)FA vs FB, (b)FA vs FC, (c)Duplicate, (d)Duplicate (images taken at least one year apart) (*Courtesy of Army Research Lab*)

person 0   person 1   person 2   person 4   person 5   person 6

digit 9   truck   car   centersign   chair   mouse

seated   cup   currency   desk   dog   doorhandle

egg   sharpener   house   hydrant   impacth   IS45sign

Figure 9: Representative images from the different classes. Images are shown without the pixel weighting, which applying a different weight to each pixel, with decreasing weight from the center to the periphery. This pixel weighting tends to suppress the background around the periphery.

Inductive Principles for Learning from Data

Vladimir Cherkassky

Department of Electrical and Computer Engineering
University of Minnesota
Minneapolis, Minnesota 55455, U.S.A.
cherkass@ece.umn.edu

Abstract. Face detection/recognition applications involve ill-defined concepts (such as 'face' or 'person') that cannot be specified a priori in terms of a small set of features. This implies the need for learning unknown class decision boundaries from data (i.e., images with known class labels). This task is a special case of a generic problem of predictive classification or pattern recognition, where the goal is to estimate class decision boundaries using available (training) data. There are many learning methods (i.e., constructive algorithms) for predictive classification. However, most approaches are heuristic, due to inherent complexity of estimation with finite data, and the lack of conceptual framework. This paper describes several principled approaches (called *inductive principles*) for estimating dependencies from data. The focus is on the general conceptual framework and on the major issues related to learning, rather than on specific learning algorithms. The following inductive principles for learning with finite data are described: penalization, structural risk minimization, Bayesian inference and minimum description length. Finally, we briefly describe a new powerful learning algorithm called Support Vector Machine, and its applications to face detection.

1   Introduction

As evidenced by many presentations at this ASI, existing approaches to face recognition fall into two groups:
(1) *Understanding / modeling of human recognition*, where the focus is on psychological models of human perception and (face) recognition process.
(2) *Statistical Learning models*, where the goal is to estimate unknown dependency from available data (samples). Specifically, the problem face detection/recognition is often formulated as the problem of *predictive classification*, where the goal is to estimate class decision boundaries (i.e., to discriminate between face and non-face images) in some input (feature) space.
   The subject of this paper is the latter approach, even though successful face recognition systems are likely to combine both approaches. Face recognition applications place particularly stringent requirements on the learning problem, since the data is high-dimensional (i.e., 100 to 1,000 -dimensional vectors corresponding to image pixels) and the number of samples (images) is large (at least a few thousand). Numerous learning approaches have been proposed and used for face recognition. These include, for example, neural network, statistical pattern recognition, wavelet, genetic optimization and fuzzy methodologies (see examples

elsewhere in this volume). However, it is difficult to objectively compare these methodologies, because most are heuristic, i.e. they lack general conceptual framework and often define the problem in terms of the solution approach. In this paper we present first the mathematical formulation of the learning problem and then describe several inductive principles. It is argued that a clear understanding of the basic issues and concepts related to learning is necessary for developing sound constructive learning methods.   Finally, we describe a new constructive method called Support Vector Machine (SVM) for implementing structural risk minimization inductive principle. This method is based on Statistical Learning Theory (aka Vapnik-Chervonenkis or VC-theory). Several recent SVM applications to face detection are also reviewed.

2 Formulation of the Learning Problem

Learning is the process of estimating an unknown (input, output) dependency or structure of a System using a limited number of observations (see Fig.1). The general learning scenario involves three components: a Generator of random input vectors, a System which returns an output for a given input vector, and the Learning Machine which estimates an unknown (input, output) mapping of the System, from the observed (input, output) samples. This formulation describes many practical learning problems such as interpolation, regression, classification, clustering and density estimation.

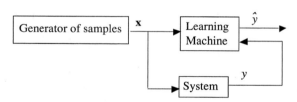

Figure 1. A Learning Machine uses observations of the System to form an approximation of its output.

 Each component of a learning system in Fig.1 can be further described in mathematical terms:

The Generator (or sampling distribution) produces random vectors $\mathbf{x} \in \Re^d$, drawn independently from a fixed probability density $p(\mathbf{x})$ which is unknown.

The System produces an output value y for every input vector $\mathbf{x}$ according to the fixed conditional density $p(y|\mathbf{x})$, which is also unknown.

The Learning Machine is capable of implementing a set of approximating functions $f(\mathbf{x}, \omega)$, $\omega \in \Omega$ where Ω is a set of parameters. The set of approximating functions of the Learning Machine should be chosen *a priori*, before the formal inference (learning) process is begun. Ideally, the choice approximating functions reflects a priori knowledge about the System (unknown dependency).

This choice is application-dependent and is outside the scope of the learning problem. Common sets of approximating functions include: multilayer perceptron networks, radial basis functions, wavelets, Fourier (harmonic) expansion etc.

There is an important distinction between two types of approximating functions: linear in parameters vs nonlinear in parameters. Learning (estimation) procedures using the former are also refered to as *linear* , whereas those using the latter are called *nonlinear* .

<u>The Learning problem</u> can be now stated as follows:
Given a set of n training samples

$$(\mathbf{x}_i, y_i), \quad (i = 1, ..., n) \tag{1}$$

produced according to (unknown) joint probability density function (pdf)

$$p(\mathbf{x}, y) = p(\mathbf{x}) p(y|\mathbf{x}) \tag{2}$$

select a function (from the set of approximating functions $f(\mathbf{x}, \omega)$) which best approximates the System's response.

The quality of an approximation produced by the Learning Machine is measured by the loss or discrepancy measure $L(y, f(\mathbf{x}, \omega))$ between the output produced by the System and the Learning Machine for a given point $\mathbf{x}$. The expected value of the loss is called the (expected or prediction) *risk functional*:

$$R(\omega) = \int L(y, f(\mathbf{x}, \omega)) \, p(\mathbf{x}, y) dx dy \tag{3}$$

Learning is the process of estimating the function $f(\mathbf{x}, \omega^*)$ which minimizes the risk functional over the set of functions supported by the Learning Machine, using only the training data ($p(\mathbf{x}, y)$ is not known). We cannot expect to find $f(\mathbf{x}, \omega^*)$ exactly, so we denote $f(\mathbf{x}, \omega)$ as the estimate of the optimal solution obtained with finite training data using some learning procedure.

The generic learning problem can be subdivided into four classes of common problems: classification, regression, density estimation, and clustering/vector quantization [Vapnik, 1995; Cherkassky and Mulier, 1998]. For each of these problems, the nature of the loss function and the output (y) differ. However, the goal of minimizing the risk functional based only on training data is common to all learning problems. Next we briefly describe classification and density estimation tasks which are directly relevant to face recognition/detection applications.

Classification
In a (two-class) classification problem, the output of the System takes on only two (symbolic) values $y = \{0, 1\}$, corresponding to two classes (i.e., face and non-face). Hence, the output of the Learning Machine need only take on two values as well, so the set of functions $f(\mathbf{x}, \omega)$, $\omega \in \Omega$ becomes a set of *indicator* functions. A commonly used loss function for this problem measures the classification error:

$$L(y, f(\mathbf{x}, \omega)) = \begin{cases} 0 & \text{if } y = f(\mathbf{x}, \omega) \\ 1 & \text{if } y \neq f(\mathbf{x}, \omega) \end{cases} \tag{4}$$

Using this loss function, the risk functional (3) quantifies the probability of misclassification. Learning then becomes the problem of finding the indicator function $f(\mathbf{x}, \omega_0)$ (classifier) which minimizes the probability of misclassification using only the training data.

Density Estimation

For estimating the density of $\mathbf{x}$, the output of the System is not used. The output of the Learning Machine now represents density, so $f(\mathbf{x}, \omega)$, $\omega \in \Omega$ becomes a set of densities. Using the loss function

$$L(f(\mathbf{x}, \omega)) = -\ln f(\mathbf{x}, \omega) \tag{5}$$

in the risk functional (3) gives

$$R(\omega) = \int -\ln f(\mathbf{x}, \omega) p(\mathbf{x}) dx \tag{6}$$

which is a common risk functional (called Maximum Likelihood) used for density estimation. Minimizing (6) using only the training data $\mathbf{x}_1, ..., \mathbf{x}_K$ leads to the density estimate $f(\mathbf{x}, \omega^*)$.

Note that a given learning task (i.e., classification or regression) can be solved by minimizing (3) directly if the density $p(\mathbf{x}, y)$ were known. Moreover, if the density is known, the training data is not even needed. This implies that density estimation is the most general and hence the most difficult type of learning problem. It leads to the fairly obvious principle for estimation problems with finite data [Vapnik, 1995]: *Do not solve a given learning problem by indirectly solving a harder problem (of density estimation) as an intermediate step.* This principle is rarely followed under statistical and neural network approaches where classification problem is solved via class density estimation, as in [Bishop, 1995; Ripley, 1996].

So far, we provided the formulation of the learning problem without describing any learning methods for obtaining an estimate $f(\mathbf{x}, \omega^*)$ of the "true dependency". The next issue is: how should a Learning Machine use training data? - The answer is given by the concept known as an *inductive principle*. An inductive principle is a general prescription for obtaining an estimate $f(\mathbf{x}, \omega^*)$ of the "true dependency" in the class of approximating functions, from the available (finite) training data. An inductive principle tells *what* to do with the data, whereas the learning method specifies *how* to obtain an estimate. Hence, a learning method is a constructive implementation of an inductive principle for selecting an estimate $f(\mathbf{x}, \omega^*)$ from a particular set of functions $f(\mathbf{x}, \omega)$. For a given inductive principle, there are (infinitely) many learning methods, corresponding to different sets of approximating functions.

There are two groups of inductive principles, depending on the amount of a priori knowledge about the true dependency. *Classical (parametric)* methods assume strong a priori knowledge, reflected in a pre-specified parametric model (comprising a set of approximating functions), so that only model parameters need to be estimated using training data. *Adaptive (or flexible)* methods use weak a priori knowledge, so that both the model structure (complexity) and its parameters need to be estimated from data.

3 Inductive Principles in Classical Statistics

The classical approach, as proposed by Fisher [1952], divides the learning problem into two portions: specification and estimation. *Specification* consists of determining the parametric form of the unknown underlying distributions, while *estimation* is the process of determining parameters which characterize the specified distributions. Classical theory focuses on the problem of estimation and sidesteps the issue of specification.

Note that the learning problem formulation does not assume that the true dependency $f(\mathbf{x}, \omega_0)$ belongs to a set of approximating functions $f(\mathbf{x}, \omega)$, $\omega \in \Omega$. Classical approaches to the learning problem depend on much stricter assumptions than those posed in the general learning formulation since they assume the true parametric form of the model is known (specified). Then available data is used to estimate the values of a parameter vector $\mathbf{w}$. The two inductive principles commonly used in the classical learning process are *Empirical Risk Minimization* (ERM) and *Maximum Likelihood* (ML). Maximum likelihood is a specific form of the more general ERM principle obtained when using particular loss function (5). ERM approach assumes that the training data is sufficiently representative of the future data (i.e., unknown distribution $p(\mathbf{x}, y)$). Hence, an estimate $f(\mathbf{x}, \omega^*)$ minimizing the empirical risk (training error)

$$R_{emp}(\mathbf{w}) = \frac{1}{n} \sum_{i=1}^{n} L\big(y_i, f(\mathbf{x}_i, \mathbf{w})\big) \tag{7}$$

would also minimize the prediction risk (3). This leads to the following ERM prescription for estimating the (parametric) model from data:

$$\mathbf{w}^* = \arg \min_{\mathbf{w}} R_{emp}(\mathbf{w}) \tag{8}$$

As an example, consider the classical formulation of classification, based on the following restricted learning model: The conditional densities for each class, $p(\mathbf{x} \mid y = 0)$ and $p(\mathbf{x} \mid y = 1)$ are estimated from data using classical (parametric) density estimation using the ML inductive principle. These estimates are denoted as $p_0(\mathbf{x}, \alpha^*)$ and $p_1(\mathbf{x}, \beta^*)$, respectively. The probability of occurrence of each class, called *prior* probabilities, $p(y = 0)$ and $p(y = 1)$, are assumed to be known or estimated, i.e. as a fraction of samples from a particular class in the training set. Using Bayes theorem it is possible to use these quantities to determine for a given observation $\mathbf{x}$, the probability of that observation belonging to each class. These probabilities, called *posterior* probabilities can be used to construct a discriminant rule that describes how an observation $\mathbf{x}$ should be classified, so as to minimize the probability of error. This rule chooses the output class which has the maximum posterior probability, as described next.

First, Bayes rule is used to calculate the posterior probabilities for each class:

$$p(y = 1|\mathbf{x}) = \frac{p_1(\mathbf{x}, \beta^*)p(y = 1)}{p(\mathbf{x})} \tag{9}$$

There is no need to compute the denominator (normalizing constant) in (9), since the decision rule is a comparison of the relative magnitudes of the posterior probabilities. Once the posterior probabilities are estimated, the following rule (discriminant function) is used to classify input $\mathbf{X}$:

$$f(\mathbf{x}) = \begin{cases} 0 & \text{if } p_0(\mathbf{x}, \alpha^*)p(y = 0) > p_1(\mathbf{x}, \beta^*)p(y = 1) \\ 1 & \text{otherwise} \end{cases} \tag{10}$$

Note that the parameters α^+ and β^+ used in (10) were estimated via ML. Therefore, the classical approach applies the ERM inductive principle *indirectly* to first estimate the densities, which are then used to formulate the decision rule. This differs from applying the ERM inductive principle *directly* to minimize the empirical risk

$$R_{emp}(\mathbf{w}) = \frac{1}{n} \sum_{i=1}^{n} I(y_i = f(\mathbf{x}_i, \mathbf{w})) \tag{11}$$

by estimating the expected risk functional for classification (3) using the empirical risk (11).

There are two problems with using ML for learning problems with finite data. First, with finite data, the classification problem should be solved directly, rather than via density estimation. Posing the problem directly will require less data samples for a given level of solution accuracy. The second problem is that with finite data the knowledge of the parametric form of a model may lead to sub-optimal solutions. For example, Fisher [1952] suggested to use a linear discriminant function even when an optimal decision boundary is known to be quadratic. The intuitive explanation is that a simpler (linear) model has fewer parameters and hence can be estimated more accurately than a more complex (quadratic) model, with small number of samples. This suggests the need for model *complexity control* for learning problems with finite data. The lack of complexity control is the main deficiency of ERM. All inductive principles for adaptive learning described later in this paper have provisions for complexity control.

4 Concepts for Adaptive Learning

All learning methods use a priori knowledge to choose a class of approximating functions of a Learning Machine, $f(\mathbf{x}, \omega)$, $\omega \in \Omega$. For example, *parametric methods* use a very *restricted set* of approximating functions of pre-specified parametric form, so that only a fixed number of parameters need to be determined from data. *Adaptive methods* use a *wide set* of functions (universal approximators) capable of approximating any continuous mapping. This class of approximating functions is very flexible (overparameterized) and allows for multiple solutions when a model is estimated with finite data. Hence, additional constraints (penalty) need to be imposed on a potential of a function (within a class $f(\mathbf{x}, \omega)$, $\omega \in \Omega$) to be a solution to the learning problem.

In summary, in order to form a *unique* generalization (model) from finite data, *any learning process* requires:

(a) a (wide, flexible) set of approximating functions $f(\mathbf{x}, \omega)$, $\omega \in \Omega$ chosen a priori.

(b) *complexity penalty* (or assumptions) used to impose constraints on a potential of each function from the class (a) to be a solution. Usually, these assumptions provide (explicitly or implicitly) ordering of the functions according to some measure of their flexibility to fit the data.

(c) *an inductive principle (or inference method)*, i.e. a general prescription for combining assumptions (b) with available training data in order to produce an estimate of (unknown) true dependency. An inductive principle specifies *what* needs to be done; it does not say *how* to do it.

(d) *a learning method,* i.e. constructive (computational) implementation of an inductive principle for a given class of approximating functions.

The distinction between inductive principles and learning methods is crucial for understanding and further advancement of the methods. For a given inductive principle, there may be (infinitely) many learning methods, corresponding to different classes of approximating functions and/or different optimization techniques. For example, under Empirical Risk Minimization (ERM) inductive principle one seeks to find a solution $f(\mathbf{x}, \omega^*)$ that minimizes the empirical risk(training error), as a substitute for (unknown) expected risk(true error). Depending on the chosen loss function and the chosen class of approximating functions, ERM inductive principle can be implemented as a variety of methods (i.e., Maximum Likelihood estimators, linear regression, polynomial methods, fixed-topology neural networks etc.). ERM inductive principle is typically used in a classical (parametric) setting when the model is given (specified) first and then its parameters are estimated from data. This approach works well only when the number of training samples is large relative to the (pre-specified) model complexity (or the number of free parameters).

Adaptive methods do not make restrictive assumptions about the unknown dependency, so they use a very flexible class of approximating functions. For example, neural network classifiers (with variable number of hidden units) can form arbitrary class decision boundaries. Hence, the problem is to estimate both the *model flexibility or complexity* (i.e., the number of hidden units) and its parameters (neural network weights). The problem of choosing (optimally) the model complexity from data is also called *model selection*. Adaptive methods differ mainly on the basis of a class of approximating functions used by a method. Most practical adaptive methods developed in statistics and neural networks use classes of functions *nonlinear* in parameters. Hence in adaptive methods estimation of model parameters is a difficult task of *nonlinear optimization*.

5 Inductive principles for learning with finite data

The main issue in adaptive learning with finite data is choosing the candidate model of the right complexity to describe the training data. Various inductive principles differ in terms of:

- representation (encoding) of a penalty (or complexity ordering) on a set of approximating functions;
- applicability (of a principle) when the true model does not belong to the set of approximating functions;
- the mechanism for combining a complexity penalty with training data;
- availability of constructive procedures (learning algorithms) for a given principle.

This section provides an overview of inductive principles for the learning problem given in section 2.

Penalization (regularization) inductive principle. Under this approach, one assumes a very flexible (i.e. with many 'free' parameters) class of approximating functions $f(\mathbf{x}, \omega)$, $\omega \in \Omega$. However, in order to restrict the solutions, a penalization (regularization) term is added to the Empirical Risk to be minimized:

$$R_{pen}(\omega) = R_{emp}(\omega) + \lambda\phi[f(\mathbf{x}, \omega)] \tag{12}$$

Here $R_{emp}(\omega)$ denotes the empirical risk (training error), and the penalty $\phi[f(\mathbf{x}, \omega)]$ is a non-negative functional associated with each possible estimate $f(\mathbf{x}, \omega)$. Parameter $\lambda > 0$ controls the strength of the penalty relative to the term $R_{emp}(\omega)$. Note that the penalty term $\phi[f(\mathbf{x}, \omega)]$ is independent of the training data. Under this framework, a priori knowledge is included in the form of the penalty term, and the strength of such knowledge is controlled by the value of regularization parameter λ. For example, if λ is very large, then the result of minimizing $R_{pen}(\omega)$ does not depend on the data; whereas for small λ the final model does not depend on the penalty functional. For many common classes of approximating functions, it is possible to develop functionals $\phi[f(\mathbf{x}, \omega)]$ which measure complexity. The 'optimal' value of λ (providing smallest prediction risk) is usually chosen using resampling methods. Thus under this approach, the optimal model estimate is found as a result of a trade-off between fitting the data and a priori knowledge (i.e., penalty term).

Many heuristic procedures can be cast (at least conceptually) in the penalization framework. For example, neural networks employ gradient-descent (stochastic optimization) techniques for minimizing the empirical risk functional. One way to avoid overfitting with over-parameterized models (such as neural networks) is to stop the training early, i.e. before reaching minimum. Such *early stopping* can be interpreted as a form of penalization, where a penalty is defined on a path (in the space of model parameters) corresponding to the successive model estimates obtained during gradient-descent training. The solutions are penalized according to the number of gradient descent steps taken along this curve, i.e. the distance from the starting point (initial conditions) in the parameter space.

Structural Risk Minimization (SRM). Under SRM, approximating functions of a Learning Machine are ordered according to their complexity, i.e. form a *nested structure:*

$$S_0 \subset S_1 \subset S_2 \subset ... \tag{13}$$

For example, in the class of polynomial approximating functions, the elements of a structure are polynomials of a given degree. Condition (13) is satisfied since polynomials of degree m are a subset of polynomials of degree $(m+1)$. The goal of learning is to choose an optimal element of a structure (i.e. polynomial degree) and estimate its coefficients from a given training sample. For approximating functions *linear* in parameters (such as polynomials), the complexity is given by the number of free parameters. For functions nonlinear in parameters, the complexity is defined as VC-dimension [Vapnik, 1995]. By definition, a structure provides ordering of its elements according to their complexity (i.e., VC dimension denoted by h):

$$h_1 \leq h_2 ... \leq h_k ...$$

The optimal choice of model complexity provides the minimum of the Prediction Risk (3). Statistical Learning Theory [Vapnik, 1995] provides *analytic* upper-bound estimates for Prediction Risk. These estimates are used for complexity control, i.e. choosing an optimal element of a structure, under SRM inductive principle.

Here we only describe *constructive distribution-independent* bounds for classification. Other types of VC generalization bounds can be found in [Vapnik, 1995]. For two-class classification problems, the following bound for generalization ability of a learning machine holds with probability of at least $1 - \eta$ simultaneously for all approximating functions of a learning machine:

$$R(\omega) \leq R_{emp}(\omega) + \frac{\varepsilon}{2}\left(1 + \sqrt{1 + \frac{4R_{emp}(\omega)}{\varepsilon}}\right) \qquad (14)$$

where

$$\varepsilon = \varepsilon\left(\frac{n}{h}, \frac{-\ln\eta}{n}\right) = a_1 \frac{h\left(\ln\frac{a_2 n}{h} + 1\right) - \ln(\eta/4)}{n} \qquad (15)$$

Statistical Learning Theory [Vapnik,1982, Vapnik,1995] proves that the values of constants a_1, a_2 must be in the range $0 < a_1 \leq 4$, $0 < a_2 \leq 2$. The values $a_1 = 4$, $a_2 = 2$ have been derived for the worst case distribution (discontinuous density function). For practical applications, smaller values for constants a_1 and a_2 should be chosen empirically. According to [Vapnik, 1995; Cherkassky and Mulier, 1998], the *confidence level* $1 - \eta$ is chosen depending on the training set size as:

$$\eta = \min\left(\frac{4}{\sqrt{n}}, 1\right) \qquad (16)$$

The bound (14) can be conveniently presented as:

$$R(\omega) \leq R_{emp}(\omega) + \Phi\left(R_{emp}(\omega), n/h, -\ln\eta/n\right) \qquad (17)$$

where the second term in the right-hand side is called the *confidence interval*, as it estimates the difference between the training error and the true error. The confidence interval Φ should not be confused with the confidence level $1 - \eta$. Let us analyze the behavior of Φ as a function of sample size n, with all other parameters fixed. It can be readily seen that the confidence interval mainly depends on ε, which monotonically decreases (to zero) with n according to (15). Hence, Φ also monotonically decreases with n , as can be intuitively expected. Moreover, detailed

analysis shows strong dependency of the confidence interval Φ on the ratio n/h, and we can distinguish two main regimes [Vapnik, 1995]:
-   small (or finite) sample size, when the ratio of the number of training samples to the VC-dimension of approximating functions is small (say, less than 20);
-   large sample size, when this ratio is large.
With small samples, there is a need to match complexity (capacity) of approximating functions to the available data. Under SRM, this is accomplished by choosing the (optimal) structure element providing minimum of the bound (14), as shown in Fig. 2.

Finally, we note that the structure (13) can be defined in various ways, i.e. via
-   *dictionary representation*

$$f_m(\mathbf{x}, \mathbf{w}, \mathbf{V}) = \sum_{i=0}^{m} w_i \, g(\mathbf{x}, \mathbf{v}_i) \tag{18}$$

where $g(\mathbf{x}, \mathbf{v}_i)$ is a set of basis functions with adjustable parameters $\mathbf{v}_i$, and $\mathbf{w}_i$ are linear coefficients. Both $\mathbf{w}_i$ and $\mathbf{v}_i$ are estimated to fit the training data. Representation (18) defines a structure, since $f_1 \subset f_2 \subset .... \subset f_k \subset .....$ For example, feedforward neural networks indexed by the number of hidden units m represent a dictionary structure (18).
-   *penalization formulation* (12);
-   *input preprocessing*;
-   *initialization* of parameters of a (nonlinear) optimization algorithm (i.e., backpropagation);
-   *stopping* conditions of an optimization algorithm.
See [Cherkassky and Mulier, 1998] for examples of these structures.

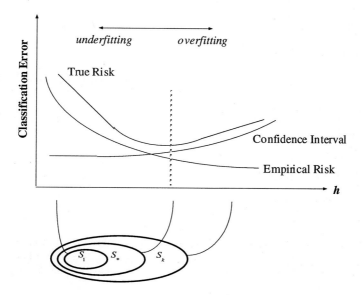

Figure 2. An upper bound on the true (expected) risk and the empirical risk as a function of h (for fixed n).

Bayesian Inference. This type of inference uses additional a priori information about approximating functions in order to obtain a unique predictive model from finite data. This knowledge is in the form of the so-called *prior probability distribution*, i.e. the probability of any function (from the set approximating functions) to be the true (unknown) function. This adds subjectivity to the design of a learning machine, since the final model depends largely on a good choice of priors. Moreover, the very notion that the prior distribution adequately captures prior knowledge may not be acceptable in many situations, i.e. when we need to estimate a constant (but unknown) parameter. On the other hand, Bayesian approach provides an effective way of encoding prior knowledge, and can be a powerful tool when used by experts.

Bayesian inference is based on the classical Bayes formula for updating prior probabilities using the evidence provided by the data:

$$P[\text{model} \mid \text{data}] = \frac{P[\text{data} \mid \text{model}]P[\text{model}]}{P[\text{data}]} \tag{19}$$

where

$P[\text{model}]$ is *prior* probability (before the data is observed)

$P[\text{data}]$ is the probability of observing training data

$P[\text{model} \mid \text{data}]$ is *a posterior* probability of a model given the data

$P[\text{data} \mid \text{model}]$ is the probability that the data is generated by a model, also known as *likelihood* .

Let us consider the general case of (parametric) density estimation, when the class of density functions supported by the learning machine is a parametric set, i.e. $f(\mathbf{x}, \omega)$, $\omega \in \Omega$ is a set of densities where $\mathbf{w}$ is an m-dimensional vector of 'free' parameters (m is fixed). It is also assumed that the unknown density $f(\mathbf{x}, \omega_0)$ belongs to this class. Given a set of i.i.d. training data $\mathbf{X} = [\mathbf{x}_1, ..., \mathbf{x}_n]$, the probability of seeing this particular data set as a function of $\mathbf{w}$ is

$$P[\text{data}|\text{model}] = P(\mathbf{X}|\mathbf{w}) = \prod_{i=1}^{n} f(\mathbf{x}_i, \mathbf{w}) \tag{20}$$

Recall that choosing the model (parameter $\mathbf{w}^*$) maximizing likelihood $P(X|\mathbf{w})$ amounts to ML.

A priori density function

$$P[\text{model}] = p(\mathbf{w}) \tag{21}$$

gives the probability of any (implementable) density $f(\mathbf{x}, \omega)$, $\omega \in \Omega$ to be the true one. Then Bayes formula gives:

$$P(\mathbf{w}|\mathbf{X}) = \frac{P(\mathbf{X}|\mathbf{w})P(\mathbf{w})}{P(\mathbf{X})} \tag{22}$$

Usually, the prior distribution is taken rather broad, reflecting general uncertainty about 'correct' parameter values. Having observed the data, this prior distribution is converted into posterior distribution according to Bayes formula. This posterior distribution will be more narrow, reflecting the fact that it is consistent with the observed data.

There are two distinct ways to use Bayes formula for obtaining an estimate of unknown p.d.f. The true Bayesian approach is to average over all possible models (implementable by a learning machine), which gives the following p.d.f. estimate:

$$\Theta(\mathbf{x}|\mathbf{X}) = \int f(\mathbf{x}, \mathbf{w}) p(\mathbf{w}|\mathbf{X}) d\mathbf{w} \qquad (23)$$

where $p(\mathbf{w}|\mathbf{X})$ is given by the Bayes formula (22). Equation (23) provides an example of an important technique in Bayesian inference called *marginalization*, which involves integrating out redundant variables (such as parameters $\mathbf{w}$). The estimator $\Theta(\mathbf{x}|\mathbf{X})$ has many attractive properties [Bishop, 1995]. In particular, the final model is a weighted sum of all possible predictive models, with weights given by the evidence (or posterior probability) that each model is correct. However, multi-dimensional integration (due to the large number of parameters $\mathbf{w}$) presents a challenging problem. Standard numerical integration is impossible, whereas analytic evaluation is feasible only under certain restrictive assumptions, i.e. when the posterior density has the same form as a prior (typically assumed to be Gaussian). When Gaussian assumptions do not hold, various forms of random sampling also known as Monte Carlo methods have been proposed to evaluate integrals (23) directly [Bishop, 1995].

Another way to implement Bayesian approach is to choose an estimate $f(\mathbf{x}, \omega^*)$ maximizing posterior probability $p(\mathbf{w}|\mathbf{X})$. This is known as the maximum a posterior probability (MAP) estimate. MAP formulation can be related to penalization formulation (12) with an explicit form of regularization parameter [Friedman,1994]. Choosing the optimal value of regularization parameter is equivalent to finding a 'good' prior. There has been some work done to tailor priors to the data, i.e. the so-called MLII techniques [Berger, 1985]. However, such empirical Bayes approach contradicts the original notion of data-independent prior knowledge.

Although the penalization inductive principle can be interpreted in terms of Bayesian formulation, they have a different motivation. The Bayesian methodology is used to encode a priori knowledge about multiple, general, user-defined characteristics of the target function. The goal of penalization is to perform complexity control by encoding a priori knowledge about function smoothness in terms of a penalty functional. Bayesian model selection tends to penalize more complex models, by choosing the model with largest evidence; but this does not guarantee the best generalization performance (or minimum prediction risk). On the other hand, formulations provided by Penalization framework and Statistical Learning Theory are based on the explicit minimization of the prediction risk.

Minimum Description Length (MDL). This principle is based on the information-theoretic analysis of the randomness concept. In contrast to all other inductive principles which use statistical distributions to describe an unknown model, the MDL approach regards *models as codes*, i.e. encodings of the training data. The main idea is that any data set can be appropriately encoded, and its *code length* represents an inherent property of the data, which is directly related to the generalization capability of the model (i.e., code).

Kolmogorov [1965] introduced the notion of *algorithmic complexity* for characterization of randomness of a data set. He defined the algorithmic complexity of a data set to be the shortest binary code describing this data. Further, the randomness of a data set can be related to the length of the binary code, i.e. the data is random if it cannot be compressed significantly. Rissanen [1978; 1989] proposed to use Kolmogorov's characterization of randomness as tool for inductive inference, known as MDL principle.

In order to illustrate the MDL principle, consider the training data set:

$$(\mathbf{x}_i, y_i), \quad (i = 1, ..., n)$$

where samples $(\mathbf{x}_i, y_i)$ are drawn randomly and independently from some (unknown) distribution. Let us further assume that training data corresponds to classification problem, where the class label $y = \{0,1\}$ and $\mathbf{x}$ is d-dimensional feature vector.

The problem of estimating dependency between $\mathbf{x}$ and y can be formulated under MDL inductive principle as follows:

Given a data object $\mathbf{X} = [\mathbf{x}_1, ..., \mathbf{x}_n]$, is a binary string $y_1, ..., y_n$ random? The binary string $\mathbf{y} = (y_1, ..., y_n)$ can be encoded using n bits. However, if there are systematic dependency in the data captured by the model $y = f(\mathbf{x})$, we can encode the output string $\mathbf{y}$ by a possibly shorter code that consists of two parts:
- the model having code length $L(\text{model})$
- the error term specifying how the actual data differs from the model predictions, with a code length $L(data \mid \text{model})$.

Hence, the total length l of such a code for representing binary string $\mathbf{y}$ is:

$$l = L(\text{model}) + L(\text{data}|\text{model}) \tag{24}$$

and the coefficient of compression for this string is:

$$K(\text{model}) = \frac{l}{n} \tag{25}$$

If the coefficient of compression is small, then the string is not random, and the model captures significant dependency between x and y.

Note that the optimal (MDL) model achieves balance between the complexity of the model and the error term in (24). It can be intuitively expected that the shortest description length model provides accurate representation of the unknown dependency and hence minimum prediction risk. Vapnik [1995] gives formal proof of the theorem that justifies the MDL principle (for classification problems). Informally, this theorem states that minimizing the coefficient of compression corresponds to minimizing the probability of misclassification (for future data).

The MDL approach provides very general conceptual framework for learning from samples. In fact, the notion of compression coefficient (responsible for generalization) does not depend on the knowledge of the codebook structure, the number of tables in the codebook, the number of training samples etc. Moreover, the MDL inductive principle does not even use the notion of a statistical distribution and thus avoids the controversy between the Bayesian and frequentist interpretation of probability. Unfortunately, the MDL framework does not tell us how to construct 'good' codebooks with a small number of tables yet accurate representation of the training data. Developing effective constructive procedures under MDL principle remains an open research problem. In practice, MDL may be used for model selection for restricted types of models which allow simple characterization of the model description length, such as decision trees [Rissanen, 1989]. However, application of MDL to other types of model, i.e. feedforward neural networks has not been successful, due to difficulty in developing optimal encoding of the network in a data-dependent fashion.

We conclude this section by summarizing properties of various inductive principles (see Table 1). All inductive principles use a (given) class of approximating functions. In adaptive methods, this class is typically flexible (overparameterized) and allows for multiple solutions when a model is estimated with finite data. A priori knowledge effectively constrains functions in this class, in order to produce a unique predictive model. Different ways to represent a priori knowledge and model complexity are indicated in the first row of the Table. The second row describes constructive procedures for complexity control. Various mechanisms for model selection are described in the third row. Finally, the last row of the table indicates applicability of each inductive method when there is a mismatch between a priori knowledge and the truth, i.e. in a situation when the set of approximating functions does not include the true dependency. In the case of a mismatch, the Bayesian inference is not applicable (since the prior probability of the truth is zero), while all other inductive principles still apply.

Major inductive principles described above form a basis for various adaptive learning procedures. An obvious question is: which inductive principle is best for learning with finite data? There seems to be no clear answer. Each major inductive principle has its own school of followers, who claim its superiority and generality over the others. For example, Bishop [1995] suggests that MDL can be viewed as an approximation to the Bayesian inference. On the other hand, Rissanen[1989] claims that MDL approach 'provides a justification for the Bayesian techniques, which often appear as innovative but arbitrary and sometimes confusing'. Vapnik [1995] suggests superiority of SRM over Bayesian inference and shows close connection between SRM and MDL inductive principle. This situation is rather surprising and clearly unsatisfactory. Meaningful (empirical) comparisons could be certainly helpful, but are not readily available, mainly because each inductive approach comes with its own set of assumptions and terminology. In this respect, the comparison in Table 1 may be helpful for developing future comparisons. Each inductive principle, when reasonably applied, usually yields an acceptable solution for practical applications. Hence, experts in a particular approach tend to promote it as the best. It should be also emphasized that in most practical problems the success is mainly due to proper encoding / utilization of the application domain knowledge, rather than learning itself. However, the use of domain knowledge is, strictly speaking, outside the formal framework of predictive learning.

In our experience, Structural Risk Minimization appears to be the most powerful inductive principle for learning problems with finite data [Cherkassky and Mulier, 1998]. In particular, SRM provides useful conceptual framework for understanding existing statistical and neural network learning methods, and for developing new methodologies such as Support Vector Machines described next.

Table 1. Comparison of inductive principles

	Penalization	SRM	Bayesian	MDL
representation of a priori knowledge or complexity	penalty term	structure	prior distr.	codebook
constructive procedure for complexity control	min. of penalized risk	opt. element of a structure	aposteriori distribution	not defined
method for model selection	resampling	analytic bound on pred. risk	marginalization	min code length
applicability when the true model does not belong to the set of approx. functions	yes	yes	no	yes

6. Support Vector Machines with Applications to Face Detection

There are two known strategies for minimizing the VC-bound (17) for classification, corresponding to two constructive implementations of the SRM inductive principle:

(1) *Keep the confidence interval fixed, and minimize the empirical risk.* This is done by specifying a structure where the value of the confidence interval is fixed for a given element S_m. Examples include all statistical and neural network methods using dictionary representation, where the number of basis functions (features) m specifies an element of a structure. For a given m, the empirical risk is minimized using numerical optimization. For a given amount of data, there is an optimal element of a structure (value of m) providing smallest estimate of expected risk.

(2) *Keep the value of the empirical risk fixed (small) and minimize the confidence interval.* This approach requires a special structure, such that the value of the empirical risk is kept small (say, zero misclassification error) for all approximating functions. Under this strategy, an optimal element of a structure would minimize the value of the confidence interval. Implementation of the second strategy leads to a new class of learning methods called Support Vector Machines (SVM).

Next we present an overview of SVM for classification problems. The goal is to explain (informally) SVM conceptual framework. For complete description of SVM, see [Vapnik, 1995; Cherkassky and Mulier, 1998]. Let us describe first a structure on a set of linear indicator functions that keeps the value of the empirical risk fixed (i.e., zero) for all approximating functions. Such a structure implements the second strategy for SRM by minimizing the confidence interval.

A linear indicator function capable of separating the training data without error is called a *separating hyperplane* (see Fig. 3). Suppose training data consisting of

n samples $(\mathbf{x}_1, y_1),...,(\mathbf{x}_n, y_n)$, $\mathbf{x} \in \Re^d$, $y \in \{+1, -1\}$ can be separated by the hyperplane decision function:

$$D(\mathbf{x}) = (\mathbf{w} \cdot \mathbf{x}) + w_0 \qquad (26)$$

with appropriate coefficients $\mathbf{w}$ and w_0. The assumption about linearly separable data will be later relaxed; however it allows clear explanation of the SVM approach. A separating hyperplane satisfies the constraints which define the separation of the data samples:

$$y_i\left[(\mathbf{w} \cdot \mathbf{x}_i) + w_0\right] \geq 1 \qquad i = 1,...,n \qquad (27)$$

For a given training data set, all possible separating hyperplanes can be represented in the form (27). Note that the formulation of the separating hyperplane allows us to solve the classification problem directly. It does not require estimation of density as an intermediate step.

The minimal distance from the separating hyperplane to closest data point is called the *margin* and denoted by τ. A separating hyperplane is called *optimal* if the margin is the maximum possible. It is intuitively clear that a larger margin corresponds to better generalization. The larger the margin, the more separation between the classes. The SVM framework presented next shows how to formally describe an optimal hyperplane in terms of the training data. The distance between the separating hyperplane and a sample $\mathbf{x}'$ is $|D(\mathbf{x}')|/\|\mathbf{w}\|$ as shown in Fig. 4. Assuming that a margin τ exists, all training samples obey the inequality:

$$\frac{y_k D(\mathbf{x}_k)}{\|\mathbf{w}\|} \geq \tau, \quad k = 1,...,n \qquad (28)$$

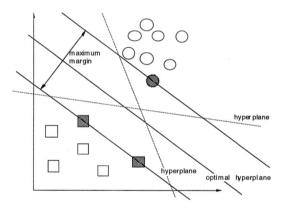

Figure 3. Separating hyperplanes in a two dimensional space. An optimal hyperplane has maximal margin. The data points at the margin (indicated in gray) are called the support vectors since they define the optimal hyperplane.

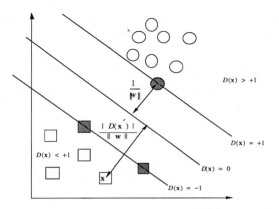

Figure 4. The decision boundary of the optimal hyperplane is defined by points **x** for which $D(\mathbf{x}) = 0$. The distance between a hyperplane and any sample **x'** is $|D(\mathbf{x}')|/\|\mathbf{w}\|$. The distance between a support vector and the optimal hyperplane is $1/\|\mathbf{w}\|$.

Determining the optimal hyperplane amounts to finding the **w** which maximizes the margin τ. Note that there are an infinite number of solutions that differ only in scaling of **w**. In order to limit solutions, fix the scale on the product of τ and norm of **w**: $\tau\|\mathbf{w}\|= 1$.

Thus, maximizing the margin τ is equivalent to minimizing the norm of **w**. An *optimal separating hyperplane* is one that satisfies condition (27) above and additionally minimizes

$$\eta(\mathbf{w}) =\|\mathbf{w}\|^2 \tag{29}$$

with respect to both **w** and $\mathbf{w}_0$. The data points that exist at the margin, or equivalently, the data points for which (27) is an *equality* are called the *support vectors* (Figure 4). Since the support vectors are data points closest to the decision surface, they determine the location of the optimal separating hyperplane. The decision surface of the optimal hyperplane can be written as a linear combination of the support vectors:

$$D(\mathbf{x}) = \sum_{i=1}^{N_s} \alpha_i^* y_i^s \left(\mathbf{x} \cdot \mathbf{x}_i^s\right) + w_0^* \tag{30}$$

where $(\mathbf{x}_i^s, y_i^s)$, $(i = 1,...,N_s)$ are the support vectors.

The generalization ability of the optimal separating hyperplane can be directly related to the number of support vectors. Assuming an optimal hyperplane can be constructed with a small number of support vectors (relative to the training set size), it will have good generalization ability, *even in high dimensional space*. This can be related to the MDL inductive principle: in order to define the optimal margin hyperplane one needs only to specify the support vectors and their class labels. Then according to [Vapnik, 1995], the test error is bounded by the compression coefficient, i.e. the ratio of the number of bits needed to encode support vectors to the number of bits to encode all training samples.

Since the hyperplane is used to implement SVM approximating functions, its VC dimension need to be estimated. The VC dimension for a set of (linear) hyperplanes is $d+1$. However, the hyperplanes with a given maximum margin form a subset of this set, and may have a smaller VC dimension. Vapnik [1995] provides the following bound:

For the hyperplane functions (27) satisfying the constraint $\parallel \mathbf{w} \parallel^2 \leq c$, the VC dimension is bounded by

$$h \leq \min(r^2 c, d) + 1 \tag{31}$$

where τ is the radius of the smallest sphere that contains the training input vectors $(\mathbf{x}_1, ..., \mathbf{x}_n)$.

Now it is possible to directly control the complexity of the hyperplane (i.e., VC dimension) *independent of dimensionality of the sample space*. Specifically, consider a structure on the set of separating hyperplanes according to increasing complexity by the norm of the weights $\parallel \mathbf{w} \parallel^2$:

$$S_k = \left\{ (\mathbf{w} \cdot \mathbf{x}) + w_0 : \|\mathbf{w}\|^2 \leq c_k \right\} \quad \text{where} \quad c_1 < c_2 < c_3... \tag{32}$$

Recall that the guaranteed risk for classification problems is the sum of the empirical risk and the confidence interval:

$$R(\mathbf{w}) \leq R_{emp}(\mathbf{w}) + \Phi \tag{33}$$

Since the separating hyperplane always has zero empirical risk, the guaranteed risk is minimized by *minimizing the confidence interval*. The confidence interval is minimized by minimizing the VC dimension h, which according to (31), corresponds to minimizing the norm of the weights $\parallel \mathbf{w} \parallel^2$.

Finding an optimal hyperplane for the separable case is a *quadratic optimization* problem of minimizing (29) with linear constraints (27) given the training data $(\mathbf{x}_i, y_i)$, $i = 1, ..., n$, $\mathbf{x} \in \Re^d$. The solution to this problem consists of $d+1$ parameters. For data of moderate dimension d, this problem can be solved using quadratic programming. For very high dimensional spaces, it is not practical to solve the problem in the present form. However, this problem can be translated into a *dual form* which is is easier to solve because in the dual formulation the problem size depends on the number of samples rather than dimension d. For precise dual SVM formulation see [Vapnik, 1995; Cherkassky and Mulier, 1998].

The SVM model described above is still not very useful, as it cannot handle *nonseparable* training data and *nonlinear* decision boundaries. So we briefly describe next SVM modifications addressing these issues.

First, consider linear separating hyperplanes for nonseparable data. In this case, some of the data samples fall inside the margin, and the SVM attempts to achieve two (conflicting) goals:
(a) maximize the margin;
(b) minimize the number of nonseparable samples, i.e. samples falling within the margin. This is (approximately) achieved by minimizing the total deviation (of nonseparable samples) from the margin boundary.

The trade-off between these two goals leads to SVM formulation called the *soft margin hyperplane* [Vapnik, 1995]. This hyperplane is defined by parameters $\mathbf{w}, \mathbf{w}_0$ which minimize the functional:

$$\frac{C}{n}\sum_{i=1}^{n}\xi_i + \frac{1}{2}\|\mathbf{w}\|^2 \tag{34}$$

where the first term is the sum of deviations ξ_i of nonseparable samples from the margin boundary, and the second term defines the margin (as in the original formulation (27) (29)). The constant C effectively controls the trade-off between SVM complexity and the proportion of nonseparable samples. Thus C is a regularization parameter which must be set by a user or selected via resampling.

The second issue (i.e., *nonlinear* decision boundary) is solved by:

(1) Mapping the input data to high-dimensional feature space via nonlinear mapping $\mathbf{x} \to \mathbf{z}$ specified a priori (see Fig. 5). Let us denote $g_j(\mathbf{x}), j = 1, ..., m$ as a set of nonlinear transformation functions defined apriori. These functions map the vector x into an m-dimensional feature space $\mathbf{z} = \{g_1(\mathbf{x}), ..., g_m(\mathbf{x})\}$.

(2) Constructing an optimal (linear) hyperplane in this feature space. The complexity of SVM decision boundary is independent of the feature space dimensionality, which can be very large (or even infinite).

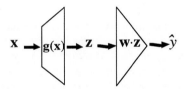

Figure 5. The SVM maps input data **x** into a high dimensional feature space **z** using a nonlinear function g. A linear approximation in the feature space (with coefficients **w**) is used to estimate the output.

Notice that SVM formulation solves the conceptual problem of constructing an *optimal linear decision boundary* in a high-dimensional **z**-space. Moreover, the high-dimensional mapping $\mathbf{x} \to \mathbf{z}$ ensures that nonlinear decision boundaries (in **x**-space) become linear boundaries (in **z**-space). For example, the functions $g_j(\mathbf{x}), j = 1, ..., m$ could correspond to polynomial terms of the components of **x** up to a certain order (including interaction terms). Linear decision boundaries in the feature space would then map to polynomial decision boundaries in the input space. For instance, a two dimensional input vector $\mathbf{x} = (x_1, x_2)$ mapped using third order polynomials, will be transformed to a 16-dimensional feature space. In practical applications, the dimensionality of the feature space is quite large. For example, mapping 100-dimensional input vectors (i.e., 10 by 10 pixel images) using third-order polynomials would yield **z**-space dimensionality over 10^6.

Hence, there is a *technical obstacle* of solving a large-size quadratic optimization problem in **z**-space. This technical problem is addressed next. The original SVM optimization formulation requires only calculation of the inner product between vectors in the **x**-space. Similarly, following mapping $\mathbf{x} \to \mathbf{z}$, solving the SVM optimization problem would require only determining inner products in the feature space defined by the basis functions $g_j(\mathbf{x})$, $j = 1,...,m$. It turns out, that for many mappings $\mathbf{x} \to \mathbf{z}$ satisfying certain mathematical conditions [Vapnik, 1995], the inner product in a high-dimensional $\mathbf{z}$-space can be calculated via inner product kernel in $\mathbf{x}$-space:

$$(\mathbf{z} \cdot \mathbf{z}') = H(\mathbf{x}, \mathbf{x}') \tag{35}$$

where the vectors $\mathbf{z}$ and $\mathbf{z}'$ are the images of vectors $\mathbf{x}$ and $\mathbf{x}'$ in the input space. So instead of computing inner products in a high-dimensional $\mathbf{z}$-space one can use their kernel representation (35) in $\mathbf{x}$-space. In the dual form, the SVM decision function has the form:

$$D(\mathbf{x}) = \sum_{i=1}^{n} \alpha_i y_i H(\mathbf{x}_i, \mathbf{x}) \tag{36}$$

Notice that this representation is same as (30) except that the kernel H takes the place of the inner product in (30).

The kernel functions corresponding to different choices of basis functions can be analytically derived [Vapnik, 1995; Vapnik et al, 1996; Cherkassky and Mulier, 1998]. Below are a few common examples:

Polynomial expansion of degree q have inner product kernel:

$$H(\mathbf{x}, \mathbf{x}') = [(\mathbf{x} \cdot \mathbf{x}') + 1]^q \tag{37}$$

Radial basis functions of the form:

$$f(x) = \text{sign}\left(\sum_{i=1}^{n} \alpha_i \exp\left\{ \frac{|\mathbf{x} - \mathbf{x}_i|^2}{\sigma^2} \right\} \right) \tag{38}$$

where σ defines the width have the inner product kernel:

$$H(\mathbf{x}, \mathbf{x}') = \exp\left\{ -\frac{|\mathbf{x} - \mathbf{x}'|^2}{\sigma^2} \right\} \tag{39}$$

Note that the number of radial basis functions, the center parameters, which correspond to the support vectors, and the coefficients α_i are all automatically determined via the optimal hyperplane. All radial basis functions have the same width parameter which is specified a priori.

Next we review several SVM applications to pattern recognition. The first study (conducted by a team of researchers at Bell Labs) is a popular handwritten character recognition problem, where ten handwritten digits represent zipcodes [LeCun, et al., 1990]. The U.S. Postal data set contains 7,300 training patterns and 2,000 test patterns from real-life postal zipcodes. Following segmentation, each character is recorded as a grey-scale image with a resolution of 16x16 pixels, so the input vector has dimensionality 256. The support vector method with three different classes of approximating functions was applied: third-degree polynomials, radial basis functions, and neural network. The best generalization performance of the

SVM model, i.e. the classification error observed on the test set is around 4% [Vapnik, 1995]. This generalization performance of SVM for this application does not depend on the type of approximating (or kernel) functions used by SVM. For comparison, the percentage error for humans classifying this data set is 2.5% [Bromley & Sackinger, 1991]. Note that SVM is a general purpose learning approach and it does rely on application-specific preprocessing. In fact, SVM would produce the same classification results following a random permutation of pixels in the original data.

Huang et al [1998] applied SVM to eye detection. They used 16x16 image vectors corrsponding to eye / non-eye images. All image data was preprocessed so that each pixel is normalized to a [-1, +1] range before training. The training data consisted of 186 eye images and 185 non-eye images. Independent test data was 100 images of each class. The best generalization performance of 4% (test error) was achieved with polynomial kernels of second degree.

Osuna et al [1997] applied SVM to face detection in natural images. That is, given an arbitrary image (i.e., scanned photo), determine whether it contains faces and locate them. The training data consisted of 19x19 images of faces and non-faces. Some generic preprocessing (illumination gradient correction, histogram equalization) was applied to this data prior to SVM training. The SVM model used second-order polynomial kernel. Following training, their SVM classifier is applied to 19x19 window subimages of an input image. The input image is presented at various scales, in order to achieve scale independent classification. Their test data used two test sets A and B. Set A contained 313 high-quality images containing exactly 1 face. Set B contained 23 'difficult' images containing multiple faces in each image. Note that even though the number of test images fairly small, they generate several million of pattern windows, i.e. overlapping subimages at different scales [Osuna et al, 1997]. Osuna et al [1997] report the following generalization performance of their SVM implementation:

for test set A face detection rate is 97.1% (with 4 false alarms);

for test set B face detection rate is 74.2% (with 20 false alarms).

These results are similar to generalization performance achieved by Sung and Poggio [1994] on the same image data. Sung and Poggio's approach relies on custom preprocessing of the input data to model the distribution of the face and non-face clusters in the feature space, followed by the neural network classifier.

Acknowledgement: this work was supported, in part, by NSF grant IRI--9618167 and by the IBM Partnership Award.

References

Berger, J.(1985) *Statistical Decision Theory and Bayesian Analysis*, Springer

Bishop, C.(1995) *Neural Networks for Pattern Recognition*, Oxford Univ. Press

Bromley, J., Sackinger, E.(1991) Neural network and k nearest neighbor classifiers, Technical Report 11359-910819-16TM, AT&T

Cherkassky, V., Mulier, F.(1998) *Learning From Data: Concepts, Theory and Methods*, Wiley (to appear)

Fisher, R.A.(1952) *Contributions to Mathematical Statistics*, Wiley, New York

Friedman, J.H.(1994) An overview of predictive learning and function approximation, in *From Statistics to Neural Networks*, Cherkassky, V., Friedman, J.H., and Wechsler, H. (Eds.), NATO ASI Series F, 136, Springer Verlag

Huang, J., Ii, D., Shao, X., and Wechsler, H.(1998) Eye Detection and Pose Estimation Using Support Vector Machines (SVM), *Face Recognition: From Theory to Applications*, Wechsler, H., Phillips, J., Bruce, V., Huang, T., and Fogelman, F. (Eds.), Springer Verlag (to appear)

Kolmogorov, A. N.(1965) Three approaches to the quantitative definitions of information, Problem of Information Transmission, 1, (1), 1-7

Le Cun, Y., Boser, B., Denker, J.S., Henderson, D., Howard, R.E., Hubbard, W., Jackel, L.J.(1990) Handwritten digit recognition with a back-propagation neural network, *Advances in Neural Information Processing Systems*, 2, 396-404

Osuna, E., Freund, R., Girosi, F., Training Support Vector Machines: an application to face detection(1997) in Proc. of CVPR'97, Puerto Rico

Rissanen, J.(1978) Modeling by shortest data description, Automatica,14, 465-471

Rissanen, J.(1989) *Stochastic Complexity and Statistical Inquiry*, World Scientific

Sung, K. and Poggio, T., Example-based learning for view-based human face detection(1994) AI memo 1521, MIT AI Lab

Vapnik, V., Golowich, S., Smola, A., Support vector method for function approximation, regression estimation, and signal processing(1996) *Advances in Neural Information Processing Systems*, 10

Vapnik, V. (1982) *Estimation of Dependencies Based on Empirical Data,* Springer Verlag, New York

Vapnik, V. (1995) *The Nature of Statistical Learning Theory*, Springer Verlag, New York

Wechsler, H. (1997) Personal communication

Phenotypic versus Genotypic Approaches to Face Recognition

John Daugman

University of Cambridge
The Computer Laboratory
Cambridge CB2 3QG England

Abstract. Performance of face recognition schemes is bounded at one limit by a *genotypic* error rate (the birth rate of identical twins), and at another limit by a *phenotypic* error rate (change in facial appearance over time). These set minimal False Accept and False Reject frequencies, by undermining the between-class variability in the first case, and increasing the within-class variability in the second. It would be preferable to base recognition decisions upon features which had very little genetic penetrance, yet high complexity, and stability over the lifetime of the individual. Phenotypic facial features do exist with exactly these properties. When imaged at a distance of up to about one meter, the population entropy (information density) of iris patterns is roughly 3.4 bits per square millimeter, and their complexity spans about 266 independent degrees-of-freedom.

Keywords. Phenotype, genotype, monozygotic twins, biometric, iris, randomness, complexity, degrees-of-freedom, 2D Gabor wavelets, demodulation, decidability.

1 Introduction

The central issue in pattern recognition is the relation between within-class variability and between-class variability. These are determined by the degrees of freedom spanned by the pattern classes. Ideally the within-class variability should be small and the between-class variability large, so that the classes are well separated. In the case of encoding faces for identity, one would like different faces to generate face codes that are as different from each other as possible, while different images of the same face should ideally generate similar codes across conditions. Several recent investigations of how well this goal is achieved have studied the invariances in face coding schemes under changes in illumination, perspective angle or pose, and expression. Their results have tended to show that there is greater variability in the code for a given face across these three types of changes, than there is among the codes for different faces when these three factors are kept constant [e.g. Adini et al., 1997]. Since reports documenting performance of particular face recognition algorithms have often been based upon trials in which these factors (pose, illumination, and expression) were held artificially constant, the performance statistics in real-world settings have been disappointing by contrast.

When there is variability across two or more dimensions (let us say both face identity and facial expression), then discriminability can benefit from variability *within* a class of the other dimension, but not *between* classes of the other dimension. For example, facial expressions are more reliably distinguished if there is large variation among the different expressions generated by a given face, but small variation in how a given expression is generated among different faces. Consequences of within-class and between-class variability, for single dimensions and across them, are noted in the following table:

Task	Within-Class Variability	Between-Class Variability
Face detection (classes: face / non-face)	bad	good
Face identification (classes: same/different faces)	bad	good
Facial expression interpretation (classes: same/different faces)	good	bad
Facial expression interpretation (classes: same/different expressions)	bad	good

Some of the forms of variation in facial appearance that have been briefly mentioned here are perhaps best summarized pictorially in the painting by Boilly, *Reunion de Têtes Diverses:*

Louis Léopold Boilly, Reunion de Têtes Diverses

2 Genotype and Phenotype

In characterizing the within-class variability and the between-class variability of faces, it is clear that over sufficient periods of time, the variability of any given face can easily outstrip the variability among contemporary faces. No one would deny that young babies look far more similar to each other, than each does to the adult that it grows into.

Even when all other factors such as pose angle, expression, illumination, and age are held constant, we can distinguish between aspects of facial variation that are genetically inherited ("genotypic features"), from those that primarily reflect development, aging, or environment ("phenotypic features").[1] Persons who are genetically identical would share all their genotypic features, such as gender, blood group, race, and DNA sequence, whereas phenotypic features can be shared among different individuals only by chance, according to their associated probability distributions.

One source of evidence about the genotypic/phenotypic ratio of facial variation arises from identical (monozygotic) twins. Obviously any pair of twins are always matched in age. Each twin's appearance changes over time in the normal dramatic way, yet the pair usually remain strikingly similar to each other in appearance at any age. Nobody would deny that identical twins look vastly more similar to each other than unrelated persons do. Since such twins are genetically identical, their similarity in appearance serves to calibrate the extent of *genetic penetrance* for facial structure.

A further, but secondary, calibration for the genetic penetrance of facial appearance is provided by persons who share only 50% rather than 100% of their genes. These include fraternal twins, full siblings, double cousins, and a given parent and offspring. Occasionally the latter pairings have virtually indistinguishable appearance at a similar age, such as Robert F. Kennedy and his son Michael in adulthood.

2.1 Genotype-Phenotype Limitations on Face Recognition

Automatic face recognition systems have two basic error rates: a False Accept Rate (accepting one person as another), and a False Reject Rate (failing to detect a valid match). It is clear that the phenotypic variation of a person's facial appearance over time imposes one limit on performance (not necessarily the lowest limit), since when such variation is great enough, it causes a False Reject. Likewise, it is clear that the high genetic penetrance for facial appearance imposes a different limit on performance (again, not necessarily the lowest such limit), since persons with identical genetic constitution look

---

[1] I am defining somewhat special terminology here. Strictly speaking, *genotype* refers to a genetic constitution, or a group sharing it, and *phenotype* refers to a feature expressed by the interaction of genotype, environment, and development. *Genetic penetrance* describes the extent to which the features expressed are genetically determined. Those that are, I call *genotypic features*.

so similar. Thus the birth rate of identical twins determines one bound on the False Accept Rate, unless it can be demonstrated that face recognition algorithms can reliably distinguish identical twins, which has not yet been done. These two performance bounds are summarized in the following table:

Type of Feature	Performance Limitation
Genotypic	False Accept Rate $\geq$ birth rate of monozygotic twins
Phenotypic	False Reject Rate $\geq$ feature variability over time

Roughly one in 80 births are twins, and about a third of these are identical (monozygotic). So a representative sample of 240 births (counting twin births as one event) usually yields 243 persons, among whom there are three pairs of twins; and one such pair of persons are genetically identical. Thus the chances are roughly one in 121 (or $2/243 = 0.82\%$) that any person selected at random has an identical twin. Unless and until face recognition algorithms can demonstrate reliable distinction of twins, it must be assumed that such persons would be confused with each other, creating a minimum False Accept Rate of 0.82% due to this birth rate alone. For face recognition applications that require higher confidence levels than 99.18% for correct rejection of false matches, this ceiling on performance is a fatal limitation. Exactly the same argument, and numbers, pertains to the maximum possible confidence levels that can theoretically be achieved by DNA tests.

It is possible, however, to base practical face recognition systems upon phenotypic facial information (not shared by identical twins) that possesses great complexity and randomness; and which furthermore shows invariance to imaging conditions, age, and expression. We will see that when such images can be acquired, they permit a massive reduction in both the False Accept and False Reject error rates compared with the genotypic error bound and phenotypic error bound noted in the above table for overall face recognition.

3 Phenotypic Facial Features with Great Complexity

By far the most numerous and dense degrees-of-freedom (forms of variability among individuals), which are both stable over time and visible in a face, are found in the complex texture of the iris of either eye. This protected internal organ, which can be imaged adequately at distances of up to about a meter, reveals about 266 independent degrees-of-freedom of textural variation across individuals. One way to calibrate the "information density" of the iris is by its human-population entropy per unit area. This works out to 3.4 bits per square millimeter on the iris, based upon 222,743 IrisCode comparisons recently collected by the British Telecom Research Laboratories using the algorithms for iris encoding and recognition to be described here.

3.1 Properties of the Iris

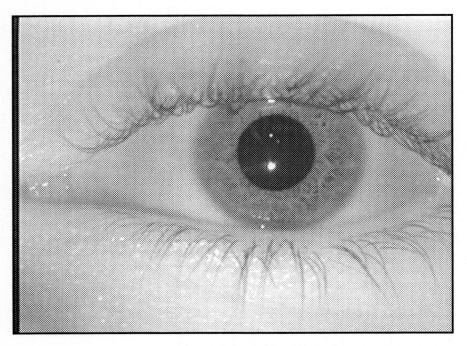

Fig. 3.1. Illustration of an iris pattern, imaged at a distance of about 50 cm.

The iris is composed of elastic connective tissue, the trabecular meshwork, whose prenatal morphogenesis is completed during the 8th month of gestation. It consists of pectinate ligaments adhering into a tangled mesh revealing striations, ciliary processes, crypts, rings, furrows, a corona, sometimes freckles, vasculature, and other features. During the first year of life a blanket of chromatophore cells usually changes the colour of the iris, but the available clinical evidence indicates that the trabecular pattern itself is stable throughout the lifespan. Because the iris is a protected internal organ of the eye, behind the cornea and the aqueous humour, it is immune to the environment except for its pupillary reflex to light. (The elastic deformations that occur with pupillary dilation and constriction are readily reversed mathematically by the algorithms for localizing the inner and outer boundaries of the iris.) Pupillary motion, even in the absence of illumination changes (termed *hippus*), and the associated elastic deformations in the iris texture, provide one test against photographic or other simulacra of a living iris in high security applications of this approach to face recognition. There are few systematic variations in the amount of iris detail with ethnic identity or eye colour; even visibly dark-eyed persons reveal plenty of iris detail when imaged with suitable wavelengths of infrared light. [Clinical reference: Adler, 1965.]

3.2 Analysis of Iris Patterns

The two-dimensional modulations which create iris patterns can be extracted by *demodulation* [Daugman and Downing, 1995], as illustrated in Figure 3.2:

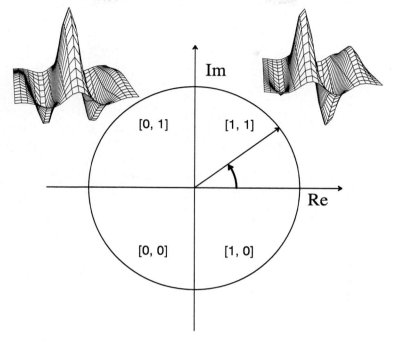

Fig. 3.2. Pattern encoding by phase demodulation using 2D Gabor wavelets.

First it is necessary to localize precisely the inner and outer boundaries of the iris, and to detect and exclude eyelids if they intrude. These detection operations are accomplished by integro-differential operators of the form

$$\max_{(r,x_0,y_0)} \left| G_\sigma(r) * \frac{\partial}{\partial r} \oint_{r,x_0,y_0} \frac{I(x,y)}{2\pi r} ds \right| \tag{3.1}$$

where contour integration parameterized by scale and location coordinates r, x_0, y_0 is performed along arc infinitesimals ds over the image data $I(x,y)$.

Then a doubly-dimensionless coordinate system is defined which maps the tissue in a manner that is invariant to changes in pupillary constriction and overall iris image size, and hence also invariant to camera zoom factor and distance to the eye. This coordinate system is pseudo-polar, although it does not assume concentricity of the inner and outer boundaries of the iris since the pupil is normally somewhat nasal, and inferior, to the iris. The coordinate system compensates automatically for the stretching of the iris

tissue as the pupil dilates. It is illustrated graphically in Figure 3.3, together
with a phase-demodulation IrisCode indicated in the top left as a bit stream.

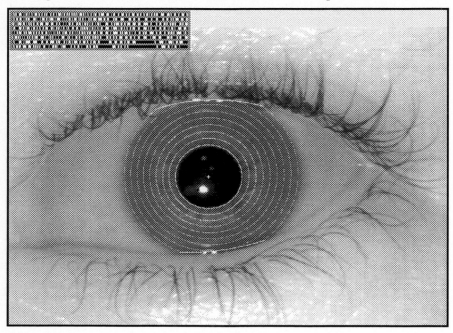

Fig. 3.3. Isolation of an iris for encoding, and its resulting "IrisCode."

The detailed iris pattern is encoded into a 256-byte "IrisCode" by demod-
ulating it with 2D Gabor wavelets [Daugman 1980, 1988], which represent the
texture by phasors in the complex plane. The phasor angle is quantized into
just the quadrant in which it lies for each local element of the iris pattern,
and this operation is repeated all across the iris, at many different scales.

$$h_{Re} = 1 \text{ if } \text{Re} \int_\rho \int_\phi e^{-i\omega(\theta_0-\phi)} e^{-(r_0-\rho)^2/\alpha^2} e^{-(\theta_0-\phi)^2/\beta^2} I(\rho,\phi)\rho d\rho d\phi \geq 0$$
(3.2)

$$h_{Re} = 0 \text{ if } \text{Re} \int_\rho \int_\phi e^{-i\omega(\theta_0-\phi)} e^{-(r_0-\rho)^2/\alpha^2} e^{-(\theta_0-\phi)^2/\beta^2} I(\rho,\phi)\rho d\rho d\phi < 0$$
(3.3)

$$h_{Im} = 1 \text{ if } \text{Im} \int_\rho \int_\phi e^{-i\omega(\theta_0-\phi)} e^{-(r_0-\rho)^2/\alpha^2} e^{-(\theta_0-\phi)^2/\beta^2} I(\rho,\phi)\rho d\rho d\phi \geq 0$$
(3.4)

$$h_{Im} = 0 \text{ if } \text{Im} \int_\rho \int_\phi e^{-i\omega(\theta_0-\phi)} e^{-(r_0-\rho)^2/\alpha^2} e^{-(\theta_0-\phi)^2/\beta^2} I(\rho,\phi)\rho d\rho d\phi < 0$$
(3.5)

3.3 Independence and the Degrees-of-Freedom in IrisCodes

It is important to establish that there exists independent variation in iris patterns, across populations and across positions in the iris. This is confirmed by tracking the probability of a bit being set, as shown in Figure 3.4. If there were any systematic correlations among irises, this plot would not be flat. The fact that it is flat at a value of 0.5 means that any given bit in an IrisCode is equally likely to be set or cleared, and so IrisCodes are maximum entropy codes [Daugman, 1993] in a bit-wise sense.

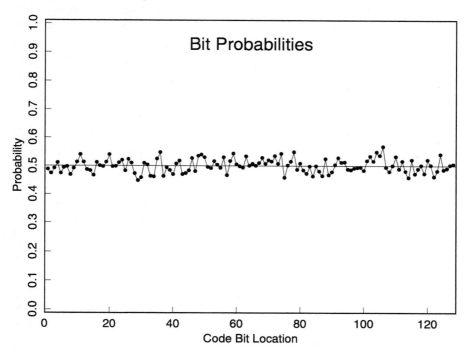

Fig. 3.4. Test for independence of code bits, across a population of IrisCodes.

The histogram in Figure 3.5 compares different eyes' IrisCodes by vector Exclusive-OR'ing them in order to detect the fraction of their bits that disagree. Since any given bit is equally likely to be set or cleared, an average Hamming Distance fraction of 0.5 would be expected. The observed mean was 0.498 in comparisons between 222,743 different pairings of IrisCodes enrolled by British Telecom. The standard deviation of this distribution, 0.0306, indicates that the underlying number of degrees-of-freedom in such comparisons is $N = pq/\sigma^2 = 266$. This indicates that within any given IrisCode, only a small subset of the 2,048 bits computed are independent of each other, due to the large correlations (mainly radial) that exist within any given iris pattern. (If every bit in an IrisCode were independent, then the distribution in Figure 3.5 would be very much sharper, with an expected standard deviation of only $\sqrt{pq/N} = 0.011$; thus the Hamming Distance interval between 0.49 and 0.51 would contain most of its area.) The solid curve fitted to the data is a binomial distribution with 266 degrees-of-freedom; this is the expected distribution from tossing a fair coin 266 times in a row, and tallying up the fraction of heads in each such run. The factorials which dominate the tails of such a distribution make it astronomically improbable that two different IrisCodes having these many degrees-of-freedom could accidentally disagree in much fewer than half their bits. For example, the chances of disagreeing in only 25% or fewer of their bits (getting an HD below 0.25, or equivalent to the chances of getting fewer than 25% heads in 266 coin tosses) are less than one in 10^{16}. Thus the observation of a match with even such poor quality is extraordinarily compelling evidence of identity.

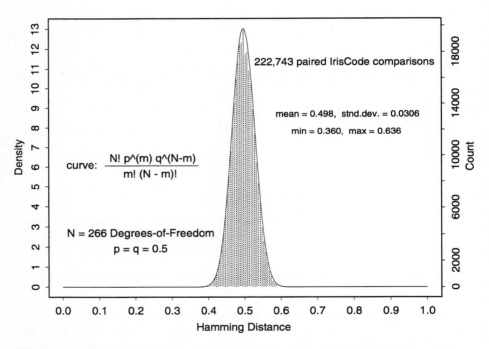

Fig. 3.5. Histogram of raw Hamming Distances between 222,743 pairs of unrelated IrisCodes. The fitted curve is a binomial distribution with 266 degrees-of-freedom.

4 Genetically Identical Irises

Just as the striking visual similarity of identical twins reveals the genetic penetrance of overall facial appearance, a comparison of genetically identical irises reveals that iris texture is a phenotypic feature, not a genotypic feature. A convenient source of genetically identical irises are the right and left pair from any given person. Such pairs have the same genetic relationship as the four irises of two identical twins, or indeed in the probable future, the $2N$ irises of N human clones. Eye colour of course has high genetic penetrance, as does the overall statistical quality of the iris texture, but the textural details are uncorrelated and independent even in genetically identically pairs. This is shown in Figure 4.1, comparing 648 right/left iris pairs from 324 persons.

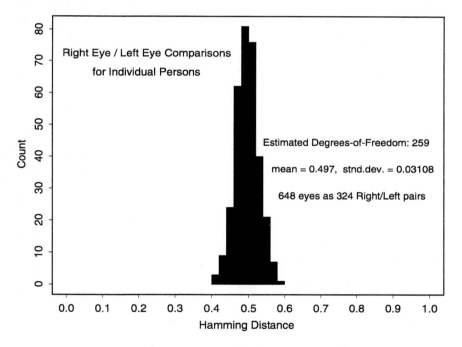

Fig. 4.1. Histogram of raw Hamming Distances between IrisCodes computed from 324 pairs of genetically identical irises (648 eyes in right/left pairs). This distribution is statistically indistinguishable from Figure 3.5, which compared unrelated irises.

The mean Hamming Distance was 0.497 with standard deviation 0.03108, indicating 259 degrees-of-freedom among genetically identical irises. These results are statistically indistinguishable from those shown in Figure 3.5 for genetically unrelated irises. This shows that the detailed phase structure extracted from irises by the phasor demodulation process is phenotypic, so performance is not limited (unlike faces) by the birth rate of identical twins.

5 Statistical Recognition Principle

The principle of operation behind this approach to face recognition using random phenotypic features of high complexity is the *failure* of a test of statistical independence. Samples from stochastic sequences with sufficient complexity need reveal only a little unexpected agreement, in order to reject the hypothesis that they are independent. For example, in two runs of 1,000 coin tosses, agreement rates between their paired outcomes higher than 56% or lower than 44% are extremely improbable: the odds against a higher or lower rate of agreement are roughly 10,000 to 1. The failure of a statistical test of independence can thereby serve as a basis for recognizing patterns with very high confidence, if they possess enough degrees-of-freedom. Combinatorial complexity of random features generates similarity metrics having binomial distributions. With so many degrees-of-freedom, iris patterns thereby allow face recognition decisions to be made with astronomic confidence levels.

5.1 Extreme-Value Distribution for Rotated IrisCodes

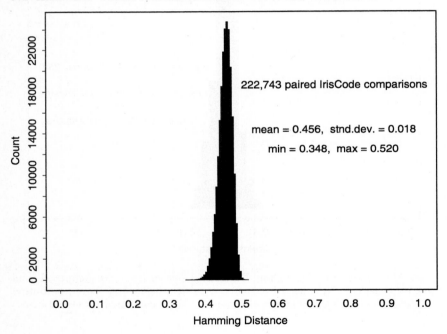

Fig. 5.1. Histogram of Hamming Distances between unrelated IrisCodes computed after comparisons in multiple (7) relative rotations, keeping only each best match.

The computed IrisCode for any eye is invariant under translations and dilations (size change), including changes in the pupil diameter relative to the iris diameter. However, the phasor information scrolls in phase as the iris is rotated, due to tilt of the head or camera or due to torsional rotation of the eye in its socket. Therefore all iris comparisons need to be repeated over a range of relative rotations, keeping only the best match. This amounts to sampling the distribution of Figure 3.5 many times and keeping only the smallest value, which leads to the extreme-value distribution of Figure 5.1.

The raw binomial distribution shown earlier in Figure 3.5 had the form:

$$f(x) = \frac{N!}{m!(N-m)!} \, p^m q^{(N-m)} \tag{5.1}$$

where $N = 266$, $p = q = 0.5$, and $x = m/N$ is the Hamming Distance. Let $F_0(x)$ be its cumulative from the left, up to x: $F_0(x) = \int_0^x f(x)dx$. When only the smallest of n samples from such a distribution is kept, the resulting extreme-value distribution has density $f_n(x)$:

$$f_n(x) = nf(x)\left[1 - F_0(x)\right]^{n-1} \tag{5.2}$$

as shown plotted in Figure 5.2 (data fit will be seen later in Figure 6.1.) The

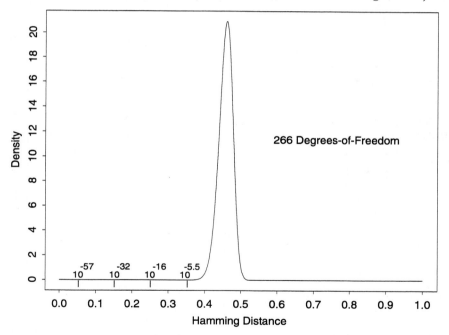

Fig. 5.2. Theoretical density function for the derived binomial distribution for best IrisCode matches after multiple relative rotations.

areas under the tail of this probability density function are shown marked off at various points, illustrating that, for example, finding accidental agreement of two unrelated IrisCodes in 75% or more of their bits (a Hamming Distance of 0.25 or lower) has extremely small probability (roughly 10^{-16}). This illustrates that we can tolerate a huge amount of corruption in iris images due to poor resolution, poor focus, occluding eyelashes and eyelids, contact lenses, specular reflections from the cornea or from eyeglasses, camera noise, etc. We can accept matches of very poor quality, say up to a third of the bits being wrong, and still make decisions about identity with very high confidence.

6 Decidability of Iris-Based Face Recognition

Finally, the overall *decidability* of the task of recognizing faces by their iris patterns is revealed by comparing the Hamming Distance distributions for "same" and "different" irises. To the degree that one can confidently decide whether an observed sample belongs to the left or the right distribution in Figure 6.1, this recognition task can be successfully performed.

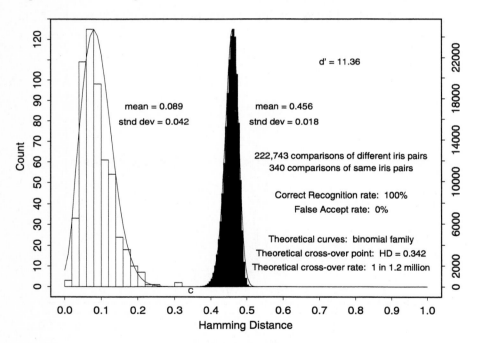

Fig. 6.1. Decision environment for face recognition based on iris patterns.

For such a decision task, the Decidability Index d' measures how well separated the two distributions are, since recognition errors are caused by their overlap. If their two means are μ_1 and μ_2, and their two standard deviations are σ_1 and σ_2, then d' is defined as

$$d' = \frac{|\mu_1 - \mu_2|}{\sqrt{(\sigma_1^2 + \sigma_2^2)/2}} \tag{6.1}$$

This measure of decidability (or detectability) is independent of how liberal or conservative is the acceptance threshold used, and it instead reflects the degree to which any improvement in (say) the False Accept error rate must be paid for by a worsening of the False Reject error rate. The measured decidability is $d' = 11.36$ for iris patterns, which is much higher than for any other reported method of face recognition.

By calculating the areas under the curves fitted to the observed distributions of Hamming Distances, we can compute the theoretical error rates as a function of the decision criterion employed. These are provided in the following Table, for various Hamming Distance acceptance thresholds:

Error Probabilities

HD Criterion	Odds of False Accept	Odds of False Reject
0.28	1 in 10^{12}	1 in 11,400
0.29	1 in 10^{11}	1 in 22,700
0.30	1 in 6.2 billion	1 in 46,000
0.31	1 in 665 million	1 in 95,000
0.32	1 in 81 million	1 in 201,000
0.33	1 in 11.1 million	1 in 433,000
0.34	1 in 1.7 million	1 in 950,000
0.342 Cross-over	1 in 1.2 million	1 in 1.2 million
0.35	1 in 295,000	1 in 2.12 million
0.36	1 in 57,000	1 in 4.84 million
0.37	1 in 12,300	1 in 11.3 million

Table 6.1. Theoretical probabilities of False Accept and False Reject errors, at various decision criteria for the acceptable Hamming Distances between enrolled and presenting IrisCodes. The cross-over point is 0.342, at which fraction of disagreeing bits the odds of either type of error are both equal to 1 in 1.2 million.

6.1 Recognition versus Verification

Because the probabilities of False Accepts are so low even at rather high Hamming Distances, as shown in the Table above, it is possible (and indeed routine) with this approach to perform exhaustive searches through very large databases for *recognition* of a presenting iris pattern, rather than merely a one-to-one comparison for *verification*. Clearly, exhaustive search recognitions are far more demanding than mere verifications, since the probabilities of a False Accept in any single comparison are increased proportionately with the size of the exhaustive search database. More precisely, if P_1 is the probability of a False Accept in a single (one-to-one) verification trial, then P_N, the probability of getting any False Accepts in recognition trials after searching exhaustively through a database of N impostors, is:

$$P_N = 1 - (1 - P_1)^N \qquad (6.2)$$

This is a terribly demanding relationship. For example, even if P_1 were 0.001 (better than any existing scheme for overall face recognition), then even after searching through a database of merely $N = 200$ impostors, the probability of getting one or more False Accepts among these impostors is $P_N = 0.181$; when the database of impostors has grown merely to $N = 2,000$ the probability of a False Accept among them will have grown to $P_N = 0.86$. However, with iris-based face recognition, the confidence levels against a False Accept are so high that we can afford to search even nationwide or planetary-sized databases exhaustively, and still suffer only minuscule chances of a False Accept. The above table of cumulatives under the fitted British Telecom distributions indicates that if we use an acceptance Hamming Distance criterion of 0.28 (i.e. allowing up to 28% of the bits in two IrisCodes to disagree while still accepting them as a match), the False Accept probability in single trials is 10^{-12}. Even after diluting down these odds by performing an exhaustive search over the total number of human irises on the planet, roughly 10^{10}, the chances of a False Accept among them would still be only 1%. This is an extraordinary statistical situation for a recognition system, and it reveals the power of combinatorics to solve pattern recognition problems by reducing them to the detection of the failure of a test of statistical independence.

6.2 Execution Speeds

On an Intel 486DX66 processor (66 MHz), the execution times for the critical steps in this process are as follows, with optimized integer code:

Operation	Execution Time
Assessing image focus	28 milliseconds
Localizing the eye and iris	408 milliseconds
Fitting pupillary boundary	76 milliseconds
Detecting and fitting eyelids	93 milliseconds
Demodulation and IrisCode creation	102 milliseconds

Once an IrisCode has been computed, it is compared exhaustively against all enrolled IrisCodes in the database, in search of a match. This search process is facilitated by vectorizing the XOR comparisons by the word-length of the machine, since two integers of such length (say 32 bits) can have all of their bits XOR'd at once in a single machine instruction. Ergodicity (representativeness of subsamples) and commensurability (universal format of IrisCodes) facilitate extremely rapid comparisons. On a 486DX66 processor the rate of raw comparisons approaches 100,000 IrisCodes per second, and this rate could be increased using dedicated PLA hardware to many millions of persons per second if such large databases of IrisCodes were ever enrolled.

6.3 Current Usage of this Technique

In addition to the British Telecom license for experimental trials, whose data were reproduced here, the algorithms described in this chapter have also been licensed in executable form to Sensar Corp. (New Jersey, USA) for installation into bank Automatic Teller Machines manufactured by NCR Corp., Diebold, Siemens AG (Munich), and Oki (Tokyo). They have also been implemented into IriScan (New Jersey, USA) products for physical access control, nuclear power station security, computer login, prison controls, electronic commerce authentication, and various Goverment applications.[2]

References

[Adini et al. 1997] Adini, Y., Moses, Y., and Ullman, S. (1997) Face recognition: the problem of compensating for changes in illumination direction. *IEEE Trans. Pattern Analysis and Machine Intelligence*, 19(7): 721-732.

[Adler 1965] Adler, F.H. (1965). *Physiology of the Eye: Clinical Application*, fourth ed. London: The C.V. Mosby Company.

[Daugman and Downing 1995] Daugman, J., and Downing, J. (1995) Demodulation, predictive coding, and spatial vision. *J. Opt. Soc. Am. A*, 12(4): 641-660.

[Daugman 1980] Daugman, J. (1980) Two-dimensional spectral analysis of cortical receptive field profiles. *Vis. Res.* 20(10): 847-856.

[Daugman 1988] Daugman, J. (1988) Complete discrete 2D Gabor transforms by neural networks for image analysis and compression. *IEEE Trans. Acoustics, Speech, and Signal Processing* 36(7): 1169-1179.

[Daugman 1993] Daugman, J. (1993) High confidence visual recognition of persons by a test of statistical independence. *IEEE Trans. Pattern Analysis and Machine Intelligence*, 15(11): 1148-1161.

[2] **Acknowledgements:** Supported by grants from British Telecom and The Gatsby Foundation. The large database of iris images from which IrisCodes were computed and compared were acquired and made available by British Telecom. Their cooperation and support are gratefully acknowledged.

Connectionists Methods for Human Face Processing

Emmanuel Viennet[1] and Françoise Fogelman Soulié[2]

[1]LIPN, Université Paris 13, 93430 Villetaneuse, France.
viennet@lipn.univ-paris13.fr
[2]Atos Ingéniérie Intégration,
1 avenue Newton, bp 207, 92 142 Clamart cedex, France.
ffogelman@atos-group.com

Abstract. We show in this paper how Neural Networks can be used for Human Face Processing. In Part I, we show how Neural Networks can be viewed as a particular class of Statistical models. We introduce learning as an estimation problem (1), then describe Multi-Layer Perceptrons and Radial Basis Function networks (2), widely used Neural Networks which we will use in Part II, for face processing. We further present Vapnik's framework for learning (3), show the capacity/generalization dilemma and discuss its implications for Neural Network training and model selection. Vapnik's ideas lead to a new interesting class of classifier, Support Vector Machines, presented in section 3.2. We then discuss the combination of models (4) and give a formalism which allows to cooperatively train multi-modular Neural Networks architectures. Finally, we present a multi-modular architecture to perform "Segmentation-Recognition in the loop" (5).

In Part II, we show how the presented models can be applied to build an efficient face localization and identification system. The face images are detected by scanning the scene with a retina feeding a hierarchical coarse-to-fine classifier. Detections are then identified in a small family of known persons.

Part I: Introduction to Connectionist Methods

Recent developments in the Neural Network (NN) field have shown the deep theoretical links between NN and Statistics [20, 41]. In practice, developing a NN requires the same care as for a statistical model. Some authors [37] have even proposed an equivalence list (table 1) trying to show that the differences between NN and statistics could be but a matter of vocabulary only.

In a way, *Neural Networks are indeed simple statistical models*: there are actually formal equivalences between some NN and conventional statistical techniques, such as Principal Component Analysis, Discriminant Analysis, Projection Pursuit, Ridge Regression...

On the other hand, *NN are not only statistical models*: they can be expressed in a unique formulation, which embodies both linear and non-linear models; it is easy to incorporate a priori knowledge into a NN architecture; NNs can be combined into complex multi-modular architectures. Yet, NN are by no means systematically better than statistical models: there is no "universaly best" model and one should always

Neural Networks	Statistics
learning	estimation
weight	parameters
knowledge	parameters value
supervised learning	regression / classification
classification	discrimination
non supervised learning	density estimation / clustering
clustering	classification / taxinomy
neural network	model
"large": 100 000 weights	"large": 50 parameters
learning set	sample
"large": 50 000 examples	"large": 200 cases

Table 1: Glossary: Neural Networks vs. Statistics.

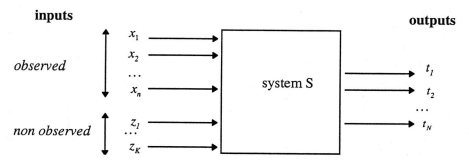

Figure 1: Input-output system.

compare various techniques in order to achieve the best performances on his problem.

In this paper, we will introduce some elements of the general statistical framework of NN, which we will then apply to face processing in Part II. The interested reader can refer to specialized books for more detailed presentations [5, 14, 37].

1 The problem

We will concentrate here on NNs trained through supervised learning.

1.1 The statistical model

Let us consider 3 random variables X, T and Z, of dimension n, N and K respectively, and an *input-output system* S (fig. 1), which, from inputs X and Z produces output T [20].

The system implements the mapping ("true" but unknown):

$$t_k = g_k(x_1, \ldots, x_n; z_1, \ldots, z_k) \quad k = 1, \ldots, N \tag{1}$$

However, since only inputs x can be observed, system S is modelled through a statistical model:

$$t_k = f_k(x_1, \ldots, x_n) + \epsilon_k \quad k = 1, \ldots, N \tag{2}$$

where ϵ_k is a random variable with (unknown) distribution P_ϵ, which models our ignorance of the non observable variable Z.

The problem consists in estimating function f_k.

1.2 Estimation

Let us suppose that we are given a *sample D*, of m observations of variables (X, T). From now on, for the sake of simplicity, we will assume that T is of dimension 1: $N = 1$. We denote f the function f_1 and $P(x, t)$ the joint distribution of (X, T):

$$D = \{(x^1, t^1), \ldots, (x^m, t^m)\} \tag{3}$$

We look for an estimator $\hat{f}$ of f. One can use $\hat{f}$ for:

1. *prediction / classification*: for any new data vector $x = (x_1, \ldots, x_n)$, one wants to predict what the output of system S will be: $t = \hat{f}(x)$.

   In this case, one will try to minimize the approximation error, i.e. $f(x) - \hat{f}(x)$.

2. *interpretation*: one wants to use $\hat{f}$ to understand the structure of system S.

NN are used mostly for prediction/classification, while statistical models are more often targetted at interpretation.

Let $L[t, g(x)]$ be the *loss function* which measures the cost resulting from replacing function f by function g. The risk R is defined as:

$$R(f, g) = \int L\,[t, g(x)]\,dP(x, t) \tag{4}$$

Risk R is the criterion used to compute estimator $\hat{f}$: $\hat{f}$ is chosen, from the set of all possible functions g, as that function which minimizes the risk:

$$\hat{f} = \arg\min_g R(f, g) \tag{5}$$

In practice, one cannot compute R since distribution P is unknown. One must thus use either of two methods:

- *density estimation*: estimate P, then replace it by its estimation in 5, and look for estimation $\hat{f}$ solution of 5;
- *regression*: define the *empirical risk*:

$$R_E(f, g) = \frac{1}{m} \sum_{k=1}^{m} L\,[t^k, g(x^k)] \tag{6}$$

which measures the average loss on sample D and find $\hat{f}$ which minimizes R_E.

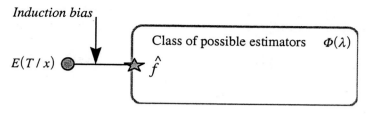

Figure 2: Estimator $\hat{f}$ is searched within space $\Phi(\lambda)$.

For example, if the loss is measured by the square error, R is the *Mean Square Error* criterion (MSE) and R_E the Empirical Mean Square Error (EMSE). That is, one have:

$$L[t, g(x)] = [t - g(x)]^2 \tag{7}$$

$$R(f, g) = \text{MSE} = E\left([t - g(x)]^2\right) = \int [t - g(x)]^2 \, dP(x, t)$$

$$R_E(f, g) = \text{EMSE} = \frac{1}{m} \sum_{k=1}^{m} [t^k - g(x^k)]^2$$

The following property holds true for any function g:

$$E\left([T - g(x)]^2\right) = \int [t - g(x)]^2 \, dP(x, t)$$

$$= E\left([T - E(T/X)]^2\right) + [E(T/X) - g(X)]^2$$

Hence, that estimator which minimizes R in the least mean square sense is:

$$\hat{f}(x) = E(T/X)$$

i.e. the conditional expectancy of T given X is the optimal estimator. Let us notice that, in the case where T is a discrete variable (e.g. in classification):

$$\hat{f}(x) = P(T/x)$$

which is the a posteriori probability of class T, given x.

1.3 Search Space for the Estimator

In practice, the estimator $\hat{f}$ is constrained to be part of a given class of functions $\Phi(\lambda)$ (where λ is the index of functions in $\Phi(\lambda)$, not necessarily a parameter). Then, when solving 5, one is restricted to searching space $\Phi(\lambda)$ and thus is not guaranteed to be able to reach the optimal solution $E(T/x)$: there is a systematic induction bias (fig. 2).

One should expect estimator $\hat{f}$ to be consistant: if class $\Phi(\lambda)$ grows, then $\hat{f}$ should become optimal.

In *non-parametric estimation*, there is no a priori assumption on the form of functions in $\Phi(\lambda)$. This is the case for example for *k-nearest neighbor* models (k-nn) or *Parzen windows*: λ is then a parameter equal to $1/k$ for k-nn and $1/\sigma$ for Parzen windows of width σ.

In *parametric estimation*, functions in $\Phi(\lambda)$ are of a given form, parameterized by a (vector) parameter W: $\Phi(\lambda, W)$. This is the case, for example, of *Gaussian mixtures*

(λ is the number of Gaussians in the mixture and $W = (\mu, \sigma)$ is the parameter of the Gaussian), or of Multi-Layer Perceptrons (λ is the number of hidden neurons, W the weight vector of the network).

In this case, the estimation problem is decomposed into two successive steps:

1. *data approximation*: data are fitted by choosing the optimal parameter W:

$$W^* = \arg\min_W \frac{1}{m} \sum_{k=1}^{m} \left[t^k - g(x^k; W; \lambda) \right]^2 \qquad (8)$$

$$\hat{f}(x; \lambda) = g(x; W^*; \lambda)$$

2. *model selection*: one compares various families $\{\Phi(\lambda), \lambda\}$ and chooses an "optimal" value of λ (we will see later how).

1.4 The Bias / Variance Dilemma

We have denoted D the data sample $\{(x^1, t^1), \ldots, (x^m, t^m)\}$ which allowed us to compute the estimator $\hat{f}$ of f. $\hat{f}$ thus depends upon sample D, which we will denote $\hat{f}(x; D)$. Let us introduce this dependency in equation 7. We have:

$$E\left(\left[T - \hat{f}(X; D) \right]^2 / X, D \right) = \int \left[T - \hat{f}(X; D) \right]^2 dP(x, t)$$

$$= E\left([T - E(T/X)]^2 / X, D \right) + \left[\hat{f}(X; D) - E(T/X) \right]^2$$

As we saw before, $\left[\hat{f}(X; D) - E(T/X) \right]^2$ is a measure of the quality of estimator $\hat{f}$. To obtain a measure independant from the particular sample D, we can average this measure on all possible data samples D (of size m). we obtain [21]:

$$E_D\left(\left[\hat{f}(X; D) - E(T/X) \right]^2 \right)$$

$$= \underbrace{\left(E_D\left[\hat{f}(X; D) \right] - E\left[T/X\right] \right)^2}_{\text{bias}} + \underbrace{E_D\left(\left[\hat{f}(X; D) - E_D\left(\hat{f}(X; D) \right) \right]^2 \right)}_{\text{variance}}$$

The *bias* measures the mean distance of $\hat{f}(X; D)$ to the optimal value $E(T/X)$, whereas the variance measures how this distance varies with D.

A "good" estimator will have a good *accuracy*, i.e. a small bias, and a good *stability*, i.e. a small variance. However, these two objectives are contradictory: when λ parameter increases (for example in the above mentionned families: k-nn, Parzen windows, Gaussian mixtures, MLP), then the bias decreases and the variance increases (fig. 3). λ is thus used to control the bias / variance balance.

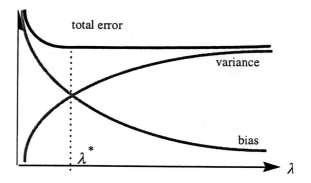

Figure 3: Bias / Variance Dilemma.

2 Multi-Layer Perceptrons

2.1 Neurons

A neuron is an elementary processor characterized by (fig. 4):
- an internal state $s_i \in \wp$;
- input signals $s_1, \ldots, s_n$;
- a state transition function g: $s_i = g(s_1, \ldots, s_n)$.

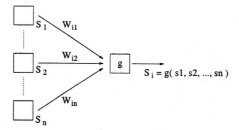

Figure 4: The neuron

There exist various sorts of neurons, in particular:
- *dot-product neuron*. Its transition function is: $s_i = f(A_i)$ with

$$A_i = \sum_{k=1}^{n} W_{ik} s_k = {}^t W_i . s \qquad (9)$$

where coefficient W_{ik} is called the connection weight from k to i.

The dot-product neuron is thus composed of two successive modules: a linear transformation (the dot-product) followed by a (generally) non-linear transformation f. Function f can be the identity, a threshold function, a sigmoid function, ...

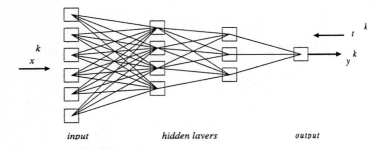

Figure 5: Multi-Layer Perceptron (MLP).

- *distance neuron.* Its transition function is again $s_i = f(A_i)$, here with

$$A_i = \|W_i - s\|^2 \qquad (10)$$

The distance neuron is thus composed of two successive module: a distance evaluation module followed by a (generally) non-linear transformation f. Function f can be the identity or a kernel function. Distance neurons compare a *prototype* (their weight vector W_i) to the input signal.

A *Neural Network* (NN) is a set of interconnected neurons. It is fully caracterized by:

- its architecture: the number of neurons and their interconnection scheme;
- the neurons transition functions: weights W_{ik} and functions f.

2.2 The Multi-Layer Perceptron (MLP)

A Multi-Layer Perceptron (MLP) (fig. 5) is a network composed of successive *layers* (a layer is a set of neurons which are not connected):

- an input layer (where the inputs to the system are presented) and an output layer (where the outputs of the system are read out);
- one or more hidden layers.

Each neuron is a dot-product neuron (eq. 9) where function f is a sigmoid function (in general). A MLP implements a transformation:

$$y = F(x_1, \ldots, x_n; W) \qquad (11)$$

MLPs can be connected in various ways, depending upon the problem (fig. 6):

- full connections: the neuron receives inputs from all neurons in the previous layer;
- local connections: a neuron receives inputs from only some of the neurons in the previous layer, called its "receptive field". The various neurons in one layer can have receptive fields of the same size, covering -possibly with some overlap- the input layer. This arrangement is similar to having a sliding "window" on the input layer.
- shared weights: all neurons in one layer are locally connected to their inputs through a receptive field of the same size, and their weights are identical. This

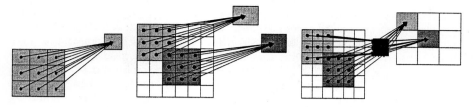

Figure 6: Connections in Multi-Layer Perceptron: full connections (left), local connections (middle) and shared weights (right).

arrangement is similar to having a filter passed through the input layer, the coefficients of the filter being the common weights vector.

It is to be noted that, depending upon the connection scheme, the number of weights can be very different: for an input layer with N neurons and a layer with P neurons, the number of weights on connections between these 2 layers will be $P \times N$ for full connections, $P \times k$ for local connections with a receptive field of size k, and just k for local connections with shared weights.

One particular case of MLP is the non-supervised or auto-associative MLP (fig. 7): its input and output layers have the same number of neurons. The desired output is identical to the input: the MLP is expected to reproduce the input at its output layer. In general, the hidden layer has less neurons than the input or output layers: the MLP thus has to encode the input signal into the hidden neurons, and thus decode it to produce the output.

In the general case where the output layer is different from the input layer, one has a hetero-associative MLP. This is, in particular the case in classification problems: the output layer then has as many neurons as there are classes; for class i, all neurons will be "off" (state 0) except neuron i which will be "on" (state 1).

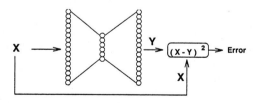

Figure 7: Multi-Layer Perceptron in auto-associative mode.

2.3 Training MLPs

An MLP is "trained" by using a data sample D (3) so as to determine those weights W^* solutions of (8) where $g(x; W; \lambda)$ is the function $F(x; W)$ implemented by the MLP:

$$W^* = \arg \min_W \frac{1}{m} \sum_{k=1}^{m} \left[t^k - F(x^k; W) \right]^2 \tag{12}$$

In order to solve (12), one uses numerical optimization techniques: gradient descent, conjugate gradients, second order methods, ..., which are called, in this context, *learning algorithms*. The most well known algorithm, the *gradient back-propagation* algorithm is based upon the following idea: in any point W, the gradient vector of the empirical risk, ∇R_E, points in the direction of increasing empirical risk. To decrease R_E, one thus has just to move in the opposite direction to the gradient ∇R_E. The back-propagation algorithm is an iterative algorithm, which consists in modifying weights according to the following rule:

$$W_{ij}(t) = W_{ij}(t-1) + \Delta W_{ij}(t) \tag{13}$$

where $\Delta W_{ij}(t)$ is proportional to the opposite of the gradient:

$$\Delta W_{ij}(t) = -\epsilon(t)\frac{1}{m}\sum_{k=1}^{m}\frac{\partial C_E(x^k;W)}{\partial W_{ij}} \tag{14}$$

where $C_E(x^k;W) = \left[t^k - F(x^k;W)\right]^2$.

This algorithm depends upon all the examples, which have thus to be made available for each weight update: this is why it is called the *off-line* algorithm. The *on-line* algorithm performs one weight update after each presentation of an example:

$$\Delta W_{ij}(t) = -\epsilon(t)\frac{\partial C_E(x^k;W)}{\partial W_{ij}} \tag{15}$$

Usually, especially when the data sample D is large, and thus redundant, the on-line algorithm is much faster than the off-line algorithm [29].

In practice, one uses the given data sample D_m as follows: it is separated in 3 sub-samples: $D = D_m^l$ is the training set used in (14) or (15). D_m^v is a validation set used for model selection, i.e. to compare the performances of models (e.g. compare MLPs with various numbers of hidden units). Finally, D_m^t is used to estimate the performances of the selected optimal model on an independent data set which has never been used during training or validation.

One should be careful when training MLPs: learning algorithms must, like every other numerical algorithms, be implemented with care. There are many tricks described in the litterature: one must be cautious and make a clear distinction between theoretical results and the results which are actually achieved after numerical training.

2.4 Radial Basis Function Network

A Radial Basis Function Network -RBF- (fig. 8) is a MLP with one hidden layer of distance neurons. It is trained in much the same way as MLPs, the parameters to be adapted through learning are W_{ij}^1 the parameters of the function used in the hidden layer (10), and W_i the weights from hidden to output layer. For example, if the hidden neurons are Gaussian:

$$F(x_1,\ldots,x_n) = \sum_{i=1}^{p} W_i \exp\left[-\frac{1}{\sigma_i^2}\sum_{j=1}^{n} n(x_j - \mu_i)^2\right] \tag{16}$$

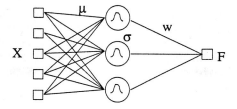

Figure 8: Radial Basis Function Network.

and $W_{ij}^1 = (\mu_i, \sigma_i^2)$.

These parameters are updated by applying (14) or (15) with the derivative of C_E being computed with respect to W_{ij}^1 and W_i. In the same way as nearest neighbor classifiers, RBFs tend to have poor performances on high-dimensional inputs.

3 Vapnik's model and Support Vector Machines

3.1 Risk and Generalization bounds

We have previously defined the risk R and the empirical risk R_E by:

$$R(f,g) = \int L\left[t, g(x)\right] dP(x,t)$$

$$R_E(f,g) = \frac{1}{m}\sum_{k=1}^{m} L\left[t^k, g(x^k)\right]$$

Since $P(x,t)$ is unknown, one cannot compute R nor thus minimize it. In practice, one thus tries to minimize R_E: this is the *minimum empirical risk principle* (MRE). Before accepting such a principle, one should be able to answer the following questions [40]:

- is the MRE principle consistant? i.e. does function $\hat{f}_m$ which minimizes R_E for sample D_m converge to function $\hat{f}$ which minimizes R?
- is convergence fast?

The answers to these questions depend upon the *Vapnik Chervonenkis dimension* (VC dimension) of the class of functions $\Phi(\lambda)$ where the solution $\hat{f}_m$ is looked for. We will not define here the VC dimension (see for instance [39, 11]): suffices it to say that it is an estimation of the class *complexity*. Denoting h this dimension, Vapnik [40] has shown that:

1. the MRE principle is consistant if dimension h is finite;

2. the speed of convergence is: $\sqrt{\ln(m/h)/(m/h)}$;

3. with probability $1 - \eta$:

$$R(f,\hat{f}) \leq R_E(f,\hat{f}) + C(m,h;\eta) \tag{17}$$

$$C(m,h;\eta) = 2\sqrt{\frac{1+\ln(2m/h)}{m/h} - \frac{\ln\eta}{m}} \tag{18}$$

These properties, and in particular (18), show that it is reasonable to minimize the empirical risk R_E instead of risk R, *as long as h is finite*. However, there is a systematic error which depends upon m, the size of sample D_m, and h the VC dimension of class $\Phi(\lambda)$. This error is bounded by $C(m, h; \eta)$ (fig. 9). However, Vapnik's result (18) is a worst case analysis: the bound is not very tight.

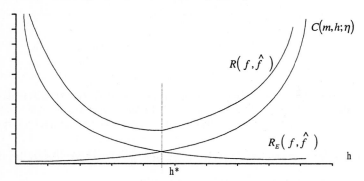

Figure 9: Risk R, Empirical risk R_E and Vapnik's bound C.

The expression of (18) shows that there exists an optimal value h^* of h. If m is fixed, then when h increases:
- the empirical risk $R_E(f, \hat{f})$ decreases;
- the error bound $C(m, h; \eta)$ increases.

This is the usual bias-variance dilemma. As h grows larger, it becomes easier to fit the data and the bias becomes smaller. However, when h grows larger, the estimator depends more on the data and the variance grows larger too. As a result there exists a class of functions $\Phi(h^*)$ of optimal complexity h^* for which $R(f, \hat{f})$ is minimal (fig. 9): h^* must be large enough to fit the data, but not too much with respect to the number m of available data.

Vapnik's results allow to apply the MRE principle, by ensuring a bound on the generalization error $C(m, h; \eta)$. However:
- this bound is not tight: as we have said before, it comes from a worst case analysis;
- the VC dimension is defined through theoretical developments [39]. Its value is known (table 2) for only a few classes $\Phi(\lambda)$, but not for the simplest classes of MLPs.

3.2 Support Vector Machines

Support Vector Machines (SVM) are new classifiers proposed by Vapnik [41] and implementing the Structural Risk Minimization principle.

In the following, we will briefly recall the SVM principles. The interested reader can find more information in the paper of V. Cherkassky in this volume, or in a tutorial by C. Burges [11]. In section 9, we will present a few preliminary results obtained with SVM on our face detection application.

Network	VC dimension	Reference
threshold neurons N neurons, W weights	$h \leq 2W \log_2 eN$	[3]
$k_0 \times k_1 \times 1$ W weights from input to others neurons	$h \geq W + 1$	[2]
$k_0 \times k_1 \times 1$	$h \leq 2W \log_2 eN$	[3]
$k_0 \times k_1 \times k_2 \times 1$ if $k_0 \geq k_1$ and $k_2 \leq \frac{2^{k_1}}{k_1^2/2 + k_1/2 + 1}$: if $k_1 > k_0 > 1$ and $k_1 \geq k_2$:	$h \geq k_0 k_1 + 1 + k_1(k_2 - 1)$ $h \geq k_0 k_1 + 1 + \frac{k_1(k_2-1)}{2}$	[2]

Table 2: Vapnik Chervonenkis Dimension for some classes of MLPs. The notation $k_0 \times k_1 \times s$ represents a MLP with k_0 input neurons, k_1 hidden neurons, and s output neurons. $k_0 \times k_1 \times k_2 \times s$ is a MLp with 2 hidden layers with k_1 and k_2 neurons.

Introduction When building a pattern classifier, one wants to minimize the *risk* R or generalization error. During learning, we can only measure the *empirical risk* R_{emp}, the error on the training sample. We mentionned above (17) a bound on the risk functional, which can also be written as follows: with probability $1 - \eta$,

$$R \leq R_{emp} + C(l/h, \eta) \tag{19}$$

where C depends on the Vapnik-Chervonenkis dimension h of the set functions implemented by the classifier and the size l of the training sample. C gives a confidence interval on the generalization error, knowing the error on the learning sample.

Empirical Risk Minimization (ERM) strategies [41] aim to minimize the bound on R by minimizing the first term R_{emp} of eq. 19. Neural Networks are good examples of ERM application. In order to control the generalization (C), a classifier with small h must be chosen. This can be achieved by data preprocessing [22], regularization techniques, or network architecture selection.

SVM implements another strategy : keep the empirical risk fixed ($R_{emp} = 0$) and minimize $C(l/h, \eta)$. A SVM is a two-class classifier which simply computes $f(x, w, b) = \text{sign}(w.x + b)$ If the set $(x_i, y_i), i = 1, ..., l$ (where $y_1 = \pm 1$ gives the class of each example) can be separated without errors by f, one can show that the VC dimension h of the family of functions f is bounded by

$$h \leq \min(R^2 A^2, n) + 1 \tag{20}$$

where n is the dimension of the input space, R is the radius of the smallest sphere enclosing all the examples x_i, and A a constant such that $\|w\| < A$.

Thus, if we minimize $\|w\|$, we also minimize the bound on the generalization error $C(l/h, \eta)$ in eq. 19. Minimizing $\|w\|$ while separating the classes has a convincing geometric interpretation : it leads to the hyperplane whose distance to the closest example (the so-called *margin*) is maximal.

Optimal Hyperplane   The problem stated above can be formulated as follows : minimize $\Phi = \frac{1}{2} w.w$ subject to the constraints : $y_i.f(x_i, w, b) \geq 1$, $i = 1...l$. By expressing the Lagrangian $L(w, b, \alpha) = \Phi - \sum \alpha_i \{f(x, w, b) - 1\}$, it can easily shown [41] that the solution w_0 is a linear combination of the examples x_i : $w_0 = \sum y_i \alpha_i x_i$. Lagrange multipliers $\Lambda = (\alpha_i)$ are maximizing the functional

$$Q(\Lambda) = \sum_{i=1}^{l} \alpha_i - \frac{1}{2} \sum_{i,j=1}^{l} \alpha_i \alpha_j y_i y_j x_i.x_j \tag{21}$$

under the constraints : $\sum_{i=1}^{l} \alpha_i^0 y_i = 0$ and $\alpha_i \geq 0$.

All constraints which are *active* in the solution lead to zero multipliers, $\alpha_k = 0$. Thus, only a few patterns appear in expression of w_0. They are called *support vectors* (SV).

The derivation above can be generalized to non-linear separators simply by changing the scalar product $u.v = K(u,v)$. Among useful scalar products, we decided to use the polynomials of degree d : $K(u,v) = (\frac{u.v}{n})^d$ which allow to draw SVM non-linear frontiers between classes.

Non separability   If the training set is not separable by the hyper-surface, the problem given by eq. 21 has no solution. Vapnik [41] suggests to use a modified formulation which leads to maximize the same functional $Q(\Lambda)$ under one more constraint $\alpha_i \leq C$. The constant C prevents divergence of Q and controls the capacity of the classifier. The choice of C is done empirically.

Optimization technique   In order to implement the SVM, we developed an optimization method based on the algorithm proposed by More and Torraldo [30]. This algorithm is oriented to solve large quadratic programming problems with bound constraints. Given a quadratic function $q : I\!\!R^n \to I\!\!R$, the problem is to find

$$\min_{x}\{q(x) : l \leq x \leq u\}, \tag{22}$$

where $l \in I\!\!R^n$ and $u \in I\!\!R^n$ define the feasible region. The idea of the algorithm is to use a conjugate gradient to search the face of the feasible region defined by the current iterate and the projected gradient method to move to a different face. It is proved that for strictly convex problems the algorithm converges to the solution in a finite number of steps.

To build a SVM, we have the minimize the quadratic form $Q(\Lambda)$ under bound constraints $0 \leq \alpha_i \leq C$ and $\sum_{i=1}^{l} \alpha_i^0 y_i = 0$. We can use a penalization technique to express this problem in the form of equation 22. This introduces a term $\frac{\gamma}{2} \left(\sum_{i=1}^{n} \alpha_i y_i \right)^2$, $\gamma > 0$ and we define q as

$$q(\Lambda) = \frac{1}{2}\Lambda'(D + \gamma F)\Lambda - \sum_{i=1}^{l} \alpha_i, \tag{23}$$

where $D_{ij} = y_i y_j K(x_i, x_j)$ and $F_{ij} = y_i y_j$ are positive matrices. As γ grows, the solution converges to the solution of the original problem (eq. 21).

Incremental optimization During optimization with l examples, we have to store a l by l matrix. In our case, the total number of examples (faces + backgrounds) reach 50 000, so we have to optimize incrementally the SVM, using the following procedure:

1. Let A be of set of N_a patterns, initialized randomly from the training set, and B the set of the remaining examples.

2. Optimize the SVM on A. A subset of the patterns of A is selected as support vectors and kept in A, while the other examples, for which $y_i.f(x_i, w, b) > 1$ are moved to B.

3. Select some patterns from B such that $y_i.f(x_i, w, b) \leq 1$, and put them in A.

4. Repeat from step 2, until convergence.

At the end of this procedure, A contains the SV. Note that N_a must be larger that the total number of SV. This number is related to the generalization error rate [11, 41].

4 Models Combination

It very often happens that we have a family of models to choose from: one can try to *select* the best one for his particular problem, or to *combine* them all. When combining models, one hopes that the errors of one model will not be done by another, so that the overall performances of the combination will be improved. There exist various ways to combine models.

- *ensemble*: all models are computed *in parallel* and the various estimations produced are then combined, e.g. by taking their average [23];
- *stacking*: all models are computed in sequence and the final estimation is the result of the last model [45, 9];
- *task decomposition*: one sequence of models is executed, depending on the input. Input space is decomposed in various "zones", each corresponding to a particular sub-task: the corresponding sequence of models is the "expert" dedicated to solving that task. The decomposition can be done by hand or obtained through training [25].

These combination methods can be used to build complex multi-modular architectures, which embody the knowledge available about the particular problem at hand.

A technique was introduced [6, 7] to train such multi-modular architectures. Let us suppose that we have an architecture composed of $M_1, \ldots, M_N$ interconnected in such a way that their interconnection graph has no cycle.

One can show that it is possible to train such an architecture through an algorithm very similar to the Gradient Back-propagation algorithm. In practice, each module is trained separately and then the whole architecture is trained cooperatively. This technique has proved very efficient in many applications [4, 42, 19].

5 Segmentation - Recognition

In many image processing problems, objects must be first localized and then identified. This is the case for example in Optical Character Recognition (OCR) and of course

138

in face recognition, but it occurs in speech processing as well. The two problems are heavily inter-twinned: one can easily segment a character which he has already identified, but isolating an object without knowing what it is is much harder. Hence the idea of "segmentation-recognition in the loop", which has been first proposed in the OCR domain [27, 28].

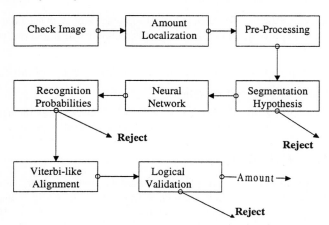

Figure 10: Segmentation-Recognition in the Loop.

For example, we have developed an OCR application for check-reading [18] with a succession of steps (fig. 10): a segmentation hypothesis is generated which is then passed for recognition to a multi-modular architecture. The result of this recognition is scored by a Viterbi algorithm: and the result with best score is chosen as the final result. The process of segmentation-recognition is thus iterative: if the score is not high enough, further segmentation hypothesis can be generated.

The multi-modular architecture has two modules (fig. 11):

- an MLP for feature extraction: the MLP is an auto-associative MLP (see fig. 7);
- an RBF for recognition: the RBF uses as input the "code" extracted in the hidden layer of the MLP.

Such an architecture is very efficient: the MLP reduces the dimensionality of the input, which allows good performances of the RBF. When the two modules have been separately trained, they are further cooperatively trained, along the process described in section 4.

Part II: Localization and identification of faces in indoor images

We have just shown that Statistics provide a theoretical framework well suited to introduce Neural networks architectures and training methodology. Multi-modular

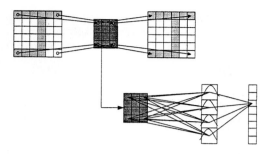

Figure 11: Multi-Modular Architecture for OCR.

architectures and "segmentation-recognition in the loop" can be used to solve problems of image processing, involving complex objects. We will now see how these techniques can be applied to Face Processing.

6 Introduction

During the last decade, a lot of research has been done on automatic face processing, leading to thousands of publications. We can see two main reasons: first, face processing is a nice academic problem, for which no satisfying solution exists but which seems tractable: there is room for a lot of improvements of current technologies. Second, there is pressure from companies wishing to develop commercial applications. Among the major applications of face processing systems, let's cite automatic surveillance, access control, teleconferencing systems, indexing, etc.

In this paper, we present a system allowing to count and identify people in a scene image. This system, developed during the last five years, is suitable for surveillance tasks and offers state of the art performances. We discuss the methodology used and compare various approaches for face/background discrimination: face-space unsupervised modelization, discriminant neural networks, hierarchical classification system. Finally, we present recent developments using Vapnik's Support Vector Machines classifiers.

6.1 Face localization methods

There are so many teams working on face processing systems that it would be difficult to cite all relevant publications in a few pages. The interested reader can find a good review in [13].

Face localization algorithms can be roughly divided in tow classes: feature-based and face-based methods. Feature based methods [15, 24, 32] looks for individual components of the face, such that eyes, mouth, face outline, and so on. The main problem with these methods is their lack of robustness: some features are often missing in faces images due to lighting conditions or hidden parts.

Face-based methods try to build global characterization of a face image, allowing to tell if an image is or not a face image. Such methods are expected to offer more robustness. They usually do not depend on explicit a-priori knowledge about faces, but make use of a set of example images (*training set*) to extract model parameters.

We proposed a few years ago [8, 43, 19, 42] to use Space Displacement Neural Networks architectures (see section 2.2) with supervised training for face detection. More recently, Rowley et al. at CMU developed a face detection system based on similar principles [33, 34].

In the following, we present various improvements of our previous system, using new hierarchical architecture. We will show how an efficient face detector can be built using several multi-modular classifiers in cascade.

6.2   The application

The goal of the application described in this paper is to count and identify the people in a scene image. We restrict the search to faces looking approximately towards the camera (with a tolerance of $\pm 40°$ in rotation). The detected faces is identified in a group of previously known persons (a *family*), or detected as unknown.

The input of the system is a digitized indoor scene image (760x580 pixels, 256 grey levels). The distance to the camera is unconstrained, the illumination and apparent size of faces are very variable. Generally speaking, the images are of poor quality : low resolution and contrast on faces.

We gathered a database of 5000 scene images, including around 6500 faces from 40 distinct persons[1]. For all the experiments described in this paper, we have used 4000 scene images to train the systems, and the remaining 1000 to evaluate the performances. All scenes have been manually labeled, registering the coordinates of boxed faces (as in figure 12).

As usual in detection problems, two kinds of errors may occur :
- *Non detection* (false negative) : face not detected;
- *Alarm* (false positive) : detection of an object which is not a face;

For any detection system, the decision usually depends on a threshold parameter Θ. All results should then be presented using "detection curves", plotting the non detection rate versus false positive rate.

6.3   System's overview

Figure 13 gives an overview of our system. As mentioned above, we adopt a global approach, and don't introduce in the algorithms any a priori knowledge about faces. In principle, the presented methodology can be applied to other object detection tasks [16].

In order to detect all faces with a single fixed-size classifier, we decompose the scene image on a multiresolution pyramid. Such a pyramid can easily be computed using a low pass filter (smoothing) associated to a sub-sampling operation (figure 14). Each resulting image is scanned by the classifier's retina. Large faces will be detected in the lower levels, while small ones will be detected in the upper ones.

---

[1] Unfortunately, this database is part of an industrial project and is currently not publicly available.

Figure 12: A labeled scene. Note that the detection should be tolerant to strong rotations (leftmost face).

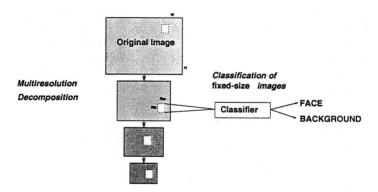

Figure 13: The input image is decomposed in a multiresolution pyramid; each level of the pyramid is scanned by the retina of a classifier.

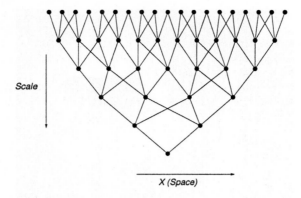

Figure 14: A multiresolution pyramid can be built using filtering and sub-sampling. For simplicity, the operation is presented here in one dimension. Points of S_i are given by local averaging of the preceding level S_{i-1}, allowing fast computation. Index i can be seen as a *scale* parameter.

7 Modelization versus Discrimination

In this section, we briefly discuss two usual ways to image detection: unsupervised modelization and supervised classification.

The (huge) set of all possible face images is called the "face space". Linear Principal Component Analysis and variants have widely been used for face detection. Turk et al. [38] proposed to use a variant of Principal Component Analysis (PCA) to modelize the face space. After computing the PCA on a training set of face images, the distance from a new image to the face space can be estimated.

These approaches suffer two weaknesses: first, the image is considered as a one dimensional vector (pixels values), so the computation does not take advantage of the bidimensional structure of the face (correlations between neighboring pixels). Second, the estimation is *unsupervised*: the face space is modelized using only examples of face images. As we will see in this section, a discriminant system trained using examples of faces and non-faces images can obtain much more accurate results.

7.1 PCA and auto-associative networks

It is well known that PCA can be implemented by an auto-associative multi layer perceptron with one hidden layer and linear transfer functions [1], as represented in figure 7. MLPs with sigmoidal transfer function are expected to slightly improve PCA. In fact several authors used auto-associative MLP networks for face detection (e.g. [17]).

In order to check the performances of this approach, we trained an auto-associative network on a set of 5000 faces. Faces are normalized to 20x25 pixels and, after a few tries, we choose a hidden layer has 48 cells.

Results measured on a separate test set (1500 faces, 100000 backgrounds images) are presented in figure 16. From the left curve, we can see that the faces images are better reconstructed that backgrounds. There's a significant overlap between the two distributions. The detection curve (right) shows that to get 1 % of non detected faces, we have to accept about 17 % of false positives. It seems that auto-associative systems are unable to deal with complex backgrounds.

PCA-like methods basically compute the distance between the input pattern and its projection on the subspace S spawned by principal axis. This subspace is estimated using examples of faces only, but may contain also other patterns, as illustrated by figure 15.

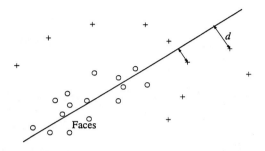

Figure 15: Why PCA doesn't work for detection: PCA subspace is the line, estimated using examples of faces (circles). The detection is then based on the distance d from a point to the line. Background images (crosses), even far from faces region, can lie very close to the subspace.

Constraints on the model must be added by using counter-examples, leading us to discriminant systems.

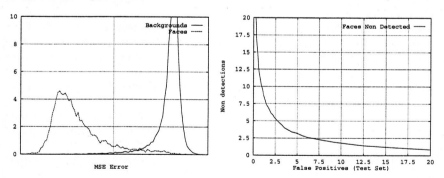

Figure 16: Results of auto-associative system. Left: reconstruction errors repartition (on test sets); right: corresponding detection curve.

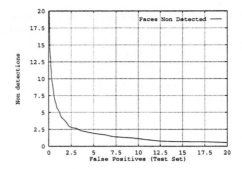

Figure 17: Detection curve obtained after supervised MLP training.

7.2 Discriminant systems

To learn a discriminant classifier, one needs a set of patterns of each class. For a detection problem, this means that we have to collect a set of background (non face) images. This set is virtually unlimited, so we have to design a strategy to collect relevant counter-examples.

In the following, we will respectively denote by N_{faces} and N_{back} the numbers of faces and non-faces (background images) examples.

A simple MLP classifier Just to put in evidence the gain obtained by using a supervised training scheme, we did a very simple experience: we *randomly* selected $N_{\text{back}} = N_{\text{faces}} = 5000$ background images and trained a classifier on the obtained examples. Here again, we normalized the images to 20x25 pixels. The classifier is a multi-layer perceptron with one hidden layer of 48 cells, 2 output cells (one per class). All layers are fully connected.

Figure 17 shows the detection curve measured on the test set. For 1 % of non detected faces, we get approximately 10 % of false positives. This is obviously a poor result, but can be compared to the 17 % of false positives obtained by the auto-associative network (figure 16). The discriminant system is clearly better, but in order to improves its performances we have to improve the selection of counter examples.

Adding more examples: modifying the cost function Before looking at more sophisticated ways to find counter-examples, let's try to add more random background images.

During learning, the average error is minimized. This error (or *cost*) for a pattern from class i is

$$E_i = \frac{1}{2} \left\| o - t_i \right\|^2$$

where o is the NN output, and t_i the desired output for class i. If the number of examples in a class is much larger than is the others classes, the training will be biased towards this class. This problem can be solved by weighting the cost :

$$E'_i = \frac{N}{4N_i} \|o - t_i\|^2$$

where N_i is the number of patterns in class i, and $N = \sum_i N_i$ the training set size. Thus, each class contributes equally to the total error, which is minimized during learning.

Experimental results are summarized in table 3 (The set of faces is the same as before, with $N_{\text{faces}} = 5000$).

NN	N_{faces}	N_{back}	Non detection	False Positive
MLP auto-associative	5000	0	1 %	17.5 %
MLP classif	5000	5000	1 %	10.0 %
MLP classif	5000	40 000	1 %	14.3 %
MLP *cost*	5000	40 000	1 %	6.5 %

Table 3: Results obtained by various simple systems, measured on the same test set.

Adding more counter-examples without modifying the cost function degrades performances. Training with a modified cost allows to reduce the false positive rate down to 6.5 %.

Remember that the classifier will be applied in each position of the multiresolution decomposition of the scene to analyze. In our case, this leads to around 100 000 calls by scene. A false positive rate of 6.5 % per call gives 6500 objects detected in the scene!

8 Hierarchical system and Incremental learning

8.1 Incremental selection of examples

Various incremental strategies have been proposed in the literature [44, 33], based on the idea of incrementally re-inject false positives in the training set during the learning procedure. The main idea is:

1. choose a classifier (e.g. NN architecture);

2. let F be the set of faces examples;

3. randomly select a set B of non face examples;

4. Repeat :
    - supervised training using F and B;
    - collect false positives on scenes images and add them to B;

   Until false positive rate $< \epsilon$.

This kind of approach raise several problems :

- Size of B grows (fast), since we only add examples. Heuristics may be used to limit the number of non faces examples, by selecting only counter examples "far" from the existing ones.
- After each step of the procedure, the classification problem gets harder ("hard" false positives are selected). This is the most serious problem. From modern learning theory [41], we know that for each given problem, one has to choose a model with a complexity related to the training set. The "complexity" of a model can be quantified by its *capacity* (or VC dimension, see section 3). After each modification of the training set, the architecture of the NN classifier should be adjusted accordingly, in order to increase its capacity.
- To get good performances, one has to choose a classifier able to solve the "harder" problem, leading to large computing times.

8.2 Hierarchical approach

A modular hierarchical system can solve the problems mentioned above. The main principle is illustrated by figure 18. Each classifier evaluates the probability that the presented image is a face, *given* that all previous classifiers consider it's a face. If the probability is below a threshold, the image is rejected as "non face". The classifier at

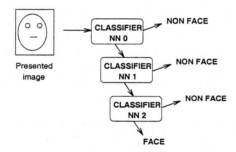

Figure 18: A 3-level hierarchical detection system.

level i is trained using only patterns (faces and non faces) selected at previous levels, in a fashion similar to incremental selection schemes discussed above. After each stage, the classification problem gets harder: only background images looking like faces are selected. The complexity of each level can be adjusted accordingly. Here, processing time considerations does not limit the choice, since the vast majority of the images will be filtered by the first classifier, which can be very quick, as we will show in next section.

8.3 The 3 stages system

In this section, we present our face detection system based on 3 hierarchical classifiers. In preliminary experiments (section 7), we used only simple multi-layer perceptrons (MLP). This kind of architectures are clearly not optimal for image classification problems. As mentioned above, they don't take advantage of the 2D structure of the input pattern.

A classifier is classically decomposed in two parts: extraction of features, and classification. For face detection, extracted features may be "low level" or "high level". Low levels features are computed by standard image processing techniques: filtering, edge detection, linear data analysis and so on. They do not carry specific knowledge about the object to detect. In contrast, high level features need a model of the object. For faces, we could use eyes positions, mouth, hair outline, etc. As stated above, such high level features are often difficult to use in real (noisy) images.

Some connectionnists architectures allow to integrate low level feature extraction with the classification process. A well known example is the Space Displacement Neural Networks (SDNN) "LeNet" proposed by Le Cun [26] for handwritten digits recognition. SDNNs use local connection patterns and shared weights (see figure 19).

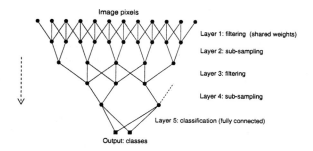

Figure 19: Part of SDNN LeNet, shown in one dimension. Processing goes downwards. This architecture uses 4 layers of "feature extraction", alternating filtering and sub-sampling to reduce dimension of the data. Last layer can be seen as a quasi-linear classifier of the features. Each set of similar weights share the same value, giving translation-invariant processing.

MLP-RBF architectures for image detection   As explained in section 2.2, MLP networks neurons compute their activies using dot-product neurons, leading to a non local behaviour. The obtained class frontiers are thus unbounded, as illustrated by figure 20. Even after an extensive training procedure, our image classifier will have to handle lots of *outliers* patterns, very distinct from all previously seen images. The RBF networks, as stated in section 2.4, are based on distance computations and localized kernels, naturaly leading to bounded activity regions: output on outliers patterns is zero.

The problem with RBF networks (and with all distance-based classifiers) is that they poorly perform on high-dimensionnal inputs (the so-called curse of dimensionality). These classifiers are usually used on low dimensionnal *features*, extracted by some algorithm, instead of raw data. We propose another solution : use a multi-modular connexionnist architecture, with a MLP module for feature extraction and dimensionnality reduction, and a RBF module for classification, taking the best of

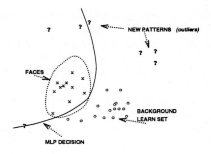

Figure 20: Multi Layer Perceptrons (MLP) separate classes using unbounded hyper-surfaces.

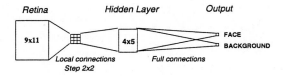

Figure 21: MLP for first stage: use a single hidden layer with local connections to the small retina.

both systems. This architecture is very similar to the one presented in section 5 for digit recognition.

Description of architectures   Let's now describe the classifiers used for our 3-stage hierarchical system:

1. *First stage* is applied to every position of the multiresolution pyramid, so it has to be very fast. We use a very simple MLP, working with a low resolution (9x11 retina), as shown in figure 21.

2. *Second stage* use a higher resolution to distinguish between faces and other objects. We use a MLP+RBF architecture: the MLP layer reduce the input dimension from 20x25 to 6x8 cells (see figure 22). Average number of calls per scene is approximately 3000.

3. *Third stage*. Various proposed systems use "high level" features search to confirm detections : presence of eyes, mouth, etc.

   Such features are often hard to detect in our images (hidden or rotated faces, low contrast due to flash), as can be seen in figure 24. Once again, we use a MLP+RBF module, but with a higher resolution and information from the body of the detected person. In effect, multimodular connexionnists architectures provide a very convenient way to combine different sources of informations and to optimize jointly the corresponding modules. In this case, we have three

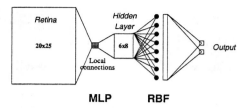

Figure 22: MLP+RBF for second stage of detection.

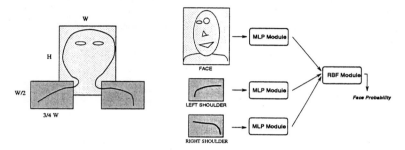

Figure 23: Third classification module uses information from face and shoulders regions. MLP modules extracts features from each regions. Those features are combined by a RBF classifier which take the final decision.

retinas (figure 23): one for the face image, and two smaller ones receiving information from the shoulders regions. Of course, these regions do not always carry useful information: the shoulders may not be observable. Nevertheless, using this source of information allowed us to reduce the false positive rate by 25%. In a first phase, each MLP module is independently trained to reconstruct the presented images (as in our standard MLP+RBF architectures), then the RBF classifier is initialized and the whole MLPs+RBF system optimized by gradient descent.

8.4 Results of the localization system

After the third stage of classification, we usually get several detections for each face. These detections are grouped by a simple clustering algorithm.

We plotted in figure 25 the detection curve measured on an independent set of 1000 scenes (test set). This curve has been obtained by varying the decision threshold of the third stage (the other threshold are fixed during the incremental learning procedure). If we allow 2% of the face to be non detected, we get less than one false positive in 100 scenes.

In the current (non-optimized) implementation, a 760x580 image is processed in 20 seconds on a 133MHz PC. Note that we do not make any assumptions on the structure of the scene and don't use any color or movement information to speed up

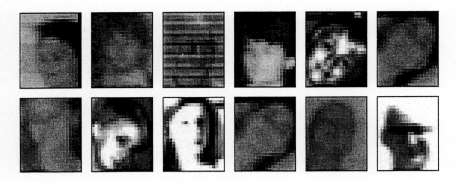

Figure 24: Some faces images of bad quality...

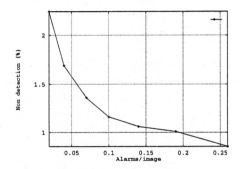

Figure 25: Non detection rate vs false positives/image, obtained with the presented MLP+RBF 3 stage system.

the search. The presented system could be used to process any complex static image.

Instead of specializing the system to gain speed, we will try in the next section to gain more accuracy (i.e. to reduce further the false alarm rate) by introducing a new type of image classifier, Support Vector Machines.

9 Improving the accuracy with Support Vector Machines

Very recently, SVM classifiers (see section 3.2) have been compared to RBF on digit image recognition, clearly demonstrating the better accuracy of SVM [36]. An application to face detection has also been presented last month [31], with interesting results.

Here, we present a few preliminary results obtained by replacing the last MLP+RBF module of our face detection system by a SVM machine. We used a Gaussian kernel as dot product.

The best machine obtained so far has about 2000 support vectors. This number can be reduced by 10% without significant loss of performance (pruning the SV associated to low values of multiplier α. The performances obtained during this preliminary experiments were very similar to our best NN classifier, which were selected after a lot of time consuming trials and errors.

Note that the technique used is quite simple and leaves room for improvements:

- invariances to translations, rotations and illumination changes should be added, either by using a specialized dot-product or with the "virtual support vector" technique [35].
- speedups by a factor 50 have been reported by reducing the number of SV via the "reduced set" method [10, 12].

During optimization, SVM extract "important" examples from the learning set. The importance of each support is quantified by its associated Lagrange multiplier α_i. This can be used to quickly inspect a large pattern database by visualizing the support vectors. For instance, incorrectly labeled pattern will almost surely be selected as support, with high α_i value. The images shown in figure 26 are faces in the training set which were originally labeled as "non-faces". Removing these patterns and re-training the system decrease the error rate while reducing the number of SV.

Figure 26: Incorrectly labeled images found among the Support Vectors.

10   Identification of detected faces

After localization, we want to identify the detected face to a member of a small group of known persons, which we called a "family". Such a system is for instance useful for automatic people tracking, in surveillance or telecommunication applications. For this kind of tasks, a large number of examples is usually available; faces images of each person can for instance be automatically extracted from a video sequence. On the other hand, images are of bad quality, the identification system need to be very robust to changes of light, rotations, imperfect segmentation, etc. Figure 27 shows some faces images.

A TDNN classifier network can get good performances on this task, if it is trained with enough examples [42]. The average generalization error rate measured for families of eleven persons is 2 %. Larger error rates are observed if a person change its appearance (e.g. hairs). A known problem with such discriminant system is their inability to accurately detect and reject patterns from unknown classes (in our case non faces images and faces from previously unknown persons) [19]. This is illustrated by the curve 28, which plots the the rejection rate on both faces and non faces as a function of the face identification error rate. With an error rate of 1 %, about 40 % of the unknown faces are accepted as images of faces from one of known classes.

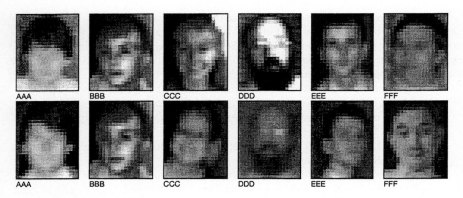

Figure 27: A typical "family". Images from the first line belongs to the training set, and from the second line to the test set.

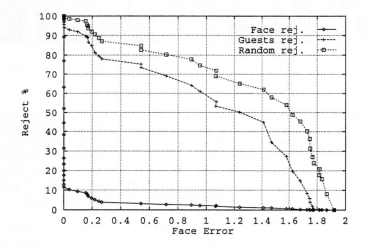

Figure 28: Rejection rate as a function of the face identification error rate, measured on three sets of images: known faces, unknown faces (labeled "Guests") and random noise images.

11 Conclusion

The results discussed in this paper clearly demonstrate that connexionnist methods allow to build robust and accurate systems for real world image processing problems. We shown how different kind of models can be combined to improve performances, both in terms of computing speed and error rates. The presented system offers very good performances for face detection in complex images, and is suitable for real world applications. Our recent results using Vapnik's Support Vector Machines lead to further reduction of error rates.

References

[1] P. Baldi and K. Hornik. Neural networks and principal component analysis: learning from examples without local minima. *Neural Networks*, 2:53–58, 1989.

[2] P. L. Bartlett. Vapnik-chervonenkis dimension bounds for two- and three-layer networks. *Neural Computation*, 5(3):371–373, 1993.

[3] E. Baum and D. Haussler. What size net gives valid generalization? *Neural Computation*, 1(1):151–160, 1989.

[4] Y. Bennani. *Approches Connexionnistes pour la Reconnaissance Automatique du Locuteur: Modélisation et Identification*. PhD thesis, Université Paris XI, 1992.

[5] C. M. Bishop. *Neural Networks for Pattern Recognition*. Oxford University Press, Oxford, 1995.

[6] L. Bottou and P. Gallinari. A formalism for neural net algorithms. In EC2, editor, *Proceedings of Neuro-Nîmes'91*, 1991.

[7] L. Bottou and P. Gallinari. A framework for the cooperation of learning algorithms. In R. Lippmann, J. Moody, and D. Touretzky, editors, *Advances in Neural Information Processing Systems*, 3, pages 781–788, 1991.

[8] H. Bouattour, F. Fogelman Soulié, and E. Viennet. Neural nets for human face recognition. In *Proceedings of IJCNN Baltimore*, volume 3, page 700, 1992.

[9] L. Breiman and J. Friedman. A new approach to multiple outputs through stacking. Technical Report LCS 114, Standford University, 1994.

[10] C. C. J. Burges. Simplified support vector decision rules. In L. Saitta, editor, 13th *International Conference on Machine Learning*, pages 71–77. Morgan Kaufman, 1996.

[11] C. J. C. Burges. A tutorial on support vector machines for pattern recognition. *Submitted to Data Mining and Knowledge Discovery*, 1997. Available from http://svm.research.bell-labs.com/SVMdoc.html.

[12] C. J. C. Burges and B. Schölkopf. Improving the accuracy and speed of support vector machines. In M. Mozer, M. Jordan, and T. Petsche, editors, *Advances in Neural Information Processing Systems*, 9, pages 375–381, 1997.

[13] R. Chellapa, C. L. Wilson, and S. Sirohey. Human and machine recognition of faces: A survey. *Proceedings of the IEEE*, 83(5):705–740, May 1995.

[14] V. Cherkassky, J. Friedman, and H. Wechsler, editors. *From Statistics to Neural Networks: Theory and pattern recognition Applications*, volume F136 of *NATO ASI Series in Computer and System Sciences*. Springer Verlag, 1994.

[15] I. Craw, H. Ellis, and J. Lishman. Automatic extraction of face-features. *Pattern Recognition Letters*, 5:183–187, Feb. 1987.

[16] R. Fernandez, E. Viennet, E. Goles, R. Barrientos, and M. Telias. On-line coarse ore granulometric analyser using neural networks. In *Proceedings of ICANN'95 Paris*, volume industrial session, Oct. 1995.

[17] M. Fleming and G. W. Cottrell. Categorization of faces using unsupervised feature extraction. In *Proceedings of IJCNN Washington*, volume 2, 1990.

[18] F. Fogelman Soulié, D. Gureghian Gastinel, J. Loncelle, M. E., and J. Gallinari. A check reading system. In F. F. Soulié and P. Gallinari, editors, *Industrial Applications of Neural Networks*, pages 363–368. World Scientific, 1997.

[19] F. Fogelman Soulié, B. Lamy, and E. Viennet. Multi-modular neural networks architectures for pattern recognition: Applications in Optical Characters Recognition and Human Face Recognition. *Int. J. Pattern Recognition and Artificial Intelligence*, 7(4), 1993.

[20] J. Friedman. Adaptive techniques for machine learning and function approximation. In Cherkassky et al. [14], page 61.

[21] S. Geman, E. Bienenstock, and R. Doursat. Neural networks and the bias/variance dilemma. *Neural Computation*, 4:1–58, 1992.

[22] I. Guyon, V. Vapnik, B. Boser, L. Bottou, and S. A. Solla. Structural risk minimization for character recognition. In J. Moody, S. Hanson, and R. Lippmann, editors, *Advances in Neural Information Processing Systems*, 4, pages 471–479, 1992.

[23] L. Hansen, C. Liisberg, and P. Salamon. Ensemble methods for handwritten digit recognition. In *NNSP'92*, pages 333–342. IEEE, 1992.

[24] C. Huang and C. Chen. Human facial feature extraction for face interpretation and recognition. *Pattern Recognition*, 25(12):1435–1444, 1992.

[25] R. A. Jacobs, M. I. Jordan, S. J. Nowlan, and G. E. Hinton. Adaptive mixtures of local experts. *Neural Computation*, 3:79–87, 1991.

[26] Y. Le Cun, B. Boser, J. S. Denker, D. Henderson, R. E. Howard, W. Hubbard, and L. D. Jackel. Handwritten digit recognition with a back-propagation network. In Touretzky, editor, *Advances in Neural Information Processing Systems*, 2, pages 396–404, 1990.

[27] G. L. Martin and M. Rashid. Recognizing overlapping hand-printed characters by centered-object integrated segmentation and recognition. In J. Moody, S. Hanson, and R. Lippmann, editors, *Advances in Neural Information Processing Systems*, 4, pages 504–511, 1992.

[28] O. Matan, C. J. Burges, Y. Le Cun, and J. S. Denker. Multi-digit recognition using a Space Displacement Neural Network. In J. Moody, S. Hanson, and R. Lippmann, editors, *Advances in Neural Information Processing Systems*, 4, pages 488–495, 1992.

[29] M. Møller. Supervised learning on large redundant training sets. *Internation Journal of Neural Systems*, 4(1):15–25, 1993.

[30] J. More and G. Toraldo. On the solution of large quadratic programming problems with bounds constraints. *SIAM Optimization*, 1(1):93–113, 1991.

[31] E. Osuna, R. Freund, and F. Girosi. Training support vector machines: an application to face detection. In *Proceedings of CVPR'97*, Puerto Rico, June 1997.

[32] N. Roeder and X. Li. Accuracy analysis for facial feature detection. *Pattern Recognition*, 29(1):143–157, 1996.

[33] H. Rowley, S. Baluja, and T. Kanade. Human face detection in visual scenes. Technical Report CMU-CS-95-158R, School of Computer Science Carnegie Mellon University, Pittsburgh, PA 15213, 1995.

[34] H. Rowley, S. Baluja, and T. Kanade. Human face detection in visual scenes. In *Advances in Neural Information Processing Systems*, 8, 1995.

[35] B. Schölkopf, C. Burges, and V. Vapnik. Incorporating invariances in support vector learning machines. In *Proceedings ICANN'96 Int. Conf. on Artifical Neural Networks*, Berlin, 1996. Springer Verlab.

[36] B. Schölkopf, K. Sung, C. Burges, F. Girosi, P. Niyogi, T. Poggio, and V. Vapnik. Comparing support vector machines with gaussian kernels to radial basis function classifiers. *IEEE Trans. Signal Processing*, 45:2758–2765, 1997. Also available from ftp://publications.mit.edu, A.I. Memo No. 1599.

[37] S. Thiria, Y. Lechevallier, O. Gascuel, and S. Canut, editors. *Statistiques et méthodes neuronales*. Dunod, 1997. (In french).

[38] M. Turk and A. Pentland. Eigenfaces for recognition. *Journal of Cognitive Neuroscience*, 3(1):71–86, 1991.

[39] V. Vapnik. *Estimation of Dependences Based on Empirical Data.* Springer-Verlag, 1982.

[40] V. Vapnik. Principles of risk minimization for learning theory. In J. Moody, S. Hanson, and R. Lippmann, editors, *Advances in Neural Information Processing Systems*, 4, pages 831–838, 1992.

[41] V. Vapnik. *The Nature of Statistical Learning Theory.* Springer-Verlag, 1995.

[42] E. Viennet. *Architectures Connexionnistes Multi-Modulaires. Application à l'analyse de scène.* PhD thesis, Université Paris XI, june 1993.

[43] E. Viennet and F. Fogelman Soulié. Multi-resolution scene segmentation using MLPs. In *Proceedings of IJCNN Baltimore*, volume 3, page 55, 1992.

[44] J. Vincent. Facial feature location in coarse resolution images by multi-layered perceptrons. In *Artificial Neural Networks*, pages 821–826. Elsevier Science, 1991.

[45] D. H. Wolpert. Stacked generalization. *Neural Networks*, 5(2):242–259, 1992.

Efficient Focusing and Face Detection

Yali Amit [1], Donald Geman [2] and Bruno Jedynak [1]

[1] Department of Statistics, University of Chicago, Chicago, Illinois 60637, U.S.A.
[2] Department of Mathematics and Statistics, University of Massachusetts, Amherst, Massachusetts 01003, U.S.A.

Abstract. We present an algorithm for shape detection and apply it to frontal views of faces in still grey level images with arbitrary backgrounds. Detection is done in two stages: (i) "focusing," during which a relatively small number of regions-of-interest are identified, minimizing computation and false negatives at the (temporary) expense of false positives; and (ii) "intensive classification," during which a selected region-of-interest is labeled face or background based on multiple decision trees and normalized data. In contrast to most detection algorithms, the processing is then very highly concentrated in the regions near faces and near false positives.

Focusing is based on spatial arrangements of edge fragments. We first define an enormous family of these, all invariant over a wide range of photometric and geometric transformations. Then, using only examples of faces, we select particular arrangements which are more common in faces than in general backgrounds. The second phase is texture-based; we recursively partition a training set consisting of registered and standardized regions-of-interest of both faces and non-faces.

The face training data consist of 30 individuals, 10 images per person, obtained from the Ollivetti data base. The processing time (on a Ultra Sparc 2) is under a second for a test image of size 100×100, and scales linearly with the size of the image. We achieve a false positive rate of about .2 per 10000 pixels; we estimate a false negative rate of 10%.

Keywords. Face detection, visual selection, training, invariance

1   Introduction

We present an algorithm for detecting instances of isolated objects against general backgrounds based on still grey level images. The algorithm is applied to detecting and localizing faces from frontal views, which is currently an active research area. Complications arise from diverse lighting, complex backgrounds, facial expressions and extra facial features (e.g., beards and glasses). One of the main applications is face recognition; indeed, most recognition algorithms assume the face is already detected or that the background is very simple.

In most existing algorithms every candidate for a "bounding box" is directly classified as "face" or "background". The gray levels are preprocessed to account for variations due to lighting and image acquisition using techniques such as histogram equalization and plane-fitting. The classifier is induced from training data, normalized in the same manner, and consisting of both face and "non-face" images;

examples include [Colmenarez and Huang, 1997; Osuna et al., 1997; Pentland et al., 1994; Rowley et al., 1995; Sung and Poggio, 1994; Yuille et al., 1992]. Most of these authors report low false positive rates and a false negative rate of less than 10%.

However, applying these algorithms directly to every candidate subimage is very costly. As a result, the more intensive processing is sometimes preceded by a fast filter designed to identify plausible locations with very few false negatives (i.e., missed faces), but at the temporary expense of a considerable number of false positives. For example, in [Rowley et al., 1995], two neural networks are developed, one for 30×30 regions which allows the face to be displaced from the center and is only applied every ten pixels, and another, more discriminating, one, trained on 20×20 subimages and only applied to the subimages filtered by the first one. The total running time is then 20 seconds (on a Sun Ultra-Sparc 2) for the 392×272 image in figure 2. Other methods are based on first extracting "interest points," especially distinguished facial features, such as an elliptical outline [Jecquin and Eleftheriadis, 1995], the eyes and mouth [Han et al., 1996; Tankus et al., 1997; Yow and Cipolla, 1995], and local extrema [Huang et al., 1996; Hoogenboom and Lew, 1996]. "Key features" are also prominent in [Bichsel, 1991; Burl et al., 1995; Yuille et al., 1992].

Efficient focusing is our primary objective. However, in contrast to the work cited above, our approach to visual selection does not utilize complex features, which might be as difficult to detect as the face itself. Instead, we use shape information derived from local primitives, basically edge fragments, which are invariant to linear gray level transformations. In addition, they are independent at distances on the order of the scale of the object, both in the "generic background" and "object" image populations. Significant differences in the density of these features in the two populations renders *global arrangements* even more discriminating and leads to efficient focusing. Final disambiguation between object and background at the flagged locations is based on texture information: After registration and standardization, the greyscale values serve as queries for constructing multiple decision trees. Other proposals for combining edge and texture information appear in [Cootes and Taylor, 1996] and [Sung and Poggio, 1994].

Another link with some prior work, notably [Bichsel, 1991; Burl et al., 1995; Cootes and Taylor, 1996; Yow and Cipolla, 1995], as well as our own previous work on shape recognition [Amit and Geman, 1997; Amit et al., 1997] and model registration ([Amit, 1997]), is the emphasis on *geometrical relationships* among selected points. In our framework, it is not the points themselves which are distinguished, but rather the global arrangements among their locations. Indeed, the localized features are generic (as in [Maurer and von der Malsburg, 1996]) and too primitive and common to be informative about shape. All the discriminating power derives from spatial arrangements.

In fact, we initially consider a virtually infinite- dimensional family of arrangements, sufficiently rich that an appropriately chosen *subfamily* can separate nearly any generic shape class from general backgrounds. The selection of specific features for selective attention is based on training data. A similar procedure was investigated in [Amit and Geman, 1997] and [Amit et al., 1997], where shape features and tree classifiers were jointly induced during learning. The work here extends that program.

The paper is organized as follows. In section 2 we define the problem more precisely and give a compact summary of the algorithm together with some experimental results. The various components are fleshed out in the ensuing sections. In section 3 we introduce the family of features and pinpoint some key assumptions regarding their joint distribution in faces and background. Training is explained in section 4. The focusing procedure is detailed in section 5 and section 6 is a brief conclusion.

2   Overview of the Algorithm

2.1   Problem Formulation

The problem of face detection can be viewed as a classification problem: Each image location must be classified as face or background. Since we will be dealing with approximately frontal views, we assume the location of the face is identified by a basis of three distinguished points or *landmarks*, taken to be the "centers" of the two eyes and the mouth. It should be emphasized that there is no explicit search for "eyes" and "mouth" in the algorithm; this is merely a way of defining the location of a face.

Let G denote a 48×48 *reference grid*; the points $l_1 = (20, 20), l_2 = (33, 20)$ and $l_3 = (27, 33)$ serve as reference points for the landmarks. Let $I = \{I(z) : z \in Z\}$ be a test image on a lattice Z. Every triple of points $\mathbf{b} = (b_1, b_2, b_3) \in Z^3$ represents a candidate *basis* for the location of a face. These points also determine a unique affine map $A_\mathbf{b}$ from G into the image, carrying (l_1, l_2, l_3) to (b_1, b_2, b_3). The reference grid G is mapped by $A_\mathbf{b}$ into a region $R_\mathbf{b} = A_\mathbf{b}(G) \subset Z$ which is called the *region-of-interest* (ROI) of the basis $\mathbf{b}$. *Note that a ROI is actually a reference frame or candidate pose rather than simply a subimage.* Each ROI $R_\mathbf{b}$ (equivalently, each basis $\mathbf{b}$) will be classified "F" or "B" based on the image data $\{I(z), z \in R_\mathbf{b}\}$.

Our goal is to detect faces at a range of distances of 10-20 pixels between the two eyes and at rotations of +/-10 degrees. Larger faces in the original image are detected by downsampling to .75, .5 and .25 the original resolution. Taking into account these variations in scale and rotation at a fixed resolution and the variability of the relative locations of the landmarks in the population of faces, we calculate on the order of 10^7 possible bases in a 100×100 image. Since errors of 2-3 pixels in the location of the eyes or mouth can be ignored, each face corresponds to approximately 15000 bases. Under the assumption of one face per 100×100 image, the prior probability that a basis corresponds to the landmarks on a face is on the order of 10^{-3}.

2.2   Training

For any basis $\mathbf{b}$, the *registered image* $RI_\mathbf{b}$ on the reference grid G is $RI_\mathbf{b}(z) = I(A_\mathbf{b}z)$. The three landmarks are marked on all training images of faces and each of these is registered to G; thus the three marked landmarks appear at l_1, l_2, l_3.

The purpose of training is to identify a collection of local binary features $X_i, i = 1, \ldots, k$, and corresponding locations $c_i \in G, i = 1, ..., k$, such that each X_i is present in a small neighborhood of c_i for approximately one-half the training images of faces. We presume these properties "generalize" to face images on arbitrary ROI's $R_\mathbf{b}$ provided, of course, that the locations c_i (and their neighborhoods) have the same *local coordinates* in $R_\mathbf{b}$. In addition, the "density" of these features in the "background population" is sufficiently low that if a randomly sampled region-of-interest is registered to G, the likelihood of finding X_i near c_i is considerably less than one-half for each $i = 1, ..., k$.

Such features are easy to identify because they are extracted from the pool of all local arrangements of edge fragments, which is enormous and which has certain invariance properties. Moreover, due to very weak statistical dependence among the features, one can then identify a collection $\{(i_1, i_2, i_3)\}$ of *triples* of local features with the property that each training image has at least one triple present, i.e., feature X_{i_j} is found at c_{i_j} for $j = 1, 2, 3$. The feature triple $X_{i_1}, X_{i_2}, X_{i_3}$ is then associated with the triangle $(c_{i_1}, c_{i_2}, c_{i_3})$ in G.

2.3   Focusing

The locations of all the local features $X_i, i = 1, ..., k$, in a test image are precomputed. For each triangle $(c_{i_1}, c_{i_2}, c_{i_3})$, a search is then carried out for triples of pixels $\mathbf{z} = (z_1, z_2, z_3), z_i \in Z$, such that feature X_{i_j} is at $z_j, j = 1, 2, 3$, and such that the two triangles defined by $\mathbf{z}$ and $(c_{i_1}, c_{i_2}, c_{i_3})$ are similar to within scale changes of +/-25%, rotations on the order of 10 degrees, and other small deviations in shape. There is a unique affine map $A_{\mathbf{z}}$ taking the locations of c_{i_j} into $z_j, j = 1, 2, 3$. The triple $b_1 = A_{\mathbf{z}} l_1, b_2 = A_{\mathbf{z}} l_2, b_3 = A_{\mathbf{z}} l_3$ is then a hypothesis for the location of a face in the image.

There are on the order of 15000 bases around the hypothesized one which would yield locations consistent with each $\mathbf{z}$. The hypothesized basis serves as a representative of this cluster. This amounts to *a posteriori* clustering of the bases as opposed to *a priori* clustering utilizing some coarser grid. As observed in other algorithms, if the bases are clustered *a priori* in order to reduce computation time then the number of false negatives increases sharply. The collection of triangles is thus a mechanism for visual attention ("focusing") by identifying plausible clusters of bases. Due to the sparsity of the local features in the background, the number of ROI's identified by the collection of triangles is on the order of several hundreds as opposed to millions.

2.4   Intensive Classification

Each hypothesized ROI $R_{\mathbf{b}}$ is then registered to G and classified as face or background based on grey-level patterns (i.e., texture) in $RI_{\mathbf{b}}^0 = \{RI_{\mathbf{b}}(z), z \in G^0\}$, where G^0 is a 20×20 subgrid G located around the landmarks (two eyes and center of mouth). The subimage $RI_{\mathbf{b}}^0$ is *standardized* by subtracting the mean of the gray level values and dividing by the standard deviation. This yields a *normalized* (i.e., registered and standardized) image $NI_{\mathbf{b}}^0$ for each basis $\mathbf{b}$ detected by a triangle. The vector $NI_{\mathbf{b}}^0$ is classified using a collection of randomized decision trees induced from a data set consisting of normalized training faces, and a collection of false positives identified on generic background images by the collection of triangles, which are also normalized. The splits in the trees are based on thresholds of the gray levels at individual pixels. These trees are aggregated to yield a classification of a detected basis.

2.5   Performance

The training data consist of 30 people, 10 images per person, obtained from the Ollivetti data base. In addition, a set of several hundred background images with no faces was downloaded from the net. We achieve a false positive rate of about .2 per 10000 pixels. A false negative rate of under 10% is estimated using an extra 100 test images from the Ollivetti data base tested at a variety of resolutions. The processing time (on a Ultra Sparc 2) is about one second for an image of size 100×100, and scales linearly with the size of the image.

In figure 1 we show the result for one image; in this case only one box is detected by the algorithm. Also shown is the corresponding basis triangle which represents an estimate on the locations of the eyes and mouth. Figures 2 and 3 show similar results for two other images. Figure 2 shows the detected boxes on an image alongside a gray-scale rendering of the *logarithm* of the number of times each pixel in the image is accessed for some form of calculation. The corresponding image for most other approaches to face detection, particularly those based on artificial neural networks, would be virtually flat.

3   A Class of Features

Our aim is to construct a very rich family of binary features. The construction is recursive, basically problem-independent, and leads to a hierarchy of shape descriptors with certain invariance properties. The selection of specific features for detecting faces is based on training data and the learning process is described in the following section.

Let $X(z)$ be a binary function denoting the presence or absence of a *local* image property in the vicinity of z. Thus $X(z)$ is a function of the image data in $I(z+N)$, where $\{I(z), z \in Z\}$ is the raw image data and N is small neighborhood of the origin. We seek invariance to gray scale transformations induced by changes in lighting (or other factors), and to spatial deformations in the range prescribed earlier, i.e. scaling of +/-25%, rotations of +/- 10 degrees and other small deformations. In particular, the local features should be largely invariant under the registration process itself.

3.1   Elementary Tests

All the features used for visual selection are based on comparisons of differences of gray levels, which we refer to as *elementary tests*. The neighborhood N is the immediate 3×3 neighborhood of the origin.
Comparison of differences: $E(z_2) = 1 \Leftrightarrow |I(z_1) - I(z_2)| < |I(z_2) - I(z_3)|$, where z_1, z_2, z_3 are adjacent pixels, either in a row, column or diagonal, or forming a right angle with z_2 at the vertex.
It is clear that these tests are strictly invariant to linear grey-scale transformations and nearly invariant under the types of geometric deformations mentioned above.

Let $R_1, R_2, \ldots, R_k$ be a collection of $r \times r$ subregions of a ROI R_b with centers $z_i, i = 1, \ldots, k$, such that $|z_i - z_j| > r$. (Typically $5 < r < 10$). Let $\mathbf{E}_i$ be the collection of all elementary tests at all locations in the region R_i. We make the following two assumptions:

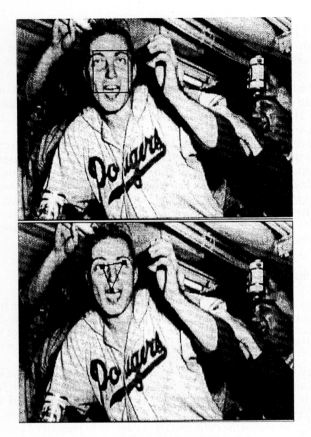

Fig. 1: The detected bounding box and the detected eyes and mouth.

Assumption One: Conditional Independence. The random vectors $\mathbf{E}_i$, $i = 1, \ldots, k$, are independent conditional on the class of the data (here face or background). In other words, given that the image data in the ROI is a face, with the two eyes near b_1 and b_2 and the center of the mouth near b_3, the random vectors $\mathbf{E}_1, ..., \mathbf{E}_k$ are statistically independent; similarly given "background." We do not believe this property holds for the actual gray level intensities $\{I(z), z \in R_i\}, i = 1 \ldots, k$, due to long range correlations induced, for example, by lighting effects.

Assumption Two: Stationarity. Realizations of each $\mathbf{E}_i$ in the "background" represent a stationary point process. That is, the probability of any particular value of $\mathbf{E}_i$ is independent of the location of R_i in the ROI. This is obviously not true if the image is a face.

Let X_R denote a binary feature which depends only on the elementary tests in an $r \times r$ support region R. There are several consequences of these two assumptions for any features $X_{R_i}, i = 1, \ldots, k$, relative to the regions R_i above.

1. $X_{R_1}, ..., X_{R_k}$ are conditionally independent given face and given background.

2. Meaningful estimates of the likelihood of the event $\{X_R = 1\}$ given background

Fig. 2: Top: The detected boxes. Bottom: A gray scale rendering, on a log-scale, of the number of times a pixel is accessed.

and given face can be obtained due to the local nature of the features and the invariance to linear gray level transformations. Due to translation invariance the statistics for background are expressed by *density per pixel*, and estimated by counting the number of pixels z in a large number of background images for which $X_R = 1$ where R is centered at z. The estimates for faces are obtained by counting the number of *registered* training images for which $X_R = 1$.

3. Any family $X_{R_i}, i = 1, \ldots, k$, which has different statistics on face and background, i.e., $P(X_{R_i} = 1|F) > P(X_{R_i} = 1|B)$, immediately yields a classical likelihood ratio test. Thresholds for rejection of the background hypothesis at various levels of false positive and false negative probabilities can be essentially calculated analytically. If the X_{R_i} were (conditionally) identically distributed, then a sufficient statistic for the likelihood ratio test would simply be $\xi = \sharp\{1 \leq i \leq k : X_{R_i} = 1\}$; the background hypothesis is rejected for $\xi > N$.

Fig. 3: Two additional detection examples.

Every feature X we consider is a disjunction (ORing) of conjunctions of elementary tests. However, we do not entertain this entire family, but rather a subfamily, still extremely rich, which is constructed in a recursive fashion. For example, the elementary tests always appear in fixed local patterns which we call "tags." The end result is an enormous family of *generic* features. Then, during training (section 4), we single out certain ones with suitable discriminating power and computational cost for detecting faces.

3.2   Tags

Tags are conjunctions of *adjacent* elementary tests in small neighborhoods of at most 4×4. These are essentially oriented "edge detectors." Given a pair of adjacent pixels z, y let $v = z - y$ and w be the 90 degree rotation of v. Denote $z_1 = z + w, z_2 = z - w, z_3 = z + v$ and $y_1 = y + w, y_2 = y - w, y_3 = y - v$. An edge is present at z if

$$|I(z) - I(y)| > \max_{i=1,2,3} \left(\max \left(|I(z) - I(z_i)|, |I(y) - I(y_i)| \right) \right).$$

The orientation of the edge is v if $I(z) > I(y)$ and $-v$ otherwise. Thus six intensity difference comparisons are involved in defining the edge. (We rule out any location where the magnitude of $|I(z) - I(y)|$ is less than 8 on a scale of 0 to 255.) There are eight tag types corresponding to four orientations matched with the sign of the center difference. Let $T_1, ..., T_8$ denote these features: $T_t(z) = 1$ if and only if there is a tag of type t at $z \in Z$.

We use "edge tags" mainly due to the importance of edges in image analysis and our familiarity with features of this nature. Furthermore, such features provide a small number of simple repeatable structures from which all higher level features can be composed. This has important implications for storage and computation. Finally since the tags involve conjunctions of adjacent elementary tests they exhibit a high degree of invariance to spatial deformations, in particular scaling. Still, it may well be that there are other, more effective functionals of the elementary tests.

3.3 Tag Arrangements

It is not efficient to terminate the "grouping process" with the tags themselves because their density in the background is high and their individual discriminating power is low. Moreover, any single, fixed spatial arrangement of tags, namely $\{T_{t_1}(z_1) = 1, ..., T_{t_m}(z_m) = 1\}$, is clearly lacking in invariance and much too rare for all but small values of m. Every feature we consider is a *disjunction* of such spatial arrangements which we continue to call a *tag arrangement* (TA), although a more appropriate description might be "flexible tag arrangement."

More formally, let $\mathbf{D} \subset Z^m$ be any subset of the m-dimensional lattice with the property that $z_1 \in W_1$ for any $(z_1, ..., z_m) \in \mathbf{D}$ where W_1 is a small neighborhood of the origin. Let $\mathbf{t} = (t_1, ..., t_m)$ $(1 \leq t_i \leq 8)$ be any sequence of tag types. The pair $Z = (\mathbf{D}, \mathbf{t})$ is called a tag arrangement. For $z \in Z$ let $\mathbf{D}_z = \{(z_1, ..., z_m) : (z_1 - z, ..., z_m - z) \in \mathbf{D}\}$. Define a binary feature $X(z)$ at $z \in Z$ by

$$X(z) = \max_{(z_1, ..., z_m) \in \mathbf{D}} \min_{1 \leq i \leq m} T_{t_i}(z_i + z) = \max_{(z_1, ..., z_m) \in \mathbf{D}_z} \min_{1 \leq i \leq m} T_{t_i}(z_i).$$

Thus, $X(z) = 1$ if and only if the arrangement $\{T_{t_1}(z_1) = 1, ..., T_{t_m}(z_m) = 1\}$ appears for some $(z_1, ..., z_m) \in \mathbf{D}_z$. Our family consists of all such binary features over choices of m, $\mathbf{t}$ and $\mathbf{D}$. We will assume that the arrangement is at the scale of the reference so that $|z_i - z_j| \leq 48$ for any $(z_1, ..., z_m) \in \mathbf{D}$.

Given an image I, each occurrence $X(z) = 1$ is referred to as an *instance* of X. *Every feature we use, from the tags to the triangles mentioned earlier, is a tag arrangement.* Notice that the types of tags in a TA are not necessarily distinct. On the contrary, some of the most invariant and discriminating TA's involve, naturally, several tags of the same type which "line up" in accordance with their orientation to form small curve-like structures.

A TA X will be called a *local tag arrangement* (LTA) if in fact *all* the spatial configurations $(z_1, ..., z_m) \in \mathbf{D}$ are confined to a fixed $r \times r$ neighborhood of the origin. In this way, the assumptions of section 3.1 are in force. The *density* of an

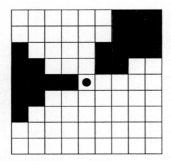

Fig. 4: An example of regions W_2, W_3 for an LTA.

LTA X in the background, is $P(X(z) = 1|B)$, which is independent of z due to stationarity.

Example 1 (LTA). $\mathbf{D} = \{0\} \times \{W_2\} \cdots \times \{W_m\}$ where $W_2, ..., W_m$ are neighborhoods of the origin of size at most $r \times r$. In other words the tags "around" t_1 are allowed to "float" over a small subregion determined by the location of t_1. In this case $X(z) \leq T_{t_1}(z)$ so that the density of such a TA is necessarily lower than that of T_{t_1}. The LTA's we use are of this form and therefore provide a filter on the tags at which they are centered. For an example of the regions defining an LTA see figure 4. The TA's used in our previous work [Amit and Geman, 1997] were also of similar form.

Example 2 (Triangle). Consider three LTA's $X_i = (\mathbf{D}_i, \mathbf{t}_i), i = 1, 2, 3$ made respectively from m_1, m_2, m_3 tags. Given three regions U_1, U_2, U_3, the binary feature corresponding to the requirement that, for each $i = 1, 2, 3$, $X_i(z) = 1$ for some $z \in U_i$, is again a TA with $m = m_1 + m_2 + m_3$, $\mathbf{t} = (\mathbf{t}_1, \mathbf{t}_2, \mathbf{t}_3)$ and $\mathbf{D} = \cup_{z \in U_1} \mathbf{D}_{1,z} \times \cup_{z \in U_2} \mathbf{D}_{2,z} \times \cup_{z \in U_3} \mathbf{D}_{3,z}$.

For the definition of tags in terms of the elementary tests there was no need for ORing because the tests were adjacent and in the range of allowable spatial deformations this adjacency is preserved. This accounts for the high degree of invariance we observe in the tags themselves. On other hand, the LTA's involve relations among more complex structures which may not necessarily be adjacent. Spatial deformations may alter the distance between such structures so that some degree of flexibility is needed in the definition to preserve invariance. The degree of invariance can be controlled by the size of the regions $W_2, ..., W_m$ in the definition. Of course increasing the size of the W increases the density of the LTA's and hence the computational cost of the algorithm.

On a set of several hundred generic background images we have observed a tag density of .034 per pixel for each type. For LTA's constructed with regions W consisting of about ten pixels, the densities corresponding to $m = 2, 3, 4$ are, respectively, .01, .006, .004. The rather gradual decrease in density is due to the high degree of dependence among nearby edge fragments. Figure 5 shows all the instances of tag '0' on the image processed in figure 1 and all the instances of an LTA centered at tag '0'. The reduction in density is apparent. On the other hand this LTA appeared on over 50% of the registered training images in a small region in the upper left hand part of the face. See figure 6 below.

Fig. 5: Top: Instances of tag type '0' on an image. Bottom: Instances of an LTA centered at tag type '0'.

4   Training

The features are selected from the family of TA's. The particular ones chosen are those with the highest discriminating power for a given classification problem and a given set of parameters controlling error rates and total computation. The classification problem at hand is separating ROI's which represent a face from all others. There are two distinct training phases corresponding to focusing, which is based on edge information, and final classification, which is based on grey level configurations in normalized data.

4.1   Selecting Dedicated TA's for Focusing

The training set consists of 300 *registered* images of faces based on 30 individuals. Our goal is identify LTA's which are relatively more common in faces *near a given location* in G than in arbitrary background images registered to G. Focusing is

168

Fig. 6: Left: The locations of one LTA aggregated over the training set; the frequency at a pixel is proportional to darkness. The three landmarks are also shown. Right: Another LTA.

then based on TA's which are constructed from the selected LTA's by the procedure outlined in Example 2 above and discussed in more detail below.

More specifically, we seek LTA's X which appear in a small, particular, $n \times n$ region $C \subset G$ in at least a fraction $1 - \alpha$ of the faces and at most a fraction δ of background ROI's registered to G. We assess the prevalence in faces by the fraction of the 300 registered training faces for which $X(C) = \max_{z \in C} X(z) = 1$. The particular parameters chosen depend on target error rates and computational load; this will be discussed below. The "false positive" rate δ is estimated by multiplying the density of the LTA by n^2, the number of pixels in C; this is a crude upper bound since in effect we are replacing the probability of the union of events by the sum of the probabilities. Figure 6 shows the sum of 300 binary images in each of which all locations of one particular LTA is marked; the dark spots indicate high frequency locations.

The search procedure is recursive and very similar to the one described in [Amit et al., 1997]. The basic idea is to add the tags one at a time based on trying to keep the faces together. For each location $z \in G$ and tag type t_1 look for pairs (t_2, W_2) such that the LTA corresponding to $\mathbf{D} = \{0\} \times \{W_2\}$ maximizes $P(X(C) = 1|F)$, where C is the $n \times n$ neighborhood of z. (the probability is estimated from the 300 images). If more than $100(1 - \alpha)\%$ of the faces stay together, add one more tag by maximizing the incidence in faces over LTA's with $m = 3$ and t_1, t_2 and W_2 fixed. If the maximizer still achieves the threshold $1 - \alpha$, then add a fourth tag, and so forth.

The whole procedure is easily automated and a set of LTA's $X_1, ..., X_k$, with regions $C_1, ..., C_k$, and with the desired α and δ, can be identified in minutes. This is possible (for virtually any shape class) due to the use of non-informative, ordinary edge fragments and the resulting extraordinary richness of the family of all local arrangements of these. In our view, a procedure based instead on *informative* and *distinguished* points, such as junctions, boundary singularities, concavities, etc., is not feasible. Special points are too scarce and too hard to identify, leading to a comparatively limited family of unstable arrangements

4.2 Parameters

The three principal "performance" parameters are of course the false negative rate, the false positive rate and the total amount of computation. Keeping the latter in check necessitates using repeatable substructures and limiting the number of ROI's which pass the "threshold test" or "triangle search," i.e., finding at least $N = 3$ of the X_i somewhere in designated regions C_i. It is only these ROI's which are considered for further processing, including normalization. The parameters α and δ defined above are the corresponding error rates for the individual LTA's $X_i(C_i)$. Since any face ROI which is "lost" during the triangle search is lost forever, we seek a very low false negative rate during focusing.

There are several "nuisance" parameters in the training algorithm, the main ones being the "depth" m of the LTA's and the number of triples, say M. We shall assume certain other parameters are fixed throughout, such as the size of the regions W (set at around ten pixels) and the threshold in the likelihood ratio test (set at $N = 3$ since this is the minimum number necessary to determine a basis). Changing m and M has a direct bearing on performance. For example, increasing m leads to rarer events and smaller densities, but then M must be increased in order to "cover" the faces, and the net effect on total computation is not obvious. We have not systematically explored the tradeoffs. The choices given below were obtained mostly by trial and error. This was possible without excessive experimentation due to certain *analytic* calculations which exploit the two assumptions of conditional independence and background stationarity. For example, the error rates of a triangle, $(X_1(C_1), X_2(C_2), X_3(C_3))$, can be computed directly from the individual α_i and δ_i by exploiting conditional independence; and these rates in turn can be approximated, at least in the background, using the densities of $X_1(z), X_2(z), X_3(z)$.

We made $k = 9$ LTA's of depth $m = 4$. Using 5×5 regions C, this yielded $\alpha_i \leq .4$ and $\delta_i \leq .1 = 25 \times .004$ for each $X_i(C_i)$. Roughly speaking, then, each LTA covers at least one-half the faces and occurs in at most one-tenth the registered background ROI's. A simple calculation using the binomial distribution yields global error rates of under 10% false positives and under 10% false negatives for the threshold test. (Due to various approximations explained in section 5, the actual number of false negatives appears to be lower.) The number of triangles we actually use is somewhat less than $\binom{9}{3} = 84$ since we reject those with small angles (i.e., not sufficiently spread out) in order to obtain stable affine mappings (see section 5).

The ten percent false positive rate should be interpreted as follows. There are 10^7 candidate bases. We predict that 10^6 survive the threshold test and are not classified as background. But these bases are very highly correlated. Indeed we know that for each basis which passes this test, approximately 15000 others in its vicinity will pass as well, and all of these bases would flag the same face if it were present. Hence there are only on the order of 100 clusters of bases which survive this test. In section 5 we explain how one can locate these clusters without actually looping through all the bases.

4.3 Classification Based on Normalized Grey Levels

Consider the subset of ROI's which are detected by the triangles. These subimages form a more homogeneous population than randomly chosen ROI's. This is due simply to the presence of certain local features at certain locations. Each such ROI has an associated basis **b**. A sample of such ROI's, $\{R_{\mathbf{b}}\}$, is obtained from a large collection of background images. Each of these is then registered and standardized to yield a "normalized" image $NI_{\mathbf{b}}^0$ (see section 2.4.).

For the face training data, the landmarks are provided manually and the corresponding normalized image $NI_{\mathbf{b}}^0$ is then determined. In order to enrich the training set of faces we randomly perturb the locations of the three landmarks. We regard the normalized ROI of a face as a robust source of information about characteristic grey level patterns in faces, i.e., about typical face textures. For example, the area around the mouth is usually darker than the area around the cheeks. Clearly the only reliable information of this nature resides in *relative* brightness values for *registered* data, which provides the justification for the normalization process.

Each normalized image is regarded as a 400 dimensional feature vector of real numbers typically lying between -2 and 2. Standard CART ([Breiman et al., 1984]) is applied to grow a classification tree from this training sample. There are two classes, "F" and "B" and the splits (questions) are elementary tests which compare a normalized grey level to a threshold. Each terminal node of this tree can also be assigned an estimate of the posterior distribution on faces and background. Note that this posterior is also conditional on the ROI having been detected by one of the triangles.

5 Focusing

Recall that $I = \{I(z) : z \in Z\}$ denotes a test image on Z and there is a region-of-interest $R_{\mathbf{b}}$ corresponding to each basis $\mathbf{b} = (b_1, b_2, b_3)$, where the family $\mathcal{B}$ of bases is limited by the allowed range of scalings, rotations, etc. This yields on the order of 10^7 ROI's, each to be classified as "B" or "F" based on the image data $\{I(z), z \in R_{\mathbf{b}}\}$.

Let X_{ij} denote the j'th LTA in the i'th triangle, $i = 1, ..., M$, and let C_{ij} be its corresponding region in the reference grid. (Of course each X_{ij} is one of the LTA's $X_1, ..., X_9$ and similarly for the C_{ij}.) Recall that $RI_{\mathbf{b}}$ denotes the data in $R_{\mathbf{b}}$ registered to G. Exact implementation of the entire detection algorithm means performing the following four steps:

1. For each $\mathbf{b} \in \mathcal{B}$, register the data in $R_{\mathbf{b}}$ to G.

2. Check whether at least one of the triangles is present in $RI_{\mathbf{b}}$, i.e., calculate $\mathcal{F}(\mathbf{b}) = \max_i \min_{j=1,2,3} X_{ij}(C_{ij})$, where i runs over triangles.

3. If $\mathcal{F}(\mathbf{b}) = 0$ (i.e., no triangle is present), classify $R_{\mathbf{b}}$ as "B" and stop.

4. If $\mathcal{F}(\mathbf{b}) = 1$, normalize the data in $RI_{\mathbf{b}}$ (as described in Section 2) and send the normalized grey-levels down each classification tree. Add the resulting distributions and classify $R_{\mathbf{b}}$ as "F" or "B" according to the higher mass, or according to some other classification rule.

The algorithm we have implemented is a much faster variation based on an image-wide search for triangles in the original coordinates. First, notice that whereas the regions C_{ij} are specified in the reference frame, the LTA's X_{ij} themselves are defined in global coordinates in a basis-independent manner. Hence, due to the (near) invariance to the registration process (as discussed in section 3), we can search for individual LTA's *directly* in $R_\mathbf{b}$ rather than in the image $RI_\mathbf{b}$. Specifically, define $C_{ij}(\mathbf{b}) = A_\mathbf{b}(C_{ij})$, where again $A_\mathbf{b}$ is the affine map taking the registered landmark locations $(l_1, l_2, l_3) \in G^3$ to $\mathbf{b} \in R_\mathbf{b}^3$. Then, with high likelihood, $\min_{j=1,2,3} X_{ij}(C_{ij}) = 1$ relative to the registered data $RI_\mathbf{b}$ if and only if $\min_{j=1,2,3} X_{ij}(C_{ij}(\mathbf{b})) = 1$ relative to the raw data on $R_\mathbf{b}$.

However, the algorithm still requires a loop over bases, even though the registration process need no longer be applied to every ROI. We can eliminate this loop by defining a tag arrangement Δ_i for each $i = 1, ..., M$ in terms of *global coordinates*, and a small basis-dependent region $S_i(\mathbf{b})$ such that: $\mathcal{F}(\mathbf{b}) \leq \mathcal{F}^*(\mathbf{b}) \equiv \max_i \max_{z \in S_i(\mathbf{b})} \Delta_i(z)$. In other words, $\mathcal{F}^*$ is more conservative filter. Let $\mathcal{B}^*$ be the set of all bases for which $\mathcal{F}^*(\mathbf{b}) = 1$. Then clearly, $\mathcal{B}^* = \bigcup_{i,z:\Delta_i(z)=1} \mathcal{B}_{iz}$ where $\mathcal{B}_{iz} = \{\mathbf{b} \in \mathcal{B} : z \in S_i(\mathbf{b})\}$. It follows directly that we can replace the original algorithm by

1. Loop over $z \in Z$

2. Loop over $i = 1, \ldots, M$, calculate $\Delta_i(z)$.

    a If $\Delta_i(z) = 0$, goto next i.

    b If $\Delta_i(z) = 1$, normalize the data in $R_\mathbf{b}$ for each $\mathbf{b} \in \mathcal{B}_{iz}$, and send the normalized grey-levels down each classification tree. Add the resulting distributions and classify $R_\mathbf{b}$ for each $\mathbf{b} \in \mathcal{B}_{iz}$ as "F" or "B" according to the higher mass, or according to some other classification rule. Goto next i.

3. Classify all remaining ROI's as "B".

A major speed-up is obtained by representing the "cluster" of bases $\mathcal{B}_{iz}$ by a single element $\mathbf{b} \in \mathcal{B}_{iz}$. This basis is easily identified by a coordinate transformation based on the locations of three image locations in the detected triangle Δ_i.

We conclude this section by describing the TA's Δ_i and the resulting search process in the full image plane. The Δ_i's are defined in order to accommodate a range of scales of +/-25%, small rotations and other deformations. Let $c_1, ..., c_9$ denote the centers of the 5×5 regions $C_1, ..., C_9$.

1. Loop over the entire image and find the locations of each of the tag types.

2. Loop through the locations of the tag types and find those which are at the center of any of the LTA's $X_1, ..., X_9$. The locations of all nine LTA's are then identified.

3. For each triangle c_{i1}, c_{i2}, c_{i3}:

    (a) For each location z_1 of X_{i1} search for X_{i2} in the 9×9 region around $z_1 + (c_{i2} - c_{i1})$.

    (b) If an instance is found, say at z_2, calculate the predicted location z of X_{i3} by mapping c_{i3} according to the translation, scale and rotation which takes c_{i1} to z_1 and c_{i2} to z_2.

(c) Search for X_{i3} in a 5×5 region around z. If it is found, say at z_3, a match $\mathbf{z} = (z_1, z_2, z_3)$ is identified for the triangle c_{i1}, c_{i2}, c_{i3}.

4. For each such triple $\mathbf{z} = (z_1, z_2, z_3)$ identify the map $A_{\mathbf{z}}$ as above and the corresponding basis $\mathbf{b} = (A_{\mathbf{z}} l_1, A_{\mathbf{z}} l_2, A_{\mathbf{z}} l_3)$. This basis is a representative of the cluster of bases mentioned above; each ROI in the cluster has the indicated triple of LTA's.

This loop is many times faster than a loop through all bases. This image-wide search also provides an *a posteriori* clustering of the bases of the image. Only representative bases are then processed by the CART trees and ultimately classified as face or background. Our attempts to accelerate the loop through the bases by clustering them in an *a priori* way, say using a coarser grid, resulted in significant increases in false negatives.

6   Conclusion

We have described a detection algorithm with two stages - focusing and intense classification. Focusing involves detecting at least one member of a family of global arrangements of local image features. This step is computationally very efficient and all but a relatively small number of potential regions-of-interest are discarded. Intensive classification involves normalizing the remaining regions-of-interest and implementing a tree-based classifier for object versus background.

The training algorithm has two corresponding steps: identifying discriminating and invariant local features based on examples of faces, and making classification trees by recursively partitioning a training set consisting of both positive and negative examples, the latter being registered and standardized false positive ROI's detected by the feature arrangements in sample background images. Although described in the specific context of face detection, the algorithm is easily ported to other problems as will be illustrated in a forthcoming paper in which we also investigate connections to selective attention in natural visual systems.

Acknowledgement: this work was supported in part by the Army Research Office under grant DAAH04-96-1-0061, the Army Research Office (MURI) under grant DAAH04-96-1-0445, by the NSF under grant DMS-9217655, and by the ONR under contract N00014-91-J-1021.

References

Amit, Y. (1997), 'Graphical shape templates for automatic anatomy detection, application to mri brain scans', *IEEE Trans. Medical Imaging* **16**, 28–40.

Amit, Y. and Geman, D. (1997), 'Shape quantization and recognition with randomized trees', *Neural Computation* **9**, 1545–1588.

Amit, Y., Geman, D. and Wilder, K. (1997), 'Joint induction of shape features and tree classifiers', *IEEE Trans. PAMI* **19(11)**.

Bichsel, M. (1991), Strategies of robust object recognition for the automatic identification of human faces, Technical report, ETH-Zurich.

Breiman, L., Friedman, J., Olshen, R. and Stone, C. (1984), *Classification and Regression Trees*, Wadsworth, Belmont, CA.

Burl, M., Leung, T. and Perona, P. (1995), Face localization via shape statistics, *in* 'Proceedings, International Workshop on Automatic Face and Gesture Recognition', pp. 154–159.

Colmenarez, A. J. and Huang, T. S. (1997), Face detection with information-based maximum discrimination, *in* 'Proceedings, CVPR', IEEE Computer Society Press, pp. 782–787.

Cootes, T. F. and Taylor, C. J. (1996), Locating faces using statistical feature detectors, *in* 'Proceedings, Second International Conference on Automatic Face and Gesture Recognition', IEEE Computer Society Press, pp. 204–209.

Han, C. C., Liao, H., Yu, L. and Hua, L. (1996), Fast face detection via morphology-based pre-processing, Technical report.

Hoogenboom, R. and Lew, M. (1996), Face detection using local maxima, *in* 'Proceedings, Second International Conference on Automatic Face and Gesture Recognition', IEEE Computer Society Press, pp. 334–339.

Huang, J., Gutta, S. and Wechsler, H. (1996), Detection of human faces using decision trees, *in* 'Proceedings, Second International Conference on Automatic Face and Gesture Recognition', IEEE Computer Society Press, pp. 248–252.

Jecquin, A. and Eleftheriadis, A. (1995), Automatic location tracking of faces and facial features in video sequences, *in* 'Proceedings, International Workshop on Automatic Face and Gesture Recognition, Zurich'.

Maurer, T. and von der Malsburg, C. (1996), Tracking and learning graphs and pose on image sequences of faces, *in* 'Proceedings, Second International Conference on Automatic Face and Gesture Recognition', IEEE Computer Society Press, pp. 176–181.

Osuna, E., Freund, R. and Girosi, F. (1997), Training support vector machines: an application to face detection, *in* 'Proceedings, CVPR', IEEE Computer Society Press, pp. 130–136.

Pentland, A., Moghaddam, B. and Starner, T. (1994), View-based and modular eigenspaces for face recognition, *in* 'Proceedings, Computer Vision and Pattern Recognition 94', pp. 84–91.

Rowley, H. A., Baluja, S. and Kanade, T. (1995), Human face detection in visual scenes, Technical Report CMU-CS-95-158R, School of Computer Science, Carnegie Mellon University.

Sung, K. K. and Poggio, T. (1994), Example-based learning for view-based human face detection, Technical Report A.I Memo 1521, Artificial Intelligence Laboratory, M.I.T.

Tankus, A., Yeshurun, H. and Intrator, N. (1997), Face detection by direct convexity estimation, *in* 'Proceedings of the First Intl. Conference on Audio- and Video-based Biometric Person Authentication, Springer, Crans-Montana, Switzerland'.

Yow, K. C. and Cipolla, R. (1995), Towards an automatic human face localization system, *in* 'Proceedings, British Machine Vision Conference', BMVA Press, pp. 701–710.

Yuille, A. L., Cohen, D. S. and Halliman, P. (1992), 'Feature extraction from faces using deformable templates', *Inter. J. Comp. Vision* **8**, 104–109.

Face Detection and Recognition

Antonio J. Colmenarez and Thomas S. Huang

Department of Electrical and Computer Engineering,
Coordinated Science Laboratory, and
Beckman Institute for Advanced Science and Technology.
University of Illinois at Urbana-Champaign
405 N. Mathews Ave,
Urbana, IL 61801, U.S.A.
http://www.ifp.uiuc.edu/~antonio

Abstract. Two of the most important aspects in the general research framework of face recognition by computer are addressed here: face and facial feature detection, and face recognition -- or rather face comparison. The best reported results of the mug-shot face recognition problem are obtained with elastic matching using jets. In this approach, the overall face detection, facial feature localization, and face comparison is carried out in a single step. This paper describes our research progress towards a different approach for face recognition. On the one hand, we describe a visual learning technique and its application to face detection in complex background, and accurate facial feature detection/tracking. On the other hand, a fast algorithm for 2D-template matching is presented as well as its application to face recognition. Finally, we report an automatic, real-time face recognition system.

Keywords. Face detection, face recognition, facial feature detection/tracking, maximum likelihood, maximum discrimination, information theory, visual learning techniques, template matching

1   Introduction

In the general framework of face recognition, a probe still-image is matched against a collection of images -- the database of the people known by the system. As a result, most of the work carried out in face recognition by computer is limited to the comparison between face images. The best reported results of the mug-shot face recognition problem are obtained with jet-based elastic matching and principal component analysis. In these approaches, the overall face detection, facial feature localization, and face comparison is carried out in a single step.

Provided that video cameras, frame grabbers, and the corresponding software support are becoming more readily available, face recognition with video sequences poses a new, interesting problem. Straightforward extension of the known face recognition approaches are not suitable, since the computational resources required for storing a video sequence for each individual in the database, and matching an input video segment with a video database are most likely prohibiting. A new representation for the face knowledge is required for the database, as well as better face-learning techniques than just keeping pictures of the people known by the system.

In this paper, we present our research progress towards face recognition with video sequences. First, we briefly describe a visual-learning technique that leads to an automatic, real-time, robust face and facial feature detection and tracking system. Such a system provides the starting point and the setup for automatic processing of video sequences with faces. We also introduce in this paper a fast algorithm for 2D-template matching, which provides an efficient way for massive image comparison; and finally, we describe a template-matching based, real-time face recognition system.

2 Face Detection

Visual pattern detection is a problem of significant importance and difficulty. Automatic detection of targets is the first step in most automatic vision systems. Most of the research carried out by the computer vision community relies on the robust detection and accurate location of objects within the tested images. In many cases, algorithms for automatic, visual detection of targets are not provided. In other cases, rather useless algorithms are used which are based on assumptions (for example, controlled environment) that are not suitable for real-life applications.

Although it seems an easy task for the human vision system, machine detection of visual patterns is difficult due to the wide range of variations present in real-live data. Aside from the intra-class variation proper of any family of objects, visual detection of patterns has to deal with other sources of image variations such as light conditions, object pose, imaging system, etc.

Considering it as a pattern, the face is a challenging object to detect and recognize. The face anatomy is rigid enough so that all faces are similar in structure, yet we are very much different from each other. In addition to individual variations and the racial variations, there are the facial expressions, which allow an individual to change his or her appearance significantly.

The main approaches for pattern recognition have been used in face and facial feature detection. However, a complete evaluation and comparison of these techniques is rather difficult since too many aspects are to be considered such as the training set, the testing set, computational requirements, and other testing conditions.

Yang and Huang [1] presented a hierarchical knowledge-based system for face detection in complex backgrounds in which the structure of the rules for discrimination is set beforehand. Pentland and Moghaddam [2] reported a maximum likelihood face detection system based on a feature vector obtained from the eigenspace decomposition (Eigenfaces). Soulie, Viennet and Lamy [3]

Sung and Poggio [4], and Rowley, Baluja and Kanade [5] have reported face detection systems based on neural networks. These systems report the best performance in term of correct-answer-false-alarm ratio; however, they are extremely computationally expensive in both the training and testing procedures. Other approaches of relevance are those based on features [6,7,8]; in these, the facial features are first detected and then, face candidates are geometrically validated with their relative feature positions.

In this section, we described a visual learning technique based on information-theoretic discrimination of patterns, and report a real-time, face and facial feature detection system that uses it.

2.1 Information-Based Maximum Discrimination

Visual pattern detection can be treated as a particular case of pattern recognition in which only two main classes are dealt with: (i) the class of views of the object to be detected and (ii) the class of all other views, background, other objects, etc. Given a training set with both positive and negative examples, the learning process is the selection of the best possible discriminant function. Such discriminant function, is later used in the detection procedure to decide whether the object in question is present or not in a given view.

The goal of the presented visual learning technique is to set up the probability model that maximizes the Kullback relative information between the two classes of the training examples. Kullback relative information, also known as Kullback divergence, or cross entropy [9], measures the "distance" between two probability measures. Although it does not satisfy the triangle inequality, this divergence is a non-negative measure of the difference between two probability functions that equals zero only when they are identical.

Images from the training set are analyzed as observations of a random process. The two classes (for example, faces and backgrounds) are characterized by two probability functions. The probability functions are build assuming a modified Markov process structure. Then, the learning procedure is turned into an optimization whose goal is to find the process structure that maximizes the Kullback divergence. The result of this optimization is a likelihood ratio function based on the obtained probability models that can be used to evaluate an image observation and decide if it belongs to one class or another. A detailed description of this learning technique and its implementation can be found in [10,11].

2.1.1 Maximum Likelihood Detection

Let us have a set of training samples of an object class - the positive examples, for instance, the class of 20x20-pixel images of up-right frontal view of human faces.

$$\mathbf{T_{positive}} = \{\mathbf{X_p}^1, \cdots, \mathbf{X_p}^N \mid \mathbf{X_p} \in \mathbf{I}^{20 \cdot 20}\}$$

Let us also have a set of examples of other classes of objects - the negative examples, for instance, a set of randomly selected 20x20 images.

$$\mathbf{T_{negative}} = \{\mathbf{X_n}^1, \cdots, \mathbf{X_n}^M \mid \mathbf{X_n} \in \mathbf{I}^{w \cdot h}\}$$

Assuming that we can construct and estimate the probability models for each class given the sets of examples, object detection can be carried out using the maximum likelihood decision rule:

$$\mathbf{X} \in \mathbf{T_{positive}} \quad \text{if} \quad L(\mathbf{X}) > L_{th}$$

where $L(\mathbf{X}) = P^{pos}(\mathbf{X}) / P^{neg}(\mathbf{X})$ is the likelihood ratio.

In the case of visual object detection, $\mathbf{X}$ is an image window of fixed size. The training set of positive examples is obtained by re-scaling images to that fixed size, while the negative examples are obtained by looking at sub-windows of randomly selected images. The detection procedure is a multi-scale search for the sub-windows that pass the likelihood decision rule. By searching over several scaled versions of the input images, objects of different sizes (scale factors of that of $\mathbf{X}$) can be detected.

2.1.2 Information-Based Learning

The Kullback relative information, defined as:

$$H_{positive|negative} = \sum_{\forall \mathbf{X}} P^{pos}(\mathbf{X}) \cdot \log L(\mathbf{X})$$

can be used as a measure of the overall discrimination capability of the likelihood ratio.

In the case that the probability models, and therefore the likelihood ratio, depend on some parameter set $\mathbf{S}$, the Kullback relative information can be used as optimization criteria to choose those parameters.

In this general framework, we define Information-Based learning as the aforementioned process of optimization of a discriminant function. It is worth noting that the complexity involved in the probability modeling, estimation, and the proposed optimization limits its application in the general form. In the following section, we described a practical solution.

2.1.3 Information-Based Learning with Modified Markov Models

Let us assume a modified 1st-order Markov process structure, and compute the probability function of the observation $\mathbf{X}$ as:

$$P(\mathbf{X}, \mathbf{S}) = P_1(X_{S_1}) \prod_{i=2,\cdots,N} P_i(X_{S_i} \mid X_{S_{i-1}})$$

where $\mathbf{S}$ is a vector of indices that defines the structure of the modified Markov sequence, and $P_i(X_{S_i} \mid X_{S_{i-1}})$ are non-parametric probability estimators based on the statistics obtained from the training set.

Using the chain rule, we can compute the Kullback divergence if the probability functions of the positive and negative examples as:

$$H_{\text{positivelnegative}}(\mathbf{S}) = H_1(X_{S_1}) \sum_{i=2,\cdots,N} H_i(X_{S_i} \mid X_{S_{i-1}})$$

where $H_i(X_{S_i} \mid X_{S_{i-1}})$ is the Kullback divergence of the conditional probability functions $P^{pos}_i(X_{S_i} \mid X_{S_{i-1}})$ and $P^{neg}_i(X_{S_i} \mid X_{S_{i-1}})$.

Note that for each pair of indices - a total of N^2, $H(X_k \mid X_l)$ can be computed using the divergence definition and the non-parametric probability estimators obtained from the training sets. Then, the learning problem is turn into an optimization where the goal is to find the vector of indices $\mathbf{S}$ that maximizes the overall Kullback divergence. Once $\mathbf{S}$ is found, the likelihood ratio:

$$L(\mathbf{X}) = L_1(X_{S_1}) \prod_{i=2,\cdots,N} L_i(X_{S_i} \mid X_{S_{i-1}})$$

is ready to be used as the discriminant function in a object detection system.

A detailed description of this optimization procedure, its implementation, and results in the context of face detection is given in [10,11]. In the following section, we describe a face detection and tracking system in which the discriminant functions for the face and eye patterns are based on this learning technique.

2.2 Face and Facial Feature Detection System

We describe in this section an automatic, real-time face and facial feature detection and tracking system implemented using the previously presented visual learning technique.

Our system runs on an SGI-ONYX with 12 R10000 processors, and a SIRIUS video acquisition board. Real-time video is grabbed from a camera to the computer memory for processing, and sent back out to a monitor with additional labeling information such as the position of the face and the facial features. The video stream consists of WxH full color frames at 15 fps; however, all the processing is carried out on gray-level images.

As it is illustrated in Figure 1, the system operates in one of two modes. In the detection-mode, the system is constantly carrying out an exhaustive search to find faces and their outer eye corners. Setup to detect faces in a range of size (actually, that is the distance between the outer eye corners) between 100 and 400 pixels, this detection loop runs on 10 processors at about 3 frames per second. Once a face is successfully detected, that is when the confidence level of the detection is above a fixed threshold, the system switch to the tracking-mode.

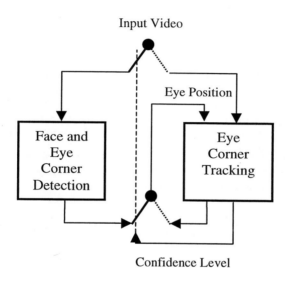

Figure 1 Overview of the face and facial detection/tracking system.

In the tracking-mode, the previous positions of the outer eye corners are used to setup normalized (in size and orientation) images with the incoming frames, so that the locations of those facial features are continuously updated. Whenever, the confidence level of the feature tracking falls under a predefined threshold, the system switch back to the detection-mode. The tracking procedure (or rather, this localized detection) is based on the likelihood models obtained with the aforementioned visual learning technique but at a much higher resolution. As a result, there is no error accumulation or inaccuracy over long video sequences. Additionally, this mode runs on one processor at full frame-rate, leaving the most of the processing power of our computer available for other applications such as face recognition.

While the detection-mode imposes constraints on the input such as near-frontal view with up-right position and relatively slow motion, the tracking-mode releases all these constraints so that any views in which the outer eye corners are not occluded can be handled.

3 Face Recognition

The main approach taken in face recognition is the comparison between the information present in a database and the probe data obtained from the person to be recognized. Early work used the feature relative sizes and positions in the comparison, while recent methods use face appearance (i.e. the gray-level intensity). Several similarity measures and pre-processing techniques have been used to deal with image variations due to light condition, head pose, and facial expression. Chellapa, Wilson, and Sirohey have reviewed the research efforts on face recognition and other related issues [12].

A major difficulty in face recognition comes from the appearance variation of the face due to facial expressions. In the particular case of the mug-shot problem, elastic-graph-matching techniques outperform other methods by allowing some deformation to deal with facial expression. However, the overall optimization involved in finding the face and the facial deformation while matching with the database, is extremely computationally expensive.

Assuming that the face and its facial feature can be accurately located so that the facial expression can be compensated, the face recognition problem comes down to matching this expression-normalized facial appearance with those of the database. Under these conditions, the straightforward Euclidean distance might be used. In this section, we described a fast algorithm for 2D-template matching and a face recognition system based on template correlation and the previously described face and facial feature detection system.

3.1 Fast Algorithm for 2D-Template Matching

Matching by template correlation is basically the search for the position within an image that minimizes the Euclidean distance between the image region and the template used. Brute-force template correlation is an exhaustive search that can be efficiently implemented using the FFT. Template matching via FFT is carried out by searching for the position with a peak of the correlation between the image and the template.

Techniques to speed it up are based on logarithmic search, coarse-to-fine approaches, etc. We describe in this section a fast algorithm for 2D-template matching. The proposed technique reduces the two-dimensional search for the peak of the correlation to two independent, one-dimensional searches. As a result, we achieve a speed up of around two orders of magnitude, and a memory size reduction of around one order of magnitude.

3.1.1 Template Matching via FFT

Let us consider an image template $y(n,m)$ $n,m \in W_y$, and a test image $x(n,m)$ $n,m \in W_x$. The correlation: $z(n,m) = x(n,m) \otimes y(n,m)$ can be computed as the inverse 2D-FFT of $Z(k,l) = X(k,l)Y^*(k,l)$, where $X(k,l)$ and $Y(k,l)$ are the 2D-FFT's of the images $x(n,m)$ and $y(n,m)$ zero-padded over a region large enough to avoid overlapping. The peak of the correlation $z(n,m)$ and the corresponding normalized correlation coefficient can be obtained straightforward using the definition.

Assuming that the image is correlated with many templates, such as in the case of face recognition, and that the 2D-FFT of the templates can be computed in advanced, most of the computation is taken by the inverse 2D-FFT. The proposed algorithm finds the location of the peak of the correlation without actually evaluating the inverse 2D-FFT; this is possible because of the energy packing property of the Fourier Transform.

3.1.2 Intuitive Description of the Algorithm

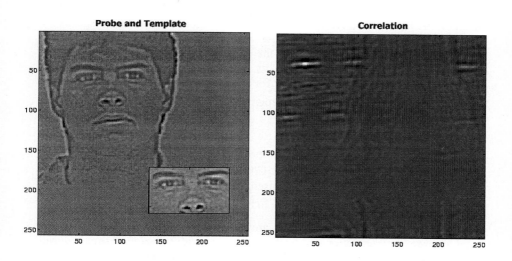

Figure 2 Example of the probe, the template, and the correlation between them.

Let us consider the images in Figure 2: (a) is the test image, (b) is the template, and (c) is the correlation between them. Note that a peak of the correlation occurs at the position (39,36) where the template would have to be shifted to match the test image. It can be shown that if two 1D-signal (lines of the test image) of similar energy are correlated with a 1D-template (a line of the template image) signal, the best matching one gives the highest correlation energy.

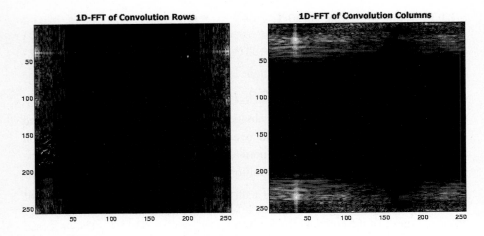

Figure 3 1D-FFT of rows of the correlation, and columns of the correlation.

Let us also consider Figure 3. (a) and (b) are obtained by computing 1D-DFT of the rows and the columns of the correlation respectively. Or similarly, they can be computed by taking inverse 1D-DFT of the columns, and the rows of $Z(k,l) = X(k,l)Y^*(k,l)$. Note that the 39th row in (a) and the 36th column in (b) have the highest response. They are shown in Figure 4 (a) and (b) respectively. Figure 4 also shows (a) the first row and (b) the first column of the auto-correlation of the template. Note that the overall shape as well as the location of the peaks is similar in both sets of plots. It can be shown that if the test signal provides a perfect match for the template, for instance: $y[n] = x[n]$ $n \in W_y \subset W_x$, and regions of support are of similar size, then

$$Y(e^{jw})^2 \approx X(e^{jw})Y^*(e^{jw}).$$

The first observation suggests that the peak of the 2D correlation can be found faster by observing only several 1D-inverse FFT of the columns and rows of $Z(k,l)$. The second observation is useful to precisely select from the template auto-correlation, the columns and rows to be used in the test.

Because only a few 1D-inverse FFTs are computed and stored per template, the total amount of computation and memory required with this algorithm is reduced. The limitations, however, are that the size of the template cannot be much smaller than that of the test image, and that the template and the image have to be highly correlated.

In the particular case of face recognition, this limitation does not pose any inconvenience. Since the faces are roughly located beforehand, the size of the template and the probe image are similar. On the other hand, only high values of the correlation coefficient between the probe image and one particular template are useful to conclude that the person in question is the same to that of the template. Therefore, even though the algorithm fails to compute the exact maximum correlation coefficient for all templates, it is still useful to find the best candidates.

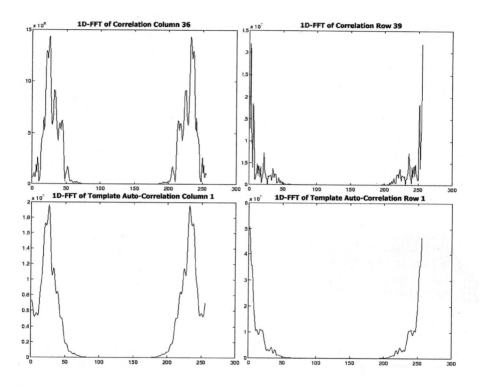

Figure 4 1D-FFT of the column and row of the correlation with highest response, and 1D-FFT of the 1st column and 1st row of the template auto-correlation.

3.1.3 Results of Face Recognition

The simplest version of the presented algorithm was tested in the context of face recognition. Only one column and one row are used to find the peak of the correlation; we chose those that maximizes the energy of the first column and row of the template auto-correlation. Once the position of the correlation peak was found the correlation coefficient between the image and the template is computed using the definition in a window of ±1 pixels around the estimated peak position and the maximum is taken.

A database of 11 people with 18 templates each was used for this test. The templates were obtained by rotating and re-scaling the mug shots of each person. Each template was then matched against the original mug shots of each person; a total of 2,178 matches were computed. The actual correlation coefficients and the ones obtained with the proposed algorithm agree remarkably on good matches. For templates with correlation coefficient greater than 0.70, our algorithm succeeded to find the peak of the correlation within ±1 pixels in 99% of the cases.

3.2 Face Recognition System

In this section, we describe a face recognition system based upon the previously described face and facial feature detection/tracking system. The recognition program, which runs a module of the face tracking system, uses template correlation to compare detected and tracked faces from the video sequence with the database.

Every time a person is successfully detected and tracked, the recognition module is launched. If the confidence level of the recognition is not higher than some threshold, a new entry is added to the database. Entries are later associate with the individual information such as the name.

A database of templates is constantly used and updated by the system. The templates are created using the outer eye corners as the reference to normalize the scale and the rotation of the input face. Note that more than one entry per person is allowed in the system, and they are automatically created if the person changes his or her appearance significantly with respect to previous entries. This way, in a very simple scheme, the system automatically learns from video and the individual changes due to facial expressions.

4 Summary

In this paper we presented our progress towards face recognition using video sequences. We described a visual learning technique that maximizes the information-based maximum discrimination. And we presented a fast algorithm for 2D-template matching. Finally, we reported an automatic, real-time face recognition system that uses video sequences continuously to: (i) detect the presence of a face in the input video, (ii) accurately locate/track the outer eye corners, (iii) match the input face with the database, and (iv) learn faces by adding entries to the database based on the confidence level of the matching and tracking procedures.

Acknowledgement

This work was supported in part by the Army Research Laboratory under cooperate agreement No DAAL01-96-2-0003, and in part by the Joint Services Electronics Program Grant ONR N00014-96-1-0129.

Bibliography

[1]   G. Yang and T.S. Huang, "Human Face Detection in a Complex Background", Pattern Recognition, Vol. 27, No 1, pp. 53-63, 1994

[2]   B. Moghaddam and A. Pentland, "Maximum Likelihood Detection of Faces and Hands", Int. Workshop on Automatic Face- and Gesture-Recognition, Zurich, 1995.

[3]   F. Soulie, E. Viennet, and B. Lamy, "Multi-Modular Neural Network Architectures: Pattern Recognition Applications in Optical Character Recognition and Human Face Recognition", Intl. Journal of Pattern Recognition and Artificial Intelligence, Vol. 7, No 4, 1993.

[4]   K. Sung and T. Poggio, "Example-Based Learning for View-Based Human Face Detection". A. I. Memo 1521, CBCL Paper 112, MIT, December 1994.

[5]   H. Rowley, S. Baluja, and T. Kanade, "Neural Network-Based Face Detection", CVPR, 1996.

[6]   M.C. Burl, and P. Perona, "Recognition of Planar Objects Classes", Computer Vision and Pattern Recognition, 1995.

[7]   K. C. Yow, and R. Cipolla, "A Probabilistic Framework for Perceptual Grouping of Features for Human Face Detection", Int. Conf. Automatic Face and Gesture Recognition, Vermont, 1996.

[8]   K. C. Yow, and R. Cipolla, "Detection of Human Faces Under Scale, Orientation, and Viewpoint Variations", Int. Conf. Automatic Face and Gesture Recognition}, Vermont, 1996.

[9]   R. M. Gray, "Entropy and Information Theory", Springer-Verlag, 1990.

[10] A. Colmenarez and T.S. Huang, "Face Detection with Information-Based Maximum Discrimination", Computer Vision and Pattern Recognition, 1997.

[11] A. Colmenarez and T.S. Huang, "Maximum Likelihood Face Detection", International Conference On Face and Gesture Recognition, 1996.

[12] R. Chellapa, C. L. Wilson, and S. Sirohey, "Human and Machine Recognition of Faces: A Survey", Proceedings of the IEEE, vol. 83, #5, May 1995.

The Bochum/USC Face Recognition System and How it Fared in the FERET Phase III Test

Kazunori Okada[1], Johannes Steffens[1,2,3], Thomas Maurer[2], Hai Hong[1], Egor Elagin[1,3], Hartmut Neven[1,3], and Christoph von der Malsburg[1,2]

[1] Computer Science Department *and* Center for Neural Engineering
   University of Southern California
   Los Angeles, CA 90089-2520, USA
   kazunori@selforg.usc.edu
[2] Institut für Neuroinformatik
   Ruhr-Universität Bochum
   D–44780 Bochum, Germany
[3] Now also at Eyematic Interfaces, Inc
   827 20th Street, Santa Monica, CA 90403, USA

Summary. This paper summarizes the Bochum/USC face recognition system, our preparations for the FERET Phase III test, and test results as far as they have been made known to us. Our technology is based on Gabor wavelets and elastic bunch graph matching. We briefly discuss our technology in relation to biological and PCA based systems and indicate current activities in the lab and potential future applications.

1. Introduction

Vision is the most important of our senses by which we establish continuity between past and present. Vision is difficult for the simple fact that present scenes never repeat past examples in detail. Bridging that difference is the challenge. Vision has many aspects among which object recognition is but one. Object recognition requires the detection of similarity in spite of image variation in terms of translation, rotation scaling, pose (rotation in depth), deformation, illumination, occlusion, noise and background. Moreover, depending on the specific task, an object may have changing attributes, e.g., surface markings.

In principle, there are three types of information as a basis for generalization from past samples to present instances. One is the information in those samples themselves. It is of extreme biological importance to generalize from minimal sample bases. A second is the structural commonality of an individual object with others. This is a prominent aspect of face recognition, but plays an important role also for more variegated objects as far as they are composed of common shape primitives [Biederman, 1987]. A third type of information is based on first principles which can be built into a system and need not be derived from experience at all. An example of first principles are the transformation laws within the image plane — translation, rotation and scaling. In general, a vision system will exploit a mixture of all three information sources.

Face recognition is a rather particular example of object recognition in that all faces are qualitatively similar to each other and the distinctions to be made are of a gradual nature. For a discussion of face recognition in distinction to other object recognition tasks see [Biederman and Kalocsai, 1997]. There is the common expectation that technical systems are potentially superior to human face recognition in being able to make precise metric measurements. Unfortunately, this is vitiated by even small variations in pose and facial expression.

We are dealing here with the problem of recognizing a person from a single photograph against a gallery of hundreds of persons, each represented again by a single photograph — the task set by the FERET program. The task as such is virtually impossible for humans to perform, due to the practical impossibility of memorizing (or repeatedly looking through) data bases of thousands of images as was required in the program's test. But even deciding whether two images presented in direct sequence do or do not refer to the same person is made difficult by variation in pose (or expression) [Kalocsai et al., 1994], [Biederman and Kalocsai, 1997]. The difficulty arises from the fact that a single photo doesn't contain enough information about a face's depth profile to predict images of different pose. The face recognition system we have developed is distinguished from others by a larger extent to which its generalization capabilities are based on general principles instead of on statistical learning. We will come back to this point at the end of the paper.

This report succinctly describes the basic system as developed previously [Lades et al., 1993], [Wiskott et al., 1997] and the particular improvements in preparation for the latest FERET test, as well as some details of our system implementation. We then discuss performance of our system resulting from in-house preparation tests and the FERET phase III test, which we have taken in March of 1997 and which has been partially reported [Phillips and Rauss, 1997]. We conclude by mentioning current activities in the lab and potential future applications of our technology, and by discussing our technology in relation to biological and PCA-based systems.

2. The System as Previously Developed

2.1 The Wavelet Transform

Previous versions of our system are described in [Lades et al., 1993],[Wiskott et al., 1997]. The basic data format of our system is the Gabor-based wavelet

$$\psi_{\mathbf{k}}(\mathbf{x}) = \frac{k^2}{\sigma^2} e^{-\frac{k^2}{2\sigma^2}x^2} \left\{ e^{i\,\mathbf{k}\,\mathbf{x}} - e^{-\frac{\sigma^2}{2}} \right\}. \tag{2.1}$$

The wavelet is a plane wave with wave vector $\mathbf{k}$, restricted by a Gaussian window, the size of which relative to the wavelength is parameterized by σ. The second term in the brace removes the DC component. A wavelet, centered at image position $\mathbf{x}$, is used to extract the wavelet component $J_{\mathbf{k}}$ from the image with gray level distribution $I(\mathbf{x})$,

$$J_{\mathbf{k}}(\mathbf{x}) = \int d\mathbf{x}'\, I(\mathbf{x}')\, \psi_{\mathbf{k}}(\mathbf{x} - \mathbf{x}'). \tag{2.2}$$

We typically sample the space of wave vectors $\mathbf{k}$ in a discrete hierarchy of 5 resolution levels (differing by half-octaves) and 8 orientations at each resolution level, thus giving 40 complex values for each sampled image point (the real and imaginary components referring to the cosine and sine phases of the plane wave). We designate the samples in $\mathbf{k}$-space by the index $j = 1, \ldots, 40$ and consider all wavelet components centered in a single image point as a vector which we call a *jet*. A jet describes the local features of the area surrounding $\mathbf{x}$. If sampled with sufficient density, the image can be reconstructed from jets within the bandpass covered by the sampled frequencies.

2.2 Graphs and Their Similarity

To describe the aspect of an object (in this context, a face) we use a labeled graph, the nodes of which refer to points on the object's aspect and are labeled by jets. Edges of the graph are labeled with distance vectors between the nodes. To compare jets and graphs, similarity functions are defined. If two graphs are of equal geometry, their similarity is the simple sum of pair-wise jet similarities. If the graphs have relative distortion, a second term can be introduced [Lades et al., 1993] to take this into account. An important feature of our system is that we use two different jet similarity functions for two different and even complementary tasks. If the components of a jet J are written in the form $J_j = a_j\, e^{i\phi_j}$, with amplitude a_j and phase ϕ_j, one form for the similarity of two jets J and J' is the normalized scalar product of the amplitude vector

$$S(J, J') = \frac{\sum_j a_j a'_j}{\sqrt{\sum_j a_j^2 \sum_j a'^2_j}}. \tag{2.3}$$

The other similarity function has the form

$$S(J, J') = \frac{\sum_j a_j a'_j \cos(\phi_j - \phi'_j - \mathbf{d}\mathbf{k}_j)}{\sqrt{\sum_j a_j^2 \sum_j a'^2_j}}. \tag{2.4}$$

This function contains the relative displacement vector $\mathbf{d}$ between the image points to which the two jets refer. When comparing two jets during graph matching, the similarity between them is maximized with respect to $\mathbf{d}$, leading to an accurate determination of jet position. This idea goes back to [Fleet and Jepson, 1990], [Theimer and Mallot, 1994]. We use it in the form developed by [Wiskott, 1995]. We are using both similarity functions, preferring the phase-insensitive version, eq. (2.3), which varies smoothly with relative position, when first matching a graph, and using the phase-sensitive version, eq. (2.4), when being interested in accurate positioning.

2.3 Elastic Graph Matching

The fundamental process with our system is elastic graph matching. In it, a *model graph* — a graph derived from a facial image with appropriate node positions — is compared to a test image. In the process, the nodes of the model graph are tentatively positioned over the image, jets are extracted from those image points and the similarity of the the thus-defined image graph to the model graph is determined. This similarity is optimized by varying node positions in the image. In an initial phase, this variation takes the form of a global move of a rigid copy of the model graph's node positions. In a second phase, image nodes are allowed to move individually, introducing elastic graph distortions. In order to *find* a decent match we use the phase-insensitive similarity function, eq. (2.3). With this similarity function, graphs and jets are attracted to their match points in the image over large distances by a smoothly ascending similarity gradient. When trying to *locate* a jet with great accuracy we use the phase sensitive similarity function, eq. (2.4), which by utilizing the phase is very sensitive to small jet displacements.

2.4 Elastic Bunch Graph Matching

When attempting to find an as yet unknown face in an image and to define a graph to represent it, we make use of a data structure called a *bunch graph* [Wiskott et al., 1995]. It is similar to the graph as described above, but instead of attaching only a single jet to each node, we attach a whole bunch of jets, each derived from a different facial image. To form a bunch graph, a collection of facial images (the *bunch graph gallery*) is marked with node locations at defined positions of the head. We call these positions *landmarks*. They are found by a semi-automatic process [Wiskott et al., 1997]. When matching a bunch graph to an image, the jet extracted from the image is compared to all jets in the corresponding bunch attached to the bunch graph and the best-matching one is selected. This process is called *elastic bunch graph matching*. Constructed with a judiciously selected gallery, a bunch graph covers a great variety of faces with different local properties.

We accomplish recognition of the input face in three stages — face finding, landmark finding, and recognition by comparison. The first two stages serve to create a scale invariant model of the face in an input image. Both stages are based on elastic bunch graph matching, although with different parameter settings corresponding to different level of detail. Faces of different pose (in the FERET test the pose was identified in the file name) are processed in the same manner but with different bunch graphs customized for the relevant poses. In the last stage, face models are compared to achieve recognition. Each stage is discussed in detail below, in the order in which they are actually performed.

2.5 Face Finding

This first stage serves to find a face in an image and determine its size. This is accomplished by a set of matches to bunch graphs of appropriate pose and of three different sizes. The detailed schedule of this match is described in [Wiskott et al., 1997]. The best matching bunch graph determines the size and position of the face. We next place a square frame around the face so that the face occupies about a quarter of the area of the frame. The resulting image is warped to a standard size (currently 128×128 pixels), and a new wavelet transform is computed, thus defining the *image frame*. The image frame is passed to the next module, the Landmark Finder. See Fig. 2.1 B for the graph placed over the facial image during face finding. The reliability of this step in letting the face fall entirely inside the image frame is crucial to the success of the system.

2.6 Landmark Finding

Although in the face finding step a set of nodes was placed over the face, the basic procedure is now repeated with a bunch graph containing more nodes and a larger bunch graph gallery. The purpose of this step is to find facial landmarks with high positional accuracy and reliability and to encode the information contained in the image as accurately as possible. This step is equally crucial since a node not correctly placed over its landmark will lead to distorted similarity values during the comparison stage. Fig. 2.1 C shows a typical result of this stage. This model graph represents all the information extracted from an image. For a face in frontal pose it contains 48 nodes, compared to the 16 nodes used during face finding.

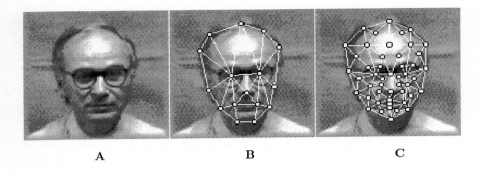

| A | B | C |

Fig. 2.1. Graph representation of a facial image. A: Input image. B: Face-finding graph. C: Model graph as defined for landmark-finding. The image frame determined by face finding is used in each case.

2.7 Graph Comparison

The model graphs produced as the result of the landmark finding step are compared pairwise to compute a similarity value. This value is computed as the sum of jet similarities between pairs of corresponding nodes divided by the number of pairs, using the phase-insensitive similarity function, eq. (2.3). Since model graphs for different poses differ in structure, a little conversion table was used to identify correspondence between nodes referring to the same landmark. The result of the graph comparison step is a complete comparison score, containing for each of the face entries in the gallery provided by ARL an ordered list of all other entries in descending order of similarity.

3. Algorithmic Improvements for FERET Phase III Test

A large part of our effort in preparation of the FERET Phase III test consisted in re-implementation of the previous system in the object-oriented program library FLAVOR (see section 3.4), as well as testing, debugging and parameter optimization.

It is a characteristic of the FERET data base that although most pairs of pictures of one person were shot in the same photo session (*same session* images), some were taken in different sessions (*duplicates*), sometimes more than a year apart. The same-session images contain a number of false cues, such as identical lighting and background, similar geometry (e.g., distance to camera) and camera settings, as well as identical clothing and hair style. We have made no effort whatsoever to exploit any of these cues. As only duplicates are relevant for practical applications of face recognition technology, we concentrated our system optimization effort on those. We also made efforts to achieve robustness with respect to at least small pose variations. With this motivation we have added three methods to our system. They are applied after the landmark finding process, section 2.6, in the following order.

3.1 Facial Histogram Equalization

In order to adjust for differences in lighting and in camera setting (which may lead to partial film saturation), we apply a technique called *histogram equalization.* In this technique, a gray value histogram is computed for an image, and depending on its shape a non-linear gray scale transfer function is computed and applied, to spread out intensity levels near histogram peaks and compress them near troughs. The particular version we apply is an adaptation of [Bates and McDonnell, 1986]. We apply histogram equalization after landmark finding. At that stage we define the smallest rectangular image segment containing the whole face as defined by the graph of landmarks. We compute the gray value histogram and the non-linear transfer function from this rectangle only (thus ignoring histogram distortions in the background) but apply the resulting equalization to the whole image frame. We then perform another Gabor wavelet transform to compute corrected jets for the model graph (actually this is the same transformation mentioned at the end of the next section).

3.2 Rescaling Gabor Filters

A coarse face size adjustment is implicit in our face finding procedure, section 2.5. The accuracy of this size determination is sufficient to define the image frame used for the landmark finding stage, but we observed that due to occasional misplacement of nodes the facial size in the image frame may still vary. This residual size variation is small enough not to compromise the reliability and accuracy of landmark finding, but it leads to distortion of the wavelet components extracted in the wavelet transform: a linear size scaling of the face translates directly into an inverse linear frequency scaling of the wavelets (only the product $\mathbf{kx}$ appears in the definition of the wavelet, eq. (2.1)).

We measure the exact facial size in the image frame by computing the mean Euclidean distance of all landmarks (nodes of the model graph) from their center of gravity, and comparing this number to the one derived from the standard graph used in the definition of the landmark finding bunch graph. The ratio of these two numbers, the *size adjustment factor,* is used to recompute wavelet components, with wavenumber $\mathbf{k}$ adjusted accordingly in eq. (2.1). In principle, scale-adjusted wavelet components can be computed by interpolation between neighboring frequency levels [Lades, 1995]. However, for the sake of higher accuracy we recomputed a wavelet transform from the image frame with the adjusted frequencies.

3.3 Jet Transformation for Face Rotation in Depth

The FERET test was to contain sub-tests with depth-rotated probe images. As all practical applications of face recognition technology will have to deal at least to some extent with pose variation, we made efforts to cope with this problem.

The FERET program insisted that a person be recognized on the basis of a single gallery image. There is no reliable method to compute the depth-profile of a face from a single image. Without exact knowledge of the three-dimensional shape of an object, the correspondence between images of different pose cannot be established accurately. This general impasse is mitigated by the fact that human faces share the general shape of their depth profile. Using an average facial depth profile it is therefore possible to predict a rotated pose to some degree of accuracy, which is perhaps a basis for improved recognition of the depth-rotated faces.

As far as a sparse set of point correspondences is concerned, this strategy is already implicit in our basic technology as described above, specifically in the average pose-specific graphs used in our bunch graphs, section 2.4, and the correspondences between nodes relating to the same landmark in different graphs. A more complicated story, however, is the adjustment of wavelet components, which contain the bulk of the information about facial identity. To some extent, Gabor-based wavelets are robust to the distortions implicit in small depth rotations of objects with generally smooth surfaces. This robustness has been the basis of our performance on depth rotation in previous FERET tests.

Here is the simple idea on which we base our approach for jet transformation [Maurer and von der Malsburg, 1995]. Assume we were dealing with a totally flat surface in three-dimensional space with some gray level distribution painted onto it, and a jet encoding this distribution around a given point. It would then be possible to accurately predict the transformation of the jet components due to depth rotation of the surface (assuming an isotropic radiance profile). Assuming the jet to be taken at the origin $\mathbf{x} = \mathbf{0}$ of the coordinate system and assuming the rotation to be about this point, the projection to the image plane of other points $\mathbf{x} = (x_1, x_2)$ is transformed according to $\mathbf{x}' = \mathbf{A}\,\mathbf{x}$, with $\mathbf{A}$ determined by the rotation angles in the image plane and in depth. This translates into the jet transformation

$$J'_{\mathbf{k}} = \int d\mathbf{x}\, I(\mathbf{A}^{-1}\mathbf{x})\, \psi_{\mathbf{k}}(\mathbf{x}) = \int d\mathbf{x}\, I(\mathbf{x})\, \psi_{\mathbf{k}}(\mathbf{A}\,\mathbf{x})\, \det(\mathbf{A}). \qquad (3.1)$$

As we want to stick to our sampling grid in $\mathbf{k}$ space, we make the Ansatz

$$\psi_{\mathbf{k}}(\mathbf{A}\,\mathbf{x})\, \det(\mathbf{A}) \approx \sum_{\mathbf{k}'} c_{\mathbf{k}\mathbf{k}'}(\mathbf{A})\, \psi_{\mathbf{k}'}(\mathbf{x}), \qquad (3.2)$$

although this can only be an approximation, with an accuracy that increases with sampling density in $\mathbf{k}$-space. Multiplication of eq. (3.2) with $\psi_{\mathbf{k}''}(\mathbf{x})$ and integration leads to a system of linear equations to determine the $c_{\mathbf{k}\mathbf{k}'}(\mathbf{A})$. All integrals can be solved analytically; details can be found in [Maurer and von der Malsburg, 1995]. Once the $c_{\mathbf{k}\mathbf{k}'}(\mathbf{A})$ are determined, the jet can be transformed according to

$$\mathbf{J}' = \mathbf{C}(\mathbf{A})\, \mathbf{J}. \qquad (3.3)$$

We can thus compute the transformation matrix $\mathbf{C}$ to transform the jet — our local visual feature vector — from one perspective into the other, given only the normal vectors of the surface before and after the rotation relative to the camera.

To apply this bit of theory to face recognition we have to assume that the surface around node points is flat to some degree of accuracy, and we have to determine the orientation of this area, i.e., its normal vector, for the two poses being compared. Once this normal vector and the geometric transformation of the face (the rotation angle) are known, the jet at this node can be transformed analytically.

As facial normal vectors are not available to us directly we have adaptively determined estimates from training galleries of 50–80 persons for each pair of poses to be compared. On these faces the flexible grids are placed automatically as described in section 2.6. For a given pair of corresponding nodes we create trial values for the normal angles, transform the jets for all persons from the rotated pose to the frontal pose and compare the two sets in terms of the recognition performance measure

$$E = \frac{1}{N^2} \sum_i \sum_j (s_{ii} - s_{ij}), \qquad (3.4)$$

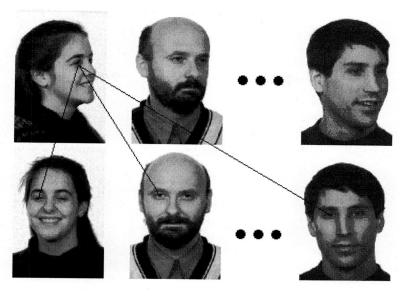

Fig. 3.1. Typical half profile and frontal faces. To learn the effective normal angles for the left eye, the left eyes of all half poses are compared with the left eyes of all frontal poses. Note the low degree of uniformity of poses labeled "half profile" in the FERET data base.

where the s_{ii} are jet similarities for the same person and s_{ij} for different persons. Stepping the trial values for normal angles through all possible orientations in steps of $5°$ horizontally and vertically, we optimize E. The procedure is repeated for all nodes of the flexible grids visible in both views, nodes having no correspondent in the other view being ignored (see Fig. 3.1). By this procedure we get an average set of effective normal vectors which determine — together with the head rotation angle — the transformation of the jets between the two poses. Let us remark here that we have only two free parameters per node (the two normal angles) for 50–80 data points (the jets of all persons at this node). As a consequence, there will be no generalization problem, which is confirmed by our tests.

After learning the transformation on a training gallery of quarter rotated faces, we obtained the following error rates on test images from the FERET training data base against a frontal gallery of 596 different persons, with a recognition attempt being counted as an error if it failed to identify the correct person as the best match:

Averaged error rates in %

Jet transformation	No	Yes
Quarter–Frontal (138 probes)	22.6	13.8
R–Frontal (237 probes)	13.5	9.2

Jet transformation thus almost halves the error rates on the quarter rotated faces ($22.5°$ rotation angle). With the same set of normal angles it reduced error rates by a third on the so-called R faces (about half-way between quarter and frontal), proving the method to be robust against pose measurement inaccuracies. Further results are reported in section 4.1.

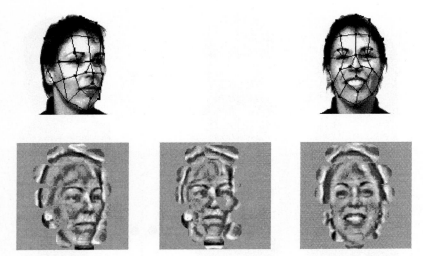

Fig. 3.2. Visualization of the pose transformation on one example. The original images together with the automatically placed grids are shown in the top row, and in the bottom row left and right the respective reconstructions. In the middle of the bottom row there is the reconstruction of the transformed face graph, which has to be compared with the right one for recognition. Only jets at nodes visible in both views are compared.

By reconstructing images from jets (see, e.g., [Pötzsch et al., 1996]), this pose transformation can be visualized, see Fig. 3.2.

One could argue that the assumption of area flatness is grossly violated in certain facial locations, such as near the eyes or the tip of the nose. However, even if that is the case the system tries, during the optimization of E, to find effective normal vectors to describe the transformation as accurately as possible.

3.4 Implementation Issues

We describe here some of the technical issues we faced for the latest FERET test, which we took in March 1997. For this test, we re-implemented the application on the basis of $FLAVOR,$[1] an extensive C++ class library of image processing algorithms designed and written by Christoph von der Malsburg's groups at the Institut für Neuroinformatik, Ruhr-Universität Bochum and at the Laboratory of Computational and Biological Vision, University of Southern California [Rinne et al., 1997]. FLAVOR provided us with all the core algorithms and a lot of support functions, e.g., for the display of results, and a user interface. We integrated the new features described above into FLAVOR and built an application program suited to the needs of the FERET test. FLAVOR thus gave us a stable starting point and a good environment for rapid prototyping and development.

We then optimized the data structures and memory allocation of our system's code in order to reduce the application's computation time. After these optimizations, the computation time to create a gallery entry was approximately one minute

---

[1] *Flexible Library for Active Vision and Object Recognition*

on a workstation with a 60 MHz SuperSPARC processor; the computation time for a recognition run was approximately ten seconds when the probe image's pose was frontal and twenty seconds when rotation in depth had to be compensated for, using the same processor with a gallery of 3816 entries.

The computation time is crucial, both for comparing our system to human performance and for fielded applications, where recognition times on the order of a few seconds are required. The computation time of our system was somewhat slow for this, though we have since improved on this: We have implemented an on-line system based on the same technology which tracks faces in real time, using a more powerful platform. This system can process 8 persons per minute without compromising much of the recognition performance [Steffens et al., 1997].

Memory requirements are another practical issue when trying to apply a system to real-world conditions. The size of a test image (256×384 pixels) in the FERET database is 96 KBytes; the size of a model graph containing 48 nodes and jets with 40 components is approximately 16 KBytes, when stored in binary. This could be considered as more than 80 % of data compression for a face model, although there are other methods which can achieve better compression factors [Turk and Pentland, 1991]. One possible way for a representation based on jets to achieve higher compression factors is to cluster jets or jet coefficients using their regularities. Krüger *et al.* proposed a clustering algorithm for reducing the number of jets in a bunch graph [Krüger et al., 1997]. Lately, Kalocsai *et al.* showed that it is possible to eliminate certain filters without sacrificing discriminative power of the representation [Kalocsai et al., 1997]. The jet and filter clustering is important not only for data compression, but also for reducing computation time.

3.5 Test Procedure

The test was administered such that, first, all 3816 images supplied by the test conductor were used to generate model graphs for later recognition purposes. This process of gallery creation consumed most of the processing time (see below). Then, the same model graphs were used as a probe set, i.e., run through the recognition process and compared against the whole gallery. The resulting matrix of similarity values is the major test result. It was then analyzed by the test conductor by restricting both gallery and probe sets to appropriate subsets, which generated the performance measurements reported in the following section (see [Phillips and Rauss, 1997] for details).

Our system was tested in two conditions — with and without coordinates of the eyes in the images supplied as additional information. Thus, for this test we actually performed two sets of gallery creation (one using the eye coordinate information, the other ignoring it) and two sets of 3816 recognition runs against the full gallery. The processing time for the entire test procedure was approximately 26 hours (22 hours for gallery creation and 4 hours for the recognition runs), for which we employed six workstations (two with 150 MHz microSPARC II and four with 60 MHz SuperSPARC processors) running in parallel.

4. Test Results

The results of the latest FERET test are described in this section. The results of in-house pre-tests for confirming the system improvement are described, followed by an evaluation of the FERET test results reported by Phillips and Rauss [Phillips and Rauss, 1997].

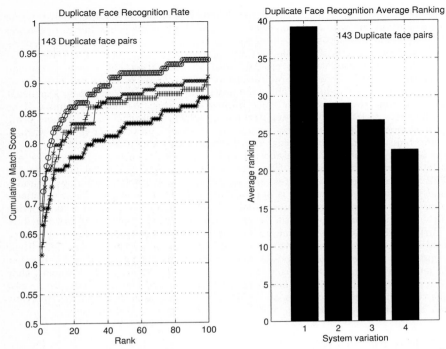

Fig. 4.1. Recognition results of FA vs FB tests in the duplicate face recognition task for various system settings. *Duplicate Face Recognition Rate* (left) shows percentage of successful duplicate face recognition. *Duplicate Face Average Ranking* (right) is an average over recognition ranks for each probe. Rank 1 corresponds to a correct recognition and a lower value means better performance. Legend: * and 1: without new functions; + and 2: histogram equalization only; × and 3: Gabor filter rescaling only; o and 4: both new functions.

4.1 Pre-test Results

To evaluate our system improvements described in section 3., we performed some in-house pre-tests with the training data consisting of 526 sets of images provided by ARL [Phillips et al., 1996]. Each set comprised pictures of the same person taken in different photo sessions. Each set from one session contained two frontal face images marked FA and FB and an optional number of the rotated face images. For some persons, images from multiple photo sessions exist which were, in some cases, taken more than a year apart (duplicate sets). A pair of images from the same set contained either slight variations in facial expression (between FA and FB) or variations in depth rotation (between FA and rotated faces). On the other hand, a pair of images from different sets but belonging to the same person (duplicates) contained greater variations of facial appearance due to changes of illumination, background, facial expression, hair style and face size on top of the variations between FA and FB or FA and rotated faces. See [Phillips et al., 1996] for a detailed description of the data set.

Our system performed very well on the same session recognition task: the recognition rate (RR) of FB probe set (526 entries) was 96.6% and RR of QR probe set

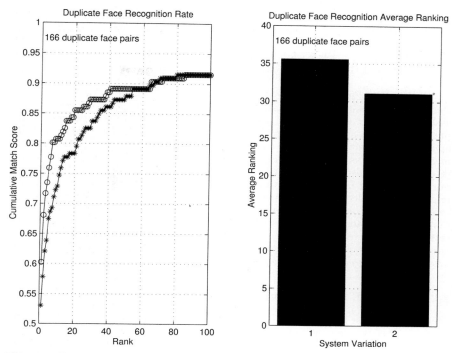

Fig. 4.2. Recognition results of the FA vs QR test in the duplicate face recognition task. Legend: o and 2: with jet transformation; * and 1: without jet transformation. The jet transformation pushes the recognition rates on the rotated duplicates close to those of the frontal ones (see Fig. 4.1); thus, rotation in depth does not seem to be the major problem on these images.

(374 entries) was 87.2%. It turned out to be difficult to evaluate improvement of our system by the same session recognition task due to the already high recognition performance. We therefore concentrated our efforts on the duplicate face recognition task. There were 143 duplicates in the FA vs FB test and 166 duplicates in the FA vs QR test.

We evaluated our system in two conditions: 1) recognition tests of a probe set with an FA gallery, in which a probe was recognized correctly if the best match in the gallery was from the same session of the probe and 2) recognition tests of the same probe set with the same gallery but correct recognition of a probe was granted if the second best match was a duplicate of the probe. Note that the latter condition is harder than the former because of the greater variations of duplicates. We will refer to the former as the same session recognition task and to the latter as the duplicate face recognition task. For both conditions, we performed two tests, one with the FB probe set and the other with a quarter rotated face (QR) probe set. The size of probe sets varied depending on the type of test and condition but the size of the gallery was always fixed at 526 entries. Eye coordinate information was not used for any of the tests.

We evaluated the performance of histogram equalization and Gabor filter rescaling by the FA vs FB test in the duplicate face recognition task. Recognition results with and without the new functions are shown in Fig. 4.1. For testing the performance of the jet transformation to compensate for rotation in depth, the FA vs QR test in the duplicate face recognition task was used. Recognition results with and without jet transformation are compared in Fig. 4.2. Both facial histogram equalization and Gabor filter rescaling were used as preprocesses for the FA vs QR tests.

Fig. 4.1 and Fig. 4.2 indicate a significant drop in recognition performance for the duplicate face recognition task when compared to the same session recognition task. This clearly shows that the great amount of face and image variations in duplicates indicates a need for improving the system further [Phillips et al., 1997]. By applying histogram equalization and Gabor filter rescaling, the recognition performance of the FA vs FB test was improved as shown by a 12% increase in recognition rate. The result also shows that improvement included not only the recognition rate but also ranks of failure cases so that average rank of all probes was significantly improved (42% decrease in average ranking). For the FA vs QR test, similar improvements were observed by correcting for face rotation in depth through application of the jet transformation described in section 3.3 (14% increase in recognition rate and 13% decrease in average ranking; see Fig. 4.2). These results suggest that our system has considerably improved, especially in the case when facial and image properties vary greatly, such as is the case with the duplicate images.

4.2 The FERET Test Result

Phillips and Rauss [Phillips and Rauss, 1997] reported results of the FERET phase III test. This test was administered in September 1996 and March 1997. There were ten groups of participants. Their report included a performance analysis of ten systems for the same session recognition and the duplicate face recognition tasks, which were explained in the previous section; however, only tests which made use of the eye coordinate information is reported there.

Our pre-test results, presented in section 4.1 and produced with a much smaller data set, were well replicated qualitatively in their report [Phillips and Rauss, 1997]. In the FA vs FB test of the same session recognition task, three systems, including ours, showed similarly high performance (approximately 95% RR). In the FA vs FB test of the duplicate face recognition task, two systems, including ours, outperformed others (approximately 60% RR), when 1196 entries in the gallery and 722 entries in the probe set were used. It is notable that on the subset of duplicates whose images were taken more than one year apart, our system was significantly better than all others: With 864 entries in the gallery and 234 entries in the probe set, our system achieved a recognition rate of approximately 52%, while the second best system scored approximately 35%.

Note that results without the use of eye coordinates were not included in Phillips and Rauss' report. This type of test was taken by only two participants, including our group. When eye coordinates are not given, a system has to find facial landmarks automatically and this adds another factor that potentially degrades recognition performance. Finding facial landmarks is a sub-category of the face recognition problem that is known to be difficult in general. Table 4.1 summarizes our results of the FERET phase III test in detail. Data in the table referring to the test with eye coordinate information correspond to the data reported by Phillips and Rauss.

In Table 4.1, we can see similar performance with or without the use of eye coordinate information; the degradation of recognition rate when eye coordinates were unavailable was at most 3%. These results can be explained by our reliable process of facial landmark finding. The FC images were introduced to the FERET tests for phase III. They are frontal images using modified illumination (taken with only natural light in a photo studio by turning off the studio lighting). Our system performed very well on this task for both categories. Our system's low recognition performance on the Quarter 2 task can be explained by the additive effects from two types of variations, depth rotation and duplicates. Some inaccuracies of pose labels which we found in our training data set (see Fig. 3.1) might also have contributed to the decrease of recognition performance for rotated face images.

The low recognition rate in the report of Phillips and Rauss, produced with the most realistic duplicate data set (Dup 3), showed that current technology is not close to solving the face recognition problem completely. Although the performance of any system using a limited data set cannot be fully translated to more realistic situations, their results highlight the quality of our technology. Our face recognition system seems to be closest to reaching the level of robust recognition of faces with realistic variations. One of our future work directions is to enhance the performance of our system in this domain.

5. Technical Applications

The technology we describe here has a wide range of applications, some of which have already been realized. In the field of security, face recognition technology can be used for access control to high-security areas, as realized in the commercial system ZN-Face [Konen and Schulze-Krüger, 1995], and the application can be easily extended to picture I.D. verification. In the area of criminal investigation, big galleries of potential suspects can be reduced, with the help of a sample image or of a composite [Konen, 1996], to a sample of 50 or so images. A witness can be expected to examine these preselected samples before losing concentration or recollection.

Table 4.1. Results for different recognition tasks. For a number of different recognition tasks, the recognition ratio (in %) for three different ranks is shown, for both the case with and without eye coordinates being supplied to the system. The sizes of the gallery and probe sets are also given. Definition of tasks following the FERET program's reports [Phillips et al., 1996], [Phillips and Rauss, 1997]: FA vs FB: same session recognition task; FA vs FC: illumination variations (see text) in FC set; Dup 1: probe set contains all duplicate images available; Dup 2: probe set contains duplicate images where difference is whether eye glasses are worn; Dup 3: probe set contains duplicate images taken at least one year apart; Quarter 1: quarter rotated images compared to FA images; Quarter 2: quarter rotated images compared to duplicate images; RB vs RC: images compared are with subject's head rotated nominally 12° to left and right, respectively.

Test	Probe/ Gallery	With Eye Coordinates			Without Eye Coordinates		
		Rank 1	10	20	Rank 1	10	20
FA vs FB	1195/1196	95	98	99	94	97	97
FA vs FC	194/1196	82	92	95	80	89	92
Dup 1	722/1196	62	72	79	61	71	79
Dup 2	176/1196	93	97	98	94	95	95
Dup 3	234/ 864	52	71	76	52	68	73
Quarter 1	32/1196	85	91	91	78	87	87
Quarter 2	126/1196	33	60	66	29	60	64
RB vs RC	94/1196	52	67	73	50	65	69

In distinction to security access control, in many situations the person to be identified cannot be expected to cooperate in the generation of a fiducial photo. Much wider application areas, such as automatic monitoring, or automatic passenger tracking and identification at airports, are opened by the PersonSpotter system we have recently developed [Steffens et al., 1997]. It is able to capture, track and recognize a person walking by a camera in real time.

On-line facial expression recognition [Hong et al., 1997] opens vistas on better human-machine communication, for instance for video games, tele-conferencing and computer-based training systems. Recognition of facial and hand gestures [Triesch and von der Malsburg, 1996] can be used to control machines more conveniently.

Fully immersive tele-conferencing requires the creation of a display that renders remote participants with correct direction of gaze independent of their spatial relation to the camera, and the creation of a realistic three-dimensional sound field. For both tasks, heads and facial features of participants (ears in the case of immersive sound) have to be accurately tracked [Maurer and von der Malsburg, 1996].

Video annotation would be an important multimedia application of our technology. Thus, by recognizing faces, facial expression and gestures, including head pose [Elagin et al., 1997], one could identify, characterize and extract human activities from video sequences on the basis of abstract descriptions.

6. Discussion

6.1 Sources of Structural Information

Perhaps the most striking feature of the visual system of higher vertebrates is its great generality and flexibility in recognizing objects and situations. This is in stark contrast to the high degree of specialization of most technical vision systems. One of our motivations for working on face recognition and in the FERET program was to expose ourselves to the requirements of a real-world vision application while working with a minimum of domain-specific structure.

In this connection we would like to return to an issue we raised in the introduction, referring to the type of information sources tapped during the storage and recognition processes. We had classified possible sources into a) individual sample data, b) statistical samples of images of the same object type ("same type" to be taken in a narrower or wider sense), or c) information in the form of first principles not instructed by sample data (at least not by object-specific samples). A previously described system [Lades et al., 1993], which might be considered a forerunner of the system we describe here, had been based entirely on individual data samples extracted from single images and on first principles. Those first principles concerned the form of visual features (Gabor-based wavelets), the data structure of labeled graphs, and a matching procedure permitting in-plane transformations (translation and deformation [Lades et al., 1993] as well as scaling and rotation [Lades, 1995]). The resulting system recognized faces by comparing stored individual samples to full test images. The system was entirely general and could recognize arbitrary objects, not just faces, if only the stored aspect was not too different from the one presented in the test image.

Specific constraints set by the FERET test forced us to build face-specific information into our system. One of these constraints was the great number, several millions, of image comparisons to be performed within a limited time period. This precluded us from comparing image pairs by elastic graph matching with its expensive examination of multiple image jets per stored jet. Instead, we extract from each image a fixed, parsimonious set of jets, centered on landmarks, and compare each jet to its one correspondent in the other image, see section 2.. Finding landmarks is only possible on the basis of information about faces in general. In our system this "general face knowledge" is constituted by the bunch graph — a small gallery of sample portraits together with semi-automatically identified landmark positions.

Another constraint set by the FERET test was the requirement to be robust with respect to differences in pose. As discussed in section 3.3, this also forced on us face-related system knowledge, in the form of pose-specific graph structures and their correspondences, and in the form of a general mechanism for jet transformation, the parameters of the latter being trained on a set of sample faces.

Although we have to admit that our system presently still relies in several places on hand-constructed scaffolding, such as the manual selection of landmarks in the bunch graph entries, it is perhaps not too far removed from one to be based entirely on first principles plus exposure to samples. This goal is not just of academic value, as vision technology will come into its own only if applications can be trained instead of being manually constructed.

6.2 Comparison to the Vertebrate Visual System

Our extensive usage of Gabor-type wavelets is the most obvious point of similarity to the visual system of higher vertebrates [Jones and Palmer, 1987]. It was Daugman [Daugman, 1988] who first pushed the idea that receptive fields in the primary visual cortical areas are most appropriately described as two-dimensional Gabor functions. It is tempting to liken simple cells [Hubel and Wiesel, 1962] to the sine and cosine components of wavelets (or intermediate phases) and to connect complex cells [Hubel and Wiesel, 1962] with Gabor magnitudes. The great utility of Gabor magnitudes, as experimentally observed in certain stages of the matching process, suggests an evolutionary mechanism for the occurrence of complex cells in our visual system. We have two mutually non-exclusive explanations for this importance of disregarding phase information during the matching process. One is that the inclusion of phases creates the danger of being caught in one of the many local optima when matching a jet to an image. The other is the surmise that perhaps the phase relationships between wavelets of different frequency in a given object location are subject to much stronger variations than amplitude relations.

The great robustness of our face recognition system with respect to image variations is to a very large extent due to properties of the wavelets we employ. Some aspects of this may be easy to understand, such as the gradual response of wavelet responses to image deformation. Another important aspect may be that many common image variations are local both in the spatial and in the frequency domain, thus affecting only some wavelet components and leaving the others intact [Biederman and Kalocsai, 1997]. Other aspects are still obscure, such as the surprisingly small effect of lighting differences on wavelet components.

Another very encouraging aspect of our system is the close correspondence of its behavior under image variation to changes in psychophysical responses [Biederman and Kalocsai, 1997], [Hancock et al., 1997]. The error rates and response times of human subjects degrade under variation of facial expression or pose very much in parallel to the degradation of image-model similarities in the earlier version [Lades et al., 1993] of our system, giving correlation coefficients of 0.90 and higher [Biederman and Kalocsai, 1997].

6.3 Comparison to the Principal Components Approach

The FERET program aims at stimulating the development of alternative face recognition technologies and testing them competitively. Our strongest competitors have based their systems on Principal Component Analysis (PCA) techniques. It is therefore important to compare our system to PCA. In its basic form, the eigenface approach [Turk and Pentland, 1991] considers the pixel array within a rectangle around the face as a vector. Such vectors are collected from a large sample of facial images, all carefully aligned relative to each other. The correlation matrix is formed for this collection of vectors and its eigenvectors, or principal components, are extracted. The original face images can be linearly combined, using the components of the eigenvectors as coefficients, to form *eigenfaces.* A small number of eigenfaces corresponding to the largest eigenvalues are used as feature vectors. These vectors conveniently help to find, encode and compare faces.

In this simple form, the PCA approach has the great advantage over our method of representing faces much more parsimoniously and requiring much less computation. On the other hand, PCA requires the collection of a large number of images before features can be defined. (This is not a problem with the specific job of face recognition, but may turn out to be a severe restriction of flexibility when attempting more general object recognition tasks.) Moreover, the sample images have to be aligned very carefully, imprecision in alignment amounting to a corresponding reduction in effective resolution.

The eigenface approach becomes problematic when facial deformation (due to alteration in expression or pose) becomes important. Two ways have been proposed to deal with this. In one, several smaller windows are defined over landmarks of the face and are independently subjected to PCA in addition to the full face [Pentland et al., 1993], [Penev and Atick, 1996]. During recognition, landmarks are found and compared independently using the local PCAs, perhaps constraining relative positions of landmarks appropriately. In the other approach [Craw and Cameron, 1991], [Vetter and Troje, 1995], [Lanitis et al., 1995] faces are first morphed to an average shape prior to running PCA. PCA may also be performed separately on the shape vectors used during morphing. The essential features of both versions, elastic deformation and local feature vectors attached at landmark nodes, make the PCA approach more similar to ours and suggest perhaps a point of convergence for both methods. A major difference remains, however, the difference in origin of (local) features, object-specific statistical samples in the case of PCA and object-independent wavelets in ours.

Unfortunately we have insufficient information on our competitor's systems to be able to attribute their strengths and weaknesses in the FERET test to specific functional aspects. However, Hancock et al. [Hancock et al., 1997] have compared our system and PCA-based systems with performance of human subjects and concluded: "Comparisons between the systems' performance with faces with and without the hair visible, and prediction of memory performance with and without alteration in face expressions, suggested that the graph-matching system was better at capturing aspects of the appearance of the *face,* while the PCA-based system seemed better at capturing aspects of the appearance of specific *images* of faces" (emphasis original).

In our opinion, the better performance of our system on subtasks of the FERET test with strong image alterations (duplicates, illumination, glasses, pose) and when compared to psychophysical data is to a large part due to properties of Gabor wavelets, which form a well regularized mapping from pixel space to feature space when it comes to slight misalignment and to variation in scale and in illumination. Their structure is determined by principles and not by the particular properties of statistical samples, and thus they are much less sensitive than the PCA approach to unexpected alterations of images.

Acknowledgement. This work was supported by the Army Research Laboratory, contracts DAAL01-93-K-0109 and DAAL01-96-K-0035. We thank Norbert Krüger, Michael Pötzsch, Michael Rinne and Jan Wieghardt for extensive help with the preparation of the FERET Phase III test, and Jan Vorbrüggen for advice and editorial work on the manuscript. For the experiments we have used the FERET database of facial images collected under the ARPA/ARL FERET program.

References

Bates, R. H. T. and McDonnell, N. J. (1986): *Image Restoration and Reconstruction.* Oxford Unversity Press, Oxford, p. 226–227.

Kalocsai, P., Biederman, I., and Cooper, E. E. (1994): *To What Extent Can the Recognition of Unfamiliar Faces be Accounted for by a Representation of the Direct Output of Simple Cell.* In: Proceedings ARVO, Sarasota, Florida, p.1627.

Biederman, I. (1987): *Recognition-by-Components: A Theory of Human Image Understanding.* Psychological Review 94:115–147.

Biederman, I. and Kalocsai, P. (1997): *Neurocomputational Bases of Object and Face Recognition.* Phil. Trans. Roy Soc.: Biological Sciences, in press.

Craw, I. and Cameron, P. (1991): *Parameterising images for recognition and reconstruction.* Proc. British Machine Vision Conference, Turing Institute Press and Springer Verlag.

Daugman, J. D. (1988): *Complete Discrete 2-D Gabor Transforms by Neural Networks for Image Analysis and Compression.* IEEE Trans. on Acoustics, Speech and Signal Processing 36:1169–1179.

Elagin, E., Steffens, J., and Neven, H. (1997): *Automatic Real-Time Pose Estimation System for Human Faces Based on Bunch Graph Matching Technology.* Proc. Intl. Conf. on Automatic Face- and Gesture- Recognition, Nara, Japan (submitted).

Fleet, D. J. and Jepson, A. D. (1990): *Computation of Component Image Velocity from Local Phase Information.* Intl. J. of Computer Vision, 5(1):77–104.

Hancock, P. J. B., Bruce, V, and Burton, A. M. (1997): *A Comparison of Two Computer-Based Face Identification Systems with Human Perceptions of Faces.* Vision Research, in press.

Hong, H., Neven, H., and von der Malsburg, C. (1997): *Online Facial Expression Recognition based on Personalized Gallery.* Proc. Intl. Conf. on Automatic Face- and Gesture- Recognition, Nara, Japan (submitted).

Hubel, D. H. and Wiesel, T. N. (1962): *Receptive Fields, Binocular and Functional Architecture in the Cat's Visual Cortex.* Journal of Physiology, 106–154.

Jones, J. and Palmer, L. (1987): *An Evaluation of the Two-Dimensional Gabor Filter Model of Simple Receptive Fields in Cat Striate Cortex.* Journal of Neurophysiology, 1233–1258.

Kalocsai, P., Neven, H., Steffens, J., and Biederman, I. (1997): *Statistical Analysis of Gabor-filter Representation.* Proc. Intl. Conf. on Automatic Face- and Gesture- Recognition, Nara, Japan (submitted).

Konen, W. (1996): *Comparing Facial Line Drawings with Gray-Level Images: A Case Study on PHANTOMAS.* Proc. ICANN'96, Springer-Verlag, Heidelberg, New York, 727–734.

Konen, W. and Schulze-Krüger, E. (1995): *ZN-Face: A System for Access Control Using Automated Face Recognition.* Proc. Intl. Workshop on Automatic Face- and Gesture- Recognition, Zürich, 18–23.

Krüger, N., Pötzsch, M., and von der Malsburg, C. (1997): *Determination of Face Position and Pose with a Learned Representation Based on Labeled Graphs.* Image and Vision Computing, 665–673.

Krüger, N. (1997): *An Algorithm for the Learning of Weights in Discrimination Funcions Using a priori Constraints.* IEEE Trans. on Pattern Recognition and Machine Intelligence, 19:764–768.

Lades, M. (1995): *Invariant Object Recognition Based on Dynamical Links, Robust to Scaling, Rotation and Variation of Illumination.* PhD. Thesis, Ruhr-Universität, Bochum, Germany.

Lades, M., Vorbrüggen, J. C., Buhmann, J., Lange, J., von der Malsburg, C., Würtz, R. P., and Konen, W. (1993): *Distortion Invariant Object Recognition in the Dynamic Link Architecture.* IEEE Transactions on Computers, 42(3):300–311.

Lanitis, A., Taylor, C. J., Cootes, T. F. (1995): *A Unified Approach To Coding and Interpreting Face Images.* Proc. Intl. Conference on Computer Vision, Cambridge, 368–373.

Maurer, T., and von der Malsburg, C. (1995): *Single-View Based Recognition of Faces Rotated in Depth.* Proc. Intl. Workshop on Automatic Face- and Gesture-Recognition, Zürich, 248–253.

Maurer, T., and von der Malsburg, C. (1996): *Tracking and Learning Graphs and Pose on Image Sequences.* Proc. Intl. Workshop on Automatic Face- and Gesture- Recognition, Vermont, 176–181.

Penev, J. S., and Atick, J. J. (1996): *Local feature analysis: a general statistical theory for object representation.* Network: computation in neural systems, 7:477–500.

Pentland, A., Moghaddam, B., and Starner, T. (1993): *View-Based and Modular Eigenspaces for Face Recognition.* Technical Report 245, MIT Media Lab Vismod.

Phillips, P. J., Rauss, P., and Der, S. Z. (1996): *FERET (Face Recognition Technology) Recognition Algorithm Development and Test Results.* US Army Research Laboratory Technical Report ARL–TR–995.

Phillips, P. J., Moon, H., Rauss, P., and Rizvi, S. A. (1997): *The FERET September 1996 Database and Evaluation Procedure.* Proc. First Intl. Conference on Audio and Video-based Biometric Person Authentication, Crans-Montana, Switzerland, 395–402.

Phillips, P. J., and Rauss, P. (1997): *Face Recognition Technology (FERET Program).* Proc. Office of National Drug Control Policy, in press.

Pötzsch, M., Maurer, T., Wiskott, L., and von der Malsburg, C. (1996): *Reconstruction from Graphs Labeled with Responses of Gabor Filters.* Proc. ICANN'96, Springer-Verlag, Heidelberg, New York, 845–850.

Rinne, M., Pötzsch, M., and von der Malsburg, C. (1997): *Designing Objects for Computer Vision (FLAVOR).* In preparation.

Steffens, J., Elagin, E., and Neven, H. (1997): *PersonSpotter - Fast and Robust System for Human Detection, Tracking and Recognition.* Proc. Intl. Conf. on Automatic Face- and Gesture- Recognition, Nara, Japan (submitted).

Theimer, W. M., and Mallot, H. A. (1994): *Phase-Based Binocular Vergence Control and Depth Reconstruction Using Active Vision.* CVGIP: Image Understanding, 60(3):343–358.

Triesch, J., and von der Malsburg, C. (1996): *Robust Classification of Hand Postures against Complex Backgrounds.* Proc. Intl. Workshop on Automatic Face- and Gesture- Recognition, Vermont, 170–175.

Turk, M., and Pentland, A. (1991): *Eigenfaces for Recognition.* Journal of Cognitive Neuroscience 3:71–86.

Vetter, T., and Troje, N. (1995): *A separated linear shape and texture space for modeling two-dimensional images of human faces.* Technical Report, MPI for biological Cybernetics, TR15.

Wiskott, L. (1995): *Labeled Graphs and Dynamic Link Matching for Face Recognition and Scene Analysis.* Reihe Physik vol. 53. Verlag Harri Deutsch, Thun, Frankfurt a. Main.

Wiskott, L., Fellous, J. M., Krüger, N., and von der Malsburg, C. (1995): *Face Recognition and Gender Determination.* Proc. Intl. Workshop on Automatic Face- and Gesture- Recognition, Zürich, 92–97.

Wiskott, L., Fellous, J. M., Krüger, N., and von der Malsburg, C. (1997): *Face Recognition by Elastic Bunch Graph Matching.* IEEE Trans. on Pattern Recognition and Machine Intelligence, 19:775–779.

Face Recognition Using Deformable Matching

Chahab Nastar

INRIA, B.P. 105, F-78153 Le Chesnay, France.
Chahab.Nastar@inria.fr

Summary. We describe flexible images, a new method for modeling images as defomable intensity (or gray) surfaces. The technique simultaneously incorporates the shape (x, y) and texture $(I(x, y))$ components of the image. Specifically, the intensity surface is modeled as a deformable 3D mesh in $(x, y, I(x, y))$ space which obeys Lagrangian dynamics. Using an efficient technique for matching two surfaces (in terms of the analytic modes of vibration), we can obtain a dense correspondence field (or *3D warp*) between two images. Furthermore, we use explicit statistical learning of the class of valid deformations in order to provide *a priori* knowledge about object-specific deformations. The resulting formulation leads to a compact representation based on both the physically-based modes of deformation as well as the statistical modes of variation observed in actual training data. We demonstrate the power of this approach with experiments with image matching, interpolation of missing data, and image retrieval in a large face database.

1. Introduction

Our goal is to present an efficient method for query-by-example retrieval from a face database. That task being quite specific, we will first position our work within the computer vision, the face recognition, and the image retrieval communities.

1.1 Background: Computer Vision Today

Computer vision is about understanding and interpreting images of the real world. It was originally intended for robot vision and navigation. Therefore, the problem of three-dimensional (3D) vision has been the core of computer vision for years.

The explosion of internet and multimedia gave birth to new issues for understanding images. Robot vision ceased to be the main focus of attention of computer vision scientists. Over the last decade, one can observe not only a serious diversification in computer vision problems, but also radical changes in the way computer vision algorithms are designed.

For example, the *bottom-up* Marr paradigm (segmentation, reconstruction, interpretation, [10]) is today controverted. For years, vision algorithms were categorized in either of these three levels, seldom solving a problem in its whole. The reason is that each of these subproblems is very complex. Consider image segmentation, the lower-level task. Segmentation algorithms often need several hard-to-tune parameters, and there is no single algorithm capable of automatically segmenting a complex scene in the general case.

Therefore, recently, attempts have been made to interpret images without segmentation or reconstruction. Our research falls into that category. It is therefore *appearance-based*, which means that it does not use any 3D information, rather trying to recognize objects out of simple 2D images, such as the images that can commonly be found on the internet.

Another remarkable evolution of computer vision is that the constraint for the algorithms to be *fully automatic* is today relaxed. In our multimedia era, user *interactivity* is accepted and encouraged, especially if it allows to make better vision algorithms (i.e. algorithms that can solve harder problems). The method described in this paper is also part of this "new tradition". We present a specific case of interactive search in a face database; we allow simple user interactivity by performing query-by-example face recognition. This will be detailed in the following sections.

1.2 Face Recognition

Computer vision scientists are interested in face recognition for over 20 years. Since the beginning of the 1990s, the subject has become a major issue in computer vision, mainly due to the important real-world applications of face recognition: smart surveillance, secure access, telecommunications, digital libraries, medicine... (a survey can be found in [4]).

On the theoretical side, face recognition is a specific and hard case of object recognition. Faces are very specific objects whose most common appearance (frontal faces) roughly look alike. Subtle changes make the faces different. Therefore, in a traditional feature space, frontal faces will form a dense cluster, and standard pattern recognition techniques will generally fail to discriminate between them.

To sum up, face recognition needs *dedicated* representations of the images and *specific* algorithms. In this paper, we will introduce a specific representation of the images ("flexible images"), and tune our matching technique to facial imagery, via statistical learning.

We will also view the face recognition problem as a face database search problem. This approach needs a short presentation of the more generic problem of content-based image retrieval, hereafter.

1.3 Content-based image retrieval

Multimedia documents are dominated by images. Thus, retrieving images based on their content, commonly called *content-based image retrieval*, has become a major issue in computer vision.

However, high-level interpretation of the scene represented in the image is next to impossible in the general case, since it actually comes down to the general vision problem. A convenient and interactive way of searching an image database is the query-by-example approach: the user selects an image and asks the computer to *find more images that look like this one*. Such an approach needs proper indexing of the images in the database. Although sometimes powerful, the traditional approach of indexing the images by key-words is time-consuming, costly, and subjective. One would rather like to perform an automatic indexing of the images, that would capture their content based on image features such as color, shape, texture etc. The system should then retrieve images whose index is similar to the index of the query image. In other words, in query-by-example image retrieval, we perform an interpretation of the content of the query image *based on pictorial similarity*.

More precisely, content-based image retrieval systems need three components:

- a representation of image features (i.e the index or image signature) conveniently chosen for their perceptual significance.
- a significant similarity metric which will measure the similarity between the query image and every other image in the database.
- a user-friendly interface for browsing, searching and visualizing the images.

For the algorithm designer, the hardest step is really the representation of the image content, i.e. the computation of image signatures. The designer has various ways of indexing a database. To begin with, he has to find out if the database is generic (i.e. with varied image content), in which case he will use generic image features, or specific (i.e. contains a single object class, e.g. faces), in which case he will rather develop dedicated algorithms.

Another question that the designer can ask himself is whether the spatial arrangement of the objects in the image is significant or not. If the answer is yes, he will encode that spatial arrangement in the signature (as a consequence, the image can be approximately reconstructed from its signature). Otherwise, he will go for global measures over the image that will lose spatial arrangement. The possible images signature categories with examples are summarized in table 1.3.

signature	generic	specific
encodes arrangement	*Fourier spectrum*	*eigenfaces*
forgets arrangement	*color histogram*	*distance ratios*

Table 1.1. Image signature categories & examples

The proposed approach in this paper is *specific* and *encodes* spatial arrangement. This is of course the most natural choice for a face database.

1.4 Related work

The main related work is the "eigenfaces" technique [19], which is a statistical texture technique based on Principal Component Analysis. It is efficient and has become very popular in face recognition.

However, no shape correspondence is performed in "eigenfaces". Only the texture of the faces are matched and represented in an eigenspace. This short-coming is the first motivation of our work: we need a better face matching technique which incorporates both shape and texture. Most of the current work in the area of image-based object modeling deals with the shape and texture components of an image in an independent manner [3, 5]. In our representation, shape and texture are unified in a single compact mathematical framework. This novel image correspondence method is used to match two images by deforming the intensity surface of one image into the another (under "physical forces" exerted by nearby mesh nodes). The resulting vector of displacements yields a pixel-dense set of correspondences which can be used for image matching, image warping, image interpolation, and image retrieval in a large database.

1.5 Organization of the paper

In section 2., the XYI representation of an image is introduced. Mathematical details about the physics-based modeling of deformable intensity surfaces, their quantitative analysis, and their warping are given. In section 3., the necessity of statistical learning of the warps is exposed. Section 4. describes how to back-project a priori knowledge of the warps of an object class into its physics-based equations, leading to increased efficiency, robustness, and speed. Section 5. presents the experimental results, including the modes of variation with simultaneous integration of shape and texture, face warps in various subspaces, interpolation of missing data, and our main application, face image retrieval from a database. We draw the conclusions in section 6..

2. Flexible images

2.1 The XYI representation

The idea of using intensity surfaces for matching and recognition comes from the observation that the transformation of shape to intensity is quasi-linear under controlled lighting conditions ; in other terms, the intensity of the 2D image reflects the actual 3D shape. This essential observation is the basis of all shape from shading methods [8] ; however, unlike those methods, our aim is not actually to reconstruct depth information from a single 2D projection, but rather keep in mind that, under controlled lighting conditions, the changes in the image intensities from one image to the other reflect changes in their actual 3D shape. Mathematically, supposing the object of interest to be a Lambertian (or matte) surface, the amount of intensity reflected when illuminated by a single light source placed at infinity, is isotropic :

$$I(x,y) = \alpha \, \boldsymbol{N}(x,y).\boldsymbol{L} \qquad (2.1)$$

where $N(x,y)$ is the surface normal vector at point (x,y), L is the light source vector, and α is a positive scalar. This equation directly links shape $N(x,y)$ and intensity surface $I(x,y)$ (figure 2.1). If the shape is relatively smooth, we can represent the image intensity as a continuous surface :

$$(x,y) \longrightarrow I(x,y) \qquad (2.2)$$

Our system focuses on recognition in the 3D space defined by $(x,y,I(x,y))$, that we will call the XYI space. We now need to match gray surfaces in 3D

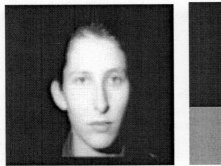

Fig. 2.1. An image and its XYI surface representation

in $(x,y,I(x,y))$ space (XYI space) allowing a quantitative measure of their similarity.

2.2 Physics-based modeling

Surface Matching (registration) is a classic vision problem. Examples include the matching the model of an object and its stereo reconstruction, or the matching of medical images for tracing down the evolution of a tumor. Surface matching can either be rigid (superimposing two surfaces via a translation and a rotation) or nonrigid (deforming one surface to closely match another one). For example, an efficient geometric method for surface matching is the the Iterative Closest Point algorithm [2, 21].

The method presented in this paper is physics-based. Specifically, the intensity surface of the "source" image is modeled as a deformable 3D mesh in XYI space which obeys Lagrangian dynamics. This surface is thus deformed to match the surface of the "target" image. We choose the physics-based matching which allows since it provides a better quantitative measure of the deformation process, as exposed in the next section.

2.3 Deformable Intensity Surfaces

The mathematical approach to our model is inspired by the one described in [15]. The intensity surface is modeled as a deformable mesh of size $N = n \times n'$ nodes (figure 2.2). It is ruled by Lagrangian dynamics [1] :

$$M\ddot{U} + C\dot{U} + KU = F(t)$$ (2.3)

where $U = [\ldots, \Delta x_i, \Delta y_i, \Delta z_i, \ldots]^T$ is a vector storing nodal displacements, M, C and K are respectively the mass, damping and stiffness matrices of the system, and F is the image force. The above equation is of order $3N$.

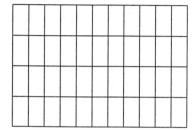 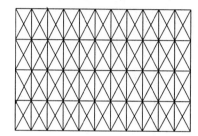

Fig. 2.2. Surface meshes

We can adapt the effective external force investigated in [15] to our problem : at each node M_i of the mesh points, the image force points to *the closest point P_i in the 3D binary image* :

$$F(t) = [\ldots, \overrightarrow{M_i P_i}(t), \ldots]^T$$ (2.4)

Euclidean distance algorithms can help us extract this force in each voxel of the 3D image, as a pre-processing [6, 20].

Note that our formulation provides an interesting alternative to optical flow methods, without the classical *brightness constraint* [9]. Indeed, the brightness constraint corresponds to a particular case of our formulation where the closest point P_i has to have the same intensity as M_i ($\overrightarrow{M_i P_i}$ is parallel to the XY plane). We do not make that assumption here: by allowing changes in XY (shape domain) and I (texture domain), our method *unifies shape and texture* similarity measurement in a single framework.

In our formulation, deforming the intensity surface of a source image into the one of a target image takes place in 5 steps :

1. Reduce, if necessary, the number of graylevels of the source and the target images down to the same number g of graylevels (e.g. $g = 32$).

2. Initialize the deformable surface S as a subsampling of the intensity surface of the source image.

3. Convert the target image to its 3D binary representation, *3D-target*.

4. Compute distance maps at each voxel of *3D-target*.

5. Let S deform dynamically in *3D-target* (equation (2.3)) with the external force derived from the distance maps created at step 4.

Note that steps 1 to 4 are pre-processing steps. Steps 1 and 2 provide respectively intensity and spatial smoothing of the image, an essential prerequisite before actually considering $I(x, y)$ as a surface.

Figure 2.3 shows a schematic representation of the deformation process. Note that the external forces (dashed arrows) do *not* necessarily correspond to the final displacement field of the surface. The elasticity of the surface provides an intrinsic smoothness constraint for computing the final displacement field.

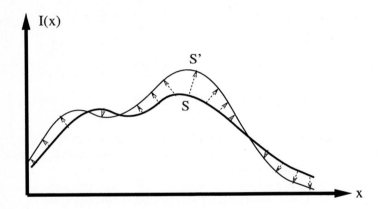

Fig. 2.3. A 1D representation of the intensity surface S being pulled towards S' by image forces. In optical flow, arrows would be constrained to be horizontal.

2.4 Quantative analysis: modes of vibration

The applicability of eigenvector decomposition methods for appearance-based object recognition has been convincingly demonstrated in [14]. For deformable surfaces, a powerful eigenvector decomposition is *modal analysis* [17, 15], which in particular allows to reduce the degrees of freedom of the full system (equation 2.3).

The vibration modes $\phi(i)$ of the previous deformable surface are the vector solutions of the eigenproblem :

$$K\phi = \omega^2 M\phi \qquad (2.5)$$

where $\omega(i)$ is the i-th eigenfrequency of the system. Solving the governing equations in the modal basis leads to scalar equations where the unknown $\tilde{u}(i)$ is the amplitude of mode i [1]:

$$\ddot{\tilde{u}}(i) + \tilde{c}_i \dot{\tilde{u}}(i) + \omega(i)^2 \tilde{u}(i) = \tilde{f}_i(t) \qquad i = 1, \dots, 3N. \tag{2.6}$$

The graph representing modal amplitudes $\tilde{u}(i)$ as a function of mode rank i is called the deformation spectrum $\tilde{U}$. The closed-form expression of the displacement field is:

$$U \approx \sum_{i=1}^{P} \tilde{u}(i)\phi(i) = \Phi\tilde{U} \tag{2.7}$$

with $P \ll 3N$, which means that only P scalar equations of the type of (2.6) need to be solved. The modal superposition equation (2.7) can be seen as a Fourier expansion with high-frequencies neglected [15].

We make use of *the analytic expressions of the modes* which are known sine and cosine functions for specific surface topologies. For quadrilateral surface meshes that have plane topology (which is the case of the intensity surfaces), the eigenfrequencies of the system are [15] :

$$\omega^2(p, p') = 4K/M \left(\sin^2 \frac{p\pi}{2n} + \sin^2 \frac{p'\pi}{2n'}\right) \tag{2.8}$$

where K is the stiffness of each spring, M the mass of each node, and p and p' are the mode parameters. The modes of vibration are :

$$\phi(p, p') = [\dots, \cos \frac{p\pi(2i-1)}{2n} \cos \frac{p'\pi(2j-1)}{2n'}, \dots]^T \tag{2.9}$$

where $i = 1, \dots, n$ and $j = 1, \dots, n'$. Note that the modes have to be normalized to unity. These analytic expressions avoid costly eigendecompositions and furthermore allow the total number of modes to be easily adjusted.

In conclusion, the deformation process is now quantitatively and concisely described by the deformation spectrum $\tilde{U}$. By neglecting high frequencies, the deformation spectrum captures a closed-form, smooth solution of the full matching process. The computation is fast by using the analytic modes.

The number of modes to be superimposed is one of the main problems of any vibration-based technique. Indeed, the optimal number cannot be adjusted *a priori* for any application; it clearly depends on the frequency components of the motion. Basically, the optimal number of modes will be *as small as possible*, but should capture *a representative sketch* of the surface deformation. A typical *a priori* value covering many types of standard deformations is the quarter of the degrees of freedom in the system [1] (see also section 5.).

2.5 XYI Warping

The above modal analysis technique represents a coordinate transform from the nodal displacement space to the modal amplitude subspace:

$$\tilde{U} = \Phi^T U \tag{2.10}$$

where Φ is the matrix of analytic modes $\phi(p, p')$ and $\tilde{U}$ is the resultant vector of modal amplitudes which encodes the type of deformations which characterize the difference between the two images. In addition, once we have solved for the resultant 3D displacement field we can then warp the original image onto the second in the XYI space and then render a resultant 2D image using simple computer graphics techniques.[1] Figure 2.4 shows an example illustrating this warping process. We note that in this paper the source-to-target warp image (1→2) is used for rendering and image interpolation whereas the deformation spectrum $\tilde{U}$ is used primarily for recognition and indexing.

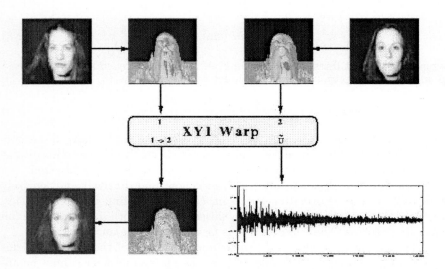

Fig. 2.4. Example of XYI warping the source image (top left) to the target image (top right). The output is the source-to-target warp image (bottom left) and the corresponding deformation spectrum (bottom right).

---

[1] Note that the equilibrium XYI manifold will not necessarily reside on a regular 3D lattice and therefore must be rendered by projection onto a regular XY lattice and resampling.

3. Statistical Analysis

In theory, our deformable intensity surface can undergo any possible deformation. Thus, it is necessary to *learn* the deformations of a specific class of objects and add them as a priori *constraints* into our system. This is an important step for guiding the deformations of our mesh when performed within a specific object class and also allows us to deal with occlusions and missing data, as we shall see later.

Our approach to learning the space of allowable manifold deformations particular to a specific object class Ω (eg., frontal faces) is that of *unsupervised learning*. Particularly, we perform PCA on a selected training set of deformations in order to recover the principal components of the warps. This approach is actually part of a more complete statistical formulation for estimating the probability density function of these warps in the high-dimensional vector space $\tilde{U} \in \mathcal{R}^P$ (see [13]). The estimated class-conditional density $P(\tilde{U}|\Omega)$ can be ultimately used in a Bayesian framework for a variety of tasks such as regression, interpolation, inference and classification [11, 12]. However, in this paper, we have concentrated mainly on the dimensionality-reduction aspect of PCA in order to obtain a lower-dimensional subspace in which to solve for the manifold correspondence field.

Principal Component Analysis

Given a training set of suitable warp vectors $\{\tilde{U}^t\}$ for $t = 1...N_T$, the principal warps are obtained by solving the eigenvalue problem

$$\Lambda = E^T \Sigma E \qquad (3.1)$$

where Σ is the covariance matrix of the training set, E is the eigenvector matrix of Σ and Λ is the corresponding diagonal matrix of eigenvalues. The unitary matrix E defines a coordinate transform (rotation) which *decorrelates* the data and makes explicit the *invariant subspaces* of the matrix operator Σ. In PCA, a partial KLT is performed to identify the largest-eigenvalue eigenvectors and obtain a principal component feature vector $\hat{U} = E_M^T (\tilde{U} - \tilde{U}_0)$, where $\tilde{U}_0$ the mean warp vector and E_M is a submatrix of E containing the principal eigenvectors. This KL transform can be seen as a linear transformation $\hat{U} = \mathcal{T}(\tilde{U}) : \mathcal{R}^P \to \mathcal{R}^L$ which extracts a lower-dimensional subspace of the KL basis corresponding to the maximal eigenvalues. These principal components preserve the major linear correlations in the data and discard the minor ones.[2]

---

[2] In practice the number of training vectors N_T is far less than the dimensionality of the data, P, consequently the covariance matrix Σ is singular. However, the first $L < N_T$ eigenvectors can always be computed (estimated) from N_T samples using, for example, a Singular Value Decomposition [7].

By ranking the eigenvectors of the KL expansion with respect to their eigenvalues and selecting the first L principal components we form an orthogonal decomposition of the vector space $\mathcal{R}^P$ into two mutually exclusive and complementary subspaces: the principal subspace (or feature space) $\{E_i\}_{i=1}^L$ containing the principal components and its orthogonal complement $\bar{F} = \{E_i\}_{i=L+1}^P$. In this paper, we simply discard the orthogonal subspace and work entirely within the principal subspace $\{E_i\}_{i=1}^L$, hereafter referred to simply by the matrix E.

4. Combining Physics and Statistics

We now wish to combine the physically-based dynamics of our deformable system with the statistical principal components computed as described in the previous section. The selected training set will therefore define our object-specific set of deformations for the problem at hand (*e.g.*, facial modeling). Our goal is to *constrain* the dynamics of the physical system to lie in the principal subspace of learned warps.

Instead of solving the unconstrained governing equation (2.3), we compute the projection of the unknown **U** (dimension : 3nn'), first into a modal subbasis (dimension P), then into a Karhunen-Loeve subspace (dimension L) :

$$U \xrightarrow{\Phi} \tilde{U} \xrightarrow{E} \hat{U} \tag{4.1}$$

The first transform is the projection into the modal subspace :

$$U = \Phi\tilde{U} \tag{4.2}$$

The second transform is a projection of the modal amplitudes into the PCA subspace :

$$\tilde{U} = E\hat{U} + \tilde{U}_0 \tag{4.3}$$

Equations (2.10) and (4.3) yield the global transform :

$$U = \Psi\hat{U} + U_0 \tag{4.4}$$

where the global transformation matrix Ψ is simply :

$$\Psi = \Phi E \tag{4.5}$$

and :

$$U_0 = \Phi\tilde{U}_0 \tag{4.6}$$

Note that Ψ is a rectangular orthogonal matrix.

By premultiplying equation (2.3) by Ψ^T and changing unknowns (equation (4.4)), we obtain :

$$\Psi^T M \Psi\ddot{\hat{U}} + \Psi^T C \Psi\dot{\hat{U}} + \Psi^T K \Psi\hat{U} = \Psi^T F(t) - \Psi^T K U_0 \tag{4.7}$$

Let :

$$\hat{M} = \Psi^T M \Psi \qquad (4.8)$$

$$\hat{C} = \Psi^T C \Psi \qquad (4.9)$$

$$\hat{K} = \Psi^T K \Psi = E^T \Omega^2 E \qquad (4.10)$$

$$\hat{F}(t) = \Psi^T F(t) - \Psi^T K U_0 = \Psi^T F(t) - E^T \Omega^2 \tilde{U}_0 \qquad (4.11)$$

Note that the new mass, damping and stiffness matrices, as well as the new external force, do not involve heavy computations because : *(i)* we make the common assumption that M and C are scalar matrices ($M = mI$, $C = cI$ where m and c are mass and damping scalars), and *(ii)* $\Omega^2 = diag[\ldots, \omega_i^2, \ldots]$ is a diagonal matrix.

We end up with the standard Lagrangian equation of unknown $\hat{U}$.

$$\hat{M} \ddot{\hat{U}} + \hat{C} \dot{\hat{U}} + \hat{K} \hat{U} = \hat{F}(t) \qquad (4.12)$$

Solving this equation for $\hat{U}$ and then changing basis back to the canonical basis (equation (4.4)) provides the estimated displacement U.

By using this double projection method, the resulting displacement U is constrained to lie along those learned deformation modes that are characteristic of the object class.

5. Experimental Results

For the learning phase, we choose a set of 50 faces to be warped into a reference face. Each of these faces has a $N = 128 \times 128$ resolution, and the manifolds are matched in a modal subspace whose dimension is suitably chosen $P = 3 \times 128^2/4^2 = 3072$ [1]. We then perform a Principal Components Analysis on the spectra of these warps.

Figure 5.1 shows the modes of variation along individual KL-eigenvectors extracted from the learning set. For example, we can see that $\overrightarrow{E_1}$ represents change in global headshape (as well as the size of the eyes). Eigenvectors $\overrightarrow{E_2}$ and $\overrightarrow{E_3}$ represent a change in the chin size and forehead, respectively. Higher-order eigenvectors, for example $\overrightarrow{E_{10}}$ represent subtler variations in facial appearance (e.g. eye shape). Note that in this figure, the variations simultaneously affect the shape and the texture of the image. By looking at the KL-eigenvalues, it is easy to draw the percentage of the data variance that is captured versus the number of eigenvalues. Figure 5.2 shows that 90% of the data is adequately captured by $L = 25$ principal eigenvectors.

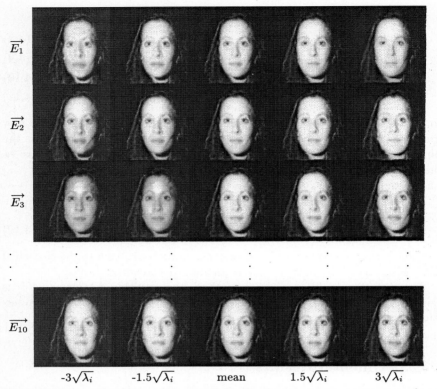

$$-3\sqrt{\lambda_i} \qquad -1.5\sqrt{\lambda_i} \qquad \text{mean} \qquad 1.5\sqrt{\lambda_i} \qquad 3\sqrt{\lambda_i}$$

Fig. 5.1. Modes of variation of the manifold. The first eigenvector represents change in global headshape (as well as the size of the eyes). The second and third eigenvectors represent a change in the chin size and forehead, respectively. Higher-order eigenvectors, for example the tenth one, represent subtler variations in facial appearance (e.g. eye shape)

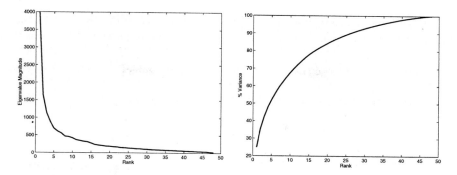

Fig. 5.2. Left : Eigenvalue spectrum of the PCA transform. Right : Cumulative eigenvalue spectrum of the PCA transform

5.1 Subspace Warps

Figure 5.3 shows an example of matching a source image to that of the target using both the unconstrained and constrained warps. This basic example illustrates how a dense correspondence field can be obtained between two images from different objects.

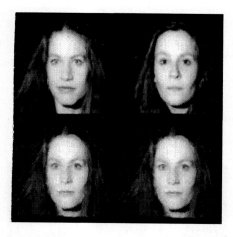

Fig. 5.3. Top Left: Source image. Top Right: Target image. Bottom Left: Unconstrained warp in modal space. Bottom Right: Constrained warp in KL-space

Figure 5.4 displays a typical deformation spectrum and its reconstruction in the KL subspace. The total reconstruction error is on the order of 4%, demonstrating that by solving the reduced-order physical system (equation

(4.7)), we have not significantly sacrificed accuracy. In addition, solving this equation requires considerably less computation. The degrees of freedom in the original mesh were $3N = 3 \times 128 \times 128 \approx 50,000$. In the modal subspace, the degrees of freedom were reduced to $P = 3 \times 32 \times 32 \approx 3,000$, and finally in the KL subspace, the degrees of freedom were further reduced to $L = 25$, thus achieving a compression factor of approximately $2000 : 1$

$$50,000 \xrightarrow{\Phi} 3000 \xrightarrow{E} 25 \tag{5.1}$$

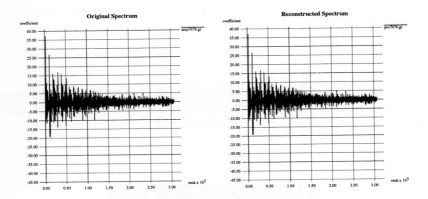

Fig. 5.4. Left: the original deformation spectrum. Right: reconstruction of the spectrum in the KL-subspace.

5.2 Interpolation of Missing Data

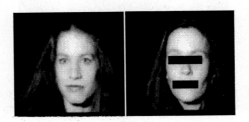

Fig. 5.5. Left: Source Image. Right: Target Image.

One of the advantages of learned warps is that, during the matching process, the deformations are constrained for a specific object. Consequently, invalid deformations arising out of missing data (e.g. object occlusion) are automatically disallowed.

The first example illustrates an experiment where regions of the face were occluded with a black bar (to simulate occlusion or incomplete data), as shown in figure 5.5. If we attempt an unconstrained warp in the modal space, an invalid reconstruction will be obtained (figure 5.6 left and center). On the other hand, if the deformation is constrained by the learned modes, we obtain a better reconstruction of the missing data as shown in figure 5.6 right. This example illustrates how our principal warp formulation effectively functions as a model-based image interpolant for a given class of objects. The second example is similar in spirit to the first, except where the missing

Fig. 5.6. Image warps. Left: in the real space. Center: in the unconstrained modal subspace. Right: in the constrained principal subspace

data is replaced by an arbitrary image region (in this case a texture), for example when one object partially occludes another. Here once again we see how the learned principal warps can yield a much better reconstruction and interpolation of non-matching image regions (figures 5.7 and 5.8).

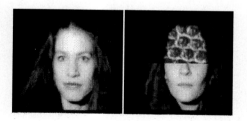

Fig. 5.7. Left: Source Image. Right: Target Image.

Fig. 5.8. Image warps. Left: in the real space. Center: in the unconstrained modal subspace. Right: in the constrained principal subspace

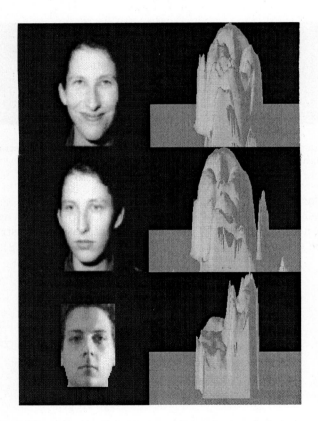

Fig. 5.9. Face images and their corresponding intensity surfaces with changes in facial expression, pose, and lighting.

5.3 Image Retrieval

The compact description obtained with the learned subspace warps leads to the main application of our work, which is face image retrieval from a database.

5.3.1 Significance. The frequency-based representation of modal analysis is especially significant for image retrieval, since a number of image appearance variations are easily described in terms of frequencies of the intensity manifold. Figure 5.9 shows three face images with specific facial expression, pose, and lighting (compare to figure 2.1). Facial expressions affect the intensity manifold locally (high frequency phenomenon)[3], while changes in pose or lighting affect the intensity manifold globally (low-frequency phenomenon). Only a change in face identity should affect all frequencies indifferently (figure 5.10).

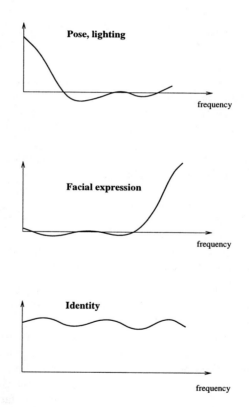

Fig. 5.10. Typical deformation spectra for face image warps.

---

[3] Occlusion is also often a local phenomenon.

5.3.2 Similarity metric. The strain energy describing the amount of energy needed to deform a surface into another is by definition [1]:

$$E_{strain} = \frac{1}{2} U^T K U \tag{5.2}$$

This expression is much simpler when developed in the modal basis of the system:

$$E_{strain} = \frac{1}{2} \tilde{U}^T \Omega^2 \tilde{U} = \frac{1}{2} \sum_{p=1}^{n} \sum_{p'=1}^{n'} \omega^2(p,p') \, \tilde{u}^2(p,p') \tag{5.3}$$

The strain energy is indeed a perceptually significant similarity metric for image retrieval: *the less strain energetic the source-to-target warp, the more similar the corresponding images.*

In a number of applications [1, 18], the low-order version of the strain energy is used:

$$E_{low} = \frac{1}{2} \sum_{p=1}^{q} \sum_{p'=1}^{q'} \omega^2(p,p') \, \tilde{u}^2(p,p') \tag{5.4}$$

with $q \times q' \ll n \times n'$.

In the specific case of face images, we observe that the typical deformation spectra have specific shapes, depending on the variation between the source and the target image (pose, lighting, facial expression, occlusion, identity). From figure 5.10, it is clear that the band-pass version of the strain energy is a particularly good similarity metric, since it should have a relatively high value for a change in identity and a much smaller value in case of occlusion, changes in expression, pose and lighting:

$$E_{band} = \frac{1}{2} \sum_{p=Low}^{Hi} \sum_{p'=Low'}^{Hi'} \omega^2(p,p') \, \tilde{u}^2(p,p') \tag{5.5}$$

where $(Hi - Low) \times (Hi' - Low') \ll n \times n'$. Note that the low-order version of the strain energy is obtained for $Low = Low' = 0$.

5.3.3 Results. We have successfully used the band-pass strain energy metric (reformulated in the reduced KL subspace) for face indexing and retrieval in a large database.

Specifically, we use the MIT Media Lab face database which contains 7,562 "mugshot" face images of approximately 3,000 people, where each person has at least 2 images in the database. The faces are roughly aligned in the same position in all images, so that no normalization against translation, rotation or scale is necessary; however, changes in lighting and facial expressions, as well as out-of-plane rotations frequently occur.

We select a reference face among the 7,562 images in the database (the most similar face to the mean face). We then warp all other faces of the database to the reference face, compute the strain energies and store them as a set of KL coefficients. The i-th face is stored as the KL spectrum $\hat{U}_i$. The relative distance between the faces labeled i and j is :

$$d(i,j) = (\hat{U}_i - \hat{U}_j)^T \, \hat{K} \, (\hat{U}_i - \hat{U}_j) \tag{5.6}$$

where $\hat{K}$ is defined in section 4..

To assess the recognition rate, we use a *nearest neighbor* rule. If the most similar face was of the same person then a correct recognition was scored. In our experiment, the system produced a recognition accuracy of 97%, which corresponds to only six mistakes in matching views of 200 people randomly chosen in the database of 7,562 images. This is significantly better than had previously been reported for this dataset [19, 16]. Examples of typical retrievals in hard cases are shown in figures 5.11,5.12, 5.13 and 5.14 .

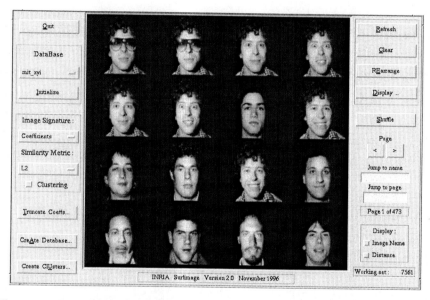

Fig. 5.11. Retrieval of the top left face. Similarity decreases from top to bottom and left to right (only the 15 best matches are represented). Note that in particular the second and third best matches are faces of the query person without sunglasses.

6. Conclusions

We have described the *flexible images* technique, a novel approach for image matching based on deformable intensity surfaces, with an application to

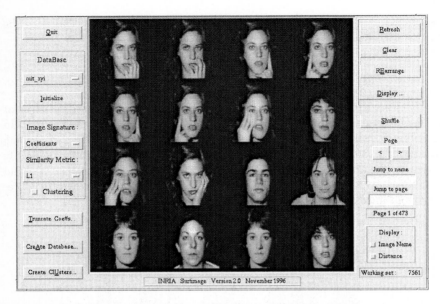

Fig. 5.12. Retrieval of the top left face. This example illustrates the robustness of the approach to important occlusions.

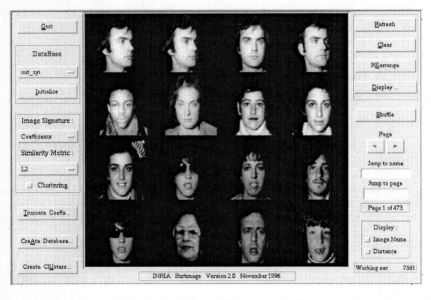

Fig. 5.13. Retrieval of the top left face. This example illustrates the robustness of the approach to wide pose variations.

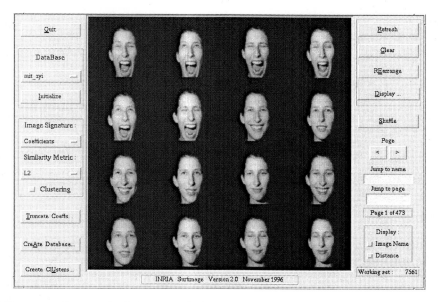

Fig. 5.14. Retrieval of the top left face. This example shows that the system is invariant to wide facial expressions.

face image retrieval. In this approach, the intensity surface of the image is modeled as a deformable surface embedded in XYI space. Our approach is thus a *generalization* of optical flow and deformable shape matching methods (which consider only changes in XY), of statistical texture models such as "eigenfaces" (which consider only changes in I an assume an already existing XY correspondence), and of hybrid methods with treat shape and texture separately and sequentially.

We have further shown how to tailor the space of allowable XYI deformations to fit the actual variation found in individual target classes. This was accomplished by a statistical analysis of observed image-to-image deformations using a Principal Components Analysis. The result is that the image deformation is restricted to the subspace of physically-plausible deformations. In the process, the dimensionality of the matching and the numerical complexity of the governing equation are drastically reduced.

By considering only the low-dimensional subspace of plausible deformations, we make the image matching process more robust and more efficient. We in effect "build in" statistical *a priori* knowledge about how the object can vary in order to obtain the best image-to-image match possible. To illustrate the power of this method we have shown that we can interpolate missing data despite significant occlusions and noise, and that we can use this method to obtain very compact image descriptions which are also useful for recognition and image retrieval.

Acknowledgements

This research has been carried out in collaboration with Dr. B. Moghaddam and Prof. A. Pentland.

References

1. K. J. Bathe. *Finite Element Procedures in Engineering Analysis*. Prentice-Hall, 1982.
2. Paul J. Besl and Neil D. McKay. A method for registration of 3D shapes. *IEEE Transactions on Pattern Analysis and Machine Intelligence*, 14(2):239–256, February 1992.
3. D. Beymer. Feature correspondence by interleaving shape and texture computations. In *IEEE Proceedings of Computer Vision and Pattern Recognition (CVPR '96)*, San Francisco, June 1996.
4. R. Chellappa, C.L. Wilson, and S. Sirohey. Human and machine recognition of faces : A survey. *Proceedings of the IEEE*, 83(5):705–740, 1995.
5. T. F. Cootes, C. J. Taylor, D. H. Cooper, and J. Graham. Active Shape Models - Their Training and Application. *Computer Vision and Image Understanding*, 61(1):38–59, January 1995.
6. P. E. Danielsson. Euclidean distance mapping. *Computer Vision, Graphics, and Image Processing*, 14:227–248, 1980.
7. G. H. Golub and C. F. Van Loan. *Matrix Computations*. Johns Hopkins Press, 1989.
8. B.K.P. Horn. *Robot Vision*. McGraw-Hill, New York, 1986.
9. B.K.P. Horn and G. Schunck. Determining optical flow. *Artificial Intelligence*, 17:185–203, 1981.
10. D. Marr. *Vision*. MIT Press, 1982.
11. B. Moghaddam, C. Nastar, and A. Pentland. Bayesian face recognition using deformable intensity surfaces. In *IEEE Proceedings of Computer Vision and Pattern Recognition (CVPR '96)*, San Francisco, June 1996.
12. B. Moghaddam, C. Nastar, and A. Pentland. A bayesian similarity metric for direct image matching. In *Proceedings of 13th International Conference on Pattern Recognition*, Vienna, Austria, 1996.
13. B. Moghaddam and A. Pentland. Probabilistic visual learning for object detection. In *IEEE Proceedings of the Fifth International Conference on Computer Vision*, Cambridge, USA, june 1995.
14. H. Murase and S. K. Nayar. Visual learning and recognition of 3D objects from appearance. *International Journal of Computer Vision*, 14(5), 1995.
15. C. Nastar and N. Ayache. Frequency-based nonrigid motion analysis: Application to four dimensional medical images. *IEEE Transactions on Pattern Analysis and Machine Intelligence*, 18(11):1067–1079, November 1996.
16. A. Pentland, B. Moghaddam, T. Starner, and M. Turk. View based and modular eigenspaces for face recognition. In *IEEE Proceedings of Computer Vision and Pattern Recognition*, 1994.

17. A. Pentland and S. Sclaroff. Closed-form solutions for physically based shape modelling and recognition. *IEEE Transactions on Pattern Analysis and Machine Intelligence*, PAMI-13(7):715–729, July 1991.

18. S. Sclaroff and A. Pentland. A modal framework for correspondence and description. In *Proceedings of the Fourth International Conference on Computer Vision (ICCV '93)*, Berlin, May 1993.

19. M. Turk and A. Pentland. Eigenfaces for recognition. *Journal of Cognitive Neuroscience*, 3(1), 1991.

20. Q.Z. Ye. The signed euclidean distance transform and its applications. In *International Conference on Pattern Recognition*, pages 495–499, 1988.

21. Z. Zhang. Iterative point matching for registration of free-form curves and surfaces. *International Journal of Computer Vision*, 13(2):119–152, 1994. also INRIA Tech. Report #1658.

Beyond Linear Eigenspaces:
Bayesian Matching for Face Recognition

Baback Moghaddam[1] and Alex Pentland[2]

[1] Mitsubishi Electric Research Lab, 201 Broadway, Cambridge, MA 02139, USA
[2] MIT Media Laboratory, 20 Ames St., Cambridge, MA 02139, USA

Abstract. We propose a novel technique for direct visual matching of images for the purposes of face recognition and database search. Specifically, we argue in favor of a *probabilistic* measure of similarity, in contrast to simpler methods which are based on standard Euclidean L_2 norms (*e.g.,* template matching) or subspace-restricted norms (*e.g.,* eigenspace matching). The proposed similarity measure is based on a Bayesian analysis of image differences: we model two mutually exclusive classes of variation between two facial images: *intra-personal* (variations in appearance of the same individual, due to different expressions or lighting) and *extra-personal* (variations in appearance due to a difference in identity). The high-dimensional probability density functions for each respective class are then obtained from training data using an eigenspace density estimation technique and subsequently used to compute a similarity measure based on the *a posteriori* probability of membership in the *intra-personal* class, which is used to rank matches in the database. The performance advantage of this probabilistic matching technique over standard Euclidean nearest-neighbor eigenspace matching is demonstrated using results from ARPA's 1996 "FERET" face recognition competition, in which this algorithm was found to be the top performer.

1. Introduction

Current approaches to image matching for visual object recognition and image database retrieval often make use of simple image similarity metrics such as Euclidean distance or normalized correlation, which correspond to a standard template-matching approach to recognition [2, 5]. For example, in its simplest form, the similarity measure $S(I_1, I_2)$ between two images I_1 and I_2 can be set to be inversely proportional to the norm $||I_1 - I_2||$. Such a simple formulation suffers from a major drawback: it does not exploit knowledge of which type of variations are critical (as opposed to incidental) in expressing similarity. In this paper, we formulate a *probabilistic* similarity measure which is based on the probability that the image intensity differences, denoted by $\Delta = I_1 - I_2$, are characteristic of typical variations in appearance of the *same* object. For example, for purposes of face recognition, we can define two classes of facial image variations: *intrapersonal* variations Ω_I (corresponding, for example, to different facial expressions of the *same* individual) and *extrapersonal* variations Ω_E (corresponding to variations between *different* individuals). Our similarity measure is then expressed in terms of the probability

$$S(I_1, I_2) = P(\Delta \in \Omega_I) = P(\Omega_I|\Delta) \tag{1.1}$$

where $P(\Omega_I|\Delta)$ is the *a posteriori* probability given by Bayes rule, using estimates of the likelihoods $P(\Delta|\Omega_I)$ and $P(\Delta|\Omega_E)$ which are derived from training data using an efficient subspace method for density estimation of high-dimensional data [9]. This Bayesian (MAP) approach can also be viewed as a generalized nonlinear extension of Linear Discriminant Analysis (LDA) [13, 3] or "FisherFace" techniques [1] for face recognition. Moreover, our nonlinear generalization has distinct computational/storage advantages over these linear methods for large databases.

2. Analysis of Image Differences

In previous work [6, 7, 11], a statistical analysis of various types of image differences was used to characterize facial variations. Two distinct mutually exclusive classes were defined: Ω_I representing *intrapersonal* variations between multiple images of the same individual and Ω_E representing *extrapersonal* variations which result when matching two different individuals. Furthermore, different inter-image representations were tested using this *dual* probabilistic eigenspace analysis: XYI-warp modal deformation spectra [11, 6, 7], XY-warp optical flow fields [7, 6] and a simplified I-(intensity)-only image-based differences [10, 7]. In this chapter, we will hereafter exclusively (but not restrictedly) focus on the latter representation, I-differences between two (pre-aligned and registered) images.

We now consider the problem of characterizing the type of differences which occur when matching two images in a face recognition task. We define two distinct and mutually exclusive classes: Ω_I representing *intrapersonal* variations between multiple images of the same individual (*e.g.*, with different expressions and lighting conditions), and Ω_E representing *extrapersonal* variations which result when matching two different individuals. We will assume that both classes are Gaussian-distributed and seek to obtain estimates of the likelihood functions $P(\Delta|\Omega_I)$ and $P(\Delta|\Omega_E)$ for a given intensity difference $\Delta = I_1 - I_2$.

Given these likelihoods we can define the similarity score $S(I_1, I_2)$ between a pair of images directly in terms of the intrapersonal *a posteriori* probability as given by Bayes rule:

$$\begin{aligned} S &= P(\Omega_I|\Delta) \\ &= \frac{P(\Delta|\Omega_I)P(\Omega_I)}{P(\Delta|\Omega_I)P(\Omega_I) + P(\Delta|\Omega_E)P(\Omega_E)} \end{aligned} \tag{2.1}$$

where the priors $P(\Omega)$ can be set to reflect specific operating conditions (*e.g.,* number of test images *vs.* the size of the database) or other sources of *a priori* knowledge regarding the two images being matched. Additionally, this particular Bayesian formulation casts the standard face recognition task (essentially an M-ary classification problem for M individuals) into a *binary* pattern classification problem with Ω_I and Ω_E. This much simpler problem is then solved using the maximum *a posteriori* (MAP) rule — *i.e.,* two images are determined to belong to the same individual if $P(\Omega_I|\Delta) > P(\Omega_E|\Delta)$, or equivalently, if $S(I_1, I_2) > \frac{1}{2}$.

2.1 Density Modeling

One difficulty with this approach is that the intensity difference vector is very high-dimensional, with $\Delta \in \mathcal{R}^N$ and $N = O(10^4)$. Therefore we typically lack sufficient independent training observations to compute reliable 2nd-order statistics for the likelihood densities (*i.e.,* singular covariance matrices will result). Even if we were able to estimate these statistics, the computational cost of evaluating the likelihoods is formidable. Furthermore, this computation would be highly inefficient since the *intrinsic* dimensionality or major degrees-of-freedom of Δ for each class is likely to be significantly smaller than N.

Recently, an efficient density estimation method was proposed by Moghaddam & Pentland [9] which divides the vector space $\mathcal{R}^N$ into two complementary subspaces using an eigenspace decomposition. This method relies on a Principal Components Analysis (PCA) [4] to form a low-dimensional estimate of the complete likelihood which can be evaluated using only the first M principal components, where $M << N$. This decomposition is illustrated in Figure 2.1 which shows an orthogonal decomposition of the vector space $\mathcal{R}^N$ into two mutually exclusive subspaces: the principal subspace F containing the first M principal components and its orthogonal complement $\bar{F}$, which contains the residual of the expansion. The component in the orthogonal subspace $\bar{F}$ is the so-called "distance-from-feature-space" (DFFS), a Euclidean distance equivalent to the PCA residual error. The component of Δ which lies *in* the feature space F is referred to as the "distance-in-feature-space" (DIFS) and is a *Mahalanobis* distance for Gaussian densities.

As shown in [9], the complete likelihood estimate can be written as the product of two independent marginal Gaussian densities

$$\hat{P}(\Delta|\Omega) = \left[\frac{\exp\left(-\frac{1}{2}\sum_{i=1}^{M}\frac{y_i^2}{\lambda_i}\right)}{(2\pi)^{M/2}\prod_{i=1}^{M}\lambda_i^{1/2}} \right] \cdot \left[\frac{\exp\left(-\frac{\epsilon^2(\Delta)}{2\rho}\right)}{(2\pi\rho)^{(N-M)/2}} \right] \tag{2.2}$$

$$= P_F(\Delta|\Omega)\,\hat{P}_{\bar{F}}(\Delta|\Omega)$$

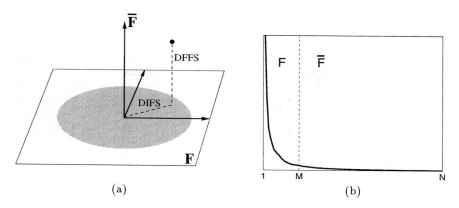

Fig. 2.1. (a) Decomposition of $\mathcal{R}^N$ into the principal subspace F and its orthogonal complement $\bar{F}$ for a Gaussian density, (b) a typical eigenvalue spectrum and its division into the two orthogonal subspaces.

where $P_F(\Delta|\Omega)$ is the true marginal density in F, $\hat{P}_{\bar{F}}(\Delta|\Omega)$ is the estimated marginal density in the orthogonal complement $\bar{F}$, y_i are the principal components and $\epsilon^2(\Delta)$ is the residual (or DFFS). The optimal value for the weighting parameter ρ is then found to be simply the average of the $\bar{F}$ eigenvalues

$$\rho = \frac{1}{N-M} \sum_{i=M+1}^{N} \lambda_i \tag{2.3}$$

We note that in actual practice, the majority of the $\bar{F}$ eigenvalues are unknown but *can* be estimated, for example, by fitting a nonlinear function to the available portion of the eigenvalue spectrum and estimating the average of the eigenvalues beyond the principal subspace.

3. Experiments

To test our recognition strategy we used a collection of images from the FERET face database. This collection of images consists of hard recognition cases that have proven difficult for all face recognition algorithms previously tested on the FERET database. The difficulty posed by this dataset appears to stem from the fact that the images were taken at different times, at different locations, and under different imaging conditions. The set of images consists of pairs of frontal-views (FA/FB) and are divided into two subsets: the "gallery" (training set) and the "probes" (testing set). The gallery images consisted of 74 pairs of images (2 per individual) and the probe set consisted of 38 pairs of images, corresponding to a subset of the gallery members. The

(a)   (b)

Fig. 3.1. Examples of FERET frontal-view image pairs used for (a) the Gallery set (training) and (b) the Probe set (testing).

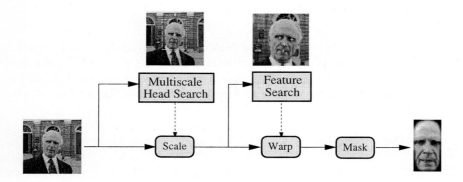

Fig. 3.2. The face alignment system

probe and gallery datasets were captured a week apart and exhibit differences in clothing, hair and lighting (see Figure 3.1).

Before we can apply our matching technique, we need to perform an affine alignment of these facial images. For this purpose we have used an automatic face-processing system which extracts faces from the input image and normalizes for translation, scale as well as slight rotations (both in-plane and out-of-plane). This system is described in detail in [9] and uses maximum-likelihood estimation of object location (in this case the position and scale of a face and the location of individual facial features) to geometrically align faces into standard normalized form as shown in Figure 3.2. All the faces in our experiments were geometrically aligned and normalized in this manner prior to further analysis.

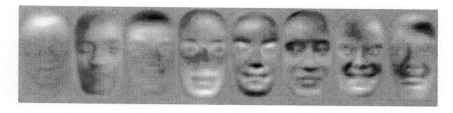

Fig. 3.3. Standard Eigenfaces.

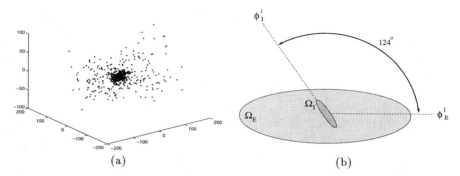

$$(a) \qquad\qquad\qquad (b)$$

Fig. 3.4. (a) Distribution of the two classes in the first 3 principal components (circles for Ω_I, dots for Ω_E) and (b) schematic representation of the two distributions showing orientation difference between the corresponding principal eigenvectors.

3.1 Eigenface Matching

As a baseline comparison, we first used an eigenface matching technique for recognition [14]. The normalized images from the gallery and the probe sets were projected onto a 100-dimensional eigenspace and a nearest-neighbor rule based on a Euclidean distance measure was used to match each probe image to a gallery image. We note that this method corresponds to a generalized template-matching method which uses a Euclidean norm type of similarity $S(I_1, I_2)$, which is restricted to the principal component subspace of the data. A few of the lower-order eigenfaces used for this projection are shown in Figure 3.3. We note that these eigenfaces represent the principal components of an entirely different set of images — *i.e.*, none of the individuals in the gallery or probe sets were used in obtaining these eigenvectors. In other words, neither the gallery nor the probe sets were part of the "training set." The rank-1 recognition rate obtained with this method was found to be 84% (64 correct matches out of 76), and the correct match was always in the top 10 nearest neighbors. Note that this performance is better than or similar to recognition rates obtained by any algorithm tested on this database, and that it is lower (by about 10%) than the typical rates that we have obtained with the FERET database [8]. We attribute this lower performance to the fact that these images were selected to be particularly challenging. In fact, using an eigenface method to match the first views of the 76 individuals in the gallery to their second views, we obtain a higher recognition rate of 89% (68 out of 76), suggesting that the gallery images represent a less challenging data set since these images were taken at the same time and under identical lighting conditions.

3.2 Bayesian Matching

For our probabilistic algorithm, we first gathered training data by computing the intensity differences for a training subset of 74 intrapersonal differences (by matching the two views of every individual in the gallery) and a random subset of 296 extrapersonal differences (by matching images of *different* individuals in the gallery), corresponding to the classes Ω_I and Ω_E, respectively.

It is interesting to consider how these two classes are distributed, for example, are they linearly separable or embedded distributions? One simple method of visualizing this is to plot their mutual principal components — *i.e.,* perform PCA on the *combined* dataset and project each vector onto the principal eigenvectors. Such a visualization is shown in Figure 3.4(a) which is a 3D scatter plot of the first 3 principal components. This plot shows what appears to be two completely enmeshed distributions, both having near-zero means and differing primarily in the amount of scatter, with Ω_I displaying smaller intensity differences as expected. It therefore appears that one can not reliably distinguish low-amplitude extrapersonal differences (of which there are many) from intrapersonal ones.

However, direct visual interpretation of Figure 3.4(a) is very misleading since we are essentially dealing with low-dimensional (or "flattened") hyperellipsoids which are intersecting near the origin of a very high-dimensional space. The key distinguishing factor between the two distributions is their relative orientation. Fortunately, we can easily determine this relative orientation by performing a separate PCA on each class and computing the dot product of their respective first eigenvectors. This analysis yields the cosine of the angle between the major axes of the two hyper-ellipsoids, which was found to be 124°, implying that the orientation of the two hyper-ellipsoids is quite different. Figure 3.4(b) is a schematic illustration of the geometry of this configuration, where the hyper-ellipsoids have been drawn to approximate scale using the corresponding eigenvalues.

3.3 Dual Eigenfaces

We note that the two mutually exclusive classes Ω_I and Ω_E correspond to a "dual" set of eigenfaces as shown in Figure 3.5. Note that the intrapersonal

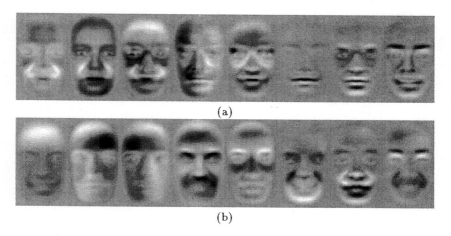

(a)

(b)

Fig. 3.5. "Dual" Eigenfaces: (a) Intrapersonal, (b) Extrapersonal

variations shown in Figure 3.5-(a) represent subtle variations due mostly to expression changes (and lighting) whereas the extrapersonal variations in Figure 3.5-(b) are more representative of general eigenfaces which code variations such as hair color, facial hair and glasses. Also note the overall qualitative similarity of the extrapersonal eigenfaces to the standard eigenfaces in Figure 3.3. This suggests the basic intuition that intensity differences of the extrapersonal type span a larger vector space similar to the volume of face-space spanned by standard eigenfaces, whereas the *intrapersonal* eigenspace corresponds to a more tightly constrained subspace. It is the representation of this intrapersonal subspace that is the critical part of formulating a probabilistic measure of facial similarity. In fact our experiments with a larger set of FERET images have shown that this intrapersonal eigenspace alone is sufficient for a simplified *maximum likelihood* measure of similarity (see Section 3.4).

Finally, we note that since these classes are not linearly separable, simple linear discriminant techniques (*e.g.*, using hyperplanes) can not be used with any degree of reliability. The proper decision surface is inherently nonlinear (quadratic, in fact, under the Gaussian assumption) and is best defined in terms of the *a posteriori* probabilities — *i.e.*, by the equality $P(\Omega_I|\Delta) = P(\Omega_E|\Delta)$. Fortunately, the optimal discriminant surface is automatically implemented when invoking a MAP classification rule.

Having analyzed the geometry of the two distributions, we then computed the likelihood estimates $P(\Delta|\Omega_I)$ and $P(\Delta|\Omega_E)$ using the PCA-based method outlined in Section 2.1. We selected principal subspace dimensions of $M_I = 10$ and $M_E = 30$ for Ω_I and Ω_E, respectively. These density estimates were then used with a default setting of equal priors, $P(\Omega_I) = P(\Omega_E)$, to evaluate the

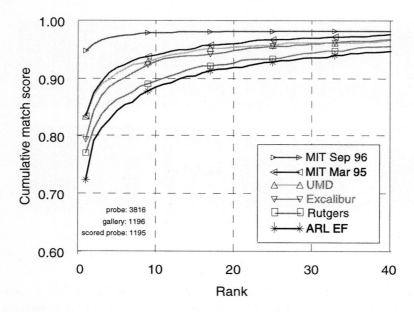

Fig. 3.6. Cumulative recognition rates for frontal FA/FB views for the competing algorithms in the FERET 1996 test. The top curve (labeled "MIT Sep 96") corresponds to our Bayesian matching technique. Note that second placed is standard eigenface matching (labeled "MIT Mar 95").

a posteriori intrapersonal probability $P(\Omega_I|\Delta)$ for matching probe images to those in the gallery.

Therefore, for each probe image we computed probe-to-gallery differences and sorted the matching order, this time using the *a posteriori* probability $P(\Omega_I|\Delta)$ as the similarity measure. This probabilistic ranking yielded an improved rank-1 recognition rate of 89.5%. Furthermore, out of the 608 extrapersonal warps performed in this recognition experiment, only 2% (11) were misclassified as being intrapersonal — *i.e.*, with $P(\Omega_I|\Delta) > P(\Omega_E|\Delta)$.

3.4 The 1996 FERET Competition

This approach to recognition has produced a significant improvement over the accuracy we obtained using a standard eigenface nearest-neighbor matching rule. The probabilistic similarity measure was used in the September 1996 FERET competition (with subspace dimensionalities of $M_I = M_E = 125$) and was found to be the top-performing system by a typical margin of 10-20% over the other competing algorithms [12] (see Figure 3.6). Figure 3.7(a) shows the performance comparison between standard eigenfaces and the Bayesian method from this test. Note the 10% gain in performance afforded by the new Bayesian similarity measure. Similarly, Figure 3.7(b) shows the recognition results for "duplicate" images which were separated in time by up to 6 months (a much more challenging recognition problem) which shows a

239

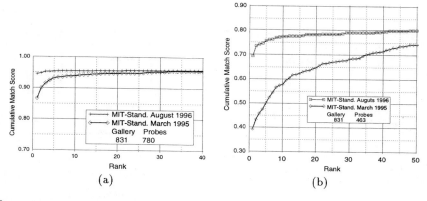

Fig. 3.7. Cumulative recognition rates for standard eigenface matching and the newer Bayesian similarity metric: (a) frontal FA/FB views, (b) frontal duplicate views.

30% improvement in recognition rate with Bayesian matching. Thus we note that in both cases (FA/FB and duplicates) the new probabilistic similarity measure has effectively *halved* the error rate of eigenface matching.

We have recently experimented with a more simplified probabilistic similarity measure which uses only the *intrapersonal* eigenfaces with the intensity difference Δ to formulate a *maximum likelihood* (ML) matching technique using

$$S' = P(\Delta|\Omega_I) \tag{3.1}$$

instead of the *maximum a posteriori* (MAP) approach defined by Equation 2.1. Although this simplified measure has not yet been officially FERET tested, our own experiments with a database of size 2000 have shown that using S' instead of S results in only a minor (2%) deficit in the recognition rate while cutting the computational cost by a factor of 1/2 (requiring a single eigenspace projection as opposed to two).

3.5 Eigenface vs. Probabilistic Matching

It is interesting to compare and contrast the conceptual and operational difference between standard eigenface matching based on Euclidean-norm type of similarity and the new probabilistic similarity computation. This is shown in Figure 3.8 which represents the signal flow graphs for the two methods. With eigenface matching both the probe and gallery images are projected onto a single "universal" set of eigenfaces, after which their respective coefficients are differenced and normed to compute a Euclidean distance metric which is the basis of the similarity score. With probabilistic matching on the other hand, the two registered probe and gallery images are **first** differenced and then projected onto **two** sets of eigenfaces which are used to compute the two likelihoods $P(\Delta|\Omega_I)$ and $P(\Delta|\Omega_E)$, from which the *a posteriori* probability $P(\Omega_I|\Delta)$ is computed by application of Bayes rule

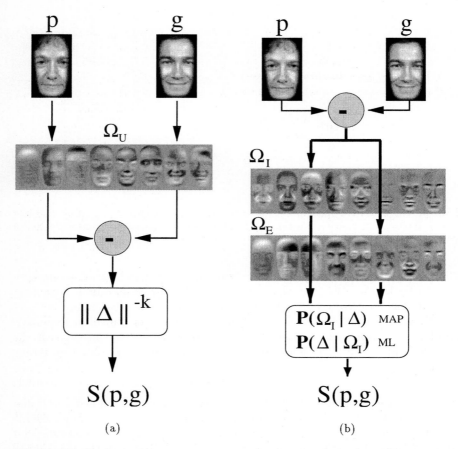

Fig. 3.8. Operational signal flow diagrams for (a) Eigenface similarity and (b) Probabilistic similarity.

as in Eq. 2.1. Alternatively, the likelihood $P(\Delta|\Omega_I)$ alone can be computed to form the more simplified similarity in Eq. 3.1. As noted in the previous section use of S' instead of S reduces the computational requirements by a factor of two, while only compromising the overall recognition rate by a few percentage points.

4. Discussion

We have proposed a novel technique for direct visual matching of images for the purposes of recognition and search in a large face database. Specifically, we have argued in favor of a *probabilistic* measure of similarity, in contrast to simpler methods which are based on standard L_2 norms (*e.g.*, template matching [2], "warped" template matching [5]) or subspace-restricted norms (*e.g.*, eigenspace matching [14]). The proposed similarity measure is based on a Bayesian analysis of image differences: we model two mutually exclusive classes of variation between two face images: *intra-personal* (variations in appearance of the same individual, due to different expressions or lighting, for example) and *extra-personal* (variations in appearance due to different identity). The high-dimensional probability density functions for each respective class are then obtained from training data using an eigenspace density estimation technique and subsequently used to compute a similarity measure based on the *a posteriori* probability of membership in the *intra-personal* class, which is used to rank and find the best matches in the database.

The performance advantage of our probabilistic matching technique has been demonstrated using both a small database (internally tested) as well as a large (800+) database with an independent double-blind test as part of ARPA's September 1996 "FERET" competition, in which Bayesian similarity out-performed all competing algorithms (at least one of which was using an LDA/Fisher type method). We believe that these results clearly demonstrate the superior performance of probabilistic matching over eigenface, LDA/Fisher and other existing techniques.

This probabilistic framework is particularly advantageous in that the intra/extra density estimates explicitly characterize the type of appearance variations which are critical in formulating a meaningful measure of similarity. For example, the deformations corresponding to facial expression changes (which may have high image-difference norms) are, in fact, *irrelevant* when the measure of similarity is to be based on *identity*. The subspace density estimation method used for representing these classes thus corresponds to a *learning* method for discovering the principal modes of variation important to the classification task. Furthermore, by equating similarity with the *a posteriori* probability we obtain an optimal non-linear decision rule for matching and recognition. This aspect of our approach differs significantly from recent methods which use simple linear discriminant analysis techniques for recognition (*e.g.*, [13, 3]). Our Bayesian (MAP) method can also be viewed as a generalized nonlinear (quadratic) version of Linear Discriminant Analysis (LDA) [3] or "FisherFace" techniques [1]. The computational advantage of our approach is that there is no need to compute and store an eigenspace for each individual in the gallery (as required with LDA). One (or at most two) eigenspaces are sufficient for probabilistic matching and therefore storage and computational costs are fixed and do not increase with the size of the database (as with LDA/Fisher methods).

Finally, the results obtained with the simplified ML similarity measure (S' in Eq. 3.1) suggest a computationally equivalent yet superior alternative to standard eigenface matching. In other words, a likelihood similarity based on the intrapersonal density $P(\Delta|\Omega_I)$ alone is far superior to nearest-neighbor matching in eigenspace while essentially requiring the same number of projections. For completeness (and a slightly better performance) however, one should use the *a posteriori* similarity S in Eq. 2.1, at twice the computational cost of standard eigenfaces.

Acknowledgements

The authors wish to thank Wasi Wahid for his help with the FERET tests and in implementing some of the experiments described in this chapter and also Tony Jebara for helpful discussions and his insights regarding the implementation of a computationally simplified form for the MAP/ML similarity measures. We would also like to acknowledge Jonathon Phillips from the US Army Research Laboratory for providing the official FERET 1996 competition performance curves used in Figures 3.6 and 3.7.

References

1. V.I. Belhumeur, J.P. Hespanha, and D.J. Kriegman. Eigenfaces vs. fisherfaces: Recognition using class specific linear projection. *IEEE Transactions on Pattern Analysis and Machine Intelligence*, PAMI-19(7):711–720, July 1997.
2. R. Brunelli and T. Poggio. Face recognition : Features vs. templates. *IEEE Transactions on Pattern Analysis and Machine Intelligence*, 15(10), October 1993.
3. K. Etemad and R. Chellappa. Discriminant analysis for recognition of human faces. In *Proc. of Int'l Conf. on Acoustics, Speech and Signal Processing*, pages 2148–2151, 1996.
4. I.T. Jolliffe. *Principal Component Analysis*. Springer-Verlag, New York, 1986.
5. M. J. Jones and T. Poggio. Model-based matching by linear combination of prototypes. AI Memo No. 1583, Artificial Intelligence Laboratory, Massachusettes Institute of Technology, November 1996.
6. B. Moghaddam, C. Nastar, and A. Pentland. Bayesian face recognition using deformable intensity differences. In *Proc. of IEEE Conf. on Computer Vision and Pattern Recognition*, June 1996.
7. B. Moghaddam, C. Nastar, and A. Pentland. A bayesian similarity measure for direct image matching. In *International Conference on Pattern Recognition*, Vienna, Austria, August 1996.
8. B. Moghaddam and A. Pentland. Face recognition using view-based and modular eigenspaces. *Automatic Systems for the Identification and Inspection of Humans*, 2277, 1994.
9. B. Moghaddam and A. Pentland. Probabilistic visual learning for object representation. *IEEE Transactions on Pattern Analysis and Machine Intelligence*, PAMI-19(7):696–710, July 1997.
10. B. Moghaddam, W. Wahid, and A. Pentland. Beyond eigenfaces: Probabilistic matching for face recognition. In *Proc. of International Conf. on Automatic Face and Gesture Recognition*, Nara, Japan, April 1998.

11. C. Nastar, B. Moghaddam, and A. Pentland. Generalized image matching: Statistical learning of physically-based deformations. In *Proceedings of the Fourth European Conference on Computer Vision (ECCV'96)*, Cambridge, UK, April 1996.

12. P. J. Phillips, H. Moon, P. Rauss, and S. Rizvi. The FERET evaluation methodology for face-recognition algorithms. In *IEEE Proceedings of Computer Vision and Pattern Recognition*, pages 137–143, June 1997.

13. D. Swets and J. Weng. Using discriminant eigenfeatures for image retrieval. *IEEE Transactions on Pattern Analysis and Machine Intelligence*, PAMI-18(8):831–836, August 1996.

14. M. Turk and A. Pentland. Eigenfaces for recognition. *Journal of Cognitive Neuroscience*, 3(1), 1991.

The FERET Evaluation

P. Jonathon Phillips[1], Hyeonjoon Moon [2], Syed Rizvi [3], and Patrick Rauss [4]

[1] National Institute of Standards and Technology
Gaithersburg, MD 20899
jonathon@magi.nist.gov

[2] Department of Electrical and Computer Engineering
State Unviversity of New York at Buffalo
Amherst, NY 14260
moon@acsu.buffalo.edu

[3] Department of Applied Sciences
College of Staten Island of City University of New York
Staten Island, NY 10314
rizvi@unlser1.unl.csi.cuny.edu

[4] U.S. Army Research Laboratory
Adelphi, MD 20783
prauss@ragu.arl.mil

Abstract. Two of the most critical requirements in support of producing reliable face-recognition systems are a large database of facial images and a testing procedure to evaluate systems. The Face Recognition Technology (FERET) program has addressed both issues through the FERET database of facial images and the establishment of the FERET tests. The FERET database is divided into two portions. The development portion is provided to researchers for algorithm development and the sequestered portion provides a set of images not seen by the researchers to test algorithms. The set of test is the third in a sequence of FERET tests. This test was administered in September 1996 and March 1997. The Sept96 test provided a detailed assesment of the state of the art, measurement of algorithm performance on large databases, and a comparison among face recognition algorithms.

Key Words: face recognition, FERET, algorithm evaluation

1 Introduction

Face recognition is a rapidly developing area of computer vision, which has advanced to the point of face recognition systems being demonstrated in real-world settings (Phillips and Rauss, 1997). The progress in face recognition has been facilitated by the FERET database of facial images and the FERET sequence of algorithm evaluation procedures (Phillips et al., 1998), with the FERET database and evaluations becoming de facto standards.

The FERET database is a standard database that is used for algorithm development and testing, which is divided into development and sequestered portions. The development portion provides a common database for designing algorithms, and relieves researchers from spending effort to collect a database of facial images. This has been made possible for researchers to develop algorithms on a common database, and to report results in the literature on a common database. Without the availability of a standard database, researchers tend to develop algorithms and report results on databases of less than 50 individuals which is not representative of real-world applications.

The sequestered portion of the database is used for testing and evaluating face recognition algorithms, and is the heart of the FERET evaluation procedures. This portion allows for the testing of algorithms on facial imagery that researchers have not seen before, which tests an algorithm's ability to generalize rather than on how well an algorithm is tuned to a particular set of images.

The independently administered FERET test allows for a scientific assessment of the relative strengths and weaknesses of different approaches. More importantly, the FERET database and tests clarify the current state of the art in face recognition and point out general directions for future research. The FERET tests allow the computer vision community to assess overall strengths and weaknesses in the field, not only on the basis of the performance of an individual algorithm, but in addition on the aggregate performance of all algorithms tested. Through this type of assessment, the community learns in an unbiased and open manner of the important technical problems to be addressed, and how the community is progressing toward solving these problems.

2 Background

The first FERET tests took place in August 1994 and March 1995 (for details of these tests and the FERET database and program, see Phillips et al., 1997; Phillips and Rauss, 1997; and Phillips et al., 1998). The FERET database collection began in September 1993 along with the FERET program.

The August 1994 test established, for the first time, as a performance baseline for face-recognition algorithms. This test was designed to measure performance on algorithms that could automatically locate, normalize, and identify faces from a database. The test consisted of three subtests, each with a different gallery and probe set. The *gallery* is the set of known individuals. An image of an unknown face presented to the algorithm is called a *probe*, and the collection of probes is called the *probe set*. The first subtest examined the ability of algorithms to recognize faces from a gallery of 316 individuals. The second was the false-alarm test, which measured how well an algorithm rejects faces not in the gallery. The third baselined the effects of pose changes on performance.

Figure 1. Duplicate images (examples of variations between collections).

The second FERET test, which took place in March 1995, measured progress since August 1994 and evaluate algorithms on larger galleries. The March 1995 evaluation consisted of a single test with a gallery of 817 known individuals. One emphasis of the test was on duplicate images in the probe set. A *duplicate* is defined as an image of a person whose corresponding gallery image was taken on a different date.

The FERET database is designed to advance the state of the art in face recognition, with the images collected directly supporting both algorithm development and the FERET evaluation tests. The database is divided into a development set, which is provided to researchers, and a set of sequestered images for testing. The images in the development set are representative of the sequestered images.

The facial images were collected in 15 sessions between August 1993 and July 1996. Sessions lasted one or two days, and the location and setup did not change during a session. In an effort to maintain a degree of consistency throughout the database, the photographer used the same physical setup in each session. However, because the equipment had to reassembled for each session, there was variation from session to session (figure 1).

Images of an individual were acquired in sets of 5 to 11 images, collected under relatively unconstrained conditions (figure 2). Two frontal views were taken (**fa** and **fb**); a different facial expression was requested for the second frontal image. For 200 sets of images, a third frontal image was taken with a different camera and different lighting (this is referred to as the **fc** image). The remaining images were collected at various aspects between right and left half profile. To add simple variations to the database, the photographers sometimes took a second set of images, for which the subjects were asked to put on their glasses and/or pull their hair back. Sometimes a second set of images of a person was taken on a later date; such a set of images is referred to as a duplicate set. Such duplicates sets result in variations in scale, pose, expression, and illimination of the face. For some people, there was nearly a year between their first and last Sittings with some subjects being photographed multiple times (figure 1).

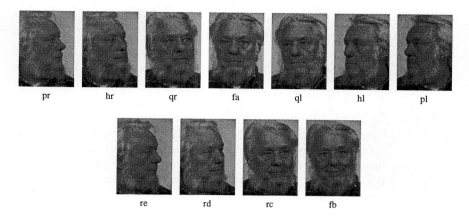

pr	hr	qr	fa	ql	hl	pl

re	rd	rc	fb

Figure 2. Image set.

By July 1996, 1564 sets of images were in the database, for 14,126 total images. The database contains 1199 individuals and 365 duplicate sets of images. For some people, over two years elapsed between their first and most recent sittings, with some subjects being photographed multiple times (figure 2). The development portion of the database consisted of 503 sets of images, which were released to researchers. The remaining images were sequestered by the Government.

3 Design of the Sept96 Test

The traditional method of testing a face-recognition algorithm is to provide the algorithm with two sets of images (Phillips et al., 1996), the gallery and the probe set, which do not intersect. Unfortunately, this method severely limits one's ability to analyze the data. To overcome this deficiency, we modified the test protocol to allow for a more detailed analysis of face-recognition algorithm performance. We designed the testing protocol so that algorithm performance can be computed for a variety of different galleries and probe sets.

In the new protocol, an algorithm is given two sets of images: the *target set* and the *query set*. We introduce this terminology to distinguish these sets from the gallery and probe sets that are used in computing performance statistics. The target set is given to the algorithm as the set of known facial images. The images in the query set are the unknown facial images to be identified. For each image q_i in the query set $\mathcal{Q}$, an algorithm reports the similarity $s_i(k)$ between q_i and each image t_k in the target set T. The key property of the new protocol, which allows for greater flexibility in scoring, is that for any two images q_i and t_k, we know $s_i(k)$.

From the output files, algorithm performance can be computed for virtual galleries and probe sets. A gallery G is a virtual gallery if G is a proper subset of the target set, i.e., $G \subseteq T$. Similarly, P is a virtual probe set if $P \subseteq Q$. For a given gallery G and probe set P, the performance scores are computed by examination of the similarity measures $s_i(k)$ such that $q_i \in P$ and $t_k \in G$.

The virtual gallery and probe set technique allows us to characterize algorithm performance by different categories of images. The different categories include (1) rotated images, (2) duplicates taken within a week of the gallery image, (3) duplicates where the time between the images is at least one year, (4) galleries containing one image per person, and (5) galleries containing more than one image per person. We can create a gallery of 100 people and estimate the algorithm's performance at recognizing people in this gallery. Using this as a starting point, we can then create virtual galleries of 200, 300, ..., 1000 people and determine how performance changes as the size of the gallery increases. Another avenue of investigation is to create n different galleries of size 100, and calculate the variation in algorithm performance with the different galleries of size 100.

Virtual galleries and probe sets allow for an algorithm to be evaluated on different images of the same person. To accomplish this, it is necessary for more than one image of a person to be placed in the target set. If such images were marked as the same person, then the algorithms being tested could use the information in the evaluation process. To avoid this happening, we require that each image in the target set be treated as an unique face. (In practice, this condition is enforced by giving every image in the target and query set a unique random identification.)

4 Test Details

In the Sept96 FERET test, the target set contained 3323 images and the query set 3816 images. All the images in the target set were frontal images. The query set consisted of all the images in the target set plus rotated images and digitally modified images. We designed the digitally modified images to test the effects of illumination and scale (Phillips et al., 1996). For each query image q_i, an algorithm outputs the similarity measure $s_i(k)$ for all images t_k in the target set. The output for each query image q_i is sorted by the similarity scores $s_i(\bullet)$.

Except for the rotated and digitally modified images, the target and query sets are the same. Thus, the test output contains every target image matched with itself. This allowed a detailed analysis of performance on multiple galleries and probe sets.

Fully automatic face recognition systems consist of two parts, face detection and normalization and face recognition. To be able to characterize the performance of the two portions and open up the testing procedure to more algorithms, we devised two versions of the September 1996 test. The target and query sets are the same for each version. The first version requires that the algorithms be fully automatic, and the testee is given a list of images in the target and query sets. In the second version of the test, the coordinates of the eyes are also provided. By comparing the performance between the two versions, one can estimate the performance of the face-locating and identifying portions of an algorithm.

The test was administered at each group's site under the supervision of one of the authors. Each group had three days to complete the test on less than 10 UNIX workstations (this limit was not reached). We did not record the time or number of workstations because execution time can vary according to machines used, machine and network configuration, and the amount of time the developers spent optimizing their code (we wanted to encourage algorithm development, not code optimization). (We imposed the time limit to encourage the development of algorithms that could be incorporated into fieldable systems.)

The images in the gallery and probe sets were from both the developmental and sequestered portions of the FERET database. Only images from the FERET database were included in the test; however, algorithm developers were not prohibited from using images outside the FERET database to develop or tune parameters in their algorithms.

5 Performance Evaluation

In this chapter, we report identification results using a closed universe model. In the closed universe, every probe is in the gallery. The complement to the closed universe is the open universe where some probes are not in the gallery. The open universe model is used in verification and authentication scenarios. The FERET results for these scenarios can be found in Rizvi et al., 1998.

The closed-universe model allows one to ask how good an algorithm is at identifying a probe image; the question is not always "is the top match correct?" but "is the correct answer in the top n matches?" This lets one know how many images have to be examined to get the desired level of performance. The performance statistics are reported as cumulative match scores. The rank is plotted along the horizontal axis, and the vertical axis is the percentage of correct matches. The cumulative match score can be calculated for any subset of the probe set. We calculate this score to evaluate an algorithm's performance on different categories of probes, i.e., rotated or scaled probes. The computation of the score is quite simple. Let P be the number of probes to be scored and R_k the number of these probes in the subset set that are in the top k. The fraction reported correctly is R_k/P.

6 The Latest Test

In this chapter, we report extensively on the identification results for the Sept96 FERET test. The Sept96 test was administerd in September 1996 and in March 1997. We evaluate the algorithms using large-gallery tests, and present the results as cumulative match scores. Performance is broken out by different categories of probes. This allows for a detailed assessment of the state of the art in face recognition.

We report the results for 10 algorithms. Table 2 lists the groups tested, verisons of the test taken, and when the test was administered. Two algorithms were developed at the MIT Media Laboratory. The first was the same algorithm that was tested in March 1995 (Moghaddam and Pentland, 1995; Pentland et al., 1994). This algorithm was retested so that improvement since March 1995 could be determined. The second algorithm was based on more recent work (Moghaddam et al., 1996). Algorithms were also tested from Excalibur Corp. (Carlsbad, CA), Michigan State University (Swets and Weng, 1996), Rutgers University (Wilder, 1994), University of Southern California (Wiskott et al., 1997; Okada et al., 1998), and two from University of Maryland (UMd) (Etemad and Chellappa, 1997; Zhao et al., 1998). The first algorithm from UMd was tested in September 1996 and a second version of the algorithm was tested in March 1997. The final two algorithms were implemented at ARL to provide a performance baseline. The ARL algorithms tested were normalized correlation, and our implementation of eigenfaces (Turk and Pentland, 1991). In our implementation of eigenfaces, all the images we scaled, masked, and histogram equalized. The training set consisted of 500 faces. Faces were represented by their projection onto the first 200 eigenvectors and were identified by a nearest neighborhood classifier using the L_1 metric. For normalized correlation, the images were scaled and masked.

Table 1. Dates and versions of test that groups took the Sept96 FERET test

Version	Group	Sep. 1996	Mar. 1997	Baseline
Fully	MIT	✓		
Automatic	USC		✓	
Eye	ARL PCA			✓
Coordinates	ARL Correlation			✓
Given	Excalibur	✓		
	MIT	✓		
	MSU	✓		
	Rutgers	✓		
	UMd	✓	✓	
	USC		✓	

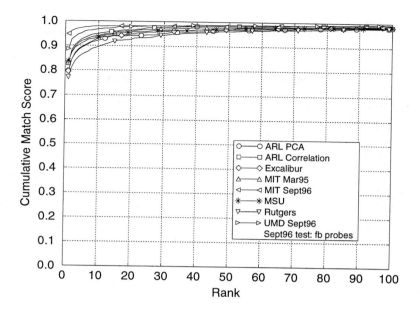

Figure 3. Sept96 Test: **fb** probes (probes scored = 1195)

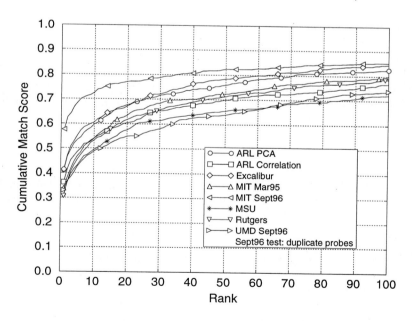

Figure 4. Sept96 test: duplicate probes (probes scored = 722)

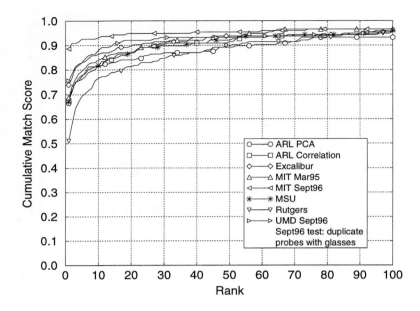

Figure 5. Sept96 test: duplicate probes with glasses (probes scored = 176)

7 The September 1996 Administered Test

In this section, we report the results of the Sept96 test administered in September 1996. To evaluate identification performance, we constructed a gallery of 1196 frontal images and scored performance against different probe categories. (For one category, a smaller gallery was constructed.) None of the people in the gallery were wearing glasses.

7.1 Eye Coordinates Given

In this subsection, we report performance when the eye coordinates were provided. In the first category, the probe set consisted of the **fb** images for 1195 of the gallery images. Figure 3 shows performance for this category.

In the second category, the probe set contained 722 duplicate images. Figure 4 shows the performance on this category for the eight algorithms that we tested.

Figure 5 shows performance against 176 duplicate probes with glasses. The scores for duplicates with glasses is higher that scores for all duplicates. This is because most duplicates with glasses were taken on the same day as the cooresponding gallery images.

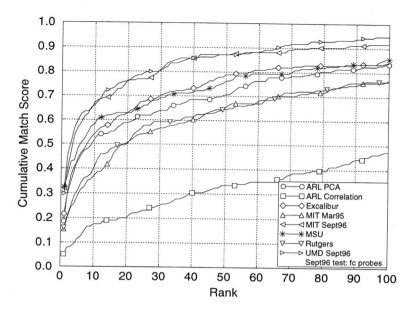

Figure 6. Sept96 test: **fc** probes (probes scored = 194)

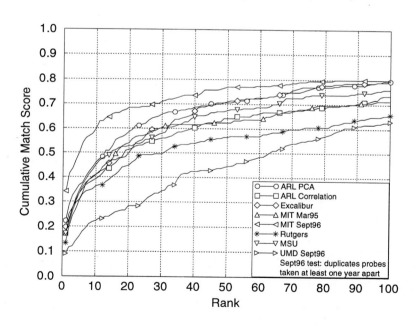

Figure 7. Sept96 test: duplicate probes taken at least one year apart
(probes scored = 234)

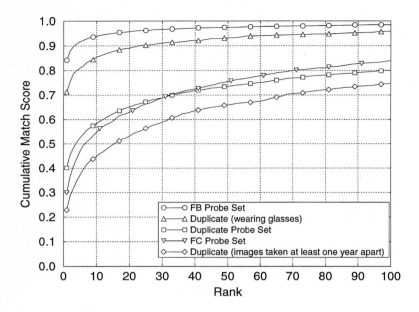

Figure 8. Comparison of difficulties of different probe sets.

Figure 6 shows performance against the 194 **fc** probes. The **fc** probes were taken on the same day as the gallery images, but had different lighting conditions.

Figure 7 shows the performance against duplicate probes taken at least one year apart. For this test, we used a gallery that consisted of 864 frontal images with one image per person, which were taken before Jan. 1995. In this test, the probe set contained 234 duplicate images, which were taken after Jan. 1996.

In figure 8, we compare the difficulty of different probe sets. Whereas figure 4 reports the performance for each algorithm, figure 8 shows a single curve that is an average of the performance of all the algorithms. For example, the first rank score for duplicate probe sets is computed from an average of the first rank score for all algorithms in figure 4. Figure 8 reports performance according to five categories of images. The first category consists of the second frontal images (**fb**) from the same set as the gallery image (section 2). The second category consists of images of people wearing glasses. The third category is the set of all duplicate images (figure 4). The fourth category consists of the frontal **fc** images (images taken on the same day, but with a different camera and lighting). The final category consists of images that were taken at least a year apart. (The gallery in this category is a subset of the gallery in the other categories.)

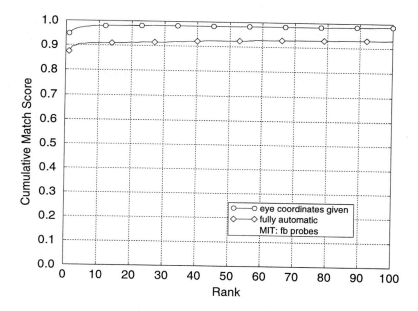

Figure 9. Sept96 test (MIT): **fb** probes

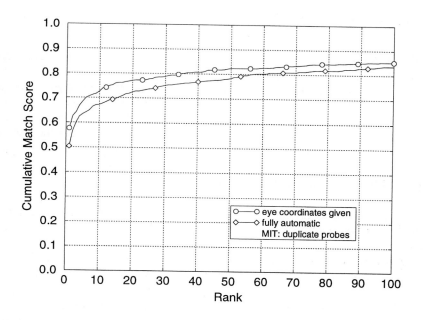

Figure 10. Sept96 test (MIT): duplicate probes

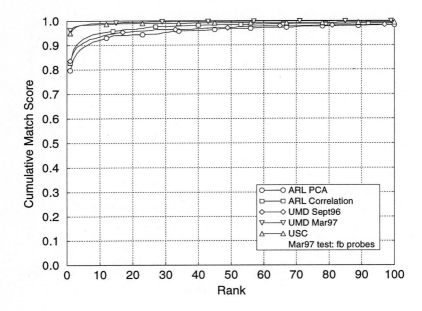

Figure 11. Mar97 test: **fb** probes

7.2 Fully Automatic Performance

In this subsection, we report performance for the fully automatic MIT Media Lab algorithm. We plot performance of the partial and fully automatic scores. This allows one to compare performance between both verisons of the algorithms. In the first category, the probe set consisted of the **fb** and performance is shown in figure 9. shows performance for this category. Figure 10 shows the performance on duplicate images. The galleries and probe sets use the same in the partial automatic results. (section 7.1)

8 March 1997 Adiminstered Tests

In this section, we report performances for the algorithms tested in March 1997 and the two ARL baseline algorithms.

8.1 Eye Coordinates Given

In this subsection, we report results when the eye coordinates are provided. Figure 11 shows performance for **fb** probes. In the second category, the probe set contained 722 duplicate images. Figure 12 shows the performance on this category for the five algorithms that we tested.

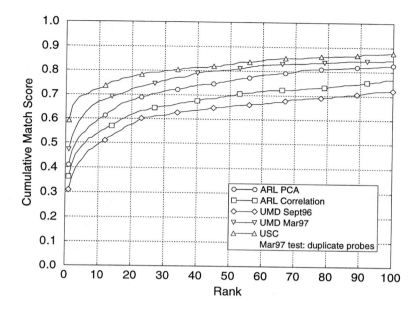

Figure 12. Mar97 test: duplicate probes

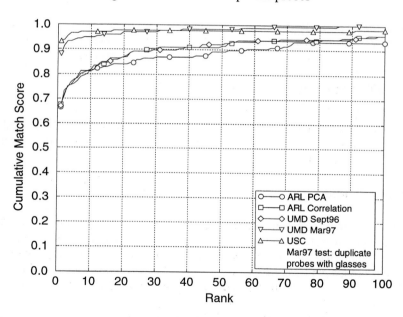

Figure 13. Mar97 test: duplicate probes with glasses

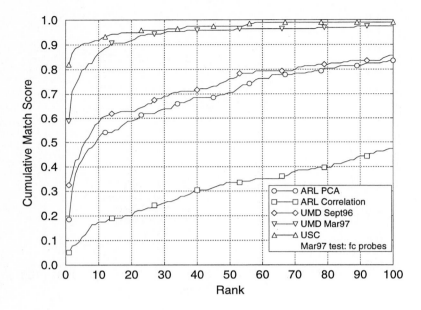

Figure 14. Mar97 test: **fc** probes

Figure 13 shows performance against 176 duplicate probes with glasses. Figure 14 shows performance against the 194 **fc** probes. Figure 15 shows the performance against duplicate probes taken at least one year apart.

8.2 Fully Automatic Performance

In this subsection, we report performance for the fully automatic USC algorithm. Figure 16 shows performance for the **fb** probes and figure 17 shows performance for the duplicate probes.

9 Conclusions

We draw a number of conclusions from the September 1996 FERET test. The first is that substantial progress has been made in face recognition. This is directly supported by the improvement in performance of the algorithms developed at the MIT Media Lab and UMd. Indirectly supporting this conclusion is the number of groups that agreed to take this test. The second is that face recognition is a dynamic and rapidly developing field. This is supported by (1) the improvement in performance of the MIT Media Lab and the UMd algorithms, and (2) the overall level of performance between the March 1995 and the Sept96

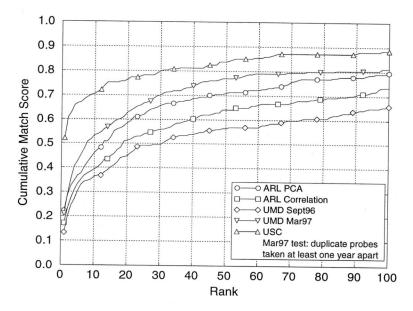

Figure 15. Mar97 test: Duplicate probes taken at least one year apart

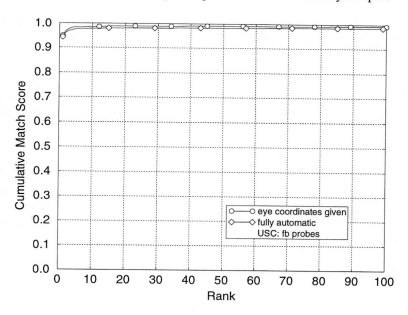

Figure 16. Mar97 test (USC): **fb** probes

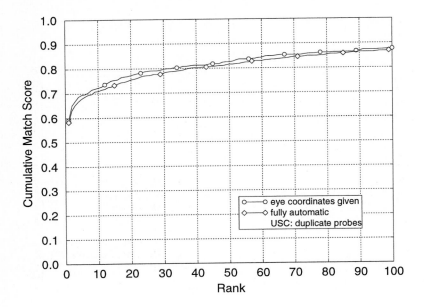

Figure 17. Mar97 (USC): duplicate probes

FERET tests. The constant improvement means that when comparing algorithms, it is necessary to note when the tests were administered.

The Sept96 FERET test shows that the upper bound in performance has not been reached. The results show that work needs to be made in recognizing faces from duplicate images and handling variations due to illumination. Work also needs to be done in understanding how changing the gallery affects algorithm performance.

10 Acknowledgements

The work reported here is part of the Face Recognition Technology (FERET) program, which is sponsored by the U.S. Department of Defense Counterdrug Technology Development Program. Portions of this work were performed while the first author was at the U.S. Army Research Laboratory, Adelphi, Md.

11 References

Chellappa R., Wilson,C. L., and Sirohey, C. (1995), Human and Machine Recognition of Faces: A Survey, *Proc. IEEE* **83**, 705-740.

Cherkassky, V. and Mulier, F. (1998), *Learning from Data : Concepts, Theory and Methods*, Wiley.

Cortes, C. and Vapnik, V. (1995), Support-Vector Networks, *Machine Learning*, 20, 273-297.

Etemad K., and Chellappa R. (1996), Discriminant Analysis for Recognition of Human Face Images, *In Proceedings of ICASSP*, 2148-2151.

Moghaddam B., Nastar C., and Pentland A. (1996), Bayesian Face Recognition using Deformable Intensity Surfaces, *In Proceedings Computer Vision and Pattern Recognition*, 638-645.

Moghaddam B. and Pentland A.(1997), Probabilistic Visual Learning for Object Detection, *IEEE Tran. PAMI*, 17(7):696-710.

Okada H., Steffens J., Maurer T., Hong H., Elagin E., Neven H., and Malsburg C. (1998), The Bochum/USC Face Recognition System, *Face Recognition: From Theory to Applications*, Springer Verlag.

Osuna, E., Freund, R., Girosi, F. (1997), Training Support Vector Machines: An Application to Face Detection, In *Proceedings Computer Vision and Pattern Recognition*.

Pentland A. and Turk M.(1991), Eigenfaces for recognition, *Journal of Cognitive Neuroscience*, 3(1):71-86.

Phillips P. J., Moon H., Rauss P., and Rizvi S. (1997), The FERET Evaluation Methodology for Face-Recognition Algorithms, *In Proceedings Computer Vision and Pattern Recognition*, 137-143.

Phillips P. J. and Rauss P (1997), The Face Recognition Technology (FERET) Program, *In Proceedings 1997 ONDCP International Technology Symposium – Harnessing Technology to Support the National Drug Control Strategy*.

Phillips P. J., Rauss P., and Der S. (1996), FERET (Face Recognition Technology) Recognition Algorithm Development and Test Report, *Technical Report ARL-TR #995, U.S. Army Research Laboratory*.

Phillips P. J., Wechsler, H., Huang, J., and Rauss, P. (1998), The FERET Database and Evaluation Procedure for Face Recognition Algorithms, *Image and Vision Computing* (to appear).

Rizvi S., Phillips P.J., and Moon H. (1998), The FERET Verification Testing Protocol for Face Recognition Algorithms, *The IEEE Third International Conference on Automatic Face and Gesture Recognition* (to appear).

Samal A. and Iyengar, P. (1992), Automatic Recognition and Analysis of Human Faces and Facial Expressions: A Survey, *Pattern Recognition* **25**, 65-77.

Swets D. and Weng J. (1996), Using Discriminant Eigenfeatures for Image Retrieval, *IEEE Trans. PAMI*, 18(8):831-836.

Wilder J. (1994), Face Recognition using Transform Coding of Grayscale Projections and the Neural Tree Network, *Artificial Neural Networks with applications in speech and vision*, 520-536, Chapman Hall.

Wiskott L., Fellous J.M., Kruger N., and Malsburg C.(1997), Face Recognition by Elastic bunch graph matching, *IEEE Trans. PAMI*, 17(7):775-779.

Zhao W., Krishnaswamy A., Chellappa R., Swets D. L., and Weng J. (1998), Discriminant Analysis of Principal Components for Face Recognition, *Face Recognition: From Theory to Applications*, Springer Verlag.

Active Vision-based Face Recognition: Issues, Applications and Techniques

Massimo Tistarelli and Enrico Grosso

University of Genoa
Department of Communication, Computer and Systems Science (DIST)
Computer Vision Laboratory
Via Opera Pia 13 - 16145 Genoa, Italy

Abstract. In the literature the recognition task has been generally considered in a *passive* perspective, where everything is static and there is no definite relation between the object and its environment.

The capability of the observer to move and to perform planned fixations, is very important to give a better description of the subject during the acquisition of the model database and also for recognition. Moreover, a selective attentional mechanism allows to reduce the amount of information needed to describe a database of objects. This is accomplished both at the task level, by performing planned fixations, and at the sensor level, by adopting an appropriate sampling of the image. In this paper, several aspects related to the application of active vision techniques to face recognition are discussed.

A practical system (currently under development within an European research project), encompassing the active vision paradigm, is described. Several experiments on face recognition and also identity verification, performed on real images, are presented.

Keywords. Face recognition, face verification, visual processing, active vision, singular value decomposition.

1 Introduction

The automatic detection of person's identity is a very interesting issue both in social and industrial environments. As an example consider the following applications:

- surveillance;
- law-enforcement;
- identity verification - secure access control;
- smart interfaces;
- home marketing (World Wide Web).

Many approaches exist for the authentication/recognition of a person's identity, like fingerprint match, retinal scan, voice recognition, hand geometry, signature comparison and also visual recognition. Few of these methods are very reliable for automated person verification and, very often, they reflect a very low social acceptability.

The recognition of individuals from images of the face has many advantages over other methods:

- a limited hardware is required (PC-based workstation, frame grabber and b/w camera);
- there is no need to make major changes to the environment;
- the response time can be very short (with low-cost computing resources);
- the social implications are very favourable and may improve the man-machine interaction.

At present, few commercial systems exist for the recognition of human faces[1]. In order to achieve an acceptable reliability level for the introduction of this technology in the industry and in social life, there is still much work to be done. This paper presents a step beyond, introducing an improvement in current techniques for face recognition.

2 Recognition and Active Vision

Recognition is possibly the final motivation for any vision system either artificial or natural (with different objectives, of course). In the literature the recognition task has been generally considered under the most general assumptions:

"recognize any object and its pose in a scene (without any other objects) or locate any object in an unknown environment (or a picture)"

This is an ill-posed problem (a unique solution does not exist and/or the search space is not continuous). Certainly the main reason for this ambitious proposal must be searched in the challenging ability of humans to recognize objects quite quickly. But, is this ability due to a particular efficiency of the search strategy in the model database? or is it due to the computational power of the inference engine (the brain)? without any doubt these are two relevant characteristics of the human brain, but these are not necessarily the primary reasons for the efficiency of the human visual system. There are other mechanisms in natural perceptual systems which are purposively designed to:

1. reduce the complexity of the visual process;
2. optimize the resources required to accomplish the task.

There are several examples in psychophysics experiments where a subject is asked to find objects in pictures within different environments [1, 2]. The recognition time always depends on the context in which the object is put. In fact, it is rather complex to understand impossible or unexpected scenes, for example to recognize a car on a roof in a picture of a landscape. Therefore, the knowledge of the environment and expectations are of central importance

---

[1] They are all based on neural networks which have the intrinsic limitation of being quite inefficient when simulated on conventional computers. Moreover, neural nets can perform a good generalization, but the performance degrade significantly as the number of images to be handled increases.

for recognition in humans and are among the primary reasons for efficient recognition.

The motivation for this mechanism is practical and pragmatic: a perceptual system and the world where it lives cannot be separated. Basically because the perception/recognition process is well tuned for survival and other activities which are performed within known environments. On the other hand, there is simply too much that can be known about "the world" for a vision system to allow the definition of a general-purpose, complete description. Therefore, we have to accept some limitations (as even the human visual system does) but with the goal of accomplishing some useful activities.

In other words, it is possible to conceive a general-purpose recognition system, but, in order to pursue a feasible application (survival in a jungle for an ape, survival in a metropolis for a human being), generalization must be viewed within a precise framework: the task to be performed.

All natural perceptual systems are capable of interacting with the environment and get as much information as needed, purposively controlling the flow of input data, but also limiting the amount of information acquired from the sensory system [3, 4, 5, 6, 7, 8]. The anatomy of the human visual system is a clear example: despite the formidable acuity in the fovea centralis (1 minute of arc) and the wide field of view (about 140×200 degrees of solid angle), the optic nerve is composed of only 1 million nerve fibers. The space-variant distribution of the cells in the retina allows a formidable data flow reduction. In fact, the same resolution would result in a space-invariant sensor of about 600,000,000 pixels [9].

Another important perceptual mechanism related to the data acquisition process, is the attention mechanism. Again, as not all (visual in our case) input data is relevant for a given task, the perceptual system must be capable of making a selection of the input signal in various dimensions: "signal space", depth, motion etc. The selection is controlled by a proper attention mechanism through ad-hoc band-limiting or focusing processes.

One example is gaze control: whenever an expected event is detected within the visual field, a motor command is given to the head-eye motor system to move the gaze toward that point in space. In the same way, the vergence of a binocular system in the primates can be adjusted to direct the gaze of both eyes on the same point in space, to put in focus an object at a given depth.

The active vision paradigm takes into account these and other considerations related to existing perceptual systems, to realize artificial visual systems which are able to perform a given task under general assumptions [10]. This challenging approach requires a multidisciplinary effort from neurobiology to control theory and from psychophysics to image analysis, and consequently the coordinated work of different research teams.

2.1 Fixation and recognition

What is the role of fixation in the recognition process? Yarbus, in his work on ocular movements [11], demonstrated that the sequence of fixations performed by the human oculo-motor system, strongly depends on the task (in this case the question asked to the subject). He also showed that the eyes perform a particular sequence of fixations, if the subject has to recognize a part or a person in the scene. The eyes are successively directed toward the parts of the scene containing the most relevant features [2]. This motion strategy suggests that the motion of the eyes is particularly important for recognition (at least in the human visual system).

2.2 Space-variant imaging

It is generally assumed that, to recognize an object, it is necessary to have a high resolution description of the most salient features of the interest object. This can be accomplished either by "capturing", in rapid succession, these parts of the scene[3] or moving an interest window on a high resolution image [14].

Certainly object features are important for recognition, but it is not said that the object itself is better characterized by the most prominent features taken in isolation, rather than by the context in which they are located. For this reason it is not sufficient to scan the scene or the image with a high resolution window, but it is also necessary to provide some information on the area around the window. A way to meet these requirements is to adopt a space-variant sampling strategy of the image, where the central part of the visual field is sampled at a higher resolution than the periphery. In this way the peripheral part of the visual field, coded at low resolution, can still be used to describe the context in which high resolution data is located.

A great advantage of this approach is the considerable data reduction with respect to adopting a uniform resolution schema, while a wide field of view (i.e. peripheral vision) is preserved [6, 15]. On the other hand, by adopting a space-variant image representation it becomes necessary to move the sensor to grab all the distinctive features within the face.

Many different models of space-variant image geometries have been proposed, like the truncated pyramid [14], the reciprocal wedge transform (RWT) [16], the complex logarithmic mapping (CLM) [17, 18] and the log-polar mapping [19, 20]. Among them, the log-polar mapping is starting to receive a considerably increasing interest. The analytical formulation of the log-polar mapping describes the mapping that occurs between the retina (retinal plane (ρ, θ)) and the visual cortex (log-polar or cortical plane (η, ξ)). The derived

---

[2] Eklundh [12, 13] demonstrated that these points can be recovered through a scale-space analysis of the image.

[3] This mechanism implies an efficient motion control to quickly direct the gaze toward different areas of the scene.

logarithmic-polar law, taking into account the linear increment in size of the receptive fields, going from the central region (fovea) towards the periphery, is given by:

$$\left\{ \begin{array}{l} \eta = q\,\theta \\ \xi = \ln_a \frac{\rho}{\rho_0} \end{array} \right. \tag{2.1}$$

where a defines the amount of overlapping among neighbouring receptive fields, ρ_0 is the radius of the innermost circle, $\frac{1}{q}$ corresponds to the minimum angular resolution of the log-polar layout (see figure 2.1) and (ρ, θ) are the polar coordinates. They are related to the conventional Cartesian reference system by:

$$\begin{array}{l} x = \rho \cos\theta \\ y = \rho \sin\theta \end{array} \tag{2.2}$$

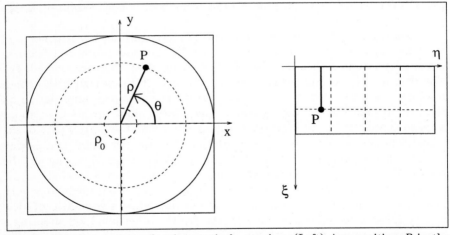

Figure 2.1. Parameters of retino-cortical mapping. (Left) Any position P in the retinal plane can be expressed in terms of (ρ, θ) or (x, y) coordinates. (Right) In the log-polar plane the same position is identified by (η, ξ).

At present the log-polar transformation is computed at frame rate by using special re-mapping software routines. Hardware boards [21] and prototypes of space variant CCD's [22, 23] have already been designed and manufactured in the last years and a compact camera using C-MOS technology will be soon available [24] .

2.3 Active Vision

The term active vision comes from the notion of an observer which is able to move and interact with the environment, to optimally accomplish a given task.

This means not only the collection of "more images" of a scene, but the development of proper mechanisms, devices and tools to control the acquisition and processing of perceptual data.

Active vision systems have mechanisms that can actively control camera parameters such as position, orientation, focus, zoom aperture, and vergence (in a binocular system) in response to the requirements of the task *and* external stimuli. They may also have features such as spatially variant (foveal) sensors. More broadly, active vision encompass *attention*, selective sensing in space, resolution and time, whether it is achieved by modifying physical camera parameters or the way data is processed after acquisition.

All these capabilities require appropriate hardware and software tools. In particular, to facilitate the development of artificial systems encompassing the active vision paradigm, mechanical devices have been designed which allow to move cameras under computer control. These devices are also called robot or camera heads.

2.4 Robot heads

There are several commercially available pan and tilt heads that can be used within an active vision system. Some of these products consist of single pan and tilt units, that can carry a camera on top. Recently however, other devices appeared in the market, that consist of a camera with pan and tilt capabilities. In the latter cases, there is no need to purchase an external camera to integrate in the robot head. Usually the motion is controlled by a computer either sending commands through a serial port or writing instructions into registers mapped in the input/output space.

There are a number of pan & tilt units that were designed for robotics applications and therefore allow accurate motion control. On the other hand, there are several models of pan & tilt units with an integrated camera, based on a well engineered design for tele-conferencing applications. Although the motion specifications are in general poorer than the other pan & tilt units, the cost (in the order of 1,000-2,000 $) is very attractive especially since a color camera is already included.

A number of advanced pan-tilt camera heads have been developed in various academic or research institutions [4].

---

[4] A comprehensive list of research institutions which developed camera heads can be found on the WEB at:
"http://www.cis.upenn.edu/ grasp/head/headpage/headpage.html"

Probably the first research camera head has been realized at the University of Rochester, the Department of Computer Science [25, 26]. This binocular head has two movable color CCD television cameras providing input to a MaxVideo pipelined image-processing system. One motor controls the tilt angle of the two-eye platform, and separate motors control each camera's pan angle, providing independent vergence control. The controllers allow both velocity and position commands and data read-back. The main feature of the camera controllers is their speed. Camera movements of 400 degrees per second can be achieved, approximating the 700 degrees per second speed of human eye movements. The actuators and cameras are hold by a Unimation PUMA 760 robot arm, to allow arbitrary translation and positioning of the head within the robot workspace.

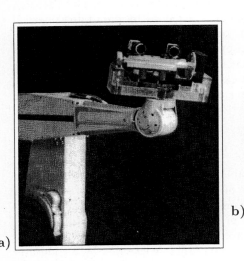

b)

a)

Figure 2.2. (a) The University of Rochester robot head. (b)The Aalborg University robot head developed within the VAP Esprit project.

Another interesting architecture is the robot head developed within the VAP (*Vision As Process*) research project of the European Union [5]. The VAP head [27, 28] includes 12 degrees of freedom, all independently controllable. That includes 2 ERNITEC zoom lenses for control of zoom, aperture, and focus. The head has also facilities for independent pan for each of the two cameras. A combined set of pan and tilt motors are used for emulation of neck movements. The eye movements may be performed at 100 deg/sec,

---

[5] The partners involved in the VAP project are: CVAP Royal Inst. of Tech. (Sweden) - Aalborg University (Denmark) - LIFIA-IMAG (France) - University of Genoa DIST (Italy) - Linkoping University (Sweden) - University of Haifa (Israel)

while neck movements have a maximum speed of 10 deg/sec. The mechanical degrees of freedom (eyes and neck) exploit NEWPORT/Micro-controle rotational stages. All the motion control hardware is interfaced to a Motorola MVME 147 computer running OS/9.

The micro robot head developed by Vision Applications inc. and Boston University has several characteristic features [22]. The camera consists of a miniature commercially available CCD image sensor and a custom lens assembly mounted on a specially designed actuator. The micro camera is driven by a *Spherical Pointing Motor*, which is a novel pan-tilt actuator using three orthogonal motor windings to achieve open-loop pan-tilt motion of the camera in a small, low-power package. The functional principle is to orient a permanent magnet to the magnetic field induced by three orthogonal coils by applying the appropriate ratio of current for the coils. The prototype camera is 4 × 5 × 6 cm and weights only 160 grams. The raw video signal coming from the CCD sensor is processed at video rate on a DSP processing board to obtain space-variant log-polar images.

a)

b)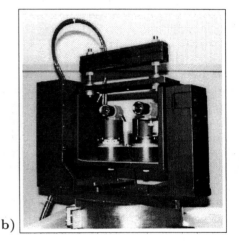

Figure 2.3. (a) The Boston University/Vision Applications miniature camera head. (b) The robot head developed at DIST.

The robot head developed at LIRA-Lab, DIST University of Genoa is shown in figure 2.3 (b). This is a binocular image acquisition system provided with four rotational degrees of freedom [29] . The two cameras have independent vergence movements and common tilt. Direct drive DC motors are used for pan and tilt while stepper motors with reduction gears are used for vergence. The whole camera platform can rotate around a common pan axis, providing the system with a mobility very similar to the human neck.

The peak velocity for pan and tilt is 190 deg/sec and the acceleration is 1300 deg/sec^2, while for the vergence the peak velocity is about 1400 deg/sec and the acceleration 80000 deg/sec^2. A Pentium-based PC hosts a Klinger MM2000 four axis control board and a Matrox IM-640 board set, which is used to perform fast image processing.

3 Visual face recognition

The identification of individuals given a database of known faces is a challenging problem which has been studied with a considerable effort in the last years. Dealing with access verification from image data, there are two distinct problems: face detection (i.e. to detect a face within an image) and identity verification (i.e. to identify a person given an image of the face). There are many approaches to face detection and verification. In general, it is possible to distinguish between feature-based and iconic-based techniques. Many algorithms have been studied and implemented based on both categories [30, 31, 32, 33, 34].

Given the rich representation required to characterize a human face, iconic data seem naturally best suited to convey all the needed information, and also to allow a sufficient degree of generalization [32]. On the contrary, image features of a face, like the edges of the eyes, eyebrows or lips are not always stable when slightly varying the illumination or the face expression [35].

The proposed face recognition system is based on an eigenvector representation of the face database, where individuals are represented by a collection of fixations rather than a single, high resolution image. In order to improve the recognition reliability, a verification step, based on the analysis of the gray level histograms, is also incorporated in the system to validate the correctness of the matching.

The proposed system has been tested on a limited database of subjects, yielding up to 98% of successful recognition.

4 The VIRSBS system

The ideas and methodologies developed in this paper are an integral part of a research project funded by the European Union involving several academic and industrial partners[6]. The main goal of the VIRSBS (*Visual Intelligent Recognition for Secure Banking Services*) project is to realize a prototype autonomous station for personal identity verification. This station will include

---

[6] The partners involved in the VIRSBS project are: DIST University of Genoa - Italy (E. Grosso and M. Tistarelli); IST ISR University of Lisbon - Portugal (J. Costeira and J. Santos Victor); LMI EPFL Lausanne- Switzerland (J. Bigun); Logitron Srl - Italy (L. Gagliardi); Maynooth College - Ireland (D. Vernon)

all the features required to be integrated into a new generation of automated security check-point along corridors, passageways or access doors, and in the next-generation of automatic teller machines (ATM).

The developed system for person identification is sketched in figure 4.1.

Figure 4.1. The VIRSBS ATM station.

The central camera is used to first acquire an image of the whole face of the subject; then 4 face features are selected on the face. The image coordinates of the selected points are used to direct the gaze, of the two cameras on the sides, toward the face features and then acquire an image for each feature Once the images of the face features have been acquired, they are re-sampled to obtain a log-polar space-variant representation of the same which is 30×64 pixels. The sampled images are used, either to build/update a face database or to recognize the subject.

5 Principal Component Analysis (PCA) and recognition in "face space"

The principal component analysis approach for recognition is aimed to the reduction in dimensionality of the data space [33, 34]. The database of face images (the set of "known" faces) is coded by the "eigen-images" computed from the original set of face images.

This method proved to be quite successful, but with one limitation: a high resolution model is used to describe every element within a face, while, as already pointed out, different areas in the face have different relevance for

Figure 4.2. Samples from the set of 152 images used in the experiments. All views with neutral and smiling expression are shown.

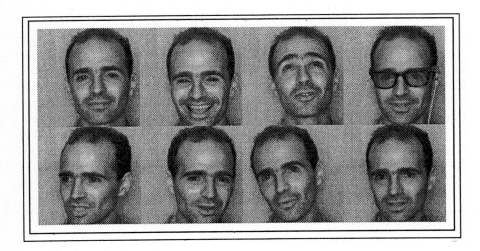

Figure 4.3. All views acquired for one subject.

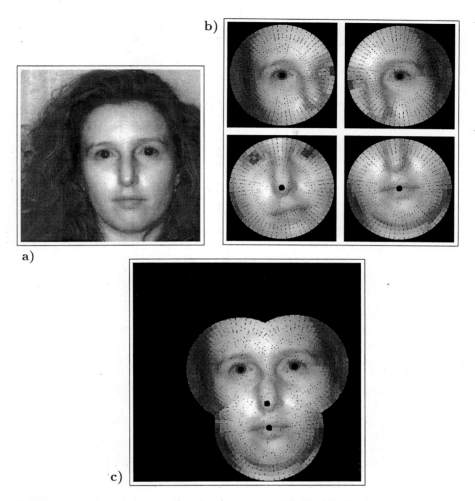

Figure 4.4. (a) First view of one subject. (b) Log-polar images (eyes, nose and lips) extracted from the subject in (a), represented in the Cartesian plane. (c) Reconstruction of the face from the 4 fixations. This view is equivalent to the information coded in the face-space.

recognition. In the human visual system this problem is overcome by collecting several pictures of the face, by directing the gaze toward different points such as the eyes, the lips and the nose. This mechanism has the consequence of limiting the bandwidth of the signal to be processed and thus reducing the time required for recognition.

The procedure adopted to build the model database of the known individuals is as follows:

1. Acquire a set of N views from each known individual (with different facial expression and slight motion), each view is composed of P space-variant images obtained by directing the gaze toward different points on the same face. From each set of P images (each image has a resolution 30×64 pixels) obtain a one-dimensional vector $\hat{\mathbf{V}}_\mathbf{k}$ and compute the difference with the average vector of all the imaged subjects

$$\begin{aligned} \mathbf{V}_k &= \hat{\mathbf{V}}_\mathbf{k} - \boldsymbol{\Psi} \\ \boldsymbol{\Psi} &= \tfrac{1}{M} \sum_i \hat{\mathbf{V}}_\mathbf{i} \end{aligned} \tag{5.1}$$

where M is equal to the number of subjects multiplied by the number of views N.

2. The M vectors $\mathbf{V}_k$ form the columns of the matrix $\mathbf{A}$. The face space is defined by the M eigenvectors of the covariance matrix $\mathbf{C} = \mathbf{A}\mathbf{A}^t$. The eigenvalues λ_k are used to rank the associated eigenvectors $\mathbf{U}_k$. The eigenvectors corresponding to the lower eigenvalues are discarded.

In order to characterize each individual in the database also the projection of each face image into the face space is computed and stored in the database.

$$\omega_l = \mathbf{U}_l \mathbf{V}_k \qquad\qquad l = 1, \cdots, M \tag{5.2}$$

The vector $\boldsymbol{\Omega}_k = (\omega_1, \cdots, \omega_M)_k$, stored for each individual, is the average of the vectors computed for each view recorded from the same person.

During the on-line recognition phase a new face image is first "normalized" (to the "dc component" $\boldsymbol{\Psi}$ of the set of known faces), then it is projected into the face space by computing the vector $\boldsymbol{\Omega}$. The face is recognized according to the Euclidean distance from the projection of each known individual:

$$\epsilon_k = ||\boldsymbol{\Omega} - \boldsymbol{\Omega}_k|| \tag{5.3}$$

The new face is recognized to belong to the individual corresponding to the minimum value of the error. An upper threshold is set to determine if the face image does not belong to any known individual.

5.1 Incremental object representation

Within a face recognition system it is desirable to have an incremental representation of the objects [36]. By using space-variant fixations, more and more detail can be added, just by moving the camera to select new features.

The Karhunen-Loève procedure (explained in the previous section) is equivalent to the singular values decomposition (SVD) of the matrix $\mathbf{A}$ whose columns are the image vectors $\mathbf{V}_i$:

$$\mathbf{A} = \mathbf{U}\, \Sigma\, \mathbf{W^t} \qquad \Sigma = \begin{bmatrix} \sigma_0 & 0 & \cdots & 0 \\ 0 & \sigma_1 & \cdots & 0 \\ \vdots & 0 & \ddots & \vdots \\ 0 & \cdots & 0 & \sigma_N \end{bmatrix} \qquad (5.4)$$

$\mathbf{U}$ is a $M \times N$ matrix whose columns are the eigenvectors of $\mathbf{A}$, Σ is a $N \times N$ diagonal matrix of the singular values σ_i of $\mathbf{A}$, and the columns of $\mathbf{W}$ represent a base for the null space of $\mathbf{A}$. The image eigenspace is defined by the r columns of $\mathbf{U}$ corresponding to the higher σ_i. From the r base vectors, 2 new matrixes $\mathbf{U'}$ and $\mathbf{W'}$ are obtained, with reduced dimensions [7]:

$$\mathbf{A'} = \mathbf{U'}\, \Sigma'\, \mathbf{W'^t} \qquad (5.5)$$

Given a new matrix $\mathbf{B}$ composed of n image vectors $\mathbf{V}_k$, the existing database can be updated simply by recomputing the SVD from the reduced matrix $\mathbf{A'}$:

$$\mathbf{A'B} = \mathbf{U'}\, \Sigma'\, \mathbf{W'^t B} = \mathbf{U''}\, \Sigma''\, \mathbf{W''^t} \qquad (5.6)$$

also in this case, a subset of the $r + n$ eigen-images can be selected, according to the singular values. The possibility to retain less eigenvectors than the number n of added images, depends from the capability of the existing eigenspace to generalize a subject (or a pose) from the already computed eigenvectors.

5.2 Histogram-based verification

In order for a new subject to be recognized, the Euclidean distance in equation (5.3) must be lower than a given threshold. Due to several reasons (motion of the head, objects occluding the face etc.), sometimes the Euclidean distance is higher than the threshold; in this case the recognition fails and it is not possible to determine which is the correct match.

---

[7] The new matrixes $\mathbf{U'}$ and $\mathbf{W'}$ are obtained by first ordering the σ_i, ranking the columns of $\mathbf{U}$ and $\mathbf{W}$ according to the order of the σ_i, and finally discarding the columns corresponding to the lower σ_i. An adaptive threshold is applied to select the higher σ_i, which depends on the highest eigenvalue and on the mean of the eigenvalues.

It has been observed that the outline of the gray level histogram of a face image is quite different for each subject, while it is generally stable under varying pose and illumination of the same face (see figure 5.1) [8]. The similarity of the histograms can be used to verify the similarity of the matched faces corresponding to the 4 lower PCA distances.

Whenever the normalized Euclidean distance is higher than 1, the value of the correlation between the histograms of the subject to be recognized and the subjects with the 4 lower distances, is used as matching score. In all other case both the Euclidean distance and the correlation are used to recognize the new subject. On the other hand, if the correlation of the histograms is lower than a defined threshold value, the subject is labeled as not recognized, or not present in the database.

6 Face recognition experiments

In order to analyze the performance of the system, a sequence of 152 views from 19 subjects was acquired. The resolution of the images is 512x512 pixels with 8 bits per pixel. For each view 4 log-polar images (30 × 64 pixels) were extracted, centered on the eyes, nose and lips. In our application each face vector is composed of 1 to 4 space-variant images, each obtained by re-sampling the original high-resolution image at a different fixation point (see figure 4.4). Each vector of the sequence differs for the expression of the face, a slight motion of the head or partial occlusion of the face (see figure 4.2 and 4.3). The vectors obtained were used to compute the eigenvectors describing the space of known faces.

The high resolution image corresponding to the first view of each subject was also used to compute the gray level histogram of the subject. Many databases composed by 16, 17 or 18 subjects have been used to test the system. One database included all 4 fixations; other 4 "modular" databases were built containing only one fixation per subject. Several recognition tests were run where each view of each subject is matched against each database. The output was categorized according to 4 classes:

A) the subject is correctly recognized as best match, corresponding to the lowest Euclidean distance;

B) the correct subject is selected among the 4 best matches, corresponding to the highest histogram correlation;

C) the correct subject is not shown among the 4 best matches;

D) a wrong subject is recognized as best match;

Some test results are summarized in table 6.1, 6.2 and 6.3. As it can be noticed, a maximum of 98% recognition score (including outputs of class "A"

---

[8] It is worth noting that a change in illumination only involves a translation along one axis of the gray level histogram, without affecting its shape.

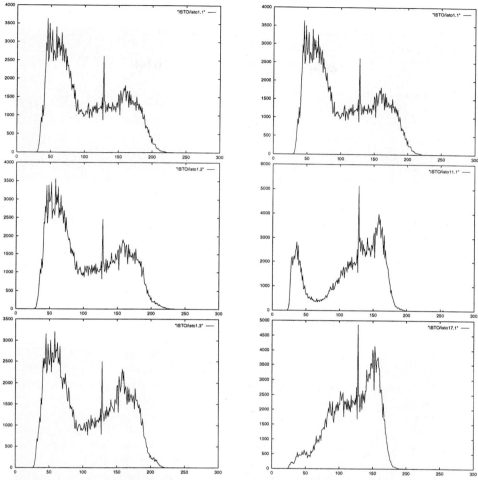

Figure 5.1. Example gray level histograms obtained: (left) from the same subject under different poses; (right) different subjects under the same pose.

a) b)

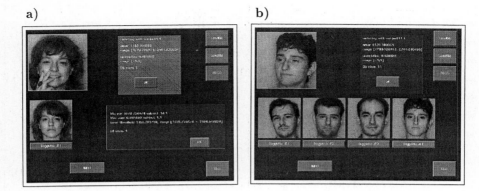

Figure 5.2. (a) Example of output of one successful recognition of class "A".
(b) Output of one successful recognition of class "B". In this case the recognition
was performed using a database including only the fixation relative to the left eye.
It is worth noting that the correct subject (4th from left in the picture) corresponds
to the highest histogram correlation score.

a) b)

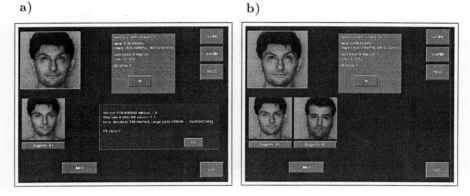

Figure 6.1. Example of recognition output for the same subject: (a) all 4 fixations
have been used, and the correct subject is recognized; (b) only the fixations centered
on the eyes have been used, and a recognition of class "B" is obtained. The correct
subject still corresponds to the highest histogram correlation score.

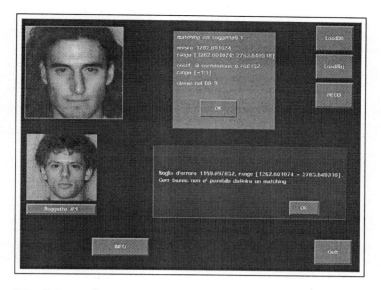

Figure 6.2. Output of one erroneous recognition of class "D". In this case the subject head was slightly rotated toward the front. The original view included in the database is shown in figure 4.2.

and "B") is obtained by using a database with two views per subject and not recognizing the profile views. smiling face is always correctly recognized. Despite of the great amount of deformation in the smiling view, it is remarkable how the system is still capable of achieving 100% correct recognition. On the contrary, the profile views can not always be generalized by the eigenspace from the one or two views included in the database.

Considering one "fail" example, reported in figure 6.2, it is worth noting that, even though the eigen-image representation is capable of generalizing slightly rotated views, it is very hard to recognize a subject with a considerable amount of motion in depth (in the example the head was rotated toward the front). In order to correct this problem, it may be useful to add more views to the database (the database used was composed of just 2 views) including "enlarged" versions of the same face. Another way to be explored, is to exploit the log-polar scale-invariance property into the eigen-image representation.

7 Visual identity verification

One of the major challenges of the VIRSBS project is to avoid the use of a bulk database including all possible bank customers. For this reason, a

Table 6.1. Recognition score obtained from 5 databases with 16 subjects, one view per subject in the database. The outputs are obtained after 128 recognition tests with the 16 subjects and 8 views per subject.

Output	DB 4 fixations	DB left eye	DB right eye	DB nose	DB mouth
A	74.3%	63.3%	68.8%	65.6%	64.8%
B	18%	27.8%	21.1%	23.4%	25%
C	4.7%	9.4%	7.8%	10%	8.6%
D	3%	1.5%	2.3%	1%	1.6%

Table 6.2. Recognition score obtained from 5 databases with 16 subjects, one view per subject in the database. The outputs are obtained after 96 recognition tests with the 16 subjects and 6 views per subject. The profile views (5 and 6) are not included in the test.

Output	DB 4 fixations	DB left eye	DB right eye	DB nose	DB mouth
A	85.4%	72.9%	80.2%	80.2%	73%
B	9.4%	18.8%	12.5%	15.7%	19.8%
C	3.1%	7.3%	5.2%	3.1%	6.2%
D	2.1%	1%	2.1%	1%	1%

Table 6.3. Recognition score obtained from 5 databases with 16 subjects, two views per subject in the database. The outputs are obtained after 96 recognition tests with the 16 subjects and 6 views per subject. The profile views (5 and 6) are not included in the test.

Output	DB 4 fixations	DB left eye	DB right eye	DB nose	DB mouth
A	88.6%	83.3%	86.5%	86.5%	80.2%
B	9.4%	7.3%	6.3%	9.4%	17.7%
C	1%	7.3%	6.2%	3.1%	2.1%
D	1%	2.1%	1%	1%	0%

representation of the user's face must be recorded on the personal ATM smart card [9], and this should be matched (verified) against the imaged subject.

In this section two techniques for addressing the face verification problem are described. The robustness of the algorithm and also the implications of the memory limitation imposed by the available smart card technology have been considered.

Face verification is related to but differs from face recognition. Therefore, methods that are successfully applied for the former may not give good results with the latter and vice-versa.

For face recognition the population of all possible subjects (not including the impostors) is known a priori (the database). This is unknown for verification: everyone can be an impostor.

7.1 Face verification by using the PCA technique

In order to apply the PCA or "eigen-images" approach for face verification, a database is built from a set of images of the same subject, showing several characteristic poses and facial expressions. The input face image is compared with this "database".

In order to test the PCA approach for face verification, a database composed of a set of images relative to the same fixation (the left eye) from the same subject under several poses was built and a recognition test performed with many different subjects. From the test set in figure 4.2 and 4.3, only the first 8 images were used in all tests.

In the first instance, a database was composed of only two eigenvectors. The diagram in figure 7.1 (a) reports the distances computed for the two poses not included in the database of the correct subject (first two points) and the same poses related to the remaining seven subjects. In order to verify the scalability of the errors with the number of eigenvectors, one and successively two more eigenvectors were added to the original database (see figure 7.1 (b)).

A very low Euclidean distance was expected when projecting images of the same subject represented in the database, while a very high distance was expected from the other individuals.

As it can be noticed, even though in both cases the correct subject corresponds to the lower Euclidean distance (5.3), there is still one subject showing a very similar error. This is probably due to the fact that two or four eigenvectors are not sufficient to make a distinction between the two subjects. On the other hand, by using 4 eigenvectors, already 8 Kbytes are being used, therefore it is still possible to improve the representation by adding more fixations and characterize better the person's identity.

---

[9] A smart card or chip card, is a bank card with a small memory on it, This is used to store data about the customer's account and also data for identification.

7.2 Face verification by using intensity matching

A much simpler technique has been tested as well where one image of the subject is simply matched with all the others. The matching is performed by computing the correlation between two images.

The images are first "normalized" to the average gray level, the pixel by pixel difference of intensities is computed and finally the integral of the differences is used as the measure of the "distance" between the two images. A *Khoros* block diagram of the algorithm is shown in figure 7.2. In figure 7.3 the results obtained by matching the first subject with the first 8 subject in the data set are shown. As in the PCA experiments the X axis represents the poses and used for each subject, while the Y axis is the computed distance from the first image of the first subject. As it can be noticed this technique is rather more stable than the PCA verification method.

There may be many reasons for this. The first one is that the PCA technique is best suited to model a face given a high number of samples, which is normally required to perform recognition. On the other hand, the generalization power of the PCA can have a counter effect if too few eigenvectors are used and, as in the tests performed, if there are not enough features or they are not sufficiently distinctive to characterize the subject.

In the future more experiments will be performed to verify if the addition of more features (two eyes and nose/mouth) can improve the performance of the PCA for verification. Another issue is the resolution of the log-polar images used to represent the fixations. Increasing the resolution may improve the discrimination power of the method. On the other hand, the 16 Kbytes limit imposed by the current smart card technology must be considered as well.

8 Conclusion

The identification of individuals by recognition of face images has been considered. The current availability of many motorized camera heads makes it feasible to design a vision system encompassing the active vision paradigm. A system has been described, based on the active vision paradigm, for the recognition of human faces.

Some advantages of the "active" approach for object recognition have been presented, such as:

— the relation between the environment and the recognition process, which is useful both to locate an object and speed up the search in the model database;

— the possibility to move and obtain a better description of the object, both during the model acquisition and in the recognition phase;

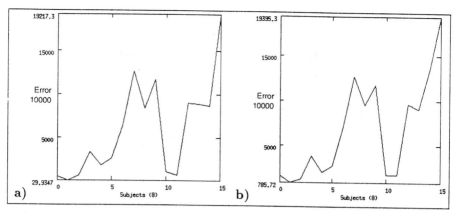

Figure 7.1. Distance computed from the PCA technique using (a) 2 and (b) 4 eigenvectors. On the X axis two poses for each of the 8 subjects are plotted. The first two abscissa represent the two poses of the subject coded in the database. The computed Euclidean distance is shown on the Y axis.

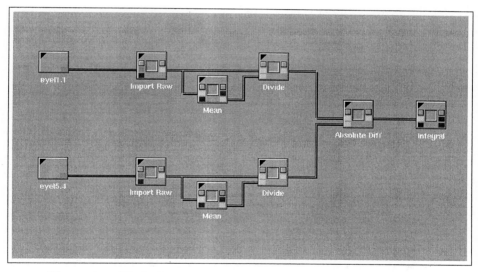

Figure 7.2. Block diagram showing the basic cell for image matching

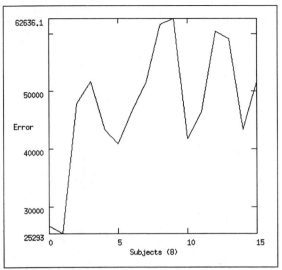

Figure 7.3. Results obtained from the matching technique. The leftmost part represents the matching score for the first subject.

— the motion of the observer associated with a space-variant representation of the images, allows a reduction in the size of the model database and consequently also the time required for recognition.

The proposed method applies a principal component analysis to an image ensemble to reduce the search space for known subjects. The images of faces are acquired and coded as a collection of space-variant fixations, obtained from a binocular camera head. The system proved to be quite successful on a set of 152 images, reaching a recognition score of up to 98%.

The PCA technique has been applied straightforwardly to perform also face verification tests. The preliminary results obtained already show that the discrimination power of the PCA may require a greater memory storage capacity than what is currently available from the smart card technology. On the other hand, a simple experiment of direct image matching suggests a greater stability requiring far less memory usage. A further investigation is required to determine whether using a different number of fixations and/or poses to represent a subject with the PCA technique, may improve the robustness and stability of the method. On the other hand, even the direct intensity matching may be successfully applied with few improvements and tests, and certainly deserves further attention.

Several aspects have been addressed explicitly and many are still under investigation. For example, one topic which is still to be more deeply investigated is the relation between the log-polar representation and the principal component analysis obtained from the eigen-face approach. This analysis

285

would be very important to further explore the advantages of a space-variant representation for recognition.

Acknowledgements

We thank D. Ferralasco and R. Ferrari and M. Perrone for their valuable contribution to the development of this paper.
This work has been partially funded by the LTR Esprit Project 21894 "VIRSBS".

References

1. A. Guzman. Analysis of curved line drawings using context and global information. *Machine Intelligence*, 6, 1971.
2. I. Biederman. Human image understanding: Recent research and theory. *CVGIP*, 32:29–73, 1985.
3. Y. Aloimonos, I. Weiss, and A. Bandyopadhyay. Active vision. *Intern. Journal of Computer Vision*, 1(4):333–356, 1988.
4. R. K. Bajcsy. Active perception. *Proc. IEEE*, 76(8):996–1005, 1988.
5. D.H. Ballard. Animate vision. *Artificial Intelligence*, 48:57–86, 1991.
6. G. Sandini and M. Tistarelli. Vision and space-variant sensing. In H. Wechsler, editor, *Neural Networks for Perception: Human and Machine Perception*. Academic Press, 1991.
7. Y. Aloimonos. Purposize, qualitative, active vision. *CVGIP: Image Understanding*, 56(special issue on qualitative, active vision):3–129, July 1992.
8. M. Tistarelli and G. Sandini. Dynamic aspects in active vision. *CVGIP: Image Understanding*, 56:108–129, July 1992.
9. E. L. Schwartz, D. N. Greve, and G. Bonmassar. Space-variant active vision: definition, overview and examples. *Neural Networks*, 8(7/8):1297–1308, 1995.
10. M. Swain and M. Stricker. Promising directions in active vision. *Intern. Journal of Computer Vision*, 11(2):109–126, 1993.
11. A.L. Yarbus. *Eye Movements and Vision*. Plenum Press, 1967.
12. K. Brunnstrom, T. Lindeberg, and J. Eklundh. Active detection and classification of junctions by foveation with a head-eye system guided by the scale-space primal sketch. In *Proc. of second European Conference on Computer Vision*, pages 701–709, S. Margherita Ligure (Italy), 1992. Springer Verlag.
13. K. Pahlavan, T. Uhlin, and J. Eklundh. Integrating primary ocular processes. In *Proc. of second European Conference on Computer Vision*, pages 526–541, S. Margherita Ligure (Italy), 1992. Springer Verlag.
14. P. J. Burt. Smart sensing in machine vision. In *Machine Vision: Algorithms, Architectures, and Systems*. Academic Press, 1988.
15. L. Massone, G. Sandini, and V. Tagliasco. Form-invariant topological mapping strategy for 2-d shape recognition. *CVGIP*, 30(2):169–188, 1985.
16. F. Tong and Z.N. Li. The reciprocal-wedge transform for space-variant sensing. In *4th IEEE Intl. Conference on Computer Vision*, pages 330–334, Berlin, 1993.
17. R.C. Jain, S.L. Bartlett, and N. O'Brian. Motion stereo using ego-motion complex logarithmic mapping. *IEEE Trans. on PAMI*, PAMI-9(3):356–369, 1987.

18. E. L. Schwartz. Spatial mapping in the primate sensory projection: Analytic structure and relevance to perception. *Biological Cybernetics*, (25):181–194, 1977.

19. C. F. R. Weiman and G. Chaikin. Logarithmic spiral grids for image processing and display. *Comp. Graphics and Image Processing*, (11):197–226, 1979.

20. G. Sandini and V. Tagliasco. An anthropomorphic retina-like structure for scene analysis. *CGIP*, 14 No.3:365–372, 1980.

21. T.E. Fisher and R.D. Juday. A programmable video image remapper. In *Proc. SPIE*, volume 938, pages 122–128, 1988.

22. B. Bederson, R. Wallace, and E.L. Schwartz. A miniature pan-tilt actuator: the spherical pointing motor. *IEEE Transactions on Robotics and Automation*, (10):298–308, 1994.

23. I. Debusschere, E. Bronckaers, C. Claeys, G. Kreider, J. Van der Spiegel, P. Bellutti, G. Soncini, P. Dario, F. Fantini, and G. Sandini. A 2d retinal ccd sensor for fast 2d shape recognition and tracking. In *Proc. 5th Int. Solid-State Sensor and Transducers*, Montreux, June 25-30 1989.

24. F. Ferrari, G. Sandini, L. Hermans, C. Guerin, A. Manganas, P. Dario, and H. Frowein. Tide project 1038 ibidem, technical annex. Technical report, Ibidem Consortium, June 1994.

25. C.M. Brown. The Rochester robot. Technical Report 257, University of Rochester, Rochester, NY, 1988.

26. D.J. Coombs and C.M. Brown. Real-time binocular smooth pursuit. *Intern. Journal of Computer Vision*, 11(2):147–164, 1993.

27. H.I. Christensen, J. Horstman, and T. Rasmussen. A control theoretical approach to active vision. In *2nd Asian Conf. on Computer Vision*, Singapore, December 1995.

28. K. Pahlavan. *Active Robot Vision and Primary Ocular Processes*. PhD thesis, Royal Institute of Technology, Stockolm, Sweden, May 1993.

29. C. Capurro, F. Panerai, E. Grosso, and G. Sandini. A binocular active vision system using space variant sensors: Exploiting autonomous behaviors for space application. In *Int. Conf. on Digital Signal Processing*, Nicosia, Cyprus, July 1993.

30. I. Craw, D. Tock, and A. Bennett. Finding face features. In *Proc. of second European Conference on Computer Vision*, pages 92–96, S. Margherita Ligure (Italy), 1992. Springer Verlag.

31. V. Bruce, A. Coombes, and R. Richards. Describing the shapes of faces using surface primitives. *Image and Vision Computing*, 11(6):353–363, 1993.

32. R. Brunelli and T. Poggio. Face recognition: Features versus templates. *IEEE Trans. on PAMI*, PAMI-15(10):1042–1052, 1993.

33. L. Sirovich and M. Kirby. Application of the karhunen-loève procedure for the characterization of human faces. *IEEE Trans. on PAMI*, PAMI-12(1):103–108, 1990.

34. M. Turk and A. Pentland. Eigenfaces for recognition. *Journal of Cognitive Neuroscience*, 3(1):71–79, March 1991.

35. G. Robertson and I. Craw. Testing face recognition systems. In *Proc. of 4th British Machine Vision Conference*, pages 25–34, University of Surrey, Guildford (UK), 1993.

36. B.S. Manjunath, S. Chandrasekaran, and Y.F. Wang. An eigenspace update algorithm for image analysis. In *Proc. of the First IEEE International Symposium on Computer Vision*, pages 551–556, Miami (FL), 1995.

Getting Facial Features and Gestures in 3D

Marc Proesmans and Luc Van Gool

Katholieke Universiteit Leuven,
Kard. Mercierlaan 94, 3001 Leuven, Belgium

Abstract In the study of face perception and face animation, there is a growing interest in using 3-D data. The advent of dedicated laser scanners has proved instrumental in this regard. The availability of 3D face models makes it easier to change viewpoints and illumination conditions in perception experiments or to build animated likenesses in graphics. Here we propose to go one step further and also capture face dynamics (visemes, epressions) in 3-D. To that end, an active 3-D acquisition system is proposed, that yields 3-D, textured snapshots from a single image. By the fact that data are captured from a single shot, the face may move during the operation. Alternatively, images can be taken at video rate and for each frame a 3-D reconstruction (still textured if required) can be made. Such 3-D movies can then be used to analyse facial expressions in 3-D, through the tracking of points or features on the face. Preliminary experiments in that direction are presented. The reported work is part of an effort to model facial expressions without taking recourse to the modeling of the underlying physiology.

1   Introduction

An ideal authentication system should allow quite some liberty in the head pose of the person to be checked. Similarly, it would be ideal if the person can be in motion during the control. Insisting on the person freezing before the system would make it rather intrusive or offensive, or at least a bit of a nuisance. It seems easier to reach such goals with 3-D measurements of the face than when only 2-D images are taken. From a 3-D description it is easier to extract viewpoint-invariant characteristics. In order to deal with moving faces, traditional active devices would pose difficulties, however, as they require scanning operations of several seconds. Moreover, only a few of such systems yield the surface texture, which is crucial for face recognition by humans. It stands to reason then to add texture extraction for the recognition of faces by computers.

In the case of face animation for virtual actors, avatars, videophone talking heads, and diverse applications of graphics, the importance of 3-D, textured face descriptions has also been recognised. Starting from such data, efforts have been made to build anatomical models, with detailed models for the skin, muscles and skull [13]. Animation is then guided by the physiological processes that govern the dynamics of this skin/muscle/skull complex. Sometimes video data are used to drive such model, based on the 2-D tracking of features. The question is whether a more phenomenological approach couldn't be more beneficial, due to its simplicity. At the end of the day, humans don't have to know about muscles pulling, pushing, and squeezing skin to 'know' all too well whether a facial expression looks natural or not. Thus, it seems interesting to model facial dynamics directly from observations. This requires measuring the 3-D changes that faces undergo during expressions and this with a sufficiently frequent, temporal sampling. Even if in the end intermediate views would be generated by the interpolation of extremal positions of the facial features, knowledge about intermediate stages may suggest the most appropriate interpolation schemes.

The paper proposes a 3-D acquisition method that fullfills several of these requirements. It extracts 3-D information ánd the corresponding surface texture from image data that can be captured at video-rate. This is the basis for its capacity to densely sample the changes that 3-D shapes undergo over time.

In section 2 the 3-D acquisition system is described. Section 3 illustrates the use of the system for the extraction of 3-D face shape and texture. Section 4 describes a first application, where the data are used to assist police forces in the identification of offenders. This work includes the derivation of a simple model for skin reflectance. Section 5 shows the use of the 3-D data for the extraction and tracking of facial features such as the lips, the mouth and the nose. This is useful e.g. to animate a virtual face from the facial expressions of an actor. The section illustrates this with a simple 'special effect' movie.

2   Three-dimensional face capture

Extracting 3-D information from scenes is a longstanding research issue in the computer vision community [9]. Two major strands have developed.

A first class are so-called 'passive' techniques, that work with normal, ambient light. The reconstruction is based on finding the projection of several points in different images taken from different viewpoints. If the images are taken simultaneously, the scene may contain moving parts and the motion can even be retrieved by processing subsequent camera frames [21]. Given the 3-D shape and the multiple views, one is in a good position to map texture onto the surface and to extract surface reflectance characteristics.

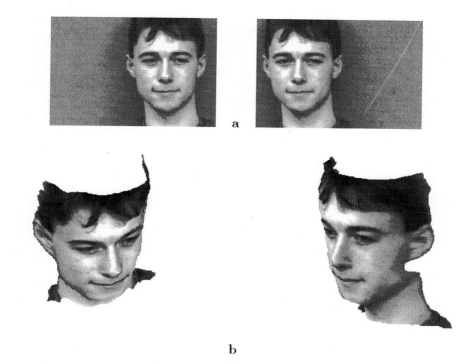

b

Figure 1: **a:** *Original stereo image pair of a face.* **b:** *Two views of the reconstructed surface.*

Passive techniques also pose problems, however. First, the correspondence problem, i.e. the search for the same points in several views, is still a weak but essential step. Even with the latest algorithms the precision of passive, 3-D reconstructions compares unfavourably with the active techniques discussed next. Figure 1 shows the results for a face using a passive technique [18]. Although convincing to some extent, accuracy is wanting when it comes to person identification or the modelling of well-known persons.

A second class of 3-D acquisition systems are 'active' in the sense that they apply a special illumination to extract the 3-D information (for a review see e.g. [1, 9]). The illumination should reduce the problem of finding correspondences. The projected patterns are often observed with two or more cameras, but also from a single view can 3-D information be gathered, with the projector replacing one of the cameras in a stereo system. On the whole, active techniques yield higher precision. Simultaneously, the image processing operations are simpler. They obviously are also more intrusive, although the pattern(s) could be projected using near-infrared light, to which CCDs are quite sensitive. The projection of the pattern can also make it more difficult to extract the underlying surface texture. As a consequence, active devices can yield misalignments between the shape and its texture, because they are captured neither simultaneously nor by the same sensor. Also – and this is particularly important for faces – active systems usually scan the object surface or use a series of subsequent projections. In such cases, the acquisition time easily gets too long to deal with object motion.

The system proposed here combines features of both approaches, making it quite appropriate for 3-D face capture. It uses a special illumination pattern to obtain good precision, but only a single image is used for the extraction of the 3-D shape ('one-shot' operation). From the same image alsso the surface texture is extracted, resulting in a perfect alignment between the two. This one-shot system is an improvement over an earlier version by our lab [23], where the spatial resolution was lower, the system more difficult to set up, and surface texture was not extracted. The improvement was possible because the illumination pattern was simplified. Fig. 2(a) shows the setup. Note that the projector and camera can be put quite close, leaving a small opening angle between the rays of viewing and projection. The advantage is that problems of occlusion are minimised and 3-D reconstruction can be performed until close to the occluding boundaries of the object's surface (as viewed from the camera). Fig. 2(b) shows a detail of the face, so that the pattern is clearly visible. It consists of a simple line grid.

¿From the perspective of active systems, an interesting novelty it that both 3-D shape and texture are extracted from a single image. As already mentioned, there is no alignment problem between the two because they are derived from the same image. Fig. 3(a) shows an image of a face, (b) the extracted 3-D shape, and (c) the result with the image texture mapped. Texture extraction is based on filtering out the grid lines from the original image or, if the person keeps very still, from a second image taken without the pattern. In all the examples shown in the paper, the former approach – filtering out the lines – was used.

The system is not actually a 'range acquisition' system. So far, 3D acquisition has been almost synonymous to range – i.e. distance – extraction. Getting shape via variations in distance might be a costly detour, however. It usually is the requirement to know absolute distance that complicates the necessary hardware and calibration. The system yields 3-D shape only up to scale. This can be easily fixed by giving a single, measured length, if there is a need...

It is also useful to note that this system is easy to calibrate. It suffices to show a scene with two dominant planes (like the corner of the room or a box for instance) and to specify the angle subtended between these planes. From there, the system autocalibrates. This makes it easy to change the setup of the camera and the projector or, generally, to transport the system toward the people or objects to be reconstructed.

The one-shot nature of this system, i.e. the extraction of the 3-D data

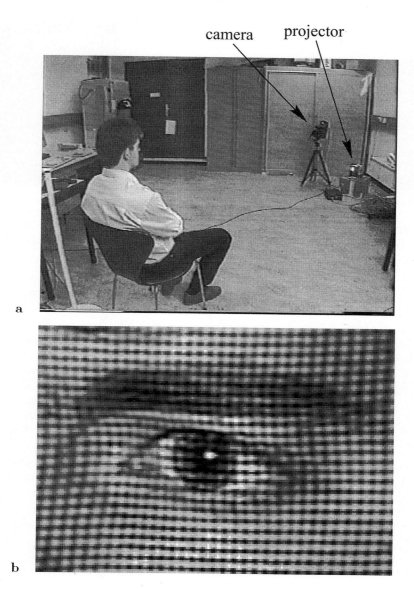

Figure 2: **a:** *Required hardware: a camera, a projector and a computer. A regular square pattern is projected on the scene (here the face of the person sitting on the chair).* **b:** *Detail of the face, with the projected pattern.*

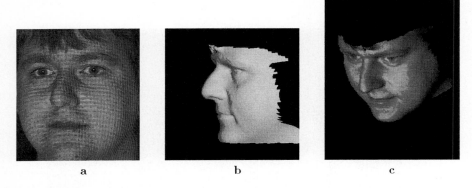

a   b   c

Figure 3: **a:** *Original image of a face;* **b:** *A profile view of the reconstruction;* **c:** *Texture mapped reconstruction. All results were obtained from the image in* **a.**

from a single image, makes it possible to take a video sequence of a face, and reconstruct every frame of it. The result is a dynamic, 3-D reconstruction. Such dynamic 3-D sequences could be of particular interest for the study of facial expressions, the extraction of visemes, etc. The one-shot nature of this system also allows to extract the 3-D shape of objects while in motion, a consideration that might be of particular importance for visual inspection along production lines. The capture of dynamic 3-D is still quite rare, but a few other systems are around. Kanade and coworkers have demonstrated the extraction of 3-D, whole body dynamics with a passive system with about 50 cameras [21]. Nayar and coworkers [25, 15] used shape from defocus. Multiple aligned cameras take images of the same scene through a system of half-translucent mirrors. Their system also uses a simple, regular illumination pattern. To the best of our knowledge, the system doesn't extract surface texture, but such an extension would seem feasible.

The system used here is also not alone in its one-shot operation. Hall *et al.* [7] developed a grid-pattern method for extracting sparse range images for simple shapes, where the identification is based on the interactive labeling of some line intersections. Vuori and Smith [24] based their line identification on the restriction that the objects have a maximal height and lines will fall in predictable stripes of the image. Therefore, the grid has to remain quite sparse. Blake *et al.* [3] use a calibrated stereo setup to observe two sets of subsequently projected lines. By having the lines intersect the epipolar lines obliquely, these intersections help narrow down the possible line identity. Again, lines must not be positioned too close in order for this strategy to work. As a result, the reconstructions obtained with these systems all have a rather low resolution.

Other systems use a "single" image of denser grids, but with some form of line coding. Boyer and Kak [4] developed a light striping concept based on colour-coding. Vuylsteke and Oosterlinck [23] use a binary coding scheme where each line neighbourhood has its own signature. Maruyama and Abe [14] introduce random gaps in the line pattern which allows to uniquely identify the lines. An exception is the work by Chia *et al.*[6]. The authors assume orthographic projection of a pattern combined with sufficient perspective distorsions in the camera image. The latter is necessary to identify the lines in the pattern. They also assume that the intrinsic camera parameters are known. We believe that the strategy behind the system proposed here is more robust, because it doesn't depend on subtle effects of perspective deformations. A unique feature is that no attempt is made to identify the lines in absolute terms. Only the relative positions of the lines in the pattern is used.

More details about the system can be found elsewhere [20].

3   Illustration of 3-D face reconstructions

This section illustrates some of the typical results obtained with the system.

Fig. 4 shows 3-D reconstructions for 5 faces. The left column shows the input images. The other three columns show the 3-D reconstructions from different viewpoints. Note the gaps in some of the views (black areas): parts of the faces that were not visible to the camera could not be reconstructed. Taking multiple views can remedy this problem. This is illustrated in fig. 5 where 2 views are taken of a face and the resulting reconstructions have been brought in registration, as shown on the right. In this case, part of the nose is hidden for each of the two camera positions. The combined reconstruction (fig. 5, image on the right) shows that the two reconstructions fit well. Bright areas are those for which data are available in the two reconstructions, dark areas correspond to data extracted from the first view exclusively. The registration was carried out using the ICP algorithm [5]. The holes in the reconstructions show that the system successfully handles depth discontinuities. A bigger problem is hair. Typically, hair is not captured well and these parts are also left open by the system.

In the previous illustration, the strategy has been to use as few images as possible for the complete reconstruction of a face. The resulting 3-D descriptions consist of approximately 8000-10000 bilinear patches. If this resolution is too low, one can project a finer grid and either take a higher resolution camera (e.g. one of the latest digital photo cameras), or zoom in and compile the 3-D model out of smaller pieces. The latter is possible by only moving the camera, and without additional calibration. On the statue, a grid was projected of 600×600 lines. This is too many to even be visible in a single image. Hence, one can 'scan' the scene by taking a series of more detailed images. While doing so, the position of the projector is kept fixed.

294

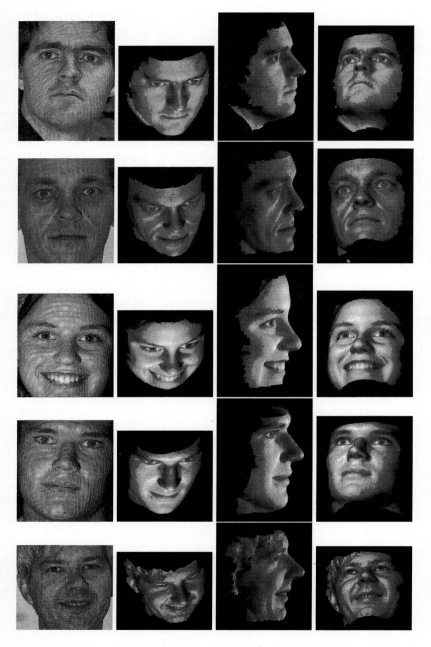

Figure 4: *3-D reconstructions of 5 faces. The left column shows the input images.*

  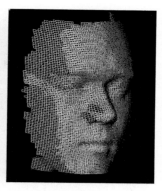

Figure 5: *The same face from two different camera viewpoints. The image on the right shows the superposition after registration of the two reconstructions.*

Only the camera is moved around, taking images of the detailed patches. The setup is calibrated only once, best for the camera position that corresponds to the most central patch. The patches have to overlap, in order to support registration afterwards. A series of such images is shown in fig. 6. For every image a reconstruction is made of the corresponding surface patch. Only the reconstruction of the patch for which the calibration was carried out will be 'correct', however. The others have – by approximation – an affine skew. Therefore, a registration step was implemented that allows them to deform affinely while being matched. Fig. 7 shows the resulting mosaic of matched patches. As all the patches are based on a single grid of lines, it is easy to integrate them into a single surface description. As to the texture, this can be extracted as a weighted sum of the overlapping image textures. Fig. 8 show the result for the statue. As these results show, because of the high resolution one can zoom in quite a bit on parts of this structure while keeping a realistic impression. Of course, the reconstruction is still only a partial one. Such large, but high resolution parts can in a second pass be registered as well, to form a complete reconstruction.

In the previous examples, the face to be capture remained still. As mentioned before, the system holds special promise for the extraction of dynamic 3-D. Fig. 9 shows a few frames of a video taken for the 3-D reconstruction of facial expressions. The grid was projected onto the face all the time. For every frame of the video, a 3-D reconstruction was made and the skin texture was extracted. Hence, not only shape but also texture dynamics are captured, which is important e.g. to include the blinking of the eyes. Fig. 10 shows the results for the frames selected in fig. 9. The reconstructions are viewed from three different directions. Armed with such dynamic 3-D data, it is tempting to use the observed changes directly as a means for driving

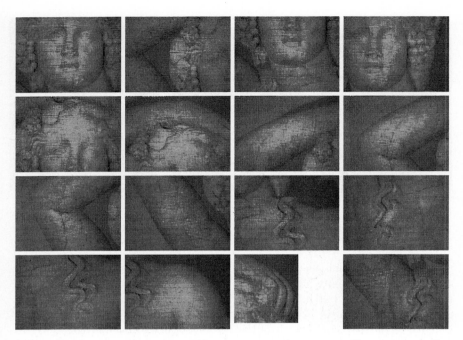

Figure 6: *A series of detailed image of a Greek statue. The corresponding patches overlap.*

Figure 7: *The mosaic of patches after registration.*

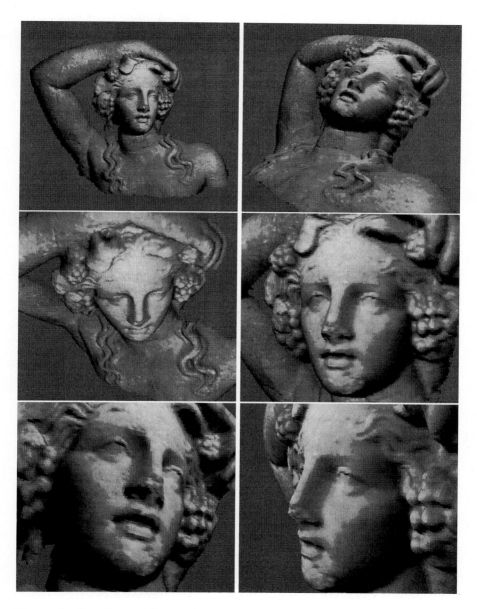

Figure 8: *Six views of the reconstructed statue. The reconstruction has been built from different patches, as explained in the text.*

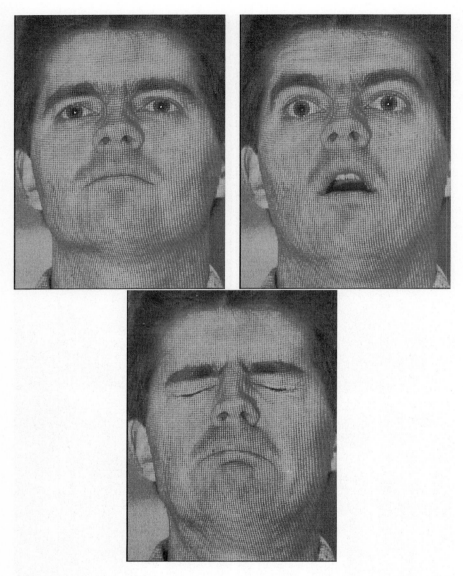

Figure 9: *Three frames out of a video sequence showing a gesturing face*

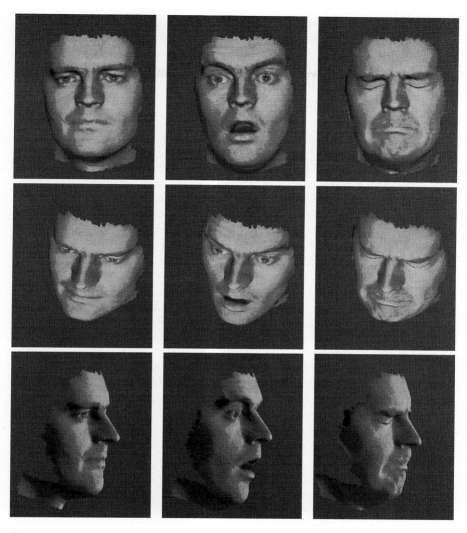

Figure 10: *Texture-mapped 3D reconstructions for the frames of fig. 9 shown from 3 different viewpoints.*

face animation suites. Rather than going through the painstaking process of modelling the skull, muscles, and skin, the 3-D optical flow of the data could be calculated, the typical motions could be extracted for different facial expressions over several individuals, and applied to the corresponding points on other faces, much in line with the approach pioneered by Thomas Vetter (cfr. same volume).

4 Forensic applications of 3-D face models

Three-dimensional face data can play a useful role in the identification of criminals. The comparision of surveillance video data and mugshots of potential offenders or suspects often is a difficult task. Surveillance cameras typically look down upon the scene, whereas mugshots usually are frontal or profile pictures. Similarly, the illumination conditions can be quite different. Sometimes the police forces will take a suspect to the scene of the crime and images can be taken with at least the same camera and from a similar viewpoint. Such procedure is time consuming, expensive and not always without risk, however.

The availability of a 3-D head model for a suspect can alleviate such problems considerably. It then becomes possible to depict a suspect's head in a similar 3-D position and to emulate the lighting that was in place at the time of the crime. It is then much easier to make direct comparisons with the surveillance data. It becomes e.g. possible to overlay a number of facial features and to check whether the rest of the faces fall in registration.

The possibility to show a 3-D face model from different relative viewpoints, including those of the original surveillance cameras, is obvious. The emulation of changing illumination is not so obvious at this point. The texture that is mapped onto the faces is obtained from the image that is used for the extraction of the 3-D shape. Image based texture does not yield the true surface reflectance, however, and this is needed to simulate changes in illumination. Therefore, from the image texture, the illumination at the time of data capture has to be decoupled from the surface reflectance characteristics. In general, this is a very difficult problem. Fortunately, the situation here is less complex, because the angle of the incoming (projected) light is calculated explicitly when the system is calibrated. Armed with the 3-D shape and the knowledge of where the light is coming from, reflectance modelling becomes much easier. Nevertheless, some problems remain, because the derivation of a BRDF would require a sufficient number of samples. To that end, assumptions have to be made on parts of the face having similar reflectance characteristics. Moreover, with the current setup the angle between viewing and projection is always small. It is also a bit naive to assume that all light is coming from a single direction, i.e. from the projector. In a typical room, there will be ambient light. So far. our work in this area has been restricted to the modelling of the latter effect.

Our preliminary experiments start with the assumption that Lambertian reflection is a good model for most of the face. This might seem far-fetched in view of the observations that have been made for diffuse reflection from real surfaces [16]. The angle between the rays of projection and viewing is quite small (typically 10° or less) and under these conditions the Lambertian model can be expected to apply rather well [28]. Assuming the face surface is Lambertian,

$$A \sim \frac{I}{\cos(\alpha)} \quad ,$$

with A the albedo, I the image intensity, and α the angle between the surface normal and the incoming light. Using this model, the resulting albedo is shown in fig. 11b. One would expect to find values that are more or less

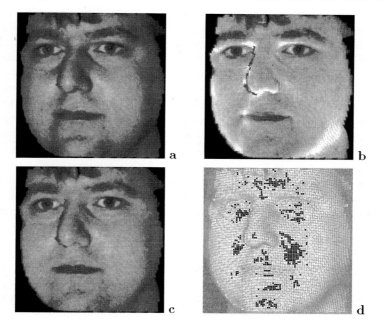

Figure 11: **a:** *Original texture mapped surface.* **b:** *'Albedo' for Lambertian surface.* **c:** *'Albedo' with the proposed lighting model.* **d:** *Black areas denote places where specular reflections may occur.*

constant over the face, but under the jaw substantially higher values are found. This clearly is not correct, but it is in line with the expectations about diffusely reflecting surfaces. It is typical that the Lambertian model yields albedos that are too high where the normal on the surface deviates strongly from the incoming light direction [27]. A second factor that could contribute is ambient light. This assumption was tested by refining the illumination model. In addition to the incoming, directed light, it was assumed that there was a constant, omnidirectional ambient component (e.g. reflections from the walls etc.). In that case

$$A \sim \frac{I}{f(\alpha)}, \quad \text{with} \quad f(\alpha) = 1 - \gamma + \gamma . \cos(\alpha) \ ,$$

with γ a number between 0 and 1 that determines the relative weight of the directional and ambient light components. In a little experiment, the value of γ was chosen as to minimize the variations in 'albedo' over the face. For the example image, the optimal value came out to be $\gamma = 0.3$ and the resulting albedo is given in fig. 11c. As can be seen, there are still substantial variations in the value of the albedo. The brighter regions correspond to specularities, which would require additional care. The regions underneath the chin and the jaw are darker now. This again is a deviation from the expectations.

It therefore seems necessary to modify the Lambertian model itself, both by refining it according to the refined models for diffuse reflection [16, 27, 28] and by adding a specular component. The places where specular reflection might occur can be predicted rather well. The strongest specularities will be caused by the directional light and its incident direction is known with respect to the surface normal and the viewpoint of the camera. Fig. 11d shows the places where the mirror conditions for incoming and outgoing light are satisfied (black dots). It is interesting to note that these positions can be found without a 3-D reconstruction. They correspond to positions where the grid looks square in the camera image. This is caused by the fact that enlarging and foreshortening effects of projection and viewing resp. cancel out, due to the mirror configurations of projecting and viewing rays.

An example of a virtual change of illumination, based on the albedo resulting from the mixed lighting model, is shown in fig. 12

5 Facial feature extraction in 3-D

Most current work on facial feature extraction takes video sequences as input. It has proved not so straightforward to achieve good robustness from such images. It can e.g. be very difficult to extract the lips, certainly if the images contain a complete face and the resolution of the mouth is not so high. In order to build stable lip detectors and trackers researchers usually had to control the viewpoint, to zoom in on the mouth area or to use lipstick to increase contrast (see e.g [11, 12, 2] for state-of-the-art contributions).

For one thing, the availability of 3-D data can help to reduce the influence of the viewpoint, through the use of viewpoint invariant geometrical features. What we propose is a kind of syntactical approach to facial feature extraction, much in the tradition of the face recognition literature but based on 3-D data. The first step is to detect the nose as the point where both principal

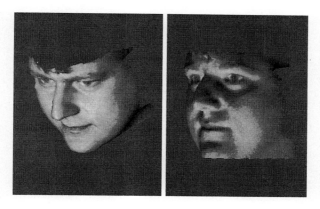

Figure 12: *A simulated change in illumination (right image) on the basis of the original view (left image).*

curvatures κ_1 and κ_2 are large. The nose tip can thus be defined as the point where one finds

$$\max(\sum_{W_x} min(\kappa_1, \kappa_2)) \ .$$

in some window with width W around it. The position of the nose tip gives a first indication of the location of the mouth area. Each lip can be modeled as a long stretched region with one large and one small principle curvature. Furthermore it is assumed that both lips have the same extent, lie almost parallel to eachother, and have approximately the same curvature. Both lips are determined simultaneously as

$$\max(\sum_{lip\ region} min(\kappa_1^{upper\ lip}, \kappa_1^{lower\ lip})) \ .$$

with κ_1 the largest principal curvature. Similar methods can be applied to find the eyebrows and the chin.

The results of the nose and mouth extraction procedures are illustrated on a series of images. A video sequence was taken of a talking face. Throughout, the reconstruction grid was projected onto the face. Fig. 13 shows 3 frames from the talking head sequence. Fig. 14 shows a part of the original images, with the position of the nose indicated with a point and the lips as two line segments. Both the nose and lips have been detected at a resolution given by the squares of the pattern. Each frame was treated separately, so no tracking was used to improve the results and the results therefore illustrate the quality that can be expected from a single view. As can be seen, the position of the nose point is stable and the lip lines nicely stick to the upper and lower parts of the upper and lower lips, also when the teeth become visible.

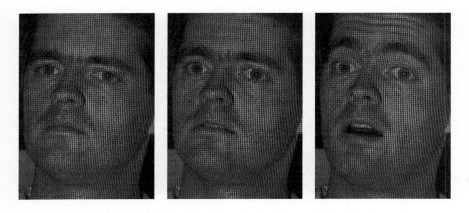

Figure 13: *Three frames of a talking head video sequence.*

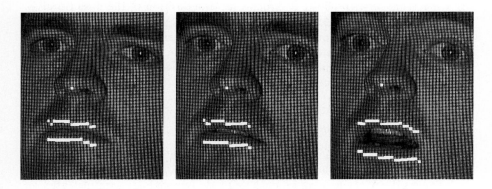

Figure 14: *Detected nose and lips, based on surface curvature. Results for every frame were obtained independently.*

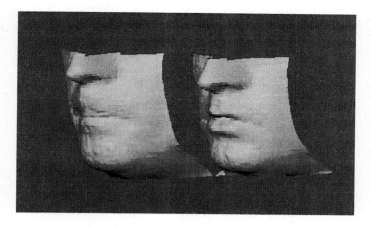

Figure 15: *3-D mouth shapes (visemes) for /m/ (left) and /n/ (right).*

Facial feature tracking is useful for several applications. One is the creation of intelligent human-machine interfaces. The machine can be made to look at the facial expressions an adapt its behaviour accordingly. Another example is 'visual speech'. In noisy environments, the performance of speech recognition systems can be improved by simultaneously looking at the mouth. Rather than apply speech recognition or lip reading in isolation, both can be used to complement each other. As an example, /m/ and /n/ sound very similar, but can be distinguished quite easily by their 'visemes', i.e. the shape of the mouth area. This is illustrated in fig. 15. A further example where facial features have a role to play is in the world of virtual actors, special effects, and related issues in the postproduction industry for broadcasting and the movies. Fig. 16 shows six frames of a small movie. The face was put through a virtual ordeal, being submerged, deformed, tossed and turned. The input was the gesturing face sequence already shown in fig. 10. In order to implement this demo, facial features like the nose and chin were automatically detected and deformed. Note how also the orientation and illumination constantly change. Achieving the same level of realism using graphics-based animation would take quite an effort.

6   Conclusions and future work

The paper focused on an active technique to generate 3-D models of faces. These were used for the extraction of basic textural and geometric features. The proposed 3-D acquisition method also allows capturing dynamic 3-D data, rendering it especially useful for the analysis and reconstruction of facial expressions and visemes. In summary, the main characteristics of the proposed acquisition method are:

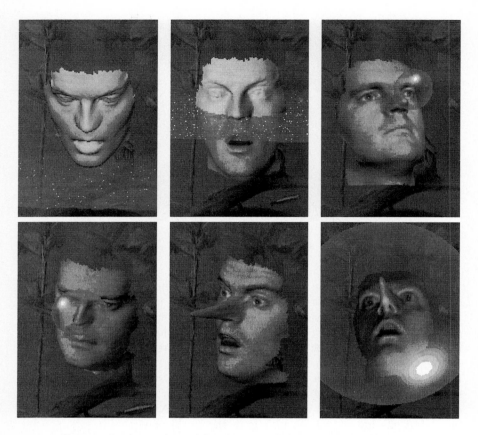

Figure 16: *A number of frames out of the VR demo sequence.*

1. the required hardware is minimal – a slide projector, a camera and a computer – and hence the system is cheap;

2. the calibration is simple, requiring no exotic calibration objects or patterns, and making the system easy to transport;

3. the acquisition time for the necessary input is that one of a single image at standard video frame rate, therefore head motion is not a problem and can be captured;

4. the spatial resolution is sufficiently high for most facial feature extraction tasks;

5. the output is a mesh of connected points, rather than a mere cloud of points, hence the topology of the surface is known;

6. it extracts realistic surface texture, in colour if required;

Planned work encompasses the following aspects:

• Speeding up the system. Currently it takes a few minutes for the extraction of the 3-D shape and texture for a single frame. A first and self-evident improvement would be to exploit the temporal continuity that exists between the shapes and textures of subsequent frames. All dynamic results shown in this paper have been obtained by carrying out the reconstruction of each frame from scratch. In fact, the stability of the reconstructions when viewed as a video testifies to the precision of the method.

• Refining the skin reflectance model. Given the rather detailed information from the image textured 3-D models, it seems worthwhile spending more time on the derivation of refined skin reflectance models.

• Combining photometric and geometric cues. For the extraction of the facial features only geometrical cues were used. Combining these with texture cues looks like a promising avenue.

• Extending the applications. We have plans to work on several applications of 3-D faces. One is building tools that assist the police forces with the identification of criminals. Another is the animation of virtual actors based on a real actor's performance, or visual speech extraction.

Acknowledgements: M.P. gratefully acknowledges a postdoctoral research grant from the Flemish Institute for the advancement of Science and Technology in Industry (IWT). The authors also gratefully acknowledge support from Esprit-LTR project 'Improofs' for the reported skin reflectance work.

References

[1] Besl, P., Active Optical Range Imaging Sensors, Machine Vision and Applications, Vol. 1, No. 2, 1988, p.127-152

[2] A. Blake, R. Curwen, and A. Zisserman, A Framework for Sptio-Temporal Control in the Tracking of Visual Contours, Int. J. Comp. Vision, Vol 11.2, pp. 127-145, 1993.

[3] A. Blake, D. McCowen, H. R. Lo, and P. J. Lindsey, Trinocular Active Range-Sensing, IEEE PAMI 15(5), pp. 477-483, 1993.

[4] K. Boyer and A. Kak, Color-encoded structured light for rapid active ranging, IEEE Trans. PAMI, Vol. 9, No. 10, pp. 14-28, 1987

[5] Y. Chen and G. Medioni, Object Modeling by Registration of Multiple Range Images. Proc. Int. Conf. on Robotics and Automation, Sacramento CA, pp. 2724-2729, 1991

[6] T. Chia, Z. Chen and C. Yueh, Curved Surface Reconstruction using a Simple Structured Light Method, Proc. Internat. Conf. Pattern Recognition, Vienna, Vol. A, pp. 844-848, 1996

[7] Hall, E.L., Measuring curved surface for robot vision, IEEE computer, Vol. 15, No. 12, p.42-54

[8] G. Hu and G. Stockman, 3-D surface solution using structured light and constraint propagation, IEEE Trans. PAMI, Vol. 11, No. 4, pp. 390-402, 1989

[9] Jarvis, A persepctive on range finding techniques for computer vision, IEEE Trans. on PAMI, Vol. 5, No 2, March 83, p.122-139

[10] A. Lanitis, N.A. Thacker, and S.W. Beet, A Unified Approach to Coding and Interpreting Face Images, Proc. ICCV, 1995.

[11] M. Kass, A. Witkin, and D. Terzopoulos, Snakes: active contour models, Int. J. Comp. Vision, pp. 321-331, 1988.

[12] R. Kaucic, B. Dalton, and A. Blake, Real-time Lip Tracking for Audio-Visual Speech Recognition Applications, Proc. ECCV, Vol II, pp. 376-387, 1996.

[13] Y. Lee, D. Terzopoulos, and K. Waters, Realistic modeling for facial animation, SIGGRAPH, pp. 55-62, 1995

[14] M. Maruyama, and S. Abe, Range Sensing by Projecting Multiple Slits with Random Cuts, IEEE PAMI 15(6), pp. 647-650, 1993.

[15] S.K. Nayar, M. Watanabe, and M. Noguchi Real-time focus range sensor, IEEE Trans. PAMI, Vol.18, No.12, pp. 1186-1197, 1996.

[16] M. Oren and S. Nayar, Generalization of the Lambertian model and implications for machine vision, Int. Journal of Computer Vision, 14(3), pp. 227-252, 1995

[17] M.A. Turk and A.P. Pentland, Face Recognition Using Eigenfaces, Proc. CVPR, pp. 586-591, 1991. 1990.

[18] M. Proesmans, L. Van Gool, and A. Oosterlinck, Determination of optical flow and its discontinuities using non-linear diffusion, Third European Conf. on Computer Vision, Stockholm, pp. 295-304, may 1994 ed.

[19] M. Proesmans, L. Van Gool and A. Oosterlinck, One-shot active range acquisition, Proc. Internat. Conf. Pattern Recognition, Vienna, Vol. C, pp. 336-340, 1996

[20] M. Proesmans and L. Van Gool, One-shot active 3D shape acquisition. Multisensor Fusion and Integration, to be held in Washington DC, Dec.'96.

[21] P. Rander, P. Narayanan, and T. Kanade, Revovery of dynamic scene structure from multiple image sequences, Proc. Int. Conf. Multisensor Fusion and Integration of Intell. Systems, pp. 305-312, 1996

[22] Rioux M., Laser range finder based upon synchronous scanners. Applied Optics 23(21), p.3837-3844, 1984.

[23] P. Vuylsteke and A. Oosterlinck, Range Image Acquisition with a Single Binary-Encoded Light Pattern, IEEE PAMI 12(2), pp. 148-164, 1990.

[24] Vuori T. A. and Smith C.L., Three dimensional imaging system with structered lighting and practical constraints, Journal of Electronic Imaging 6(1), pp. 140-144, 1997.

[25] M. Watanabe and S. Nayar, Telecentric optics for computational vision, Proc. European Conf. Computer Vision, Vol. II, pp. 439-451, 1996.

[26] Will P.M. and Pennington K.S. Grid coding: a novel technique for image processing, Proceedings IEEE, 60(6), pp. 669-680, 1972.

[27] L. Wolff, On the relative brightness of specular and diffuse reflection, Proc. CVPR, pp. 369-376, 1994.

[28] L. Wolff, Generalizing Lambert's Law For Smooth Surfaces, Proc. ECCV, pp. 40-53, 1996.

Generalization to Novel Views from a Single Face Image

Thomas Vetter and Volker Blanz

Max-Planck-Institut für biologische Kybernetik
Spemannstr. 38
72076 Tübingen – Germany
thomas.vetter@tuebingen.mpg.de
volker.blanz@tuebingen.mpg.de

Abstract. When only a single image of a face is available, can we generate new images of the face across changes in viewpoint or illumination? The approach presented in this paper acquires its knowledge about possible image changes from other faces and transfers this prior knowledge to a novel face image. In previous work we introduced the concept of linear object classes (Vetter and Poggio, 1997; Vetter, 1997): In an image based approach, a flexible image model of faces was used to synthesize new images of a face when only a single 2D image of that face is available.

In this paper we describe a new general flexible face model which is now "learned" from examples of individual 3D-face data (Cyberware-scans). In an analysis-by-synthesis loop the flexible 3D model is matched to the novel face image. Variation of the model parameters, similar to multidimensional morphing, allows for generating new images of the face where viewpoint, illumination or even the expression is changed.

The key problem for generating a flexible face model is the computation of dense correspondence between all given example faces. A new correspondence algorithm is described, which is a generalization of existing algorithms for optic flow computation to 3D-face data.

1   Introduction

"Can you imagine?"
"Yes, I see ......"
In human language mental imagery seems to be a natural ability. Imagery is often discussed as one of the basic forms of human cognition for the analysis of situations or scenes (Kosslyn, 1994).

A similar concept is developed in machine intelligence for the problem of pattern analysis and image understanding. In order to separate or compensate for the many factors that can change the image of an object, image models are built that allow the influence of each of these imaging factors to be simulated. So in computer vision imagery is directly translated into image synthesis and an image analysis is performed by matching an image model to a novel image, thereby parameterizing the novel image in terms of a known model.

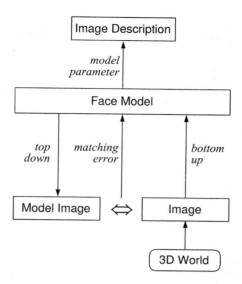

Figure 1: *A simple analysis by synthesis schema. To analyze an image if it represents a face, the face model generates a model image which is compared with the input image. After minimizing the matching error, the internal model parameters lead to the description of the input image.*

Analysis by synthesis
The requirement of pattern synthesis for pattern analysis has often been proposed within a Bayesian framework (Grenander, 1978; Mumford, 1996) or has been formulated as an alignment technique (Ullman, 1989). This is in contrast to pure of *bottom-up* techniques which have been advocated especially for the early stages of visual signal processing (Marr, 1982). Here a standard strategy is to reduce a signal to a feature vector and to compare this vector with those expected for signals in various categories. A crucial problem of these algorithms is that they cannot explicitly describe variations between or within the categories and therefore have difficulty separating unexpected noise from the variations within a particular category.

In contrast, the algorithm described in this paper works by actively reconstructing the signal to be analyzed. In an additional *top-down* path an estimated signal is generated and compared to the present input signal. Then by comparing the real signal with its reconstruction it is decided if the analysis is sufficient to explain the signal or not. Clearly, such an approach has the additional problem of defining a model function to reconstruct the input signal.

This paper focuses on the analysis and synthesis of images of a specific object class – that is on images of human faces. For object classes, such as faces or cars, where all objects share a common similarity, such a model function could be learned from examples. That is, the image model for the whole object class is derived by exploiting some prototypical example images.

Models developed for the analysis and synthesis of images of a specific class of objects must solve two problems simultaneously:

- The model must be able to synthesize images that cover the whole range of possible images of the class.

- It must be possible to match the model to a novel image. Formally, this leads to an optimization problem with all of the associated requirements that a global minimum can be found.

In recent years, two-dimensional image-based face models have been constructed and applied for the synthesis of rigid and nonrigid face transformations (Choi et al., 1991; Beymer et al., 1993; Lanitis et al., 1995). These models exploit prior knowledge from example images of prototypical faces and work by building flexible image-based representations (*active shape models*) of known objects by a linear combination of labeled examples. These representations are applied for the task of image search and recognition or synthesis (Lanitis et al., 1995). The underlying coding of an image of a new object or face is based on linear combinations of the two-dimensional shape (warping fields) of examples of prototypical images as well as the linear combinations of their color values at corresponding locations (texture).

For the problem of synthesizing novel views to a single example image of a face we developed over the last years the concept of *linear object classes* (Vetter and Poggio, 1997; Vetter, 1997). This image-based method allows us to compute novel views of a face from a single image. On the one hand, the method draws on a general flexible image model which can be learned automatically from examples images, and on the other hand, on an algorithm that allows for matching this flexible model to a novel face image. The novel image now can be described or coded through the internal model parameters which are necessary to reconstruct the image. The design of the model allows also for synthesizing new views of the face.

In this paper we replace the two-dimensional image model by a three-dimensional flexible face model. A flexible three-dimensional face model will lead on the one hand to a more efficient data representation and on the other hand to a better generalization to new illumination conditions.

In all these techniques, it is crucial to establish the correspondence between each example face and single reference face, matching image points in the two-dimensional approach, and surface points in the three-dimensional case. Correspondence is a key step posing a difficult problem. However, for images of objects which share many common features, such as faces all seen from a single specific viewpoint, automated techniques seem feasible. The techniques applied in the past can be separated in two groups, one which establishes the correspondence for a small number of feature points only and into the techniques computing the correspondence for every pixel in an image. For the first approach usually models of particular features like the eye corners or the whole chin line are developed off line and then matched to a new image (Lanitis et al., 1995; Herpers et al., 1996). The second technique computes the correspondence for each pixel in an image by comparing this image to a reference image using methods derived from optical flow computation(Beymer et al., 1993; Beymer and Poggio, 1996). In this paper we will extend this method of dense correspondence which we already applied successfully to face images (Vetter and Poggio, 1997; Vetter et al., 1997), to the three-dimensional face data.

The paper is organized as follows. First, we describe the flexible three-dimensional face model and compare it to the two-dimensional image models we used earlier. Second we describe an algorithm to compute dense correspondence between individual 3D models of human faces. Third we describe an algorithm that allows to match the flexible face model to a novel image. Finally we show examples for synthesizing new images from a single image of a face and describe future improvements.

2   Flexible 3D face models

In this section we will give the formulation of a flexible three-dimensional face model which captures prior knowledge about faces exploiting the general similarity among faces. The model is a straight forward extension of the linear object class approach as described earlier(Vetter and Poggio, 1997; Vetter, 1997). Prototypical examples of an object class like faces are linked to a general class model that captures the similarity and regularities specific for this object class.

Three-dimensional models

In computer graphics, presently the most realistic three-dimensional face representations consist of a 3D mesh describing the geometry and a texture map capturing the color data of a face. These representations of individual faces are obtained either by three-dimensional scanning devices or through photogrammetric techniques from several two-dimensional images of a specific face (Parke, 1974; Akimoto et al., 1993). The synthesis of new faces by interpolation between such face representation was already demonstrated in the pioneering work of Parke (1974). Recently this idea of forming linear combinations of faces was used and extended to a general three-dimensional flexible face model for the analysis and synthesis of two-dimensional facial images (Choi et al., 1991; Poggio and Vetter, 1992; Vetter and Poggio, 1997).

Shape model: The three-dimensional geometry of a face is represented by a shape-vector $\mathbf{S} = (X_1, Y_1, Z_1, X_2, ..., Y_n, Z_n)^T \in \Re^{3n}$, that contains the X, Y, Z-coordinates of its n vertices. The central assumption for the formation of a flexible face model is that a set of M example faces $\mathbf{S}_i$ is available. Additionally, it is assumed that all these example faces $\mathbf{S}_i$ consist of the same number of n consistently labeled vertices, in other words all example faces are in full correspondence (see next section on correspondence). Usually this labeling is defined on an average face shape, which is obtained iteratively and which is often denoted as reference face $\mathbf{S}_{ref}$. Additionally, all faces are assumed to be aligned in an optimal way by rotating and translating them in three-dimensional space. Under this assumptions a new face geometry $\mathbf{S}_{model}$ can be generated as a linear combination of M example shape-vectors $\mathbf{S}_i$ each weighted by c_i

$$\mathbf{S}_{model} = \sum_{i=1}^{M} c_i \, \mathbf{S}_i \, .$$

(1)

The linear shape models derived in equation (1) allows for representing a new shape $\mathbf{S}$ as its approximation through the M example shapes $\mathbf{S}_i$: $\mathbf{S} \approx \sum_{i=1}^{M} c_i \, \mathbf{S}_i$. In other words, the example shapes represent a shape basis onto which a new shape $\mathbf{S}$ is projected. The coefficients c_i of the projection then define a coding of the original shape vector in this vector space which is spanned by all examples. A common strategy for increasing the efficiency of such a coding schema is to reduce the statistical redundancy within the example space. Principal component analysis (PCA) also known as Karhunen-Loeve expansion, is the standard procedure to obtain an optimal reduction of the dimensionality in data (for more details see (Duda and Hart, 1973)). While an optimization of the data representation is essential for any application, here, however, it will not be further discussed since it does not affect the basic idea of this paragraph which is the modeling of faces in a linear vector space.

Texture model: The second component of a flexible three-dimensional face or head model is texture information, which is usually stored in a *texture map*. A texture map is simply a two-dimensional color pattern storing the brightness or color values, ideally only the *albedo* of the surface is stored. This pattern can be synthetically generated or can be a scanned image.

A u, v coordinate system is introduced to associate the texture map with the modeled surface. The texture map is defined in the two-dimensional u, v coordinate system. For polygonal surfaces as defined through a shape vector $\mathbf{S}$, each vertex has an assigned u, v texture coordinate. For points on the surface between vertices, the u, v coordinates are interpolated. For convenience we assume that the total number n of stored values in such a texture map is equal to the total number of vertices in a shape vector $\mathbf{S}$.

The linear texture model, described in (Choi et al., 1991), starts from a set of M example face textures $\mathbf{T}_i$. Equivalent to the shape model described earlier it is assumed that all M textures $\mathbf{T}_i$ consist of the same number of n consistently labeled texture values that is all textures are in full correspondence. For texture synthesis linear models are used again. A new texture $\mathbf{T}_{model}$ is generated as the weighted sum of M given example textures $\mathbf{T}_i$ as follows

$$\mathbf{T}_{model} = \sum_{i=1}^{M} b_i \mathbf{T}_i, \tag{2}$$

Equivalent to the linear expansion of shape vectors (equation 1) the linear expansion of textures can be understood and used as an efficient coding schema for textures. A new texture can be coded by its M projection coefficients b_i in the 'texture vector space" spanned by M basis textures. Again, these basis textures can be just some prototypical example textures or can be derived from a large example set through an data optimization technique like PCA.

Cylindrical Coordinates

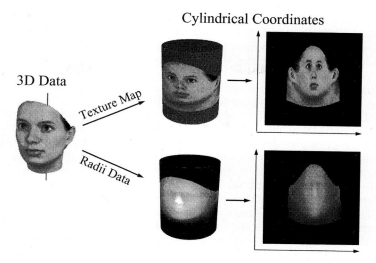

Figure 2: *Three-dimensional head data represented in cylindrical coordinates result in a data format which consists of two 2D-images. One image is the texture map (top right), and in the other image the geometry is coded (bottom right).*

3   3D Correspondence with Optical Flow

The key assumption of the flexible face model is the correspondence between all three-dimensional example data sets. That is, we have to find for every vertex location in one face data set, e.g. a vertex located on the nose, the corresponding vertex location on the nose in a reference face. This is in general a hard problem. However, assuming that all face data sets are roughly aligned and they are not categorical different like having a beard or not, an automatic technique is feasible for computing the correspondence. The key idea of the work described in this paragraph is to modify an existing optical flow algorithm to match points on the surfaces of three-dimensional objects instead of points in 2D-images. While establishing correspondence between three-dimensional objects has only recently become an issue, matching correspondent structures in two-dimensional images has been studied for many years.

Optical Flow Algorithm
In video sequences, in order to estimate the velocities of scene elements with respect to the camera it is necessary to compute the vector-field of optical flow, which expresses at each point $p_1 = (x_1, y_1)$ in the first image the displacement $(\delta x, \delta y) = (x_2 - x_1, y_2 - y_1)$ to the corresponding point $p_2 = (x_2, y_2)$ in the following image. A variety of different optical flow algorithms have been designed to solve this problem (for a review see (Barron et al., 1994)). Unlike temporal sequences taken from one scene, a comparison of images of

completely different scenes or faces may violate a number of important assumptions made in optical flow estimation. However, it was shown that some optical flow algorithms can still cope with this more difficult matching problem, opening up a wide range of applications in image analysis and synthesis (Beymer et al., 1993).

For building flexible image models of faces (Vetter and Poggio, 1997) we used a coarse-to-fine gradient-based method (Bergen et al., 1992) applied to the Laplacians of the images and followed an implementation described in (Bergen and Hingorani, 1990). The Laplacian of the images were computed from the Gaussian pyramid adopting the algorithm proposed by (Burt and Adelson, 1983). For every point x, y in an image $I(x, y)$, the algorithm attempts to minimize the error term $E = \sum (I_x \delta x + I_y \delta y - \delta I)^2$ for $\delta x, \delta y$, with I_x, I_y being the spatial image derivatives of the Laplacians and δI the difference of the Laplacians of the two compared images. The coarse-to-fine strategy starts with low resolution images and refines the computed displacements when finer levels are processed. The final result of this computation $(\delta x, \delta y)$ is used as an approximation of the spatial displacement of each pixel between two images.

Three-dimensional face representations.

The adaptation and extension of this optical flow algorithm to the three-dimensional head data is straight forward due to the fact that the cylindrical representation of a head model is analogous to images (see figure 2). Instead of grey-level values in image coordinates x, y here we store the radius values and the color values for each angle ϕ and height h. A parameterization of a three-dimensional head in cylindrical coordinates results therefore in two 'images', one representing the geometry of the head and the other containing the texture information. In order to compute the correspondence between different heads, both texture and geometry were considered simultaneously. The optical flow algorithm as described earlier had to be modified in the following way. Instead of comparing a scalar grey-level function $I(x, y)$, our modification of the algorithm attempts to find the best fit for the vector function

$$\vec{F}(h, \phi) = \begin{pmatrix} radius(h, \phi) \\ red(h, \phi) \\ green(h, \phi) \\ blue(h, \phi) \end{pmatrix}$$

$$\text{in a norm } \left\| \begin{pmatrix} radius \\ red \\ green \\ blue \end{pmatrix} \right\|^2$$

$$= w_1 \cdot radius^2 + w_2 \cdot red^2 + w_3 \cdot green^2 + w_4 \cdot blue^2.$$

The coefficients $w_1 ... w_4$ correct for the different energies [contrasts] in range and color values, and they assign roughly the same weight to shape as to all color channels taken together.

For representing the geometry, radius values can be replaced by other surface properties such as Gaussian curvature or surface normals.

The system's output, at this stage, is a surface flow-field or correspondence function

$$C(h, \phi) = \begin{pmatrix} dh(h, \phi) \\ d\phi(h, \phi) \end{pmatrix}. \tag{3}$$

After computing the correspondence between all individual faces of the training set to the reference face, the T_i and S_i of the flexible face model can be computed.

4 Matching the flexible 3D model to a 2D image

Based on an example set of faces which are already in correspondence, new 3D shape vectors S^{model} and texture maps T^{model} can be generated by varying the coefficients c_i and b_i in equations (1) and (2). Combining model shape and model texture results in a complete 3D face representation which now can be rendered to a new model image I^{model}. This model image is not only a function of the model parameters c_i and b_i, it also depends on some projection parameters p_j and on the surface reflectance properties and illumination parameters r_j used for rendering. For the general matching problem of the model to a novel image I^{novel} we define the following error function

$$E(\vec{c}, \vec{b}, \vec{p}, \vec{r}) = \frac{1}{2} \sum_{x,y} \left[I^{novel}(x, y) - I^{model}(x, y) \right]^2 \tag{4}$$

where the sum is over all pixels (x, y) in the images, I^{novel} is the novel image being matched and I^{model} is the current guess for the model image for a specific parameter setting $(\vec{c}, \vec{b}, \vec{p}, \vec{r})$. Minimizing the error yields the model image which best fits the novel image with respect to the L_2 norm.

However, the optimization of the error function in equation (4) is extremely difficult for several reasons. First, the function is not linear in most of the parameters, second, the number of parameters is large (> 100) and additionally, the whole computation is extremely expensive since it requires the rendering of the three-dimensional face model to an image for each evaluation of the error function.

In this paper we will simplify the problem by assuming the illumination parameters $\vec{r}$ and also the projection parameters $\vec{p}$, such as view point, are known. This assumptions allows us to reduce the amount of rendering and also to use image modeling techniques developed earlier (Jones and Poggio, 1996; Vetter et al., 1997). By rendering images from all example faces under fixed illumination and projection parameters, the flexible 3D model is transformed into a flexible 2D face model. This allows us to generate new model images all depicting faces in the requested spatial orientation and under the known illumination. After matching this flexible 2D model (see below) to the novel image the optimal model parameters are used within the flexible 3D model to generate a three-dimensional face representation which best matches the novel target image.

4.1   Linear image model

To built the flexible 2D model we first render all 3D example faces under the given projection and illumination parameters to images $I_0, I_1, \ldots, I_M$. Let I_0 be the reference image which defines the topology for the whole model, and positions within I_0 are parameterized in (u, v). The 2D correspondence s_j between each pixel in the rendered reference image I_0 and its corresponding location in each rendered example image I_i, can be directly computed as the projection P of the 3D shapes between all 3D faces and the reference face, as $s_j = PS_j - PS_0$ with $s_o \equiv 0$.

These pixelwise correspondences between I_0 and each example image are mappings $s_j : \mathcal{R}^2 \rightarrow \mathcal{R}^2$ which map the points of I_0 onto I_j, i.e. $s_j(u, v) = (x, y)$ where (x, y) is the point in I_j which corresponds to (u, v) in I_0. We refer to s_j as a *correspondence field* and interchangeably as the *2D shape vector* for the vectorized I_j. Warping image I_j onto the reference image I_0 we obtain t_j as:

$$t_j(u, v) = I_j \circ s_j(u, v) \Leftrightarrow I_j(x, y) = t_j \circ s_j^{-1}(x, y).$$

So, $\{t_j\}$ is the set of shape normalized prototype images, referred to as *texture vectors*. They are normalized in the sense that their shape is the same as the shape of the chosen reference image.

The flexible image model is the set of images I^{model}, parameterized by $\vec{c} = [c_0, c_1, \ldots, c_M], \vec{b} = [b_0, b_1, \ldots, b_M]$ such that

$$I^{model} \circ \left(\sum_{i=0}^{M} c_i s_i\right) = \sum_{j=0}^{M} b_j t_j. \tag{5}$$

The summation $\sum_{i=0}^{M} c_i s_i$ constrains the 2D shape of every model image to be a linear combination of the example 2D shapes. Similarly, the summation $\sum_{j=0}^{M} b_j t_j$ constrains the texture of every model image to be a linear combination of the example textures.

For any values for c_i and b_i, a model image can be rendered by computing $(x, y) = \sum_{i=0}^{M} c_i s_i(u, v)$ and $g = \sum_{j=0}^{M} b_j t_j(u, v)$ for each (u, v) in the reference image. Then the (x, y) pixel is rendered by assigning $I^{model}(x, y) = g$, that is by warping the texture into the model shape.

4.2   Matching a 2D face model to an image

For matching the flexible image model to a novel image we used the method described in (Jones and Poggio, 1996; Vetter et al., 1997). In 2D the error function as defined earlier in equation (4) is reduced to a function of the model parameters $\vec{c}$ and $\vec{b}$.

$$E(\vec{c}, \vec{b}) = \frac{1}{2} \sum_{x,y} \left[I^{novel}(x, y) - I^{model}(x, y)\right]^2$$

In order to compute I^{model} (see equation (5)) the shape transformation

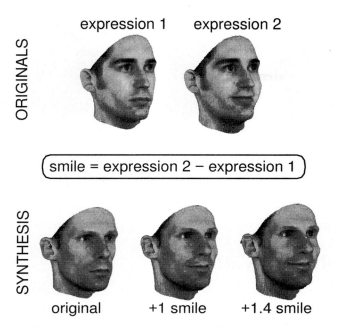

ORIGINALS

expression 1   expression 2

smile = expression 2 − expression 1

SYNTHESIS

original   +1 smile   +1.4 smile

Figure 3: *Correspondence between faces allows to map expression changes from one face to the other. The difference between the two expressions in the top row is mapped on the left face in the lower row multiplied by a factor of 1 (center) or by 1.4 (lower right)*

($\sum c_i s_i$) has to be inverted or one has to work in the coordinate system (u, v) of the reference image, which is computationally more efficient. Therefore, the shape transformation (given some estimated values for $\vec{c}$ and $\vec{b}$) is applied to both I^{novel} and I^{model}. From equation (5) we obtain

$$E = \frac{1}{2} \sum_{u,v} [I^{novel} \circ (\sum_{i=0}^{M} c_i s_i(u, v)) - \sum_{j=0}^{M} b_j \mathbf{t}_j(u, v)]^2.$$

Minimizing the error yields the model image which best fits the novel image with respect to the L_2 norm. The optimal model parameters $\vec{c}$ and $\vec{b}$ are found by a stochastic gradient descent algorithm (Viola, 1995), a method that is fast and has a low tendency to be caught in local minima.

The robustness of the algorithm is further improved using a coarse-to-fine approach (Burt and Adelson, 1983). In addition to the textural pyramids, separate resolution pyramids are computed for displacement fields s in x and y.

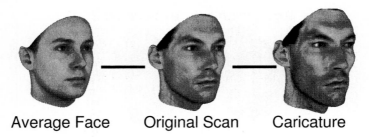

Average Face Original Scan Caricature

Figure 4: *The comparison the 3D model of an individual face to the average face allows for exaggerating the characteristics of that face. After establishing correspondence between all example faces (200), the average face can be computed. Here a caricature of the face was obtained by increasing the difference of its shape and of texture vectors to the average face by a factor of two.*

5 Novel view synthesis

After matching the 2D image model to the novel image, the 2D model parameters $\vec{c}$ and $\vec{b}$ can be used in the three-dimensional flexible face model as defined in equations (1) and (2). The justification of this parameter transfer is discussed in detail under the aspect of *linear object classes* in (Vetter and Poggio, 1997). The output of the 3D flexible face model should be seen as an estimate of the three-dimensional shape from the two-dimensional image. Since this result is a complete 3D face model new images can be rendered from any viewpoint or under any illumination condition.

5.1 Non rigid face transformations

The correspondence between all faces within this flexible model allows for mapping non rigid face transitions 'learned' from one face onto all other faces in the model.

Facial expressions: In figure 3 the transformation for a smile is extracted from one person and then mapped onto the face of a different person. By computing the correspondence between two examples of one persons face, one example showing the face smiling and the other showing the face in a neutral expression, this results in a correspondence field or deformation field which captures the spatial displacement for each vertex in the model according to the smile. This expression specific correspondence field is formal identical to the correspondence fields between different persons described earlier. Such a 'smile-vector' now can be added or subtracted from each face which is in correspondence to one of the originals, making a neutral looking face more smily or giving a smiling face a more emotionless expression.

In the following, we will describe two procedures that evaluate the characteristics of an individual face in respect to the other faces in the data base.

321

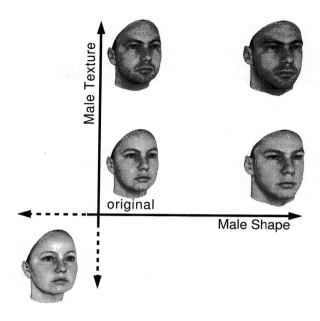

Figure 5: *Varying the perceived sex of a face. An original face is modified with respect to its shape (horizontal) and its texture (vertical). A sex specific vector is added or subtracted to the 3D-model of that face. The vector is defined by the difference between the male and the female average face where each average is computed over 100 faces.*

Caricaturing: Automated algorithms to enhance the characteristics of an individual face in images are well known (Brennan, 1985; Benson and Perrett, 1993). Typically, such algorithms operate as follows: First, a measure of the average value of a set of "features" across a large number of faces is computed. These features are defined, usually, as a set of facial landmark locations (e.g., corners of the eye and other points that are reasonably easy to localize/match on all faces) in the two-dimensional image. Next, to create a caricature of an individual face, a measure of the deviation of the face from the average two-dimensional configuration is computed. Finally, "distinctive" or unusual features of the face are exaggerated to produce the caricature. This generic algorithm applied to images, easily transfers to three-dimensional head representations (see also O'Toole et al., 1997) . Instead of using localized features we computed the average head shape by averaging over all shape vectors S_i and computed the average texture over all texture vectors T_i. Now individual 3D-models of faces can be directly compared with this average at each vertex position. By increasing the difference (distance) to the average the characteristics of a face can be exaggerated, for example a relatively big nose, compared to the average, becomes even bigger and a small nose will shrink even more. In figure 4 a caricature of a face is shown, the caricature is generated by doubling the distance of the original face to the average.

A different question to ask is, how are male and female faces distributed in our flexible face model, are there simple parameters in the model that correlate with the sex of a face. Such a question can not be answered in advance, since the sex of faces did not influence our design of the flexible model. To answer this question we performed a simple classification experiment on our faces, which were represented through their shape and texture vectors. Surprisingly, already a very simple linear classifier separated female and male faces to more than 90% correct. The classifier we used was a hyperplane in our model space, which was between the female and the male average and additionally perpendicular to the vector that is defined as the direction between the female and the male average. In other words, the projection of an individual face onto the vector, defined through the direction between the female and the male average, is already a good indicator for the sex of a face. *Manipulating the sex of a face:* The capability of our face model to synthesize new faces, can be used to modify the sex specific appearance of a face. The vector, defined by the direction between the male and female average, added or subtracted to an individual face, generates a new face which is more female or male. In figure 5 such a manipulation is shown. The original face of a female person is modified separately in its texture and shape components by adding or subtracting this sex specific vector.

6   Data set

We used a 3D data set obtained from 200 laser scanned $(Cyberware^{TM})$ heads of young adults (100 male and 100 female).

The laser scans provide head structure data in a cylindrical representation, with radii of surface points sampled at 512 equally-spaced angles, and at 512 equally spaced vertical distances. Additionally, the RGB-color values were recorded in the same spatial resolution and were stored in a texture map with 8 bit per channel. All faces were without makeup, accessories, and facial hair. After the head hair was removed digitally (but with manual editing), individual heads were represented by approximately 70000 vertices and the same number of color values.

The data set of 200 human faces was split randomly in a test and in a training set (100 faces each). The training set was used to built the flexible face model while the images to reconstruct were rendered from the test set .

Images were rendered showing the faces 30° from frontal using mainly ambient light. The image size used in the experiments was 256-by-256 pixel and 8 bit per color channel.

7   Results

The correspondence between all 3D example face models and a reference face modell was computed automatically. The results were correct (visual inspection) for almost all 200 faces, only in 7 cases obvious correspondence errors occurred.

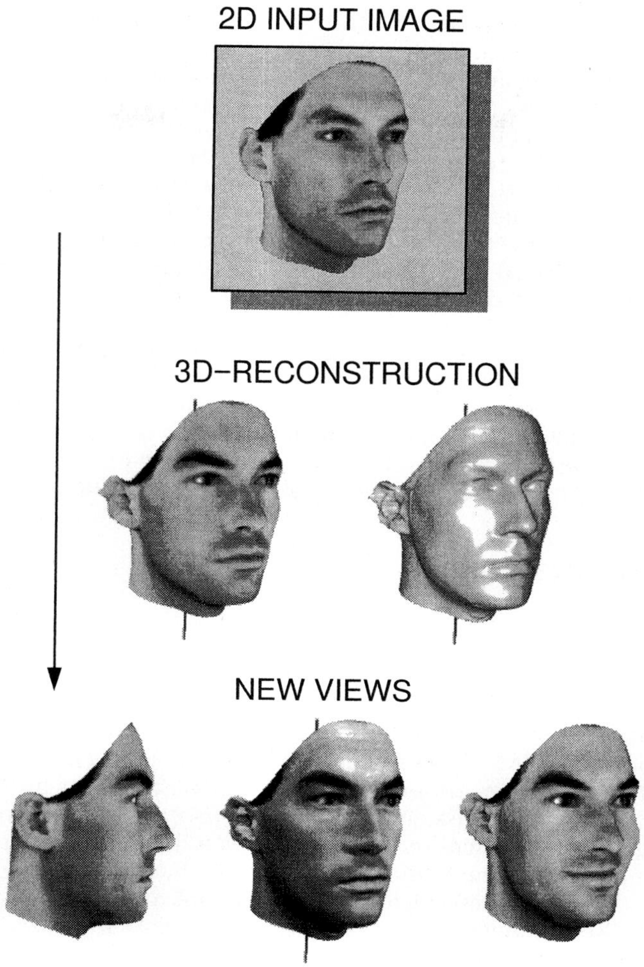

323

Figure 6: *Three-dimensional reconstruction of a face (center row) from a single two-dimensional image of known orientation and illumination (top row). The prior knowledge about faces was given through a training set of three-dimensional data of 100 faces different from the input face. The lower row shows new views generated by the flexible face model. From the left to the right, the face is shown from a new view point, under a changed illumination and smiling.*

Figure 6 shows an example of a three-dimensional face reconstruction from a single image. For the view synthesis we split our data set of 200 faces randomly into a training and a test set, each consisting of 100 faces. The training set was used to 'learn' a flexible model, where as test images of known orientation and illumination were rendered from the test set. After matching the model to the test image the model parameters were used to generate a complete three-dimensional face reconstuction. Presently, evaluation of the three-dimensional face reconstructions from single images is only based on visual inspection. Out of 100 reconstructions, 43 faces were highly similar and often hard to distinguish from the original. In 29 cases the shape reconstructions were good but texture showed obvious deficiencies in color. For the remaining 28 faces the reconstructions showed no similarity to the original. Still, face shape was natural and in only one case not human like, while texture problems were more severe. Figure 6 shows an example of a three-dimensional face reconstruction from a single image. We rated this example as highly similar but within this category it is lower average. The figure shows, beside the reconstruction in the center row, images where the view point, the illumination or the facial expression is changed.

8 Conclusions

We presented a method for approximating the three-dimensional shape of a face from just a single image. In an analysis-by-synthesis loop a flexible 3D-face model is matched to a novel image. The novel image now can be described or coded through the model parameters reconstructing the image. Prior knowledge on the three-dimensional appearance of faces derived from an example set of faces allows for predicting new images of a face. The results presented in this paper are preliminary. We hope the color problem can be resolved by appropriate constraints in color space. We also plan to apply a more sophisticated evaluation of reconstruction quality based on ratings by naive human subjects and automated similarity measures.

Clearly, the present implementation with its intermediate step of generating a complete 2D face model can not be the final solution. Next, we plan for each iteration step to form linear combinations in our 3D-representation first, render an image from this model and then perform the comparison to the target image. This requires several changes in our matching procedure to keep the computational costs tolerable.

Also, the present approach is restricted to images of faces where projection parameters and illumination conditions are known. The extension of the method to face images taken under arbitrary conditions will need several improvements. One the one hand, adding more free parameters into the matching procedure will require more sophisticated model representations especially in terms of the statistical dependence of the parameters. On the other hand, the linear model depends on the given example set. In order to represent faces from a different race or a different age group, the model will need examples of these, an effect also well known in human perception (cf. e.g. (O'Toole et al., 1994)).

A final judgment and comparison of the presented 3D-model approach with our 2D-image models presented earlier (Vetter and Poggio, 1997; Vetter,

1997) is currently difficult. At present, the two-dimensional linear object class approach seems to be more reliable in terms of its ability of match novel images. The number of wrong reconstuctions is less, however, for faces where the input image could be reconstructed, the 3D model showed a much better ability to generalize to new images. The implicit estimate of the surface normals in the image allowed for modifying the illumination conditions in the same image.

References

Akimoto, T., Suenaga, Y., and Wallace, R. (1993). Automatic creation of 3D facial models. *IEEE Computer Graphics and Applications*, 13(3):16–22.

Barron, J., Fleet, D., and Beauchemin, S. (1994). Performance of optical flow techniques. *Int. Journal of Computer Vision*, pages 43–77.

Benson, P. J. and Perrett, D. (1993). Perception and recognition of photographic quality caricatures : implications for the recognition of natural images. *European Journal of Cognitive Psychology*, 3:105–135.

Bergen, J., Anandan, P., Hanna, K., and Hingorani, R. (1992). Hierarchical model-based motion estimation. In *Proceedings of the European Conference on Computer Vision*, pages 237–252, Santa Margherita Ligure, Italy.

Bergen, J. and Hingorani, R. (1990). Hierarchical motion-based frame rate conversion. Technical report, David Sarnoff Research Center Princeton NJ 08540.

Beymer, D. and Poggio, T. (1996). Image representation for visual learning. *Science*, 272:1905–1909.

Beymer, D., Shashua, A., and Poggio, T. (1993). Example-based image analysis and synthesis. A.I. Memo No. 1431, Artificial Intelligence Laboratory, Massachusetts Institute of Technology.

Brennan, S. E. (1985). The caricature generator. *Leonardo*, 18:170–178.

Burt, P. and Adelson, E. (1983). The Laplacian pyramide as a compact image code. *IEEE Transactions on Communications*, (31):532–540.

Choi, C., Okazaki, T., Harashima, H., and Takebe, T. (1991). A system of analyzing and synthesizing facial images. In *Proc. IEEE Int. Symposium of Circuit and Syatems (ISCAS91)*, pages 2665–2668.

Duda, R. and Hart, P. (1973). *Pattern classification and scene analysis*. John Wiley & Sons, New York.

Grenander, U. (1978). *Pattern Analysis, Lectures in Pattern Theory*. Springer, New York, 1 edition.

Herpers, R., Michaelis, M., Lichtenauer, K. H., and Sommer, G. (1996). Edge and keypoint detection in facial regions. In *Proc. International Conference on Automatic Face and Gesture Recognition*, pages 22–27, Killington, VT.

Jones, M. and Poggio, T. (1996). Model-based matching by linear combination of prototypes. A.i. memo no., Artificial Intelligence Laboratory, Massachusetts Institute of Technology.

Kosslyn, S. M. (1994). *Image and Brain*. MIT Press, Cambridge, MA.

Lanitis, A., Taylor, C., Cootes, T., and Ahmad, T. (1995). Automatic interpretation of human faces and hand gestures using flexible models. In M.Bichsel, editor, *Proc. International Workshop on Face and Gesture Recognition*, pages 98–103, Zurich, Switzerland.

Marr, D. (1982). *Vision,*. W. H. Freeman, San Fancisco.

Mumford, D. (1996). Pattern theory: A unifying perspective. In Knill, D. and Richards, W., editors, *Perception as Bayesian Inference*. Cambridge University Press.

O'Toole, A., Deffenbacher, K., Valentin, D., and Abdi, H. (1994). Structural aspects of face recognition and the other-race effect. *Memory and Cognition*, 22:208–224.

O'Toole, A., Vetter, T., Volz, H., and Salter, E. (1997). Three-dimensional caricatures of human heads: distinctiveness and the perception of facial age. *Perception*, in press.

Parke, F. (1974). A parametric model of human faces. Doctoral thesis, University of Utah, Salt Lake City.

Poggio, T. and Vetter, T. (1992). Recognition and structure from one 2D model view: observations on prototypes, object classes, and symmetries. A.I. Memo No. 1347, Artificial Intelligence Laboratory, Massachusetts Institute of Technology.

Ullman, S. (1989). Aligning pictorial descriptions: An approach for object recognition. *Cognition*, 32:193–254.

Vetter, T. (1997). Synthestis of novel views from a single face image. *International Journal of Computer Vision*, (in press).

Vetter, T., Jones, M. J., and Poggio, T. (1997). A bootstrapping algorithm for learning linear models of object classes. In *IEEE Conference on Computer Vision and Pattern Recognition – CVPR'97*, Puerto Rico, USA. IEEE Computer Society Press.

Vetter, T. and Poggio, T. (1997). Linear objectclasses and image synthesis from a single example image. *IEEE Transactions on Pattern Analysis and Machine Intelligence*, 19(7):733–742.

Viola, P. (1995). Alignment by maximization of mutual information. A.I. Memo No. 1548, Artificial Intelligence Laboratory, Massachusetts Institute of Technology.

Modular Forensic Architectures

Srinivas Gutta and Harry Wechsler

Department of Computer Science
George Mason University
Fairfax, VA 22030-4444, U.S.A.
{sgutta, wechsler)@cs.gmu.edu

Abstract. We describe modular (hybrid) forensic architectures for verification ('surveillance'), gender and ethnic classification of human faces and show their feasibility using a collection of 3,006 face images corresponding to 1,009 subjects from the FERET database. The hybrid approach consists of two modules : an ensemble of connectionist networks - radial basis functions (RBF) - and an inductive decision tree (DT). The specific functionalities of our hybrid architecture include (**a**) query by consensus provided by the ensemble of networks to cope with the inherent variability of the image formation and data acquisition process, (**b**) categorical classification provided by decision trees, and (**c**) flexible and adaptive thresholds as opposed to *ad hoc* and hard thresholds provided by DT as well. Experimental results prove the feasibility of our approach as they yield (**i**) 96 % accuracy, for the verification task, (**ii**) 96 % accuracy on gender classification, and (**iii**) 94 % accuracy on the ethnic classification task.

Keywords. Decision Trees (DT), Ethnic Classification, Face Recognition, FERET, Gender Classification, Hybrid Classifiers, Network Ensembles, Radial Basis Functions (RBF), Surveillance

1 Introduction

Multimedia applications, like the Digital Library Initiative (DLI), are accessing increasing amounts of data across 'Information Highways'. The future growth of multimedia is predicated on 'intelligent' storage, search, processing, and retrieval of information from large and heterogeneous databases through user friendly interfaces. In particular, as multimedia applications in wide-ranging fields - from photo-journalism to medical technology - include pictorial information, the need for data compression and for querying large on-line image databases will significantly increase. Another application area is biometrics technology, where both face recognition, analysis and discrimination of facial expressions is important for (video) applications related to forensics, telecommunication, HDTV, and medicine. Key issues to be addressed in this context should include derivation and computation of attributes of images and objects that provide useful query functionality, retrieval methods based on similarity as opposed to exact match, query by image example or user drawn image, query refinement and navigation, and high dimensional data base indexing [Niblack, 1993].

One of the most important technologies needed to expand the frontiers of computing is the management of visual information. Grand challenges like space exploration and weather prediction are expanding human frontiers, but the grandest challenge is the exploration of how we as human beings recognize each other, react to the world and interact with each other. Faces are accessible 'windows' into the mechanisms that govern our emotional and social lives [Jain, 1992]. The face is a unique feature of human beings. Even the faces of 'identical twins' differ in some respects. Humans can detect, identify and analyze faces in a scene with little or no effort. This skill is quite robust, despite large changes in the visual stimulus due to viewing conditions, expression, aging, and distractions such as glasses or changes in hairstyle. Building automated systems that accomplish this task is, however, very difficult. There are several related sub problems: (i) detection of a pattern as a face, (ii) recognition, (iii) analysis of facial expressions, and (iv) classification based on physical features [Samal and Iyengar, 1992]. A system that performs these operations will find countless applications, e.g. criminal identification and retrieval of missing children, workstation and building security, credit card verification, and video-document retrieval. In particular one could start to address tasks ranging from tagging ('annotating') video frames characterized by specific facial landmarks - like specific faces wearing glasses - to retrieving all the frames where same person shows up.

Facial analysis is a difficult task mostly because of the inherent variability of the image formation process in terms of image quality and photometry, geometry, occlusion, change, and disguise. Two recent surveys on facial analysis discuss these challenges in some detail [Samal and Iyengar, 1992; Chellappa et. el., 1995]. All face analysis systems available today can only perform on restricted databases of images in terms of size, age, gender, and/or race, and they further assume well controlled environments. There are additional degrees of variability ranging from those assuming that the position/cropping of the face and its environment (distance and illumination) are totally controlled, to those involving little or no control over the background and viewpoint, and eventually to those allowing for major changes in facial appearance due to factors such as aging and disguise (hat and/or glasses).

As intelligent highways and multimedia applications are being developed it becomes imperative to develop robust classification and retrieval schemes. This chapter addresses those concerns by considering hybrid classifier architectures and showing their feasibility for forensic tasks on large databases consisting of facial images. The hybrid architectures, consisting of an ensemble of connectionist networks - radial basis functions (RBF) - and an inductive decision tree (DT), combine the merits of 'holistic' template matching with those of 'discrete' features using both positive and negative learning examples. The specific functionalities of our hybrid architecture include (a) query by consensus provided by the ensemble of networks to cope with the inherent variability of the image formation and data acquisition process, (b) categorical classification provided by decision trees, and (c) flexible and adaptive thresholds as opposed to *ad hoc* and hard thresholds provided by DT as well.

The above issues are addressed in full detail through the remainder of this chapter where fully automated solutions for face recognition and analysis tasks are presented using as a test bed images from the FERET facial database. Section 2 provides a brief background on the face processing problem. Motivation for hybrid classifiers is presented in Section 3, while the methodology for classification in the context of the face recognition problem is discussed in Section 4. The system and the tools developed to implement the modular forensic architecture are described in Section 5. The image acquisition process and the FERET database are briefly described in Section 6. Extensive experiments were carried out to validate the hybrid classifier architecture and they are described in Section 7. The paper concludes in Section 8 with an assessment of our results and with a look towards future developments.

2 Facial Analysis

For social interaction people must be able to process faces in a variety of ways. There is a vast amount of literature on social and cognitive psychology attesting to the impressive capabilities of humans at identifying familiar faces, as well as extracting information from both familiar and unfamiliar faces, including gender, race, and emotional state of the person [Valentin et. al., 1994]. Facial analysis is a difficult task, mostly because of the inherent variability of the image formation process in terms of image quality and photometry, geometry, occlusion, change, and disguise.

Identifying people seems straightforward -- people do it all the time in business and in social encounters. Automated recognition, however, requires computer systems to look through large prestored sets of characteristics ('the gallery') and pick the one that matches best the features of the unknown individual ('the probe'). In most practical scenarios there are two possible recognition tasks to be considered [Phillips et. al., 1998]:

- MATCH: An image of an unknown individual is collected ('probe') and the identity is found searching a large set of images ('gallery'). Matching becomes especially difficult when the probe is a duplicate rather than the same (counterpart) image from the gallery. The duplicate image involves variability due to both the image acquisition process and to changes in physical appearance. Robust matching should allow for the possibility that there is no match for the probe in the existing gallery.

- SURVEILLANCE: Rather than identifying a person, the system is now involved with verification and checks if a given probe belongs to a relatively small gallery, sometimes labeled as a set of intruders. The surveillance system is usually flooded with a large set of face images (e.g. video frame retrieval and/or airport security) and most of the faces, if not all of them, correspond to false positives.

There are two major approaches for automated recognition of human faces. The first approach, the abstractive one, extracts (and measures) discrete *local* features 'indexes' for retrieving and identifying faces, so subsequently standard statistical pattern recognition techniques can be employed for probing amongst faces using these measurements. The other approach, the holistic one, conceptually related to template matching, attempts to recognize faces using *global* representations. Characteristic of this approach are connectionist methods such as back propagation ('holons'), principal component analysis (PCA), and singular value decomposition (SVD) using eigenfaces [Turk and Pentland, 1991].

Face recognition starts with the detection of face patterns, proceeds by normalizing the face images to account for geometrical and illumination changes, possibly using information about the facial landmarks, identifies the faces using appropriate classification algorithms, and post processes the results using model-based schemes and logistic feedback. The variety of methods published in the literature show that there is not a unique or generic solution to the face recognition problem. Consequently, a taxonomy of face recognition technology cannot identify clear cut algorithms, but consider instead processing strategies describing (i) face detection and normalization, (ii) feature extraction, (iii) coding and internal representation, and (iv) classification and recognition. The first stage, that of face detection, involves attention mechanisms similar to those used by the human visual system (HVS) to screen out the visual field and to focus on salient input characteristics. Some recent work would model the human head as an elliptical structure in order to segment it [Sirohey, 1993]. As the human face is an elastic object, Arad et al [1994] suggest modeling facial expression and learning the resulting image warping using RBF in order to achieve image normalization. As another example, the novel dynamic and multiresolution (DMA) scheme introduced by Takacs and Wechsler [1995] is mostly concerned with the aspects involved in selecting (information loaded) fixation points and the early detection of salient facial landmarks needed for the (geometrical) normalization stage.

The basic question, relevant for face classification and still begging an answer, is what form should the structural code (for encoding the face) take to achieve face recognition. Recent experiments performed by Brunelli and Poggio [1993a] suggest that the optimal strategy for face recognition is still holistic and corresponds to template matching. Although recognition by matching raw images has been successful under limited circumstances [Baron, 1981], it suffers from the usual shortcomings of straightforward correlation-based approaches, such as sensitivity to face orientation, size, variable lighting conditions, and noise. The reason for this vulnerability of direct matching methods lie in their attempt to carry out the required classification in a space of extreme high dimensionality. To overcome the curse of dimensionality, the connectionist equivalent of data compression methods are employed first. It has been successfully argued, however, that the resulting principal component (feature) dimensions do not necessarily retain the structure needed for classification, and that more general and powerful method for feature extraction such as projection pursuit [Huber, 1981] are required [Phillips, 1994]. The basic idea behind projection pursuit is to pick 'interesting' low dimensional projections of a high dimensional point cloud, by maximizing an objective function such as the deviation from normality. In other words, one should seek features not only in terms of large variance but whose probability density function (pdf) is multimodal.

One can also consider a hybrid strategy, using both local and global concepts, as it is the case with the Dynamic Link Architecture (DLA) [Buhmann et. al., 1992]. DLA starts by first extracting local (feature) information and then performs matching using global information describing the connecting geometry of significant local features. The Gabor and/or wavelet defined local (feature) representations, labeled as jets, are augmented by their intrinsic global spatial structure. Face recognition is the result of graph matching employing optimization techniques based on diffusion processes. The corresponding cost (fitness) function consists of two terms, one measuring the resemblance between the jets corresponding to an unknown face and those describing the database, and the other term measuring the resemblance between the corresponding spatial structures linking the jets.

Few attempts have been made to perform gender classification and the ones made used very small data sets. At the same time we are not aware of publications related to ethnic classification. An early example of gender classification system (SEXNET) is due to Golomb et. al. [1990]. In SEXNET, a back propagation network was trained to discriminate the gender of human faces, yielding an accuracy of 91.9% on a data set of 90 exemplars corresponding to 45 male and 45 female subjects. The training set was composed of 80 exemplars and only the remaining 10 exemplars were used for testing. Brunelli and Poggio [1993b] report an accuracy of 87.5% using cross validation on a data set of 168 images corresponding to 21 male and 21 female subjects and based on 18 geometrical features. The system consists of a hyper basis function network trained on the data sets of all minus one subject and then tested on the excluded one. Using a discriminant function analysis Burton et. al. [1993] report an accuracy of 85.5% on a data set of 91 male and 88 female images respectively. Tamura et. al. [1996] use a backpropagation network on a data set of 60 low resolution face images corresponding to 30 male and 30 female subjects, yielding an accuracy of 90%. The training set was composed of 30 faces (15 male and 15 female) and the testing set consists of the remaining 30 faces. Recently Wiskott [1997] reported an accuracy of 92% on a data set of 111 faces corresponding to 72 male and 39 female faces using Dynamic Link Matching (DLM).

As the size of the data sets used in the experiments reported above is quite restricted, no conclusions can be drawn about the ability of such methods to generalize and to scale up for large image databases, possibly consisting of several hundreds or thousands of images. Towards that end, we describe hybrid classification architectures for verification, gender and ethnic classification of human faces and show their feasibility using a collection of 3,006 face images from the FERET database corresponding to 1,906 images of gender male and 1,100 images of gender female. The same database consists of 1,934 images of Caucasian origin, 362 images of Asian origin, 474 images of Oriental origin and 236 images of African origin, respectively.

3 Hybrid Classifiers

The hybrid approach is based on a psychologically plausible distinction between two types of cognitive operations: automatic, reflexive or low level (e.g., perception) *vs* controlled, deliberative or high level (e.g., reasoning). The concept of reductionism is a common practice in the development of intelligent systems - to design solutions to complex problems through a stepwise decomposition of the task into successive modules. Typically, in hybrid systems, reflexive tasks are assigned to the connectionist subsystem and deliberative tasks to the symbolic subsystem. In the context of facial analysis, hybrid architectures, consisting of connectionist networks and symbolic methods, would thus combine the merits of 'holistic' template matching' with those of 'discrete' methods using numerical and symbolic values, respectively.

The hybrid approach for classification involves specific levels of knowledge where the hierarchy is defined in terms of concept granularity and specific interfaces. As one moves upward in the hierarchical structure, we witness a corresponding degree of data compression so more powerful ('reasoning') methods can be employed but on reduced amounts of data. Connectionism can handle the whole range of sensory inputs and their variability ('noise'). Its distributed nature provides for fault tolerance to missing and incomplete data. The output of such modules, known to have a well-defined maximum likelihood (ML) probabilistic meaning, can be then combined across an ensemble of such networks. Symbolic methods are compact and can fuse data from different sensory modalities and cognitive modes. As a consequence one can make sense of the sensory input and interpret ('explain') it using meaningful coding units.

An early example of using an ensemble of neural networks is due to Hamshire and Waibel [1992]. The Meta - Pi classifier is a connectionist pattern classifier that consists of a number of source-dependent sub networks that are integrated by a combinational Time Delay Neural Network (TDNN) superstructure. The TDNN combines the outputs of the modules, trained independently, in order to provide a global classification. Lincoln and Skrzypek [1990] have proposed multiple back propagation networks for improved performance and fault tolerance. Following training, a 'cluster' is created by computing the average of the outputs generated by the individual networks. The output of the 'cluster' is used as the desired output during training by feeding it back to the individual networks. The reason behind using such a strategy comes from the assumption that while it is possible to 'fool' a single BP network all of the time one cannot mislead all the networks all the time. Battiti and Colla [1994] have proposed means to combine the outputs of different neural network classifiers to improve the rejection-accuracy (ROC) rates and to make the combined performance better than that obtained from the individual components. The suggested concept of democracy is analogous with the human way of reaching a pondered decision - query by consensus. Flocchini et al., [1992], have proposed a complex architecture based on a hierarchy of neural networks with a self-referencing structure. The system is structured as a tree in which nodes correspond to neural networks, each one having different tasks. Each leaf is a recognition module defined as a network with different characteristics. These networks are coordinated by a supervisor in a self-referencing structure. During the training phase, the Meta-Net supervisor observes the behavior of recognition nets and learns which net is more reliable in what task. During the test phase the Meta-Net decides, given an input image, what weights to assign to each network and how to modify their output in order to obtain the final result. Soulie et. al. [1993] have proposed Multi-Modular Architectures (MMA) that integrate various neural networks to realize feature extraction and recognition in successive stages that are cooperatively trained.

Hybrid architectures, whose task is to integrate the connectionist and symbolic ('rule-based') levels are discussed by Greenspan [1991] using unsupervised and supervised learning, respectively. The approach, conceptually similar to learned vector quantization (LVQ), was used for pattern recognition tasks. Towell and Shavlik [1994] present a methodology for the transfer of symbolic knowledge into a neural network (KBANN) and for the extraction of rules from the trained neural network (NOFM) in order to interpret the operation of the system. KBANN translates a collection of rules into a neural network by individually translating each rule into a small subnetwork that accurately reproduces the behavior of the translated rule. These small sub networks are then assembled to form a single neural network that mimics the behavior of the whole rule. KBANN uses a knowledge base of domain-specific inference rules, in the form of propositional Horn clauses, to define what is initially known about the topic. Once the KBANN network has been trained, the NOFM method, forms groups of similarly weighted links with each hidden and output unit and sets link weights of all group members to the average of the group. In the next step NOFM eliminates any groups that do not significantly affect whether the output unit will be active or not. Holding all link weights constant, NOFM optimizes biases of all hidden and output units using the backpropagation algorithm and forms a single rule for each hidden and output unit. The rule consists of a threshold given by the bias and weighted antecedents specified by the remaining links, and finally the rules are simplified by eliminating weights and thresholds. Recently, Morgan and Boulard [1995] have suggested hybrid methods for automatic speech recognition. Specifically, it is suggested that back propagation (BP) should estimate emission probabilities for the global decoder encoded as a Hidden Markov Model (HMM).

An important consideration for anyone developing classification schemes, hybrid or otherwise, is the way the system is trained. Valid assumptions about performance in terms of generalization ability can be made only when the data used to train the system is representative of that likely to be encountered later on during field operation and that appropriate strategies, such as crossvalidation (CV), would partition the data into training, tuning, and testing sets, respectively. If one were to define ambiguity as the variation of the output ensemble members over unlabeled ('test') data, the disagreement between networks can be quantified and corrective training takes place [Krogh and Vedelsby, 1995]. An active learning scheme, corresponding to corrective training, would retrain on those test examples for whom the ensemble strongly disagrees.

The hybrid approach pursued in this chapter consists of connectionist and symbolic modules. The connectionist stage is further defined in terms of an ensemble of Radial Basis Function (RBF) networks, while the symbolic stage consists of Decision Trees (DT). The CV ensemble implements active learning schemes leading to decreased ambiguity by employing different topologies for the networks themselves and training the networks on different data sets corresponding to variations of the original data.

4 Methodology

The hybrid classifier architecture for face recognition tasks is shown below in Fig. 1. The motivation for this architecture comes from (a) the apparent need to process imagery at different levels of granularity, like those provided by connectionist and symbolic approaches, and (b) integration of local and global processes. As it was discussed earlier, face recognition starts through the detection of a pattern as a face and boxing it, proceeds by normalizing the face image to account for geometrical and illumination changes using information about the box surrounding the face and/or eyes location, and finally it identifies the face using appropriate image representation and classification algorithms. The results reported later on assume that the patterns corresponding to face images have been detected and normalized. The specific face recognition tasks considered herein include (**i**) surveilling a gallery of images for the presence of specific probes (see Section 7.1), (**ii**) gender classification (see Section 7.2), and (**iii**) ethnic classification (see Section 7.3). The tools needed to detect face patterns and normalize them are discussed elsewhere [Gutta, et. al., 1998; Huang, et. al., 1996], while this chapter describes only the tools developed to realize and implement those stages of face recognition involved in classification tasks. The hybrid classifiers used consist of an ensemble of radial basis functions (ERBF) networks and decision trees (DT).

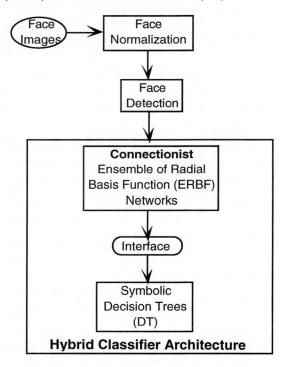

Figure 1. Automated face Recognition (AFR)

5 Hybrid Classifier Architecture

The hybrid classifiers consist of an ensemble of connectionist networks - radial basis functions (RBF) - and an inductive decision tree (DT). The reasons behind using RBF are their ability for clustering similar images before classifying them and the potential for developing in the future hierarchical rather than linear classifiers where faces will be iteratively discriminated in terms of gender, race, and age, before final recognition takes place. Decision trees (DT) implement the symbolic stage using RBF outputs because they provide for flexible and adaptive thresholds, and can interpret ('explain') the way classification and retrieval are eventually achieved. We describe next Ensembles of RBFs (ERBF) and hybrid classifiers consisting of ERBF and DT.

5.1   RBF

The construction of the RBF network involves three different layers. The input layer is made up of source nodes (sensory units). The second layer is a hidden layer whose goal is to cluster the data and reduce its dimensionality. The output layer supplies the response of the network to the activation patterns applied to the input layer. The transformation from the input space to the hidden-unit space is *non-linear,* whereas the transformation from the hidden-unit space to the output space is *linear.* In particular, we note that a RBF classifier can be viewed in two ways [Lippmann and Ng, 1991]. One is to interpret the RBF classifier as a set of kernel functions that expand input vectors into a high-dimensional space, trying to take advantage of the mathematical fact that a classification problem cast into a high-dimensional space is more likely to be linearly separable than one in a low-dimensional space. Another view is to interpret the RBF classifier as a function-mapping interpolation method that tries to construct hypersurfaces, one for each class, by taking a linear combination of the Basis Functions (BF). These hypersurfaces can be viewed as discriminant functions, where the surface has a high value for the class it represents and a low value for all others. An unknown input vector is classified as belonging to the class associated with the hypersurface with the largest output at that point. In this case the BFs do not serve as a basis for a high-dimensional space, but as components in a finite expansion of the desired hypersurface where the component coefficients (weights) have to be trained.

An RBF classifier has architecture very similar to that of a traditional three-layer back-propagation network (Fig. 2). Connections between the input and middle layers have unit weights and, as a result, do not have to be trained. Nodes in the middle layer, called BF nodes, produce a localized response to the input using Gaussian kernels Each hidden unit can be viewed as a localized receptive field (RF). The hidden layer is trained using k-means clustering.

The most common basis function (BF) used are Gaussians, where the activation level y_i of the hidden unit i is given by:

$$y_i = \Phi_i\left(\|X - \mu_i\|\right) = \exp\left[-\sum_{k=1}^{D}\frac{(x_k - \mu_{ik})^2}{2h\sigma_{ik}^2 o}\right]$$

where h is a proportionality constant for the variance, x_k is the kth component of the input vector $X = [x_1, x_2, \ldots, x_D]$, and μ_{ik} and σ_{ik}^2 are the kth components of the mean and variance vectors, and o is the overlap factor between BFs. The outputs of the hidden unit lie between 0 and 1, and could be possibly interpreted as fuzzy memberships; the closer the input to the center of the Gaussian, the larger the response of the node. The activation level Z_j of an output unit is given by:

$$Z_j = \sum_i w_{ij} y_i + w_{0j}$$

where Z_j is the output of the jth output node, y_i is the activation of the ith BF node, w_{ij} is the weight connecting the ith BF node to the jth output node, and w_{0j} is the bias or the threshold of the jth output node. The bias comes from the weights associated with a BF node that has a constant unit output regardless of the input. An unknown vector X is classified as belonging to the class associated with the output node j with the largest output Z_j.

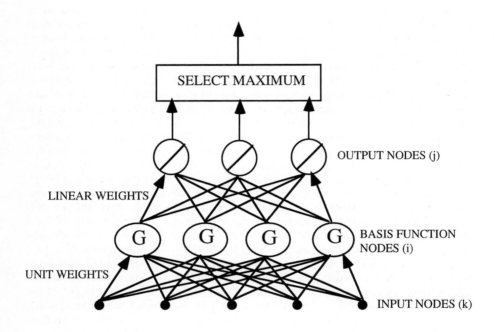

Figure 2. RBF Architecture

The RBF input consists of **n** normalized face images fed to the network as 1D vectors. The hidden (unsupervised) layer, implements an enhanced **k**-means clustering procedure, where both the number of Gaussian cluster nodes and their variance are dynamically set. The number of clusters varies, in steps of 5, from 1/5 of the number of training images to **n**, the total number of training images. The width of the Gaussian for each cluster, is set to the **maximum** {the distance between the center of the cluster and the farthest away member - within class diameter, the distance between the center of the cluster and closest pattern from all other clusters} multiplied by an overlap factor **o**, here equal to 2. The width is further dynamically refined using different proportionality constants **h**. The hidden layer yields the equivalent of a functional facial base, where each cluster node encodes some common characteristics across the face space. The output (supervised) layer maps face encodings ('expansions') along such a space to their corresponding ID(entity) classes and finds the corresponding expansion ('weight') coefficients using pseudoinverse techniques. Note that the number of clusters is frozen for that configuration (number of clusters and specific proportionality constant **h**) which yields 100 % accuracy on the ID identification task when tested on the same training images.

5.2 Ensemble of Radial Basis Function (ERBF) Networks

For a connectionist architecture to be successful it has to cope with the variability available in the image acquisition process. One possible solution to the above problem is to implement the equivalent of query by consensus using an ensemble of Radial Basis Functions (ERBF), where each RBF network acts as an individual jury member and the ERBF collectively reaches some classification decision. Network ensembles are defined in terms of their specific topology (connections and RBF nodes) and the data they are trained on. Specifically, both original data and their induced distortions, caused by geometrical changes and blur, are used for training. Two different versions of ERBF are proposed and described below.

5.2.1 ERBF1

The first model integrates three RBF components and it is shown in Fig. 3. Each RBF component is further defined in terms of three RBF nodes, each of which specified in terms of the number of clusters and the overlap factors. The overlap factors **o**, defined earlier, for the RBF nodes RBF(11, 21, 31), RBF(12, 22, 32), and RBF(13, 23, 33) are set to (standard) 2, 2.5, and 3, respectively. The same RBF nodes were trained on original face images, and on the same original face images with either some Gaussian noise added or subject to some degree of geometrical ('rotation'), respectively. The intermediate nodes C1, C2, and C3 act as buffers for the transfer of the normalized face images to the various RBF components. Training is performed until 100 % recognition accuracy is achieved for each RBF node. The nine output vectors generated by the RBF nodes are passed to a judge *who* would make a decision on whether the probe ('input') belongs to the gallery or not. The specific decision is {**if** the norm of the average of all the nine outputs is greater than threshold θ **then** accept **else** reject}, where the threshold θ is empirically set.

5.2.2 ERBF2

ERBF2 is derived from ERBF1 by increasing the number of images (3) used to train each class and by decreasing the number of RBF nodes from nine to three (Fig. 4). Each RBF node is now trained on a mix of face images consisting of original ones and their distorted variations. As it was the case with ERBF1, the overlap factor **o** for RBF1, RBF2, and RBF3 were set to (standard) 2, 2.5, and 3, respectively. Training is performed until 100 % recognition accuracy is achieved for each RBF node. During testing, nine output vectors are generated, corresponding to the Cartesian product between the kind of input {original, variation with Gaussian noise, variation with rotation}and the kind of RBF node, and they are passed to a *judge* who would make a decision on whether the probe ('input') belongs to the gallery or not. The specific decision is { **if** the norm of the average of all the nine outputs is greater than threshold θ **then** accept **else** reject}, where the threshold θ is empirically set.

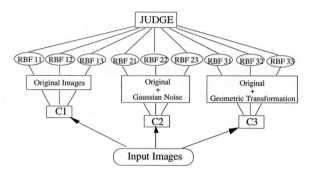

Figure 3. ERBF1 Architecture

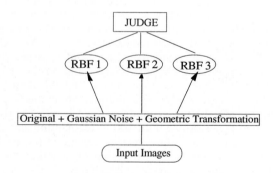

Figure 4. ERBF2 Architecture

5.3 Decision Tree (DT)

The basic aim of any concept-learning symbolic system is to construct rules for classifying objects given a *training set* of objects whose class labels are known. In the formalism used here all objects are described by a fixed collection of attributes, each with its own set of discrete values and each object ('face') belongs to one of two classes. The two classes correspond to the gallery (positive example / 'CORRECT') and the complement of the gallery (negative example /

'INCORRECT'). The decision tree (DT) realizes the rules needed for the above classification.

The decision tree employed is Quinlan's C4.5 [1986] and it uses an information-theoretical approach based on entropy. C4.5 builds the decision tree using a top-down, divide-and-conquer approach: select an attribute, divide the training set into subsets characterized by the possible values of the attribute, and follow the same procedure recursively with each subset until no subset contains objects from more than one class. The single-class subsets correspond then to leaves of the decision tree. The entropy based criterion that has been used for the selection of the attribute is called the *gain ratio criterion* .

The information theory that underpins the criterion responsible for attribute selection is as follows. Assume that S is any set of events ('cases') and let *freq* (C_i, S) stand for the number of events in S that belong to some class C_i while $|S|$ denotes the total number of events in the set S. Define now the message ('event') *m* as the one corresponding to the case when one event is selected at random from S and it belongs to some class C_j. The message *m* has then the probability $p = freq (C_j, S) / |S|$ and the information ('entropy') it conveys is $- \log_2 p$ bits. The information for events coming from all the *k* classes, *info (S),* is then $- \Sigma p \log_2 p$.

Let X now be a possible test ('attribute selection') with *n* outcomes that partitions the set S of training cases into subsets $S_1, S_2, ..., S_n$ and define

$$\text{info } (X, S) = \Sigma \left(|S_i| / |S| \right) \text{info } (S_i)$$

$$\text{gain } (X) = \text{info}(S) - \text{info } (X, S)$$

The *gain criterion* selects that test X for whom *gain (X)* achieves maximum. This criterion has, however, a serious deficiency, namely, it has strong bias in favor of those tests yielding many outcomes. This bias can be, however, accounted for by normalization where apparent gains, attributable to tests with many outcomes, are properly adjusted. Towards that end define *split info (X)* as the entropy of an event where information is given in terms of outcomes, rather than classes as it was the case with *info (S)* , and redefine *gain(X)* as *gain ratio (X)* :

$$\text{split info } (X) = - \Sigma \left(|T_i| / |T| \right) \log_2 \left(|T_i| / |T| \right)$$

$$\text{gain ratio } (X) = \text{gain } (X) / \text{split info } (X)$$

If the split is trivial, split information will be small and the gain ratio will be unstable. To avoid this, the *gain ratio* criterion selects a test to maximize the ratio subject to the constraint that the information gain must be at least as large as the average gain over all tests examined.

5.4 ERBF (1,2) and DT (C4.5) Hybrids

Inductive learning, when used to build decision trees requires a special interface for numeric-to-symbolic data conversion. The ERBF output vector (X1, ... ,X9) chosen for training is tagged for example, as 'CORRECT' (positive example) or 'INCORRECT' (negative example) for the surveillance task and quantized to values ranging from 1 to 10. The input from ERBF to the C4.5 consists of a string of learning (positive and negative) events, each event given as a vector of discrete ('quantized') attribute values. Training involves choosing a random set of positive and negative events. C4.5 builds the classifier as a decision tree whose structure consists of

- *leaves*, indicating class identity, or
- *decision nodes* that specify some test to be carried out on a single attribute value, with one branch for each possible outcome of the test.

The decision tree is used to classify an example by starting at the root of the tree and moving through it until a leaf is encountered. At each branch point an attribute is evaluated and a decision on how to move down the tree is made.

6 FERET

For the most part, the performance of face recognition systems reported in the literature has been measured on small databases, with each research site carrying out experiments using their own database and thus making meaningful comparisons and drawing conclusions impossible [Robertson and Craw, 1994]. The majority of those databases were collected under very controlled situations and consisted of a relatively small number of subjects and corresponding images. To overcome such shortcomings, we have been developing over the last several years the FERET facial database so a standard tested for face recognition applications can become available [Phillips, et. al., 1998]. The FERET data base consists now of 1,934 sets comprising 14,075 images. Since large amounts of images were acquired during different photo sessions, the lighting conditions and the size of the facial images can vary. The diversity of the FERET data base is across gender, race and age, and includes duplicates as well.

Specific software and hardware requirements have to be met in order to accomplish the goals of the FERET program in terms of data collection, communication and sharing of resources, data processing and benchmarking, and specific graphical user interfaces (GUIs). Computational requirements are extensive, even more so when one contemplates processing and/or making available hundreds of images at one time. 1,934 facial image sets - including 494 duplicate sets taken at different times and possibly wearing glasses - consisting of several poses and totaling 14,075 images have been collected so far. Acquisition of duplicate sets is very important if one wants to assess how robust is a given face recognition system when tested on images shot at different times, which are likely to be different. The facial image sets were acquired without any restrictions imposed on expression and with two frontal images shot at different times during the photo session.

7 Experiments

The database for our experiments comes from the standard FERET facial database and comprises 3,006 frontal images whose resolution is 256 x 384 encoded using 256 gray scale levels. The frontal images come from 1,009 unique subjects. It is to be noted that each subject appears in the database as an original pair ('fa' and 'fb'). An image of a subject taken on a different date is called a duplicate. Specifically, an image of a subject appearing in the database taken at a different date is labeled as 'duplicate1', while the modified (scaled up version of original) image of a subject is labeled as 'duplicate2'. These images are then resized to standard resolution of 256 x 384. The database now includes 494 ('duplicate1' + 'duplicate2') subject duplicate pairs. The images were acquired within a span of 3 years. These images are then passed to a Face Detection and Normalization system [Gutta, et. al., 1998; Huang, et. al., 1996] and made available at a standard resolution of 64 x 72. The total number of images of gender 'Male' is 1,906 and of gender 'Female' is 1,100 images. The same database consists of 1,932 images of Caucasian origin, 362 images of Asian origin, 474 images of Oriental origin and 238 images of African origin, respectively.

In Section 7.1, we report on the experiments conducted for the surveillance task, in Section 7.2 we report on the experiments conducted for the gender classification task, while in Section 7.3 we report the results for the ethnic classification task. A sample set of face images is shown in Fig. 5.

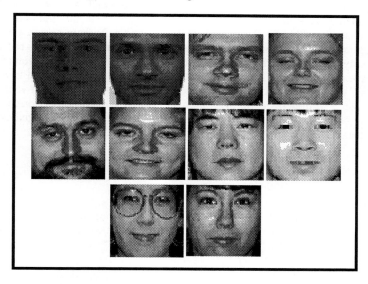

Figure 5. Sample Set of Face Images

7.1 Surveillance

First we report on experiments where, possibly for security reasons, the automatic face recognition (AFR) system screens a large number of probes against some predefined gallery it has already been trained on. The experiments were carried out on 904 images drawn randomly from the FERET images, and the hybrid classifier consists of ERBF and C4.5, as described in Section 6. In order to achieve improved generalization, the training and testing strategy used is a modified form of k - fold cross validation (CV) [Weiss and Kulikowski, 1991]. Specifically, the cases are randomly divided into k mutually exclusive partitions of approximately equal size. Cases coming from one partition are used for training, while the remaining cases corresponding to (k-1) partitions are used for testing. The average error rate when the training set iterated across each one of the k partitions is the CV error rate. To take advantage of available data and the specifics of the image acquisition process, each CV cycle consists of two rounds. As an example, the first CV cycle on its first round trains the connectionist (ERBF) component using the first 50 'fa' frontal images. Once training is successful, the resulting ERBF network is frozen, and the hybrid system proceeds by learning the DT. Towards that end, one randomly samples positive and negative examples from the corresponding 50 'fb' images and the remaining 402 'fa' and 402 'fb' images, and the DT is built according to the outputs generated for those examples using the ERBF network. On the second iteration, the connectionist (ERBF) component is trained on the corresponding 50 'fb' frontal images, while learning the decision tree is accomplished by randomly sampling positive and negative examples from the corresponding 50 'fa' images and the remaining 402 'fa' and 402 'fb' images. Note that images corresponding to subjects drawn from the gallery can be drawn from both the corresponding 'fa' or 'fb' images and also from the set of (102) duplicate (fa and fb) images available. The two iterations suggested above yield a sample space of 1708 ERBF output vectors (of size 9) from whom one would randomly sample the positive and negative examples required to train C4.5. Specifically, one now randomly selects 30 output (ERBF) quantized vectors tagged as positive examples and 100 output (ERBF) quantized vectors tagged as negative examples. The remaining 1578 output vectors are then tagged as test vectors. As an example, a sample decision tree, obtained using the above procedure, is shown in Fig. 6. Note that all what it takes to determine whether a face image belongs to the gallery or not is a simple test on the fifth attribute value of ERBF.

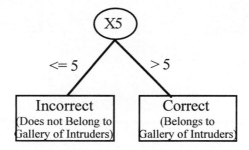

Figure 6. Decision Tree for the Surveillance Task

Table 1 gives the average CV results for the hybrid classifiers consisting of ERBF1 and C4.5 or of ERBF2 and C4.5. To assess the relevance of using hybrid classifiers we performed similar experiments where the classifier consists now only of the ERBF connectionist level. Tables 1 shows the average CV results for the case when ERBF1 and ERBF2, respectively, are used and the empirical threshold is set to 0.65. We have also experimented with the case when RBF has been used by itself on the surveillance task and listed the average CV results in Table 1 when the empirical threshold is again set to 0.65.

Table 1. Results for the Surveillance Task

Classifier Type	Correct Classification %	False Negative %	Correct Rejection %	False Positive %
RBF	76	24	73	27
ERBF 1	82	18	99	1
ERBF 2	86	14	98	2
ERBF 1 with C4.5	90	10	99	1
ERBF 2 with C4.5	96	4	100	0

The results reported in Table 1 indicate that when the connectionist ERBF model is coupled with an Inductive Decision Tree - C4.5 - the performance improves over the case when only the connectionist ERBF module is used. Specifically, we observe that the accuracy rate on the surveillance task increased on the average by 7% while the false negative rate decreased by about 8%. Another observation one can make is that the ERBF2 model is better than the ERBF1 model. The plausible explanation is that training using more examples (see Section 5.2.2) leads to better performance. We also note that the ERBF models outperform single RBF networks. The reason for this last observation comes from ERBF models implementing the equivalent of a 'query by consensus' paradigm.

7.2 Gender Classification

The cross validation strategy used is similar to that described in the preceding section and involves 20 CV cycles. Each cross validation cycle divides 3,006 images into one set of 2,886 images and two sets of 60 images each. The sets of 60 images are used for training the ERBF and DT, respectively, while the set consisting of 2,886 images is used for testing. We report on experiments when only a single RBF network is used, followed by the case when either one of the ERBF ensembles is used, and finally the case when the hybrid classifier is used. Table 2 gives the average CV results over 20 cycles.

Table 2. Results for Gender Classification

Classifier Type	Correct Classification %	Mis-Classification %
RBF	70	30
ERBF1	79	21
ERBF2	82	18
ERBF1 with C4.5	90	10
ERBF2 with C4.5	96	4

7.3 Ethnic Classification

The cross validation strategy used is similar to that used for both surveillance and gender classification. Each cross validation cycle divides 3,006 images into one set of 2,826 images, one set of 60 images and one set of 120 images. The set containing 60 images is used for training the DT, while the set containing 120 images is used for training the ERBF. The remaining set consisting of 2,826 images is used for testing. The composition of the set used for training the DT is 30 Caucasian, 10 Asian, 10 Oriental and 10 African, while the composition of the set used for training the ERBF is 30 Caucasian, 30 Asian, 30 Oriental and 30 African. The test set consists then of 1,872, 322, 434 and 198 images corresponding to Caucasian, Asian, Oriental and African origins, respectively. We report on experiments when only a single RBF network is used, followed by the case when either one of the ERBF ensemble is used, and finally the case when the hybrid classifier is used. Table 3 gives the average CV results over 20 cycles.

Table 3. Results for Ethnic Classification

Classifier Type	Correct Classification %	Mis-Classification %
RBF	62	38
ERBF1	74	26
ERBF2	82	18
ERBF1 with C4.5	86	14
ERBF2 with C4.5	94	6

From the results reported in the above tables one observes that when the connectionist ERBF model is coupled with an Inductive Decision Tree - C4.5 - the performance improves over the case when only the connectionist ERBF module is used. Specifically, we observe that the classification rate increased on the average by 14% and 12% for the gender and ethnic tasks respectively. Another observation one can make is that the ERBF2 model is better than the ERBF1 model. The plausible explanation is that training using more examples ('multiple displays') (see Section 5.2.2) leads to better performance. We also note that the ERBF models reported above outperform single RBF networks. The reason for this last observation comes from ERBF models implementing the equivalent of a 'query by consensus' paradigm. Improved ERBF (vs RBF) performance can be also traced to the fact that the range for test images is (slightly) different from those encountered during training and that using more but slightly different nets ('referees') adds to the strength of the decision.

8 Conclusions

We have advanced in this chapter modular forensic architectures for face surveillance, gender and ethnic classification, all within the context of face recognition. Experimental data shows the feasibility of such architectures using a collection of 3,006 face images corresponding to 1,009 subjects from the FERET database. Cross Validation (CV) results yield an average accuracy rate of - (a) 96% on the surveillance task, (b) 96% on the gender classification task and (c) 94% on the ethnic classification task. The hybrid (modular) architectures, consisting of an ensemble of connectionist networks - radial basis functions (RBF) - and an inductive decision tree (DT), combine the merits of 'holistic' template matching with those of 'discrete' features based classifiers using both positive and negative learning examples.

The classifier architecture presented in this chapter could serve in the building of hierarchical classifiers where faces would be sequentially discriminated in terms of gender, ethnicity and age before final recognition would take place.

Acknowledgments: This work was partly supported by the DoD Counterdrug Technology Development Program, with the US Army Research Laboratory as Technical Agent, under contract DAAL01-97-K-0018.

References

Arad, N., Dyn, N., Reisfeld, D., and Yeshurun, Y. (1994) Image Warping by Radial Basis Functions: Application to Facial Expressions, *CVGIP: Graphical Models and Image Processing* 56, No 2, 161-172.

Baron, R. J. (1981) Mechanisms of Human Facial Recognition, *International Journal of Man-Machine Studies* 15, 137-178 (1981).

Battiti, R., and Colla, A. M. (1994) Democracy in Neural Nets: Voting Schemes for Classification, *Neural Networks* 7, No. 4, 691-707.

Brunelli, R., and Poggio, T. (1993a) Face Recognition: Features versus Templates, *IEEE Trans. on Pattern Analysis and Machine Intelligence* 15, No. 4, 1042-1052.

Brunelli, R., and Poggio, T. (1993b) Caricatural Effects in Automated Face Perception, *Biol. Cybern.* 69, 235-241.

Buhmann, J., Lange, J., Malsburg, C., Vorbruggen, J. C., and Wurtz, R. P. (1992) Object Recognition with Gabor Functions in the Dynamic Link

Architecture, in *Neural Networks for Signal Processing*, B. Kosko, (Ed.), Vol. 1, 121-159, Prentice Hall.

Burton, A. M., Bruce, V., and Dench, N. (1993) What's the Difference between Men and Women? Evidence from Facial Measurement, *Perception* 22, 153-176.

Chellappa R., Wilson, C. L., and Sirohey, S. (1995) Human and Machine Recognition of Faces: A Survey, *Proc. IEEE* 83, 705-740.

Flocchini, P., Gardin, F., Mauri, G., Pensini, M. P., and Stofella, P. (1992) Combining Image Processing Operators and Neural Networks in a Face Recognition System, *International Journal of Pattern Recognition and Artificial Intelligence (IJPRAI)* 6, 446-467.

Golomb, B. A., Lawrence, D. T., and Sejnowski, T. J. (1990) SEXNET: A Neural Network Identifies Sex from Human Faces, in *Advances in Neural Information Processing Systems (NIPS)*, Vol. 3, 572-577, Lippmann, R. P., Moody, J. E. and Touretzky, D.S., (Eds.), Morgan Kaufmann.

Greenspan, H., Goodman, R., and Chellappa, R. (1991) Texture Analysis via Unsupervised and Supervised Learning, in *Proc. of the International Joint Conference on Neural Networks*, Vol. 1, 639-644.

Gutta, S., Huang, J., Kakkad, V., and Wechsler, H. (1998) Face Surveillance, *International Conference on Computer Vision (ICCV)*, Mumbai, India.

Gutta, S., Huang, J., Singh, D., Shah, I., Takacs, B., and Wechsler, H. (1995) Benchmark Studies on face Recognition, *Proc. of International Workshop on Automatic Face - and Gesture Recognition (IWAFGR)*, 227-231, Zurich, Switzerland.

Hampshire, J. B., and Waibel, A. (1992) The Meta-Pi Network: Building Distributed Knowledge Representations for Robust Multisource Pattern Recognition, *IEEE Trans. on Pattern Analysis and Machine Intelligence* 14, No. 7, 751-769.

Huang, J., Gutta, S., and Wechsler, H. (1996) Detection of Human Faces Using Decision Trees, in *Proc. International Conference on Automated Face and Hand Gesture Recognition (ICAFGR)*, 248-252.

Huber, P. J. (1981) *Robust statistics* , John Wiley, New York.

Jain, A. (1992) Final Report to NSF of the Workshop on Visual Information Management.

Krogh, A., and Vedelsby, J. (1995) Neural Network Ensembles, Cross Validation and Active Learning, in *Advances in Neural Information Processing Systems (NIPS)*, Vol. 2, 231-238, Touretzky, D.S., (Ed.), Morgan Kaufmann.

Lincoln, W. P., and Skrzypek, J. (1990) Synergy of Clustering Multiple Back Propagation Networks, in *Advances in neural Information Processing Systems (NIPS)*, Vol. 2, 650-657, Touretzky, D.S., (Ed.), Morgan Kaufmann.

Lippmann, R. P., and Ng, K. (1991) A Comparative Study of the Practical Characteristic of Neural Networks and Pattern Classifiers , Technical Report 894, Lincoln Labs., MIT.

Morgan, N., and Bourlard, H. (1995) Continuous Speech Recognition, *IEEE Signal Processing Magazine* , 25-42.

Niblack, W. (1993) The QBIC project: Querying images by content using color, texture, and shape, RJ 9203, IBM San Jose Research Division.

Phillips, P. J. (1994) Matching Pursuit Filter Design, *Proc. of the International Conference on Pattern Recognition (ICPR)*, Vol. 3, 57-61, Jerusalem, Isreal.

Phillips, P. J., Wechsler, H., Huang, J., and Rauss, R. (1998) The FERET Database and Evaluation Procedure for Face Recognition Algorithms, *Image and Vision Computing*, (to appear).

Quinlan, J. R. (1986) The Effect of Noise on Concept Learning, in *Machine Learning: an Artificial Intelligence Approach* 2, 149-166 R.S. Michalski, J.G. Carbonell and T.M. Mitchell, (Eds.), Morgan Kaufmann.

Robertson, G., and Craw, I. (1994) Testing Face Recognition Systems, *Image and Vision Computing* 19, 609-614.

Samal A., and Iyengar, P. (1992) Automatic Recognition and Analysis of Human faces and Facial Expressions: A Survey, *Pattern Recognition* 25, 65-77.

Sirohey, S. A. (1993) Human Face Segmentation and Identification, Computer Vision Laboratory, University of Maryland CS-TR-3176.

Soulie, F. F., Viennet, E., and Lamy, B. (1993) Multi-Modular Neural Network Architectures for Pattern Recognition: Applications in Optical Character Recognition and Human Face Recognition, *International Journal of Pattern Recognition and Artificial Intelligence (IJPRAI)*.

Takacs B., and Wechsler, H. (1995) Face Location Using a Dynamic Model of Retinal Feature Extraction, *Proc. of International Workshop on Automatic Face- and Gesture Recognition (IWAFGR)*, 243-247, Zurich, Switzerland.

Tamura, S., Kawai, H., and Mitsumoto, H. (1996) Male/Female Identification from 8 x 6 Very Low Resolution Face Images by Neural Network, *Pattern Recognition* 29 No. 2, 331-335.

Towell, G. G., and Shavlik, J. W. (1994) Refining Symbolic Knowledge using Neural Networks, in *Machine Learning: A Multistrategy Approach* , Vol. 4, 405-438, Michalski, R.S. and Tecuci, G. (Eds.), Morgan Kaufmann Publishers.

Turk M., and Pentland, A. (1991) Eigenfaces for Recognition, *Journal of Cognitive Neuroscience* 3, 71-86.

Valentin, D., Abdi, H., Toole, A., and Cottrell, G. W. (1994) Connectionist Models of Face Processing: A Survey, *Pattern Recognition* 27, No. 9, 1209-1230.

Weiss, S. M., and Kulikowski, C. A. (1991) *Computer Systems That Learn*, Morgan Kaufmann.

Wiskott, L. (1997) Phantom Faces for Face Analysis, Pattern Recognition 30, No. 6, 837-846.

Eye Detection and Face Recognition
Using Evolutionary Computation

Jeffrey Huang, Chengjun Liu, and Harry Wechsler

Department of Computer Science
George Mason University
Fairfax, VA 22030
{rhuang, cliu, wechsler}@cs.gmu.edu
http://www.chagall.gmu.edu/

Abstract. This chapter introduces evolutionary computation (EC) and genetic algorithms (GAs) for face recognition tasks. We first address eye detection as a visual routine and show how to implement it using a hybrid approach integrating learning and evolution. The goals of the novel architecture for eye detection are twofold: (i) derivation of the saliency attention map using consensus between navigation routines encoded as finite state automata (FSA) evolved using GAs and (ii) selection of optimal features using GAs and induction of DT (decision trees) for possibly classifying as eyes the most salient locations identified earlier. Experimental results, using 30 face images from the FERET data base show the feasibility of our hybrid approach. We then introduce the Optimal Projection Axes (OPA) method for face recognition. OPA works by searching through all the rotations defined over whitened Principal Component Analysis (PCA) subspaces. Whitening, which does not preserve norms, plays a dual role: (i) counteracts the fact that the Mean Square Error (MSE) principle underlying PCA preferentially weights low frequencies, and (ii) increases the reachable space of solutions to include non-orthogonal bases. As the search space is too large for any systematic search, stochastic and directed ('greedy') search is undertaken using again evolution in the form of Genetic Algorithms (GAs). Evolution is driven by a fitness function defined in terms of performance accuracy and class separation ('scatter index'). Experiments carried out using 1,107 facial images corresponding to 369 subjects (with 169 subjects having duplicated images) from the FERET data base show that OPA yields improved performance over the eigenface and MDF (Most Discriminant Features) methods.

Keywords: Active Vision, Attention, Behavior-based AI, Collective Behavior, Evolutionary Computation, Decision Trees (DT), Eye Detection, Face Recognition, Genetic Algorithms (GAs), Most Discriminant Features (MDF), Principal Component Analysis (PCA), Optimal Projection Axes (OPA), Saliency Map, Scatter, Visual Routines, Whitening

1 Introduction

Automated face recognition is becoming important for applications such as forensics, biometrics, telecommunication and HDTV, and medicine. The face is a unique feature of human beings. Even the faces of "identical" twins differ in some respects. Humans can detect and identify faces in a scene with little or no effort. This skill is quite robust, despite large changes in the visual stimulus due to viewing conditions, expression, aging, and distractions such as glasses or changes in hair style. Building automated systems that accomplish this task under significant variability in the image formation process is, however, very difficult. There are several related (face recognition) subproblems: (i) detection of a pattern as a face (in the crowd), (ii) detection of facial landmarks, (iii) identification of the faces, and (iv) analysis of facial expressions (Samal et al., 1992).

Face recognition starts with the detection of face patterns (Rowley et al, 1995) in sometimes cluttered scenes, proceeds by normalizing the face images to account for geometrical and illumination changes, possibly using information about the location and appearance of facial landmarks, identifies the faces using appropriate classification algorithms, and post processes the results using model-based schemes and logistic feedback. The ability to detect salient facial landmarks is an important component of any face recognition system, in particular for normalization purposes and for the extraction of the image features to be used later on by the face classifiers. The detection of facial landmarks underlies attention mechanisms similar to those used by the human visual system (HVS) to screen out the visual field and to focus its attention on salient input characteristics. Among the many facial landmarks available it appears that the eyes plays the most important role in face normalization and facilitates further localization of other facial landmarks. As both the position of the eyes and the interocular distance are relatively constant for most people, eye detection provides an excellent framework for further image normalization and restricts the search for other facial landmarks. The requirement for robust face recognition despite variability in the image formation process can be achieved through adaptive 'eye' classification schemes.

As the facial landscape to be explored is quite large it becomes necessary to assess the saliency of each region in terms of the likelihood that it covers one of the two eyes. Towards that end Active and Selective Vision (ASV) plays a major role. ASV has advanced the widely-held belief that intelligent data collection rather than image recovery and reconstruction is the goal of visual perception. It involves a large degree of adaptation and it provides a mobile and intelligent observer with the capability to decide *where* to seek information, *what* information to pick up, and *how* to process it, so eventually the perceptual system can successfully interpret the surrounding environment.

The design of eye detection routines has to address both attention mechanisms and recognition schemes, and one has thus to address the twin problems of optimal feature selection and classifier design. As searching a non-linear space is both complex and expensive we introduce a novel and hybrid adaptive methodology for developing eye detection routines drawing on both learning and evolutionary components. The goals of the novel architecture for eye detection are twofold: (i) derivation of the saliency attention map using consensus between navigation routines encoded as finite state automata (FSA) evolved using GAs and (ii) selection of optimal features using GAs and induction of DT (decision trees) for possibly classifying as eyes the most salient locations identified earlier.

Face recognition, a difficult but fundamental task for intelligent systems, depends heavily on the particular choice of the features used by the (pattern) classifier. Feature selection in pattern recognition involves the derivation of salient features from the raw input data in order to reduce the amount of data used for classification and simultaneously to provide enhanced discriminatory power. The selection of an appropriate set of features is one of the most difficult tasks in the design of pattern classification systems. At the lowest level, the raw feature data is derived from noisy sensor data, the characteristics of which are complex and difficult to characterize. In addition, there is considerable interaction among low level features which must be identified and exploited. The typical number of possible features, however, is so large as to prohibit any systematic exploration of all but a few possible interaction types (e.g., pairwise interactions). In addition, any sort of performance oriented evaluation of feature subsets involves building and testing the associated classifier, resulting in additional overhead costs.

As a consequence, a fairly standard approach is to attempt to pre-select a subset of features using abstract measures which indicate important properties of good feature sets such as orthogonality, infomax, large variance, multimodality of marginal distributions, high kurtosis, low entropy, and/or sparse coding. This approach has been recently dubbed the "filter" approach (Kohavi and John, 1995) and it is generally much less resource intensive than building and testing the associated classifiers, but may result in suboptimal performance if the abstract measures do not correlate well with actual performance. It is still difficult, however, to develop abstract feature space measures of optimality which guarantee optimality in classification performance. In practice this is best achieved by including some form of performance evaluation of the feature subsets while searching for good subsets. This approach, recently dubbed the "wrapper" approach (Kohavi and John, 1995), typically involves building a classifier based on the feature subset being evaluated, and using the performance of the classifier as a component of the overall evaluation. This approach should produce better classification performance than the filter approach, but it adds considerable overhead to an already expensive search process. This in turn usually restricts the number of alternative feature subsets one can afford to evaluate, and thus may also produce suboptimal results. Towards that end we introduce the Optimal Projection Axes (OPA) method for face recognition which enjoys the merits of both the filter and wrapper approaches.

OPA works by searching through all the rotations defined over whitened Principal Component Analysis (PCA) subspaces. Whitening, which does not preserve norms, plays a dual role: (i) counteracts the fact that the Mean Square Error (MSE) principle underlying PCA preferentially weights low frequencies, and (ii) increases the reachable space of solutions to include non-orthogonal bases. As the search space is too large for any systematic search, stochastic and directed ('greedy') search is undertaken using evolution in the form of Genetic Algorithms (GAs). Evolution is driven by a fitness function defined in terms of performance accuracy and class separation ('scatter index').

2 Active and Selective Vision (ASV)

The flow of visual input consists of huge amounts of time-varying information. It is crucial for both biological vision and automated systems to perceive and comprehend such a constantly changing environment within a relatively short processing time. To cope with such a computational challenge one should locate and analyze only the information relevant to the current task by quickly focusing on selected areas of the scene as per need. One would think that the vast amount of input data reaching the sensors must be processed in parallel by the human visual system (HVS) in order to obtain reasonable performance, but due to architectural constraints this is hardly feasible. Attention mechanisms thus balance between computationally expensive parallel techniques and time intensive serial techniques to simplify computation and reduce the amount of processing. Besides complexity reasons (Culhane et al., 1992) efficient attention schemes are needed also to form the basis for behavioral coordination (Allport, 1989).

Active and selective vision leads directly to issues of attention. Sensory, perceptual, and cognitive systems are space-time limited, while the potential information available to each of them is potentially infinite. Much of attentional selectivity, explained as filter theory in terms of system limitation with respect to both storage and processing capabilities, is mostly concerned with early selection of spotlights and late but selective processing of control and recognition. Selective processing of regions with restricted location (or motion) is thus necessary for achieving almost real-time and enhanced performance with limited resources. As an example, restricted but enhanced processing becomes possible and it implements the equivalent of foveal perception.

Various computational models of visual *attention* have been proposed to filter out some of the input and thus not only reduce the computational complexity of the underlying processes but possibly provide a basis to form invariant and canonical object representations as well. Several biologically motivated models of attentional mechanisms and visual integration have appeared in the literature. For most of these models every point in the visual field competes for control over attention based on its local conspicuity and the history of the system. A high level feature integration mechanism is then implemented to select the next center of gaze or fixation point. Koch and Ullman (1987) have proposed using a number of elementary maps encoding conspicuous orientation, color, and direction of movements, which then would be merged into a single representation, called the *saliency map*. The most active location of this map is computed by a *winner take-all* (WTA) mechanism and selected as the next focus of interest. In this chapter corresponding attention mechanisms supporting the derivation of the saliency map are derived using a hybrid adaptive approach which evolves Finite State Automata (FSA) searching for functionally salient ('eye') facial areas.

3 Behavior-Based AI and Visual Routines

As part of behavior-based AI, Maes (1992) has proposed autonomous agents (animats) as sets of reactive modules, each of them having its own specific but limited competence. Behavior-based AI has advanced the idea that for successful operation (and survival) an intelligent and autonomous agent should (**i**) consist of multiple competencies ('routines'), (**ii**) be "open" or "situated" in its environment, and (**iii**) monitor the domain of application and figure out, in a competitive fashion, what to do next while dealing with many conflicting goals simultaneously. A similar behavior-based like approach for pattern classification and navigation tasks is suggested by the concept of visual routines (Ullman, 1984), recently referred to as a visual routine processor (VRP) by Horswill (1995). The VRP assumes the existence of a set of visual routines that can be applied to base image representations (maps), subject to specific functionalities, and driven by the task at hand. Moghaddam and Pentland (1995) have suggested that reactive behavior be implemented in terms of "perceptual intelligence" so the sensory input is directly coupled to a (probabilistic) decision-making unit for the purpose of control and action. An autonomous agent is then essentially a Finite-State Automata (FSA) or Hidden-Markov Model (HMM) whose feature inputs are chosen by sensors connected to the environment and/or are derived from it, and whose actions operate on the same environment. The automata decides its actions based on inputs and/or features it 'forages', while the behavior of the controller is learned. It is up to evolution and learning to collectively define and hardwire such purposeful automata.

Eye detection can be then viewed as a face recognition (routine) competency, whose inner workings include screening out the facial landscape to detect ('pop-out') salient locations for possible eye locations, and labeling as eye only those salient areas whose feature distribution 'fits' what the eye classifier has been trained to recognize. In other words, the first stage of the eye detection routine would implement attention mechanisms whose goal is to create a saliency 'eye' map, while the second stage processes the facial landscape filtered by the just created saliency map for actual eye recognition.

A difficult and still open question regarding the concept of visual routines introduced earlier is the extent to which their design could be automated. Brooks (1985), for example, has shown that much of his initial success has been due to carefully but manually chosen behaviors and cleverly designed interactions among the modules. In order to scale up to more complex behavior and greater robustness, Brooks (1985) and others are looking to machine learning techniques and evolutionary algorithms to tune and properly adapt such behavioral routines. The important question for the VRP mentioned earlier is how to automatically craft such visual routines and how to integrate their outputs. Early attempts, developed using manual design, involved simulations lacking low-level (base) representations and operating on bitmaps only. Ramachandran (1985), an advocate of the utilitarian theory of perception, has suggested as an alternative that one could craft such visual routines by evolving a "bag of perceptual tricks" whose survival is dependent on functionality and fitness. This approach, which can be directly traced to the earlier "Neural Darwinism" theory of neuronal group selection as a basis for higher brain function (Edelman,1987), suggests natural selection as the major force behind the automatic design of visual routines and their integration. Another possibility for evolving visual routines would employ genetic algorithms (GAs).

4 Evolutionary Computation and Genetic Algorithms

The process of natural selection leads to evolution as a result of adaptive strategies being continuously tested for their fitness as it is the case for closed-loop control. Reasoning by analogy, one attempts then to emulate computationally the 'survival of the fittest' for complex and difficult problems as those encountered in detection and homing. Evolutionary Computation (EC) in general, and Genetic Algorithms (GAs) in particular, mimic what nature has done all along and it does that using similar principles. GAs are further defined when one provides a specific strategy for choosing the offsprings and/or the next generation. Simulated breeding is one of the possible strategies where offsprings are selected according to their fitness. Note also that simulated breeding is conceptually similar to stochastic search in general, and to simulated annealing in particular, for the case when the size of the offspring population is limited to one individual only.

GAs (Goldberg, 1989), as examples of evolutionary computation, are nondeterministic methods, similar to stochastic approximations, that employ cross-over and mutation as selection strategies for behavioral optimization and adaptation. GAs work by maintaining a constant-sized population of candidate solutions known as individuals. The power of a genetic algorithm lies in its ability to exploit, in a highly efficient manner, information about a large number of individuals. The search underlying GAs is such that breadth and depth - exploration and exploitation - are balanced according to the observed performance of the individuals evolved so far. By allocating more reproductive occurrences to above average individual solutions, the overall effect is to increase the population's average fitness.

Further advances in pattern analysis and classification require the integration of various learning processes in a modular fashion. Adaptive systems that employ several strategies can potentially offer significant advantages over single-strategy systems. Since the type of input and acquired knowledge are more flexible, such hybrid systems can be applied to a wider range of problems. The integration of genetic algorithms and decision tree learning advocated in this chapter is also part of a broader issue being actively explored, namely, that evolution and learning can work synergistically (Hinton and Nowlan, 1987). The ability to learn can be shown to ease the burden on evolution. Evolution (genotype learning) only has to get close to the goal; (phenotype) learning can then fine tune the behavior (Mühlenbein and Kinderman, 1989). Although Darwinian theory does not allow for the inheritance of acquired characteristics, as Lamarck hinted to, learning (as acquired behaviors) can still influence the course of evolution. Towards that end, the Baldwin effect suggests that local search could change the fitness of chromosome strings and thus the course of evolution (Bala et al, 1996).

We advance later in this chapter a hybrid and adaptive architecture for developing visual detection routines using fixed length representations ('chromosomes'). Johnson et al (1994) have suggested using Genetic Programming (GP) for evolving visual routines whose perceptual task is finding the left and right hand of a person in a black and white silhouette of a person. Variable length programs were used as candidates for visual routines while restrictions were placed by presuming that some other universal routines have already detected the largest connected component and returned its bounding box and centroid. Our approach is instead based on GAs and it operates on real imagery data rather than bitmaps as it was the case with Johnson et al (1994). The reason for us using GAs in terms of fixed-length strings ('chromosomes') rather than GP comes from our belief that a compact way to evolve a successful problem-solving strategy rather than the elaborate code for implementing the same strategy is more efficient. It should be easier to craft behaviors, such as visual routines, when natural selection is confined to finding only optimal problem-solving strategies (encoded as FSAs) rather than writing the genetic instructions for actuating it, i.e., for expressing the phenotype.

5 Collective Behavior and Consensus Methods

Collective intelligence considers the scenario when several agents work together towards solving a specific problem such as detection. State transitions are now determined not only by internal but also by external excitatory and inhibitory connections linking the individual agents. It is through those connections that information is exchanged and actions are then performed. The internal connections, correspond to 'local/autonomous' information, while the external connections enforce 'global/coordination' constraints. Fukuda et al (1994) discuss the concept of a 'society of robotic' system. The distributed robotic system is not one in which individual robots carry out separate tasks, but rather one in which many robots carry out several tasks, possibly similar, but using meaningful coordination. The emergent collective behavior, the result of an incremental and opportunistic problem solving style, is chararcteristic of what Minsky (1985) defines as the "Society of Minds".

In our case the test bed for the collective behavior of a multi-agents society is the cooperation of eye detection routines towards building the saliency 'eye' map. Several animats ('agents'), each of them specialized on the same eye detection task, cooperate by exchanging information about their activities and findings. One possible solution to coordinate amongst different agents is based on consensus methods and query by consensus. An early example of using such an approach is the ensemble of neural networks (Hamshire and Waibel, 1992). Their Meta - Pi classifier is a connectionist pattern classifier that consists of a number of source-dependent subnetworks that are integrated by a combinational Time Delay Neural Network (TDNN) superstructure. The TDNN combines the outputs of the modules, trained independently, in order to provide a global classification. In our case, the inherent variability of the facial landscape input will be handled by starting the eye detection routines from close by points (near the chin). The motivation behind a consensus strategy is based on the assumption that while it is possible to 'fool' a single agent all of the time one cannot mislead all of the agents all of the time.

6 Learning and Decision Trees

The basic aim of any concept-learning symbolic system is to construct rules for classifying objects given a *training set* of objects whose class labels are known. The objects are described by a fixed collection of attributes, each with its own set of discrete values and each object belongs to only one class. The rules derived using C4.5, the most commonly used algorithm for the induction of decision trees (Quinlan, 1986), form the decision tree (DT). The C4.5 algorithm uses an information-theoretical measure, the entropy , for building the decision tree. The entropy is a measure of uncertainty ('ambiguity') and characterizes the intrinsic ability of a set of features to discriminate between classes of different objects. The entropy E for a feature set $\{f\}$ is given by:

$$E(f) = \sum_{k=1}^{n} \sum_{i=1}^{m} \left[-x_{i,k}^{+} \log_2 \left(\frac{x_{i,k}^{+}}{x_{i,k}^{+} + x_{i,k}^{-}} \right) - x_{i,k}^{-} \log_2 \left(\frac{x_{i,k}^{-}}{x_{i,k}^{+} + x_{i,k}^{-}} \right) \right] \tag{1}$$

where n is the number of classes and m_j is the number of distinct values that feature f can take on. $x_{i,k}^{+}$ is the number of positive examples in class k for which feature f takes on its ith value. Similarly $x_{i,k}^{-}$ is the number of negative examples in class k for which feature f takes on its ith value.

In an iterative fashion C4.5 determines the feature which is most discriminatory and then it dichotomizes (splits) the data into classes categorized by this feature. The next significant feature of each of the subsets is then used to further partition them and the process is repeated recursively until each of the subsets contain only one kind of labeled data. The resulting structure is called a decision tree, where nodes stand for feature discrimination tests while their exit branches stand for those subclasses of labeled examples satisfying the test. An unknown example is classified by starting at the root of the tree, performing the sequential tests and following the corresponding branches until a leaf (terminal node) is reached indicating that some class has been decided on. Decision trees are disjunctive, since each branch leaving a decision node corresponds to a separate disjunctive case. After decision trees are constructed a tree pruning mechanism is invoked. Pruning is used to reduce the effect of noise in the learning data. It discards some of the unimportant sub-trees and retains those covering the largest number of examples. The tree obtained thus provide a more general description of the learned concept.

7 Eye Detection

The ability to detect salient facial landmarks is an important component of any face recognition system. Among the many facial features available it appears that the eyes play the most important role in automated visual interpretation and human face recognition. As both the position of the eyes and the interocular distance are relatively constant for most people, detecting the eyes serves first of all as an important role in face normalization and thus facilitates further localization of facial landmarks. It is eye detection that allows one to focus attention on salient facial configurations, to filter out structural noise, and to achieve eventual face recognition. There are two major approaches for automated eye detection. The first approach, the *holistic* one, conceptually related to template matching, attempts to locate the eyes using global representations. Although detection by matching raw images has been successful under limited circumstances, it suffers from the usual shortcomings of straightforward correlation-based approaches, such as sensitivity to eye orientation, size, variable lighting conditions, and noise. The reason for this vulnerability of direct matching methods lie in their attempt to carry out the required classification in a space of extremely high dimensionality. Characteristic of the holistic approach are also connectionist methods such as backpropagation ('holons') and principal component analysis (PCA) using eigen-representations (Pentland et al, 1994).

To overcome the curse of dimensionality, the connectionist equivalent of data compression methods and contextual information should be employed as well. As an example, Samaria (1994) employs stochastic modeling, using Hidden Markov Models (HMMs), to holistically encode face information. When the frontal facial images are sampled using top-bottom raster scanning, the natural order in which the facial landmarks would appear is encoded using a HMM. The HMM lead to the efficient detection of eye strips but still leave the task of homing on the eyes unsolved. Note that all the eye detection methods available assume a prespecified face size or have to operate at several grid resolutions. Our adaptive strategy overcomes this drawback and achieves invariance through the evolution of 'navigation' routines geared to identify salient facial areas as promising eye locations.

The second approach for eye detection, the *abstractive* one, extracts (and measures) discrete local features, while standard pattern recognition techniques are then employed for locating the eyes using these measurements. Yuille (1991) describes a complex but generic strategy, characteristic of the abstractive approach, for locating facial landmarks such as the eyes using the concept of deformable templates. The template is a parameterized geometric model of the face or part of it (mouth and/or eyes) to be recognized, together with a measure of how well it fits the image data, where variations in the parameters correspond to allowable deformations. Lam and Yan (1996) extended Yuille's method for extracting eye features by using corner locations inside the eye windows which are obtained using average anthropometric measures after the head boundary is located first. Deformable templates and the closely related elastic snake models are interesting concepts, but using them can be difficult in terms of learning and implementation, not to talk about their computational complexity. Eye features could also be detected using their symmetrical characteristics. As an example, Yeshurun et al (1991) developed a generalized symmetry operator for eye detection. As another example, Ducottet et al (1994) detects the eyes as objects with circular symmetry and variable size using orthonormal wavelet transform of an image. The optimization process involved in symmetry detection can be sped up using evolutionary computation (EC). As an example, Gofman et al (1996) have introduced a global optimization approach similar to EC for detecting the local reflectional symmetry in gray level images using 2D Gabor decomposition.

8 Eye Detection Using GAs and DTs

Active and Selective Vision (ASV) works by systematically organizing the visual tasks in such a manner that as visual processing progresses in time the volume of data to attend to is reduced and computing resources are focused on salient regions of the (time varying) imagery. There is some analogy to biological visual processing to support the goals of the architecture mentioned above. We know that the two major visual pathways, the *magnocellular* (M) and *parvocellular* (P) streams, originate within the retina and project to low level cortical areas. The M and P pathways ('channels'), which exhibit very different characteristics in terms of sampling properties, spatio-temporal and spectral differentiation as well as processing strategies, form the basis of analyzing *motion* and *form*. The two pathways process different aspects of the same input. They are not independent and in fact there is considerable cross-talk even in stages beyond the level of the retina and LGN. The information entering the eye is processed by the M and P subsystems in parallel. Two overlapping sampling grids represent the input stimuli at different resolutions. M ganglion cells form a lower resolution lattice, while P ganglion cells receive higher resolution input. The M and P pathways seem to have complementary properties, thus supporting the idea of functional duality. The M pathway, which evolutionary developed much earlier than the P pathway, is primarily viewed to be responsible for the analysis of motion. There are results, however, indicating that the M pathway may have a more global function of interpreting spatial organization, such as deciding which visual elements edges and discontinuities belong to and defining individual objects on the scene (Livingstone, 1988). The P pathway, on the other hand, performs *recognition tasks* and the detailed analysis of form and color. These two fundamental visual tasks of *object localization* and *object identification* are often referred to as the *where* and *what* problems in the computer vision literature, and would correspond here to eye saliency and recognition, respectively.

8.1 System Architecture

The overall architecture, shown in Fig. 1, consists of two components whose tasks are those of eye saliency and eye recognition, respectively. The ('sensory-reactive') saliency component has to discover the most likely eye locations, while the ('model-based') eye recognition component probes the suggested locations ('candidates') for actual eye detection. The saliency and recognition components are described in Sect. 8.1.1 and 8.1.2, respectively.

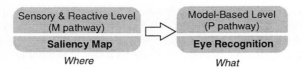

Figure 1. Architecture for Eye Detection

8.1.1 Saliency and Navigation

The derivation of the saliency map (see Fig. 2) is described in terms of tasks involved, computational models, and corresponding functionalities. The tasks involved include feature extraction and data compression, conspicuity derivation, and integration of outputs from several visual routines. The corresponding computational model has access to feature maps, while GAs are used to generate finite state automata (FSA) as appropriate policy (action) functions. Consensus methods achieve the integration of the visual routines, characteristic of distributed multi-agent's collective behavior, as the individual routines ('agents') navigate across the facial landscape trying to filter out non-eye regions and home towards what appears as most promising ('salient') eye locations.

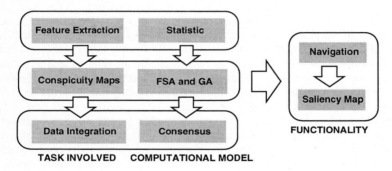

Figure 2. Derivation of the Saliency Map

8.1.2 Feature Selection and Pattern Classification

Pattern recognition, a difficult but fundamental task for intelligent systems, depends heavily on the particular choice of the features used by the classifier. One usually starts with a given set of features and then attempts to derive an optimal subset of features leading to high classification performance. A standard approach involves ranking the features of a candidate feature set according to some criteria involving second order statistics (ANOVA) and/or information theory based measures such as "infomax", and then deleting lower ranked features. Ranking by itself is usually not enough because the criteria used do not capture possible non-linear interactions among the features, nor do they measure the effectiveness of the features selected on the actual recognition task.

The fitness functions for feature subsets, based on information content, orthogonality, etc., however, can still provide baseline feedback to stochastic search methods characteristic of evolutionary computation (EC), resulting in enhanced performance. As an example, GAs can search the space of all possible subsets of a large set of candidate discrimination features, capture important non-linear interactions, and thus improve on the quality of the feature subsets produced by using ranking methods only. The effectiveness of the features selected on the actual pattern recognition task can be then assessed by learning appropriate classifiers and measuring their observed performance. Learning has the ability to smooth the fitness landscape, thus facilitating evolution, and eventually what is learned becomes clamped ('phenotype rigidity'). Fig. 3 shows how the interplay between learning and evolution takes place in the context of pattern recognition.

Feature subsets selected by the GA module for evaluation are used by the filter sub-module ('Feature Mask') to preprocess the training data and describe it only in terms of those features. The filter sub-module also divides the learning examples into the training and testing data, respectively. The training data is used by the learning sub-module, while the testing data is used by the evaluation module to assess the (local) fitness of what has been learned so far. As the amount of training examples increases, there is more opportunity for learning and an increased potential effect on evolution. Too much learning ('overfit'), however, can result in loss of generality and negatively affect the overall robustness of the results.

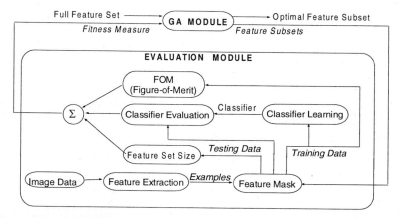

Figure 3. Eye Recognition: Symbiotic Adaptation for Pattern Classification Using Learning and Evolution

8.2 Experimental Results

This section describes in detail how the tasks of feature extraction (and data compression), evolution of visual routines for conspicuity (map) derivation, <u>and</u> the integration of the output from the visual routines for defining the saliency map, characteristic of collective behavior, are mapped into computational models. The goals of the novel architecture for eye detection are twofold: (i) derivation of the saliency attention map using consensus between navigation routines encoded as finite state automata (FSA) evolved using GAs and (ii) selection of optimal features for eye classification using GAs and induction of DT (decision trees) for classifying the most salient locations identified earlier as eye vs non-eye regions. Specifically, we describe what the image base representations are, how visual routines are encoded as FSA and evolved, and how consensus methods can integrate ('fuse') visual routine outputs during testing on unseen facial images. Experimental results are provided in a stepwise fashion as we describe our particular implementation. The facial imagery used is drawn from the FERET facial database. Since large amounts of FERET images were acquired during different photo sessions, the lighting conditions and the size of the facial images can vary. The diversity of the FERET data base is across gender, race, and age.

8.2.1 Saliency Map

This subsection provides a detailed description regarding feature representation, derivation of FSA through evolution, and the use of consensus methods to integrate conspicuity outputs from several animats.

Feature Maps
The input consists of 256 gray level (facial) images whose resolution is 192x192 (see Fig. 4a). To account for illumination changes, the original images are processed using 5x5 Laplacian masks. The Laplacian, filters out small changes due to illumination, and detects those image transitions usually associated with changes in image contents or contrast. Three feature maps corresponding to the mean, entropy, and standard deviation are then computed over 6x6 windows and then compressed to yield 32x32 images, each map encoded using four gray levels (2 bits) only. Examples of such feature maps are shown in Fig. 4b below.

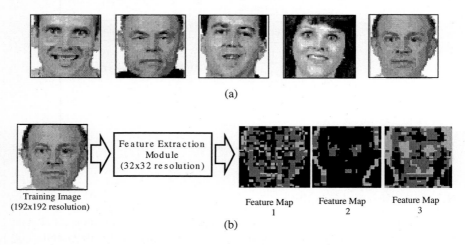

(a)

(b)

Figure 4. (a) Face Images, and (b) Feature Maps

Finite State Automata (FSA) ('Animats')
The FSA implements an animat (autonomous agent) exploring 32x32 feature maps in order to generate trajectories consisting of conspicuous points on the path to

salient eye locations. The animat searches the features landscape starting from some defined initial point, in our case the chin. The FSA encoding, string-like, resembles a chromosome, the basic unit evolution would operate later on. If PS and NS stand for the present and next state, the FSA is defined in terms of f: {PS, INPUT} → {NS, ACTION}, known as the transition function. The FSA is assumed to start from some initial state IS. The animat (FSA) exploring the features landscape consists of eight states, and as it moves around it measures ('forages') three precomputed feature maps, whose composite range is encoded using 6 bits for 64 levels. As measurements are taken, the animat decides on its next state, and an appropriate course of action ('move'). As it is shown in Fig. 5a, both the present state (PS) and the composite feature being sensed are *implicitly* represented using 8 consecutive (state) fields <0> through <7> <u>and</u> 64 corresponding (feature) subfields <0> through <63> for each state, respectively. The *explicit* contents of the FSA consist of the next state (NS) and move (see Fig. 5b). The animat never moves backwards and it can choose from five possible directional moves for a total of eight possible moves. Two of the moves are sideways (left and right), while two moves each are allocated to left 45°, straight on, and right 45°. The shaded blocks in Fig. 5b transition table, corresponding to the next state and directional move, together with the initial state, are subject to learning through evolution as described in the next section.

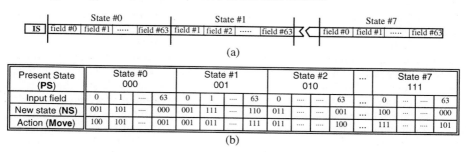

(a)

Present State (PS)	State #0 000				State #1 001				State #2 010				...	State #7 111			
Input field	0	1	....	63	0	1	....	63	0	....	....	63	...	0	...	....	63
New state (NS)	001	101	....	000	001	111	....	110	011	....	....	001	...	100	...	....	000
Action (Move)	100	101	....	001	001	011	....	111	011	....	....	100	...	111	...	....	101

(b)

Figure 5. (a) FSA Chromosome (b) State Transition Table for FSA

Evolution of FSA Animats

Learning an FSA is known as a difficult and complex computational problem. As one expects that autonomy of behavior is the result of evolutionary pressures it becomes natural to evolve the FSA using GAs. Evolution is driven by fitness, where fitness is here defined as the ability of the FSA to find its way to the left or right eye within a limited number of moves (less than 64) and home on the eye within 2 pixels from its center. The GA component is implemented using GENESIS (Grefenstette, 1991) using standard default parameter settings from the GA literature. This results in a constant population size of 50 FSAs, a crossover rate of 0.6 and a mutation rate of 0.001. It takes on the order of about 2,000 generations before evolution yields successful animats (100% accurate performance on training data). As FSAs become more fit, corresponding LEFT and RIGHT animats eventually learn to locate the corresponding eyes. Fig. 6

shows the conspicuous paths followed by the animats searching for the LEFT or RIGHT eye locations using some of the images shown in Fig. 4 above.

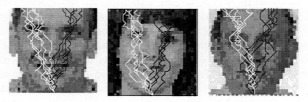

Figure 6. Conspicuous Paths Leading to the Left and Right Eye Locations Found during Training

Consensus Methods and Derivation of the Saliency Map
So far we have shown how one can train FSAs as successful autonomous agents for exploring the facial ('features') landscape. As several animats (FSAs) search the landscape in parallel, one has to collect and integrate their conspicuous outputs so eventually most salient eye locations are determined. The motivation for such an approach comes from the fact that if one were to deploy trained animats it is likely that areas of major traffic, subject to model constraints, would correspond to the eye regions. Towards that end we trained many different animats on similar tasks, **LEFT** and **RIGHT** eye detection, using random seeds for starting the FSA animat described in the previous subsection. Once the (**L** and **R**) animats end their travel, on the upper boundary of the face image, **L** and **R** traffic density across the facial landscape is collected, and one generates (**L** - **R**) traffic with the expectation that the eyes will show up as areas of increased image saliency, the nose regions will cancel out, and the other facial areas will show only insignificant saliency.

The consensus method implemented here consists of the following steps. Left and Right local but conspicuous traffics are counted for a number of different Left and Right animats, the (**L** - **R**) traffic map is generated and its significant local maxima are then detected using hystheresis and thresholding. This procedure, stepwise illustrated in Fig. 7, shows how animats detect what appears as most promising eye locations on an unseen face image using 20 Left and 20 Right trained FSAs and consensus as described above.

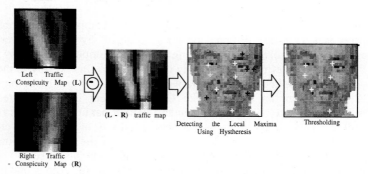

Figure 7. Derivation of Saliency Map Using Conspicuous Traffic and Consensus

The goal for the derivation of the saliency map is to screen out most of the facial landscape as possible eye locations so the recognition channel ('pathway') can be asked to classify as eye regions only a reduced area of the facial landscape. This goal, as it can be seen from Fig. 8, has been achieved to a large degree. At the same time one has yet to find the means for discarding salient but false positive eye locations. while not missing any of the eye locations. Both eyes are correctly identified as salient candidates in Figs. 8a, 8b, and 8c, while for the test images shown in Figs. 8d and 8e, one eye has not been yet declared as a salient candidate.

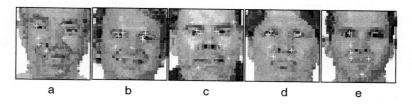

a   b   c   d   e

Figure 8. Examples of Saliency Map

In order to overcome the problem of missing eye locations, we expand on the consensus method and start the animats ('swarm') from five adjacent locations (close-by to the chin) and collect the corresponding traffic. Consensus then proceeds as before to identify salient eye locations. The result of such an approach is shown in Fig. 9. As it can be seen all the eye locations are now correctly identified as salient while several false positive eye locations are still maintained.

Figure 9. Salient Eye Location Using Multiple Starting Positions

8.2.2   Eye Recognition

This section describes the stage of eye recognition (activated only on salient eye locations) (see Fig. 3). The section includes the hybrid GA-DT architecture, its underlying learning strategy, and the final results for the eye detection task.

Genetic Algorithms
The first step in applying GAs to the problem of feature selection for (eye) recognition is to map the search space into a representation suitable for genetic search. Since the main interest is in representing the space of all possible subsets of the original feature list, the simplest form for image base representations would consider each feature as a binary gene. Each individual chromosome is then

represented as a fixed-length binary string standing for some subset of the original feature list. A chromosome corresponds to an N dimensional binary feature vector X, where each bit represents the absence or inclusion of the associated feature. The advantage of this representation is that the classical GAs operators described earlier (binary mutation and crossover) can be easily applied to this representation without any modification.

The choice of an appropriate evaluation procedure is an essential step for the successful application of GAs to any problem domain. Evaluation procedures provide GAs with feedback about the fitness of each individual in the population. GAs use this feedback to bias the search process and improve the population's average fitness. Fitness evaluation becomes available once performance of the decision trees - C4.5 (see Sect. 6) being induced is assessed. For the experiments reported later on, both parents and offspring compete to be included in the next generation.

Hybrid GA-DT

The training strategy, conceptually akin to cross-validation (CV) and bootstrapping, draws randomly from the original list of examples, both positive and negative, and generates two labeled sets consisting of training and tuning data. The training data is used to induce trees, while the tuning data is used to evaluate the trees and generate appropriate fitness measures. Once the evolution stops the best tree is frozen and it would be used for testing on salient eye locations. The decision tree induction process is applied to *training data* and it generates decision trees for each of the given (eye and non-eye) classes. The evaluation procedure assesses the fitness of each feature subset, as given by its corresponding induced tree, using now *tuning data* sets and employing an integrated measure consisting of both the number of features used and the error rate. This measure of fitness is then passed to the GA module to further evolve optimal candidate feature subsets. The whole process is initialized by randomly selecting subsets of feature and making them available to C4.5.

We describe next the image data used, the original list of possible features, and the classification scheme run on salient eye locations. The facial images are normalized to 64x64 resolution. The data base for training consists of 120 positive (+) eye examples and 480 negative ('non-eye') (-) examples, randomly drawn from across the facial landscape. The resolution for both the positive and negative eye examples is 24x16. The feature list for each 24x16 window consists initially of one hundred and forty seven features $\{x_1, x_2,..., x_{147}\}$. The set of features, each of them measured over 6x4 windows and using two pixels overlap, is:

- x_1 to x_{49}: means for each window
- x_{50} to x_{98}: entropies for each window
- x_{99} to x_{147}: means for each window after applying the Laplacian over 24x16 frames

Fig.10 illustrates the feature extraction process for training and tuning examples.

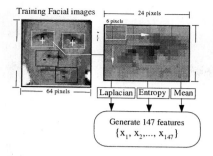

Figure 10. Feature Extraction for Decision Trees

During evolution, each generation consists of a constant population of fifty individuals, and the crossover rate and mutation rate are 0.6 and 0.001, respectively. The set of six hundred examples, 120 (+) eye and 480 (-) non-eye examples, is divided into three equal subsets for cross validation (CV) training and tuning, and a tournament consisting of three sets of CV rounds takes place. The corresponding error rates - false positives : false detection of eyes and false negatives : missing the eyes, are added to define the fitness function (see Fig. 11). The feature subset corresponding to the tree derived from the third CV round, which achieved the smallest - 4.87% - total error rate, consists of only 60 of the original 147 features. This feature subset would be the one used to evaluate the overall performance on the eye detection task using all the candidate regions suggested by the saliency maps (See Sect. 8.1.1).

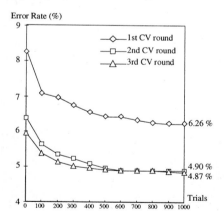

Figure 11. Fitness Measures

Once training for DT is completed the eye locations suggested by the saliency map are tested across 20 face images for being possibly classified as eyes. Fig.12 displays the 24x16 windows, centered at interesting eye locations as indicated by the saliency map, which are used as testing cases for eye recognition. The classification results are shown in Fig. 13.

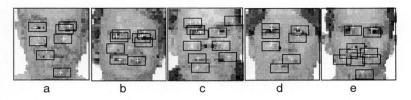

Figure 12. Salient Eye Locations

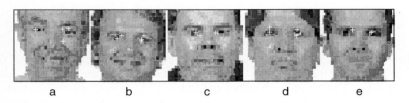

Figure 13. Eye Recognition

Winner Take All (WTA) and Final Eye Detection

Clusters of candidates are detected as it has been shown in Fig. 13. No false negatives, i.e., missing eye locations, have been observed for all 20 test images. Due to the coarse resolution of the saliency map the salient locations classified as eyes overlap. As a consequence post processing is warranted and WTA (Winner Take All) is used. Post processing starts by clustering adjacent candidates, find their corresponding centers, and filters out those who fail pairwise (horizontal and vertical) interocular distance constraints. The WTA would then choose the eye pair which yields maximum (horizontal) interocular distance and minimizes the vertical distance between the centers of the two eyes. Post processed results using WTA are shown in Fig. 14 and they indicate the final decisions made regarding eye detection. Evolution modulated by learning appears to be beneficial to eye detection as we missed only one eye in two of the 20 test images.

Figure 14. Final Results for Eye Detection

9   Evolution of Optimal Projection Axes (OPA) for Face Recognition

The non-accidental spatiotemporal properties of the world surrounding us have much to do with the design of visual systems. This viewpoint formulated by Barlow (1989) (adaptation and decorrelation in the cortex) and more recently by Ruderman (1994) amongst others, has led to a growing interest in (i) how the statistical properties of natural images enter into the optimization of the visual system, and (ii) the statistical characterization of the natural images themselves. The regularities of the surrounding world have been encoded mostly in terms of 2nd order statistics or corresponding spectral information, even that most recently there is a growing and justified interest in using higher order statistics as well. Methods based on decorrelating 2nd order statistics belong to the class of PCA (Principal Component Analysis) methods, while those concerned with independent higher order statistics belong to the class of ICA (Independent Component Analysis) methods.

Optimization of the visual system would include design criteria such as (i) redundancy minimization - decorrelation and independent component analysis (ICA), (ii) minimization of the reconstruction error (rms), (iii) maximization of information transmission (infomax), and (iv) sparseness of the neural code (Olshausen and Field, 1996). While there has been a growing interest concerning natural scene statistics and building the neural code to capture them (Rao and Ballard, 1995), the range of imagery which could be of interest goes much beyond natural scenes. One should add within the context of face recognition an important functionality related to successful pattern classification, referred to by Edelman (1987) as neural Darwinism. Successful pattern classification amounts to the wrapper approach using subsets of features suggested by the filter approach.

9.1   Optimal Projection Axes (OPA)

Sirovich and Kirby (1987) were first to apply PCA for representing face images. They showed that any particular face can be economically represented along the eigenpictures coordinate space, and that any face can be approximately reconstructed by using just a small collection of eigenpictures and the corresponding projections ('coefficients') along each eigenpicture. Since eigenpictures are fairly good in representing face images, one can also consider using the projections along them as classification features to recognize faces. As for face recognition accurate reconstruction of the image is not a requirement, a smaller subset of the eigenpictures should be sufficient. As a result, Turk and Pentland (1991) developed a well known face recognition method, known as *eigenfaces*, which corresponds to the eigenvectors associated with the dominant eigenvalues of the face (patterns) covariance matrix. The eigenfaces define a feature space which drastically reduces the dimensionality of the original space, and face detection and identification are carried out in this small space.

Further research has revealed that the leading principal components (PCs) can be effectively used for recognition only when the variations of within and between classes have the same dominant directions. If this is not the case, other PCs corresponding to smaller eigenvalues may be more useful for recognition (Jolliffe, 1986). Swets and Weng (1996) have pointed out recently that the eigenfaces derived using PCA are only the most expressive features (MEF), which are unrelated to actual face recognition. To derive the most discriminating features (MDF), one needs a subsequent discriminant analysis projection. Their procedure, similar to Linear Discriminant Analysis (LDA) involves the simultaneous diagonalization of the two within- and between- class scatter matrices (Fukunaga, 1991). The MDF space is superior to the MEF space for face recognition only when the training images are representative of the range of face image class variation; otherwise, the performance difference between the MEF and MDF is not significant.

As the integration of evolution and learning should be useful for capturing the non-accidental spatiotemporal properties ('regularities') of the world surrounding us, we advance its use for face recognition. Towards that end we have developed a novel approach called Optimal Projection Axes (OPA) for face recognition by searching through all the rotations defined over whitened PCA subspaces. Evolution is driven by a fitness function defined in terms of performance accuracy and class separation ('scatter index'). Accuracy indicates the extent to which learning has been successful so far, while the scatter index gives an indication of the expected fitness on future trials. Experimental results using a large date set (1107 facial images from the US Army FERET database) and comparative studies with other methods (eigenfaces and MDF - see above) demonstrate the feasibility of our approach.

The OPA approach integrates the techniques of PCA, whitening and rotation transformations, and GA. First, PCA projects the face images into a lower dimensional space while keeping most of the expressive (representational) information of the original images. Then, the whitening transformation counteracts the fact that the mean square error (MSE) principle underlying PCA preferentially weights low frequencies. Directed but random rotations of the lower dimensional (whitened PCA) space are guided by evolution and use domain specific knowledge ('fitness'). The fitness behind evolution and the one used to find OPA as optimal bases would consider both recognition rates and the scatter index which are derived using the projections of the face images onto the optimal bases. Note that the reachable space of GAs is increased as a result of using a non-orthonormal (whitening) transformation. Under the whitening transformation the norms (distances) are not preserved. One can expect better performance from non-orthogonal bases over orthogonal ones as they lead to an overcomplete and robust representational space (Daugmann, 1990). Our experimental results showed that when whitening was not performed the face recognition results were worse than when using it.

9.1.1 Dimensionality Reduction

PCA generates a set of orthonormal bases known as principal components. Let $X=[X_1,X_2,...,X_n]$ be the sample set of the original images. After normalizing the images to unity norm (so the inner product is equal to 1) and substracting the grand mean a new image set $Y=[Y_1,Y_2,...,Y_n]$ is obtained. Each Y_i represents a normalized image with dimensionality N, $Y_i = (y_{i_1}, y_{i_2}, \cdots, y_{i_N})^t$, ($i$=1,2,...,$n$). The eigenvector and eigenvalue matrices Φ, Λ are computed as

$$(YY')\Phi = \Phi\Lambda \tag{2}$$

Note that YY' is an NxN matrix while $Y'Y$ is an nxn matrix. If the sample size n is much smaller than the dimensionality N, then the following computation method saves some computation (Turk and Pentland, 1991)

$$(Y'Y)\Psi = \Psi\Lambda_1 \tag{3}$$
$$\Im = Y\Psi \tag{4}$$

where $\Lambda_1 = diag\{\lambda_1, \lambda_2, \cdots, \lambda_n\}$, and $\Im = [\Phi_1, \Phi_2, \cdots, \Phi_n]$. If one assumes that the eigenvalues are sorted in decreasing order, $\lambda_1 \geq \lambda_2 \geq \cdots \geq \lambda_n$, then the first m leading eigenvectors define matrix P

$$P = [\Phi_1, \Phi_2, \cdots, \Phi_m] \tag{5}$$

The new feature set Z with lower dimensionality m (m<<N) is then computed as

$$Z = P'Y \tag{6}$$

9.1.2 Whitening Transformation

The low dimensional feature set Z is now subject to the whitening transformation, $\Gamma = diag\{\lambda_1^{-1/2}, \lambda_2^{-1/2}, \cdots, \lambda_m^{-1/2}\}$, leading to another feature set V

$$V = \Gamma Z \tag{7}$$

The reason why the whitening procedure can lead to non-orthogonal bases of the overall transformation is as follows. Let Q be a mxm rotation matrix ($Q'Q = QQ' = I$) and apply Q to the feature set V. Combined with Eqs. 6 and 7 one obtains the overall transformation matrix Ξ

$$\Xi = P\Gamma Q \tag{8}$$

Let us assume the basis vectors in Ξ are orthogonal,

$$\Xi'\Xi = \Delta \tag{9}$$

where Δ is a diagonal matrix. From Eqs. 8 and 9 it follows that

$$\Gamma^2 = \Delta = cI \tag{10}$$

where c is a constant. Eq. 10 holds only when all the eigenvalues are equal, and when this is not the case the basis vectors in Ξ are not orthogonal.

9.1.3 Rotation Transformations

After the whitening transformation, the feature set V lies in an m dimensional space. Let $\Omega = [\varepsilon_1, \varepsilon_2, \cdots, \varepsilon_m]$ be the basis of this space where $\varepsilon_1, \varepsilon_2, \cdots, \varepsilon_m$ are the unit vectors. The method presented here tries to search the optimal subset of some basis vectors rotated from $\varepsilon_1, \varepsilon_2, \cdots, \varepsilon_m$. The rotation procedure is carried out by pairwise axes rotation. In particular, let us suppose the basis vectors ε_i and ε_j need to be rotated by α_k, then a new basis $\xi_1, \xi_2, \cdots, \xi_m$ is derived by

$$[\xi_1, \xi_2, \cdots, \xi_m] = [\varepsilon_1, \varepsilon_2, \cdots, \varepsilon_m]Q_k \tag{11}$$

where Q_k is a rotation matrix. There are $M = m(m-1)/2$ rotation angles in total corresponding to the M pairs of basis vectors to be rotated. For the purpose of evolving optimal basis for recognition, it makes no difference if the angles are confined to $(0, \pi/2)$, since the positive directions and the order of axes are not important. The overall rotation matrix Q is defined by

$$Q = Q_1 Q_2 \cdots Q_{m(m-1)/2} \tag{12}$$

9.1.4 Face Recognition Using Optimal Projection Axes

Corresponding to different sets of rotation angles, different basis vectors are formed. We want to pick up the best subset from a particular basis set in terms of its discriminant power. Let Q in (12) define this particular basis set (remember $\varepsilon_1, \varepsilon_2, \cdots, \varepsilon_m$ are unit vectors), and let the column vectors in Q be $\Theta_1, \Theta_2, \cdots, \Theta_m$. Now let $\Theta_{i_1}, \Theta_{i_2}, \cdots, \Theta_{i_l}$ be the optimal projection axes T which is evolved by GA (will be discussed in next section).

$$T = [\Theta_{i_1}, \Theta_{i_2}, \cdots, \Theta_{i_l}] \tag{13}$$

where $i_j \in \{1, 2, \cdots, m\}$, $i_j \neq i_k$ for $j \neq k$, and $l < m$. Then the feature set U is obtained

$$U = [U_1, U_2, \cdots, U_n] = T'V \tag{14}$$

where $U_1, U_2, \cdots, U_n$ are the feature vectors corresponding to different sample images.

Let U_k^0 (k=1, 2, ..., n) be the prototypes of class k, and the classification rule is expressed as

$$\|U_i - U_k^0\| = \min_j \|U_i - U_j^0\|, \quad U_i \in \omega_k \tag{15}$$

9.2 Search of Optimal Projection Axes (OPA) Using Genetic Algorithm

The problem of identifying and exploiting non-linear interactions among features can be addressed through the use of sophisticated search techniques such as genetic algorithms (GAs) which provide efficient methods for searching large spaces. Genetic Algorithms (Goldberg, 1989), as examples of evolutionary computation, are nondeterministic methods, similar to stochastic approximations, that can cope with large search spaces by employing cross-over and mutation strategies for behavioral optimization and adaptation. GAs work by maintaining a constant-sized population of candidate solutions known as individuals ('chromosomes'). The power of a genetic algorithm lies in its ability to exploit, in a highly efficient manner, information about a large number of individuals. The search underlying GAs is such that breadth and depth - exploration and exploitation - are balanced according to the observed performance of the individuals evolved so far.

By allocating more reproductive occurrences to above average individual solutions, the overall effect is to increase the population's average fitness.

9.2.1 Chromosome Representation and Genetic Operators

The optimal projection axes $\Theta_{i_1}, \Theta_{i_2}, \cdots, \Theta_{i_l}$ in Eq.13 is picked up from a larger vector set rotated from a basis $\varepsilon_1, \varepsilon_2, \cdots, \varepsilon_m$ in the m dimensional space by a set of rotation angles $\alpha_1, \alpha_2, \cdots, \alpha_{m(m-1)/2}$ with each angle in the range of $(0, \pi/2)$. If the angles are discretized with small enough steps, then we can use GA to search the discretized space. GA requires the solutions to be represented in the form of bit strings or chromosomes. If we use 10 bits (resolution) to represent each angle, then each discretized (angle) interval is less than 0.09 degree, and we need $10*[m(m-1)/2]$ bits to represent all the angles. As we have m basis vectors to choose from, another m bits should be added to the chromosome to facilitate that choice. Fig.15 shows the chromosome representation, where a_i $(i = 1, 2, \cdots, m)$, having the value 0 or 1, indicate whether the i-th basis vector is chosen or not.

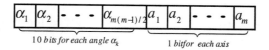

Figure 15. Chromosome representation

Let N_s be the number of different choices of basis vectors in the search space. The size of genospace, too large to search it exhaustively, is

$$N_s = 2^{5m(m-1)+m} \tag{16}$$

GA specifies the choice of various actions as functions of particular probability distributions via genetic operators: selection, crossover, and mutation operators. In our experiments, we use the (i) proportionate selection: preselection of parents in proportion to their relative fitness; (ii) two point crossover: exchange the sections between the crossover points; and (iii) fixed probability mutation: each position of a chromosome is given a fixed probability of undergoing mutation (flipping the corresponding bit).

9.2.2 Fitness Function

Fitness values guide GA on how to choose offsprings for the next generation from the current parent generation. The fitness function f has the form

$$f(Q, a_1, a_2, \cdots, a_m) = a * C_1 + D_b \tag{17}$$

where a is a constant, C_1 is the number of faces correctly recognized as the top choice after the rotation and selection of a subset of axes, and D_b denotes the scatter measurement among different classes. a is chosen such that C_1 contributes more to the fitness than D_b does and the scatter's role is to refine the decision surfaces.

Let the rotation angle set be $\alpha_1^{(k)}, \alpha_2^{(k)}, \cdots, \alpha_{m(m-1)/2}^{(k)}$, and the basis vectors after the transformation be $\xi_1^{(k)}, \xi_2^{(k)}, \cdots, \xi_m^{(k)}$ according to Eqs.11 and 12. If GA chooses l vectors $\eta_1, \eta_2, \cdots, \eta_l$ from $\xi_1^{(k)}, \xi_2^{(k)}, \cdots, \xi_m^{(k)}$, then the new feature set is specified as

$$W = [\eta_1, \eta_2, \cdots, \eta_l]^t V \tag{18}$$

Let $\omega_1, \omega_2, \cdots, \omega_L$, and $N_1, N_2, \cdots, N_L$ denote the classes and number of images within each class respectively. Let $M_1, M_2, \cdots, M_L$ and M_0 be the means of each class and the grand mean in the new feature space $span[\eta_1, \eta_2, \cdots, \eta_l]$, then D_b is obtained as

$$D_b = \sqrt{\sum_{i=1}^{L} (M_i - M_0)^2} \tag{19}$$

9.3 Experimental Results

1107 facial images corresponding to 369 subjects used for the experiments are from the US Army FERET database (Phillips et al, 1998). 600 out of the 1107 images correspond to 200 subjects with each subject having three images -- two of them are the first and the second shot, and the third shot is taken under low illumination. For the remaining 169 subjects there are also three images for each subject, but two out the three images are duplicates taken at different time. Two images of each subject are used for training with the remaining image for testing. Normalized images are cropped to the size of 64x96.

First, PCA, from Eq. 6, reduces the dimension of the original image space from N (64x96) to m and whitening procedure, Eq. 7, transforms the new features in the m dimensional space. Then GA, guided by the fitness value from Eq.17, evolves optimal projection axes in this lower dimensional space by rotating each pair of basis vectors by an angle between 0 and $\pi/2$. Finally, Eqs. 13, 14, and 15 implement the actual recognition. For comparison purposes, the Eigenface and MDF methods were implemented and experimented with as well. Table 1 shows the recognition results obtained during training using the above procedure.

Table 1. Training Performances

methods	18 features	26 features
Eigenface Method	78.05%	81.30%
MDF Method	100%	100%
OPA Method	83.47%	82.66%

Table 2 shows the recognition results for different methods on 369 test images (not used during training). PCA first reduces the space dimension to $m = 20$, and

GA would evolve the optimal projection axes in this 20 dimensional space. Top 1 recognition rate means the accuracy rate for the top response being correct, while top 3 recognition rate represents the accuracy rate for the correct response being included among the first three ranked choices. OPA evolves 18 vectors as the optimal axes with top 1 recognition rate 87.80% compared to 81.57% for the Eigenface method and 79.95% for the MDF method. Table 3 shows the results when GA evolves OPA in the 30 dimensional PCA space, resulting in 26 optimal axes with 92.14% top 1 recognition rate, compared to 87.26% for Eigenface and 86.45% for MDF method. From Tables 1, 2 and 3 it becomes apparent that MDF does not display good generalization abilities, while PCA and OPA do. The range of training data is quite large as it consists of both original and duplicate images acquired at a later time. As a consequence, during training, MDF performs better than both PCA and OPA because it overfits to a larger extent its classifier to the data. OPA yields, however, improved performances over the other two methods, during testing.

Table 2. Comparative Face Recognition Results with GA Evolving Optimal Projection Axes (OPA) in m=**20** Dimensional Space (Testing Performances)

methods	# features	top 1 recognition rate	top 3 recognition rate
Eigenface Method	18	81.57%	94.58%
MDF Method	18	79.95%	87.80%
OPA Method	18	87.80%	95.93%

Table 3. Comparative Face Recognition Results with GA Evolving Optimal Projection Axes (OPA) in m=**30** Dimensional Space (Testing Performances)

methods	# features	top 1 recognition rate	top 3 recognition rate
Eigenface Method	26	87.26%	95.66%
MDF Method	26	86.45%	93.77%
OPA Method	26	92.14%	97.02%

10   Conclusions

This chapter introduces evolutionary computation (EC) and genetic algorithms (GAs) for face recognition tasks. We first addressed eye detection as a visual routine and showed how to implement it using a hybrid approach integrating learning and evolution. The goals of the novel architecture for eye detection are twofold: (i) derivation of the saliency attention map using consensus between navigation routines encoded as finite state automata (FSA) evolved using GAs and (ii) selection of optimal features using GAs and induction of DT (decision trees) for possibly classifying as eyes the most salient locations identified earlier. Experimental results, using 30 face images from the FERET data base show the feasibility of our hybrid approach. We then introduced the Optimal Projection

Axes (OPA) method for face recognition. OPA works by searching through all the rotations defined over whitened Principal Component Analysis (PCA) subspaces. Whitening, which does not preserve norms, plays a dual role: (i) counteracts the fact that the Mean Square Error (MSE) principle underlying PCA preferentially weights low frequencies, and (ii) increases the reachable space of solutions to include non-orthogonal bases. As the search space is too large for any systematic search, stochastic and directed ('greedy') search is undertaken using evolution in the form of Genetic Algorithms (GAs). Evolution is driven by a fitness function defined in terms of performance accuracy and class separation ('scatter index'). Experiments carried out using 1,107 facial images corresponding to 369 subjects (with 169 subjects having duplicated images) from the FERET data base show that OPA yields improved performance over the eigenface and MDF (Most Discriminant Features) methods.

The hybrid approach for eye detection results hold promise for behavior-based AI in general, and the evolutionary development of attention mechanisms, visual routines, and eventual coordination of visual and navigation routines, in particular. In terms of forensic applications this approach holds promise for tasks such as facial landmark detection and surveillance. The OPA method opens new directions for future research on feature selection for face recognition tasks. Additional problems to be investigated within the EC framework include the relative merits of PCA vs Independent Component analysis (ICA) methods and the development of natural bases for face representation and recognition.

Acknowledgements: The work described here was partly supported by the US Army Research Lab under contract DAAL01-97-K-0118.

References

Allport, A. (1989). Visual Attention, in E. Posner (Ed.), *Foundations of Cognitive* Science, MIT Press.

J. Bala, K. DeJong, J. Huang, H. Vafaie, and H. Wechsler (1996), Using Learning to Facilitate the Evolution of Features for Recognizing Visual Concepts, *Evolutionary Computation*, **4**(3), 297-312.

Barlow, H. B. (1989). Unsupervised Learning, *Neural Computation*, Vol. 1, 295-311.

Brooks, R.A. (1985). Visual map making for a mobile robot, *IEEE Int. Conference on Robotics and Automation*, 819-824.

Brooks, R.A. (1986). A robust layered control system for a mobile robot, *IEEE Journal of Robotics and Automation*, Vol. 2, 14-22

Culhane, S. M. and Tsotso, J. K. (1992). An Attentional Prototype for Early Vision, *Proc. of the 2nd European Conf. on Computer Vision*, Santa Margherita Ligure, Italy.

Daugman, J. G. (1990). An information-theoretic view of analog representation in striate cortex., in *Computational Neuroscience*, Ed. E. L. Schwartz, 403-424, MIT Press.

DePersia, A. T. and Phillips, P. J. (1995). "The FERET Program: Overview and Accomplishments".

Ducottet, C., J. Daniere, M., Moine, Schon, J. P., and Courbon, M. (1994). Localization of Objects with Circular Symmetry in a Noisy Image Using Wavelet Transforms and Adapted Correlation, *Pattern Recognition*, Vol.27, No. 3, pp.351-364.

Edelman, G. M. (1987). *Neural Darwinism*, Basic Books.

Fukuda, T., et al. (1994). Optimization of group behavior on cellular robotic system in dynamic environment, *IEEE Int. Conference on Robotics and Automation,* 1027-1032.

Fukunaga, K. (1991). *Introduction to Statistical Pattern Recognition*, 2nd Edition, Academic Press.

Gofman, Y. and Kiryati, N. (1996). Detecting Symmetry in Gray Level Images: The Global Optimization Approach, *Proceeding of ICPR '96*, pp.889-894.

Goldberg, D. E. (1989) *Genetic Algorithms in Search, Optimization, and Machine Learning*, Addison-Wesley.

Goldberg. D. (1989). *Genetic Algorithms in Search, Optimization and Machine Learning*, Addison - Wesley.

Grefenstette, J. J. (1984). Genesis: A system for using genetic search procedures, *Proc. Conf. Intelligent Systems and Machines*, 161-165.

Hampshire, J. B. and Waibel, A. (1992). The Meta-Pi network: Building distributed knowledge representations for robust multisource pattern recognition, *IEEE Trans. on Pattern Analysis and Machine Intelligence* Vol. 14, No. 7, 751-769.

Hinton, G. E. and Nolan, S. J. (1987). How learning can guide evolution, *Complex Systems*, Vol. 1, pp.495-502.

Holland, J.H. (1975). *Adaptation in Neural and Artifical Systems*, University of Michigan Press, Ann Arbor, MI.

Horswill, I. (1995). Visual routines and visual search, *Int. Joint Conf. on Artificial Intelligence*, Montreal, Canada.

Johnson, M., Maes, P., and Darell, T. (1994). Evolving visual routines, in *Artificial Life IV*, edited by R.A. Brooks and P. Maes, MIT Press.

Jolliffe, I. T. (1986). *Principal Component Analysis*, Springer, New York.

Koch, C. and S. Ullman (1987). Shifts in Selective Visual Attention: Towards the Underlying Neural Circuitry, in Vaina (Ed.), Matters of Intelligence, Rediel Publishing.

Kohavi, R. and John, G. (1995). Wrappers for Feature Subset Selection. Technical Report, Computer Science Department, Stanford University.

Koza, J.R. (1992), *Genetic Programming I*, MIT Press.

Lam, K. M. and Yan, H. (1996). Locating and Extracting the Eye in Human Face Images, *Pattern Recognition*, Vol.29, NO. 5, pp.771-779.

Livingstone, M. S. and Hubel, D. H. (1988). Segregation of Form, Color, Movement, and Depth: Anatomy, Psychology, and Perception, *Science*, 240, 740-749.

Maes, P. (1992). Behavior-based AI, in J. A. Meyer, H. L. Roitblat, and S. W. Wilson (Eds.), *From Animals to Animats 2,* MIT Press.

Minsky, M. (1985). *The Society of Mind*, Simon & Schuster Inc., N.Y.

Moghaddam, B. and Pentland, A. (1995). Probabilistic visual learning for object detection, *5th Int. Conf. on Computer Vision*, Cambridge, MA.

Mühlenbein, H., and Kinderman, J. (1989). The dynamics of Evolution and Learning. Toward Genetic Neural Networks, in R. Pfeifer, Z. Schreter, F. Fogelman-Soulie, and L. Steels (Eds.), *Connectionism in Perspective*, Elsevier Science, pp. 173-197.

Olshausen, B. A. and Field, D. J. (1996). Emergence of Simple-cell Receptive Field Properties by Learning a Sparse Code for Natural Images, *Nature*, Vol. 381, 13, 607-609.

Pentland, A.P., Moghaddam, B. and Starner, T. (1994). "View-based and Modular Eigenspaces for Recognition", *Proceedings of Computer Vision and Pattern Recognition*, Seattle, USA.

Phillips, P. J., Wechsler, H., Huang, J., and Rauss, P. (1998). The FERET Database and Evaluation Procedure for Face Recognition Algorithms, *Image and Vision Computing* (to appear).

Quinlan, J. R. (1993). *C4.5: Programs for Machine Learning*, Morgan Kaufmann, San Mateo, CA.

Quinlan, J.R. (1986). The effect of noise on concept learning, in *Machine Learning: an Artificial Intelligence Approach*, edited by R.S. Michalski, J.G. Carbonell and T.M. Mitchell, Morgan Kaufmann, San Mateo, CA, pp.149-166.

Ramachandran, V.S. (1985), Apparent motion of subjective surfaces, *Perception*, 14, pp.127-134.

Rao, R. P. N. and Ballard, D. (1995). Object Indexing Using an Iconic Sparse Distributed Memory, *5th. Int. Conf. on Computer Vision*, Boston, MA, 24 - 31.

Rechenberg, I. (1973), *Evolution strategies: Optimierung Technischer Systeme nach Prinzipien der Biologischen Evolution*, Frommann-Holzboog Verlag.

Rowley, H. A., Baluja, S. and Kanade, T. (1995). Human Face Detection in Visual Scenes, *Technical Report*, CMU-CS-95-158.

Ruderman, D. (1994). The statistics of Natural Images, *Network : Computation in Neural Systems*, Vol. 5, 598-605.

Samal, A., and P. Iyengar (1992). Automatic recognition and analysis of human faces and facial expressions: A Survey", *Pattern Recognition*, Vol. 25, 65-77.

Samaria, F. S., and A. C. Harter (1994). Parameterisation of a Stochastic Model for Human Face Identification, *2nd IEEE Workshop on Applications of Computer Vision,* Sarasota, Florida.

Sirovich, L. and Kirby, M. (1987). Low-dimensional Procedure for the Characterization of Human Faces, *J. Opt. Soc. Am. A*, Vol. 4, No. 3, 519-524.

Swets, Daniel L. and Weng, John (1996). Using Discriminant Eigenfeatures for Image Retrieval, *IEEE Trans. on PAMI*, Vol. 18, No. 8, 831-836.

Turk, M. and Pentland, A. (1991). Eigenfaces for Recognition, *Journal of Cognitive Neuroscience*, Vol. 3, No. 1, 71-86.

Ullman, S. (1984). Visual routines, *Cognition*, Vol. 18, pp.97-159.

Vafaie, H., and De Jong, K. (1994). Improving a Rule Induction System Using Genetic Algorithms, in R.S. Michalski and G. Tecuci (Eds.), *Machine Learning: A Multistrategy Approach, Vol. IV*, Morgan Kaufmann, San Mateo, CA., pp. 453-469.

Yeshurun, Y., D. Reisfeld, and Wolfson, H. (1991). Symmetry: A Context Free Cue for Foveated Vision, *Neural Networks for Pattern Recognition (Vol. 1.)*, H. Wechsler, ed., Academic Press.

Yuille, A.L. (1991). Deformable Templates for Face Recognition, *J. Cognitive Neuroscience*, vol. 3, no. 1, pp. 59-70.

Part II

Participant Presentations

Learning Viewpoint Invariant Face Representations from Visual Experience by Temporal Association

Marian Stewart Bartlett[1] and Terrence J. Sejnowski[2]

[1]Departments of Cognitive Science and Psychology, UCSD, San Diego, CA 92093 and The Salk Institute, La Jolla, CA 92037. marni@salk.edu
[2]Department of Biology, UCSD, San Diego, CA 92093, and Howard Hughes Medical Institute at The Salk Institute, La Jolla, CA 92037. terry@salk.edu

Abstract. In natural visual experience, different views of an object or face tend to appear in close temporal proximity. A set of simulations is presented which demonstrate how viewpoint invariant representations of faces can be developed from visual experience by capturing the temporal relationships among the input patterns. The simulations explored the interaction of temporal smoothing of activity signals with Hebbian learning (Foldiak, 1991) in both a feed-forward system and a recurrent system. The recurrent system was a generalization of a Hopfield network with a lowpass temporal filter on all unit activities. Following training on sequences of graylevel images of faces as they changed pose, multiple views of a given face fell into the same basin of attraction, and the system acquired representations of faces that were approximately viewpoint invariant.

1 Introduction

Cells in the primate inferior temporal lobe have been reported that respond selectively to faces despite substantial changes in viewpoint (Perrett, Mistlin, & Chitty, 1989; Hasselmo, Rolls, Baylis, & Nalwa, 1989). A small proportion of cells gave responses that were invariant to angle of view, whereas other cells had tuning curves that were quite broad. Perrett et al. (1989) reported broad coding for five principal views of the head: Frontal, left profile, right profile, looking up, and looking down, and the pose tuning of these cells was on the order of $\pm 40^0$. The retinal input changes considerably under these shifts in viewpoint.

This model addresses how receptive fields with such broad pose tuning could be developed from visual experience. The model touches on several issues in the psychology and neurophysiology of face recognition. Can general learning principles account for the ability to respond to faces across changes in pose, or does this function require special purpose, possibly genetically encoded mechanisms? Is it possible to recognize faces across changes in pose without explicitly recovering or storing the 3-dimensional structure of the face? What are the potential contributions of temporal sequence information to the representation and recognition of faces?

Until recently, most investigations of face recognition focused on static images of faces. The preponderance of our experience with faces, however, is not with static faces, but with live faces that move, change expression, and pose. Temporal sequences contain information that can aid in the process of representing and recognizing faces and objects (eg. see V. Bruce, this volume). This model explores how a neural system can acquire invariance to viewpoint from visual experience by accessing the temporal structure of the input. The appearance of an object or a face changes continuously as the observer moves through the environment or as a face changes expression or pose. Capturing the temporal relationships in the input is a way to automatically associate different views of an object without requiring three-dimensional representations (Stryker, 1991).

Temporal association may be an important factor in the development of transformation invariant responses in the inferior temporal lobe of primates (Rolls, 1995). Neurons in the anterior inferior temporal lobe are capable of associating patterns by temporal proximity. After prolonged exposure to a sequence of randomly generated fractal patterns, correlations emerged in the sustained responses to neighboring patterns in the sequence (Miyashita, 1988). Macaques were presented a fixed sequence of 97 fractal patterns for 2 weeks. After training, the patterns were presented in random order. Figure 1 shows correlations in sustained responses of the AIT cells to pairs of patterns as a function of the relative position of the patterns in the training sequence. Responses to neighboring patterns were correlated, and the correlation dropped off as the distance between the patterns in the training sequence increased. These data suggest that cells in the temporal lobe can modify their receptive fields to associate patterns that occurred close together in time.

Temporal relationships can be captured by Hebbian learning (Foldiak, 1991). Hebbian learning is an unsupervised learning rule that was proposed as a model for the modification of synaptic strengths between neurons (Hebb, 1949). In Hebbian learning, the connections between simultaneously active units are strengthened. With a lowpass temporal filter on output unit activities, Hebbian learning will strengthen the connections between active inputs and *recently* active outputs. This mechanism can learn transformation invariant representations when different views of an object are presented in temporal continuity (Foldiak, 1991; Weinshall, Edelman & Bulthoff, 1991; Rhodes, 1992; O'Reilly & Johnson, 1994). Such learning mechanisms have recently been shown to learn transformation invariant of responses to complex inputs such as images of faces (Bartlett & Sejnowski, 1996, 1997; Wallis & Rolls, 1997; Becker, 1997).

There are several mechanisms by which receptive fields could be modified to perform temporal associations. The NMDA channel is an activity dependent gate in the neural membrane thought to be involved in long-term potentiation of synaptic strengths. A temporal window for Hebbian learning could be provided by the 0.5 second open-time of the NMDA channel after the neuron fires (Rhodes, 1992; Rolls, 1992). Reciprocal connections between cortical regions (O'Reilly & Johnson, 1994) or lateral interconnections within cortical regions could sustain activity over longer time periods and allow temporal associations across larger time scales.

The time course of the modifiable state of a neuron, based on the open time of the NMDA channel, has been modeled by a lowpass temporal filter on the post-synaptic unit activities (Rhodes, 1992). This paper examines the contribution of such temporal smoothing to the development of viewpoint invariant responses in both a feedfor-

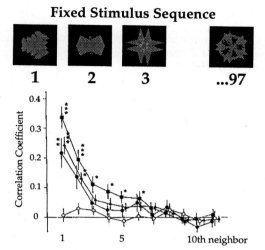

Fixed Stimulus Sequence

Figure 1: Evidence of temporal associations in IT. Top: Samples of the 97 fractal pattern stimuli in the fixed training sequence. Stimuli were in color. Bottom: Autocorrelograms on the sustained firing rates of AIT cells along the serial position number of the stimuli. Abscissa is the relative position of the patterns in the training sequence. Triangles are mean correlations in responses to the learned stimuli for 57 cells. Open circles are correlations in responses to novel stimuli for 17 cells, and closed circles are responses to learned stimuli for the same 17 cells. Squares are mean correlations for the 28 cells with statistically significant response correlations, according to Kendall's correlation test. Adapted from Miyashita (1988). Reprinted with permission from *Nature*, copyright 1988, MacMillan Magazines Ltd.

ward and a recurrent system. In the feedforward system, the Competitive Learning rule (Rumelhart & Zipser, 1985) is extended to incorporate an activity trace on the output unit activities (Foldiak, 1991). The recurrent component of the simulation examines the development of temporal associations in an attractor network. Perceptual representations have been related to to basins of attraction in activity patterns across an assembly of cells (Amit, 1995; Freeman, 1994; Hinton & Shallice, 1991). The simulation performed here shows how viewpoint invariance can be captured in an attractor network representation. The recurrent system was a generalization of a Hopfield network with a lowpass temporal filter on all unit activities (Hopfield, 1982). We show that the combination of basic Hebbian learning with temporal smoothing of unit activities produces a generalization of an attractor network learning rule that associates temporally proximal input patterns into basins of attraction (Griniasty, Tsodyks, & Amit, 1993). Following training on sequences of graylevel images of faces as they changed pose, multiple views of a given face fell into the same basin of attraction, and the system acquired representations of faces that were approximately viewpoint invariant.

2 Simulation

Stimuli for these simulations consisted of 100 images of faces undergoing a change in pose, from Beymer (1994). There were twenty individuals at each of five poses, ranging from $-30°$ to $30°$. The faces were automatically located in the frontal view image by using a feature-based template matching algorithm (Beymer, 1994). The images were normalized for luminance and scaled to 120 x 120.

Images were presented to the model in sequential order as the subject changed pose from left to right (Figure 2). The first layer of processing consisted of an oriented energy model related to the output of V1 complex cells (Daugman, 1988; Lades et al., 1993; Heeger, 1991). The images were filtered by a set of sine and cosine Gabor filters at 4 spatial scales (32, 16, 8, and 4 pixels per cycle), and at four orientations (vertical, horizontal, and $\pm45°$.) The outputs of the sine and cosine Gabor filters were squared and summed, and the result was sampled at 8 pixel intervals.

The set of V1 model outputs projected to a second layer of 70 units labeled "complex pattern units" to characterize their receptive fields after learning. The 70 units were grouped into two pools, and there was feedforward inhibition between all of the units in a pool. The complex pattern unit activities were passed through a lowpass temporal filter, described below. The third stage of the model was an attractor network produced by lateral interconnections among all of the complex pattern units. The feedforward and lateral connections were updated successively.

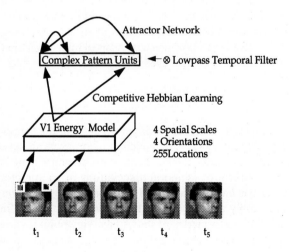

Figure 2: Model architecture.

2.1 Competitive Hebbian learning of temporal relationships

The learning rule for the feedforward connections of the model was an extension of the Competitive Learning Algorithm (Rumelhart & Zipser, 1985; Grossberg, 1976) in which the output unit activities were passed through a lowpass temporal filter. This manipulation gave the winner in the previous time steps a competitive advantage for winning, and therefore learning, in the current time step.

Let y_j^t be the weighted sum of the feedforward inputs. The output activity of unit j at time t, $\overline{y_j}^{(t)}$, is determined by the trace, or running average, of its input activity:

$$\overline{y_j}^{(t)} = (1 - \lambda)y_j^t + \lambda\overline{y_j}^{(t-1)} \tag{1}$$

The output unit activity, V_j, was subject to a step-nonlinear competition function.

$$V_j = \begin{cases} 1 & \text{if } j = max_j[\overline{y_j}^{(t)}] \\ 0.1 & \text{otherwise} \end{cases} \tag{2}$$

The connections were updated according to the following learning rule:

$$\Delta w_{ij} \propto V_j\left(\frac{x_{iu}}{\sum_k x_{ku}} - w_{ij}\right) \tag{3}$$

The weight change from input i to output j was proportional to x_{iu}, the input activity at unit i for pattern u, normalized by the total input activation for pattern u, minus a weight decay term. The weight to each unit was constrained to sum to one. Note that the output unit with the most activity for the current input pattern learned an order of magnitude more than the other units. One face image was input to the system per time step. The temporal smoothing was subject to a line process. There was no temporal smoothing across time steps in which the magnitude of the difference between subsequent input images was large.

The competitive learning rule alone, without the temporal smoothing, partitioned the set of inputs into roughly equal groups by spatial similarity. With the temporal smoothing, this learning rule clustered the input by a combination of spatial similarity and temporal proximity, where the relative contribution of the two factors was determined by the parameter λ. This learning rule is related to spatio-temporal principal component analysis. Competitive Hebbian learning can find the principal components of the input data (Oja, 1989; Sanger, 1989). The low-pass temporal filter on output unit activities in Equation 1 causes Hebbian learning to find axes along which the data covaries over recent temporal history.

2.2 Temporal association in an attractor network

The lateral interconnections in the output layer formed an attractor network. After the feedforward connections were established, the weights of the lateral connections were trained with a basic Hebbian learning rule. Hebbian learning of lateral interconnections, in combination with the lowpass temporal filter on the unit activities in (1), produced a learning rule that associated temporally proximal inputs into basins of attraction.

This is demonstrated as follows. We begin with a basic Hebbian learning rule:

$$W_{ij} = \frac{1}{N}\sum_{t=1}^{P}(y_i^t - y^0)(y_j^t - y^0) \tag{4}$$

where N is the number of units, P is the number of patterns, and y^0 is a baseline activity rate which we define as the mean activity over all of the units. Replacing y_i^t with the activity trace $\overline{y_i}^{(t)}$ defined in Equation 1, substituting $y^0 = \lambda y^0 + (1-\lambda)y^0$ and multiplying out the terms produces the following learning rule:

$$W_{ij} = \frac{1}{N}\sum_{t=1}^{P}(1-\lambda)^2(y_i^t - y^0)(y_j^t - y^0)$$

$$+\lambda(1-\lambda)\left[(y_i^t - y^0)(\overline{y_j}^{(t-1)} - y^0) + (\overline{y_i}^{(t-1)} - y^0)(y_j^t - y^0)\right]$$

$$+\lambda^2\left[(\overline{y_i}^{(t-1)} - y^0)(\overline{y_j}^{(t-1)} - y^0)\right] \tag{5}$$

This learning rule is a generalization of an attractor network learning rule that has been shown to associate random input patterns into basins of attraction based on serial position in the input sequence (Griniasty, Tsodyks & Amit, 1993). The first term in this equation is basic Hebbian learning. The weights are proportional to the covariance matrix of the input patterns at time t. The second term performs Hebbian association between the patterns at time t and $t-1$. The third term is Hebbian association of the trace activity for pattern $t-1$.

The following update rule was used for the activation V of unit i at time t from the lateral inputs (Griniasty, Tsodyks, & Amit, 1993):

$$V_i(t+\delta t) = \phi\left[\sum W_{ij}V_j(t) - \theta\right] \tag{6}$$

Where θ is a neural threshold and $\phi(x) = 1$ for $x > 0$, and 0 otherwise. In these simulations, $\theta = 0.007$, $N = 70$, $P = 100$, $y^0 = 0.03$, and $\lambda = 0.5$.

2.3 Results

The feedforward and the lateral connections were trained successively. Sequences of face images were presented to the network in order as each subject changed pose from left to right. The feedforward connections were updated by the learning rule in Equation 3, with $\lambda = 0.5$. Competitive interactions were among two pools of 35 units, such that two units were active for any given face.

After training the feedforward connections, the representation of each face was a sparse representation consisting of the two active output units of the 70 complex pattern units. Network output was evaluated with the temporal filter removed. "Pose tuning" of the feedforward system was assessed by comparing correlations in the population activities for different views of the same face to correlations across faces of different people (Figure 3 Left). Pose tuning is shown both with and without the temporal lowpass filter on unit activities during training. The temporal filter broadened the pose tuning of the feedforward system, producing a response that was more selective for the individual and less dependent on viewpoint.

The feedforward system trained with $\lambda = 0.5$ provided a sparse input to the attractor network. After the feedforward connections were established, the feedforward weights were held fixed, and sequences of face images were again presented to the network as each subject gradually changed pose. The lateral connections among the

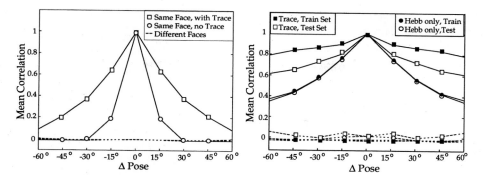

Figure 3: Left: Correlation of the outputs of the feedforward system as a function of change in pose. Correlations across different views of the same face (–) are compared to correlations across different faces (– –) with the temporal trace parameter $\lambda = 0.5$ and $\lambda = 0$. Right: Correlations in sustained activity patterns in the attractor network as a function of change in pose. Results obtained with Equation 5 (Hebb plus trace) are compared to Hebb only. Closed symbols are training set results and open symbols are test set results.

output units were updated by the learning rule in Equation 5. After training the attractor network, each face was presented to the system, and the activities in the output layer were updated until they arrived at a stable state. Following learning, the patterns of sustained activity in the attractor network were approximately viewpoint invariant.

Figure 3 (Right) shows the correlations in the sustained activity patterns as a function of change in pose. The graph compares correlations obtained with Equation 5, using $\lambda = 0.5$, to that obtained with $\lambda = 0$, which is straight Hebbian learning. Test image performance was evaluated by alternately training on four poses and testing on the fifth, and then averaging the five test performances.

2.4 Weight structure and fixed points of the attractor network

The weight structure and fixed points of the attractor network are illustrated in Figure 4 using an idealized data set in order to facilitate visualization. The idealized data set contained 25 input patterns, where each pattern was coded by activity in a single bit (Figure 4, Top). The patterns represent 5 individuals with 5 views each. The middle graph in Figure 4 shows the weight matrix obtained with the attractor network learning rule, with $\lambda = 0.5$. Note the approximately square structure of the weights along the diagonal, showing positive weights among most of the 5 views of each individual. The inset shows the actual weights between views of individuals 3 and 4. The weights decreased with the distance between the patterns in the input sequence. The bottom graphs show the fixed points attained for each input pattern. Note that the same sustained pattern of activity was obtained no matter which of the 5 views of an individual was input to the network. For this idealized representation, the attractor network produced responses that were entirely viewpoint invariant.

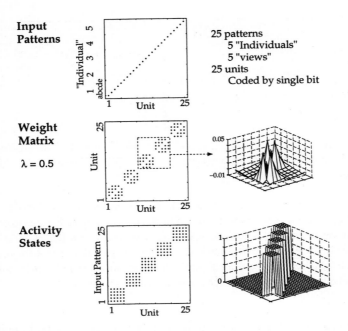

Figure 4: Demonstration of attractor network with idealized data. Top: Idealized data set. The patterns consist of 5 "individuals" (1,2,3,4,5) with five "views" each (a,b,c,d,e), and are each coded by activity in 1 of the 25 units. Center: The weight matrix obtained with equation 3. Dots show the locations of positive weights, and the inset shows the actual weights among the 5 views of two different individuals. Bottom: Fixed points for each input pattern. Unit activities are plotted for each of the 25 input patterns.

3 Discussion

Many cells in the primate anterior inferior temporal lobe and superior temporal sulcus maintain their response preferences to faces or three dimensional objects over substantial changes in viewpoint (Hasselmo, Rolls, Baylis, & Nalwa, 1989; Perrett Mistlin & Chitty, 1989; Logothetis & Pauls, 1995). This set of simulations demonstrated how such viewpoint invariant representations could be developed from visual experience through unsupervised learning.

This simulation began with structured inputs similar to the responses of V1 complex cells, and explored the performance of unsupervised learning mechanisms that can transform these inputs into pose invariant responses. We showed that a lowpass temporal filter on unit activities, which has been related to the time course of the modifiable state of a neuron (Rhodes, 1992), cooperates with Hebbian learning to (1) increase the viewpoint invariance of responses to faces in a feedforward system, and (2) create basins of attraction in an attractor network which associate temporally proximal inputs. This simulation demonstrated how viewpoint invariant representations of complex objects such as faces can be developed from visual experience by accessing the temporal structure of the input. The model addressed potential roles for both feedforward and lateral interactions in the self-organization of object representations, and demonstrated how viewpoint invariant responses can be learned in an attractor network.

Temporal sequences contain information that can aid in the process of representing and recognizing faces and objects. This model presented a means by which temporal information can be incorporated in the representation of a face. The learning rule in the feedforward component of this model extracted information about how the Gabor filter outputs covaried in recent temporal history in addition to how they covaried over static views. The processing in this model was related to spatio-temporal principal component analysis of the Gabor filter representation.

In this model, pose invariant face recognition was acquired by learning associations between 2-dimensional patterns, without recovering 3-D coordinates or structural descriptions. It has been proposed that 3-D object recognition may be performed through exposure to multiple 2-dimensional views and may not require the formation of internal 3-dimensional models, as was previously assumed (Poggio & Edelman, 1990; Ullman & Basri, 1991; Bulthoff, Edelman & Tarr, 1995). Such view-based representations may be particularly relevant for face processing, given the psychophysical evidence presented in this volume for face representations based on low-level filter outputs (see Biederman, Bruce, this volume).

In example-based models of recognition such as radial basis functions (Poggio & Edelman, 1990), neurons with view-independent responses are proposed to pool responses from view-dependent neurons. This model suggests a mechanisms for how this pooling could be learned. Logothetis and Pauls (1995) reported a small percentage of viewpoint invariant responses in the AIT of monkeys that were trained to recognize wire-framed objects across changes in view. The training images in this study oscillated $\pm 10^0$ from the vertical axis. The temporal association hypothesis presented in this paper suggests that more viewpoint invariant responses would be recorded if the monkeys were exposed to full rotations of the objects during training.

Acknowledgments

This project was supported by Lawrence Livermore National Laboratory ISCR Agreement B291528, and by the McDonnell-Pew Center for Cognitive Neuroscience at San Diego.

References

Amit, D. (1995). The Hebbian paradigm reintegrated: Local reverberations as internal representations. *Behavioral and Brain Sciences* 18:617-657.

Bartlett, M. Stewart, & Sejnowski, T., 1996. Unsupervised learning of invariant representations of faces through temporal association. *Computational Neuroscience: Int. Rev. Neurobio. Suppl. 1* J.M Bower, Ed., Academic Press, San Diego, CA:317-322.

Bartlett, M. Stewart, & Sejnowski, T., 1997. Viewpoint invariant face recognition using independent component analysis and attractor networks. In M. Mozer, M. Jordan, & T. Petsche, Eds., *Advances in Neural Information Processing Systems 9*. Cambridge, MA: MIT Press, p. 817-823.

Becker, S. (1997). Learning temporally persistent hierarchical representations. In M. Mozer, M. Jordan, & T. Petsche, Eds., *Advances in Neural Information Processing Systems 9*. Cambridge, MA: MIT Press, p. 824-830.

Beymer, D. 1994. Face recognition under varying pose. In *Proc. IEEE Conf. on Computer Vision and Pattern Recognition*. Los Alamitos, CA: IEEE Comput. Soc. Press: 756-61.

390

Biederman, I. (in press). Neural and psychophysical analysis of object and face recognition. In H . Wechsler and V. Bruce, Eds., *Face Recognition: From Theory to Applications.* Springer-Verlag.

Bulthoff, H.H. Edelman, S.Y., & M.J. Tarr (1995). How are three-dimensional objects represented in the brain? *Cerebral Cortex* 3 247-260.

Bruce, V. (in press). Human face perception and identification. In H . Wechsler and V. Bruce, Eds., *Face Recognition: From Theory to Applications.* Springer-Verlag.

Daugman, J.G. (1988). Complete discrete 2D Gabor transform by neural networks for image analysis and compression. *IEEE Transactions on Acoustics, Speech, and Signal Processing* 36: 1169-1179.

Foldiak, P. 1991. Learning invariance from transformation sequences. *Neural Computation* 3:194-200.

Freeman, W.J. 1994. Characterization of state transitions in spatially distributed, chaotic, nonlinear, dynamical systems in cerebral cortex. *Integrative Physiological and Behavioral Science,* 1994 29(3):294-306.

Griniasty, M., Tsodyks, M., & Amit, D. 1993. Conversion of temporal correlations between stimuli to spatial correlations between attractors. *Neural Comp.* 5:1-17.

Hasselmo M. Rolls E. Baylis G. & Nalwa V. 1989. Object-centered encoding by face-selective neurons in the cortex in the superior temporal sulcus of the monkey. *Experimental Brain Research* 75(2):417-29.

Hebb, D. (1949). *The organization of behavior.* New York: Wiley.

Heeger, D. (1991). Nonlinear model of neural responses in cat visual cortex. *Computational Models of Visual Processing,* M. Landy & J. Movshon, Eds. MIT Press, Cambridge, MA.

Hinton, G. & Shallice, T. (1991). Lesioning an attractor network: Investigations of acquired dyslexia. *Psychological Review* 98(1):74-75.

Hopfield, J. (1982). Neural networks and physical systems with emergent collective computational abilities. *Proceedings of the National Academy of Sciences, USA* 79 2554-2558.

Lades, M., Vorbruggen, J., Buhmann, J., Lange, J., Konen, W., von der Malsburg, C., and Wurtz, R. (1993): Distortion invariant object recognition in the dynamic link architecture. *IEEE Transactions on Computers* 42(3): p. 300-311.

Oja, E. (1989). Neural networks, principal components, and subspaces. *International Journal of Neural Systems* 1(1): 61-68.

Perrett, D. Mistlin, A. & Chitty, A. (1989). Visual neurones responsive to faces. *Trends in Neuroscience* 10: 358-364.

Poggio, T. & Edelman, S. (1990). A network that learns to recognize 3-dimensional objects. *Nature* 343: 263-266.

Miyashita, Y. (1988). Neuronal correlate of visual associative long-term memory in the primate temporal cortex. *Nature* 335(27); p.817-820.

Logothetis, N. & Pauls 1995. *Cerebral Cortex* Psychophysical and physiological evidence for viewer-centered object representations in the primate. *Cerebral Cortex* 3: 270-288.

O'Reilly, R. & Johnson, M. 1994. Object recognition and sensitive periods: A computational analysis of visual imprinting. *Neural Computation* 6:357-389.

Rhodes, P. 1992. The long open time of the NMDA channel facilitates the self-organization of invariant object responses in cortex. *Soc. Neurosci. Abst.* 18:740.

Rolls, E.T. (1995). Learning mechanisms in the temporal lobe visual cortex. *Behav. Brain Research* 66; p. 177-185.

Rumelhart, D. & Zipser, D. 1985. Feature discovery by competitive learning. *Cognitive Science* 9: 75-112.

Sanger, T. (1989a). Optimal unsupervised learning in a single-layer linear feedforward neural network. *Neural Networks* 2, 459-473.

Stryker, M. 1991. Temporal Associations. *Nature* 354:108-109.

Tsodyks M. & Feigel'man M. (1988). The enhanced storage capacity in neural networks with low activity level. *Europhysics Letters* 101-105.

Wallis, G; Rolls, E T. (1997). Invariant face and object recognition in the visual system. *Progress in Neurobiology (Oxford),* 51(2): 167-194.

Weinshall, D.& Edelman, S. 1991. A self-organizing multiple view representation of 3D objects. *Bio. Cyber.* 64(3):209-219.

Visible Speech Perception and Robustness in Face Processing[1]

CHRISTOPHER S. CAMPBELL and DOMINIC W. MASSARO

Department of Psychology, University of California - Santa Cruz, Santa Cruz, CA 95064[2]

Abstract. We present a series of empirical studies supporting the claim that visible speech perception (speechreading) is robust in conditions representative of face-to-face communication. Speechreading was relatively resistant to the influence of uniform degradation, inversion, oblique angles of view, and distance. Because speechreading is a process of pattern recognition, robustness was claimed to be a general property of face perception. Finally, we suggest that artificial systems should be based on theories of human face perception to improve performance.

Keywords. Visible speech perception, speechreading, human performance, face perception, pattern recognition

1. Introduction

The goal of this paper is to present empirical work showing that visible speech perception (speechreading) by humans remains robust or relatively insensitive to potential degradation present in everyday face-to-face communication. Although visible speech perception is only one specific task out of several others involving face perception, it should nevertheless yield outcomes that inform face perception more generally. Face perception is a general area of study that includes person recognition, gender recognition, visible speech perception, and facial affect perception.

The focus of this paper is the robustness of a system (human or machine) to variability (noise). Because we are concerned with real world situations, only

---

[1] Acknowledgments: This research was supported, in parts, by grants from the Public Health Service (PHS R01 DC00236), the National Science Foundation (BNS 8812728), and the University of California, Santa Cruz.

[2] [ccampbel,massaro]@fuzzy.ucsc.edu, URL: http://mambo.ucsc.edu/psl/

those types of noise that are common and natural will be considered. Robustness is typically understood to be the reliability or stability of a system in noise or variability (Lea, 1989), or a relative insensitivity to adverse conditions.

2. Visible Speech Perception

Experience and experiments have revealed that speechreading is not an arcane art practiced by a few trained lipreaders. All normal-sighted individuals use information from a speaker's face in addition to speech sounds in face-to-face communications. Visible speech information certainly supplies an additional source of information when the speech sounds are degraded or ambiguous. The influence of visible speech is so strong that in some instances it can change the perception of normally clear auditory speech (McGurk & McDonald, 1976). For example, if the auditory word *mice* is dubbed onto a videotape of a talker saying *nice*, a viewer will often perceive *nice*.

Although the speaker's face influences speech perception, the robustness of this influence has yet to be shown. It is possible that the reported effects are based on observations in optimal laboratory conditions when subjects may view stimuli at a close distance and from a direct frontal viewpoint. To test the robustness of visible speech perception, subjects should be presented with a range of conditions. Many natural situations involve transformations that degrade or occlude the speakers face. To explore these influences, a series of experiments was conducted to test visible speech perception under conditions of uniform degradation, inversion, different angles of view, and varying distances

In these experiments we used a computer generated talking head who we call Baldi because he has no hair (see figure 1). Baldi has a polygon topology made with a wire frame model of about 900 connected polygons and smooth shaded. Baldi is generated in real time and his animated visible speech is controlled by 36 control parameters (Cohen & Massaro, 1990).

3. Automatic Face Processing

Given the remarkable skill shown by humans in face perception, building automatic face processing systems is a particularly challenging task in the area of image processing. In general, machines have failed to approach levels seen in human performance. Current systems are befuddled by even small changes in shading/lighting, size variation, and gross occlusions (i.e. glasses or a beard).

Systems based solely on eigenvectors (eigenfaces) suffer the greatest problems. Since matches are based on a direct transform of the pixels in an image, changes in lighting, size (distance), translation, rotation, angle of view, expression, or occlusion can be serious. Feature detection and face normalization techniques have been added to many eigenvector based systems in an effort to sidestep these problems. While face normalization techniques demonstrate varying degrees of success, they are ad hoc and tend to create further problems. One such problem is the additional processing time necessary to first detect some facial feature (e.g. eyes), normalize the face image, and finally compare the face to the gallery. Another problem occurs when a landmark facial feature is difficult to locate due to the angle of view or by occlusion from, for example, a beard or hairstyle.

One move towards a biologically based solution to the automatic face recognition problem has been the use of self-organizing connectionist networks that model the neural properties of the human visual system. Neural networks can perform as well as eigenvector based systems while tolerating noise and occlusion. However, many neural network systems also use some type of preprocessor to normalize size, orientation, and lighting. Neural networks must also be trained on each face in its database at great computational cost.

4. Human Face Recognition

A great deal of psychological research has shown that human face recognition is very efficient and robust to natural transformations. A common situation occurs when the face to be recognized is distorted in a manner that filters high spatial frequencies. Such a situation could result from environmental conditions such as smoke, haze, or darkness. This situation could also result from a peripheral or distant view of the face when contrast sensitivity is reduced.

Harmon's 1973 experiment was the first to explore the effects of image degradation on face recognition. Using the method of spatial quantization, he filtered high spatial frequency information from pictures of faces. Identification results showed that the faces were still recognizable with only 16×16 pixels/face (8 cycles/face). The robustness of human face recognition was again confirmed by more recent experiments (Bachmann, 1991; Costen, Parker, & Craw, 1994, 1996).

An even more common transformation experienced in natural settings is change in viewpoint and expression. Research has confirmed that human performance is almost unaffected by viewpoint change. Learning a face from a frontal view transfers easily to a face rotated forty-five degrees in depth existent (Davies, Ellis,

& Shepherd, 1978; Patterson & Baddeley, 1977; Hill, Schyns, & Akamatsu, 1997), although somewhat poorer transfer has been found when the face is rotated ninety degrees (Bruce, 1988; Hill et al., 1997). It has also been shown that face recognition is quite good when facial expression is different at test than at learning (Bruce, 1988; Galper and Hochberg, 1971).

4.1. Image Degradation

Our first experiment employed the method of spatial quantization to produce uniform degradation of the speaker's face. Previous research has shown that spatial quantization reduces accuracy in a speechreading task (Campbell & Massaro, 1997). The current experiment expands on previous work by combining five levels of spatial quantization with two levels of orientation (upright and inverted) in a fully factorial design.

Spatial quantization degrades stimuli by averaging the image over local square areas of pixels thus reducing the resolution of the image. When the squares are large they make the image blocked or pixelated. Spatial quantization was manipulated across five levels with a normal display of 145 cycles/face and with 31, 16, 8, and 4 cycles/face (see figure 1).

Participants were presented with nine possible consonant-vowel syllables without sound and asked to identify each presentation as accurately as possible. The nine syllables were /ba/, /va/, /ða/, /da/, /za/, /la/, /ra/, /ja/, and /wa/. These syllables are members of nine viseme classes, which are visually distinct in spoken English (Massaro, 1998). The syllables were presented in either normal upright orientation or were rotated 180 degrees.

Figure 2 gives mean speechreading accuracy as a function of spatial quantization and orientation. The relationship between speechreading accuracy and spatial quantization is described by a positively decelerated function. Accuracy peaked at 69% (upright) and 53% (inverted) dropping to 15% at 4 cycles/face. Chance performance (11%) was nearly reached in the highest degradation condition. A within-subject analysis of variance indicated spatial quantization reduced speechreading accuracy ($F(4,44) = 118.37$, $p < 0.001$), orientation reduced accuracy ($F(1,11) = 133.21$, $p < 0.001$) and the effect of orientation differed across levels of spatial quantization (interaction) ($F(4,44) = 10.05$, $p < 0.001$). Inversion reduced accuracy by 16% in the normal display, 32, and 16 cycles/face. Inversion reduced accuracy by a lesser extent (11%) at 8 cycles/face and 0% at 4 cycles/face.

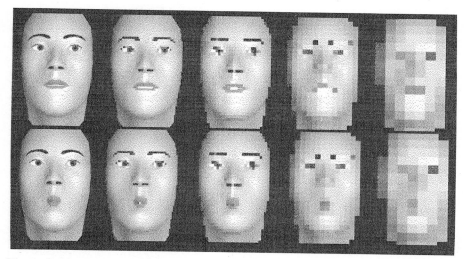

Fig. 1. Baldi with the normal display (145 cycles/face) at far left through the highest level of degradation (4 cycles/face) at far right. Points of extreme articulation during the consonant are shown for two visemes, /va/ (top) and /wa/ (bottom). The inverted view can be experienced by inverting the page.

Figure 3 shows that spatial quantization greatly reduced accuracy for /la/, /za/, and /ða/ but hardly influenced /wa/, /ja/, /va/, and /ba/. Quantization had little effect on /da/ and /ra/ because accuracy started off at very low levels. Inversion seemed to reduce accuracy most for /va/ followed by /ða/, /za/, and /ja/. Visemes that were robust with respect to spatial quantization were not necessarily robust with respect to inversion and vice-versa. For example, /va/ was relatively unaffected by quantization but when inverted, performance dropped almost to chance. Conversely, accuracy for /la/ dropped rapidly with increasing quantization but inversion produced little effect. Accuracy for /wa/ was decreased only slightly by quantization and not at all by inversion.

These results show that speechreading performance overall was fairly robust with respect to image degradation. In both upright and inverted conditions, accuracy remained relatively stable across intermediate levels of quantization to about 16 cycles/face (Fig. 2). Our robustness hypothesis would have been falsified in the case that a linear relationship was found between quantization and performance. A linear relationship would indicate that quantization directly and proportionately alters performance. Our hypothesis also would have been falsified if a negatively decelerated function described the relationship between quantization and performance. In this case, speechreading performance would

SPATIAL QUANTIZATION

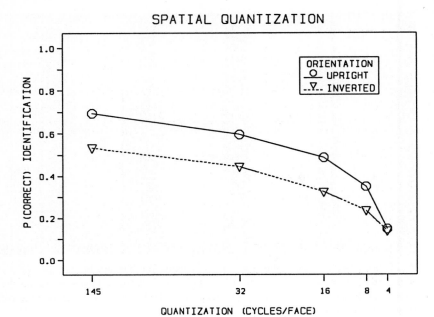

Fig. 2. Mean percent correct identification at each level of spatial quantization and orientation

have been overly sensitive to increasing quantization.

These results support our more general claim that human face perception is robust in real world conditions. Since all face perception tasks are part of the same process of pattern recognition, we should see converging evidence from other domains. Research in face recognition has shown that performance is very robust to spatial quantization. In many of these studies, accuracy remains high to 8-9 cycles/face (Harmon, 1978; Bachmann, 1991). Face recognition might be even more robust than speechreading since performance in speechreading declines at about 16 cycles/face. Research in facial affect perception also shows fairly robust performance. (Wallbott, 1992).

Unlike face recognition, however, speechreading is slightly robust to inversion. Accuracy dropped by 16% in the non-distorted condition when Baldi was inverted. This is somewhat greater than the 12% decrease in accuracy seen in a similar experiment in which four visemes were used (Massaro & Cohen, 1996). Although the decrease in accuracy reported here is significant, performance losses are considerably greater for face recognition. Decrements in face recognition accuracy due to inversion have ranged from 19% (Diamond and Carey, 1986) to

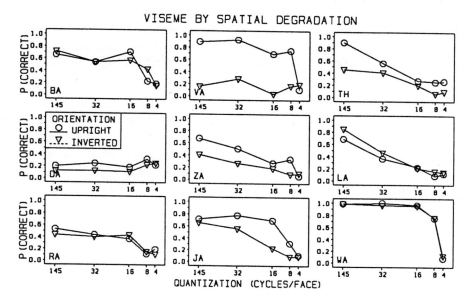

Fig. 3. Mean percent correct identification for each viseme as a function of quantization and inversion

25% (Yin, 1969; Rhodes, Brake, and Atkinson, 1993) Moreover, inversion does not influence most visemes. Accuracy for /ba/, /da/, /ra/, /la/, and /wa/ was virtually unchanged by inversion.

4.2. Viewpoint Variations

A large percentage of face perception experiments use faces in a frontal view only. One exception is an experiment by Erber (1974) showing that visible speech is informative from vertically rotated faces. However, we know of no studies that evaluated speechreading of horizontally rotated faces. In the real world, speakers' faces are viewed from many different angles. The second experiment examined how speechreading performance is influenced by changes in the angle of view. We simulated viewpoint by rotating Baldi around the horizontal and vertical axis. Participants were presented with Baldi articulating the nine visemes from nine different viewpoints. The test items were the nine visemes used in experiment 1. The nine viewpoints were a factorial combination of three vertical and three horizontal degrees of rotation. Baldi was rotated horizontally at 0, 45, and 90 degrees and vertically at 5.4, 35.4 and -24.6 degrees.

The mean percent correct identification across visemes for each angle of view is shown in figure 4. Most of the graphs show largely horizontal lines indicating only small changes in performance resulting from different horizontal angles. One notable exception was /la/ where accuracy was reduced by about 60% for the horizontal angle and about 25% for the vertical angle. Many of the lines are clustered together showing that vertical angle of regard had little influence on speechreading performance. The exceptions were /ba/, /ða/, /la/, and /ja/ showing that accuracy was much worse when Baldi was viewed from 35.4 degrees above. Of course, viewing a head from above obscures the lower half of the face making it more difficult to get important visible speech information. Consistent with our hypothesis, most of the visemes were highly robust to the influence of different viewing angles.

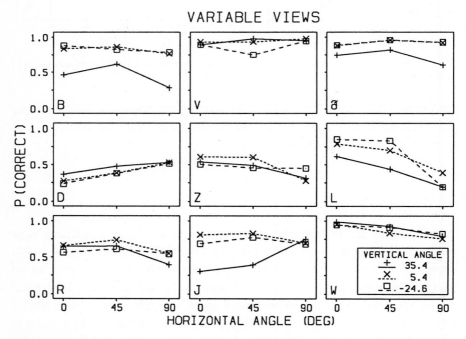

Fig. 4. Mean percent correct identification for each viseme as a function of horizontal and vertical angles of presentation. Negative numbers refer to a view from below

4.3. Viewing Distance

The third experiment examined the influence of increasing distance on speechreading performance. Baldi's head was reduced to depict distances of 2, 4, and 8 meters from the participant. In the baseline condition, Baldi's head was at its normal size simulating a distance of 1 meter (the actual distance between the screen and the participant).

As in experiment 1, participants were presented with Baldi articulating one of nine visemes without sound. The results indicated that distance reduced speechreading accuracy for the visemes overall (F(3,39) = 76.21, p < 0.001) and the influence of distance was significantly different for the different visemes (F(24,312) = 3.88, p< 0.001). Most visemes (/ba/, /va/, /za/, /la/, /ra/, and /ja/) showed about a 20% reduction in accuracy. Two visemes, /wa/ and /da/, showed no decrease at all. Distance influenced /ða/ the greatest with performance dropping by more than 50%.

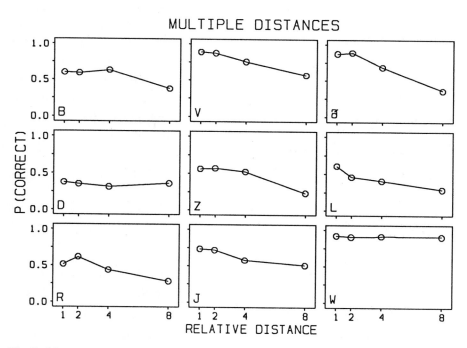

Fig. 5. Mean percent correct identification for each viseme as a function of distance in meters

The results of this experiment further support our hypothesis that speechreading is robust. The mean percent correct identification for all visemes and participants was 68% at 1 meter, 65% at 2 meters, 58% at 4 meters, and 44% at 8 meters. Thus, relatively small declines in speechreading accuracy were observed.

5. Conclusion

The goal of this paper was to present experimental support for the robustness of human face perception. The results of all experiments support our hypothesis by showing that speechreading is resistant to the influence of uniform degradation, inversion, viewpoint variations, and distance. Consistent with our findings, face recognition is robust to many real world conditions including uniform degradation, viewpoint variations, and expression changes on the face. Certainly, our understanding of human face perception would provide clues to making automatic systems more reliable. Future research will yield valuable insights into the nature of robust information processing.

Robust human face perception has three implications for face processing systems. First human performance is a benchmark by which face processing systems can be evaluated. This benchmark allows for a relative assessment of system performance and provides an attainable goal. Second, systems can maximize performance by incorporating those elements of human perception that are effective while avoiding elements that are less robust. Third, human perception is a very good model of a system that performs well in dynamic real world conditions. The demand for more natural computer interfaces could spur a need for systems that interact with humans in natural situations. To effectively process complex human communication, these systems will need to tolerate many common transformations such as lighting, viewpoint variations, and distance.

6. References

Bachmann, T. (1991). Identification of spatially quantized tachistoscopic images of faces: How many pixels does it take to carry identity? Special Issue: Face Recognition. *European Journal of Cognitive Psychology, 3,* 87-103.

Bruce, V. (1988). *Recognizing faces.* Hove, UK: Lawrence Erlbaum Assoc. Ltd.

Campbell, C. S., & Massaro, D. W. (1997). Visible speech perception: Influence of spatial quantization *Perception, 26,* 627-644.

Cohen, M. M. & Massaro, D. W. (1990). Synthesis of visible speech. *Behavior Research Methods, Instruments, & Computers, 22,* 260-263.

Costen, N. P., Parker, D. M., & Craw, I. (1994). Spatial content and spatial quantization effects in face recognition. *Perception, 23,* 129-146.

Costen, N. P., Parker, D. M., & Craw, I. (1996). Effects of high-pass and low-pass spatial filtering on face identification. *Perception & Psychophysics, 58,* 602-612.

Davies, G. M., Ellis, H. D., & Shephard, J. W. (1978). Face recognition accuracy as a function of mode of representation. *Journal of Applied Psychology, 63,* 180-187.

Diamond, R. & Carey, S. (1986). Why faces are and are not special: An effect of expertise. *Journal of Experimental Psychology: General, 115,* 107-117.

Erber, N. P. (1974). Effects of angle, distance, and illumination on visual reception of speech by profoundly deaf children. *Journal of Speech and Hearing Research, 17,* 99-112.

Galper, R. E. & Hochburg, J. (1971). Recognition memory for photographs of faces. *American Journal of Psychology, 84,* 351-354.

Harmon, L. D. (1973). The recognition of faces. *Scientific American, 229(5),* 71-82.

Hill, H., Schyns, P. G., & Akamatsu, S. (1997). Information and viewpoint dependence in face recognition. f2Cognition, 62, 201-222.

Lea, W. A. (1989). Defining, measuring, and pursuing *Towards Robustness in Speech Recognition.* Apple Valley, MN: Speech Science Publications.

Massaro, D. W. (1998). *Perceiving talking faces: From speech perception to a behavioral principle.* Cambridge, MA: MIT Press.

Massaro, D. W. & Cohen, M. M. (1996). Perceiving speech from inverted faces. *Perception & Psychophysics, 58,* 1047-1065.

McGurk, H. & MacDonald, J. (1976). Hearing lips and seeing voices. *Nature, 264,* 746-748.

Patterson, K. & Baddeley, A. D. (1977). When face recognition fails. *Journal of Experimental Psychology: Human Learning and Memory, 3,* 406-417.

Rhodes, G., Brake, S. & Atkinson, A. (1993). What's lost in inverted faces? *Cognition, 47,* 25-57.

Wallbott, H. G. (1992). Effects of distortion of spatial and temporal resolution of video stimuli on emotion attributions. *Journal of Nonverbal Behavior, 16,* 5-20.

Yin, R. K. (1969). Looking at upside-down faces. *Journal of Experimental Psychology, 81,* 141-145.

Practical Application of Facial Recognition: Automated Facial Recognition Access Control System

Julian L. Center, Jr.

Lau Technologies, Littleton, MA 01460, USA and
Creative Research Corp., Andover, MA 01810, USA
jcenter@world.std.com

Abstract A prototype for an Automated Facial Recognition Access Control System was built to research the feasibility of using such a system, in conjunction with bar-coded identification cards, to reduce manpower requirements for guarding sensitive areas. Testing of the prototype system showed that the concept is feasible and that the achieved accuracy is adequate for most access control applications.

1 Introduction

At present, access to many sensitive areas is controlled by a human facial recognition system; a human guard compares a picture on an identification card to the face of the person requesting entry. After verifying that the identification card matches the person, the guard consults information on the card or some form of database to determine if the person should be granted entry. This type of human-based access control system is very labor intensive and can be prone to error in situations where the guard can become distracted or overloaded. Automating this process could save manpower and improve security.

In 1996, the Defense Manpower Data Center (DMDC), which is under the United States Office of the Secretary of Defense, sponsored a research project to determine the feasibility of using automated facial recognition in conjunction with existing bar-coded military identification cards to control access to sensitive areas. DMDC selected Lau Technologies to develop an Automated Facial Recognition Access Control System (AFRACS) as a prototype and test vehicle for such a system.

2 System Architecture and Concept of Operation

The system architecture was chosen to minimize manpower requirements while providing easy system expansion and maintaining highly-secure and reliable operation. Figure 1 shows the architecture chosen for AFRACS. The system consists of four major parts: (1) Checkpoint, (2) Guard's Workstation, (3) Security Administrator's workstation, and (4) Master Database Server. All of these elements communicate with each other over a Local Area Network (LAN) or Wide Area Network (WAN).

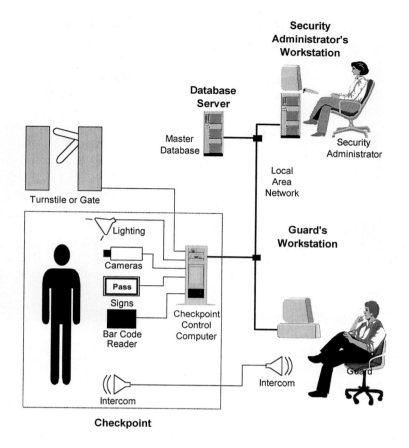

Figure 1. AFRACS Overview. AFRACS uses a distributed computing architecture to provide high reliability and easy expansion.

The AFRACS Checkpoint, shown in Figure 2, is the portion of the system seen by a person requesting entry to the facility. A Checkpoint is located at each entry portal. A person requesting entry goes to the Checkpoint, passes a bar-coded identification card through a reader, and then looks into a mirror to have his picture taken (Figure 3).

The Checkpoint controls the lights and camera needed to capture a picture of the person and then performs facial recognition analysis to determine if the picture of the person matches reference pictures in its database. If there is a match, the Checkpoint opens a door or turnstile.

Figure 2. The Checkpoint is designed for unattended operation at a remote site.

Figure 3 To use the checkpoint, the user simply enters an ID number and looks at himself in a mirror.

If the picture does not match, the Checkpoint can be programmed to give the person a chance to take another picture. If the second picture does not match, the checkpoint alerts a human guard, who may be located anywhere that can be reached by the computer network.

The guard is alerted to an entry failure by a sound from the Guard's Workstation, which then displays the location of the Checkpoint and the picture taken at the Checkpoint. It also displays the name of the holder of the entry card and the reference picture for that person. If the guard determines that the person at the Checkpoint is the card holder, he clicks an on-screen button. This button sends a message across the computer network to the Checkpoint telling it to release the gate. Both the Checkpoint and the Guard's Workstation log this override event for later review by the security administrator.

At some convenient time, the security administrator reviews all override events. If the administrator agrees that the picture is of the right person, she can enter it into the AFRACS database. This teaches AFRACS to accept variations in that person's appearance.

The security administrator also controls changes to access privileges and enrollment of new people into the system. To enroll a new person, the security administrator enters the person's demographic information into the system. This alerts a designated Checkpoint to take enrollment pictures the first time the subject appears. The security administrator then checks the pictures and enables the person's access privileges.

3 System Design Considerations

AFRACS is intended to reduce manpower requirements while maintaining a high level of physical security. Therefore, AFRACS operates totally unattended under most circumstances. However, the system also allows for human intervention in the event that a person is not recognized. Handling these overrides can be integrated into the normal duties of a single guard at a remote location. Also to minimize manpower requirements, the system is designed so that a single security administrator at a central location can maintain the master database.

The system is also designed to be highly fault tolerant, so that loss of any one element will not shut down the facility. Each Checkpoint operates autonomously, so that even if the computer network goes down, people can still gain access to the facility. Checkpoints can even be installed in remote locations without continuous access to the computer network. Communication is only needed to update access privileges and deal with access failures.

AFRACS was designed for high throughput, that is, a large number of people gaining access in a short period of time. Therefore, the Checkpoint was designed to complete a recognition transaction in less than seven seconds, including the time it takes a person to get into position, insert his ID card, take his picture, be recognized, and go through the portal. To achieve this short transaction time, the Checkpoint must deal with subjects who are standing in front of it rather than sitting down. Thus, the system was designed for personnel from 4 feet 10 inches tall to 6 feet 6 inches tall. The mounting height of the system can be changed to accommodate the full range of human height, including people in wheelchairs.

We also did not want to require people to remove their eye glasses before using the system. This makes facial recognition more difficult because the system sometimes has trouble seeing the eyes due to glare. However, we felt that the increase in user convenience was worth the reduction in accuracy for most installations.

4 Facial Recognition Technology

The AFRACS system uses facial recognition technology based on eigenface analysis methods developed by Turk and Pentland [Turk and Pentland, 1989] at the MIT Media Lab. This approach starts with a statistical analysis of a large number of facial images to understand the variations in human faces. For this analysis, principal component analysis is used to determine the facial characteristics that are key to distinguishing between people. The result of this analysis is a set of eigenfaces that capture the important variations that distinguish one human face from another. Currently, we use 128 eigenfaces to characterize these variations.

During the enrollment process, which is performed under the control of the security administrator using the Security Administrator's Workstation, reference images taken at one of the Checkpoints are analyzed and the results are stored in the reference database. The first step in analyzing each image is to find the person's eyes in the image. In the current AFRACS implementation, this is done manually by the security administrator.

The eye locations are used to determine the person's eye characteristics, which are stored in the AFRACS database, and to establish reference points for standardizing the image. Using the eye locations, AFRACS automatically produces a standardized image by rotating, scaling, and masking so that only the important facial features are included. Brightness or contrast variations, which may be due to the camera settings, are also removed.

Finally, the masked image is compared to all of the eigenfaces. Each of these comparisons produces a number between -1.0 and +1.0. All 128 of these numbers constitute the "signature" of the face seen in that picture. These coefficients, which summarize the key characteristics of the face, are stored in the AFRACS database. To achieve greater accuracy, AFRACS can account for variations in a person's appearance by storing multiple sets of eigenface coefficients for each person.

The verification process is performed in real time at a Checkpoint to determine whether a person should be granted admission or not. The first step is to retrieve the eye characteristics and reference eigenface coefficients associated with the ID number. The Checkpoint software uses the eye characteristics to locate the eyes in the new image. Once the eyes have been located, the same process used during enrollment is used to extract the eigenface coefficients from the new image. These coefficients are compared to the reference eigenface coefficients retrieved from the AFRACS database. An algorithm is used to determine a single number that represents the distance between the coefficients.

This distance measure is then compared to a decision threshold. If the distance is less than the threshold, the person is accepted (admitted). If the distance is greater than the threshold, the person is rejected. Thus, the threshold acts as a tuning parameter that can be used to adjust the security level of the system. A low threshold will provide tighter security because it will require a closer match between the new image and the reference. However, it will also result in more false rejections.

5 Test Results

One of the most critical issues in developing the prototype system was achieving high accuracy. Therefore, we performed extensive testing of AFRACS accuracy at the Lau Technologies facility. The accuracy testing was conducted over a period of ten months with a total of 84 people using the system repeatedly and producing a total of 2245 valid access attempts.

The AFRACS Checkpoints were totally unattended during data collection. The test subject entered an ID number into the system, either by using a bar-coded badge or by typing the number into a small key pad. The system then turned on lights, prompted the subject with audio cues, took the subject's picture, and attempted to identify the subject. The Checkpoints also stored the pictures for subsequent analysis. We used the images gathered during the entire test in off-line statistical analyses to assess system accuracy.

Figure 4 shows the AFRACS test results. In this figure, the probability of false rejection and the probability of false acceptance are each plotted as a function of the threshold used to make the decision. The solid curve in this figure shows the effect of varying the decision threshold on the false rejection probability.

We determined the false rejection curve by comparing the database of images gathered during the AFRACS testing to the reference database constructed during the test. The distance between the reference images and the access image was measured by the Euclidean distance between the eigenface coefficient vectors, i.e., the square root of the sum of the squares of the differences in corresponding coefficients. As the decision threshold is raised, the probability of rejection goes down because we are not requiring such a close match between the images. For example, at a threshold level of 0.60, the false rejection rate is approximately 1.8 percent. Increasing the threshold to 0.7 lowers the false rejection rate to approximately one percent.

The verification process has two failure modes that can result in a false rejection. First, the software may fail to properly find the person's eyes in the new image. In this case, the image will not be standardized properly before comparison

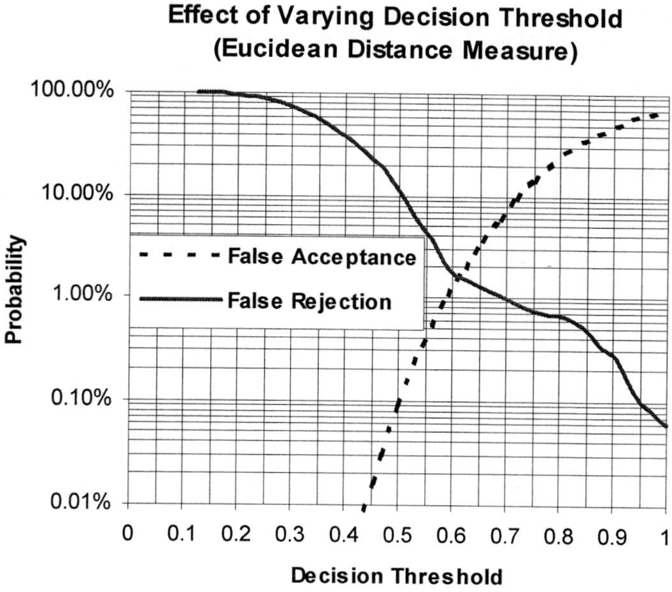

Figure 4. By adjusting the decision threshold, we can trade user convenience (increasing the false rejection rate) for tighter security (reducing the false acceptance rate).

and the distance will be relatively large. The second failure mode results from variations in the person's appearance or variations in the lighting that cause too great a difference between the new image and the reference image.

Detailed examination of the test data showed that eye finding errors occurred approximately 0.5 percent of the time. This shows in the curve of Figure 4 as the small bump at the 0.8 threshold level.

The false rejection probability computed in this analysis was the probability of being rejected on a single attempt to use the system. The analysis did not account for repeated access attempts after a failure. In practice, we found that if the system failed to recognize a valid user, the user would usually be recognized on a second attempt. However, it was too difficult to perform a valid statistical analysis of repeated access attempts using the stored images. Therefore, the false rejection probability estimates quoted here are conservative in the sense that multiple access attempts should produce much lower false rejection rates.

To determine the false acceptance rate, we drew upon a very large database of driver's license pictures. From this database, we randomly selected 10 000 images. We then used an automated eye finding algorithm to find the eyes in the images. Images for which eye finding failed were detected automatically by the software and were discarded.

The result was a database of 7386 images of different people. These images were enrolled into a database of eigenface coefficient vectors. All possible pairs of these coefficient vectors were compared, and a histogram of the results was compiled. The results are plotted as the dashed line in Figure 4.

This approach gave us a large number of images of different people. All of these images were taken under similar conditions; however, the conditions were not absolutely identical. Minor variations in lighting could have caused additional dispersion in the images, which would make these results optimistic. During this initial test, we did not have enough images of different people taken under tightly controlled lighting conditions to fully verify these results. Subsequent testing should provide us with images of enough different people to check these results.

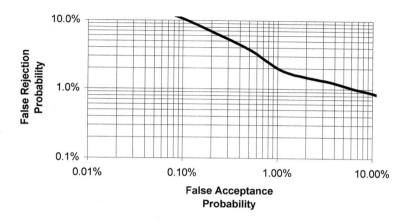

Figure 5. The Receiver Operating Characteristic (ROC) curve shows the possible combinations of probability of false rejection and probability of false acceptance that are attainable by suitably adjusting the system tuning parameter.

The tradeoff between false acceptance and false rejection is perhaps better illustrated by what is called the Receiver Operating Characteristic (a term borrowed from radar target detection theory). The ROC found in the AFRACS tests is shown in Figure 5. This curve plots the attainable combinations of false acceptance and false rejections rates as the decision threshold is varied. For example, this curve shows that the combination of a 1.0 percent false rejection rate and 2.0 false acceptance rate can be achieve by properly setting the decision threshold.

During the course of analyzing the AFRACS test data, we evaluated the use of the angular distance between the eigenface coefficient vectors [Phillips and Moon, 1997] as the distance measure for recognition decisions. Figure 6 shows the performance curves for the angular distance measure. Each of the curves in Figure 6 moves to the right relative to the curves in Figure 4, but the false acceptance curve moves farther than the false rejection curve. Therefore, it is possible to choose a new distance threshold that improves system performance.

Figure 7 shows the system ROC curve using this distance measure. Here it can be seen that setting the threshold for a 1.0 percent false rejection rate gives less than a 0.5 percent chance of false acceptance. The equal error rate (the point where the false acceptance rate equals the false rejection rate) is 0.7 percent.

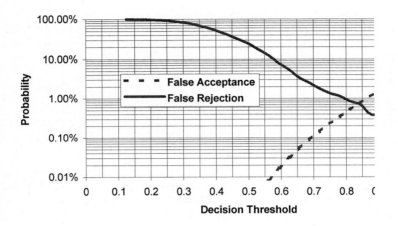

Figure 6. Although the angular distance measure shifts both curves to the right, the false acceptance curve moves farther and the performance improves.

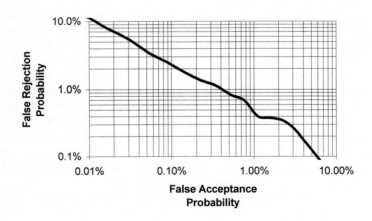

Figure 7. The ROC curve with the angular distance measure is always superior to the ROC curve with the Euclidian distance measure.

Comparing the two ROC curves (Figures 5 and 7) shows that, at least in this application, the angular distance measure is always superior to the Euclidean distance measure. In other words, for any choice of false rejection rate, the angular distance measure will give a smaller false acceptance rate.

Admittedly, these test conditions were somewhat controlled, and the results may not extrapolate to field conditions. Additional testing under more realistic conditions is currently underway at two locations chosen by DMDC.

6 Conclusions

The AFRACS Prototype System met all of its objectives. The system functionality conformed to the system specification developed early in the project. The system was easy to operate with very little user training. The system accuracy demonstrated during testing was quite adequate for most physical access control needs. A low false rejection rate can be set so that the system is convenient to use, and at the same time, a low false acceptance rate can be maintained to achieve high security. Initial test results were encouraging enough that the prototype system moved on to field testing at two locations chosen by DMDC.

Test results indicate that, in this application, the distance between eigenface component vectors is better measured by the angular distance than by the Euclidean distance. With the angular distance measure, an equal error rate of 0.7 percent was observed under the test conditions.

References

[Turk and Pentland, 1989] Turk, M. and Pentland, A., "Face Processing: Models for Recognition," SPIE Vol. 1192 Intelligent Robots and Computer Vision VIII: Algorithms and Techniques (1989).

[Phillips and Moon, 1997] Phillips, P. J. and Moon, H., "Comparison of Projection-Based Face Recognition Algorithms," Proceedings of 1997 International Conference on Systems, Man, and Cybernetics, Orlando, Florida, October 12-15, 1997.

Estimating 3D Facial Pose Using the EM Algorithm

Kwang Nam Choi, Marco Carcassoni and Edwin R. Hancock

Department of Computer Science
University of York
York, Y01 5DD, UK
email: {knchoi,carcas,erh}@minster.york.ac.uk

Summary. This paper describes how 3D facial pose may be estimated by fitting a template to 2D feature locations. The fitting process is realised as projecting the control points of the 3D template onto the 2D feature locations under orthographic projection. The parameters of the orthographic projection are iteratively estimated using the EM algorithm. The method is evaluated on both contrived data with known ground-truth together with some more naturalistic imagery. These experiments reveal that under favourable conditions the algorithm can estimate facial pitch to within 3 degrees.

1. Introduction

Facial pose estimation is a key task for many practical computer vision applications. Specific examples include visual surveillance, camera assisted user interfaces [7] and user identification verification [6]. In essence, the problem revolves around the fitting of a generic 3D template to labelled facial features located in a 2D image. Once the template has been fitted to the feature data, then 3D pose parameters may be used to manipulate the face. Viewed in this way pose estimation may be regarded as an essential pre-requisite to detailed facial verification.

There have been many attempts at efficiently recovering the 3D facial pose. Most of these use domain specific cues to limit the search-space of the 3D model. Typically, the generic facial template must be translated, scaled and subjected to Eulerian rotation. One of the most powerful cues is to use the baseline of the eyes to estimate the gaze direction [4]. In this way the tilt-direction may determined prior to rotation estimation. Based on the known ratio of the inter-eye separation and the distance to other axial features such as the tip of the nose or the lips, then the rotation angle may also be estimated. In fact, the idea of using domain-specific cues to restrict the search-space is quite generic and has been used in a number of 3D object registration applications. One notable example is the fitting of 3D models to 2D images of vehicles [10].

The observation underpinning this paper is that although specific constraints can be effectively used to restrict the search process, the underlying statistical methodology employed in the registration process is extremely limited. The aim of the work reported here is to exploit the framework of the expectation-maximisation algorithm of Dempster, Laird and Rubin to learn the 3D pose parameters subject to constraints provided by the location of the bilateral symmetry axis of the face and the orientation of the line connecting the two eyes. Our motivation in adopting the EM algorithm as a registration engine is provided by recent in-house work where we have successfully matched both line-templates [8] and 3D perspective models [2]. Here we commence by constructing a generic 3D template of the facial features. The template is quite simple. It assumes that the eyes and lip are approximately co-planar and that the tip of the nose resides at some significant height above the plane. The eyes are assumed to be symmetrically placed either side of the axis defined by the nose-tip and the lips. In keeping with the philosophy of the EM algorithm we construct a mixture model over the set of missing correspondences between the 2D facial features and the projections of the 3D template features. By assuming a Gaussian model for the registration errors, the template has freedom to deform under both uncertainties in the positions of the feature points due to inaccuracies in the template model together with the intrinsic variability of natural faces. The parameters underpinning our model are the six degrees of freedom of the orthographic projection. These are the two translation parameters on the image plane, an overall object scale together with the three Euler angles for the bary-centric (object-centred) model rotation. We reduce the parametric complexity of the 3D template registration process by centering and aligning the template at a fixed point on the bilateral facial symmetry axis. This removes the three degrees of freedom associated with two template translation parameters on the image plane together with an Euler rotation of the template symmetry axis in the bary-centred co-ordinate system.

The outline of this paper is as follows. In Section 2 we outline the geometry of our 3D facial template and explain how it is projected onto the 2D image data. Section 3 reviews the EM algorithm and explains how it may be used to estimate the parameters of orthographic projection. Experiments and sensitivity analysis are presented in section 4. Finally, Section 5 offers some conclusions and outlines our future plans.

2 Geometric Model

Our basic aim is to register the control points in a 3D facial template against a set of 2D facial feature locations. The template is constructed as follows. We commence by assuming that the left and right eyes, the lips and the chin are coplanar. These planar features are symmetric about the axis defined by the centre-points of the lip and the chin. The tip of the nose is assumed to elevated at some height h above the plane and to fall on the perpendicular plane through facial symmetry axis. The basic geometry of the template is shown in Figure 1.

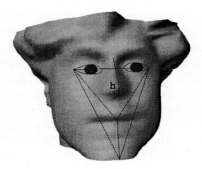

Fig. 1. The basic geometry of the face template.

The projection of the template onto the locations of the 2D facial feature points has six degrees of freedom. These correspond to the two translation parameters on the 2D image plane, the overall isotropic model scale together with the three Euler angles that define the 3D rotation of the model points. However, the complexity of the projection can be simplified using constraints provided by the 2D geometry of the labelled feature points. For instance the direction on the bilateral facial symmetry axis is easily computed by finding the perpendicular bisector of the line connecting the centres of the eyes. An alternative is to connect the centres of the lips and chin.

The 3D template control points are represented by co-ordinate vectors $\underline{v}_j = (x_j, y_j, z_j)^T$, where the index j is drawn from the set of facial feature labels $\mathcal{M}$. The available facial features are represented by 2D co-ordinate vectors $\underline{w}_i = (x_i, y_i)^T$ whose index i is drawn from the set of data-items $\mathcal{D}$. We represent the projection of the template control points into the image co-ordinate system in the following manner

$$\underline{u}_j(\Phi) = sUR_\phi S_\psi T_\theta \underline{v}_j - X_o \tag{1}$$

Here s is the overall model scale parameter and $X_o = (x_o, y_o)^T$ is the translation of the origin in the image co-ordinate system. The matrices R_ϕ, S_θ and T_ψ represent Euler rotations of the model about its bary-centre. The 3x2 matrix U selects the two x-y components from the three x-y-z components of the transformed template control points.

The sequence of Euler rotations is defined as follows. The first step is to rotate the template about the normal to the facial-plane by an angle θ. Recall that in our template, this plane is defined by the eyes, lip and chin. The net effect of this rotation is tilt the head to the left or the right. In other words, it rotates the bilateral axis of facial symmetry by an angle θ in the image plane. The rotation matrix is given by

$$T_\theta = \begin{pmatrix} 1 & 0 & 0 \\ 0 & \cos\theta & \sin\theta \\ 0 & -\sin\theta & \cos\theta \end{pmatrix} \tag{2}$$

The next step is to rotate by an angle ψ about the z-axis of the template. In our representation, the z-axis is parallel to the bilateral symmetry axis of the face and passes through the bary-centre of the template. The corresponding rotation matrix is given by

$$S_\psi = \begin{pmatrix} \cos\psi & \sin\psi & 0 \\ -\sin\psi & \cos\psi & 0 \\ 0 & 0 & 1 \end{pmatrix} \tag{3}$$

Finally, there is a rotation about the new template normal by an angle ϕ. The matrix representation of this rotation is

$$R_\phi = \begin{pmatrix} 1 & 0 & 0 \\ 0 & \cos\phi & \sin\phi \\ 0 & -\sin\phi & \cos\phi \end{pmatrix} \tag{4}$$

The parametric complexity of the projection can be reduced using some simple constraints provided by the geometry of the facial feature points on the 2D image plane. In the first instance, we can remove the translational degrees of freedom by placing the origin of the template co-ordinate system at a salient point. Here we place the origin at a fixed distance along the projection of the chin-lip line. This point corresponds to the perpendicular projection of the nose onto the bilateral symmetry axis of the face. Once the origin has been established, the angle θ, i.e. the rotation of the symmetry axis about the z-axis defined by the nose, can be estimated from the orientation of bilateral symmetry axis on the image plane. Once these constraints have been exploited, the orthographic projection can be viewed as slanting and tilting the planar component of the template by angles ψ and ϕ. The net effect is just to subject the eye-lip-chin plane to affine shear. In other words we have only to recover the slant and tilt parameters ϕ and ψ together with the overall scale s. In the next section, we explain how the resulting three degrees of freedom facial template may be registered by using the EM algorithm to iteratively estimate the parameter vector $\Phi = (s, \phi, \psi)^T$.

3 Registration Process

In this Section we detail our model registration process and describe how the underlying set of transformation parameters can be recovered using the EM algorithm. The EM algorithm was first introduced by Dempster, Laird and Rubin as a means of fitting incomplete data [3]. The algorithm has two stages. The expectation step involves estimating a mixture distribution using current parameter values. The maximisation step involves computing new parameter values that optimise the expected value of the weighted data likelihood. This two-stage process is iterated to convergence. Although the EM algorithm has been exploited in the recovery of object pose by Hornegger and Nieman [5], the main contribution of the this paper is to demonstrate the effectiveness of the algorithm in matching generic facial templates to poorly localised feature-points.

3.1 Expectation

Basic to our philosophy of exploiting the EM algorithm is the idea that every facial feature-point can in principle associate to each of the points in the 3D model template with some *a posteriori* probability. This modelling ingredient is naturally incorporated into the fitting process by developing a mixture model over the space of potential matching assignments which represent the "missing data" in our application. The expectation step of the EM algorithm provides an iterative framework for computing the *a posteriori* matching probabilities using Gaussian mixtures defined over a set of transformation parameters.

The EM algorithm commences by considering the conditional likelihood for the 2D facial feature locations $\underline{w}_i$ given the current set of transformation parameters, $\Phi^{(n)}$. The algorithm builds on the assumption that the individual data items are conditionally independent of one-another given the current parameter estimates, i.e.

$$p(\mathbf{w}|\Phi^{(n)}) = \prod_{i \in \mathcal{D}} p(\underline{w}_i|\Phi^{(n)}) \tag{5}$$

Each of the component densities appearing in the above factorisation is represented by a mixture distribution defined over a set of putative model-data associations

$$p(\underline{w}_i|\Phi^{(n)}) = \sum_{j \in \mathcal{M}} p(\underline{w}_i|\underline{v}_j, \Phi^{(n)}) P(\underline{v}_j|\Phi^{(n)}) \tag{6}$$

The ingredients of the above mixture density are the component conditional measurement densities $p(\underline{w}_i|\underline{v}_j, \Phi^{(n)})$ and the mixing proportions $P(\underline{v}_j|\Phi^{(n)})$. The conditional measurement densities represent the likelihood that the 2D facial feature location $\underline{w}_i$ originates from the 3D template control point indexed j under the prevailing set of transformation parameters $\Phi^{(n)}$. We use the shorthand notation $\alpha_j^{(n)} = P(\underline{v}_j|\Phi^{(n)})$ to denote the mixing proportions. These quantities provide a natural mechanism for assessing the significance of the individual template control points in explaining the current data-likelihood.

Conventionally, maximum-likelihood parameters are estimated using the complete log-likelihood for the available data

$$L(\Phi^{(n)}, \mathbf{w}) = \sum_{i \in \mathcal{D}} \ln p(\underline{w}_i|\Phi^{(n)}) \tag{7}$$

In the case where the conditional measurement densities are univariate Gaussian, then maximising the complete likelihood function corresponds to solving a system of least-squares equations for the transformation parameters. By contrast, the expectation step of the EM algorithm is aimed at estimating the log-likelihood function when the data under consideration is incomplete. In our 3D template-matching example this incompleteness is a consequence of the fact that we do not know how to associate feature tokens in the image and their counterparts 3D face template. In other words we need to average the log-likelihood over the space of potential correspondence matches. In fact, it was Dempster, Laird and Rubin [3] who observed that maximising the weighted log-likelihood was equivalent to maximising the conditional expectation of the log-likelihood for a new parameter set given an old parameter set. For our matching problem, maximisation of the expectation of the conditional likelihood, i.e. $E[L(\Phi^{(n+1)}, \mathbf{w})|\Phi^{(n)}, \mathbf{w})]$, is equivalent to maximising the weighted log-likelihood function

$$Q(\Phi^{(n+1)}|\Phi^{(n)}) = \sum_{i \in \mathcal{D}} \sum_{j \in \mathcal{M}} P(\underline{v}_j|\underline{w}_i, \Phi^{(n)}) \ln p(\underline{w}_i|\underline{v}_j, \Phi^{(n+1)}) \tag{8}$$

The *a posteriori* probabilities $P(\underline{v}_j|\underline{w}_i, \Phi^{(n)})$ play the role of matching weights in the expected likelihood. We interpret these weights as representing the probability of match between the facial feature point indexed i and the template control-point indexed j. In other words, they represent model-datum affinities. Using the Bayes rule, we can re-write the *a posteriori* matching probabilities in terms of the components of the conditional measurement densities appearing in the mixture model in equation (6)

$$P(\underline{v}_j|\underline{w}_i, \Phi^{(n)}) = \frac{\alpha_j^{(n)} p(\underline{w}_i|\underline{v}_j, \Phi^{(n)})}{\sum_{j' \in \mathcal{M}} \alpha_{j'}^{(n)} p(\underline{w}_i|\underline{v}_{j'}, \Phi^{(n)})} \tag{9}$$

The mixing proportions are computed by averaging the *a posteriori* probabilities over the set of facial feature points, i.e.

$$\alpha_j^{(n+1)} = \frac{1}{|\mathcal{D}|} \sum_{i \in \mathcal{D}} P(\underline{v}_j|\underline{w}_i, \Phi^{(n)}) \tag{10}$$

In order to proceed with the development of the facial template registration process we require a model for the conditional measurement densities, i.e. $p(\underline{w}_i|\underline{v}_j, \Phi^{(n)})$. Here we assume that the required model can be specified in terms of a multivariate Gaussian distribution. The random variables appearing in these distributions are the error residuals for the 2D position predictions of the jth template point delivered by the current estimated transformation parameters. Accordingly we write

$$p(\underline{w}_i|\underline{v}_j, \Phi^{(n)}) = \frac{1}{(2\pi)^{\frac{3}{2}}\sqrt{|\Sigma|}} \exp\left[-\frac{1}{2}\epsilon_{i,j}(\Phi^{(n)})^T \Sigma^{-1}\epsilon_{i,j}(\Phi^{(n)})\right] \tag{11}$$

In the above expression Σ is the variance-covariance matrix for the vector of error-residuals $\epsilon_{i,j}(\Phi^{(n)}) = \underline{w}_i - \underline{u}_j(\Phi^{(n)})$ between the components of the predicted template point positions $\underline{u}_j(\Phi^{(n)})$ and the facial feature locations in the data, i.e. $\underline{w}_i$. Formally, the matrix is related to the expectation of the outer-product of the error-residuals i.e. $\Sigma = E[\epsilon_{i,j}(\Phi^{(n)})\epsilon_{i,j}(\Phi^{(n)})^T]$. Accordingly, we compute the following estimate of Σ,

$$\tilde{\Sigma} = \frac{\sum_{i \in \mathcal{D}} \sum_{j \in \mathcal{M}} P(\underline{v}_j|\underline{w}_i, \Phi^{(n)})\epsilon_{i,j}(\Phi^{(n)})\epsilon_{i,j}(\Phi^{(n)})^T}{\sum_{i \in \mathcal{D}} \sum_{j \in \mathcal{M}} P(\underline{v}_j|\underline{w}_i, \Phi^{(n)})} \tag{12}$$

With these ingredients, and using the shorthand notation $q_{i,j}^{(n)} = P(\underline{v}_j | \underline{w}_i, \Phi^{(n)})$ for the *a posteriori* matching probabilities, the expectation step of the EM algorithm simply reduces to computing the weighted squared error criterion

$$Q'(\Phi^{(n+1)}|\Phi^{(n)}) = -\frac{1}{2}\sum_{i\in\mathcal{D}}\sum_{j\in\mathcal{M}} q_{i,j}^{(n)}\epsilon_{i,j}(\Phi^{(n)})^T \tilde{\Sigma}^{-1}\epsilon_{i,j}(\Phi^{(n)}) \qquad (13)$$

In other words, the *a posteriori* probabilities $q_{i,j}^{(n)}$ effectively regulate the contributions to the likelihood function. Matches for which there is little evidence contribute insignificantly, while those which are in good registration dominate.

3.2 Maximisation

The maximisation step aims to locate the updated the parameter-vector $\Phi^{(n+1)}$ that optimises the quantity $Q(\Phi^{(n+1)}|\Phi^{(n)})$, i.e.

$$\Phi^{(n+1)} = \arg\max_{\Phi} Q'(\Phi|\Phi^{(n)}) \qquad (14)$$

We solve the implied weighted least-squares minimisation problem using the Levenberg-Marquardt technique [9]. This non-linear optimisation technique offers a compromise between the steepest gradient and inverse Hessian methods. The former is used when close to the optimum while the latter is used far from it. In other words, when close to the optimum, parameter updating takes place with step-size proportional to the gradient $\nabla_\Phi Q'(\Phi|\Phi^{(n)})$. When far from the optimum the optimisation procedure uses second-order information residing in the Hessian, H, of $Q'(\Phi|\Phi^{(n)})$; the corresponding step-size for the parameter vector Φ is $H^{-1}\nabla_\Phi Q(\Phi|\Phi^{(n)})$.

4 Experiments

The evaluation of our pose estimation procedure involves experiments on both contrived and natural imagery. The contrived data is provided by various camera views of a plaster bust. Here the ground-truth pose angle is measured in the laboratory and the facial feature points are marked by hand. The natural data is provided by 15 different camera views for each of eight different individuals. Here we experiment with both hand-labelled together with automatically segmented and labelled feature points. The segmentation process uses Fourier-domain matched filters to characterise each of eight facial features (left and right eyebrows, left and right eye centres, hairline, nose, lips and chin) [1]. When averaged over the eight feature types, the feature localisation error is about 5 pixels. However, for certain features (e.g. the eye centres) the localisation error is about 3 pixels. These sensitivity systematics are summarised in Figure 2 which shows the localisation error as a function of facial pose and camera direction (fronto-parallel, oblique from above, oblique from below).

We commence our study by considering the contrived data. Figure 3 shows a series of views of a plaster bust. There are three camera directions. These

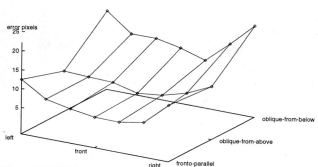

Fig. 2. The positional accuracy of automatically segmented points.

are approximately fronto-parallel, oblique from above and oblique from below. Under each of the views we list the ground truth rotation angle for the bust. This angle is measured with a protractor attached to the base of the bust. Zero rotation angle corresponds to the case when the nose points straight towards the camera. Also listed below the different views is the pose angle computed using our EM algorithm. For pose angles of up to 40 degrees in both the clockwise and counterclockwise senses, there is good agreement between the ground-truth and recovered angles.

This feature of the data is illustrated more directly in Figure 4. Here we show the difference between the ground-truth and recovered pose angles as a function of the ground-truth angle. There are three features of this plot that deserve further comment. Firstly, for moderate rotation angles the average error is approximately 3 degrees. Secondly, the error increases dramatically for rotation angles greater than 4 degrees. Finally, there appears to be a positive bias to the computed error. This is attributable to the fact that we initialise our face-template in a fronto-parallel configuration at zero rotation angle. In other words, the model must always make a positive rotation on to the data. Local optima or premature convergence in the fitting process may therefore bias the method to under-estimate the rotation angle.

To illustrate the iterative qualities of the algorithm, Figure 5 shows the feature template converging on the labelled feature points. The two examples are for the plaster-bust and the natural image. The first image shows the initial template alignment using constraints on the position of the origin co-ordinates and the direction of the bilateral symmetry axis. The second image shows the final position of the template after convergence of the EM algorithm.

Turning our attention to the real-world data, Figure 6 shows a sequence of views with the computed rotation angles appended. In this figure, the feature points are hand labelled. Here our experiments have focussed on how the template registration method degrades when automatically segmented, rather than labelled feature points, are used. Figure 7 shows a plot of the difference in com-

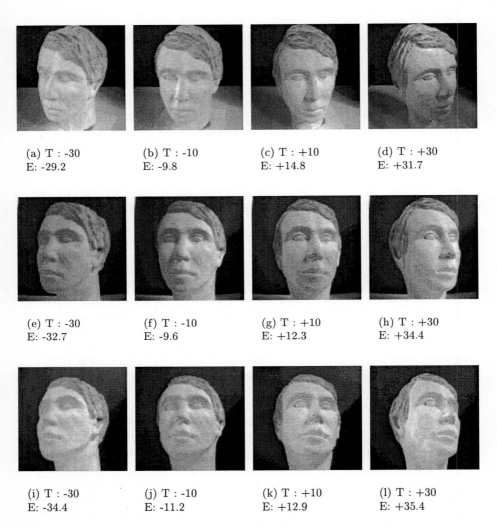

(a) T : -30
E: -29.2

(b) T : -10
E: -9.8

(c) T : +10
E: +14.8

(d) T : +30
E: +31.7

(e) T : -30
E: -32.7

(f) T : -10
E: -9.6

(g) T : +10
E: +12.3

(h) T : +30
E: +34.4

(i) T : -30
E: -34.4

(j) T : -10
E: -11.2

(k) T : +10
E: +12.9

(l) T : +30
E: +35.4

Fig. 3. A series of views of a plaster bust in which the camera direction is approximately fronto-parallel, oblique from above and oblique from below. The ground-truth angles are denoted by "T" and the estimated angles by "E".

puted rotation angle for the hand-labelled and automatically segmented points. Each entry in the plot is averaged over eight different individuals. The main feature to note from the plot is that the error increases with the rotation angle. However, for moderate rotation angles, the error is only about 3 degrees.

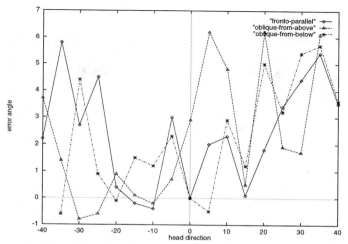

Fig. 4. The difference between the ground-truth and recovered pose angles as a function of the ground-truth angle.

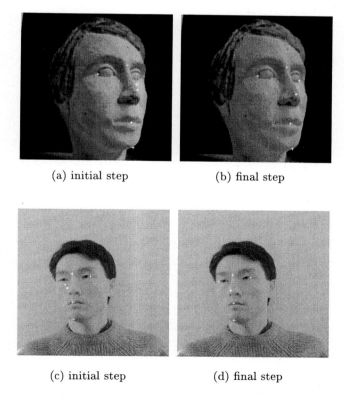

(a) initial step   (b) final step

(c) initial step   (d) final step

Fig. 5. The 3D feature template converging on the labelled feature points.

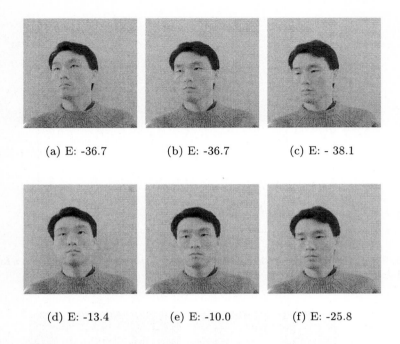

(a) E: -36.7   (b) E: -36.7   (c) E: - 38.1

(d) E: -13.4   (e) E: -10.0   (f) E: -25.8

Fig. 6. Examples of the estimated rotation angles for various facial poses.

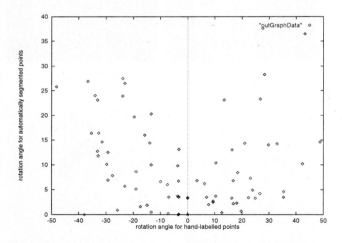

Fig. 7. The difference in computed rotation angle for the hand-labelled and automatically segmented points.

5 Conclusions

The main contribution in this paper is to present a statistical framework for iteratively registering 3D facial templates against 2D feature points. The iterative procedure is based on the EM algorithm and allows the parameters of orthographic projection between the 3D model and the 2D data to be estimated. An analysis on ground-truthed data reveals that the method is capable of recovering the rotation angle of the head to within 3 degrees provided that the overall rotation does not exceed 40 degrees. The main limitation of the method is the need for accurately located feature points. Our next steps will be focussed on improving the robustness of localisation process. Here we aim to couple the feature segmentation and pose estimation steps of the algorithm.

References

1. Choi K.N., Cross A.D.J. and Hancock E.R., "Localising Facial Features with Matched Filters", *First International Conference on Audio- and Video-based Biometric Person Authentication, Lecture Notes in Computer Science, 1206*, pp. 11-20, 1997.
2. Cross A.D.J. and Hancock E.R., "Recovering Perspective Pose with a Dual Step EM Algorithm, *Advances in Neural Information Processing Systems 10, Editted by M. Jordan, M. Kearns and S. Solla*, MIT Press to appear, 1998.
3. Dempster A.P., Lairdand N.M. and Rubin D.B., "Maximum-likelihood from incomplete data via the EM algorithm", J. Royal Statistical Soc. Ser. B (methodological),**39**, pp 1-38, 1977.
4. Gee A.H.and Cipolla R., "Determining the Gaze of Faces in Images", *Image and Vision Computing*, **12**, pp. 639–647, 1994.
5. Hornegger J. and Niemann H., "Statistical Learning Localisation and Identification of Objects" *Proceedings Fifth International Conference on Computer Vision*, pp. 914–919, 1995.
6. Kotropoulos C., Pitas I., Fischer S. and Duc B., "Face Authentication Using Morphological Dynamic Link Architecture", *LNCS 1206*, pp. 169-176, 1997.
7. Moghaddam B. and Pentland A., "Probabilistic Visual Learning for Object Detection", *Proceedings of the Fifth International Conference on Computer Vision*, pp. 786–793, 1995.
8. Moss S. and Hancock E.R., "Registering Incomplete Radar Images with the EM Algorithm", Image and Vision Computing, **15**, pp. 637–648. 1997.
9. Phong T.Q., Horaud R., Yassine A. and Tao P.D., "Object Pose from 2-D to 3-D Point and Line Correspondences", *International Journal of Computer Vision*, **15**, pp. 225–243, 1995.
10. Sullivan G.D., Baker K.D., Worrall A.D., Attwood C.I. and Remagnino P.M., "Model-based vehicle detection and classification using orthographic approximations", *Image and Vision Computing*, **15**, pp. 649-654, 1997.

PCA, Neural Networks and Estimation for Face Detection

Raphaël Feraud

France-Télécom CNET, 2, av Pierre Marzin, 22307 Lannion, France

abstract. A generative neural network model, constrained by non-face examples chosen by an iterative algorithm, is applied to face detection. To extend the detection ability in orientation and to decrease the number of false alarms, different combinations of networks are tested: ensemble, conditional ensemble and conditional mixture of networks. The use of a conditional mixture of networks obtains better results on different benchmark face databases than *state-of-the-art*.

1 Motivation

Our purpose is to classify an extracted window x from an image as a face ($x \in \mathcal{V}$) or non-face ($x \in \mathcal{N}$). The set of all possible windows is $\mathcal{E} = \mathcal{V} \cup \mathcal{N}$, with $\mathcal{V} \cap \mathcal{N} = \emptyset$. Two types of statistical model can be applied to face detection: discriminant model and generative model. Since collecting a representative set of non-face examples is impossible, our approach to face detection is to use a generative model. A principal components analysis (PCA) [Turk, M. and Pentland, A., 1991] can be used as a generative model to detect faces in an image. An autoassociative network, using three layers and linear activation functions performs a PCA [Baldi, P. and Hornik, K., 1989]. Using five layers of non-linear neurons, the compression neural network is able to perform a non-linear dimensionnality reduction [Kramer, 1991]. The distance between the input and the output of the neural network is computed to classify an extracted windows x:

$$\text{if } \|x - \hat{x}\| \leq \tau \text{ then } x \in \mathcal{V}$$

However, its use as an estimator, to classify an extracted windows as face or non-face, raises two problems (Figure 1.1):

1. $\mathcal{V}'$, the obtained sub-manifold can contain non-face examples ($\mathcal{V} \subset \mathcal{V}'$),
2. owing to local minima, the obtained solution can be close to the linear solution: the principal components analysis.

2 A Constrained Generative Model

Our approach is to use counter-examples in order to approximate the projection $\mathcal{P}$ of a point x of the input space $\mathcal{E}$ on $\mathcal{V}$. Each non-face example

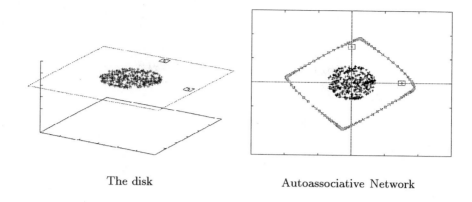

The disk   Autoassociative Network

Figure 1.1. The elements of the class $\mathcal{V}$ belong to a disk, and as in the case of face detection a non-representative set of the class $\mathcal{N}$ is collected. The obtained solution by the PCA is the principal plane. All of the points of this plane are recognized as elements of the class $\mathcal{V}$. The use of a compression neural network delimits a region in the principal plane.

is constrained to be reconstructed as the mean of the n nearest neighbours of the nearest face example [Feraud, R. et al., 1997]:

- if $x \in \mathcal{V}$, then $\mathcal{P}(x) = x$,
- if $x \notin \mathcal{V}$: $\mathcal{P}(x) = \arg\min_{y \in \mathcal{V}}(d(x, y))$, where d is the Euclidian distance. When training the neural network, the projection $\mathcal{P}$ of x on $\mathcal{V}$ is approximated by:
  $\mathcal{P}(x) \sim \frac{1}{n}\sum_{i=1}^{n} v_i$, where $v_1, v_2, \ldots, v_n$, are the n nearest neighbours, in the training set of faces, of v, the nearest face example of x.

The goal of the learning process is to approximate the distance $\mathcal{D}$ of an input space element x to the set of faces $\mathcal{V}$:

- $\mathcal{D}(x, \mathcal{V}) = \|x - \mathcal{P}(x)\| \sim \frac{1}{M}(x - \hat{x})^2$, where M is the size of input image x and $\hat{x}$ the image reconstructed by the neural network,
- let $x \in \mathcal{E}$, then $x \in \mathcal{V}$ if and only if $\mathcal{D}(x, \mathcal{V}) \leq \tau$, with $\tau \in I\!R$, where τ is a threshold used to adjust the sensitivity of the model.

In the case of non-linear dimensionnality reduction, the reconstruction error is related to the position of a point to the non-linear principal components in the input space. Nevertheless, a point can be near to a principal component and far from the set of faces. With the algorithm proposed, the reconstruction error is related to the distance between a point to the set of

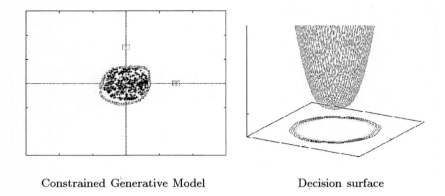

Constrained Generative Model   Decision surface

Figure 2.1. Using only two counter-exemples, our algorithm determines the boundary between the class $\mathcal{V}$ and the class $\mathcal{N}$. This boundary is not obtained by a fine tuning of the threshold (see the decision surface).

faces. As a consequence, if we assume that the learning process is consistent [Vapnik, 1995], our algorithm is able to evaluate the probability that a point belongs to the set of faces. Let y be a binary random variable: $y = 1$ corresponds to a face example and $y = 0$ to a non-face example, we use:

$$P(y = 1|x) = e^{-\frac{(x-\hat{x})^2}{\sigma^2}} \text{ , where } \sigma \text{ depends on the threshold } \tau$$

Figure 2.2. On the left some enhanced and smoothed front view faces ($[0°, 20°]$). On the right some enhanced and smoothed turned faces ($[20°, 60°]$).

The size of the training images is 15x20 pixels. The faces are normalized in position and scale (Figure 2.2). The images are enhanced by histogram equalization to obtain a relative independence to lighting conditions, smoothed to remove the noise and normalized by the average face of the training set. Three face databases are used: after vertical mirroring, B_{f1} is composed of 3600 different faces with orientation between 0 degree and 20 degree, B_{f2} is composed of 1600 different faces with orientation between 20 degree and 60 degree and B_{f3} is the concatenation of B_{f1} and B_{f2}, giving a total of 5200 faces. All of the training faces are extracted from *usenix face database*(**), from the test set B of CMU(**), and from 100 images containing faces and complex backgrounds.

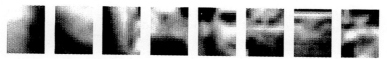

Figure 2.3. Left to right: the counter-examples successively chosen by the algorithm are increasingly similar to real faces (iteration 1 to 8).

The non-face databases (B_{nf1}, B_{nf2}, B_{nf3}), corresponding to each face database, are collected by an iterative algorithm similar to the one used in [Sung, K. and Poggio, T., 1994] or in [Rowley, H. et al., 1995]:

1. $B_{nf} = \emptyset$, $\tau = \tau_{min}$,
2. the neural network is trained with $B_f + B_{nf}$,
3. the face detection system is tested on a set of background images,
4. a maximum of 100 subimages x_i are collected with $\mathcal{D}\ (x_i, \mathcal{V}) \le \tau$,
5. $B_{nf} = B_{nf} + \{x_0, \dots, x_n\}$, $\tau = \tau + \mu$, with $\mu > 0$,
6. while $\tau < \tau_{max}$ go back to step 2.

After vertical mirroring, the size of the obtained set of non-face examples is respectively 1500 for B_{nf1}, 600 for B_{nf2} and 2600 for B_{nf3}. Since the non-face set ($\mathcal{N}$) is too large, it is not possible to prove that this algorithm converges in a finite time. Nevertheless, in only 8 iterations, collected counter-examples are close to the set of faces (Figure 2.3). Using this algorithm, three elementary face detectors are constructed: the front view face detector trained on B_{f1} and B_{nf1} (CGM1), the turned face detector trained on B_{f2} and B_{nf2} (CGM2) and the general face detector trained on B_{f3} and B_{nf3} (CGM3).

To obtain a non-linear dimensionnality reduction, five layers are necessary. Since the coordinates of a point in the principal sub-manifold are not needed to classify an extracted window, our architecture uses only four layers. The first and last layers both consist of 300 neurons, corresponding to the image size 15x20. The first hidden layer has 30 neurons and the second hidden layer 50 neurons. In order to reduce the false alarm rate and to extend the face detection ability in orientation, different combinations of networks are tested. The use of ensemble of networks to reduce the false alarm rate was shown by [Rowley, H. et al., 1995]. However, considering that to detect a face in an image, there are two subproblems to solve, detection of front view faces and turned faces, a modular architecture can also be used.

3 Ensemble of CGMs

Generalization error of an estimator can be decomposed in two terms: the bias and the variance [Geman, S. et al., 1992]. The bias is reduced with prior knowledge. The use of an ensemble of estimators can reduce the variance when these estimators are independently and identically distributed [Raviv, Y. and Intrator, N., 1996]. Each face detector produces:

$$E_i[y|x] = P_i(y = 1|x)$$

Assuming that face detectors (CGM1,CGM2,CGM3) are independently and identically distributed (iid), the ouput of the ensemble is:

$$E[y|x] = \frac{1}{3} \sum_{i=1}^{3} E_i[y|x]$$

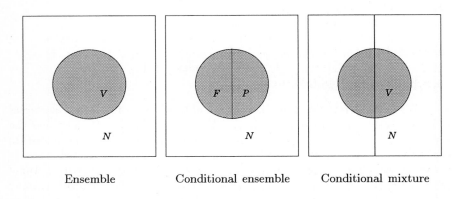

Ensemble   Conditional ensemble   Conditional mixture

Figure 3.1. The corresponding hypothesis for each combination of CGMs. The use of an ensemble of estimators supposes that there is no partition of the input space. In the case of the conditional ensemble, the set of faces is separated in two parts (front view and turned faces) and there is no partition in the set of non-faces. The use of a conditional mixture supposes that the whole input space is separated in two parts.

4 Conditional mixture of CGMs

To extend the detection ability in orientation, a conditional mixture of CGMs is tested. The training set is separated in two subsets: front view faces and the corresponding counter-examples ($\theta = 1$) and turned faces and the corresponding counter-examples ($\theta = 0$). The first subnetwork (CGM1) evaluates the probability of the tested image to be a front view face, knowing the label equals 1 ($P(y = 1|x, \theta = 1)$). The second (CGM2) evaluates the probability of the tested image to be a turned face, knowing the label equals 0 ($P(y = 1|x, \theta = 0)$). A gating network is trained to evaluate $P(\theta = 1|x)$, supposing that the partition $\theta = 1, \theta = 0$ can be generalized to every input:

$$E[y|x] = E[y|\theta = 1, x]f(x) + E[y|\theta = 0, x](1 - f(x)) \text{ , where } f(x) = \hat{P}(\theta = 1|x)$$

This system is different from a mixture of experts introduced by [Jacobs, R. A. et al., 1991]: each module is trained separately on a subset of the training set and then the gating network learns to combine the outputs.

5 Conditional ensemble of CGMs

To reduce the false alarm rate and to detect front view and turned faces, an original combination, using (CGM1,CGM2) and a gate network, is proposed. Four sets are defined:

- $\mathcal{F}$ is the front view face set,
- $\mathcal{P}$ is the turned face set, with $\mathcal{F} \cap \mathcal{P} = \emptyset$,
- $\mathcal{V} = \mathcal{F} \cup \mathcal{P}$ is the face set,
- $\mathcal{N}$ is the non-face set, with $\mathcal{V} \cap \mathcal{N} = \emptyset$,

Our goal is to evaluate $P(x \in V|x)$. Each estimator computes respectivly:

- $P(x \in F|x \in \mathcal{F} \cup \mathcal{N}, x)$ $(CGM1(x))$,
- $P(x \in P|x \in \mathcal{P} \cup \mathcal{N}, x)$ $(CGM2(x))$,

Using the Bayes theorem, we obtain:

$$P(x \in \mathcal{V}|x) = P(x \in \mathcal{N})|x)[CGM1(x) + CGM2(x)] \text{ (1)}$$
$$+P(x \in \mathcal{P})|x)CGM2(x) + P(x \in \mathcal{F})|x)CGM1(x) \text{ (2)}$$

The, we can deduce the behaviour of the conditional ensemble:

- in $\mathcal{N}$, as in the case of ensembles, the conditional ensemble reduces the variance of the error (first term of the right side of the equation (1)),
- in $\mathcal{V}$, as in the case of the conditional mixture, the conditional ensemble permits to combine to different tasks (second term of the right side of the equation (2)): detection of turned faces and detection of front view faces.

The gate network $f(x)$ is trained to calculate the probability of the tested image is a face ($P(x \in \mathcal{V}|x)$), using the following cost function:

$$C = \sum_{x_i \in \mathcal{V}} ([f(x_i)MGC1(x) + (1 - f(x_i))]MGC2(x) - y_i)^2 + \sum_{x_i \in \mathcal{N}} (f(x_i) - 0.5)^2$$

5 Discussion

Each 15x20 subimage is extracted and normalized by enhancing, smoothing and substracting the average face, before being processed by the network. The detection threshold τ is fixed for all the tested images. To detect a face at different scales, the image is subsampled.

The first test allows to evaluate the limits in orientation of the face detectors. The *sussex face database*(**), containing different faces with ten orientations betwen 0 degree and 90 degrees, is used (Table 1). The general face detector (CGM3) uses the same learning face database than the different mixtures of CGMs. Nevertheless, CGM3 has a smaller orientation range than the conditional mixtures of CGMs, and the conditional ensemble of CGMs. Since the performances of the ensemble of CGMS are low, the corresponding hypothesis (the CGMs are iid) seems to be invalid. Moreover, this test shows that the combination by a gating neural network of CGMs, trained on different training set, allows to extend the detection ability to both front view and rotated faces. The conditional mixture of CGMs obtains results in term of orientation and false alarm rate close to the best CGMs used to contruct it (see Table 1 and Table 2).

Table 1: Results on *Sussex face database*.

	CGM1	CGM2	CGM3	Ensemble (1,2,3)	Conditional ensemble (1,2,gate)	Conditional mixture (1,2,gate)
0^0	100.0 %	100.0 %	100.0 %	100.0 %	100.0 %	100.0 %
10^0	62.5 %	100.0 %	87.5 %	100.0 %	100.0 %	100.0 %
20^0	50.0 %	100.0 %	87.5 %	87.5 %	100.0 %	100.0 %
30^0	12.5 %	100.0 %	62.5 %	62.5 %	100.0 %	100.0 %
40^0	0.0 %	100.0 %	50.0 %	12.5 %	62.5.0 %	87.5 %
50^0	0.0 %	75.0 %	0.0 %	0.0 %	37.5 %	62.5 %
60^0	0.0 %	37.5 %	0.0 %	0.0 %	0.0 %	37.5 %
70^0	0.0 %	37.5 %	0.0 %	0.0 %	0.0 %	25.0 %

The second test allows to evaluate the false alarm rate and to compare our results with the best results published so far on the test set A (**) [Rowley, H. et al., 1995] of the CMU, containing 42 images of various quality. First, these results show that the estimation of the probability distribution of the face performed by one CGM (CGM3) is more precise than the one obtained by [Rowley, H. et al., 1995] with one RCNN (see Table 2). The conditional ensemble of CGMs and the conditional mixture of CGMs obtained a similar detection rate than an ensemble of RCNNs [Rowley, H. et al., 1995], but with a false alarm rate two or three times lower.

Since the results of the conditional ensemble of CGMs and the conditional mixture of CGMs are close on this test, the detection rate versus the number of false alarms is plotted (Figure 6.1). The conditional mixture of CGMs curve is above the one for the conditional ensemble of CGMs.

Table 2: Results on the CMU test set A: CGM1: face detector, CGM2: turned face detector, CGM3: general face detector. RCNN: retinally connected neural network. Considering that our goal is to detect human faces, non-human faces and rough face drawings have not been taken into account.

Model	Detection rate	False alarm rate
CGM1	77 % ± 5 % 127/164	1.4/1,000,000 ± 0.42/1,000,000 47/33,700,000
CGM2	85 % ± 5 % 139/164	6.3/1,000,000 ± 0.37/1,000,000 212/33,700,000
CGM3	85 % ± 5 % 139/164	1.36/1,000,000 ± 0.41/1,000,000 46/33,700,000
Ensemble (CGM1,CGM2,CGM3)	74 % ± 5 % 121/164	0.71/1,000,000 ± 0.43/1,000,000 24/33,700,000
Conditional Ensemble (CGM1,CGM2,Gate)	82 % ± 5 % 134/164	0.77/1,000,000 ± 0.38/1,000,000 26/33,700,000
[Rowley,1995] (three RCNNs)	85 % ± 5 % 144/169	2.13/1,000,000 ± 0.42/1,000,000 47/22,000,000
Conditional mixture (CGM1,CGM2,Gate)	87 % ± 5 % 142/164	1.15/1,000,000 ± 0.35/1,000,000 39/33,700,000

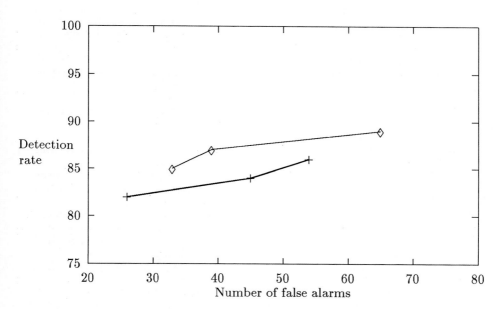

Figure 6.1. Detection rate versus number of false alarms on the CMU test set A. In bold line conditional ensemble and in solid line conditional mixture.

6 Conclusion

The conditional mixture of CGMs improves both the face detection rate ability in orientation and the false alarm rate. The obtained results are better than [Rowley, H. et al., 1995] and the other tested models. Nervertheless, the conditional ensemble of CGMs performs well too. This algorithm is used in an application called LISTEN [Collobert, M. et al., 1996]: a camera detects, tracks a face and controls a microphone array towards a speaker. The small size of the subimages (15x20) processed allows to detect a face far from the camera (with an aperture of 60 degrees, the maximum distance to the camera is 6 meters). To detect a face in real time, the number of tested hypothesis is reduced by motion and color analysis.

(**) *usenix face database, sussex face database* and CMU test sets can be retrieved at www.cs.rug.nl/ peterkr/FACE/face.html.

References

[Baldi, P. and Hornik, K., 1989] Baldi, P. and Hornik, K. (1989). Neural networks and principal components analysis: Learning from examples without local minima. *Neural Networks*, 2:53–58.

[Collobert, M. et al., 1996] Collobert, M., Feraud, R., Le Tourneur, G., Bernier, O., Viallet, J.E, Mahieux, Y., and Collobert, D. (1996). Listen: a system for locating and tracking individual speaker. In *Second International Conference On Automatic Face and Gesture Recognition*.

[Feraud, R. et al., 1997] Feraud, R., Bernier, O., and Collobert, D. (1997). A constrained generative model applied to face detection. *Neural Processing Letters*.

[Geman, S. et al., 1992] Geman, S., Bienenstock, E., and Doursat, R. (1992). Neural networks and the bias-variance dilemma. *Neural Computation*, 4:1–58.

[Jacobs, R. A. et al., 1991] Jacobs, R. A., Jordan, M. I., Nowlan, S. J., and Hinton, G. E. (1991). Adaptative mixtures of local experts. *Neural Computation*, 3:79–87.

[Kramer, 1991] Kramer, M. (1991). Nonlinear principal component analysis using autoassociative neural networks. *AIChE Journal*, 37:233–243.

[Raviv, Y. and Intrator, N., 1996] Raviv, Y. and Intrator, N. (1996). Bootstrapping with noise: An effective regularization technique. *Connection Science*, 8:355–372.

[Rowley, H. et al., 1995] Rowley, H., Baluja, S., and Kanade, T. (1995). Human face detection in visual scenes. In *Neural Information Processing Systems 8*.

[Sung, K. and Poggio, T., 1994] Sung, K. and Poggio, T. (1994). Example-based learning for view-based human face detection. Technical report, M.I.T.

[Turk, M. and Pentland, A., 1991] Turk, M. and Pentland, A. (1991). Eigenfaces for recognition. *Journal of Cognitive Neuroscience*, 3(1):71–86.

[Vapnik, 1995] Vapnik, V. (1995). *The Nature of Statistical Learning Theory*. Springer-Verlag New York Heidelberg Berlin.

3D Pose Estimation of the Face from Video

Gaile G. Gordon

Interval Research Corporation[1]
1801 Page Mill Road, Bldg. C
Palo Alto, CA 94304
gggordon@interval.com

Abstract. Face pose information is valuable for a variety of applications including unconstrained face recognition, natural human computer interfaces, and video database indexing. 3D pose estimation is a critical requirement for accurate face recognition using view varying representations, such as 2D intensity images. 3D pose extraction in this context requires 3D information, which is present in image sequences if we assume the moving objects in the sequence are primarily rigid. This paper presents a motion based pose estimation system which computes the 3D pose of the head in each frame of a video sequence. Generic low level features, such as corners, are identified and tracked in the video stream. The feature tracks are processed by a shape from motion algorithm which produces estimates of 3D geometry and pose. The geometry and pose estimates are considered together with facial structure constraints, temporal constraints, and initial pose estimates to refine knowledge of the specific face structure and its pose. We describe this system and show that it works on human faces. This is significant because the face has many smooth surfaces which make it difficult to extract dense intensity features.

1 Introduction and Motivation

Knowing the pose of the face is important in many applications including interactive human computer interfaces, and video database indexing. However, we highlight in particular the importance of pose in the context of facial recognition. In the context of recognition, knowing the pose of the face is important if the representation of the face used for comparison is not view invariant. For instance, 2D intensity data is not view invariant, whereas surface curvature data is.

In this paper, we first discuss in detail the importance of face pose in 2D face recognition. Pose estimation from a single 2D image is ill-posed, however, several authors propose pose estimation methods using a single 2D image and a general 3D face model. In section 1.2, we provide several examples showing that the error source this approach introduces can be significant in the context of face recognition. The remainder of the paper describes a pose estimation method based on structure from motion. The 3D information present in a sequence of video images of a moving face is sufficient to compute an accurate pose estimate consistent with the 3D structure of an individual's face. The algorithm is described in section 2, stressing novel contributions involving the elimination of non-rigid feature points. Results are presented in section 3 which show that this structure from motion technique is effective for human faces despite the fact that it requires trackable intensity features which can not be easily extracted on smooth surfaces. Conclusions and future work are presented in section 4.

---

[1]Much of this work was done while the author was at TASC in Reading, MA. and was supported by the FERET program of the Army Research Lab under contract DAAL01-93-C-0118.

1.1 Face pose in 2D face recognition

The term *pose* is given different meanings in many different contexts, so we begin by defining pose in the context of human faces. In general, face pose provides the position and orientation of the face. This is also analogous to the *view* of the face if one thinks of the face as stationary. More precisely, we define the 3D face pose as the six degrees of freedom which specify the relationship between the camera or sensor coordinate system and a face centered coordinate system. A face centered coordinate system is defined in terms of locations of specific facial landmarks. The choice of landmarks is not critical, except that their location must be reliable so different datasets of the same individual can be compared in a repeatable way.

Recognition from 2D intensity data is an attractive idea. The data is easy to obtain, and in many scenarios is already available. There are also several popular recognition methods using intensity data which work well under certain conditions[Moghaddam et al., 1996, Pentland et al., 1994, Wiskott et al., 1997]. However, one common property of these 2D methods is that similarity measures decrease as the difference in pose between two faces increases (see Figure 1). Correct recognition occurs when the relative difference in similarity scores for different individuals is larger than for the same individual with different poses. However, as pose misalignment increases, more recognition errors are likely to occur. Additional factors which also degrade similarity scores, such as lighting variation, and expression variation, only compound the problem. Currently we have no way of knowing what degree of pose mismatch exists, so we can't detect whether a low recognition score is due to pose misalignment error or actual identity mismatch.

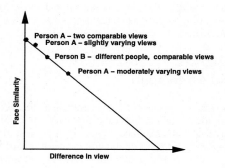

Figure 1. Similarity scores are a function of view similarity for 2D intensity face recognition systems. If the relative difference between scores of different individuals is sufficiently large compared to scores of the same individual over different views, correct recognition occurs (first three examples will produce correct ranking). Larger view misalignment or the presence of other factors which also degrade recognition (lighting variation, expression variation, crowded database) create a higher number of recognition errors.

Explicit knowledge face pose makes it possible to detect pose misalignment error. Once detected, it is possible to minimize its effect by either choosing a closer matching pose, if alternatives are available (e.g. from a video stream), or, potentially, by transforming the available images to a better pose alignment.

1.2 Pose Computation from a Single 2D View

Computation of 3D pose requires 3D information. 3D pose can be computed from a single 2D image only when there is a set of landmarks visible in the image which have a known 3D relationship [2] (as is available in the case of model based recognition). This type of information is not available in the case of face recognition based on a single set of intensity data, which is inherently 2D. If 3D relationships on the individual's face are known from some other source, we can build a model specific to the person's face shape to compute pose in a novel 2D image.

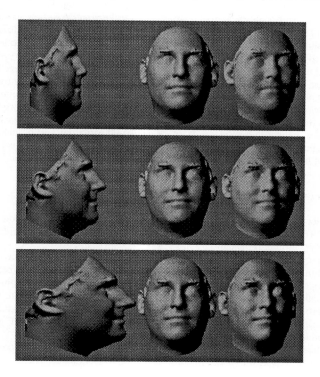

Figure 2. Illustrates the Bas Relief Ambiguity [Belhumeur et al., 1997] which confounds depth and view. The pose of the faces in the right column actually varies by several degrees (rotation about the vertical axis is $5.0°$, $7.1°$, $3.5°$ respectively). These tradeoffs between depth and view are impossible to distinguish from a single 2D image. (Reproduced by permission of Peter Belhumeur.)

Approaches have been suggested to deal with pose computation and construction of novel views from a single 2D view of the face using 3D information derived from *average* or *prototype* face shape [Aizawa et al., 1989, Beymer and Poggio, 1995, Vetter, 1997]. Since the shape of individual faces varies quite a bit, using a general face shape model introduces an

---

[2] The solution to the 3 point perspective pose estimation problem has been known since 1841 [Haralick et al., 1991]. This solution provides the 3D coordinates of each vertex of a known triangle from the perspective projection of the three points in a single 2D image.

inherent error into the pose computation. Although this source of error may be smaller when using a large set of prototype face models (assuming that there is truly a closer relationship between the actual face shape and one of the prototype face shapes), one would still expect pose computed using shape specific to the individual to be more accurate because it does not include this modeling error.

We provide two more visual arguments against the use of general face shape in computing face pose from a single image. The first is from [Belhumeur et al., 1997]. Figure 2 shows a nice example of how depth (and therefore shape) and view are confounded. The images in the middle and right columns all look exactly like the same face in the same pose, yet the pose of the faces in the right column actually varies by several degrees (rotation about the vertical axis is $5.0°$, $7.1°$, $3.5°$ respectively). The difference is pose is balanced by a difference in 3D shape (left column). These tradeoffs between depth and view are impossible to distinguish from a *single* 2D image.

The use of a general face shape to analyze the intensity data of a specific face is equivalent to mapping the intensity of one face onto the shape of another. Figure 3 shows a specific example of this type of mapping, with the bottom row of images being composed of the shape from the second row and the intensity from the first row. Does the last row represent either the first or second individual? It seems clear that a *perceptually independent* face can be produced in this manner. Novel views of a face generated using this sort of technique would therefore bring up many issues in the context of a recognition system. This effect is obviously subjective, but merits formal psychophysical testing.

1.3 Pose Computation from 3D Data

When an object is represented by 3D data, accurate estimation of pose is a simple geometric computation. The only requirement is that the features which define the object coordinate system can be identified in the data.

There are quite a number of methods to obtain 3D description of a face. On one end of the spectrum, there are laser range scanners (such as those made by Cyberware which were used to generate the data in Figure 3). These collect high spatial resolution data (in an absolute scale), but require expensive and non-portable sensing equipment. In past work [Gordon, 1991b, Gordon, 1992, Gordon, 1991a] we have used automatic feature extraction to perform pose computation and normalization on these types of data sets. Figure 4 shows the points which define the face centered coordinate system in this work.

At the other end of the spectrum, three dimensional descriptions can be computed from 2D intensity images using stereo or structure from motion techniques. These techniques provide lower resolution depth, balanced by the advantage of less expensive and more portable sensors. In particular, structure from motion is attractive because it requires only a single uncalibrated camera. The remainder of the paper describes a pose extraction algorithm using structure from motion on video sequences.

2 Pose Computation from Video Sequences

Pose extraction from video has been demonstrated in the general case. Our algorithm is based on the work of [Tomasi and Kanade, 1992]. Faces, with their smoothly varying surfaces, are not at the outset ideal candidates for these algorithms, which are based on tracking features defined by contrast events. Their surfaces can also exhibit elastic deformation, which violates the rigid motion assumptions. Similarly, the head and the torso can move independently. We use domain specific knowledge to successfully compute face pose from video despite these potential problems. The contribution of this work involves automatically limiting the feature selection to the central portion of the head through independent initial pose estimation, and

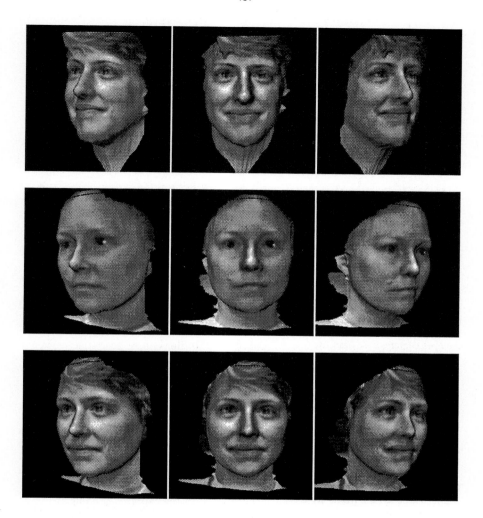

Figure 3. The top two rows of images are rendered 3D models of two different people based on actual shape and color scans (using a Cyberware scanner) of their heads. The bottom row shows the intensity data from the first person, mapped onto the shape data of the second person. The new synthetic face is perceived as a different (new) person.

438

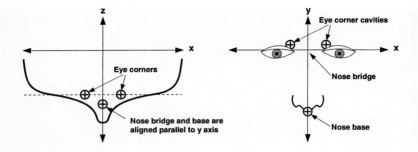

Figure 4. The face centered coordinate system defined for pose computation with range data based on features automatically extracted from surface curvature.

through careful elimination non-rigid feature points via modeling of the occluding countour and residual error analysis. Both of these issues are discussed in section 2.1.

[Azarbayejani and Pentland, 1995] presents related work on pose computation of faces from video sequences. This work represents an interactive rather than batch mode algorithm, but is based on similar rigid motion assumptions. The emaphasis of this work is on stability in the domain of recursive estimation, whereas our emphasis is on automated feature selection to avoid non-rigid phenomena. Their face pose estimates include only 6 or 7 features such as the eyes centers, nose base, etc.

The pose extraction algorithm includes these key steps:
- Computation of initial view (frontal view)
- Feature selection
- Feature tracking
- Estimation of occluded feature positions
- Computation of structure and pose at each frame

The last step, a structure from motion algorithm, is addressed first because its requirements drive the design of the other steps. The structure from motion algorithm used is based on the factorization method presented by [Tomasi and Kanade, 1992]. The algorithm takes as input a set of feature tracks. Each track consists of an array of 2D image locations, one for each frame, showing the path which a 3D point on the surface of a rigid object takes from frame to frame. These feature tracks are assembled into a $2N \times F$ matrix, where N is the number of frames and F is the number of features. After adjustment to separate the effects of translation, the track matrix is factored into two matrices, one providing the 3D location of the feature points (structure) and other providing the rotational relationship between the object and the camera at each frame (full pose results from the combination of the rotation and translation data). The pose given at each frame is relative to the first frame of the sequence. The center of mass of all feature points is used as the origin of the coordinate system. This algorithm uses orthogonal projection and assumes that 1) the correspondence of the features points from frame to frame is known, 2) occlusion events are known, and 3) the motion represented by the feature tracks is that of a rigid object.

The job of *automatically* selecting and tracking the points for input to the factorization algorithm is complex. The features tracked must correspond to surface points on a rigid object. Image features corresponding to occluding boundaries, shadows, and motion independent from the head (e.g., torso or other objects in the scene) violate this assumption and act as sources of error. This becomes even more critical when using this algorithm on faces, because the total number of features which can be extracted in low contrast areas is small, and there are large low contrast regions on the face. We discuss the feature selection first, followed by the feature tracking. The following section discusses avoiding non-rigid features.

The basic feature selection method [Shi and Tomasi, 1994] identifies local image patterns containing edges in more than one direction. These are identified by examining the eigenvalues of the G matrix used in tracking (equation 3). Two strong eigenvalues of G are a good indication of strong gradients in multiple directions and hence corner-like features. A threshold on the minimum eigenvalue of G is used as a specific selection criteria.

Once the features have been selected, they are tracked by modeling the motion of the feature window as a simple translation. The displacement of the feature window, d, is computed by minimizing the error residue, e, between frames based on this model [Lucas and Kanade, 1981].

$$Gd = e \tag{1}$$

$$G = \sum_W \begin{bmatrix} x'^2 & x'y' \\ x'y' & y'^2 \end{bmatrix} \tag{2}$$

$$e = \sum_W \begin{bmatrix} \frac{dI}{dt}x' \\ \frac{dI}{dt}y' \end{bmatrix} \tag{3}$$

where W is a small local image region (15x15 pixels). If this solution does not converge quickly, tracking stops for that specific feature. Although the translation model is more simplistic than the actual image change expected over time (e.g. it doesn't include rotation or scale changes), it is quite effective over the small inter-frame distances typical in video rate sequences.

2.1 Avoiding Non-rigid Features

This low level feature selection and tracking algorithm has several additional steps aimed at reducing the number of features selected and tracked which do not correspond to points on a rigid surface. In some cases, we take advantage of our knowledge of the application domain.

Identifying where the head is in the image is an important step. An initial pose selection algorithm provides an estimate of likely frontal views in the image stream, and also identifies the center and scale of the face. This estimate is used to locate the head initially, and limit the feature selection to the central head region, rather than the torso or the background.

Initial frontal pose is selected via a multi-resolution template matching algorithm. A small number of templates are used consisting of the central portion of generic frontal view faces at varying scales. The matching is performed at a reduced spatial and temporal resolution to lower computation time. The maximum of all correlation scores in any frame or scale is used to determine the face scale. Frames which represent local maxima in the correlation score for the selected template are identified and sorted in descending order. The highest value in the list determines frame number of the frontal views from which pose computation begins. Figure 5 shows an example of typical correlation scores over an image sequence of a rotating head. The head passes through frontal view twice.

Object occluding contours are a common source of bad feature points. Many corner features which are not true surface features can be found along the occluding contour, and can even be consistently tracked. Often these are caused by an intersection between an edge in the background and the object, or a concavity in the occluding silhouette which is visible over several frames (e.g. the intersection of the base of the ear and the neck). Assuming that the background is not moving, we compute a mask based on local frame differences indicating a liberal region contiguous to the occluding contour. We then insure that new features are not selected within this region, and similarly we stop tracking existing features when we reach this zone.

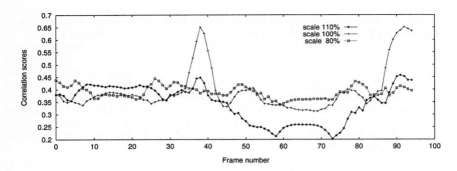

Figure 5. The selection of frontal view frame based on multiresolution correlation with generic frontal view face.

Two further steps are taken to minimize the inclusion of points not representative of rigid surface motion. The first is an affine criteria used to monitor longer term changes in the feature window [Shi and Tomasi, 1994]. Including affine transformations allows for a more realistic tracking model. To examine the likelihood that a feature window has been tracked correctly, we can compare its original values with those of its final tracked position. The affine transform which best models the relationship between the two windows is computed. This transform is applied to the original window, and the result is compared with the window in the actual tracked position. Low similarity is indicative of occlusion. A threshold can be used to remove these features from further consideration.

In addition to the affine similarity criteria, nonrigid features are identified by comparing the actual observed tracks with those estimated by the computed pose and structure [Gordon and Lewis, 1995]. Average residual for feature f is

$$\epsilon(f) = \sum_{i=1}^{N} \frac{\|observation(f, i) - prediction(f, i)\|}{N}$$

The predicted location at frame i is the orthogonal projection of the 3D feature location transformed by $pose(i)$. Features with large position residuals are removed and the pose and structure are recomputed. This method is effective at removing features not well modeled by the computed structure and pose parameters. It requires one additional recomputation of the tracking matrix factorization.

2.2 Occlusion Events

In the above description, a number of different methods are discussed to identify features which are no longer being tracked successfully This will often occur because a point being tracked becomes occluded. Since the structure from motion algorithm requires a complete feature track matrix, we must either eliminate a partially tracked feature from the matrix in all frames or attempt to fill in the undefined feature locations via estimation. It is clearly an advantage to be able to keep as many features in the tracking matrix as possible. Also, with an effective estimation procedure, new feature sets can also be selected during the tracking process to incorporate new portions of the object which come into view during the sequence. When new feature sets are selected, their locations can only be tracked forward in time from the point where they were identified. Thus, feature locations must be estimated for the frames before the selection occurred.

Estimating an Individual Point Location

The estimation procedure repeatedly examines complete submatrices of the sparsely filled track matrix [Lucas and Kanade, 1981]. To estimate any given feature location, the algorithm starts with a complete submatrix, $2F$ rows $\times P$ columns, and two partial rows each $P - 1$ in length. These partial rows represent tracks for the first $P - 1$ points in a new frame, $F + 1$. From this information, the coordinate of the point P in frame $F + 1$ is estimated.

The first step in the estimation process is to perform factorization of the dense submatrix, which establishes shape information for all P points, and the rotation and translation information for F frames.

To compute the rotational axes for frame $F + 1$, we use the $2(F + 1) \times (P - 1)$ system for which, between the matrix and partial rows data, all point locations are available. The computation of the shape coordinates was originally based on the centroid of all P points and must be first adjusted with respect to the centroid the first $P - 1$ points in each frame. As long as there are at least 4 total points, the traditional $\tilde{W} = RS$ equations will then provide an over-determined system (solved with least squares) for the two missing rotation vectors.

The translation vector for frame $F + 1$ is computed algebraically, using the original shape coordinates for $P - 1$ features, the rotation information for the new frame, and the tracking coordinates of the $P - 1$ points in the new frame.

The missing track coordinates for the point P in frame $F + 1$ are now a straight forward solution of the $W = R * S + T$ equation.

Fill Order

The control structure of our estimator is responsible for selecting the order of estimation of new points. The estimator is invoked once in each frame for each point which has an unknown location. New features are selected in groups every 8 or 10 frames. The general looping scheme processes the sparse matrix by feature selection group in several passes. Before the first pass, the columns (points) in each feature selection group are shuffled so that the number of valid frames is decreasing as point index increases. Features which are detected in less than four total frames are eliminated. An example this operation is shown graphically in Figure 6(A) and (B). Figure 6(A) represents the fill pattern of the original sparse matrix. In this example features were selected twice after the initial feature selection. Figure 6(B) shows the same information with a different point index order.

During the first pass, each of the feature selection groups is processed, filling forward in time and in increasing order of point index. For this example, the points in the original feature selection group have values over all frames at the completion of this pass. However, for any subsequent feature selection groups, there are invalid values in all frames earlier than the selection frame. The resulting track matrix is shown in Figure 6(C). The second pass fills backward in time and in increasing order of point index, as shown by the completely filled matrix in Figure 6(D). In this example there were a number of features which were valid in all frames. If this were not the case, the columns would be reshuffled and a third pass would fill in the remaining points, filling forward in time and in increasing order of point index.

442

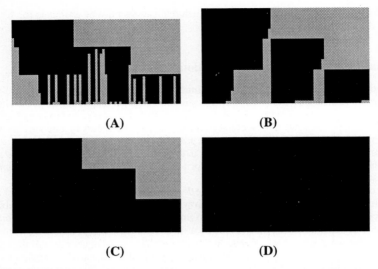

(A) (B)

(C) (D)

Figure 6. Filling in the track matrix by feature point estimation. Example shows the fill pattern of a track matrix at various stages of processing. Black squares indicate valid feature locations. Gray squares indicate unknown values. Each row represents a frame (first at the top) and each column represents a feature points. (A) After the tracking is completed, (B) after change of feature point order, (C) after first stage of estimation, and (D) after second stage of estimation.

3 Results

The pose extraction algorithm has been tested using the FERET Program video database. Each video sequences is 5 to 10 seconds and shows approximately 180° of rotation of the head primarily about the vertical (Y) axis, e.g. including both profiles and frontal views.

A frontal view frame is identified automatically as described above, and a segment of the sequence is chosen for processing such that the front view frame is essentially in the middle. Subsequences ranged from 30 to 60 frames.

Sequences were processed to produce pose estimates at each frame, as well as the 3D locations of all the feature points. A polygonal model can be generated from this data using 2D Delaunay triangulation (we used the frontal view frame) to provide the topology of the 3D points. Image data from the frontal view frame was texture mapped onto the polygonal model for visual evaluation. An example of this type of model is shown in Figure 7 at different viewing angles. Since we have computed 3D coordinates only at the extracted feature locations, there are several areas (e.g. along the bridge of the nose) which will not be described well. However, this shows that even a sparse model is useful to provide the general structure of the face. In particular, the eye sockets are set back with respect to the nose, and the overall face shape is gently curved.

To evaluate pose we visually compare our computed model transformed by a specific computed pose to the actual image in the corresponding frame. Figure 8 shows this comparison at the start and end of a sequence covering 36 frames and consisting of 40 tracked features. Relative pose between the two frames shown is 2.4° rotation about the x axis (horizontal), 70.3° rotation about the y axis (vertical), and 0.7° rotation about the z axis (out of the image plane). Visual alignment between the frames and modeled pose is very close, despite

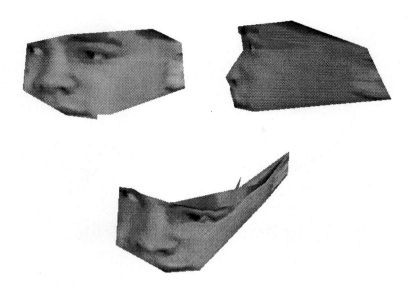

Figure 7. Different views of the same face model.

the fact that the texture which is mapped onto the model is from the frontal view frame, and is not expected to be a good map for a frame $\pm 30°$ away from this view.

4 Conclusions and Future Work

This paper presents a concrete demonstration of the use of structure from motion algorithms to compute the pose change and 3D structure of a human face as seen in a video sequence. This successful demonstration is significant particularly because of the many challenges presented by facial images with respect to structure from motion computation. These challenges include an uneven distribution of intensity features, many smooth surfaces, potential elastic movement, and the existence of multiple motion fields. The use of this capability enables accurate face recognition based on representations which are not view invariant, such as 2D intensity images.

In the context of face recognition, pose information can be used for extracting key poses from video (e.g. building reference databases), and, similarly, to select views during comparison whose pose best match those in the reference database. Since pose mismatch is a key source of error in recognition systems based on view variant representations, the comparison of pose provides an explicit confidence measure in the recognition process. It may also be possible to use the pose information to further transform available images to better match existing pose examples.

Face pose can be valuable in many other application domains including video database management, facial expression analysis, and human computer interface.

Despite this successful demonstration, there are remaining issues which form the basis of future work. A key issue is the use of *a priori* knowledge of face structure to register

444

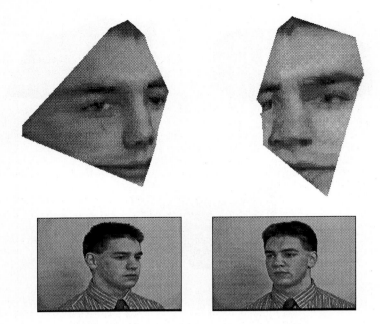

Figure 8. The model computed is shown in the computed pose of the first and last frames of the subsequence. This is compared to the actual video image at the corresponding frames demonstrating a close alignment.

the pose computed to a head centered coordinate system. At the moment, the algorithm tells us only pose relative to the the frontal view, but the exact initial pose is not determined with respect to a face centered coordinate system. This can be done via combination of this structure from motion approach with feature location algorithms [Covell and Bregler, 1996], thus relating the generic corner features selected for tracking with the semantic understanding of the facial feature locations. Once this relationship is understood, the motion computed can be transformed to the face centered coordinate system. The goal of this registration is to produce pose estimates comparable across all data sets and repeatable within data sets of the same individual.

References

[Aizawa et al., 1989] Aizawa, K., Harashima, H., and Saito, T. (1989). Model-based analysis synthesis image coding system for a person's face. *Signal Processing: Image Communications*, 1(2):139–152.

[Azarbayejani and Pentland, 1995] Azarbayejani, A. and Pentland, A. (1995). Recursive estimation of motion, structure, and focal length. *IEEE Transactions on Pattern Analysis and Machine Intelligence*, 15(6):561–575.

[Belhumeur et al., 1997] Belhumeur, P. N., Kriegman, D. J., and Yuille, A. L. (1997). The bas-relief ambiguity. In *Proceedings of the IEEE Computer Society Conference on Computer Vision and Pattern Recognition*, pages 1060–1066, Puerto Rico.

[Beymer and Poggio, 1995] Beymer, D. and Poggio, T. (1995). Face recognition from one example view. In *Proceedings of the International Conference on Computer Vision*, pages 500–507, Cambridge, MA.

[Covell and Bregler, 1996] Covell, M. and Bregler, C. (1996). Eigen-points. In *Proceedings of the IEEE International Conference on Image Processing*, volume 3, pages 471–474, Lausanne, Switzerland.

[Gordon, 1991a] Gordon, G. G. (1991a). *Face Recognition from Depth and Curvature*. PhD thesis, Harvard University, Division of Applied Sciences.

[Gordon, 1991b] Gordon, G. G. (1991b). Face recognition from depth maps and surface curvature. In *Proceedings of SPIE Conference on Geometric Methods in Computer Vision*, volume 1570, San Diego, CA.

[Gordon, 1992] Gordon, G. G. (1992). Face recognition based on depth and curvature features. In *Proceedings of the IEEE Computer Society Conference on Computer Vision and Pattern Recognition*, pages 808–810, Champaign, Illinois.

[Gordon and Lewis, 1995] Gordon, G. G. and Lewis, M. E. (1995). Face recognition using video clips and mug shots. In *Proceedings of the Office of National Drug Control Policy (ONDCP) International Technical Symposium*, volume 2, pages 13.45–13.51, Nashua, NH.

[Haralick et al., 1991] Haralick, R., Lee, C., Ottenberg, K., and Nolle, M. (1991). Analysis and solutions of the three point perspective pose estimation problem. In *Proceedings of the IEEE Computer Society Conference on Computer Vision and Pattern Recognition*, pages 592–598, Maui, Hawaii.

[Lucas and Kanade, 1981] Lucas, B. D. and Kanade, T. (1981). An iterative image registration technique with an application to stereo vision. In *International Joint Conference on Artificial Intelligence*, pages 674–679.

[Moghaddam et al., 1996] Moghaddam, B., Nastar, C., and Pentland, A. (1996). Bayesian face recognition using deformable intensity surfaces. In *Proceedings of the IEEE Computer Society Conference on Computer Vision and Pattern Recognition*, pages 638–645, San Francisco, CA.

[Pentland et al., 1994] Pentland, A., Moghaddam, B., and Starner, T. (1994). View-based and modular eigenspaces for face recognition. In *Proceedings of the IEEE Computer Society Conference on Computer Vision and Pattern Recognition*, pages 84–91, Seattle, WA.

[Shi and Tomasi, 1994] Shi, J. and Tomasi, C. (1994). Good features to track. In *Proceedings of the IEEE Computer Society Conference on Computer Vision and Pattern Recognition*, Seattle, WA.

[Tomasi and Kanade, 1992] Tomasi, C. and Kanade, T. (1992). Shape and motion from image streams under orthography: a factorization method. *International Journal of Computer Vision*, 9(2):137–154.

[Vetter, 1997] Vetter, T. (in press, 1997). Synthesis of novel views from a single face image. *International Journal of Computer Vision*.

[Wiskott et al., 1997] Wiskott, L., Fellous, J.-M., Kruger, N., and von der Malsburg, C. (1997). Face recognition by elastic bunch graph matching. *IEEE Transactions on Pattern Analysis and Machine Intelligence*, 19(7):775–779.

Characterising Virtual Eigensignatures for General Purpose Face Recognition

Daniel B Graham and Nigel M Allinson

Image Engineering and Neural Computing Group
Department of Electrical Engineering and Electronics
University of Manchester Institute of Science and Technology.
Manchester M60 1QD, UK.

Abstract. We describe an eigenspace manifold for the representation and recognition of pose-varying faces. The distribution of faces in this manifold allows us to determine theoretical recognition characteristics which are then verified experimentally. Using this manifold a framework is proposed which can be used for both familiar and unfamiliar face recognition. A simple implementation demonstrates the pose dependent nature of the system over the transition from unfamiliar to familiar face recognition. Furthermore we show that multiple test images, whether real or virtual, can be used to augment the recognition process. The results compare favourably with reported human face recognition experiments. Finally, we describe how this framework can be used as a mechanism for characterising faces from video for general purpose recognition.

1 Introduction

One of the fundamental problems that challenge face recognition systems, whether human or machine, is that natural behaviour and conditions can significantly change the appearance of a facial image. Given a sufficient change in conditions it is most probable that, in the representation of the faces, the in-condition change will be greater than the in-person change and so lead to an incorrect identification or, at best, an incorrect rejection. The human face recognition system, whilst not invariant to such changes, can usually accommodate the most frequently occurring changes with reasonable success - the performance often decaying once condition changes tend towards the extreme. Many psychological experiments have attempted to capture the extent of the human ability to recognise faces under such changes as illumination, planar rotation, depth rotation, expression, disguise, photographic inversion and occlusion. This paper will describe a system which models the characteristic manner in which faces change over pose and a method for developing an individuals' characteristic which is dependent upon the degree of familiarity of that individual.

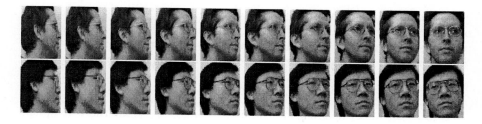

Figure 1: Pose Varying Images

2 Face Representation

2.1 Pose Varying Eigenspace

The use of eigenspace methods for facial image analysis has been common since early papers by Sirovich and Kirby [9] and, the more often cited, Turk and Pentland [10]. The majority of such systems have shown that separating the shape information (e.g. by morphing) from the texture information yields additional performance enhancements as in Costen et al.[2]. The view-based eigenspaces of Moghaddam and Pentland [4] have also shown that separate eigenspaces perform better than using a combined eigenspace of the pose-varying images. This approach is essentially several discrete systems (multiple-observers) and so highly dependent upon the number of views chosen to sample the viewing sphere and of the accuracy in the alignment of the views. Producing an eigenspace from all of the different views (a pose varying eigenspace), could continuously describe an individual through an eigenspace in the form of a convex curve. This has been shown by McKenna et al.[3] for faces and Murase and Nayar [6] for 3D objects. We state simply the standard eigenvalue formulation for an image set, $\mathbf{X}$, where $\mathbf{X}$ is formed by concatenating the rows of each image to produce a single column vector for each image which are then placed into the rows of the vector $\mathbf{X}$ (i.e. transposed).

The eigenvectors μ_a of $\mathbf{X}$ are described by the following equation:

$$\mathbf{X'X}\mu_{\mathbf{a}} = \lambda_{\mathbf{a}}\mu_{\mathbf{a}} \tag{1}$$

where λ_a is the corresponding eigenvalue to the eigenvector μ_a, and $\mathbf{X'X}$ is the covariance matrix of the image set $\mathbf{X}$. The eigenvectors of this matrix can be obtained by diagonalising $\mathbf{X'X}$. However, for image-sized matrices it is generally computationally easier to compute the eigenvectors of the alternative covariance matrix $\mathbf{XX'}$ which is of order N^2 where N is the number of images in the set and use the relationship:

$$\mu_a = \frac{1}{\sqrt{\lambda_a}}\mathbf{X'}\nu_{\mathbf{a}} \tag{2}$$

where ν_a is the eigenvector of the covariance matrix $\mathbf{XX'}$. The eigenvectors of the covariance matrix $\mathbf{XX'}$ are readily computable for small image sets in a reasonable amount of time as algorithms are available to achieve the required diagonalisation. The eigenvalues of a novel image Ψ are then given by:

$$\psi_a = \Psi \mu_a \tag{3}$$

It is in the space spanned by these eigenvalues, ψ_a, that the consequent analysis is performed and we will refer to this space as the *eigenspace.*

Our pose varying eigenspaces are constructed from images like those shown in Figure 1. An eigenspace constructed from such images captures that manner in which faces change over pose. Figure 2 shows the mean face and the effect of the first eigenvector (as in Valentin and Abdi [11]). As can be seen the first eigenvector indicates the major face orientation with negative values of the first eigenvector giving a more profile-oriented face and positive values a frontal view. This effect can be used as the basis of a *pose determination* system as in [3].

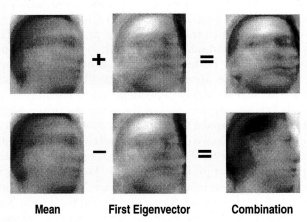

Mean   **First Eigenvector**   **Combination**

Figure 2: The effect of the first eigenvector

Figure 3 shows the characteristic curves of the two individual faces in Figure 1 in this eigenspace as they rotate from profile to frontal view. Note that these curves are represented here by ten 3D points corresponding to the first three eigenvalues of the images in an eigenspace constructed from 40 images randomly sampled from a database of 563 pose varying images of 20 people.

We have called these loops in the eigenspace *eigensignatures* as each one corresponds uniquely to a specific individual.

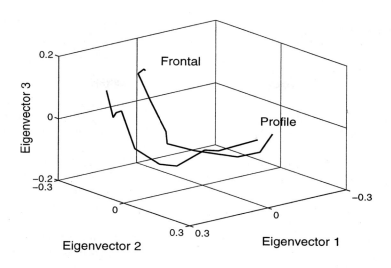

Figure 3: Eigensignatures of two people.

2.2 Properties of this Manifold

We have seen in Section 2.1 that the faces in our database are represented in the pose-varying eigenspace as a convex curve. The properties of the distribution of faces in this manifold are of interest.

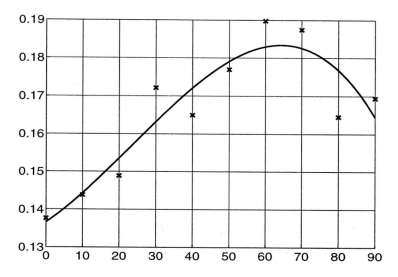

Figure 4: Average Distance between faces over Pose

In particular the distance between faces over pose allows us to predict the pose dependency of a recognition system that uses this manifold. If faces are further apart they will be easier to recognise using distance measures in the eigenspace. Those measures can be used to set thresholds or confidence limits upon the identity of a test face.

Figure 4 shows the average Euclidean distance between the people in the database over the pose angles sampled (cubic fit). From this we can predict that faces should be most easy to recognise around the 60° range and, consequently, the best pose samples to use for an analysis should be concentrated around this range. Additionally we would expect that faces are easier to recognise at the frontal view than the profile. The experiments of Section 3 will attempt to confirm these predictions.

2.3   Virtual Eigensignatures

If we consider the pose varying eigenspace described in Section 2.1, where a unified pose/identity subspace is generated which captures the manner in which faces change over varying pose and quantifies the extent of that change in terms of distances in the subspace. It can be seen in Figure 3 that individuals all differ in this subspace but that each subject undergoes a characteristic motion through the subspace. As the motion we are capturing is the same in each case and the 3D structures of each subject are closely related, it is not unreasonable to assume that the general nature of these characteristic curves can be obtained, and that a curve may be estimated from a single given point.

Formally, the recognition of faces in previously unseen views requires a function Γ which maps a real point p to a virtual eigensignature Υ. This virtual eigensignature has a confidence factor $\delta(p)$ which depends upon the initial point p. That is:

$$\Gamma(p) = \Upsilon, \delta(p) \tag{4}$$

Given further real points p_i we can generate further virtual eigensignatures Υ_i each with their own confidence factor $\delta(p_i)$. We can then combine virtual eigensignatures to produce a *refinement* of the virtual eigensignature which approaches the true eigensignature Ω. Given that the confidence factors $\delta(p_i)$ lie in the range $\{0,1\}$ we can define the weight function ω_i for each virtual eigensignature:

$$\omega_i = \frac{\delta(p_i)}{\sqrt{\sum_{i=0}^{N}(\delta(p_i))^2}} \tag{5}$$

We can combine the eigensignatures to produce:

$$\Omega \cong \sum_{i=0}^{N} \omega_i \Upsilon_i \tag{6}$$

Note that this framework is independent of the chosen representation of the eigensignatures, the confidence factors and the weight function. Additionally, the weight deduction (eqn 5) is sub-optimal, in that real points in the eigenspace ($\delta(p_i) = 1.0$) should remain in the eigensignature and not be influenced by other points. The development of an algorithm for effectively combining multiple eigensignatures will be described in a later paper.

In order to investigate the above formulation we define an eigensignature as consisting of ten points in the eigenspace sampled from profile to frontal view in $\sim 10^o$ degree steps. Virtual eigensignatures Υ_i are generated from a test point p_i using a Radial Basis Function Network (RBFN - see Moody and Darken [5]) as the mapping function Γ. The RBFN was trained on one view (p_i) to produce the full eigensignature Υ_i. The output from the RBFN thus gives ten points in the eigenspace for an individual which estimates the characteristic curve of that face in the eigenspace. Each RBFN is trained on 19 of the subject's true eigensignatures and the remaining subject's eigensignature was generated from the RBFN to form a virtual eigensignature - this was repeated for each of the 20 subjects (leave-one-out cross-validation) to produce 20 virtual eigensignatures. To investigate the pose dependent nature of the method an RBFN was trained using each of the ten views (producing ten virtual eigensignatures per person) and the performance of each of these eigensignatures was compared. In total 200 virtual eigensignatures were produced.

Recognition is performed by matching a test image (i.e a test point in the eigenspace) to one of the virtual eigensignatures using a nearest neighbour Euclidean distance. Different metrics in this eigenspace, such as the Mahalanobis distance, have also been investigated and found to perform similarly. It should be noted that simple point matching in this formulation describes the base-level performance achievable. Matching with multiple, ordered, points - whether *real* or *virtual* - would improve the performance of such systems. See Section 3.4 for an example of this.

3 Experimental Results

3.1 Train/Test View Interaction

The performance of this approach is dependent on several factors as described in Section 2.3. Here we establish the baseline performance of the system by matching the real eigensignatures (omitted during the RBFN training) with the virtual eigensignatures generated by the RBFN. Table 1 shows the percentage of correct identifications at each train/test view. It can be seen from the **Mean** row that there is a clear advantage to testing at the 40° to 50° view. This is normally referred to as the *3/4 view* and is often reported as the best performing pose in human face recognition experiments e.g. Bruce et al.[1], Valentin et al.[12] and partially in Patterson and Baddeley [7].

Table 1: Train/Test View Interaction (Pose 0 = Profile, 90 = Frontal)

Training View	Test View									
	0	10	20	30	40	50	60	70	80	90
0	100	90	60	40	20	20	20	15	15	15
10	90	100	70	60	50	45	50	40	15	15
20	35	65	100	70	30	20	30	20	20	25
30	35	75	85	100	70	60	25	25	20	20
40	35	25	40	70	100	80	55	50	25	30
50	25	30	40	65	95	100	60	55	30	30
60	15	15	30	30	60	85	100	80	55	45
70	10	10	25	30	45	55	90	100	75	50
80	15	20	35	20	20	30	45	70	100	65
90	20	10	10	20	20	15	25	30	60	100
Mean	38	44	49.5	50.5	**51**	**51**	50	48.5	41.5	39.5

A similar result would be observed for an average over testing view to determine the relative performances of each training view but it was felt that such an interpretation would be biased in favour of the central views by the window effects of the data around the end views of 0° and 90°. As such it is difficult to determine the optimal training view. However, were we to assume that *all tests* were to be carried out in this pose range, we would have reason to suppose the 3/4 view as the preferred training view.

3.2   Multiple Training Images

Recognition of a face when having only seen one previous image of that face is classed as *unfamiliar face recognition*. As the number of images increases the process tends towards *familiar face recognition*. The system presented in Section 2.3 provides a general purpose formulation for these two types of recognition. Section 3.1 has shown the base-line performance for unfamiliar face recognition and examined the pose dependent nature of the system. Here we examine the effect of increasing the number of training images used to form the refined eigensignature according to eqns 5 & 6. In a simple experiment we show the effect of increasing N (the number of virtual eigensignatures) and the pose dependency of this increase. For this evaluation we have used a confidence factor, centered around a test pose p_i, which decays sharply with distance from p_i. Namely:

$$\delta(p_i, p_j) = \frac{1}{1+ \parallel p_i - p_j \parallel} \tag{7}$$

where p_i is the pose used to train the RBFN.

Table 2 shows the performance of this system as N increases, and how this performance varies over pose. The results shown are the percentage of

Table 2: Refined Eigensignature Performance (%)

N	Test View p_j										
	0	**10**	**20**	**30**	**40**	**50**	**60**	**70**	**80**	**90**	$\overline{m_j}$
1	27.0	32.0	40.5	45.0	45.5	54.5	49.5	48.0	43.5	36.0	42.1
2	36.9	43.7	53.0	57.8	58.2	69.1	66.0	64.3	61.2	49.6	56.0
3	44.5	52.9	61.5	65.4	68.3	78.3	75.8	74.8	73.9	59.4	65.5
4	50.3	59.7	67.2	69.2	76.5	84.7	82.2	81.2	82.8	68.3	72.2
5	56.1	65.5	72.0	72.3	83.1	89.3	86.6	85.7	87.7	76.0	77.4
6	62.1	71.0	77.2	74.8	88.3	92.4	90.1	89.4	90.8	82.2	81.8
7	68.4	77.2	82.8	78.3	92.7	95.1	92.8	92.4	93.0	87.6	86.0
8	75.9	84.4	87.9	84.2	95.7	97.3	94.3	94.6	94.0	92.0	90.0
9	81.0	89.5	93.0	91.5	98.0	98.5	94.5	95.5	93.5	96.0	**93.1**
$\overline{m_N}$	55.8	64.0	70.6	70.9	78.5	**84.4**	81.3	80.6	80.0	71.9	

correct identifications at each pose for every possible combination of N virtual eigensignatures from ten. As in Section 3.1 it can be clearly seen that, on average $(\overline{m_N})$, the 50° test view outperforms all other views. There is also a clear trend of performance increasing with N $(\overline{m_j})$. Furthermore we see a preference for testing at frontal views over profile views - another common observation in human face recognition experiments [1]. This preference is more pronounced for unfamiliar faces (low N) than for familiar faces (high N) - also noted in [1].

These results show the maximum performance increase obtainable with multiple training views as the multiple views are all pose-aligned on the test views. However, we would expect similar improvements in local test areas for non-aligned images due to the nature of the eigensignature combination (eqns 5 & 6) and the confidence factor (eqn 7).

3.3 Multiple Testing Images

The experiments described in Sections 3.1 & 3.2 have demonstrated the use of virtual eigensignatures for recognition, including the case where multiple training images are available. Conversely, in real world systems, the number of training images may be low and fixed whereas the number of test images may be large and variable (e.g. video monitoring). We show here the simple situation where multiple training images are used to produce a total Euclidean distance from which we again attempt recognition. There were 363 test images of the same twenty people in the database; none of which were used at any stage during the RBFN training. These images were taken at the same time and setting as the previous images but were considered to lie in intermediate views to the 10° views used in the previous experiments.

Figure 5 shows the recognition improvements gained by using increasing numbers of test images for each of the virtual eigensignatures. The lines shown indication the percentage of correct identifications for all possible combinations of N test images of the same subject where N is shown below each line.

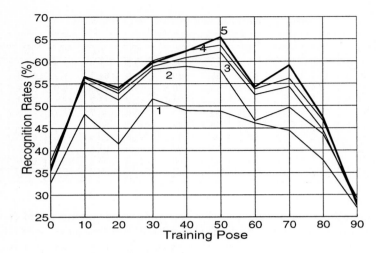

Figure 5: Use of Multiple Test Images

The solid line represents the best case of $N = 5$. As would be expected, there is a clear improvement in using additional test images. It can be seen there is little change in the performance of the system at the frontal and profile areas of the training views for increasing numbers of images. However there is a marked improvement (as N increases from 1 to 5) at the 50° training view by some 17% (compared with 2-3% at the extremes), providing further evidence for the preference of this view as the best training view to use, but with the same reservations as in Section 3.1. Conversely, we see that the performance is marginally better at profile than at frontal. It is thought that the manual alignment procedure and the actual quality of pose from each subject affects the performance at the frontal view.

3.4 Virtual Test Images

Section 3.3 has shown the minimum improvement available from the use of multiple real images which are not considered to be in any particular order. If we have, or can generate, multiple test images that are of known relative pose then we may begin to utilise the nature of each eigensignature over a local region for recognition purposes. In this case we may calculate the total Euclidean distance between the ordered test images with an ordered section of the eigensignature.

To demonstrate this we take the 363 test images as used in Section 3.3 and, for each image, generate a further two *virtual images* by rotating the image $\pm10^o$ using a cylindrical model of face shape. We then calculate the total Euclidean distance between these three images and each set of three ordered points for the true eigensignatures.

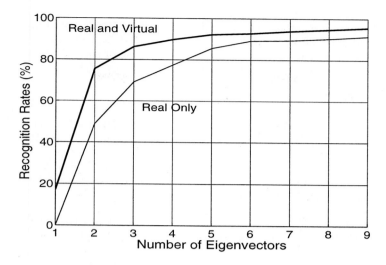

Figure 6: Use of Ordered Virtual Test Images

Figure 6 shows the performance of this approach compared to simple point matching for increasing numbers of eigenvectors. From the graph we can see a clear improvement at all points - especially when using a small number of eigenvectors. For ten eigenvectors (as used in all other experiments in this paper) we see an improvement of approximately four percent.

4   Conclusion

We have described a manifold for the recognition of pose-varying faces and examined its properties. Experiments have shown that the proposed framework performs face recognition in a manner similar to reported human face recognition. The basis of the technique does not depend upon the the sampling viewpoints - as long as the eigenspace constructed is sufficiently representative of the test viewpoints. Furthermore, as long as the eigenspace is representative of the test viewpoints, it does not necessarily mean that a individual face image must be well represented in the eigenspace. This is evident in the above experiments where only ten eigenvectors are needed for near-ideal performance.

Future work on the technique will concentrate on the automatic construction of eigensignatures, image acquisition, eigenspace optimisation and intelligent matching algorithms. Given these components we can effectively construct an automatic visual system which could continually adapt using eqn 6 in an unconstricted manner. This approach will be used as the basis for a video surveillance system for monitoring and characterising individuals

456

from their motion and behaviour. Initial experiments in this direction have shown that automatically constructed eigensignatures can classify as well as recognise and further experiments will test the use of such eigensignatures.

References

[1] Bruce, V., Valentine, T., Baddeley, A. (1987) The Basis of the 3/4 View Advantage in Face Recognition. *App. Cog. Psych.*, **1,** 109-120

[2] Costen, P., Craw, I., Robertson, G., Akamatsu, S. (1996) Automatic face recognition: What representation? *Computer Vision, ECCV'96,* LNCS, Springer-Verlag, **1064,** 504-513

[3] McKenna, S., Gong, S. Collins, J. (1996) Face Tracking and Pose Representation. *British Machine Vision Conference,* Edinburgh

[4] Moghaddam, B. and Pentland, A. (1994) Face Recognition using view-based and modular eigenspaces. *SPIE,* **2277,** 12-21

[5] Moody, J. and Darken, C. (1989) Fast Learning in Networks of Locally-Tuned Processing Units. *Neural Computation,* **1,** 281-294

[6] Murase, H. and Nayar, S. (1993) Learning Object Models from Appearance. *Proc. of the AAAI,* Washington, 836-843

[7] Patterson, K. and Baddeley, A. (1977) When Face Recognition Fails. *J. of Exp. Psychology: Learning Memory and Cognition,* **3**(4), 406-417

[8] Pentland, A., Moghaddam B., Starner, T. (1994) View-Based and Modular Eigenspaces for Face Recognition. *IEEE Conf. CVPR,* 84-91

[9] Sirovich, L. and Kirby, M. (1987) Low Dimensional procedure for the characterisation of human faces. *J.O.S.A,* **4**(3), 519-525

[10] Turk, M. and Pentland, A. (1991) Eigenfaces for Recognition. *J. of Cognitive Neuroscience,* **3**(2), 71-86

[11] Valentin, D. and Abdi, H. (1996) Can a Linear Autoassociator Recognize Faces From New Orientations. *J.O.S.A,* **13**(4), 717-724

[12] Valentin, D., Abdi, H., Edelman, B. (1997) What Represents a Face: A Computational Approach for the Integration of Physiological and Psychological Data. *Perception,* **26**

[13] Vetter, T and Poggio, T. (1995) Linear Object Classes and Image Synthesis from a Single Example Image. *TR 16,* Max-Planck-Institut für biologische Kybernetik

An Attentive Processing Strategy for the Analysis of Facial Features*

R. Herpers[1,2] and G. Sommer[1]

[1] Institut für Informatik, Lehrstuhl für Kognitive Systeme, Universität Kiel
Preußerstr. 1-9, 24105 Kiel, Germany,   Email: herpers@gsf.de
[2] GSF–Institut für Medizinische Informatik und Systemforschung, MEDIS
Ingolstädter Landstr. 1, 85764 Oberschleißheim, Germany

Abstract. Facial landmarks such as eye corners, mouth corners or nose edges are important features for many applications in face recognition. The exact detection of these landmarks, however, is not an easy task because of the high individual variability of facial images and therefore, of the tremendous complexity of all the low-level features existing within the image. For instance, a precise and reliable detection of the eye corners has not been successfully solved until now. However, the knowledge of the exact position of these landmarks in the facial image is important for many matching and face processing tasks. For the classification and discrimination of dysmorphic facial signs a precise and reliable detection of a certain set of anatomical facial landmarks is particularly necessary. For this, an attentive processing strategy has been developed which puts the focus of the processing on only those salient image areas which are really needed to solve the several subtasks. The fundamental idea of the approach presented is to concentrate the artificial attention upon only a small fraction of the existing low-level features within a spatially well restricted image area.

Keywords. Attentive Vision, Face Recognition, Image Processing

1 Introduction

Motivated by the eye movement strategies of the human visual system, a computer-based attentional strategy has been developed to detect the prominent facial features in portrait images. The attentive processing system is structured into three main components (fig. 1):

- the *localization of salient regions*,
- the *classification of foveated regions* and
- the *structural analysis of foveated regions*.

In a first processing step, the most salient facial regions such as the eye, nose, and mouth region are localized, based on a saliency representation, which is established by deriving several attentive visual cues [2]. Subsequently, the detected and now spatially limited regions are classified to evaluate the benefit of applying more detailed and expensive analysis methods [6, 7]. Furthermore, a first semantic interpretation of the foveated region is processed.

---

*This work is partially supported by the DFG, Grants So·320\1-2 and Ei 322\1-2.

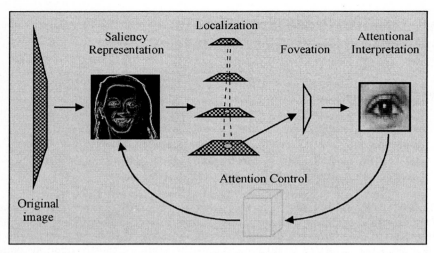

Figure 1: The attentive processing scheme. Attentive visual cues are derived from facial grey level images to build up a saliency representation. Prominent facial regions are selected and a decision is made to apply more detailed processing methods. The attentive processing is supervised by a control strategy essentially based on model knowledge and recently derived information. Applying this procedure, all salient image regions are located, selected, and analyzed in detail.

During the detailed analysis step the exact positions of relevant keypoints or anatomical landmarks such as eye corners and mouth corners are determined [3] and evaluated [5].

Fundamental to the approach presented is the common use of the processing principle: the consideration and evaluation of only salient image features. In other words, based on this processing strategy only those image features are processed and analyzed further for which evidence exist in the local arrangement of the image area considered. During the region localization only the most attentive cues are derived and represented. For the subsequent classification module an object representation is established which is composed of a small number of point representations located only at prominent image positions of the object such as prominent corners or intersection points. During the third processing step, where a structural analysis of the foveated facial region is performed, only prominent image structures such as characteristic edge and line segments are detected and considered in more detail applying stepwise adaptive detection and tracking methods.

A high degree of efficiency is achieved using an uniform or common comprehensive filtering scheme during all processing steps. While in the first processing step only simple features are required, in the subsequent processing steps more detailed information is needed. The filtering scheme developed is incorporated into a unified processing strategy based on a common attentive framework [12].

The attentional processing mechanisms developed are used as an essential component in building an image processing system to classify facial images of children with dysmorphic signs. Dysmorphic signs in facial images are minor anomalies which, by definition, do not lead to functional disturbances [13, 14] (fig. 2). In this context, dysmorphic signs in faces play an important role in syndrome identification because in most cases they are visible and prominent in the facial image. It has been shown, that particular phenotypic combinations are typical for distinct dysmorphic syndromes [13, 14]. Therefore, the detection of particular keypoint positions (fig. 2) in facial images is of high diagnostic value. For this, the localization of the keypoints or landmarks should be very accurate, reproducible, and should correspond to the anatomical definition of the keypoint positions.

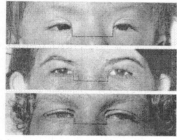 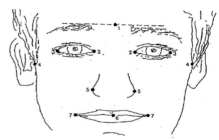

Figure 2: Example of different intercanthal distances (left). A very enlarged intercanthal distance and an epicanthus are typical examples of dysmorphic signs in the frontal facial image (first eye strip) (from [14, p. 42]). Important anthropometrical landmarks in a frontal face image (right).

2 Localization of salient regions

In general, the bottom-up visual search task in real world images is an NP-complete problem depending on the image size and the number of objects to be searched. However, a task-directed search based on selective attentional mechanisms can be computed in linear time complexity which depends on the number of objects to be searched in the image [15]. These complexity considerations suggest that attentional mechanisms are necessary to successfully solve an image analysis problem in real-time. Thus, image processing with attention control reduces computational load and focuses the computation to only those image regions which are important to solve the current task.

In the HVS elementary visual cues such as motion, color, orientation, edge information etc. are derived from the sensed input. These features establish an attentive representation upon which the control of the visual attention is based. The evaluation of this representation provides different salient image regions which are foveated in a sequential order. By adopting these gaze control principles for developing artificial image processing systems, a complex image analysis problem P is reduced to a number of subproblems P_i that can be solved individually in a simpler way [8]:

$$P(I, M) := \{P_1(I_1, M_1), \ \ldots \ , P_n(I_n, M_n)\} \tag{1}$$

where $n = 2, \ldots, N$ is the number of subproblems, $I_i \subseteq I$ are image parts of the image I and $M_i \subseteq M$ are model assumptions and other parameters. In other words, only that information, which is really essential for a given task, has to be extracted and processed further. Irrelevant image regions may be excluded as far as possible to avoid additional processing effort. The processing of several subproblems P_i is a dynamic process based on the results obtained from the subproblems processed before (fig. 1). The analysis of the results obtained and the integration of top-down knowledge may be used to determine the next subproblem and methods to solve it.

Saliency representation

The attentive processing strategy is based on a saliency representation $S(t)$ carrying all the information which is necessary to compute the selective attention (fig. 1). In the realization this saliency representation is a 2D saliency map $S(t)$ in which the spatial distribution of the salient cues from the underlying image is encoded (fig. 3). The saliency representation $S(t)$ is generated from a 'feature representation' $U(I)$ and a time dependent 'control representation' $C(t)$; $S(t) := U(I) \times C(t)$. The feature representation $U(I)$ is defined as the weighted sum of several filters f_l applied to the image $I(\vec{x})$:

$$U(I) := \sum_l a_l \ (f_l \otimes I(\vec{x})) \tag{2}$$

The control representation $C(t)$ is needed to control the attentive processing. It is defined as $C(t) := SR(t) \times A(t)$. The first component of the control map $C(t)$ is the suspension map $SR(t)$ generated to suspend already foveated and analyzed regions from further processing steps and the second component is the anticipation map $A(t)$.

To enable the computation of additional salient regions, previously selected regions have to be suspended from the subsequent processing. Therefore, a locally parameterized 2D Gaussian function, called 'suspension functions', is calculated at the center of the already detected region. The suspension of the already detected regions is represented by a suspension map $SR(t)$ (see the darkened right eye in fig. 3c) (for more details see [2, 8]).

Control representation

The control representation $C(T)$ also enables the integration of top-down information into the low-level analysis process. The knowledge integration is realized by slightly emphasizing the derived salient cues of those image regions which are intended to be localized in the next localization steps. Therefore, a spatially restricted 2D Gaussian function is calculated for each expected region and encoded in the anticipation map $A(t)$ (see the left eye in fig. 3c).

The content of the saliency representation $S(t)$ can be summarized in two parts, one part contains the regular attentive or salient cues of the underlying image and therefore, it is fixed for all following processing steps. This feature representation $U(I)$ can be processed in advance applying fast and parallel convolution methods. The second part of the saliency representation $S(t)$ the control representation $C(t)$ influences the selection of the salient features during the processing of the several attentive regions and, therefore, is time variant. It can be viewed as an integration process or an instrument for decreasing the saliency of regions which are already detected and for increasing the saliency of regions which are intended to be localized based on model assumptions and a priori knowledge.

Evaluation of the scale hierarchy

The saliency representation $S(t)$ is represented in a scale hierarchy to provide a high degree of invariance and robustness during the evaluation of the spatially distributed salient image cues. It forms the basis of all subsequent localization steps. The selection of a salient facial region starts at the coarsest scale of the hierarchy, employing a maximum search algorithm (fig. 3a). Subsequently, this initial salient map element is expanded dependent on the underlying local saliency distribution. For this, a 2D Gaussian function is fitted to the local saliency distribution (fig. 3b) and a certain contour line h is taken to fix the boundary of an elliptical region given by the following ellipse equation:

$$(\vec{x} - \bar{m})^T Cov^{-1}(\vec{x} - \bar{m}) = h = const. \tag{3}$$

where $\bar{m}$ is the expectation of the 2D Gaussian function and Cov is the covariance matrix of all map elements or pixels of the localized region.

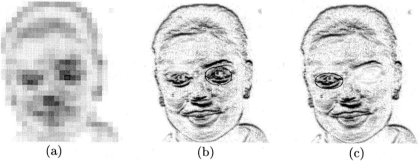

| (a) | (b) | (c) |

Figure 3: Processing of the region localization by evaluating a multi-scale representation of the saliency map. Maximum search of that element with the highest saliency (a). The maximum element is expanded optimally to the local extension of the feature representation at each scale (figs. inverted). Subsequently the computed region is projected to the next higher resolution level (b). To compute further attentive regions, regions already considered are suspended from the following localization steps (right eye in (c)). In addition, the integration of model knowledge enables an anticipation of that region which is to be detected (left eye in (c)).

After an iteration step to optimally match the ellipse to the underlying saliency representation the computed region is projected to the next higher resolution level (fig. 3b) and the region adaptation is computed again until the highest resolution level is reached. The computed region is selected at the highest resolution level and it is well adapted to the extent and the orientation of the underlying local saliency distribution (fig. 4). To enable the localization of further facial regions all previously detected regions have to be suspended from the following localizations steps. For this the suspension representation $SR(t)$ is introduced as mentioned before (fig. 3c). Applying this procedure, all salient facial image regions can be located and further processing modules can be applied to them.

Results of the region localization

The region localization has been tested on more than 100 frontal facial images with slightly different illumination conditions and camera positions. Some faces were tilted or slightly rotated in different directions. The scales and the brightness of the facial images recorded also differed from image to image (fig. 4). Within the first 3 foveation steps both eye regions were detected correctly in more than 98% of the face images considered.

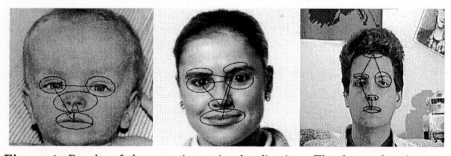

Figure 4: Results of the attentive region localization. The detected regions are spatially well adapted to scale, extent and orientation of the facial regions. The attentive localization algorithm was also applied successfully to face images of the face database of A. Pentland[1] although the resolution of the images was too low to apply all subsequent processing modules (right).

3   Region classification

After the attentive localization of the different prominent facial regions, it has to be decided whether the foveated region should be investigated in more detail or not. The subsequent detailed analysis methods (described in chapter 4) are very precise and specially developed for the particular facial part to be investigated. Since the eyes contain the most attentive cues in the facial image they are selected during early foveation steps [8]. Assuming that just one eye region is located after three foveation steps the complexity of the

---

[1] available at ftp: vismod.www.media.mit.edu/pub/images

general classification task can be reduced to the verification of the question "does the foveated region contain an eye region ?". After the successful classification of one eye region further processing steps can be chosen and model knowledge about the spatial relations between the facial regions can be integrated.

Point representations

To make this decision a neural classifier has been developed which is motivated by the dynamic link architecture introduced by the Malsburg group [1, 10]. In contrast to their work, where initially particular subjects are identified, we have to compute a discrimination task which distinguishes between different classes of facial regions. Therefore, besides the intraindividual also the interindividual variability has to be considered during the construction of the uniform classifier. For the recognition of an eye in a facial region a set of point descriptions is established. These point descriptions are located at particular characteristic image positions (e.g. significant corners or intersection points) (see fig. 5).

Figure 5: Point descriptions connected by a graph demonstrated for an artificial eye region (left). The descriptions at the circled keypoints and the spatial relationship between them are used to clearly represent the characteristic features of the considered class of region. Model graph used for eye regions (right).

The spatial relationship between the several image points is maintained by establishing a 2D graph consisting of nodes for the several point descriptions and of edges for the connections between them. In contrast to the related work, object adapted graphs are applied. In detail, the eye pattern is represented by 12 point descriptions positioned by the nodes of the graph at characteristic object positions or landmarks (fig. 5). Fundamental to this design is that the nodes are positioned only at image positions for which evidence of the local structure exists. To ensure a reliable representation of the underlying image structure at the characteristic image positions orientation selective edge and line detection filters as well as polar separable filters all based on Gaussian derivatives are applied [6, 7].

Graph matching

By applying a two step graph-matching algorithm different facial regions can be distinguished very reliably. In the first processing step the initial starting position is computed to fit the undistored model graph to the most appropriate position. In the second step the graph is distorted and the nodes are moved independently by applying a simulated annealing approach.

For the determination of the initial starting position, the similarity of the graph is calculated for all image positions in the considered image part and that image position which matches best indicates the initial starting position. During the computation of the best starting position the shape of the graph is kept rigid (fig. 6). No distortion of the graph is allowed, only the scale and orientation of the graph is varied, to achieve better invariance properties.

 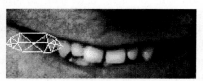

Figure 6: Results of the calculation of the initial starting position of the model graph for an eye region (left) and a non eye region (right). The calculation will terminate at that position with the greatest similarity to the represented edge information of the model graph.

After the determination of the initial starting position the model graph has to be adapted independently of its topology to achieve an optimal correspondence for each constituent node. The solution of such a high dimensional problem, considering graph sizes with 12 nodes, cannot be calculated completely. For this optimization problem, a heuristic numerical approach is applied which is able to determine an acceptable approximation of the optimal solution. In the realization a simulated annealing approach [9] is employed to compute the best match of the model graph to the test patterns (for more details we refer the reader to [6, 7]).

 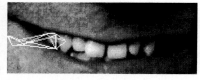

Figure 7: Results of the simulated annealing algorithm demonstrated for an eye region (left) and a non eye region (right).

Regarding eye regions the adaptation of each node to the corresponding image structure enhances the similarity to the model representation by maintaining simultaneously the spatial relationship between the nodes. For non eye regions the spatial relations will be distorted more severely, which causes higher distortions of the connecting edges (fig. 7). By applying a cost function this property can be used to distinguish reliably between facial regions. With this classification module all eye regions can be classified successfully as eye regions (sensitivity of 100%). For non eye regions the classification performance is not quite as good (95.5%).

4   Structural analysis

In the third processing step of the attentive processing strategy the foveated regions are analyzed in more detail. In the following we will take the eye region as an example, but figure 10 shows that characteristic facial features and anatomical landmark positions may also be successfully computed for other facial regions. The approach starts by detecting the most prominent and reliable features in the facial region considered. Given our task and image recording conditions these are the strong vertical step edges of the iris in eye regions. Subsequently, the complete iris and the eyelids are tracked to finally detect the eye corners. At each step the detection and tracking is controlled by integrated model knowledge [3, 4]. Additionally the assumptions are used to check the consistency of previously detected edges and to predict the edge structures searched for in the next processing step.

Basic filter operations

A very flexible filtering scheme is applied which produces many different low-level features thus providing an expressive data-driven basis for the keypoint detection [3, 4]. The detection of the image structures in the facial regions is based on a sequential search and tracking of the characteristic edges and line segments. The detection and tracking is realized by three different **basic filter operations** (fig. 8) that make extensive use of steerable edge and line detection filters which are used several times during the processing [11].

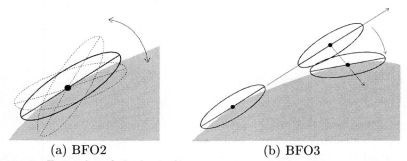

      (a) BFO2   (b) BFO3

Figure 8: Examples of the basis filter operations. BFO2: Determination of the orientation (a). BFO3: Stepwise tracking (b).

Integration of model knowledge

The approach presented for the keypoint detection essentially uses model knowledge to establish a sequential search strategy for a stepwise detection of the main characteristic structures in the image part considered. The derivation of a large number of features and the integration of model knowledge are mutually dependent.

On the one hand, the large number of features that are derivable by the filtering scheme does not allow a 'classical' computational detection strategy.

466

Therefore, a sequential strategy is introduced that integrates model knowledge into the low-level analysis processes. The model knowledge provides the 'global overview' for the confusing wealth of features. We call such a strategy 'attentive' because it focuses only on those types of features, which may be present as dictated by the model, or in other words, which are expected to be present.

On the other hand, an attentive processing requires a flexible and probably complete representation of all included features. Therefore, the filtering scheme must allow for an efficient on-line choice of the type and the quality of the features needed. In other words, there is a potential need for many features, but during the processing only a small fraction of all the features is required to solve the current problem. Therefore, more expensive and time consuming filtering is applied only to certain image positions where it is really worthwhile [11].

Sequential search strategy

The detection of the keypoints in the facial regions is achieved by a sequential search or tracking of the edge and line structures where each step consists of several applications of the basic filter operations (fig. 9). The selection of the different operations and their parameters for each step is controlled by the already derived information together with the model knowledge. The model knowledge used consists of the relevant edge and line structures, their scales and geometrical relations of the considered facial region. This information is used to search for reliable edges at specific positions, orientations, and scales in each processing step. Furthermore, different kinds of edges (white-to-black versus black-to-white edges or edges against lines etc.) can be distinguished very reliably.

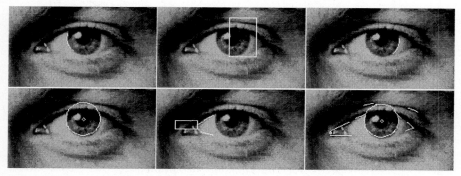

Figure 9: Example steps of the sequential search strategy for the detection of keypoints and prominent structures in an example eye region. First, a prominent vertical bright-to-dark edge is detected (first row). After the detection of the corresponding right edge segment, the final segmentation of the iris is computed. The eyelid edges are searched, tracked, and finally that edge segment which is strongly curved is detected to determine the eye corners (second row).

5 Conclusion

Fundamental to the attentive processing strategy presented is that all processing modules consider and process only prominent and really characteristic image structures. Only those image structures are considered which are relevant to the following processing task. Beginning with the region localization these are distributed edge and line structures. In the following processing steps more detailed structures need to be detected and therefore, more sensitive and expensive methods are applied locally.

The presented approach combines a cyclic as well as a hierarchical procedure which is essentially supported by appropriate model knowledge. The proposed strategy realizes an efficient integration of high-level information into mainly low-level processes.

The attentive processing strategy presented has a notably high degree of scale invariance, achieved using different resolution levels adapted to the requirements of the particular processing module and to the task to be solved. The detection and analysis of the prominent facial regions is independent of the exact position and the orientation of the face and the facial components within the image. The search algorithms proposed are able to cope with different variations due to the illumination, brightness, and contrast of the studied facial images.

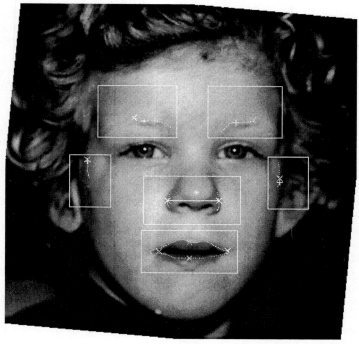

Figure 10: Result of the structural analysis demonstrated for the other facial regions. All important anthropometrical landmarks which are relevant to our medical application (see fig. 2) have been detected.

Acknowledgments

We appreciate the support of Prof. S. Stengel–Rutkowski of the Institute for Social Paediatrics and Youth Medicine. The work is partially supported by the DFG grants So 320/1-2 and Ei 322/1-2.

References

[1] J. Buhmann et al., *Distortion invariant object recognition by matching hierarchically labeled graphs*, Proc. Int. Joint Conf. on Neural Networks, IJCNN, IEEE, pp. 155-159, 1989.

[2] R. Herpers et al., *GAZE: An attentional processing strategy to detect and analyze the prominent facial regions*, In: Proc. of the Int. Workshop on Autom. Face- and Gesture-Rec., Zurich, M. Bichsel (ed.), pp. 214-220, 1995.

[3] R. Herpers et al., *Edge and keypoint detection in facial regions*, In: Proc. of the 2. Int. Conf. on Automatic Face and Gesture Recognition, Killington, IEEE, pp. 212-217, 1997.

[4] R. Herpers, et al., *Context Based Detection of Keypoints and Features in Eye Regions*, In: Proc. of the 13th int. Conf. on Pattern Recognition, 13th. ICPR, Vienna, Austria, IEEE Computer Society Press, Vol. B, pp. 23-28, 1996.

[5] R. Herpers et al., *Dynamic cell structures for the evaluation of keypoints in facial images*, In: Int. Journal of Neural Systems, Special Issue Neural Networks for Computer Vision Applications, pp. 27-39, 1997.

[6] R. Herpers et al., *Invariant classification of image parts using a dynamic grid of point representations*, In: Proc. of 3rd int. Conf. on Engineering Applications on Neural Networks, EANN'97, Neural Networks in Engineering Systems, A.B. Bulsari et al. (eds.), pp. 41-45, 1997.

[7] R. Herpers et al., *Discrimination of facial regions based on dynamic grids of point representations*, to be published in Int. Journal of Pattern Recognition and Artificial Intelligence, Special Issue on "Neural Networks in Computer Vision Applications", 1998.

[8] R. Herpers, *GAZE: A common attentive processing strategy for the detection and investigation of salient image regions*, PhD thesis, Christian-Albrechts-Universität, Kiel, Germany, 1997.

[9] S. Kirkpatrick et al., *Optimization by simulated annealing*, Science, Vol. 220, pp. 671-680, 1983.

[10] M. Lades et al., *Distortion invariant object recognition in the dynamic link architecture*, IEEE Trans. on Computers, Vol. 42, pp. 300-311, 1993.

[11] M. Michaelis, *Low level image processing using steerable filters*, PhD thesis, Christian-Albrechts-Universität, Kiel, Germany, 1995.

[12] M. Michaelis et al., *A common framework for preattentive and attentive vision using steerable filters*, In: Proc. of the CAIP'95, Prague, V. Hlavac et al. (eds.), Springer-Verlag, LNCS 970, pp. 912-919, 1995.

[13] S. Stengel-Rutkowski et al., *Anthropometric definitions of dysmorphic facial signs*, In: Hum. Genet., Vol. 67, pp. 272-295, 1984.

[14] S. Stengel–Rutkowski et al., *Chromosomale und nicht-chromosomale Dysmorphiesyndrome*, Enke Verlag, Stuttgart, 1985.

[15] J.K. Tsotsos, *Analyzing vision at the complexity level*, Behavioral and Brain Sci., Vol. 13, pp. 423-469, 1990.

Face Location in Real Backgrounds

Harold Hill

Department of Psychology
University of Stirling
Stirling, FK9 4LA
UK.

Abstract. Five experiments are reported which tested face location in images of real scenes by humans. Observers were better at locating faces than random patches. However, inverted faces and upright and inverted kettles were also well located, suggesting that the effect was not face specific. High bandpass filtering the images did not reduce performance although low bandpass filtering did, suggesting that the sritical information for the task is at a relatively high spatial frequency. When location performance for faces and kettles was directly compared under conditions of reduced presentation time, some advantage for faces and for upright images was found. It is argued that the results do not suggest face specific detection mechanism but that the face may provide a particularly effective signal for the human visual system.

Keywords. Face detection, location, face specific.

1 Introduction

Face detection and location are the necessary first stages of most if not all face processing tasks including recognition. Fundamentally the problem is one of image segmentation in that the area of the image corresponding to the face must be identified and segmented from the background so that subsequent processing can be directed to the appropriate area. In the experiments reported here human performance was tested on a task similar to that used for testing automatic face detection algorithms, that is detection and location of faces in images of real scenes.

Previous research in Psychology suggests that we may be especially good at detecting faces (Purcell & Stewart, 1988). In a 2-AFC detection task observers were found to be better at detecting upright faces than either jumbled or inverted faces made up of the same physical components. One suggestion is that this is because there are cells specifically dedicated to detecting faces. However, there does not appear to be evidence for "pop-out" of upright faces from arrays of distractors (Nothdurft, 1993), which would be expected if there was a population of face detector cells operating in parallel over the whole visual field.

Both of these previous studies were conducted using highly artificial or schematic stimuli on a blank or artificial background. In the experiments reported here pictures of real faces in real backgrounds were used, as has been more normally the case in the automatic face detection literature (Sung & Poggio, 1994;

Yang & Huang, 1994), although here there was only ever one face in each scene. In such real scenes properties of the background, for example "clutter", may be as important in determining performance as properties of the face itself. As the effect of the background was not the question of interest here it was treated as a random variable with a variety of different scenes being used so that the results would generalise across this variable. Observers were required to indicate the actual location of the face, not just to detect it, again as required when testing automatic face detection algorithms.

In order to test between different possible mechanisms underlying human face location, performance was compared in a number of conditions. Initially location performance was compared for faces and random patches in order to test if simple pattern matching is sufficient. Images were also presented upright and inverted in order to test whether familiarity/object knowledge is critical. Performance was also tested for another class of object, a kettle, for which there are unlikely to be specific detectors, in order to further address the issue of face specificity. Filtered images were also used in order to provide information as to the nature of the visual signal involved.

Figure 1. Examples of the stimuli used in Experiment 1.

2 General methods

2.1 Observers

Observers were recruited from the University of Stirling and all had normal or corrected to normal vision. Observers only took part in one experiment with any particular set of images.

2.2 Materials

Pictures were taken of a variety of indoor and outdoor scenes (e.g. carpark, lecture theatre, wood) both with a person in and without (See Figure 1). All the faces shown were in full-face view. Some or all of the person's body was also often visible. Pictures were taken using a Sony Handicam with automatic focus. Images were scaled so that all faces had an inter ocular distance of 8 pixels. 256 x 256 pixel areas were then extracted from the original images at random to avoid compositional cues and so that the face could occur anywhere in the image. Images measured 9.3 x 9.3 pixels when presented on the screen and were viewed from a distance of 45 cm., giving a 12° viewing angle.

2.3 Procedure

For experiments 1-4 observers were first shown a 40 x 40 pixel patch which either contained a face or was a random part of the image. The patch remained on the screen for 1 s. after which the picture it was taken from was shown, also for 1 s. This was replaced by a grey square of the same size, 256 x 256, and the observer's task was to indicate by pointing and clicking with the mouse where in the picture the patch had come from. The distance between the actual and the indicated centre of the patch was recorded automatically. Face and random patch trials were interleaved in a random order.

2.4 Design

Mixed factorial designs were used with all observers doing both face and random patches but the stimuli were presented at different orientations for different groups. The distance between indicated and actual patch centres was used as a measure of performance.

3 Experiment 1

3.1 Introduction

In this experiment observers had to locate a 40 x 40 patch taken from a 256 x 256 image. The patch either contained a face or was a random part of a similar image which did not contain a face. If general pattern matching is sufficient for the task no difference would be expected between the different patch types. However, any face specific advantage would be expected to result in an advantage for the patches containing faces. In order to test if performance depends on familiarity with upright faces or is dependent on image properties alone, stimuli were presented upright and inverted. Any face specific advantage would be expected to result in a large effect of inversion similar to that found for recognition (Yin, 1969; Valentine, 1988).

3.2 Method

The method was as described in the general methods section with patch type, face or random, as the within subjects factor and orientation, upright or inverted, as the between subjects factor. Ten observers took part in the experiment.

3.3   Results

As can be seen from Figure 2 there was a clear advantage for locating faces compared to random patches but little effect of orientation.   A 2(Patch) x 2(Orientation) repeated measures ANOVA gave a main effect of Patch ($F_{1,8}=56.5$, $p<<0.05$) but no effect of inversion or any interaction ($p's > 0.1$).

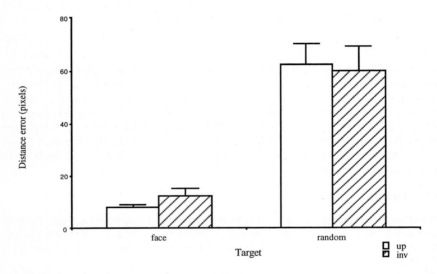

Figure 2.   Location performance as a function of patch type an orientation in Experiment 1

3.3   Discussion

In this experiment there was a clear advantage for locating patches containing faces, which would be consistent with a face specific advantage and face detector cells.   It does show that something more than pattern matching is determining performance.   The lack of an effect of inversion is uncharacteristic of face specific processing, as this normally shows a *disproportionate* effect of inversion (Valentine, 1988).   Results for the upright stimuli may have been close to ceiling, masking any differences between conditions.   However, the high performance even when inverted cannot have been mediated by orientation specific detectors or templates.   Instead it seems likely that there are low level image properties, unaffected by inversion, that allow the face to be segmented from the background. This is despite the fact that the faces in the different scenes appeared very different due to individual differences and effects such as lighting.

The difference between face and random patches may also have reflected specific disadvantages associated with location of the random patches.   For example, some of the patches were inherently ambiguous in that they came from parts of the image with a high degree of similarity, for example patches of sky or grass, making their precise location inherently difficult. This contrasts with the faces which all had a clearly defined location. This possibility was examined in the second experiment which tested location performance for a different, but equally locatable, object.

4 Experiment 2

4.1 Introduction

This experiment was identical to Experiment 1 except that the images contained kettles instead of faces (See Figure 3). The kettle was chosen as a discrete, locatable object of approximately the same size of the face for which there are highly unlikely to be specific detector cells. It was thought that the kettle's visual simplicity and relative brightness would make it easy to locate, and thus bias against finding any face specific advantage. The kettle, unlike the face, was not symmetric in the views shown. There is no ideal control for the face in terms of factors that are likely to be important such as visual complexity and familiarity but the kettle did allow a further test of whether the advantage was specific to faces.

4.2 Method

The method was the same as Experiment 1 except that the pictures used were of scenes with and without a kettle in. These were obtained in the same way and in similar situations as the faces used in Experiment 1.

Figure 3. Examples of the stimuli used in Experiment 2

4.3 Results

As can be seen from Figure 4 the pattern of results was very similar to that for Experiment 1; patches containing scenes were better located than random patches and there was little or no effect of inversion. Again there was a main effect of Patch type, kettle or random, ($F_{1,8}=711.6$, $p \ll 0.05$) but no effect of inversion or any interaction ($p > 0.1$).

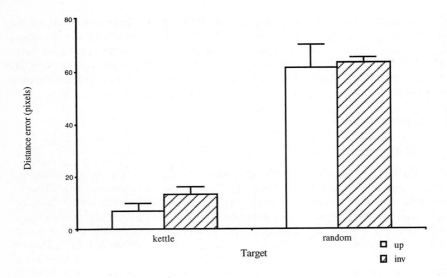

Figure 4. Location performance as a function of patch type and orientation in Experiment 2.

4.4 Discussion

The results of this experiment show that the advantage found in Experiment 1 for faces compared to random patches is not unique to faces but is also found for a very different class of object for which there are unlikely to be specific detecting mechanisms. One possibility the results suggest is of a general object detector able to locate objects likely to be of interest and separate them from the background. However, as mentioned in Experiment 1, the difference between patch types may also have been because the random patches were inherently difficult. A general object detector may take advantage of this homing in on unique areas of the image, limited in extent. Again the lack of an effect of inversion suggests that location performance does not depend on object or scene specific knowledge, although performance may again have been close to ceiling. However, the high level of performance with inverted images does again suggest that low level image properties may allow objects to be separated from the background. In the next experiment filtered images were used in order to investigate the nature of this information.

5 Experiments 3 & 4

5.1 Introduction

In these experiments low (Experiment 3) or high bandpass (Experiment 4) filtered images were used (See Figure 5). Two fairly extreme levels of filtering were used in order to provide a first approximation of the frequency of the information involved. There is evidence that particular spatial frequency bands are important for particular task like recognition (e.g. Costen, Parker & Craw, 1996) and it would be interesting if this is also the case for location and detection. In particular it was of interest to see if faces and/or kettles resulted in a coarse scale blob which was sufficient to distinguish them from the background or whether high spatial frequency information is also necessary.

Figure 5. Examples of the filtered images used in experiment 3 and 4. The images are bandpass filtered using Laplacian of Gaussian filters, the low band pass image on the left with a width of 8 pixels and the high bandpass image on the right with a width of 1 pixel.

5.2 Methods

The methods were the same as for previous experiments except for the stimuli. For this experiment the images from Experiments 1 and 2 were filtered using a Laplacian of a Gaussian with a width characterised by a "standard deviation" of 8 pixels (low bandpass) or 1 pixel (high bandpass). The Laplacian of a Gaussian models the characteristics of retinal x-ganglion cells.

5.3 Results

As can be seen from Figure 6 random patches were located equally well in low and high spatial frequency filtered images, but location of both faces and the kettle was better in the high spatial frequency images. In both high and low spatial frequency images faces and kettles were located better than random patches. The F values for these comparisons are given in Table 1.

Table 1. F values for comparisons of location performance for target and random patches in high and low bandpass filtered images.

Frequency	Target type	
	Face	Kettle
Low	($F_{1,4}=37.4$, $p<<0.05$)	($F_{1,4}=122.0$, $p<<0.05$)
High	($F_{1,8}=58.5$, $p<<0.05$)	($F_{1,8}=26.7$, $p<<0.05$)

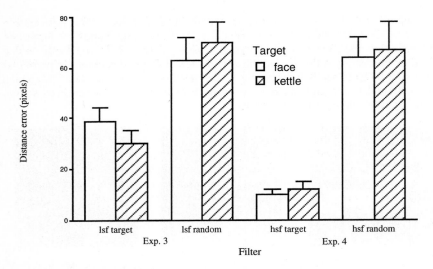

Figure 6. Location performance as a function of filter and patch and target types in Experiment 3 and 4. Key: lsf - low spatial frequency, hsf - high spatial frequency.

Comparisons with performance for unfiltered images, Experiment 1, showed a main effect of filtering for low bandpass images, Faces ($F_{1,8}=58.5$, $p<<0.05$) and Kettles ($F_{1,8}=26.7$, $p<<0.05$), but not for high bandpass images (p's >0.1).

5.4 Discussion

These experiments showed that object, including face, location is sensitive to the spatial frequency content of images although there was no difference in the accuracy of locating random patches. That high spatial frequency filtered images were as well located as unfiltered images suggests that this information may be sufficient for this task. Again, the results were similar for faces and kettles again suggesting that faces do not appear to be processed in a radically different manner, at least at the early stages of processing. Performance did appear to be slightly better for low frequency filtered kettles perhaps because there is less high spatial frequency detail to be lost. In the final experiment performance for faces and kettles was directly compared in order to further test for any differences.

6 Experiment 5

6.1 Introduction

In this experiment face and kettle location performance was compared directly in upright and inverted orientations in order to further test for any advantage associated with upright faces. In order to make the task more difficult and eliminate the possibility of ceiling effects presentation time was reduced to 100 ms. Images were also forward and backward masked. No patch was shown and observers were told that each image would contain either a face or a kettle and that their task was to indicate where this object was located. The unfiltered images from Experiments 1 and 2 were used.

6.2 Method

The images from Experiments 1 and 2 which contained a target object were used in this experiment. Observers were told that each image would contain either a face or a kettle and that their task was to indicate the location of whichever object was in each picture. Each trial consisted of an isotropic noise mask with even spatial frequency distribution, followed by the image, followed by another noise mask and then the grey square for responses, as in the previous experiments.

6.3 Results

As can be seen from Figure 7 there were effects of target type (Face/Kettle) and orientation (Upright/Inverted) in this experiment. Analysis of variance showed main effects of Target ($F_{1,22}=55.3$, $p<<0.05$) and Orientation ($F_{1,8}=15.4$, $p<0.05$) but no interaction ($p>0.1$).

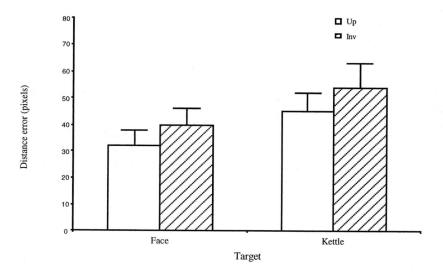

Figure 7. Distance error as a function of orientation and target type in Experiment 5.

6.4 Discussion

Under the modified conditions of this experiment faces in upright images were found to be most accurately located. This may have been masked in previous experiments because performance was close ceiling. However, the pattern of results still does not suggest face specific detection mechanisms. In particular the effect of inversion was independent of target type meaning that there was no disproportionate effect of inversion on faces, as might have been expected if face specific processing was involved. One possible explanation for the advantage, consistent with the other results reported here and previous work, is that the face constitutes a particularly effective signal for the human visual system making it easy to locate. The effect of inversion found here, which affected both faces and kettles, may make the scene more difficult to interpret making objects more difficult to locate. Previous work has reported that when the parts of an image a jumbled so they do not form a coherent whole objects are more difficult identify although their image properties are unchanged (Biederman, 1972). Similar work also suggests that performance for coherent scenes reaches ceiling with display times of 100 ms and greater, reducing differences between coherent and jumbled conditions (Biederman, Teitelbaum & Mezzanotte, 1983), and perhaps explaining why no effect of inversion was found in experiments 1 or 2.

7   General discussion

In the experiments reported the detection and location of faces did not appear to be qualitatively different from that for other objects. While faces were better located than random parts of the image this was also true for inverted faces and for upright and inverted kettles. It seems that we have a general ability to locate distinct "objects" in backgrounds. In the final experiment an advantage for upright faces was shown. However, this was not disproportionately disrupted by inversion, as might have been expected if face specific mechanisms were involved. Instead, the result suggests that the face may be a particularly effective stimulus for the human visual system. This would also explain how a face superiority effect could be found (Purcell & Stewart, 1988) in the absence of evidence for pop-out (Nothdurft, 1993) -- the face is an especially effective stimulus for detection but, as there do not appear to be specific detectors, you would still have to search for it in an array of distractors. The results of Experiments 3 and 4 suggest that the visual information that makes the face may be at relatively high spatial frequencies, detail within the face rather than an overall difference between the face and the rest of the scene. The results are somewhat difference to those that might be expected to be exhibited by many of the current automatic algorithms on this task (Sung & Poggio, 1994; Huang & Wang, 1994). In particular these, when trained on upright images, would not be expected to do as well on inverted images. Instead of template based approaches a search for easily distinctive, non orientation specific low level image properties characteristic of faces and other objects but not of backgrounds, probably at relatively high spatial frequencies, might be productive.

Acknowledgements. Many of the ideas and methods in this paper were developed in association with Roger Watt and Patricia Carlin. Vicki Bruce commented on an earlier draft.

References

Biederman, I (1972). Perceiving real world scenes. *Science*, **177**, 77-80.

Biederman, I., Mezzanotte, R.J. & Rabinowitz, J.C. (1982). Scene perception: Detecting and judging objects undergoing relational violations. *Cognitive Psychology*, **14**, 143-177.

Biederman, I, Rabinowitz, J.C., Glass, A.L. & Stacy, E. W. (1974). On the information extracted from a glance at a scene. *Journal of Experimental Psychology*, **103**, 597-600.

Costen, N.P., Parker, D.M. & Craw, I. (1996). Effects of high-pass and low-pass spatial-filtering on face identification. Perception & Psychophysics, **58**, 602-612.

Nothdurft, H. (1993). Faces and facial expressions do not pop out. *Perception*, **22**, 1287-1298.

Purcell, D.G. & Stewart, A.L. (1988). The face-detection effect: Configuration enhances detection. *Perception and Psychophysics,* **43**, 355-366.

Sung, K. & Poggio, T. (1994). Example-based learning for view-based human face detection. *Proceedings of the ARPA workshop '94*, II: 843-850.

Valentine, T. (1988). Upside-down faces: a review of the effects of inversion on face recognition. *British Journal of Psychology*, **61**, 471-491.

Yang, G. & Huang, T.S. (1994). Human face detection in a complex background. *Pattern Recognition*, **27**, 53-63.

Yin, R. (1969). Looking at upside-down faces. *Journal of Experimental Psychology,* **81**, 141-145.

Recognising People and Behaviours

A. Jonathan Howell and Hilary Buxton

School of Cognitive and Computing Sciences,
University of Sussex, Falmer, Brighton BN1 9QH, UK
{jonh,hilaryb}@cogs.susx.ac.uk

Abstract. Radial Basis Function (RBF) networks are compared with other neural network techniques on a face recognition task for applications involving identification of individuals using low resolution video information. The RBF networks have been shown to exhibit useful shift, scale and pose (y-axis rotation) invariance after training, when the input representation is made to mimic the receptive field functions found in early stages of the human vision system. Extensions of the techniques to the case of image sequence analysis are described and a Time Delay (TD) RBF network is used for recognising simple movement-based gestures. Finally, we discuss how these techniques can be used in real-life applications that require recognition of faces and gestures using low resolution video images.

1 Introduction

We are tackling the unconstrained face recognition problem and the main issue discussed in this paper is how a face can be effectively recognised once it has been localised in an image or image sequence. This problem of automatic face recognition has stimulated lively debate and research in computer vision for many years, but it is only recently that techniques have become sufficiently robust to allow useful application systems to be developed.

The real-life problems we want to solve are related to identifying individuals and their intentions in a domestic setting. The development of intelligent environments has been highlighted recently by the 'Smart Rooms' projects (Pentland, 1996) at the MIT Media Lab, which enable novel forms of interactive control for computer systems. Our particular focus is the role of adaptive learning techniques in recognising the individuals and simple movement-based gestures like head rotation. The unconstrained appearance of faces of individuals in the videoed scenes makes this a particularly difficult problem.

We know that recognising a face poses several severe tests for any visual system, such as the high degree of similarity between different faces, the great extent to which lighting conditions and expressions can alter the face, and the large number of different views from which a face can be seen. Indeed, variations in facial appearance due to lighting, pose and expression can be greater than those due to identity (Moses et al., 1994). However, there must be some sufficiently invariant set of features that allow us to recognise familiar faces. Our automated face recognition systems must be robust with respect to variability and generalise over a wide range of conditions to capture essential similarities in the views of a given individual. In our work, we use adaptive learning techniques to solve this problem of finding sets of invariant features for face classification. In addition, we use preprocessing schemes that can overcome the problem of lighting variation and multiple scales.

Our adaptive learning component is based on radial basis function (RBF) networks, which have been identified as valuable model by a wide range of researchers (Moody & Darken, 1988; Poggio & Girosi, 1990b; Girosi, 1992; Musavi et al., 1992; Ahmad & Tresp, 1993; Bishop, 1995). Their main advantages are computational simplicity and robust generalisation, supported by a well-developed mathematical theory. RBFs are seen as ideal for practical vision applications by (Girosi, 1992) as they are good at handling sparse, high-dimensional data and because they use approximation to handle noisy, real-life data. RBF networks are claimed to be more accurate classifiers than those based on Back-Propagation (BP), and they provide a guaranteed, globally optimal solution via simple, linear optimisation. For example, an RBF interpolating classifier (Edelman et al., 1992), was effective and gave performance error of only 5-9% on generalisation under changes of orientation, scale and lighting. This compares favourably with other state of the art systems such as the Turk and Pentland scheme (Pentland et al., 1994).

Cognitive studies of the way human faces are perceived can contribute to the design of systems that automate face recognition. There is evidence that we use some kind of "face recognition unit" (FRU) to recognise familiar faces (Bruce & Young, 1986; Bruce, 1988). In addition, primate vision systems seem to use view-based representations for recognition (Perrett & Oram, 1993). These ideas are partially captured by the standard RBF techniques described next where the first layer of the network maps the inputs with a hidden unit devoted to each view of the face to be classified. The second layer is then trained to combine the views so that a single output unit corresponds to the individual person.

In this paper, we first describe the RBF network model and then compare recent studies of neural network classification on the standard "Olivetti" database of faces. The RBF networks provide fast effective performance on this task. We then go on to test invariance when the pose, scale and shift is varied using input representations based on Difference of Gaussian (DoG) filtering and Gabor wavelet analysis. We extend the techniques to tackle image sequence data and use a Time-Delay RBF (TDRBF) network to recognise simple gestures. Finally, we discuss progress towards our target application of unconstrained face and gesture recognition from low resolution video data.

2 The RBF Network Model

We employed a Gaussian RBF network (Moody & Darken, 1988, 1989), which has a supervised layer from the hidden to the output units, and an unsupervised layer, from the input to the hidden units. Individual radial Gaussian functions for each hidden unit simulate the effect of overlapping and locally tuned receptive fields. This is applied to the vector norm distance, $|\mathbf{i} - \mathbf{c}|$ between the input vector **i** and hidden unit centre **c**. The output for the hidden layer is normalised (Moody & Darken, 1989; Hertz et al., 1991).

Each training example was assigned a corresponding hidden unit, the image vector is used as its centre, as seen in recent work by (Beymer & Poggio, 1996). This approach should not lead to overfitting because each image in the dataset contains unique 3-D information. Each hidden unit is given an associated σ width or scale value which defines the nature and scope of the unit's receptive field response; we use the mean Euclidean distance to all other units (Musavi et al., 1992). This gives an activation that is related to the relative proximity of the test data to the training data with a direct measure of confidence in the output of the network for a particular pattern. Patterns more than slightly different to those trained will produce very low (or no) output. The weights between the hidden and output layers are calculated using the matrix pseudo-inverse method (Poggio & Girosi, 1990a) which allows an almost instantaneous 'training' of the network, regardless of size.

A major advantage of the RBF over other network models, such as the multi-layer perceptron (MLP), is that a direct level of confidence is reflected in the level of each output unit. A discard measure was used on the tests to exclude low-confidence output; the proportion discarded and the subsequent generalisation rate are shown in the results. Low-confidence output was identified when the ratio between the highest and second highest outputs was below a certain value, i.e. the network exhibited "confusion" in the classification.

3 Comparing Face Recognition Techniques

The RBF network has been shown to provide robust classification even where data is noisy or partially missing (Ahmad & Tresp, 1993). Can this ability be used with complex 3-D objects such as faces, where the data varies in lighting, expression and pose?

We wanted to make sure that the RBF network could distinguish a useful number of classes to ensure that it would be a practical technique for future applications. A suitable source of data to test this is the Olivetti Research Laboratory (ORL) database of faces (available at `http://www.cam-orl.co.uk/facedatabase.html`). This contains 400 images of 40 people, greyscale at a resolution of 92×112. Variations allowed in the image included lighting, facial expressions (such as open or closed eyes and smiling or not smiling) and facial details (such as glasses or no glasses). All the images were taken against a plain background, with tilt and rotation up to $20°$, and scale variation up to 10%.

As this data has been used for a variety of face recognition techniques, it is possible to compare our results with other common approaches. Table 3.1 summarises the results from these papers, plus our own tests. Performance

Table 3.1. Test generalisation (% correct) and processing times for various face recognition techniques used by various researchers using ORL Face Database of 40 people, averaged over several selections.

Group	Technique	Images per Person					Processing Time	
		1	2	3	4	5	Training	Classification
Samaria	HMM	?	?	?	?	87	?	?
& Harter	pseudo 2-D HMM	?	?	?	?	95	?	4min
Lawrence	Eigenfaces	61	79	82	85	89	?	?
et al.	PCA + MLP	?	?	?	?	59	?	?
	SOM + MLP	?	?	?	?	60	?	?
	PCA + CN	66	83	87	88	92	?	?
	SOM + CN	70	83	88	93	96	4hr	<0.5sec
Lin *et al.*	PDBNN	?	?	?	?	96	20min	<0.1sec
Lucas	n-tuple	54	68	75	78	81	0.9sec	0.025sec
	cont n-tuple	73	84	90	93	95	0.9sec	0.33sec
	1-NN	?	?	?	?	97	0sec	1sec
Howell	RBF before discard	49	65	72	80	86	8sec	0.01sec
& Buxton	after discard	84	90	91	95	95	8sec	0.01sec

for systems with differing numbers of training images are given, together with times for the train and test (classification) stages (where available).

3.1 Results

Samaria initially used the ORL database, and used **Hidden Markov Models** (HMMs) to encode feature information (Samaria & Harter, 1994). This approach used several subjective parameter selections, and gave a top performance around 87% for a system trained with 200 images. Further work using pseudo 2-D HMMs was able to improve this to 95%, but the complexity of this approach seems to count this out as a useful real-time technique.

Two groups (Samaria & Harter, 1994; Lawrence et al., 1997) tested the ORL database with the **'eigenface'** (Kirby & Sirovich, 1990; Turk & Pentland, 1991) approach. Both report performance of around 90%, though the latter found that they could only get this by using separate training vectors for each image. This is in contrast to (Turk & Pentland, 1991), who averaged the eigenfaces for all images of each person in their tests. When tested with ORL data, this latter approach gave 74% for 5 training images per person (Lawrence et al., 1997). That this is much lower than the MIT results (where results over 90% are common) would seem to indicate that the ORL database represents a much harder task than the MIT face database (assuming the implementations were equivalent).

Lawrence et al. used a self-organising map (SOM) to reduce the dimensions of the input representation, and a five-layer **convolutional network**

(CN) to give translation and deformation invariance (Lawrence et al., 1997). This was faster than the previous HMM approach, but still required several hours training time. They compared the SOM's dimension-reducing abilities with PCA, and the CN with a multi-layer perceptron (MLP). This latter approach gave very poor results, especially when several hidden layers were used (Table 3.1 shows the best results from all combinations (which came from a MLP with one hidden layer) rather than average results (which are given for the other approaches from other groups).

A **probabilistic, decision-based neural network** (PDBNN) (Lin et al., 1997), a modular network structure with non-linear basis functions (each sub-network similar to a HyperBF (HBF) network (Poggio & Girosi, 1990b)) was able to train and classify much faster than the CN approach of (Lawrence et al., 1997), while reaching a similar level of performance.

The **continuous n-tuple classifier** (Lucas, 1997) has been able to train and classify quickly and provide a high level of performance. The figures shown are for tests with 200 3-tuples (600 values) per image. Using 500 4-tuples (2000 values) per image improved recognition to 86% and 97% for the n-tuple and continuous n-tuple classifier respectively.

Very high performance can even be obtained using a simple **1-nearest-neighbour** (1-NN) classifier (Lucas, 1997). The success of simple matching indicates how constrained the database is in terms of lighting and pose, as such techniques will not be invariant to such factors.

To use the ORL data with the **RBF network**, we subsampled each image to 25×25 and applied 'A3' Gabor filter preprocessing (Howell & Buxton, 1995). A simple discard measure, based on the relative magnitudes of the output units, was used to remove low confidence classifications (these being those where the highest output value was less than a certain ratio below the next highest).

The RBF network approach was fast in training and the fastest in classification of all the published techniques. Our experiments were conducted on a moderately fast Sun SPARC 20 workstation. Test generalisation before discard was fairly poor in comparison to the other approaches, though the results were well above random (2.5%). For 5 training examples per person, discarding 39% of results allowed performance to be improved from 84% to 95%, which was comparable with the best of the other techniques. The results after discard for the RBF network were especially good where lower numbers of training examples per person were provided.

3.2 Discussion

Table 3.1 shows that although, in pure generalisation terms, the RBF is not the overall top performer, it does have a sufficient level of performance (95% after discard) for our target application where it will have to deal with image sequences. In this type of application, training data is relatively sparse (compared to the large range of variation in real-life images) and test data is abundant. The success of the RBF discard measure, which makes it the best approach where low numbers of training examples are available, indicates its suitability for image sequence applications. Although discarding does reduce the number of useful classifications, a significant amount of data remains in images sequences (see Sect. 5).

A particularly important point is that most other face recognition techniques took much longer than the RBF network in the training and testing of data. It is apparent that the RBF network provides a solution which can process test images in inter-frame periods on low-cost processors. The rest of this paper will be concerned with how to apply this network to our target application of identity recognition in unconstrained domestic environments.

4 Learning Invariance

Having established the RBF network as a suitable technique for our unconstrained face recognition task, we investigated its invariance characteristics. How well can the RBF network learn identity, especially where the pose varies? For instance, can profile images, where eye information from the far side of the face is occluded, be generalised to front views? We also look at how 2-D shift and scale variations in the image affect this process. Our invariance experiments used the 'Sussex Database' (Howell & Buxton, 1996a), designed to test recognition abilities for faces in widely varying poses. The database has ten images of ten individuals showing the head and shoulders and taken in 10° steps from face-on to profile of the left side, 90° in all.

The results showed that not only can the RBF network learn identity in spite of pose variations, but it can continue to be invariant to pose in the presence of other variations. In addition, it can learn an invariance to scale variation more easily than shift as shown by both the better classification performance and the lower discard rates. The training data for these tests provided examples of the variations we want the network to learn. We were able to show that the RBF network, especially with the Gabor preprocessing, has good scale invariance even without this type of explicit training. This is a very useful property, as it reduces the total number of training examples required.

5 The RBF Network with Image Sequences

We have been able to show that the RBF network can learn to be invariant to certain types of variations that can be expected in real-life face images. We would also like to be able to use these abilities in a less constrained environment using image sequences. As mentioned before, we are computationally constrained to the inter-frame period determined by the frame grabber and the localisation software. Offsetting this limitation is the enormous abundance of data from image sequences, which suits any technique that can discard low-confidence output to leave a high ratio of correct classifications. In the context of videos of people moving around a room, which produces large numbers of images of each person in the environment, even high discard ratios of 80-90% are acceptable if the remaining output is of sufficiently high quality. We were able to collect suitable image sequences as a result of collaboration with Stephen McKenna and Shaogang Gong at Queen Mary and Westfield College, London, who are researching real-time face detection and tracking (McKenna et al., 1996).

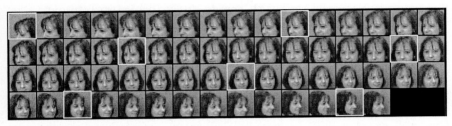

Fig. 5.1. A complete image sequence, after segmentation but before preprocessing (boxes indicate frames used for training: selection interval=10).

The sequence database is still under development, but encouraging results have been collected from preliminary experiments (Howell & Buxton, 1996b) where the RBF network is trained with the Primary sequences and tested with the provisional Secondary sequence. The investigation of the adaptive learning component with the real-time face tracker developed by QMW (McKenna et al., 1996) is an important component.

We are currently working on a 'time window' integration level with the raw output. As we are using image sequences from real life, where individuals will be present for significant periods, it is appropriate to use techniques which take advantage of temporal coherence can be used to improve performance. The idea here is that periods of low confidence output can be "patched" into a coherent stream by some kind of moving average rather than a full belief-based mechanism, for example (Buxton & Gong, 1995).

6 The RBF Network and Temporal Behaviour

To extend the investigation into temporal learning, we then asked whether the RBF could learn actions through time? To answer this, we treated our original 100-image database as 10 image sequences of a person rotating their head from side to side. We trained the network to distinguish the presence and direction of movement in simple fixed sequences.

We adapted our network model to use time-delays in order to process temporal context. This Time-Delay version of the RBF (TDRBF) network is similar to that used by Berthold (1994) for speech recognition and combines data from a fixed time 'window' into a single vector as input, details in

Howell and Buxton (1997). Berthold, however took a constructive approach, combining the idea of a sliding input window from the standard TDNN network with a training procedure for adding and adjusting RBF units when required. We have used a simpler technique, successful in previous work with RBF networks, which uses a fixed number of units, one for each example, and the pseudo-inverse process to calculate weights, as discussed above.

The network was trained with sequences of images from five people and tested with sequences of images from the other five people, so that generalisation will reflect learning of the temporal task rather than identity.

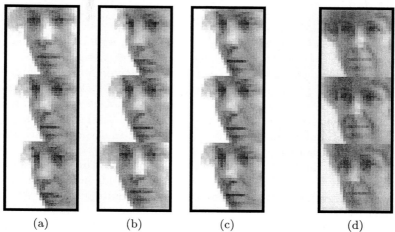

(a)   (b)   (c)   (d)

Fig. 6.1. Example image sequences of three side to side head rotations used for training the RBF network (time window of 3 frames): (a) LR training (frames 2, 3 and 4) (b) RL training (frames 4, 3 and 2) (c) Static training (frame 3 repeated) (d) LR test (frames 2, 3 and 4 of different person).

Three types of rotation sequence were created. 1) **LR sequences** simulate a left to right head rotation, and are taken from a 'window' from all ten frames of five people, as shown in Fig. 6.1(a). 2) **RL sequences** are identical to LR, except with the reverse rotation, as shown in Fig. 6.1(b). 3) **Static sequences** simulate a fixed head position through time, illustrated by Fig. 6.1(c).

Table 6.1 shows that the TDRBF network can learn the different types of movement and generalise with sequences from individuals not encountered during training. The mid-length time window gave the best generalisation performance and lowest discard proportions.

6.1 Discussion

The temporal task we used is very simplistic, as each image sequence only contains one standard-length movement. We have tested our trained network

Table 6.1. Effect of time window size on generalisation for a TDRBF network in a 3 class problem, distinguishing LR, RL and static sequences. The test sequences contain people not seen during training.

Time Window	Initial %	% Discarded	% after Discard
10	87	20	100
8	89	13	100
6	83	21	100
4	77	37	100
2	63	56	93

on a less constrained sequence, similiar to Fig. 5.1, with some success. It is difficult to assess the performance using such data at present, as it is not yet clear how real-life behaviours will need to be segmented for meaningful analysis. Most human gestures consist of combinations of movements of several part of the body. To make things harder, these are not necessarily in unison, but choreographed with each other at specific times. To signal that a specific gesture has occured recognition will have to occur over time, linking output from multiple recognisers.

The issue of the *time base* of actions, i.e. how fast or slow actions occur, would have to be taken into account in any real-life image sequences, as any movement would occur at a variety of speeds quite naturally. Although (Berthold, 1994) used the integration layer to cope with shifts in time, the scale (time base) of events was not discussed. This type of variation can be handled by a recurrent network, or by training data which explicitly demonstrated the different classes of motion-based behaviour at a variety of speeds.

7 Conclusions

In Sections 1 and 2, we described the background to our investigations of the role of adaptive learning in face recognition. In section 3, we showed that Radial Basis Function (RBF) networks performed well on the ORL comparison face recognition task, delivering both fast training and exceptionally rapid classification times. We were able to obtain 95% correct classification after training on half the views if a simple confidence metric is included. This is comparable with other state of the art techniques.

In Section 4, we briefly discussed the invariance capabilities of the RBF networks with variations in pose, translation (shift) and scale. In Section 5, we briefly outlined the extensions required to tackle real-time video from a general purpose motion tracker.

In Section 6, we considered extensions to simple motion-based behaviour and our preliminary results seem very promising. The main points here are 1) the simple, deterministic 'training' of the TDRBF networks means that they are highly suited to on-line learning, 2) the shift invariance and ability to recognise features in time means they are capable of recognising simple behaviours, and 3) high levels of performance on the generalisation to new datasets that behave in similar ways means they are very useful for such practical dynamic vision tasks. The limitations of this technique are 1) the problem of the time-base which was not fully overcome even with the addition of an integration layer, and 2) the problem of defining the simple behaviours. The TDRBF networks are capable of distinguishing a 'quick turn' from a 'slow turn' as well as distinguishing whether the turn was to the right or the left, but it seems that more qualitative definitions of behaviour would best be tackled using more general recurrent networks. This issue is discussed further by (Mozer, 1994) and by (Psarrou & Buxton, 1994). It is clear, however, that the TDRBF networks are able to perform extremely well where there is a straightforward quantitative relationship between the data and the simple behavioural pattern to be learnt.

Future work will concentrate on the integration of the face tracking mechanism with the adaptive learning techniques discussed in this paper to progress to a full prototype system and extend to more general gestural and behavioural analysis (Bobick, 1996; Nagaya et al., 1996). The key capability here is face and gesture recognition from low-resolution video sequences where there is a small set of known users. This seems to be a realistic goal if we use RBF techniques combined with good image representations as discussed in the main sections of this and the accompanying papers we have cited. It also clearly has great commercial potential for use in many interactive systems as well as in security and monitoring applications.

References

Ahmad, S., & Tresp, V. (1993). Some solutions to the missing feature problem in vision. In Hanson, S. J., Cowan, J. D., & Giles, C. L. (Eds.), *Advances in Neural Information Processing Systems*, Vol. 5, pp. 393–400 San Mateo, CA. Morgan Kaufmann.

Berthold, M. R. (1994). A time delay radial basis function network for phoneme recognition. In *Proceedings of IEEE International Conference on Neural Networks*, Vol. 7, pp. 4470–4473 Orlando, FL. IEEE Computer Society Press.

Beymer, D. J., & Poggio, T. (1996). Image representations for visual learning. *Science*, *272*, 1905–1909.

Bishop, C. M. (1995). *Neural Networks for Pattern Recognition*. Oxford University Press, Oxford, UK.

Bobick, A. F. (1996). Computers seeing action. In Fisher, R. B., & Trucco, E. (Eds.), *Proceedings of British Machine Vision Conference*, pp. 13–22 Edinburgh. BMVA Press.

Bruce, V. (1988). *Recognising Faces*. Lawrence Erlbaum Associates, London.

Bruce, V., & Young, A. (1986). Understanding face recognition. *British Journal of Psychology, 77*, 305–327.

Buxton, H., & Gong, S. (1995). Advanced visual surveillance using Bayesian nets. In Mundy, J. L., & Strat, T. (Eds.), *Proceedings of IEEE Workshop on Context-Based Vision, International Conference on Computer Vision* Cambridge, MA. IEEE Computer Society Press.

Edelman, S., Reisfeld, D., & Yeshurun, Y. (1992). Learning to recognize faces from examples. In Sandini, G. (Ed.), *Proceedings of European Conference on Computer Vision, Lecture Notes in Computer Science,* Vol. 588, pp. 787–791 Santa Margherita Ligure, Italy. Springer-Verlag.

Girosi, F. (1992). Some extensions of radial basis functions and their applications in artificial intelligence. *Computers & Mathematics with Applications, 24*(12), 61–80.

Hertz, J. A., Krogh, A., & Palmer, R. G. (1991). *Introduction to the Theory of Neural Computation.* Addison-Wesley, Redwood City CA.

Howell, A. J., & Buxton, H. (1995). Receptive field functions for face recognition. In *Proceedings of 2nd International Workshop on Parallel Modelling of Neural Operators for Pattern Recognition*, pp. 83–92 Faro, Portugal. University of Algarve.

Howell, A. J., & Buxton, H. (1996a). Face recognition using radial basis function neural networks. In Fisher, R. B., & Trucco, E. (Eds.), *Proceedings of British Machine Vision Conference*, pp. 455–464 Edinburgh. BMVA Press.

Howell, A. J., & Buxton, H. (1996b). Towards unconstrained face recognition from image sequences. In *Proceedings of International Conference on Automatic Face & Gesture Recognition*, pp. 224–229 Killington, VT. IEEE Computer Society Press.

Howell, A. J., & Buxton, H. (1997). Recognising simple behaviours using time-delay RBF networks. *Neural Processing Letters, 5*, 97–104.

Kirby, M., & Sirovich, L. (1990). Application of the Karhunen-Loève procedure for the characterization of human faces. *IEEE Transactions on Pattern Analysis & Machine Intelligence, 12*, 103–108.

Lawrence, S., Giles, C. L., Tsoi, A. C., & Back, A. D. (1997). Face recognition: A convolutional neural network approach. *IEEE Transactions on Neural Networks, 8*, 98–113.

Lin, S.-H., Kung, S.-Y., & Lin, L.-J. (1997). Face recognition/detection by probabilistic decision-based neural network. *IEEE Transactions on Neural Networks, 8*, 114–132.

Lucas, S. M. (1997). Face recognition with the continuous n-tuple classifier. In Clark, A. F. (Ed.), *Proceedings of British Machine Vision Conference*, pp. 222–231 Colchester, UK. BMVA Press.

McKenna, S., Gong, S., & Collins, J. J. (1996). Face tracking and pose representation. In Fisher, R. B., & Trucco, E. (Eds.), *Proceedings of*

British Machine Vision Conference, pp. 755–764 Edinburgh. BMVA Press.

Moody, J., & Darken, C. (1988). Learning with localized receptive fields. In Touretzky, D., Hinton, G., & Sejnowski, T. (Eds.), *Proceedings of 1988 Connectionist Models Summer School*, pp. 133–143 Pittsburgh, PA. Morgan Kaufmann.

Moody, J., & Darken, C. (1989). Fast learning in networks of locally-tuned processing units. *Neural Computation*, *1*, 281–294.

Moses, Y., Adini, Y., & Ullman, S. (1994). Face recognition: the problem of compensating for illumination changes. In Eklundh, J. O. (Ed.), *Proceedings of European Conference on Computer Vision, Lecture Notes in Computer Science*, Vol. 800, pp. 286–296 Stockholm, Sweden. Springer-Verlag.

Mozer, M. C. (1994). Neural net architectures for temporal sequence processing. In Weigend, A. S., & Gershenfeld, N. A. (Eds.), *Time Series Prediction: Predicting the Future and Understanding the Past*, pp. 243–264. Addison-Wesley, Redwood City, CA.

Musavi, M. T., Ahmad, W., Chan, K. H., Faris, K. B., & Hummels, D. M. (1992). On the training of radial basis function classifiers. *Neural Networks*, *5*, 595–603.

Nagaya, S., Seki, S., & Oka, R. (1996). A theoretical consideration of pattern space trajectory for gesture spotting recognition. In *Proceedings of International Conference on Automatic Face & Gesture Recognition*, pp. 72–77 Killington, VT. IEEE Computer Society Press.

Pentland, A. (1996). Smart rooms. *Scientific American*, *274*(4), 68–76.

Pentland, A., Moghaddam, B., & Starner, T. (1994). View-based and modular eigenspaces for face recognition. In *Proceedings of IEEE Conference on Computer Vision & Pattern Recognition*, pp. 84–91 Seattle, WA. IEEE Computer Society Press.

Perrett, D. I., & Oram, M. W. (1993). Neurophysiology of shape processing. *Image & Vision Computing*, *11*, 317–333.

Poggio, T., & Girosi, F. (1990a). Networks for approximation and learning. In *Proceedings of IEEE*, Vol. 78, pp. 1481–1497.

Poggio, T., & Girosi, F. (1990b). Regularization algorithms for learning that are equivalent to multilayer networks. *Science*, *247*, 978–982.

Psarrou, A., & Buxton, H. (1994). Motion analysis with recurrent neural nets. In *Proceedings of International Conference on Artificial Neural Networks*, pp. 54–57 Sorrento, Italy. Springer-Verlag.

Samaria, F. S., & Harter, A. C. (1994). Parameterisation of a stochastic model for human face identification. In *Proceedings of 2nd IEEE Workshop on Applications of Computer Vision* Sarasota, FL.

Turk, M., & Pentland, A. (1991). Eigenfaces for recognition. *Journal of Cognitive Neuroscience*, *3*, 71–86.

Differences of Face and Object Recognition in Utilizing Early Visual Information

Peter Kalocsai and Irving Biederman

Department of Psychology and Computer Science
University of Southern California
Los Angeles, California 90089, U.S.A.
{kalocsai, ib}@selforg.usc.edu

Abstract. The first cortical stage in both object and face recognition by humans is generally presumed to be a filtering of the image by cells which can be approximated as oriented spatial frequency kernels. Are the outputs of these filters mapped in the same manner to the separate patches of tissue in extrastriate cortex presumed to code faces and objects? Complementary images of objects and faces were produced by dividing the Fourier spectrum of each image into 8 frequency bands and 8 orientation bands. In the inverse Fourier transform, half the 8 x 8 values (analogous to all the red squares of a checkerboard in a row by column representation of frequency and orientation) were contained in one member of a complementary image pair and the remaining combinations of values (e.g., black squares) were contained in the other member. In a naming task original and complementary images produced equivalent priming (equal RTs and error rates) for objects, but name verification for famous faces showed less priming for the complementary image. One possible explanation for these results is that faces are represented as a direct mapping of the outputs of early filter values whereas objects are recognized by means of intermediate primitives (e.g., parts), in which the same primitives can be activated by many patterns of filter activations. Two additional experiments using nonface but highly similar shaped objects (chairs) and unfamiliar faces confirmed the above hypothesis.

Keywords. Face recognition, object recognition, complementary pairs, Fourier filtering

1 Introduction

Four experiments will be described which were designed to assess whether the identification or matching of faces and objects would be directly dependent on the early spatial filter representation (V1) of the visual system. There is considerable evidence in the literature that the priming of objects cannot be dependent on a representation that retained the similarity space of the activation values of spatial filters (Fiser, Biederman, & Cooper, 1997). For example, if contour is deleted from a line drawing of an object so that the geons cannot be recovered from the image, recognition becomes impossible (Biederman, 1987). The same amount of contour deletion, when it permits recovery of the geons, allows ready recognition. Fiser et al showed that the Lades et al. (1993) model recognized the two kinds of stimuli equally well. Similarly, the Lades et al. (1993) model failed to capture the differences in matching objects that did or did not differ in a NAP in the Cooper and Biederman (1993) experiment.

Biederman and Cooper (1991) showed that members of a complementary pair of object images in which every other line and vertex was deleted from each part (so that each image had 50% of the original contour) primed each other as well as they primed themselves. The measure of priming was the reduction in the naming reaction times and error rates from the first to the second brief exposure of an object picture. The priming was visual, and not just verbal or conceptual, because there was much less priming to an object that had the same name but a different shape (e.g., two different shaped chairs). In this case, humans treated the members of a complementary pair as equivalent although the two members would have different spatial filter activation patterns (Fiser, Biederman, & Cooper, 1997).

To test whether faces retain and objects do not retain the original spatial filter activation pattern, the first two experiments employed a similar design comparing the magnitude of priming of identical to complementary images. Rather than deletion of lines as in the Biederman and Cooper experiment, complementary pairs of gray-level images of objects and faces of celebrities were created by having every other Fourier component (8 scales X 8 orientations) in one member and the remaining 32 components in the other, as illustrated in Fig. 1[1].

2 Object naming experiment

Subjects named pictures of common objects on two blocks of trials (Exp. I). On the second block, for each object viewed on the first block, subjects would see either the identical filtered image that was shown on the first block, its spatial complement, or a different shaped exemplar with the same name, as illustrated in Fig. 2. The results of this experiment are shown in Fig. 3. Visual priming was evidenced on the second block of trials because the same shaped object was named more quickly and accurately that an image with the same name but a different shape. However, naming RTs and error rates for identical and complementary images were virtually equivalent, indicating that there was no contribution of the original Fourier components compared to their complements to the magnitude of visual priming.

---

[1] Complementary image pairs were created by the following procedure: 8-bit gray scale images were Fourier transformed and bandpassed filtered cutting off the highest (above 181 cycles/image) and lowest (below 12 cycles/image) spatial frequencies. The remaining part of the Fourier domain was divided into 64 areas (8 orientations x 8 spatial frequencies). The orientation borders of the Fourier spectrum were set up in succession of 22.5 degrees. The spatial frequency range covered 4 octaves in step of 0.5 octaves. By this operation the two complementary images had no common information about the objects in the Fourier domain.

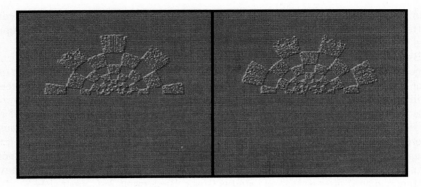

Fig. 1. Illustration of how the 8 scales X 8 orientations were distributed to the members of a complementary pair. If arranged as a checkerboard with rows the spatial frequencies and the columns the orientations, one image would have the specific scale-orientation values of the red squares, the other member the values of the black squares. Here the checkerboard is shown as two half radial grids, with scale varying with distance from the origin (low to high SF and orientation varying as shown. (The lower half would continue the upper half.)

◄— **Complements** —►

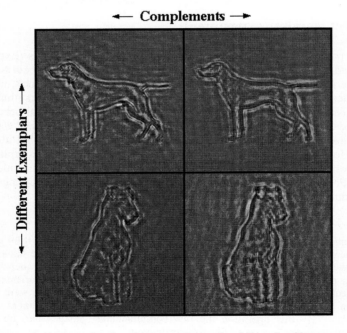

↑ **Different Exemplars** ↓

Fig. 2. Example images for the object naming task of Exp. I. Shown are the four images (2 exemplars X 2 complements) created for the entry level object "dog." In the priming paradigm one of the four images was displayed on the first block of trials and either the identical image, its complementary pair or a different exemplar image was displayed on the second block of trials.

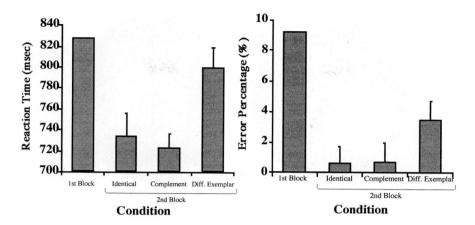

Fig. 3. Mean correct naming RTs and mean error rates for the object naming task of Exp. I. The second block data are for those trials where the object was correctly named on the first block. The second block data are for those trials where the object was correctly named on the first block.

3 Face verification experiment

Experiment II (face verification) employed the general priming design of Exp. I except now the stimuli were images of famous people and subjects verified rather than named the images. Before each trial the subject was given the name of a famous person. If the image was that person the subjects were to respond 'same'. On half the trials the picture did not correspond to the target. In these cases the picture was a face of the same general age, sex, and race as the target and the subjects were to respond 'different'. The verification task was used, rather than a naming task, because the naming of faces is slow and error prone. As in experiment I, two pictures with the same name but a different shape (differences in pose, expression, orientation, etc.), as illustrated in Fig. 4, were used to assess that the priming would be visual and not just verbal or conceptual. As in experiment I, for the 'same' trials on the second block, for each face viewed on the first block, subjects would see either the identical image, its complement or the different image of the same person as illustrated in Fig. 5. In contrast to the result for object naming, in this experiment complementary images were verified significantly more slowly and less accurately than those in the identical condition, as shown in Fig. 6. The difference between the complementary and the different exemplar faces was not significant, indicating that the visual system represented complementary face images almost as differently from the original as it did the different exemplar images. This result indicates that the representation of a face, unlike that of an object, is specific to the original filter values.

Fig. 4. Example of two original gray level images of a famous person (O. J. Simpson). illustrating differences in expression and pose used in the face verification task of Exp. II. The images were collected such that the expression and/or the orientation of the two face images of a person were different.

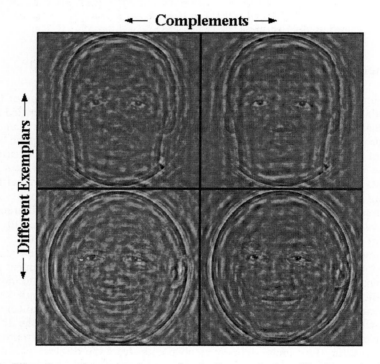

Fig. 5. Filtered complementary images for the famous face verification task of Exp. II. Shown are the four images (2 exemplars x 2 complements) created for the images of O. J. Simpson' shown in Fig. 12. In the priming paradigm one of the four images was displayed on the first block of trials and either the identical image, its complementary pair, or a different exemplar image was displayed on the second block of trials.

← Complements →

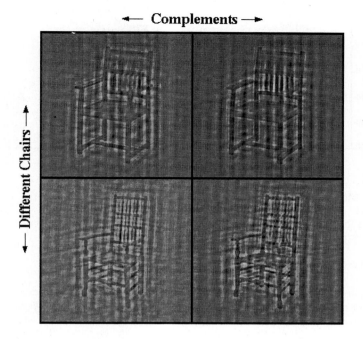

Fig. 7. Same images for the chair matching task of Exp. III. Shown are the four images (2 exemplars X 2 complements) created for two chair images from the stimuli set.

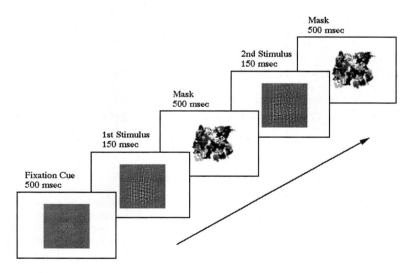

Fig. 8. Sequence of images presented in the chair matching task of Exp. III. The correct response to this sequence is 'same' because both pictures are of the same chair, though different members of a complementary pair.

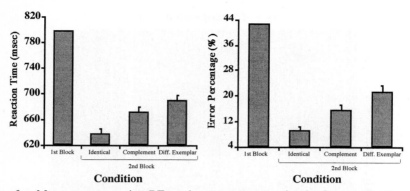

Fig. 6. Mean correct naming RTs and mean error rates for the face verification task of Exp. II. The second block data are for those trials where the object was correctly named on the first block. The second block data are for those trials where the face was correctly verified on the first block.

4 Same-different judgment of chairs and faces

One possible explanation for the above results is what we have been positing: Face representations preserve the activation pattern of early filter values, whereas object representations do not. Alternatively it could be that it is the necessity for distinguishing among highly similar entities, such as faces, that produces a dependence on the original early filter outputs. Two additional experiments were conducted to assess whether the dependence on the precise filter values were a consequence of the greater similarity of the face stimuli (or the verification task, itself) as opposed to being a phenomenon specific to the representation of faces. In these experiments, subjects viewed a sequence of two highly similar chairs (Experiment III, Figures 7 and 8 or two highly similar faces (Experiment IV) (Fig. 9). Subjects performed a same-different matching task in which they judged, 'same' or 'different,' whether the two chairs or persons were the same, ignoring whether the image was identical or complementary. The mean similarity of the complementary pairs of faces and objects were approximately equivalent as was the mean similarity of target and distractor faces and objects as assessed by the Lades et al. (1993) model[2] (Table 1). In both experiments III and IV, on half the same trials the second presented image was identical to the first and in the other half the trials it was the complementary image.

---

[2] A recent study (Subramaniam, Biederman & Kalocsai, 1997) provides strong documentation that the Lades et al. (1993) system can provide an a priori measure of shape similarity when the pairs of shapes only differ in metric properties. In a same-different sequential matching task, subjects judged whether two highly similar, blobby, asymmetric toroidal free-form shapes were identical or not. A family of 81 such shapes had been generated by Shepard and Cermack (1973). On different trials the shapes varied in similarity as assessed by the Malsburg system. For intermediate to highly similar shapes, RTs and error rates in judging that two shapes were different correlated .95 with the Malsburg similarity measure.

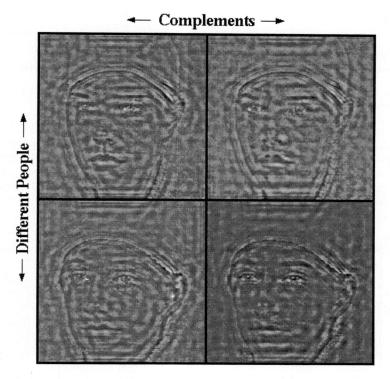

Fig. 9. Example images (from the Faces I set) for the unfamiliar face matching task of Exp. IV. Shown are the four images (2 exemplars x 2 complements) created for two face images from the stimuli set.

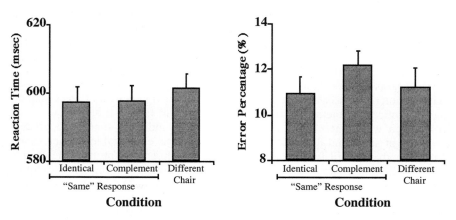

Fig. 10. Mean correct RTs and mean error rates for the chair matching task of Exp. III.

	Chairs	Faces I	Faces II
Complements	.73	.75	.78
Different ("No" trials)	.75	.76	.78

Table 1. Average similarity for stimuli in the three same-different judgment experiments (1.0 similarity would indicate perfect match).

Performance on identical and complementary chair images on same trials was virtually identical, as shown in Fig. 10, indicating that there was no effect of changing the specific spatial components of the chair images. However, for faces the complementary images were significantly more difficult to match than identical ones (Fig. 11), indicating a strong contribution of the specific spatial components in the image.

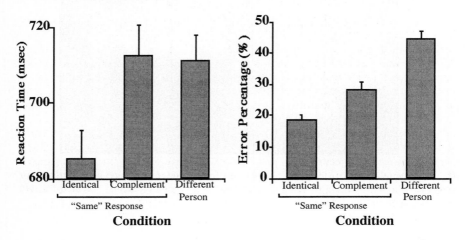

Fig. 11. Mean correct RTs and mean error rates for the unfamiliar face matching task of Exp. IV.

However, as Figures 10 and 11 shows subject made significantly more errors and their reaction time was also slower on the same-different judgment of faces than of chairs. Notice that the error percentage for Different Person trials was close to 50% which would be chance performance. This indicates that although the similarity of same and different chairs and faces was comparable to each other (Table) subjects still found the face judgment task a much more difficult one which could have altered the result. In order to test this possibility an additional experiment was run with a new set of face images (Faces II) with the purpose of making the same-different judgment of faces an easier task. As Fig. 12 indicates subject were faster and also made less error on this face judgment task compared to the previous one, but the difference between performance on the Identical and Complement conditions remained constant showing that the observed effect can not be contributed to the difficulty of the task.

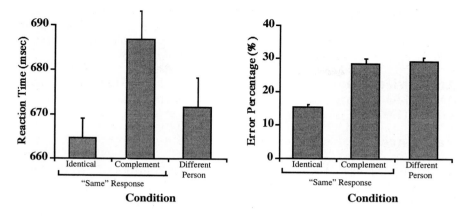

Fig. 12. Mean correct RTs and mean error rates for the unfamiliar face matching task of Exp. IV (version 2).

In summary this set of experiments showed equivalent priming and matching performance for identical and complementary images of objects. However, faces revealed a striking dependence on the original filter values. There was virtually no visual priming across members of a complementary pair of faces and face complements were far more difficult to match than identical images. These results indicate that faces are represented as a more direct mapping of the outputs of early filter values. One likely reason why the objects were unaffected by varying the filter values is that object representations employ nonaccidental characterization of parts or geons based on edges at depth or orientation discontinuities. Different spatial filter patterns can activate the same units coding edges, nonaccidental characteristics, part structures, and relations, as discussed by Hummel and Biederman (1992).

5 Conclusion

A series of experiments demonstrated that the recognition or matching of objects is largely independent of the particular spatial filter components in the image whereas the recognition or matching of a face is closely tied to these initial filter values. These results reveal crucial differences in the behavioral and neural phenomena associated with the recognition of faces and objects. Readily recognizable objects can typically be represented in terms of a geon structural description which specifies an arrangement of viewpoint invariant parts based on a nonaccidental characterization of edges at orientation and depth discontinuities. The parts and relations are determined in intermediate layers between the early array of spatially distributed filters and the object itself and they confer a degree of independence between the initial wavelet components and the representation. Individuation of faces, by contrast, requires specification of the fine metric variation in a holistic representation of a facial surface. This can be achieved by storing the pattern of activation over a set of spatially distributed filters. Such a representation would also evidence many of the phenomena associated with face recognition such as holistic effects, unverbalizability, and great susceptibility to metric variations of the face surface, as well as to image variables such as rotation in depth or the plane, contrast reversal, and direction of lighting.

Acknowledgements This research was supported by ARO NVESD grant DAAH04-94-G-0065. Parts of this paper are excerpted from Biederman and Kalocsai (1997).

References

Biederman, I. (1987). Recognition-by-components: A theory of human image understanding. *Psychological Review, 94,* 115-147.

Biederman, I. & Cooper, E. E. (1991). Priming contour-deleted images: Evidence for intermediate representations in visual object recognition. *Cognitive Psychology, 23,* 393-419.

Biederman, I., & Kalocsai, P. (1997). Neurocomputational bases of object and face recognition. *Philosophical Transactions of the Royal Society of London B*, 352, 1203-1219.

Cooper, E. E., & Biederman, I. (1993). Metric versus viewpoint-invariant shape differences in visual object recognition. *Investigative Ophthalmology & Visual Science*, 34, 1080.

Fiser, J., Biederman, I., & Cooper, E. E. (1997). To what extent can matching algorithms based on direct outputs of spatial filters account for human shape recognition? *Spatial Vision*, 10, 237-271.

Hummel, J. E., & Biederman, I. (1992). Dynamic binding in a neural network for shape recognition. *Psychological Review*, 99, 480-517.

Lades, M., Vortbrüggen, J. C., Buhmann, J., Lange, J., von der Malsburg, C., Würtz, R. P., & Konen, W. (1993). Distortion Invariant Object Recognition in the Dynamic Link Architecture. *IEEE Transactions on Computers, 42,* 300-311.

Shepard, R. N., & Cermak, G. W. (1973). Perceptual-cognitive explorations of a toroidal set of free-from stimuli. *Cognitive Psychology*, 4, 351-377.

Subramaniam, S., Biederman, I., & Kalocsai, P. (1997). Predicting nonsense shape similarity from a V1 similarity space. Unpublished ms., University of Southern California.

Pulse Images for Face Recognition

Jason M. Kinser

Institute for Biosciences, Bioinformatics, and Biotechnology, George Mason University, Fairfax, VA 22030-4444

Abstract. Recent advances in the understanding of the visual cortex of small mammals have led to new image segmentation procedures. These processes create a set of pulse images for a static input. These processes contain higher-order neurons that communicate through autowaves. For multi-channel images, such as RGB face images, the autowaves are allowed to cross channels and create a set of multi-channel pulse images. The inherent segmentation of these pulse images allows for easy location of the eyes and automated feature selection to create a lattice structure for face image processing.

Keywords. Pulse-Coupled Neural Network, Pulse Images, segmentation, image fusion

1 Introduction

Pulse image technology is based upon knowledge of the visual cortex of small mammals. For a static input a pulse image generator will create a series of pulse images in which all of the elements of the output images are binary. The useful quality of pulse images is that the generators inherently segment the input image. Thus, for a given input the objects in that input will appear as solid segments in one of the pulse images.

Face image processing can benefit from this quality of image segmentation. For example, two of the tasks that are useful in face image processing are to locate the eyes and to create a lattice structure based upon the standard features of the face. The location of the eyes is one of the first tasks for almost all face recognition algorithms. While the lattice construction is necessary for operations such as morphing.

Since the concept of pulse images is still relatively new the theory of pulse image generation will be reviewed towards its application to face image processing. Then a few examples will be presented. It should be noted that the pulse image generator is a non-training system. Therefore, it is not a recognition engine. However, due to its inherent segmentation ability it can greatly improve the performance of other recognition systems.

2. Pulse Image Theory

Pulse image generation is based upon recent models of the visual cortex. The most influential is the model of the cat visual cortex presented by Eckhorn [1990]. Other models that behave similarly have been presented by Gray *et al.* [1990], Rybak *et al.*[1992], and Parodi *et al.*[1996]. The accuracy to which the models replicate the cortex is of little importance here. The concern here is merely the application of a useful algorithm.

2.1 The Biological Foundation

The model of the visual cortex consists of two major input compartments, a higher order combination of their results and the comparison of these results to a dynamic threshold. A simple model is shown in Fig. 1. The Feed and the Link are the stimulating compartments (with only the Feed receiving an outside stimulus). They are combined and compared to a dynamic threshold to generate a binary output.

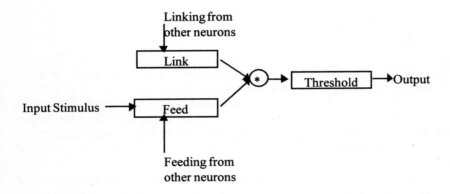

Fig. 1. Logical flow of the cortical model.

2.2 The Pulse Coupled Neural Network

The particular model used here is a popularization of Eckhorn's model known as the PCNN (Pulse Coupled Neural Network) [Johnson,1994].

2.2.1 PCNN Theory

This model stimulates the system with **S** and proceeds to iteratively compute the Feed, **F**, the Link, **L**, the internal activity, **U**, the pulse output, **Y**, and finally the dynamic threshold, Θ. The operations are described by,

$$F_{ij}[n] = e^{-\alpha_F \Delta t} F_{ij}[n-1] + S_{ij} + V_F \sum_{kl} M_{ijkl} Y_{kl}[n-1] \tag{1}$$

$$L_{ij}[n] = e^{-\alpha_L \Delta t} L_{ij}[n-1] + V_L \sum_{kl} W_{ijkl} Y_{kl}[n-1] \tag{2}$$

$$U_{ij}[n] = F_{ij}[n]\left(1 + \beta L_{ij}[n]\right) \tag{3}$$

$$Y_{ij}[n] = \begin{cases} 1 & if \ U_{ij}(t) > \Theta_{ij}[n] \\ 0 & Otherwise \end{cases} \tag{4}$$

$$\Theta_{ij}[n] = e^{-\alpha_\Theta \Delta t} \Theta_{ij}[n-1] + V_\Theta Y_{ij}[n] + \Theta_0 \ , \tag{5}$$

where β is the linking strength and V_Θ is a large value compared to V_F and V_L.

2.2.2 An Example

This system receives an image stimulus and iteratively generates pulse output images. The image in Fig. 2 is an example input image. Figs. 3 displays a few of the outputs generated by the PCNN.

In the output images segments of the original image can be seen. In this particular example the intent was to isolate the face to make it easier for a system to locate the face. It is far easier to locate the face in either of the two pulse images than in the original image. Most image recognition systems rely on the frequency components of the image. The face in Fig. 3a is quite solid in the interior (no noisy deletions) and its edges are crisp. This means that the information of the face will be widely spread in the frequency space compared to that of the original image.

Fig. 2. An original input image.

Figs. 3. Two outputs from the PCNN.

The second pulse image shows sharp edge outline of the face. For the task of finding a generic face within a scene this image is not as useful as its predecessor. However, it would be useful for purposes of discrimination. This could be useful if the scene contained other non-face objects that had similarities to a face.

Again, it should be emphasized that this system did not find the face in the scene. It is merely a segmentor that has no knowledge of the final task of a system in which it is embedded. It is suggested that the use of pulse images would significantly benefit a recognition engine. Certainly, it would be easier to find the face in the pulse image than in the original image.

2.2.3 Hardware Implementation

The PCNN has another beneficial quality in that the neurons only communicate with nearby neighbors. Thus, it can be employed in parallel hardware. Such implementations have been performed. Optical [Johnson & Ritter,1993] as well as SIMD [Kinser, and Lindblad,98] implementations have already been constructed.

2.3 Multi-Channel PCNN

Face images can readily be three channel color images. A multi-channel PCNN [Kinser,1997] has been created to manipulate multi-channel images. This system allows intra- and inter-channel communications. The system operates by modeling each channel, ε, by its own system, but it also allows for inter-channel communications though $\mathbf{W}^{\varepsilon}$.

$$F_{ij}^{\varepsilon}[n] = e^{\alpha_F \delta n} F_{ij}^{\varepsilon}[n-1] + S_{ij}^{\varepsilon} + V_f \sum_{kl} M_{ijkl} Y_{kl}^{\varepsilon}[n-1]$$

(6)

$$L_{ij}^{\varepsilon}[n] = e^{\alpha_L \delta n} L_{ij}^{\varepsilon}[n-1] + V_L \sum_{kl} W_{ijkl}^{\varepsilon} Y_{kl}^{\varepsilon}[n-1]$$

(7)

$$U_{ij}^{\varepsilon}[n] = F_{ij}^{e}[n] \left\{ 1 + \beta L_{ij}^{\varepsilon}[n] \right\}$$

(8)

$$Y_{ij}^{\varepsilon}[n] = \begin{cases} 1 & \text{if } U_{ij}^{\varepsilon}[n] > \Theta_{ij}^{\varepsilon}[n] \\ 0 & \text{Otherwise} \end{cases}$$

(9)

$$\Theta_{ij}^{\varepsilon}[n] = e^{\alpha_\Theta \delta n} \Theta_{ij}^{\varepsilon}[n-1] + V_\Theta Y_{ij}^{\varepsilon}[n]$$

(10)

Figs. 4 contain the gray-encoded versions of the three channel system. There are up to 7 gray levels in this image (plus black). Three of the gray levels are indicative of the three channels and the others are for cases when a neuron pulses in a combination of channels. The brightest pixels indicate all three channels pulsing simultaneously.

Figs. 4. Gray encoded outputs from a 3 channel PCNN.

3. The Application of Pulse Images to Face Images

In face image processing there are many operations that are desired. Of these some of the most popular are detecting the eyes and feducial points for constructing a lattice structure. Brief demonstrations of these abilities are shown in this section.

3.1 Segmentation and Eye Location

The pulse images inherently segment an image. The result of this is that the eyes will pulse in a different iteration than the rest of the face. Not only are the eyes segmented from the image cleanly they are also presented as bright pixels. In the original image the eyes are amongst the darkest objects. Most image filters detect objects by the presence of their intensity. Thus, it is more difficult to detect darker objects. However, the pulse image containing the eyes presents them in a high intensity mode making it easier for these algorithms to detect the eyes.

Fig. 5. Presents another image and Figs. 6 present some of the pulse outputs. It is clearly seen that the eyes are segmented cleanly from the rest of the face.

Fig. 5. An original input image.

3.2 Foveation Points

Humans do not stare at images, but rather their eyes continually change their focal points. These focal points are usually edges and corners within the image. These same features appear as edges and corners in the segments of the pulse images. Therefore it becomes possible to extract foveation points by simply passing the pulse regions through a low pass filter and searching for the largest intensities [Kinser,1998]

These foveation points are also (not so coincidentally) points commonly used for constructing a lattice structure over the face. Many researchers still perform the lattice construction manually. Foveation points, on the other hand, can be used as automatically determined lattice points.

Figs. 7 display two images each corresponding to a pulse image. Overlaid on the original face are the foveation points selected from the pulse images. To create a lattice structure several pulse images would need to be analyzed in this fashion. Also spurious foveation points are possible (see the bottom of Fig. 7b) and these need to be automatically eliminated.

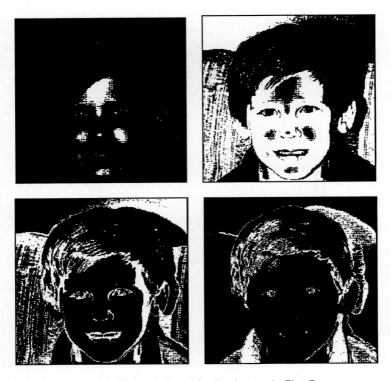

Figs. 6. Pulse outputs for the image in Fig. 5.

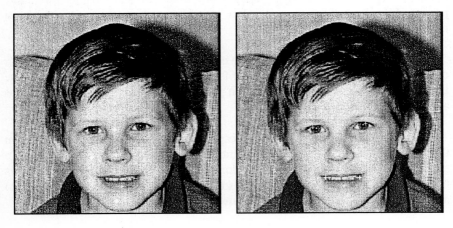

Figs. 7. Foveation points overlaid on the original image.

One final possible use of the foveation points is to create images that have focussed attention through the use of barrel transformations at the foveation points. These are useful in that more information is available about the center of the points similar to the fashion in which humans process images. Such operations based on the information contained in the pulse images has been useful in the detection of handwritten characters [Srinivasan & Kinser,1998].

Figs.8 display these foveated images based on the information in Figs. 7.

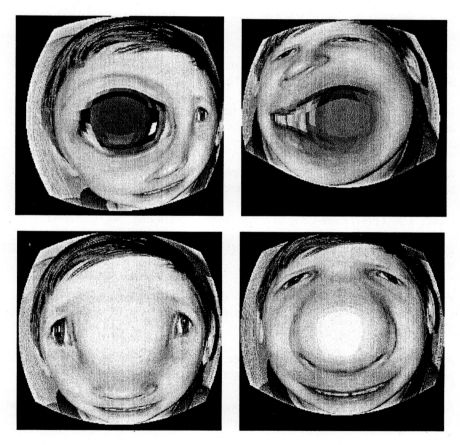

Figs. 8. Some of the foveated images using points from Figs. 7.

References

Eckhorn, R., Reitboeck, H. J., Arndt, M., Dicke, P., (1990) Feature Linking via Synchronization among Distributed Assemblies: Simulations of Results from Cat Visual Cortex, Neural Computation **2**, 293-307.

Gray, C. M., Engel, A. K., König, P., Singer, W. (1990) Oscillations in Cat Visual Cortex: Receptive Field Properties and Feature Dependence, Eur. J. Neurosci. **2**, 607-619.

Johnson, J. L., Ritter, D. (1993) Observation of periodic waves in a pulse-coupled neural network, Opt. Lett. **18**(15) 1253-1255.

Johnson, J. L. (1994) "Pulse-coupled neural nets: translation, rotation, scale, distortion, and intensity signal invariances for images, Appl. Opt. **33**(26), 6239-6253.

Kinser, J. M., Lindblad, Th., (1998) Implementation of the Pulse-Coupled Neural Network in a CNAPS Environment, accepted by IEEE Trans. on Neural Nets.

Kinser, J. M. (1997) Pulse-Coupled Image Fusion, Optical Eng., **36**(3), 737-742.

Kinser, J. M. (1998) Foveation by a Pulse-Coupled Neural Network, accepted by IEEE Trans. on Neural Nets.

Parodi, O., Combe, P., Ducom, J-C. (1996) Temporal Encoding in Vision: Coding by Spike Arrival Times Leads to Oscillations in the Case of Moving Targets, Biol. Cybern. **74**, 497-509.

Rybak, I. A., Shevtsova, N. A., Sandler, V. A. (1992) The Model of a Neural Network Visual Processor, Neurocomputing **4**, 93-102.

Srinivasan, R., Kinser, J. M. (1998) A Foveating - Fuzzy Scoring Target Recognition System, accepted by Pattern Recognition.

Faceless Identification

Lena Klasén[1] and Haibo Li[2]

[1] Swedish National Laboratory of Forensic Science, S-581 94 Linköping, SWEDEN, email: lena@isy.liu.se,
[2] Department of Electrical Engineering, Image Coding Group, Linköping University, S-581 83 Linköping, SWEDEN, email: haibo@isy.liu.se.

Abstract. Face recognition algorithms require visible faces, which normally can be obtained in a controllable and cooperative environment. In a non-cooperative environment it is not obvious that the face will appear in the images. Further, in the non-cooperative environment many parameters are out of control, such as pose, lightning conditions and resolution, affecting the accuracy of an analysis result. In the non-cooperative environment where such control can't be obtained, other cues have to be used for identification. High confidence methods for recognising persons have many potential applications. Crime scene recordings become more and more common as the number of surveillance system increases, and there is a great need for applications covering the case of recognising a person who definitely wants to remain anonymous, illustrated in figure 1.1. The work of identifying a crime suspect recorded in such a non-cooperative environment is often based on the human visual systems ability to recognise the person in the crime scene. This work is an attempt to deal with the problem of identifying persons on these "faceless" images, by using other cues than faces. A 3D deformable model is used as a platform to handle the nonrigid information of the human body and to integrate the static anthropometrical measures from each image and to estimate the dynamic motion parameters. A recursive method for estimating local shape variations and global motion is presented, using two recursive feedback systems, one loop based on analysis-by-synthesis and the other loop based on Extended Kalman-filtering technique.

1 Introduction

People mainly employ two kinds of information when exchanging information; *visual* and *audio information*. The visual language used by humans contains *body language, gestures* and *facial expressions*. A human in an image sequence can be characterised by his/her geometrical shape, texture and motion. There are many reasons for understanding how humans communicate, and there are several applications to automatically interpret the human behaviour e.g. for a more natural interaction with computers[Li (1997)], but in this work person identification is in focus. Person identification is here defined

514

Figure 1.1. An illustration of a masked robber.

as the process of distinguishing a particular person from all other individuals. In our opinion recognition is a general process, which normally contains both detection and identification. Further, authentication/verification is the process of determining whether a claimed identity matches the true identity. In the forensic case, the persons to be identified normally form a set of single or multiple images of a few crime suspects, and the image database contains a limited set of digitised crime scene images of a few persons. The question is whether the identity of the persons in the crime scene is equal to the identity of the suspects. In the forensic case it is important to remember that identification always is the decision of physical persons in the process of justice, and that methods for person identification only are tools to obtain a decision that maximises the objective part and minimises the subjective part of the decision.

The technique of using biometric methods for identification is not a new idea. The criminal justice system is in fact dominated by the identification problem. In [Champod (1993)] it can be read about Alphonse Bertillion who was employed at the Police Headquarter in Paris and invented the "Bertillion System" 1912. This method was further developed over several years, describing each recidivist by *body measurements, iris colorations, photography, "portrait parlé" including a standardised language for description, and a description of individual particularities including fingerprints.*

Quoting [Champod (1993)] (that includes the following translation of Bertillion [Bertillion (1893)], Bertillion in 1893 stated that;

"The solution to the problem of forensic identification consists less in the search for new characteristic elements of the individual than in the discovery of a means of classification"

Identification by fingerprints was introduced, and anthropometry was successively abandoned for the benefit of dactoyloscopy. Today the technology of analysing images provides methods that was out of reach for Bertillion, Galton e al.

2 Technical Approach

The technical approach is based on the idea of using the human body as the carrier of information. This is motivated by the fact that persons in a crime scene, such as a bank robbery, are more or less faceless. There are also a number of factors other than masks that set the limit for person identification[Klasén (1996A)], [Klasén (1996B)]. In this case, the static information, such as body height, the length of the legs and arms may become very useful. However, in practical cases, factors such as the non-rigidity of the human body, poor image resolution, noise, or improper camera angles seriously limit the accuracy of measurements taken from single frames, which motivates the use of image sequences rather than single frames. A digitised and calibrated sequence from a single, fixed CCD-camera is used to recover the shape and motion parameters of the human body.

The outline is to use an analysis-by-synthesis method based on a virtual 3D parameterised model of the human body to reconstruct the person in the video sequence as a nonrigid moving deformable object. There are several advantages in using such a full 3D model of the human body: *it has the ability of handling nonrigid deformation of the human body, the model provides a platform for integrating the estimated shape and motion from each single video-frame,* and *the model contains a rich set of anthropometric measures as well as information describing the 3D motion.* A block diagram of the system can be seen in figure 2.1.

2.1 Preprocessing

Image sequences similar to surveillance system recordings have been chosen as input, inspired by the lack of analysis methods at many forensic laboratories for investigating crime scene recordings. The technique used for surveillance recordings is not an optimal way to capture the event in a scene for image processing[Klasén (1996B)], but these systems will still be in use several more years although there is an ongoing process of improving the technology and several conferences on the subject e.g [Proceedings (1996)] and [Proceedings (1995)]. The image sequences are divided into subsequences, where each subsequence can be seen as an output from a single fixed camera with full video resolution sampled in the temporal domain.

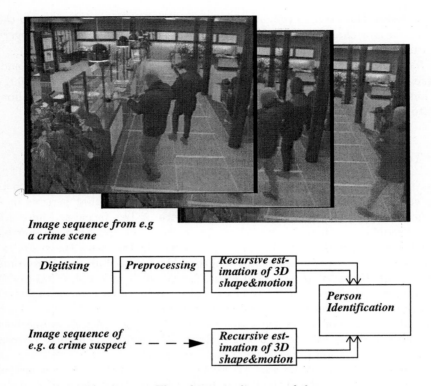

Figure 2.1. The schematic diagram of the system.

The video sequences are digitised and calibrated using the ImageLab at The National Laboratory of Forensic Science. Video sequences are digitised using a Hollywood DPS Digitising Board. Each frame is stored at 25 frames/sec and split into its fields of size 288 x 720 pixels. TrackEye 500 Motion Analysis System is used for tracking 2D points in image sequences. The tracking technique is a normalized correlation based technique which successfully tracks a small object in near real time. Rollei Metric Inc. software and camera are used for calibrating the videocamera and optics and for creating the 3D wireframe model of the human body.

2.2 Nonrigid motion estimation

The estimation of the 3D motion of a nonrigid object is a difficult problem. The difficulty arises partly from the lack of a flexible motion model which can characterize the nonrigid nature of the 3D motion. Therefore, the first step in estimating 3D motion is to build a tractable 3D motion model.

A. Nonrigid Motion Model

Assume that a point p in the body part is represented by a vector $\mathbf{s} = (x, y, z)^T$. After body movement it moves to a new position $\mathbf{s}' = (x', y', z')^T$; the change in position of this point can be written as follows according to the Helmholtz theory on nonrigid motion[Sommerfield (1950)]

$$\mathbf{s}' = \mathbf{Rs} + \mathbf{T} + \mathbf{Ds} \tag{2.1}$$

Where $\mathbf{R}$ is called the rotation matrix. $\mathbf{T}$ is the translation matrix. $\mathbf{D}$ is a deformation matrix which represents the deformation caused by muscle or clothing variations.

Unfortunately, although the mathematical form of the above motion model is simple, it is impossible to directly use the model (2.1) to estimate 3D motion of a body part. This is because $\mathbf{R}$, $\mathbf{T}$, and $\mathbf{D}$ are in general point-dependent. Fortunately, body motion can be treated as a special type of nonrigid motion. It can be viewed as *dominantly rigid motion plus a slight nonrigid motion*. Therefore $\mathbf{R}$ and $\mathbf{T}$ can be considered as global motion parameters, which become point-independent. They can be described by 6 unknown parameters. It is worth noticing that the deformation matrix still contains 9 unknown parameters which are point-oriented! But we should keep in mind that the local nonrigid motion is mainly caused by the muscles. This implies that the motion of any point in a body part is not free or independent, it is constrained by muscle and skin. If these inherent constraints are utilized, the number of unknown motion parameters will be dramatically reduced.

In order to find these inherent constraints, we must consider two aspects: the first is which points will influence a certain point, and secondly how much the point will be influenced. To answer the two questions, we need a body model in which the position and movement of points are given in the parametric form. We will introduce such a wireframe model for body part in the following subsection.

B. A 3D Wireframe Body Model

Our Candide model[Rydfalk (1987)] has been extended from containing the facial shape and facial expressions only, to a full body model. The model contains a full 3D description of the body as a nonrigid object as well as parameters for controlling the movement of the body parts. At present the body model consists of 19 nodal points, [Klasén (1996A), Hatze (1983)], connected by 16 separate body parts: head, neck, upper and lower torso, upper and lower arm and leg, hands and feet. Each body part is modelled by a small and closed set of triangles, forming a triangular wireframe mesh to model the surface. Global motion is controlled by the global motion parameters $\mathbf{R}$ and $\mathbf{T}$ for each of the bodyparts. Points at the vertices are controllable, and the displacement of a vertex point will affect the movement of its surrounding points controlling the local shape variations.

3 3D Motion Model of a Body Part

To estimate body motion, we must first build a body motion model. The motion of a body part is a composite nonrigid motion which can be described as: *the local muscle or clothing variations* $\mathbf{M_l}$ *followed by the global body motion* $\mathbf{M_g}$. Assume a point p in the body part is represented by a vector $\mathbf{s} = (x, y, z)^T$. After body motion it moves to a new position $\mathbf{s}'' = (x'', y'', z'')^T$. The change in position can be described as

$$\mathbf{s}'' = \mathbf{M_g}(\mathbf{M_l}(\mathbf{s})) \tag{3.1}$$

In the following we will formalize in more detail the local and global body motion.

3.1 Local Motion Model

Local body variations will cause the point p to move to an intermediate position $\mathbf{s}' = (x', y', z')^T$.

$$\mathbf{s}' = \mathbf{M_l}(\mathbf{s}) \tag{3.2}$$

Now we want to specify the expression of $M_l(s)$.

Assume that the triangular patches of the employed wireframe model are small enough, a linear model can be used to model arbitrarily 3D local affine deformation,

$$\delta \mathbf{s} = \mathbf{As} \tag{3.3}$$

The linear deformation model is reasonable since its 2D projection corresponds to a local affine flow, on which the texture mapping technique is based.

Assume that three vertices of a triangle are $\mathbf{s_a}$, $\mathbf{s_b}$ and $\mathbf{s_c}$, then a point $\mathbf{s}$ in the plane can be represented by

$$\mathbf{s} = \alpha \mathbf{s_a} + \beta \mathbf{s_b} + \gamma \mathbf{s_c} \tag{3.4}$$

Taking the additional constraint $\alpha + \beta + \gamma = 1$ into account, the coefficients can be determined by solving the following linear constraints

$$\begin{bmatrix} x \\ y \\ z \\ 1 \end{bmatrix} = \begin{bmatrix} x_a & x_b & x_c \\ y_a & y_b & y_c \\ z_a & z_b & z_c \\ 1 & 1 & 1 \end{bmatrix} \begin{bmatrix} \alpha \\ \beta \\ \gamma \end{bmatrix} \tag{3.5}$$

Combining (3.3) and (3.4), we have

$$\delta \mathbf{s} = \alpha \delta \mathbf{s_a} + \beta \delta \mathbf{s_b} + \gamma \delta \mathbf{s_c} \tag{3.6}$$

This equation tells that the displacement field of a triangle can be linearly represented by that of vertices of the triangle.

Since the body part is covered by a triangular mesh instead of simply by a large triangle, we have to consider the situation that adjacent triangles share a common vertex. Therefore, the constraint (3.6) has to be extended to the mesh case. Following the approach developed for the 2D case [Li (1993A)], we can rewrite Equation (3.6) as

$$\delta \mathbf{s} = \mathbf{p} \begin{bmatrix} \delta \mathbf{s_a} \\ \delta \mathbf{s_b} \\ \delta \mathbf{s_c} \end{bmatrix} \tag{3.7}$$

where $\mathbf{p}$ is constructed as

$$\mathbf{p} = [\bar{\alpha}, \bar{\beta}, \bar{\gamma}] = \begin{bmatrix} \alpha & 0 & 0 & \beta & 0 & 0 & \gamma & 0 & 0 \\ 0 & \alpha & 0 & 0 & \beta & 0 & 0 & \gamma & 0 \\ 0 & 0 & \alpha & 0 & 0 & \beta & 0 & 0 & \gamma \end{bmatrix} \tag{3.8}$$

where $\bar{\alpha}, \bar{\beta}, \bar{\gamma}$ are three 3×3 matrixes.

We then build a local motion vector $\Phi = [\delta \mathbf{s_a}, \delta \mathbf{s_b}, \ \delta \mathbf{s_c}, \delta \mathbf{s_d}, ...]^{\mathbf{T}}$ which lists all displacements of the vertices.

Then the formula (3.8) can be extended to a large matrix equation as

$$\begin{bmatrix} \delta \mathbf{s_1} \\ \delta \mathbf{s_2} \\ . \\ \delta \mathbf{s_m} \end{bmatrix} = \begin{bmatrix} \bar{\alpha}_1 & \bar{\beta}_1 & \bar{\gamma}_1 & 0 & .. & 0 \\ \bar{\alpha}_2 & \bar{\beta}_2 & \bar{\gamma}_2 & 0 & .. & 0 \\ . & . & . & . & .. & . \\ \bar{\alpha}_m & \bar{\beta}_m & 0 & 0 & .. & \bar{\gamma}_m \end{bmatrix} \begin{bmatrix} \delta \mathbf{s_a} \\ \delta \mathbf{s_b} \\ \delta \mathbf{s_c} \\ \delta \mathbf{s_d} \\ . \\ . \end{bmatrix} \tag{3.9}$$

where $\mathbf{0}$ is not a scalar zero but a 3×3 zero matrix.

Let $\mathbf{P}$ denote the matrix in the middle of the equation, $\Delta \mathbf{s}$ represents the left vector, then equation (3.9) can be written in more compact form

$$\Delta \mathbf{s} = \mathbf{P} \Phi \tag{3.10}$$

The constraint (3.10) is linear, an LS solution can be obtained as

$$\Phi = (\mathbf{P}^T \mathbf{P})^{-1} \mathbf{P}^T \Delta \mathbf{s} \tag{3.11}$$

if $\Delta \mathbf{s}$ is available. This is a globally optimal solution for the displacement of the vertices.

The equation (3.11) is the local motion model, which states that the displacement of a point as a weighted linear combination of displacements of its surrounding vertices. The change in position of this point can be written

$$\mathbf{s}' = \mathbf{M_l}(\mathbf{s}) = \mathbf{s} + \mathbf{P_s} \Phi \tag{3.12}$$

where n local movement parameters have been collected in the vector Φ. The $3 \times n$ matrix $\mathbf{P_s}$ determines how a certain point s is affected by Φ.

$$\mathbf{P_s} = \begin{bmatrix} . & \alpha & 0 & 0 & \beta & 0 & 0 & \gamma & 0 & 0 & . \\ . & 0 & \alpha & 0 & 0 & \beta & 0 & 0 & \gamma & 0 & . \\ . & 0 & 0 & \alpha & 0 & 0 & \beta & 0 & 0 & \gamma & . \end{bmatrix} \tag{3.13}$$

3.2 Global Motion Model

Global body motion can be modelled as a rotation followed by translation. This can be described as

$$s'' = \mathbf{M_g}(s') = \mathbf{R}s' + \mathbf{T} \tag{3.14}$$

Where $\mathbf{R}$ is the rotation matrix and $\mathbf{T}$ is the translation vector. The movement of the point p from s' to s'' is assumed to be caused by the global motion.

Considering that the body motion is normally large, therefore, the incremental rigid motion assumption, which is widely used in facial motion estimation, is no longer valid. The rotation matrix becomes nonlinear in three angular velocities ω_x, ω_y, and ω_z,

$$\mathbf{R} = \begin{pmatrix} a_{11} & a_{12} & a_{13} \\ a_{21} & a_{22} & a_{23} \\ a_{31} & a_{32} & a_{33} \end{pmatrix} = \begin{pmatrix} 1 & 0 & 0 \\ 0 & cos(\omega_x) & sin(\omega_x) \\ 0 & -sin(\omega_x) & cos(\omega_x) \end{pmatrix}$$

$$\bullet \begin{pmatrix} cos(\omega_y) & 0 & -sin(\omega_y) \\ 0 & 1 & 0 \\ sin(\omega_y) & 0 & cos(\omega_y) \end{pmatrix} \begin{pmatrix} cos(\omega_z) & sin(\omega_z) & 0 \\ -sin(\omega_z) & cos(\omega_z) & 0 \\ 0 & 0 & 1 \end{pmatrix} \tag{3.15}$$

The translation vector $\mathbf{T}$ is

$$\mathbf{T} = [t_x, t_y, t_z]^T \tag{3.16}$$

where t_x, t_y, and t_z are the three velocity components of the translation motion.

3.3 General Motion Model

Inserting (3.12) into (3.14), we have

$$s'' = \mathbf{R}s + \mathbf{T} + \mathbf{R}\mathbf{P_s}\Phi \tag{3.17}$$

This is a general model of 3D body motion, which is specified by the motion parameters $\mathbf{U} = [\omega_x, \omega_y, \omega_z, t_x, t_y, t_z, \Phi]$.

4. Two-View Motion Estimation

Since we are assuming that only 2D projections of the scene are available we cannot directly measure 3D body motion. Instead we will infer the 3D motion from its projection to the 2D image plane. In particular, we will study what happen in the time interval between two consecutive frames.

The general model of 3D body motion is a highly nonlinear constraint for motion parameters. A large number of local motion parameters further make the estimation of motion parameters more difficult. Therefore, it is not mathematically tractable to attempt to recover both global and local parameters simultaneously. Based on the observation that body motion is a specific nonrigid motion, global and local motion can be sequentially estimated. That is, under the assumption that only rigid motion exists, the global motion is estimated first. The estimated motion parameters are used to compensate the global motion. Finally, the local motion is estimated from the compensated frame and the current frame. This strategy has been successively used in facial motion estimation[Li (1994)].

4.1 Projection Model

Assuming the geometry projection is the perspective projection. We have

$$X = f\frac{x}{z}$$
$$Y = f\frac{y}{z} \tag{4.1}$$

where f is the focal length of the camera, (X, Y) is the projection of 3D point (x, y, z) on the image plane.

4.2 3D Motion Parameter Estimation

Inserting (3.14) into (4.1), we have

$$X'' = \frac{a_{11}X' + a_{12}Y' + a_{13}f + ft_x/z}{a_{31}X'/f + a_{32}Y'/f + a_{13} + t_z/z}$$
$$Y'' = \frac{a_{21}X' + a_{22}Y' + a_{23}f + ft_y/z}{a_{31}X'/f + a_{32}Y'/f + a_{13} + t_z/z} \tag{4.2}$$

This equation reflects how the global motion affects the 2D movement of a 3D point.

Eliminating z from (4.2), we obtain

$$(ft_y - Y''t_z)[X''(a_{31}X'/f + a_{32}Y'/f + a_{13}) - (a_{11}X' + a_{12}Y' + a_{13}f)]$$
$$= (ft_x - X''t_z)[Y''(a_{31}X'/f + a_{32}Y'/f + a_{13}) - (a_{21}X' + a_{22}Y' + a_{23}f)] \tag{4.3}$$

Equation (4.3) is nonlinear in the six unknowns t_z, t_z, t_z, ω_x, ω_y, and ω_z. Several linear and nonlinear methods have been developed to solve this problem[Tsai (1981)].

4.3 Shape Parameter Estimation

The 2D movement of a 3D point due to the shape deformation can be computed as follows:

Differentiating the equation (4.1) with respect to time we have

$$u = \frac{dX}{dt} = f \frac{\frac{dx}{dt} z - x \frac{dz}{dt}}{z^2}$$

$$v = \frac{dY}{dt} = f \frac{\frac{dy}{dt} z - y \frac{dz}{dt}}{z^2} \tag{4.4}$$

Where (u, v) is normally referred to as the *displacement field* or the *optical flow field*.

If we normalize the frame interval to be 1, then equation (4.4) can be written as

$$\begin{bmatrix} u \\ v \end{bmatrix} = \begin{bmatrix} f/z & 0 & -X/z \\ 0 & f/z & -Y/z \end{bmatrix} \begin{bmatrix} \delta x \\ \delta y \\ \delta z \end{bmatrix} = \mathbf{Q} \delta \mathbf{s} \tag{4.5}$$

where $\mathbf{Q}$ is the middle matrix.

Inserting (3.12) into (4.5) yields

$$\begin{bmatrix} u \\ v \end{bmatrix} = \mathbf{Q} \mathbf{P_s} \Phi \tag{4.6}$$

We assume that the intensity of a moving point remains constant, then we have the normal optical flow constraint equation[Horn (1986)]

$$I_x u + I_y v + I_t = 0 \tag{4.7}$$

This constraint can be written as vector form

$$[I_x, I_y] \begin{bmatrix} u \\ v \end{bmatrix} = -I_t \tag{4.8}$$

Combining (4.6) with (4.8), we have a linear constraint

$$\mathbf{G_s} \Phi = -I_t \tag{4.9}$$

where $\mathbf{G_s} = [I_x, I_y] \mathbf{Q} \mathbf{P_s}$. If we concatenate all constraints of the points belonging to the same body part, we have

$$\mathbf{G} \Phi = -\mathbf{I_t} \tag{4.10}$$

Local motion parameters can be estimated by using the LS algorithm,

$$\Phi = -(\mathbf{G}^T \mathbf{G})^{-1} \mathbf{G}^T \mathbf{I_t} \tag{4.11}$$

Formula (4.11) shows that the 3D local motion can be directly recovered from image intensities.

5 Long Sequence Motion Tracking

To track a moving person, we have to dynamically estimate his/her movement and shape variations. The two-view motion estimation algorithm described in previous section provides only the relative motion between two successive frames. The absolute motion can be obtained in the following way:

$$\mathbf{U(t + 1)} \approx \mathbf{U(t)} + \Delta \mathbf{U} \tag{5.1}$$

where $\mathbf{U(t)}$, $\mathbf{U(t + 1)}$ are the absolute motion at time instant t and $t + 1$, respectively. $\Delta \mathbf{U}$ is the two-view motion between frame $t + 1$ and frame t, which can be computed from (4.3) and (4.11).

The motion parameters obtained from the two-view case are inherently noisy. Obviously, with an increasing number of frames, the error in the estimated motion parameters will be accumulated. This will result in divergence in the motion estimation, the *"error accumulation"* problem, associated with long sequence motion tracking[Li (1993B)]. There are many works that have addressed this problem. These include the pioneer works of Broida and Chellappa[Broida (1990)] and recent works of Pentland et al [Azarbayejani (1995)]. The most basic strategy of these works lies in the combination of local techniques with Kalman filtering techniques. However, this type of technique only works well for estimating motion and structure of sparse feature points. Inspired by the idea of Kalman filtering, a recursive estimation method based on analysis-by-synthesis (ABS) strategy was proposed in our group[Li (1993B)]. This recursive estimation technique can be used for computing motion and estimation of dense points. In this paper, we integrate these two estimation techniques into a new recursive estimator: Kalman-filtering technique is used for estimating global motion and the structure of feature points, while the ABS technique for handling local shape variations. A complete recursive estimator is illustrated in Figure 5.1, in which these two feedback systems closely interacts.

5.1 Recursive Estimation By Kalman Filters

As in [Azarbayejani (1995), Broida (1990)], the 3D motion and structure of a body part can be recursively estimated by using Kalman filtering techniques. A dynamic process is defined as

$$A_{t+1} = f(A_t) + \xi \tag{5.2}$$

where the state vector A_t consists of motion and structure parameters, $A_t = (\omega_x, \omega_x, \omega_x, t_x, t_y, t_z, \mathbf{s}_a, \mathbf{s}_b, ...)$. The function f models the dynamic evolution of the state vector A_t at time t. The function f can be directly built by modelling 3D motion of the body part as a discrete-time Newtonian physical model and incorporating structure transition (3.14).

The measurement process is

$$Y_t = h(A_t) + \eta \qquad (5.3)$$

where the observation vector Y_t contains the image locations $\{X_i", Y_i"\}$ of all the tracked features in a new frame. The function h is characterized by the projection model (4.3).

Note that both ξ and η are white noise processes having known spectral density matrices.

Since the measurement process is nonlinear, the Extended Kalman Filter has to be used. Using extended Kalman filtering, we can obtain the optimal linear estimate $\hat{A}_t$ of the state vector A_t

$$\hat{A}_t = A_t^* + K_t(Y_t - h(A_t)) \qquad (5.4)$$

where A_t^* is the prediction of the state vector A_t.

Since only global motion is considered here, the local shape variation has to be handled by the second feedback loop, analysis-by-synthesis (ABS) one.

5.2 Recursive Estimation By ABS

Due to the immeasurability of local shape variations, it is impossible to directly compute local motion parameters. However, image intensity provides us with an indirect measurement of local shape variations. Therefore, in order to evaluate the closeness of the actual structure parameters $\mathbf{S} = (\mathbf{s_a}, \mathbf{s_b}, ...)$ and the predicted structure parameters $\hat{\mathbf{S}}$, we synthesize an image frame $\hat{I}(x, y, t)$ by the image synthesis module using the predicted structure parameters. Obviously, this corresponds to motion compensation [Li (1993A)]. If the predicted structure parameters are equal to the actual ones, then $I(x, y, t) = \hat{I}(x, y, t)$ disregarding for the moment optical effects such as shading.

If there is a difference between $\mathbf{S}$ and $\hat{\mathbf{S}}$, then $I(x, y, t) \neq \hat{I}(x, y, t)$. In this case we can use the local structure estimation module to estimate the relative motion $\delta\mathbf{S}$ between the synthesized image $\hat{I}(x, y, t)$ and the original image $I(x, y, t)$. Refined structure parameters can be obtained by simply adding the predicted motion parameters $\hat{\mathbf{S}}$ and the structure error $\delta\mathbf{S}$. The refined structure is then sent to the Kalman filtering loop for updating next estimation of motion and structure.

6 Person Identification

The relations between two models can finally be analysed, using the shape $\mathbf{s}$ and motion estimate $\mathbf{R}$ and $\mathbf{T}$ from the system illustrated in figure 5.1, using a technique inspired by [Hatze (1983)] among other related work. Identifying a person tends to be a multi-modality problem. Intra class variations, such as the movements of the spine, aging, varying body weight and muscles affects

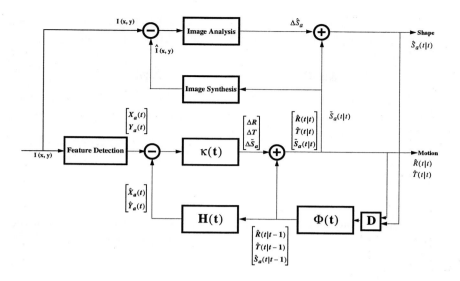

Figure 5.1. Schematic diagram of recursive estimation of global motion and local shape variations.

the accuracy of the inter class comparisons and motion analysis. Additional problems are raised by clothes and shoes, although an interesting cloth model to estimate cloth draping recently was presented [Jojic (1997)]. Combining information from a set of cues is for some applications proved to be better than relying on the result from one single method [Bigün (1997)]. This work points in the direction of the hypothesis that the intra variations among human anthropometry and motion are too large to obtain secure identification results, restricted by the surveillance technique among other parameters. Bearing in mind that in the forensic area the investigation materials are seldom restricted to images, and a potential application for this work is to be used e.g. as one module in a multi modality system. In practice, this is how investigation materials, e.g from a crime scene, are treated today. Several forensic specialists and experts perform separate analyses of traces, such as shoeprints, toolmarks, DNA or fibres. The "fusing" process is embedded in the process of justice. Another aspect that motivates this work is that exclusion of an innocent suspect is as important as identification.

7 Summary

In this work we suggest a technique to parameterise the anthropometry and 3D motion (action) of a person from an image sequence by recursive estimation of global motion and local shape variations. Finding a model representation for a human body as a nonrigid moving object and trying to quantify the anthropometry and motion in a way that allows us to separate the intra- and inter variation in such a way that a person can be rapidly recognised with high accuracy, is actually not the aim of this approach. Instead this is an attempt to try to deal with the real problem as one way of adding cues to the rather tricky process of identifying a "faceless" person, using the cues available in a non-cooperative environment.

References

Ali Azarbayejani and Alex P. Pentland, "Recursive Estimation of Motion, Structure and Focal Length", IEEE Transaction on Pattern Analysis and Machine Intelligence, Vol 17, No 6, June 1995.

A. Bertillion, "Identification Anthropométrique-Instructions signalétiques", 2nd Edition, Impremierie Administrative, Melun, 1893.

E. S. Bigün, J. Bigün, B. Duc and S. Fischer, "Expert Conciliation for Multi Modal Person Authentication Systems by Bayesian Statistics", Proceedings of the First International Conference on Audio- and Video-Based Biometric Person Authentication, pp 291-300, Crans-Montana, Switzerland, March 1997.

T. J. Broida, S. Chandrashekhar and R. Chellappa, "Recursice 3-D Motion Estimation from a Monocular Image Sequence", IEEE Transaction on Aerospace and Electronic Systems, Vol 26, No 4, July 1990.

C. Champod, C. Lennard, P. Margot, "Alphonse Bertillion and Dactyloscopy", Special Report, Journal of Forensic Identification, pp 604-625, 43(6) 1993.

H. Hatze, "Computerised Optimization of Sport Motion: An Overview of Possibilities, Methods and Recent Developments", Journal of Sports Science, 1, 3-12, 1983.

B.K. Horn, Robot Vision, MIT Press, 1986.

Nebojsa Jojic and Thomas S. Huang, "Estimating Cloth Draping Parameters from Range Data", Proccedings of International Workshop on Synthetic-Natural Hybrid Coding and Three Dimensional Imaging, Greece, 1997.

Tadahiko Kimoto and Yasuhiko Yasuda, "Hierarchical Representation of the Motion of a Walker and Motion Reconstruction for Model Based Image Coding", Optical Engineering, Vol 30, No. 7, July 1991.

Lena Klasén and Olov Fahlander, "Using Videogrammetry and 3-D Image Reconstruction to Identify Persons in Crime Scenes", SPIE Proceedings Vol. 2942-17, Boston, 1996.

Lena Klasén and Olov Fahlander, "Video Coding for Next Generation Surveillance Systems", SPIE Proceedings Vol. 2942, paper 05, Boston, 1996.

Haibo Li and Robert Forchheimer, "Two-View Facial Movement Estimation", IEEE Transaction on Circuits and Systems for Video Technology, Vol.4, No.3, 1994.

Haibo Li, Low Bitrate Image Sequence Coding, Ph.D. thesis, Linköping University, 1993.

Haibo. Li, L. Klasén, J. Ahlberg, J. Ström, A. Lundmark, F. Davoine and Robert Forchheimer, "Understanding of Human Images", Proceedings of Swedish Symposium on Image Analysis", pp 36-40, Stockholm, Sweden, March 1997.

527

Haibo Li, Pertti Rovanen and Robert Forchheimer, "3-D Motion estimation in Model-Based Facial Image Coding", IEEE Transaction on Pattern Analysis and Machine Intelligence, Vol 15, No 6, June 1993.

Proceedings from "Surveillance and Assessment Technologies for Law Enforcement", SPIE Proceedings Vol. 2935, Boston, 1996.

Proccedings from European Convention on Security and Detection, 16-18 May 1995, UK.

Mikael Rydfalk, "Candide, a Parameterised Face", Internal Report, LiTH-ISY-I-0866, Linköping University, Sweden, 1987.

A. Sommerfield, Mechanics of Deformable Bodies, 1950.

R. Tsai and T. Huang, "Estimating 3D motion Parameters of a Rigid Planar Patch", IEEE Trans. ASSP, ASSP-29, No.6, Dec. 1981.

Pose Discriminiation and Eye Detection Using Support Vector Machines (SVM)

Jeffrey Huang [1], David Ii [2], Xuhui Shao [3], and Harry Wechsler [1]

[1] Department of Computer Science
George Mason University
Fairfax, VA 22030
{rhuang, wechsler}@cs.gmu.edu
[2] Lochheed Martin
9500 Godwin Dr.
Manassas, VA 20110
david.ii@lmco.com
[3] Department of Electrical Engineering
University of Minnesota
Minneapolis, MN 55455
xshao@ece.umn.edu

Abstract. Most face recognition systems assume that the geometry of the image formation process is frontal. If additional poses, beyond the frontal one, are possible, then it becomes necessary to estimate the actual imaging pose. Once a face is detected and its pose is estimated one proceeds by normalizing the face images to account for geometrical and illumination changes, possibly using information about the location and appearance of facial landmarks such as the eyes. This paper describes a novel approach for the problem of pose estimation and eye detection using Support Vector Machines (SVM). Experimental results using frontal, and 33.75° rotated left and right poses, respectively, demonstrate the feasibility of our approach for pose estimation. The image (face) data comes from the standard FERET data base, the training set consists of 150 images equally distributed among frontal, 33.75° rotated left and right poses, respectively, and the test set consists of 450 images again equally distributed among the three different types of poses. The accuracy observed on test data, using both polynomials of degree 3 and Radial Basis Functions (RBFs) as kernel approximation functions, to determine the SVM separating hyperplanes, has been 100%. On the eye detection task, the training data consisted of 186 eye images and 186 non-eye images. SVM was tested against 200 test examples (eye and non-eye). The best generalization performance of 4% was achieved using polynomial kernels of second degree as the set of approximating functions. SVM appear to be robust classification schemes and this suggests their use for additional face recognition tasks, such as surveillance.

Key Words: eye detection, face recognition, FERET, pose estimation, predictive learning, Radial Basis Functions (RBFs), Support Vector Machines (SVMs).

1 Introduction

There are several related (face recognition) sub problems: (i) detection of a pattern as a face (in the crowd) and its pose, (ii) detection of facial landmarks, (iii) face recognition - identification and/or verification, and (iv) analysis of facial expressions (Samal et al., 1992). Face recognition starts with the detection of face patterns in sometimes cluttered scenes, proceeds by normalizing the face images to account for geometrical and illumination changes, possibly using information about the location and appearance of facial landmarks, identifies the faces using appropriate classification algorithms, and post processes the results using model-based schemes and logistic feedback (Chellappa et al, 1995). Most face recognition systems assume that the geometry of the image formation process is frontal. If additional poses, beyond the frontal one, are possible, then it becomes necessary to estimate the actual imaging pose. Pose information can then be used in a variety of ways, ranging from specific normalization and facial landmark detection procedures, to face recognizers trained for some specific pose only. This paper addresses the problems of pose estimation and eye detection using Support Vector Machines (SVM), a novel pattern classification algorithm (Cortes and Vapnik, 1995; Vapnik, 1995).

2 Predictive Learning

The goal of predictive learning is to develop a computational relationship for estimating the values for the output variables given only the values of the input variables. Different taxonomies are available for predictive learning, among them that including regression and density estimation, and classification, corresponding to the input variables being continuous and discrete / categorical, respectively, even that any classification problem can be reduced to a regression problem. Pose detection is a classification problem and this paper describes novel and robust means for solving it. Predictive learning can be thought of as a relationship $y = f(x) + error$, where the error is due both to (measurement) noise and possibly to 'unobserved' input variables. The main issues one has to address are related to prediction (generalization) ability, data and dimensionality reduction (complexity), explanation / interpretation capability, and possibly to biological plausibility.

In the framework of predictive learning, estimating ('learning') a model ('classifier') from finite data requires specification of three concepts: a set of approximating functions (i.e., a class of models : dictionary), an inductive principle and an optimization (parameter estimation) procedure. The notion of inductive principle is fundamental to all learning methods. Essentially, an inductive principle provides a general prescription for what to do with the training data in order to obtain (learn) the model. In contrast, a learning method is a constructive implementation of an inductive principle (i.e., an optimization or parameter estimation procedure) for a given set of approximating functions in which the model is sought (such as feed forward nets with sigmoid units, radial basis function networks etc.) (Cherkassky and Mulier, 1998). There is just a handful of known inductive principles (Regularization, Structural Risk Minimization (SRM), Bayesian Inference, Minimum Description Length), but there are infinitely many learning methods based on these principles. It is the prediction risk, the expected performance of an estimator ('classifier') for new (future) samples, which determines to what degree adaptation has been successful so far.

Accurate estimation of prediction risk from available training data is crucial for the control of model complexity (model selection). Classical methods for model selection are usually based on asymptotic results for linear models. Non-asymptotic (guaranteed) bounds on the prediction risk based on VC-theory have been proposed by Vapnik (1995) as part of Statistical Learning Theory (SLT). Prediction risk, for regression problems in general, and classification problems in particular, is usually estimated as a function of the empirical risk (training error) penalized (adjusted) by some measure of model complexity (see also the known tradeoffs between bias and variance). Once an accurate estimate of the prediction risk is found it can be used for model selection by choosing the model complexity which minimizes the estimated prediction risk. The Support Vector Machines (SVM), discussed in the next section, build pattern classifiers using SRM as the inductive principle, Radial Basis Functions (RBFs) or polynomial splines (as possible sets of approximating functions), and dual quadratic optimization. The constructive implementation of the SRM principle used by SVM is to keep the value of the empirical risk fixed (small) and minimize the confidence interval of the predicted risk.

3 Support Vector Machines (SVM)

For the case of two-class pattern recognition, the task of predictive learning from examples can be formulated as shown below (Vapnik, 1995). Given a set of functions

$$\{f_\alpha : \alpha \in \Lambda\}, \quad f_\alpha : R^N \to \{-1,+1\}$$

(the index set Λ not necessarily being a subset of R^n), and a set of l examples

$$(x_1, y_1), \cdots (x_i, y_i), \cdots, (x_l, y_l), \quad x_i \in R^N, \quad y_i \in \{-1,+1\},$$

each one generated from an unknown probability distribution $P(x,y)$, we want to find a function f_{α^*} which provides the smallest possible value for the risk

$$R(\alpha) = \int |f_\alpha(x) - y| \, dP(x, y).$$

$R(\alpha)$ is unknown since $P(x,y)$ is unknown. Therefore an induction principle for risk minimization is necessary. The straightforward approach, ERM (empirical risk minimization) which seeks to minimize

$$R_{emp}(\alpha) = \frac{1}{l} \sum_{i=1}^{l} |f_\alpha(x_i) - y_i|$$

turns out not to guarantee a small actual risk (i.e. a small error on the training set does not imply a small error on a test set), if the number l of training examples is limited. To make the most out of a limited amount of data, SVM would use Structural Risk Minimization (SRM) rather than ERM as the underlying inductive principle. SRM controls the (model) complexity of the SVM classifier via regularization tradeoffs between empirical risk, to be observed during training, and the size of the confidence interval to be expected during testing. The regularization tradeoffs are specified through the regularization parameter C. The above regularization tradeoff is well known in literature as the bias vs variance tradeoff. One can show that for any $\alpha \in \Lambda$ with a probability of at least 1-η, the bound

$$R(\alpha) \leq R_{emp}(\alpha) + \Phi\left(\frac{h}{l}, \frac{\log(\eta)}{l}\right)$$

holds, Φ being defined as

$$\Phi\left(\frac{h}{l}, \frac{\log(\eta)}{l}\right) = \sqrt{\frac{h\left(\log\frac{2\eta}{h} + 1\right) - \log\left(\frac{\eta}{4}\right)}{l}} \ .$$

For the case when the VC - dimension h is low compared to the number of examples l being learned the confidence interval is narrow and one is prevented from finding a good solution by accident. The VC-dimension stands for the complexity of the classifier used and it seeks to narrow the guaranteed risk bounds by seeking 'simplicity' in the design of the classifier. Specifically, SVM seeks to find those learning examples - Support Vectors (SV) - responsible for setting the decision boundaries. It is usually the case that M, the number of SV, is less that the total number of learning examples, as most of the training examples are 'far' away from the decision (hyperplanes) boundaries. Vapnik (1995) also shows that, if the number of learning samples is N, the probability of error on future trials $P(e)$ is bounded by

$$P(e) < \frac{M}{N} \qquad \text{for large } N$$

The actual SVM implementation seeks separating hyperplanes $D(\mathbf{x})$ defined as

$$D(\mathbf{x}) = (\mathbf{w} \cdot \mathbf{x}) + w_0$$

by mapping the input data $\mathbf{x}$ into a higher dimensional space $\mathbf{z}$ using a nonlinear function g. Low weights $\mathbf{w}$ defining the class boundaries imply low VC-dimension and lead to high separability between the class patterns. The reason for mapping the input into a higher dimensional space is that this mapping leads to better class separability. The complexity of SVM decision boundary, however, is independent of the feature $\mathbf{z}$ space dimensionality, which can be very large (or even infinite). SVM optimization takes advantage of the fact that the evaluation of the inner products between the feature vectors in a high dimensional feature space is done indirectly via the evaluation of the kernel H between support vectors and vectors in the input space

$$(\mathbf{z} \cdot \mathbf{z}') = H(\mathbf{x}, \mathbf{x}')$$

where the vector z and z' are the vectors **x** and **x'** mapped into the feature space. In the dual form, the SVM decision function has then the form:

$$D(\mathbf{x}) = \sum_{i=1}^{M} \beta_i y_i H(\mathbf{x}_i, \mathbf{x}')$$

The RBFs kernels **H** are given by

$$H(\mathbf{x}_i, \mathbf{x}') = \exp\left\{ -\frac{|\mathbf{x} - \mathbf{x}_i|^2}{\sigma^2} \right\}$$

and the corresponding SVM hyperplanes are defined then as

$$f(x) = sign\left(\sum_{i=1}^{M} \beta_i \exp\left\{ -\frac{|\mathbf{x} - \mathbf{x}_i|^2}{\sigma^2} \right\} + b \right)$$

and can be fully specified using dual quadratic optimization in terms of the number of kernels used - M - and their width. The polynomial kernels **H** of degree q are given by

$$H(\mathbf{x}, \mathbf{x}') = \left[(\mathbf{x} \cdot \mathbf{x}') + 1 \right]^q$$

and the corresponding SVM hyperplanes are defined then as

$$f(x) = sign\left(\sum_{i=1}^{M} \beta_i \left[(\mathbf{x} \cdot \mathbf{x}') + 1 \right]^q + b \right)$$

Note that the number M of RBFs, the kernel centers, which correspond to the support vectors, and the coefficients β_i are all automatically determined as a result of quadratic optimization with linear constraints.

The two class classifier described above can be expanded to an c class classifier by constructing c two class classifiers of the type { class i } vs { class 1...c / except i } and making the classification be the class k that yields the maximum value amongst the c classifiers.

4 Experiments

A face has to be first detected (Osuna et al, 1997) and its pose estimated before one proceeds by normalizing the face images to account for geometrical and illumination changes, possibly using information about the location and appearance of facial landmarks such as the eyes. The experiments described in this section are concerned thus with pose estimation and eye detection, respectively. Pose estimation, as described in Sect. 4.1, is a full fledged three class recognition problem. Eye detection, as described in Sect. 4.2, is a two class detection problem, and it requires exhaustive search as the SVM classifier scans for possible eye locations across the whole face.

4.1   Pose Estimation

600 facial images corresponding to 200 subjects from the FERET database (Phillips et. al, 1998) are used to assess the performance on pose estimation using SVMs. Each subject has three different poses corresponding to frontal, 33.75° rotated left and right, respectively. 600 images are randomly divided into two data sets - 150 images (50 images/pose) for training and the remaining 450 image (150 image/pose) for testing. The histogram for both training and test images is equalized using 256 gray levels. Using as constant the interoccular distance between the two eyes, the images covering facial region are cropped and normalized to size 32 x 32 to yield an input vector whose dimensionality is 1024. Some training and test images after face cropping and normalization are shown in Fig. 1.

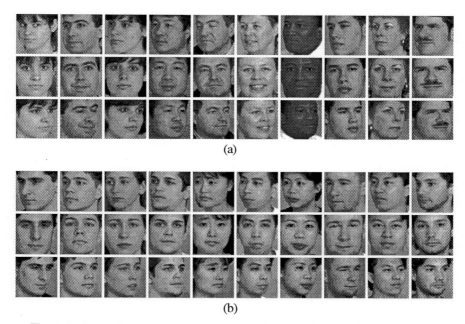

(a)

(b)

Figure 1. Examples for (a) training images and (b) test images with three poses

We report now on two SVM experiments using as approximating functions polynomial and RBF kernels, respectively. Each experiment has three classifiers corresponding to the pose of frontal (+1) vs. other (-1) poses, 33.75° rotated left (+1) vs. other poses (-1), and 33.75° rotated right (+1) vs. other poses (-1). The unseen test examples are first used for each classifier separately while the final classification result is done according to the maximum output from the three classifiers. For the experiment using polynomial kernels, we have constructed a 3th degree polynomial classifier. The performance of the classifiers and the number of support vectors chosen from 150 training examples are shown in Table 1. All the polynomial classifiers set the regularization parameter C to 100.

Table 1. Experiment results using polynomial kernels

Classifiers Type	No. of Support Vectors	Training Accuracy on 150 exs.	Testing Accuracy on 450 exs.	Testing Accuracy Using max. Output from the Three Classifiers
1. Frontal vs Others	33	100 %	99.33 %	
2. Left 33.75^o vs Others	25	100 %	99.56 %	100 %
3. Right 33.75^o vs Others	37	100 %	99.78%	

The performance of the classifiers on pose estimation using RBF kernels and the number of the support vectors chosen from 150 examples are shown in Table 2. The first RBF classifier sets the regularization parameter C = 200, while the last two will set C = 100.

Table 2. Experiment results using RBF kernels

Classifiers Type	No. of Support Vectors	Training Accuracy on 150 exs.	Testing Accuracy on 450 exs.	Testing Accuracy Using max. Output from the Three Classifiers
1. Frontal vs Others	47	100 %	100 %	
2. Left 33.75^o vs Others	38	100 %	100%	100 %
3. Right 33.75^o vs Others	43	100 %	100%	

The number of support vectors used by polynomial kernels is less than that used by RBF kernels, while the performance obtained using RBF kernels is slightly better than that obtained using polynomial kernels. RBF kernel should perform usually better for several reasons: (i) it has better boundary response as it allows for extrapolation, (ii) most high-dimensional data sets can be approximated by Gaussian-like distributions similar to that used by RBFs.

4.2   Eye Detection

Our experiment on eye detection used 16x16 image vectors corresponding to eye / non-eye images. All the image data was preprocessed so that each pixel has been normalized to a [-1, +1] range before training. The training data consisted of 186 eye images and 186 non-eye images. Test data consisted of 100 images of each class (eye and non - eye). In Table 3, the results are listed for the 3 SVM kernels with various parameter settings. The polynomial kernels utilized for the test were 2nd, 3rd and 4th order. Each SVM was tested against 200 unseen data vectors.

Table 3. Experiment results using polynomial kernels in eye detection

Polynomial Kernel	No. of Support Vectors	Testing Accuracy on 450 exs.
n=2	68	96.00 %
n=3	83	93.50 %
n=4	144	92.00 %

The best generalization performance of 4% (error on test data) was achieved using polynomial kernels of second degree as the set of discriminating functions.

5   Conclusions

This paper addresses the problems of pose estimation and eye detection using Support Vector Machines (SVM), a novel pattern classification algorithm (Cortes and Vapnik, 1995; Vapnik, 1995). Experimental results using frontal, and 33.75° rotated left and right poses, respectively, demonstrate the feasibility of our approach for pose estimation. The accuracy observed on test data, using both polynomials of degree 3 and Radial Basis Functions (RBFs) as kernel approximation functions, to determine the SVM separating hyperplanes, has been 100%.   On the eye detection task, SVM achieves an accuracy of 96 % using polynomial kernels of second degree as the set of approximating functions. SVM thus appear to be a robust classification scheme and this suggests their use for additional face recognition tasks, such as surveillance.

6   Acknowledgements

This work was partially supported by the DoD Counterdrug Technology Development Program, with the U.S. Army Research Laboratory as Technical Agent, under contract DAAL01-97-K-0118.

7   References

Chellappa R., Wilson,C. L., and Sirohey, C. (1995), Human and Machine Recognition of Faces: A Survey, *Proc. IEEE* **83**, 705-740.

Cherkassky, V. and Mulier, F. (1998), *Learning from Data : Concepts, Theory and Methods*, Wiley.

Cortes, C. and Vapnik, V. (1995), Support-Vector Networks, *Machine Learning*, 20, 273-297.

Phillips, P. J., Wechsler, H., Huang, J., and Rauss, P. (1998), The FERET Database and Evaluation Procedure for Face Recognition Algorithms, *Image and Vision Computing* (to appear).

Osuna, E., Freund, R., Girosi, F. (1997), Training Support Vector Machines: An Application to Face Detection, *Proc. of Computer Vision and Pattern Recognition (CVPR)*, San Juan, Puerto Rico.

Samal A. and Iyengar, P. (1992), Automatic Recognition and Analysis of Human Faces and Facial Expressions: A Survey, *Pattern Recognition* **25**, 65-77.

Vapnik, V. (1995) *The Nature of Statistical Learning Theory*, Springer Verlag,

A Practical Automatic Face Recognition System

Qi Bin Sun, Chian Prong Lam and Jian Kang Wu
RWC-ISS Lab
Institute of Systems Science
National University of Singapore
Singapore 119597
Email: qibin, prong, jiankang@iss.nus.sg

Abstract. This paper presents an automatic face recognition system targeted at practical applications. From a series of color images, ROIs (region of interest) which may contain faces are obtained from color segmentation. Meanwhile motion regions are detected using temporal convolution. Based on the combined color and motion information, faces are identified by ellipse fitting. Through symmetry detection operation, the frontal face images are selected from those identified faces and the eye locations are determined using gradient and geometry information. After normalization of size and rotation based on eye locations, the normalized faces are fed into the recognition engine whose kernel is a new recognition paradigm called recognition by recall. The whole processing procedure is fully automatic. Experimental results have demonstrated its validity and potential.

Keywords. Recognition by recall, Face and facial feature detection, Color segmentation, Motion analysis

1 Introduction

With requirements targeted at some practical applications such as security access control, human-computer interface etc., the research on developing face recognition system should focus not only on the recognition accuracy but also on the recognition time, meanwhile tolerating some reasonable imaging conditions. Based on the above considerations, we have developed a fully automatic face recognition system in our lab. In this practical system, we use color and motion information jointly as well as a model-based approach to detect faces from the input image sequences; Symmetry detection operations are used to select frontal faces from the detected faces before eyes are located based on gradient and geometry information; Finally the face recognition engine is started which mainly comprises recall[1] from multiple features extracted and face database modules, and obtain the output result on who the person is.

In the following sections, we will first introduce the whole system and its basic specifications, then describe its technical details and present some experimental results. We will also discuss our experiences in designing and developing this system and the work we need to do in the future.

2. System overview

Basically our system comprises three modules: face detection, facial feature detection and face recognition (Fig.1). A color image sequence input (currently 8 frames) enters two sub-system simultaneously in which one is to perform two phase color segmentation frame by frame and the other one is to extract motion information from two consecutive frames. Face candidates are then obtained through combining color segmentation and motion extraction information. Actual faces are then identified by ellipse fitting (model-based). Through symmetry detection operations, only frontal face images are selected from those identified faces and the eye locations are determined using gradient and geometry information. After a normalization process based on eyes' locations, the normalized faces are fed into the recognition engine whose kernel is a new recognition paradigm called recognition by recall. The whole processing procedure is fully automatic and the pipeline system structure is suitable for real time implementation.

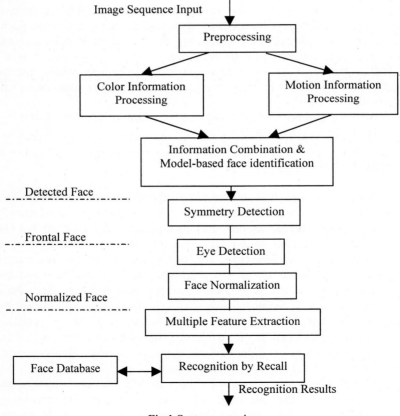

Fig.1 System overview

Currently the imaging conditions we can handle are as follows: Changes in lighting condition (with uncontrolled lighting) due to variations in position. Tilts of less than 15 degrees, such as the person facing slightly away from the camera or looking up or down slightly. Facial changes such as getting thinner or fatter, growing beard or mustache, change of hairstyle or changes in facial expression.

3. Technical detail description

In this section we will describe the technical implementation details. Basically the system is divided into three modules: face detection, facial feature detection and face recognition by recall. All techniques adopted are based on its potential in real time implementation and can reduce the effects of imaging conditions. For example, the color segmentation can be implemented by look-up tables; Furthermore the procedures of color normalization and motion extraction are also the procedures of luminance elimination.

3.1 Face detection & identification

Face detection is based on combined color and motion information. These two kinds of information have been widely used for face or gesture understanding[2][3], but they are mainly used for tracking and not for identification.

It is reported that face color is a 2-D Gaussian distribution[2] even in different races after normalizing color values from RGB space to r-g space:

$$r = \frac{R}{R+G+B}, \qquad g = \frac{G}{R+G+B} \qquad (1)$$

Where R, G, B are the three primary colors, red, green and blue respectively. r, g are normalized color values. So we can develop a face color model which can be represented by a 2-D Gaussian model $N(m, \Sigma^2)$, where $m = (\bar{r}, \bar{g})$ with

$$\bar{r} = \frac{1}{N}\sum_{i=1}^{N} r_i, \qquad \bar{g} = \frac{1}{N}\sum_{i=1}^{N} g_i, \qquad \text{and} \qquad \Sigma = \begin{bmatrix} \sigma_{rr} & \sigma_{rg} \\ \sigma_{gr} & \sigma_{gg} \end{bmatrix} \qquad (2)$$

where σ_{**} is the covariance of the 2D Gaussian distribution model.

Hence given a sequence of color images, using the Gaussian face color model produced previously, face candidates can be segmented roughly. But because this normalization process is actually an information compression process, it is unavoidable that some non-face regions are introduced during the color normalization process. Therefore, we need to perform the color segmentation again based on the result of the first color segmentation operation. The second color segmentation is conducted in L-a-b color space and based on the histograms on L, a, b dimensions. The transformations from RGB to L-a-b are:

$$L = 116 \times \left(\frac{Y}{Y_n}\right)^{\frac{1}{3}} - 16, \quad for \quad \frac{Y}{Y_n} > 0.008856, \quad L = 903 \times \frac{Y}{Y_n}, \quad for \quad \frac{Y}{Y_n} \leq 0.008856$$

$$a = 500 \times \left(f\left(\frac{X}{X_n}\right) - f\left(\frac{Y}{Y_n}\right) \right) \qquad b = 200 \times \left(f\left(\frac{Y}{Y_n}\right) - f\left(\frac{Z}{Z_n}\right) \right) \qquad (3)$$

where

$$f(t) = t^{1/3}, \quad for \quad t > 0.008856$$
$$f(t) = 7.787 \times t + \frac{16}{116}, \quad for \quad t \le 0.008856 \qquad , \qquad \begin{bmatrix} X \\ Y \\ Z \end{bmatrix} = \begin{bmatrix} 0.431 & 0.342 & 0.178 \\ 0.222 & 0.707 & 0.071 \\ 0.020 & 0.130 & 0.939 \end{bmatrix} \begin{bmatrix} R \\ G \\ B \end{bmatrix}$$

$$X_n = 0.951, \quad Y_n = 1.000, \quad Z_n = 1.089$$

It is noted that all transformations among different color spaces are done by look-up tables.

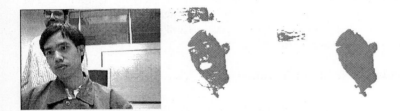

(a) Original image   (b) Color segmentation   (c) Region selecting & growing

Fig. 2 The procedure of color processing

After these two phases of color segmentation, reliable face candidates are obtained by selecting and grouping these segmented regions (Fig. 2). While doing color segmentation, the motion extraction process also starts. Firstly, locations of moving edges are found using temporal convolution:

$$M_x(x,y,t) = \frac{\partial I}{\partial x}(x,y,t) \bullet \frac{\partial I}{\partial t}(x,y,t) \quad , \qquad M_y(x,y,t) = \frac{\partial I}{\partial y}(x,y,t) \bullet \frac{\partial I}{\partial t}(x,y,t) \qquad (4)$$
$$= S_x \otimes I(x,y,t) \bullet D(x,y,t) \qquad\qquad = S_y \otimes I(x,y,t) \bullet D(x,y,t)$$

where S_x and S_y are the x and y directional Sobel operators. $I(x,y,t)$ is the intensity value of point (x,y) at time t, $D(x,y,t)$ is the difference between consecutive frames:

$$D(x,y,t) = I(x,y,t) - I(x,y,t+1)$$

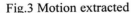

Fig.3 Motion extracted   Fig.4 Combined information

These moving edges are clustered to get a consistent motion field (Fig. 3). Once we obtain the results of color segmentation and motion extraction, the information combination process will start. Considering that the hair and clothes are helpful to separate face from background, the motion information should be weighed more on the middle parts of the face candidates while the color information should be weighed more on the upper and lower parts of the face candidates (Fig. 4). Finally faces are identified by ellipse fitting based on the data combined (Fig. 5). The ellipse fitting involves five parameters which are center point (x_0, y_0), semi-major axis a, semi-minor axis b and the tilt angle θ.

Given a set of points (x_i, y_i), $i = 1, 2, \ldots, N$, assuming that there is an ellipse passing through them, we have

$$\frac{\overline{X}_i^2}{a^2} + \frac{\overline{Y}_i^2}{b^2} = 1, \quad \text{for all } i = 1, 2, \ldots, N. \quad (5)$$

Where

$$\overline{X}_i = (x_i - x_0)\cos\theta + (y_i - y_0)\sin\theta$$
$$\overline{Y}_i = -(x_i - x_0)\sin\theta + (y_i - y_0)\cos\theta$$

The above equation is multiplied by a^2 on both sides and rearranged in the following manner. The assumption that $a \neq 0$ is used. Then

$$2xC_0 - y^2 C_1 - 2xy C_2 + 2y C_3 - C_4 = x^2 \quad (6)$$

where

$$C_0 = \left(b^2 x_0 \cos^2\theta + b^2 y_0 \cos\theta \sin\theta + a^2 x_0 \sin^2\theta - a^2 y_0 \cos\theta \sin\theta\right) / \left(b^2 \cos^2\theta + a^2 \sin^2\theta\right)$$

$$C_1 = \left(b^2 \sin^2\theta + a^2 \cos^2\theta\right) / \left(b^2 \cos^2\theta + a^2 \sin^2\theta\right)$$

$$C_2 = \left(b^2 \cos\theta \sin\theta - a^2 \cos\theta \sin\theta\right) / \left(b^2 \cos^2\theta + a^2 \sin^2\theta\right)$$

$$C_3 = \left(b^2 x_0 \cos\theta \sin\theta + b^2 y_0 \sin^2\theta - a^2 x_0 \cos\theta \sin\theta + a^2 y_0 \cos^2\theta\right) / \left(b^2 \cos^2\theta + a^2 \sin^2\theta\right)$$

$$C_4 = (b^2 x_0^2 \cos^2\theta + 2b^2 x_0 y_0 \cos\theta \sin\theta + b^2 y_0^2 \sin^2\theta + a^2 x_0^2 \sin^2\theta - 2a^2 x_0 y_0 \cos\theta \sin\theta$$
$$+ a^2 y_0^2 \cos^2\theta - a^2 b^2) / \left(b^2 \cos^2\theta + a^2 \sin^2\theta\right)$$

Thus, an ellipse can be fitted as follows:

$$\begin{pmatrix} 2x_1 & -y_1^2 & -2x_1 y_1 & 2y_1 & -1 \\ 2x_2 & -y_2^2 & -2x_2 y_2 & 2y_2 & -1 \\ \vdots & \vdots & \vdots & \vdots & \vdots \\ 2x_{N-1} & -y_{N-1}^2 & -2x_{N-1} y_{N-1} & 2y_{N-1} & -1 \\ 2x_N & -y_N^2 & -2x_N y_N & 2y_N & -1 \end{pmatrix} \begin{pmatrix} C_0 \\ C_1 \\ C_2 \\ C_3 \\ C_4 \end{pmatrix} = \begin{pmatrix} x_1^2 \\ x_2^2 \\ \vdots \\ x_{N-1}^2 \\ x_N^2 \end{pmatrix} \quad (7)$$

The above equation is of the form $\mathbf{AX} = \mathbf{C}$, where $\mathbf{A}$ is $n \times 5$, $\mathbf{C}$ is $n \times 1$, and $\mathbf{X}$ is 5×1, it can be solved using the pseudo inverse method[8]:

$$\mathbf{X} = (\mathbf{A'A})^{-1} \mathbf{A'C} \quad (8)$$

where $\mathbf{A'}$ is the transpose of $\mathbf{A}$. $\mathbf{A'A}$ and $\mathbf{A'C}$ are as follows:

Fig.5 Identified faces   Fig.6 Detected eyes

$$
\mathbf{A'A} = \begin{pmatrix}
4\sum_{i=1}^{N} x_i^2 & -2\sum_{i=1}^{N} x_i y_i^2 & -4\sum_{i=1}^{N} x_i^2 y & 4\sum_{i=1}^{N} x_i y_i & -2\sum_{i=1}^{N} x_i \\
-2\sum_{i=1}^{N} x_i y_i^2 & \sum_{i=1}^{N} y_i^4 & 2\sum_{i=1}^{N} x_i y_i^3 & -2\sum_{i=1}^{N} y_i^3 & \sum_{i=1}^{N} y_i^2 \\
-4\sum_{i=1}^{N} x_i^2 y & 2\sum_{i=1}^{N} x_i y_i^3 & 4\sum_{i=1}^{N} x_i^2 y_i^2 & -4\sum_{i=1}^{N} x_i y_i^2 & 2\sum_{i=1}^{N} x_i y_i \\
4\sum_{i=1}^{N} x_i y_i & -2\sum_{i=1}^{N} y_i^3 & -4\sum_{i=1}^{N} x_i y_i^2 & 4\sum_{i=1}^{N} y_i^2 & -2\sum_{i=1}^{N} y_i \\
-2\sum_{i=1}^{N} x_i & \sum_{i=1}^{N} y_i^2 & 2\sum_{i=1}^{N} x_i y_i & -2\sum_{i=1}^{N} y_i & N
\end{pmatrix}
\quad
\mathbf{A'C} = \begin{pmatrix}
2\sum_{i=1}^{N} x_i^3 \\
-\sum_{i=1}^{N} x_i^2 y_i^2 \\
-2\sum_{i=1}^{N} x_i^3 y_i \\
2\sum_{i=1}^{N} x_i^2 y_i \\
-\sum_{i=1}^{N} x_i^2
\end{pmatrix}
\quad (10)
$$

Once we get the values of C_0, C_1, C_2, C_3, C_4, then we can obtain the values of x_0, y_0, a, b, θ using the equation (6):

$$
y_0 = (C_3 - C_0 C_2)/(C_1 - C_2^2) \qquad x_0 = C_0 - C_2 y_0
$$

$$
\theta = 0.5 \tan^{-1}(2C_2/(1 - C_1)) \qquad u = \sqrt{(1 - C_2/\tan\theta)/(1 + C_2/\tan\theta)}
$$

$$
a = \sqrt{(x_0^2 + 2x_0 y_0 C_2 + C_1 y_0^2 - C_4)(1 + u\tan^2\theta)/(1 + \tan^2\theta)} \qquad b = a/u \qquad (11)
$$

Whether an ellipse fits face could be decided by the aspect ratio a/b and θ. The typical ranges are $1.3 \leq a/b \leq 2.0$ and $-30° \leq \theta \leq 30°$. A detailed description is in [4].

3.2 Facial feature detection

After the faces are identified from the input image sequence, we need to select the frontal faces from those identified faces and locate the eyes for face recognition.

The symmetry attribute of human face is a useful cue for us to choose frontal faces. For instance, all we have are two eyes and two ears which are symmetrical about the face middle line, as well as one nose and one mouth which are both located at the middle line. After the identified faces are normalized rotationally by the parameters of ellipse fitting (Fig. 8), symmetry detection is done using gradient and intensity information in the face region. If the difference between the left side and right side of a face is within a preset threshold (Eq (12)), the face is considered to be a frontal face.

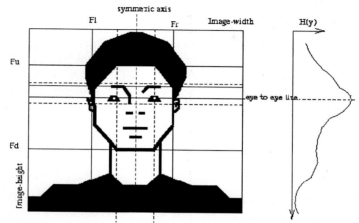

Fig.7 The illustration of symmetry detection and eye location

$$T = \left| \sum_{(x_i,y_i)\in LEFT}\left(w_1 I(x_i,y_i) + w_2 D(x_i,y_i)\right) - \sum_{(x_i,y_i)\in RIGHT}\left(w_1 I(x_i,y_i) + w_2 D(x_i,y_i)\right) \right| \quad (12)$$

where I is image intensity value and D is the norm of image gradient value.

Fig. 8 The normalized face for symmetry   Fig. 9. The located eyes

Once a frontal face is obtained, the next step is to find the eye locations. The method adopted for eye detection is a modification of [5] and the detection is conducted based on the resulted image shown in Fig.8. The algorithm firstly finds out the possible eyes-connecting lines which are located at the maximums of the filtered vertical histogram (Fig. 7), and select one as the eyes-connecting line using the previous information of color segmentation and geometry assumptions. Then the search is on the expected zones" around this line. Their exact location is then obtained by computing the horizontal and vertical coordinates of a pixel belonging to the corresponding pupils through a pixel-growing procedure (Fig. 9). The detected eyes are shown in Fig. 6.

3.3 Face recognition by recall

Before starting face recognition, the identified face must be normalized so that it is suitable for feature extraction. Based on the eye positions obtained previously, the face is rotated and resized such that the positions of the eyes are fixed at pre-set coordinates. From this normalized image, various feature extraction techniques, regardless of whether they are size or rotation invariant can be applied. Currently our proposed new paradigm on recognition, recognition by recall, utilizes features extracted by PCA. Proposed by Pentland[6], PCA has been successfully used to extract vectors for individual facial features in our earlier work on face database system (CAFIIR)[7]. However we are still looking into other feature extraction method such as auto-correlation to improve recognition accuracy.

Recognition by recall is most suitable for the recognition of complex images such as faces. It is based on the fact that when we recognized a familiar face of our friends, we do not do so by matching every single facial features but rather recall the unique features of the face which has been remembered in memory for comparison. It means that we recognize them by recall from our memory. The recall process is performed by evaluating the similarity between the person we try to recognize and the prior knowledge of our memory. It is like a content-based database. Here similarity function plays an important role and can be written as:

$$S = g\left(h_1\left(f_{11}, f_{11}^s; f_{12}, f_{12}^s; \ldots\right), h_2\left(f_{21}, f_{21}^s; f_{22}, f_{22}^s; \ldots\right), \ldots\right)$$

where h_i is the similarity function for feature measure, and g is the overall similarity measure. f^s stands for feature measures of the learning samples. h can be distance measure, correlation, or more complicated functions. For facial images, it can be characterized by facial features such as chin, eyes, nose, mouth. Both such unique facial features and similarity functions are learned from continuous exposure to the various aspects of the faces. Hence, the longer the learning cycle, the greater the ease with which we can recognize a person. To model the learning capability of the human face recognition system proposed, we use a three layer neural network. The first layer is the comparison layer which extracts the various distance measures between the input and the database sample feature vectors. The second layer, a hidden layer, is a learning module which is triggered on or off depending on the feedback. The third layer, a recognition/output layer, computes the degree of similarity between the input and the sample face in the database. If the degree of similarity is above a threshold, a face is recognized and the identity of the person is announced. Otherwise, the identity of the new face will be sought, corresponding feature vectors of the various faces of the same person stored in the database as well as the new vectors

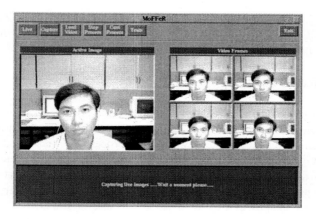

Fig. 10 The GUI platform of the face recognition system.

Fig.11 The result of face segmentation   Fig.12 The result of eye detection

Fig.13 The result of learning   Fig.14 The final recognition result

will be fed into the learning module to fine-tune the weights. The new feature vector as well as the identity of the person will be stored in the database. A detailed description is given in [1].

4 Experimental results

In this section, we shall present the experimental results obtained from our proposed method. The input color image sequence includes 8 frames with a 384*288 size, Fig.10~Fig.14 shows some processing results during face recognition. Fig.10 is the GUI platform of our face recognition system. Fig.11 is the results of face segmentation and fig.12 is the result of eye detection. Fig.13 shows the UI prompting for the identity of a face, and the final recognition result of a new set of images of the same person is shown in Fig.14. The average recognition time is less than one minute.

5 Conclusions and future work

We have proposed a fully automatic face recognition system. The selection of system structure and the techniques is based on the consideration that they are suitable for real time implementation and reduces the effects of imaging conditions. During the implementation of this system, we use as much information produced by each module as possible to enhance system performance, meanwhile keeping a reasonable processing time.

Now we are upgrading this system to detect face and facial features accurately and robustly and extend the recognition ability to multiple views.

References

[1] Jian Kang Wu, Recognition by recall, *1997 Real World Computing Symposium*, pp.142-147, Tokyo, Japan, 1997
[2] J. Yang and A. Wailbel, Tracking human faces in real-time, *Technical Report*, CMU-CS-95-210, Carnegie Mellon Univ., 1995.
[3] Feancis K.H. Quek, Eyes in the interface, *Image and vision computing*, Vo.13, No.6, pp.511-525, 1995.
[4] Q.B. Sun, C.P. Lam and J.K. Wu, Face and facial feature detection using multiple information, *Technical Report*, ISS, National Univ. of Singapore, 1996.
[5] L. Stringa, Eyes detection for face recognition, *Applied Artificial Intelligence*, Vol.7, pp.365-382, 1993.
[6] A. Pentland, Eigenface for recognition, *Journal of Cognitive Neuroscience*, Vol.3, No.1, pp.59-70, 1991.
[7] J. K. Wu and A. D. Narasimhalu, Identifying faces using multiple retrievals, *IEEE Multimedia*, pp.27-38, Summer, 1994.
[8] Saad Ahmed Sirohey, Human face segmentation and identification, *Technical Report*, CAR-TR-695, Univ. Of Maryland, 1993.

Feature Processing from Upright and Inverted Faces

Helmut Leder[1] and Vicki Bruce[2]

[1]University of Fribourg & Psychologisches Institut, FU Berlin, Habelschwerdter Allee 45, D-14195 Berlin *
[2]Department of Psychology, University of Stirling, FK8 4LA Stirling, UK

Abstract. Faces are particularly difficult to recognize when they are presented in the unusual upside down orientation. Understanding this face-inversion-effect (FIE) reveals which kind of information processing is used in the usually very efficient upright face recognition. Recent research is discussed which indicates that configural information is disrupted by inversion more than local information in faces. Moreover, the nature of configural information is investigated by means of experiments which test whether configural information consists of discrete spatial relationships or more holistic information. Empirical studies favor the former position. It is concluded that face processing relies significantly on the processing of relational information such as distance between the eyes.

1 Introduction

Human face recognition is of an immense and growing importance in modern Psychology and computer vision. Psychological investigations of the human face are challenging because of the properties of faces as dynamic objects that are recognized despite their similarity to a huge number of similar exemplars. In computer science it is investigated how the image of the human face can be treated in information processing to develop tools for automatic face recognition and human-machine-interaction (see for example the chapter of T. Huang). Human face recognition is quite reliable over a number of natural variations such as lighting, movement (see for example Christie & Bruce, *in press*) and changes over time such as hairstyle, aging and expression. However, there is one situation in which face recognition seems to be particularly disrupted: when faces are presented in an unusual upside-down orientation (Yin, 1969). Yin provided the first systematic investigation of the face-inversion-effect (FIE). Yin presented three experiments in which

---

* This paper is based on work that the authors conducted while the first author was staying at the University of Stirling with a Grant from the Swiss National Foundation in 1995. From November 1997 the first Author will be at the FU Berlin.

inversion deficits were investigated for faces and other mono-oriented object to prove that inversion is *particularly* disruptive for faces. In the first experiment recognition rates were compared when the stimuli were presented in the same orientation at study and test, either upright or inverted. Stimuli were photographs of male faces or houses, caricatures of airplanes and "men in motion". In a pairwise old-new recognition test the error rates revealed a general effect of inversion, but inversion was also more disruptive for faces than for any of the other materials. Inversion did not affect the recognition rates of the drawings of airplanes. In a second experiment the orientation varied between study and test, but the results were not as clear (see Kemp, 1996). To exclude the possibility that the results of Experiment 1 were due to the higher performance with upright faces compared to other material presented upright, Yin conducted a third experiment in which faces showed a larger inversion effect than drawings of headless costume figures which actually were easier than faces to recognize when presented upright. Yin summarized his results as having shown that inverted objects are harder to recognize when turned upside down but that the "inverted face is especially difficult to remember because ... of a general factor involving only the faces"(page 145). The FIE has been replicated frequently (see Valentine, 1988, for a review). Thus Valentine (1988) concluded nearly two decades later that the effect appeared to be robust to several experimental settings and tasks[1].

2 General versus Specific Deficits

This FIE was the target of several theoretical explanations that are sometimes hard to distinguish empirically. While one line of explanation proposes that the inversion effect is due to a component which affects any kind of information in the "inverted face" compared to the "upright face" (Valentine, 1991) other approaches explain the effect in terms of a specific processing deficit for a certain kind of information from inverted faces (Diamond & Carey, 1986; Farah, Tanaka & Drain, 1995). Valentine (1991) proposed a framework which was presented to explain (and illustrate) how faces might be encoded in memory and how face specific effects, among them the FIE, might be explained. His "face space" model proposes that faces are encoded along a number of dimensions that unfold a space in which faces are represented as vectors which are determined by the values that each face has on the different dimensions of the space. Face recognition fails if faces are confused with

---

[1] However, Valentine (1988) also concluded that the FIE might require a memory component, a hypothesis that was in accordance with some studies in which simultaneous matching tasks were used and the FIE was not found. Recent studies provide additional evidence to this hypothesis. Leder and Bruce (1997b) found that sensitivity to configural aspects is reduced in inverted presentation - but only if the comparison requires memory.

nearby neighbors or if faces cannot be matched with vectors in the face-space. According to Valentine (1991) the FIE is due to noise in the encoding process which adds noise to the location of faces in the multidimensional space and therefore causes the difficulty in recognizing it.

Although face space is a fairly general metaphor, nonetheless the predictions of the model are testable as we will demonstrate. Valentine (1991) was rather vague concerning the dimensions of the face-space. He stated (page 166) that "the dimensions of the space represent the physiognomic features that are used to encode faces". He also proposes some candidates derived from earlier studies on facial features (see Shepherd, Davies & Ellis, 1981). However, other face research has proposed likely candidates.

The present paper focuses on two broad classes of facial information. Faces contain a variety of different sorts of visually distinguishable information, such as the apparent constituting elements of the two eyes, the nose and mouth, which might differ in color, size, contrast etc. These examples represent the class of local face information. Another class of information consists of relational properties such as the distance between the eyes and the mouth-nose distance. All faces share a common arrangement of their main local features, but they differ individually in the relational as well as in their higher-order properties. For example, as the eyes are placed horizontally above the nose their distance from each other varies between individual faces as well as their placement relative to the tip of the nose.

The present paper focusses on this broad distinction between local features, such as eyes and nose, and relational - or configural- features. Taking these classes to represent specific face information Valentine's (1991) explanation of the FIE can be directly tested. While Valentine proposed a general mechanism by which inversion impaired recognition ("error associated with all dimensions") the alternative hypotheses claim that specific information is disrupted by inversion. Empirically it can be asked whether local and configural information are disrupted by inversion to the same amount or differently. Two recent studies by Searcy and Bartlett (1996) and Leder and Bruce (in press) directly tested this.

Searcy and Bartlett (1996) investigated whether inversion impaired the processing of configural information more than processing of other kind of information such as local features. In their first experiment they produced grotesque faces by either manipulating local features such as blackening teeth or whitening eyes, or by manipulating configural features by creating unnaturally grotesque configurations. When compared with the original versions both versions were rated to be grotesque in an upright orientation - but when turned upside-down this effect nearly vanished for the configural - but not for the local versions. However, these effects are based on strong and unnatural exaggeration of facial information. Moreover (see Footnote 1) it remains open, whether these perceptual effects actually affect the recognisabilty of inverted faces (which is what the FIE refers to). Leder and Bruce (in press) used a very similar design but used much more moderate manipulations and measured their effect both on ratings of the distinctiveness of the faces and on their recognition. A set of faces was created which systematically differed according to the two sorts of information. In all their experiments, subjects saw one of three versions of a face: Original faces, that had been rated as average in distinctiveness in a previous study (Hancock, Burton & Bruce, 1996), a more distinctive version in which local features had been changed, and a more distinctive version in which relational features had been changed. In the third experiment of their study subjects saw the set (which contained one third of Originals, one third relational and one third locally accentuated faces) in a distinctiveness-rating phase (9-point scale), in either upright or inverted orientation. Compared to the Originals an increase in distinctiveness was found for both manipulated versions in upright orientation. When faces were presented upside down, however, then the increase in distinctiveness vanished for the "relational" faces but the local versions retained their increased distinctiveness. In a second phase of this experiment effects on the recognisability of the different versions of faces were tested, in both orientations. Participants who provided the rating data to the upright versions provided hit-rates, other participants saw a different set of faces first and provided false-alarm rates to the three versions. Presented upright, both versions revealed higher performance compared to the originals but in upside-down presentation, the local versions showed a much stronger distinctiveness advantage. Effects of distinctiveness are generally found to be more prominent in terms of false-alarm rates (Shapiro & Penrod, 1986). In the false-alarm rates, the relationally manipulated faces lost their "advantage" over the Original versions in inverted presentation.

The results in terms of inversion effects found in the rating phases in both studies are presented in Table 1. In Table 1 the change in rated grotesqueness (Searcy & Bartlett, 1996) or distinctiveness (Leder & Bruce, in press) of the two manipulated versions is calculated as the proportion of change when the stimuli have been turned upside-down.

	local information	configural inf.
Searcy & Bartlett (1996, Exp.1)	-0.007	0.375
Leder & Bruce (in press, Exp.3)	0.063	0.204

Table 1: Size of inversion deficits (in proportion of the upright performance) of local and configural information in terms of perceived grotesqeness (Searcy & Bartlett, 1996) or rated distinctiveness (Leder & Bruce, in press)

The results of these studies suggest that at least two dimensions of facial information contribute to a face's appearance as being distinctive, but that these sources of information are differentially affected by turning the face upside-down. These findings are in accordance with a face processing model in which face inversion effects occur because a specific type of information processing is disrupted, rather than because of a general disruption of performance. Moreover, it was the configural information that was disrupted by inversion. This is in agreement with other theories and studies about the cause of the inversion effect. The rest of the present paper deals with the question what the nature of the disrupted configural information is.

3   The FIE is caused by the Disruption of Configuration

The conclusions drawn from Searcy and Bartlett (1996) and Leder and Bruce (in press) are in accordance with a number of authors who suspected that it is 'configural' processing which is particularly disrupted when faces are inverted. For example, Young, Hellawell and Hay (1987) found that subjects were better at identifying parts of composite faces when these were shown inverted compared with upright; and Bartlett and Searcy (1993) were able to show that the "Thatcher illusion" (Thompson, 1980) arises because of deficient processing of relationships between features in upside-down faces.

However, it is sometimes difficult to distinguish clearly between configural and local features, as the former rely on the availability of the latter. Even in the studies which were discussed above there has always been some confounding between local and configural information, for example, since moving the nose away from the mouth both increases the spatial distance between these two features (a "configural" change), and changes the nose into a shorter nose (a "feature" change). To overcome this difficulty it is necessary to create faces that differ in terms of one sort of information - without differing on the other. Furthermore, it is not clear what 'configural' processing refers to. In some accounts, it is the processing of the spatial relationships between different face features, yet in other accounts (e.g. Martha Farah and colleagues) it refers to the processing of a pattern as a whole, without decomposition into parts at all (holistic processing).

Farah, Tanaka and Drain (1995) attempted to distinguish local from configural processing of faces by testing the recognition of faces which were encoded either as whole faces or "part-based". In the latter case facial features were presented individually during the study phase. While the complete faces showed a significant FIE, the recognition of the part-based version did not show a significant decrease when the stimuli had been presented upside-down. Farah et al. used this condition to test a hypothesis about holistic processing, however the nature of the part-based stimulus condition in their experiments makes it impossible to differentiate the holistic from a more simple 'configural' hypothesis, as the part-based stimuli lack relational as well as holistic properties. Moreover the dissociation in the Farah et al. (1995, second experiment) study was also due to a high performance in the whole upright faces. Their results therefore need further examination to specify more clearly the source of the FIE.

Another approach was recently proposed by Leder and Bruce (1997a). If the face-inversion effect arises because faces cannot be distinguished on the basis of configural information in an inverted orientation, then faces that can be distinguished on local information only should not produce an inversion-effect. Leder and Bruce used two sets of faces which either differed only in terms of local information (eye-color, hair color etc.) or which could be individuated in terms of configural information alone (e.g. nose-mouth-distance). Faces were made using the same local features from a schematic face reconstruction set - which differed from each other in combinations of feature colors for the local versions, and which differed in the spatial arrangement of face features for the configural versions. In a first experiment of their study each participant learned both stimulus sets (six different faces) until each face could be correctly named in a familiarization phase. A recognition test included presentation of the faces in upright and inverted orientation. When faces differed in local information only, then the recognition was as good in upright as in inverted orientation. However, faces that could be distinguished in terms of configural aspects only revealed an FIE of more than 30%. From these results Leder and Bruce (1997a) concluded that the occurrence of an inversion effect in face recognition seems to require that faces differ individually in terms of their configural aspects. Moreover, the experiment revealed that the ease of distinguishing individual faces on the basis of configural information was indeed disrupted when faces were turned upside-down. In an additional experiment it was shown that the size of the inversion effect was determined by the extent to which the stimuli could be distinguished on the basis of configural properties.

4   Relational versus Holistic Information

Farah, Tanaka and Drain (1995) suggested that the inversion effect is caused by the disruption of holistic processing in inverted faces. As discussed above the empirical support for this conclusion often is associated with a confounding of holistic and relational aspects. The experiment described from Leder and Bruce (1997a) was informative concerning this point because the "local" versions alone did not give any inversion effect - despite the fact that these versions were intact whole faces. This result seems surprising if all faces would elicit "holistic" processing. Thus the strong holistic version seems to be unlikely.

The stimulus material used by Leder and Bruce (1997a) allows an even more direct test of the holistic-versus relational hypothesis. If a set of faces is available in which faces differ only in terms of relational information then it is possible to test directly whether faces are encoded in terms of the spatial relationships between different features, or in terms of higher-order holistic information.

The stimuli were used in an preliminary experiment at the University of Fribourg which investigated whether single distances are encoded from faces or whether the sensitivity to relational changes is due to a holistic, higher order representation. Retrieval of relational features was tested either in isolation or in a highly redundant context.

The 18 Participants in this study learned to name each stimulus by a randomly assigned name. The set of stimuli differed in terms of specific spatial relationships. At test the participants either saw the critical relational feature only, e.g. two eyes that were slightly closer, or a specific nose-mouth distance, and their task was to identify by name which of the faces was being probed. In a different version the relational features was embedded in a facial outline in which all other features had been deleted. Moreover, the complete versions were also tested in both orientations, upright and inverted, to check that the conditions of this experiment were sufficient to produce an FIE. The results are presented in Table 2.

	complete	relations	relations+redundant context
upright	72.7	54.5	61.3
inverted	45.4	–	–

Table 2: Identification rates for the different versions

Table 2 shows that participants were able to recognize the faces from the relational features when these were presented in isolation (e.g. the two eyes which preserved the specific "narrow eye-distance" of one of the faces). However, adding a relatively redundant context which was included to favor holistic processing also increased the performance.

Thus the results show that configural information consists of rather locally encoded relational aspects but that face recognition also might include a component of holistic processing. In additional experiments reported in Leder and Bruce (1997a) this question was further investigated. In one experiment it was found that the presence of context did not help to retrieve face identities when probed by local features which had been studied as part of a critical spatial relationship. For example, if a face was distinguished by its interocular distance, then showing the left eye alone, even within the context of the rest of the face, did not yield recognition rates as high as when just the pair of eyes with their critical separation was presented. These results do support a view of configural infromation in faces that is cast in terms of the processing of discrete spatial relationships rather than in terms of holistic processing.

Another formulation of the holistic position is that that holistic processing is marked by interdependence of the processing of facial features can be refuted in the study by Macho and Leder (in press). Macho and Leder used faces which were made of three features (eye-distance, width of the nose, and size of the mouth) with three values (respectively two features with five values) in complete designs in which all feature combinations were used. The eye-distance represented configural information in these experiments. When participants judged for each face whether it was more similar to one of the extreme exemplars the results did not show interactive influences of features. The absence of an interactive influence on participants' performance is a strong indication of non-interactive processing of facial features.

Thus, the empirical evidence suggests that it is more probable that the relational features are the atoms of configural processing, which themselves are processed quite locally. The debate of holistic processing versus relational processing might lean towards the latter - however the way that faces are perceived might rely on several aspects that might also include higher-order combinations of features.

References

Bartlett, J. C., & Searcy, J. H. (1993). Inversion and configuration of faces. *Cognitive Psychology*, *25*, 281-316.

Christie, F. & Bruce, V. (in press). The role of dynamic information in the recognition of unfamiliar faces. *Memory & Cognition*.

Diamond, R. & Carey, S. (1986). Why faces are and are not special: an effect of expertise. *Journal of Experimental Psychology: General*, *115*, 107-117.

Farah, M.J., Tanaka, J.W. & Drain, H.M. (1995). What causes the face inversion effect? *Journal of Experimental Psychology: Human Perception and Performance, 21*, 628-634.

Hancock, P.J.B., Burton, A.M. & Bruce, V. (1996). Face processing: human perception and principal components analysis. *Memory and Cognition*, *24 (1)* 26-40, 1996.

Kemp, R. (1996). Face perception: Sensitivity to feature displacement in normal, negative and inverted images. University of London: Unpublished Thesis.

Leder, H. & Bruce, V. (In press). Local and global aspects of face distinctiveness. *Quarterly Journal of Experimental Psychology*.

Leder, H. & Bruce, V. (1997a). When inverted faces are recognized: the role of configural information in face recognition. *Manuscript under revision*.

Leder, H. & Bruce, V. (1997b). Features in the context of upright and inverted faces. *Manuscript in preparation*.

Macho, S. & Leder, H. (In press). Your eyes only? A test of interactive influence in the processing of facial features. *Journal of Experimental Psychology: Human Perception and Performance*.

Searcy, J.H. & Bartlett, J.C. (1996). Inversion and processing of component and spatial-relational information in faces. *Journal of Experimental Psychology: Human Perception and Performance*, 22, 904-915.

Shapiro, P.N. & Penrod, S. (1986). Meta-analysis of facial identification studies. *Psychological Bulletin, 100*, 139-156.

Shepherd, J., Davies, G. & Ellis, H. (1981). Studies of cue saliency. In: Davies, G., Ellis, H. & Shepherd, J. (Eds.), *Perceiving and Remembering Faces.* London: Academic Press.

Thompson, P. (1980). Margaret Thatcher: A new illusion. *Perception, 9*, 483-484.

Valentine, T. (1988). Upside-down faces: A review of the effect of inversion upon face recognition. *British Journal of Psychology, 79*, 471-491.

Valentine, T. (1991). A unified account of the effects of distinctiveness, inversion and race on face recognition. *Quarterly Journal of Experimental Psychology, 43A*, 161-204.

Yin, R.K. (1969). Looking at upside-down faces. *Journal of Experimental Psychology, 81*, 141-145.

Young, A.W., Hellawell, D. & Hary, D.C. (1987). Configural information in face perception. *Perception, 16*, 747-759.

Using Differential Constraints to Generate a 3D Face Model from Stereo

Richard Lengagne[1], Olivier Monga[1], and Pascal Fua[2]

[1] INRIA Rocquencourt-Domaine de Voluceau, BP105 78153 Le Chesnay Cedex, FRANCE
[2] Computer Graphics Laboratory (LIG), EPFL, CH-1015, Lausanne, SWITZERLAND

Summary. We propose a way to incorporate a priori information in a 3D stereo reconstruction process from a pair of calibrated face images. A 3D mesh modeling the surface is iteratively deformed in order to minimize an energy function. Differential information about the object shape is used to generate an adaptive mesh that can fulfill the compacity and the accuracy requirements. Moreover, in areas where the stereo information is not reliable enough to accurately recover the surface shape, because of inappropriate texture or bad lighting conditions, we incorporate geometric constraints related to the differential properties of the surface, that can be intuitive or refer to predefined geometric properties of the object to be reconstructed. They can be applied to scalar fields, such as curvature values, or structural features, such as crest lines. Therefore, we generate a 3D face model using Computer Vision techniques that is compact, accurate and consistent with the a priori knowledge about the underlying surface.

1. Introduction

3D face modeling is currently receiving a lot of attention among the Computer Vision and Computer Graphics communities and is a thriving research field that can yield to various applications such as virtual reality, animation, face recognition, etc... In all these applications, the reconstructed face needs to be compact and accurate, especially around significant areas like the nose, the mouth, the orbits, etc... These areas can often be characterized in terms of differential properties of the surface, and a great effort has to be done in order to accurately reconstruct those features. Several attempts have been made in order to deal with that problem. In [DF94], the differential properties of the surface are inferred from a disparity map and used to modify the shape of a correlation window. In [LTM96], crest line extraction is achieved on a 3D model and is used to improve the reconstruction around sharp ridges. These methods improve the accuracy of the reconstruction but cannot be very powerful if the initial depth map is not reliable. For instance, it is well known that bad lighting conditions, or some lack of texture can make correlation-based stereo fail. Consequently, the image information is sometimes not sufficient to reconstruct the object shape. In [FB96], constraints on the depths of a given set of points on a surface mesh are applied in order to improve terrain reconstruction. In [LMF97], curvature information and structural features such as crest lines are extracted from the 3D model or interactively specified in order to generate an anisotropic surface mesh that reflects the geometric properties of the object. In this paper, we propose a further step towards the incorporation of a priori information in the reconstruction process from a pair of calibrated face images. Differential information is used to constrain the topology of a mesh modeling the surface and the parameters of an analytical surface model, through the specification of low(high)-curvature areas, or structural features. Mathematically, this incorporation is achieved via constrained mesh optimization. We show preliminary results of this ongoing research, whose purpose is to build 3D face models from Computer Vision techniques, that are as compact and accurate as possible and are consistent with a priori constraints about the face geometry.

2. The reconstruction process

2.1 An energy minimization scheme

Our reconstruction process is based on the iterative deformation of a 3D triangular mesh (i.e. a collection of vertices, triangular faces and edges) modeling the face in order to minimize an energy function E. The reconstruction process is thus considered as an optimization problem as in the snake theory ([KWT88, FL95, LTM96]).

The initial mesh is given by the triangulation of the depth map provided by a standard correlation algorithm, as the one described in [Fua93]. The energy function is the weighted sum of two terms: one external term E_{ext}, whose minimization makes the model fit to the data, and one internal term E_{int}, whose minimization constrains the model to be smooth enough.

The external term E_{ext} is derived from the stereo information. We assume that the projections of a given 3D point in the 2 image planes have the same intensities (see fig. 2.1). The purpose is thus to minimize the intensity difference between the two projections (see [FL95] or [LTM96] for more details). Notice that this process will behave the same way as the correlation algorithm, i.e. it will fail in the same cases: lack of texture, lighting problems,...

If M_1 and M_2 denote the projections of a 3D point X on the left and the right image and if I_1 and I_2 denote the intensities of these projections, then the stereo term attached to X is defined as:

$$E_{int}(X) = \frac{(I_1 - I_2)^2}{4} \tag{2.1}$$

Each facet is sampled into 3D points and the global stereo term is the sum of all the stereo terms attached to each point. This term can also be expressed in case of multi-image stereo. It is in fact slightly modified in order to only take into account the facets that are visible from the viewpoints of the image planes.

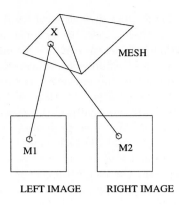

Fig. 2.1. The computation of the stereo term

The internal term E_{int} is a regularization term which tends to minimize the deviation of the mesh from a plane. It is a quadratic term (which helps the convergence of the optimization process) and a function of the second order derivatives of the surface, whose purpose is to minimize the global curvature of the surface, and to restrict the set of all possible solutions to the most "regular" ones.

If $(x, y) \rightarrow z(x, y)$ is a parameterization of the surface, this regularization term can be written as follows:

$$E_{int} = \int \int_{\omega} \mid \frac{\partial^2 z}{\partial x^2} \mid^2 + 2 \mid \frac{\partial^2 z}{\partial x \partial y} \mid^2 + \mid \frac{\partial^2 z}{\partial y^2} \mid^2 dx dy \qquad (2.2)$$

Consequently, we minimize $E = \lambda_{ext} E_{ext} + \lambda_{int} E_{int}$. We thus have to find a trade-off between data-fitting (through the stereo term) and the smoothness of the solution (through the regularization term).

For this optimization, a finite-element scheme has been implemented. Consequently, for each facet of the mesh, we have an analytical expression of the surface. The depth Z of each surface point is expressed as a polynomial function of the two other coordinates X and Y. This polynomial is of degree 5, which guarantees that the surface is piecewise C^1 (see [Neuen95], [ZT88]). The parameters of the optimization process are the depths of each vertex, as well as the partial derivatives of the depth with respect to X and Y. Consequently, if the mesh is composed of n vertices, we come up with a $6n$-variable state vector:

$$(Z_1, ..., Z_n), (\frac{\partial Z_1}{\partial X}, ..., \frac{\partial Z_n}{\partial X}), (\frac{\partial Z_1}{\partial Y}, ..., \frac{\partial Z_n}{\partial Y}),$$

$$(\frac{\partial^2 Z_1}{\partial X^2}, ..., \frac{\partial^2 Z_n}{\partial X^2}), (\frac{\partial^2 Z_1}{\partial X \partial Y}, ..., \frac{\partial^2 Z_n}{\partial X \partial Y}), (\frac{\partial^2 Z_1}{\partial Y^2}, ..., \frac{\partial^2 Z_n}{\partial Y^2}).$$

We take as initial values of the Z_i the depth values given by the triangulation of the depth map. To estimate the initial values of the partial derivatives, we have locally approximated the surface by a quadric and computed the partial derivatives of the surface as being the partial derivatives of the corresponding quadric. These values define the polynomial approximation of the surface. Reciprocally, we can compute the partial derivatives and differential properties of the surface from the analytical expression of the surface.

2.2 Adaptive meshes

The computation time can be very high if we keep a very large number of vertices. Moreover, if we further want to use our 3D model for animation purposes, for instance, a large number of points can very soon become intractable. Therefore, we have to reduce the number of vertices and to keep the points in the most significant areas of the face. Furthermore, this has to be achieved with as much automation as possible. For instance, we would like to keep many points in the nose area, the orbits, the mouth, i.e. areas which are likely to act as landmarks in an animation process. All these areas can be characterized by geometrical properties of the surface, especially differential properties. Indeed, areas like the nose ridge, the orbits, can be expressed in terms of high curvature areas, or crest lines, whereas the cheeks, the forehead (where we would like a small number of facets) can be described as low curvature areas.

We have thus chosen to refine the 3D model according to the differential properties of the surface that can be easily inferred from the analytical expression of the surface or estimated by a local quadric approximation. The surface described by the finite element model is C^{∞} inside each facet, and C^1 between two facets. Besides, the second order partial derivatives are uniquely defined at each vertex, since they belong to the set of parameters of the optimization problem. Consequently, it is meaningful to compute the surface curvatures at each vertex (see 2.2). This computation is straightforward: we can easily compute the first and the second fundamental forms associated to the surface, respectively denoted by their matrices M_1 and M_2, and the Weingarten endomorphism $W = -M_1^{-1}M_2$ (see [DoCar76, MB95]). The principal curvatures and the principal curvature directions are respectively the eigenvalues and the eigenvectors of W. Here, we just briefly describe the computation of the principal curvatures:

If k_{max}, k_{min}, K, and H respectively denote the maximum curvature, the minimum curvature, the gaussian curvature ($= k_{max}k_{min}$) and the mean curvature ($= \frac{1}{2}(k_{max} + k_{min})$) of the surface at a given vertex, and if Z_x denotes the partial derivative of Z with respect to X at this vertex, we can write:

$$K = \frac{Z_{xx}Z_{yy} - Z_{xy}^2}{\left(1 + Z_x^2 + Z_y^2\right)^2}$$

$$H = \frac{1}{2} \frac{(1 + Z_x^2)Z_{yy} - 2Z_x Z_y Z_{xy} + (1 + Z_y^2)Z_{xx}}{(1 + Z_x^2 + Z_y^2)^{\frac{3}{2}}}$$

$$k_1 = H + \sqrt{H^2 - K}$$

$$k_2 = H - \sqrt{H^2 - K}$$

If $\mid k_1 \mid \leq \mid k_2 \mid$, $k_{min} = k_1$ and $k_{max} = k_2$.

Otherwise, $k_{min} = k_2$ and $k_{max} = k_1$.

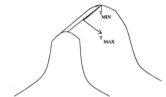

Fig. 2.2. A ridge and the principal curvature directions

As described in [LMF97], we generate an adaptive mesh governed by the principal curvatures and the principal curvature directions of the surface. The algorithm can be described as follows:

- compute at each vertex of the initial mesh the principal curvatures k_{max} and k_{min} and the principal curvature directions t_{max} and t_{min}.
- specify for each vertex of the initial mesh the three parameters (two scalar values h_1 and h_2 and an angle θ) of an ellipse centered on the vertex which governs the generation of a new mesh.
- optimize the new mesh with minimizing the energy function $E = \lambda_{int} E_{int} + \lambda_{ext} E_{ext}$.

We use for that purpose a mesh generation software developed for the Computational Field Simulations ([BCGHM96]). The algorithm completely remeshes a 2D domain, which is here a frontal projection of the face. Therefore, the vertices will not be at the same locations anymore and the surface will be sampled according to the sets of h_1, h_2 and θ. These values govern the local topology of the new mesh in the vicinity of the old vertex they are attached to. As shown in fig. 2.3, the angle θ determines in which direction the new facet in the remeshed surface will be "elongated". This direction will be given by t_{min}. In other terms, the edges of the new facets will be longer in the minimum curvature direction than in the maximum curvature direction (those two directions are orthogonal). This is rather intuitive: for instance, if we consider the case of the nose ridge, the minimum curvature direction lies along this ridge. Moreover, we want to capture as many details as possible in the direction orthogonal to this ridge, since there is a high curvature variation in that direction. Consequently, it is natural to generate longer edges in the minimum curvature direction (i.e. along the ridge) than in the maximum curvature direction (i.e. across the ridge). The scalar values h_1 and h_2 determine the average lengths of the edges in those two directions. They are decreasing functions of k_{min} and k_{max} respectively, since we want more facets in low curvature areas. Typically, they are chosen as inverses of a second order polynomial function.

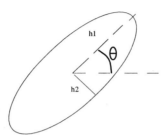

Fig. 2.3. The ellipse defining the local topology of the new mesh

We show in figures 2.4 to 2.6 some experimental results we obtained using this method. Fig. 2.4 shows a stereo pair of a face in a rectified position (here, the horizontal disparities are zero) and the initial depth map obtained by a correlation algorithm. Figure 2.5 shows the triangulation of the depth map in high resolution (4627 vertices). Such a number of vertices is much too large for any kind of subsequent applications. Our purpose is thus to selectively reduce the number of vertices while keeping a good reconstruction accuracy and, if possible, improve the reconstruction in significant areas. We then show two anisotropic curvature-governed meshes with different resolutions. The last result shows a good recovery of the nose shape. The upper part of the forehead has been cut in the last experiments.

We can also constrain the topology of the mesh using some structural information about the surface. For example, the nose ridge or the orbits are crucial features that we must reconstruct with a good accuracy. If we are able to detect those features reliably on the 3D model, we can constrain the mesh topology using these features. From a geometric point of view, these features can be described as crest lines. Crest lines are differential properties of order 3 of the surface ([MB95, MLD94]). They are defined as the sets of zero-crossings of the derivative of the maximum curvature in the maximum curvature direction, which can be expressed by the equation: $dk = \nabla k_{max}.\boldsymbol{t}_{max} = 0$, where

Fig. 2.4. A stereo pair of a face (512*512 images) and the depth map.

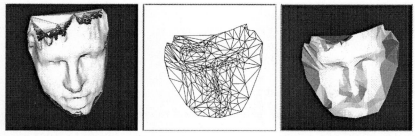

Fig. 2.5. The initial mesh (4627 vertices), the low-resolution anisotropic mesh (248 vertices) and the result of its deformation.

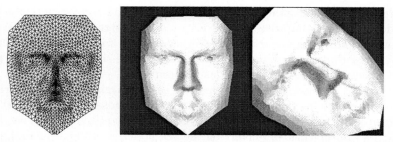

Fig. 2.6. A higher resolution anisotropic mesh governed by curvature information (1574 vertices): the mesh after deformation and two shaded views.

$\nabla k_{max} = (\dfrac{\partial k_{max}}{\partial x}, \dfrac{\partial k_{max}}{\partial y}, 0)$. As we showed above, k_{max} and t_{max} can be directly expressed in terms of the variables of the optimization process. If we want to compute higher-order derivatives, which is the case for crest lines, we have to use the analytical expression of the surface. For example, when we compute $\dfrac{\partial k_{max}}{\partial x}$ at a given vertex V, we must take as the local surface approximation the one attached to the facet corresponding to a local displacement from V in the direction of $x > 0$.

Once we have computed for each vertex the values of dk, we locate the zero-crossings of dk on the edges of the mesh and draw the crest lines using a technique close to the Marching lines algorithm ([TG92]).

Using structural information such as crest lines can be an alternative to the use of curvature fields as mentioned above. In [LFM96, LTM96], we presented an algorithm that iteratively detects crest lines on the mesh and deforms it so that the edges coincide with the crest lines. In this scheme, at each iteration, the algorithm uses both the differential information inferred from the 3D model and the image information. However, this method can only be applied if the initial mesh is not too far from the true one and can provide some rather reliable information about the differential properties of the underlying surface. As we will mention afterwards, this is not always the case. Moreover, since crest line extraction requires the computation of high order derivatives, we need rather smooth 3D data. Otherwise, the crest line extraction may not be very stable and spurious zero-crossings may appear, creating crest lines where there are none. Therefore, it seems more reasonable to generate an adaptive mesh governed by crest line information, that can be potentially filtered: the user can choose to only keep some crest lines according to their number, length, spatial organization, ..., or he can suppress the ones that he does not consider as reliable, valid or useful for his purpose. Then, the algorithm remeshes the surface, generating more facets in the vicinity of each crest line. We display in fig. 2.7 the automatic extraction of crest lines on the reconstructed face and a new mesh whose topology is driven by crest line information. The new mesh is then itself reoptimized.

2.3 Limitations of the scheme

We have therefore generated a new mesh which is more compact than the initial one and which preserves the high curvature areas. However, this method can only be used if the initial 3D model is good enough to yield reliable curvature information. In many cases, the initial model is too far from the true surface to produce such information. For instance, in the example we showed above, the 3D shape of the forehead cannot be recovered accurately from stereo information alone because of the presence of hair, which will make the correlation process fail in this area. This is analogous to the case of terrain reconstruction in presence of vegetation, which will make the recovery of the

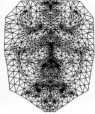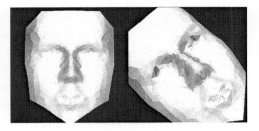

Fig. 2.7. Some crest lines automatically detected on the face, and an anisotropic mesh governed by crest line information: the mesh after deformation and two shaded views.

3D shape impossible. In other cases, bad lighting conditions will produce the same undesirable effects. Therefore, it seems necessary to incorporate in the reconstruction process extra information that can help the recovery of the 3D shape. Mainly, this incorporation has two goals:

— compensate the reduction of the number of vertices in order to preserve a good reconstruction accuracy.
— compensate the insufficiency or the inadequateness of the information contained in the image to accurately reconstruct the 3D shape.

3. The incorporation of a priori knowledge

3.1 A priori knowledge and differential properties

When we want to reconstruct an object, we have a rough idea about its shape, especially the location of typical features like crest lines, the spatial relation between these lines or the existence of patches that we can describe as "flat", "spherical", "cylindrical", etc... This kind of a priori knowledge can be of great interest where the classical stereo methods fail because of the reasons expressed above.

The a priori knowledge that a user can have about the shape he wants to reconstruct can be intuitive ("This region is flat", or "spherical") or can rely on well-known geometric properties, which can come from anthropometry in case of face reconstruction, or geology, in case of terrain reconstruction, etc... In any case, this a priori knowledge can very often be expressed in terms of differential properties. For instance, the knowledge "This area is flat" is obviously "translated" as:

at each vertex, $k_{max} = k_{min} = 0$.

"This area is spherical" means:

at each vertex, $k_{max} = k_{min} (\neq 0)$.

We can also express "structural" knowledge such as "There is a crest line here", and interactively outline the crest on the depth map (or, ideally, on the images). The location of the crest on the depth map gives its location on the 3D mesh. The line goes through several facets and separates areas where $dk > 0$ from areas where $dk < 0$. Imposing a constraint on the location of the crest line is thus equivalent to imposing $dk < 0$ on several vertices and $dk > 0$ on others.

The incorporation of a priori knowledge in the reconstruction process can be expressed in our framework as a constrained optimization process. All the constraints are expressed in terms of the partial derivatives which are the parameters of the optimization process. We use for that purpose a constrained optimization software especially designed for large systems [LZT96] (which is our case, since we have 6 parameters per vertex).

3.2 First results

So far, we have tested our constrained on synthetic data (reconstruction of a sphere from a noisy initial state, using the constraint of equal curvatures, and reconstruction of a ridge with outlining the crest line). We have also reconstructed the forehead of the face shown in the previous section, using the a priori assumption that the part of the skull above the orbits is roughly spherical.

In the latest example, we first constrain the topology of the mesh to be rather uniform and isotropic ($h_1 = h_2$ and $\theta = 0$ with the notations of the previous section), since the curvatures are globally the same on this area. Notice that in the previous section, the program had generated many facets in some areas of the forehead, since the correlation algorithm providing the initial depth map had failed in reconstructing a smooth surface. We then minimize $E = \lambda_{ext}E_{ext} + \lambda_{int}E_{int}$ under the following constraints:

$$\forall i \in \{1, .., n\}, k_{max}(i) = k_{min}(i) \tag{3.1}$$

where i denotes the i-th vertex.

In this example, we showed that we could achieve our three goals:

- produce a compact and accurate reconstruction
- get rid of some problems induced by stereo methods
- be consistent with the a priori knowledge about the object shape and about its differential properties

Let us notice that, if our goal had only been to flatten this area, we could have merely minimized $E = \lambda_{ext}E_{ext} + \lambda_{int}E_{int}$ with setting λ_{int} to a very large value, thus constraining the shape to converge to a plane. The sets of properties 3.1 would have been fulfilled as well, but the weight of the image information would have been too little to make the model converge towards the real shape, i.e. a sphere. On the contrary, in our constrained optimization scheme, the image information is still present, that makes the global shape look like a sphere, and the differential constraints act locally to

Fig. 3.1. The reconstructed forehead without differential constraints: the mesh (left) and a shaded view (middle), and the final reconstruction after incorporating differential constraints(right)

avoid some undesirable behaviors such as the one due to the presence of hair. These experiments are still preliminary, but our purpose is to build a general framework that could be applied to different cases when conventional stereo fails.

4. Conclusion

We have proposed a way of interactively reconstructing from stereo a complex 3D object like a face using a priori information about its shape and its differential properties. This kind of information can be of great interest when dealing with objects whose texture generally make conventional stereo algorithms fail, or captured in bad lighting conditions. Our long-term purpose is to develop an interactive image-based modeling software that takes into account some a priori knowledge that a user can have about the differential properties of the object to reconstruct.

5. Acknowledgements

We would like to thank H. Borouchaki from INRIA-Rocquencourt for providing us with his mesh generation software "BL2D". Moreover, the constrained optimization part is being carried on with the use of "CFSQP" software provided by Prof. Tits from University of Maryland. Finally, the face images were obtained from the Web server of ROBOTVIS project, INRIA Sophia-Antipolis.

References

[BCGHM96] H. Borouchaki, M. J. Castro-Diaz, P. L. George, F. Hecht and B. Mohammadi: Anisotropic Adaptive Mesh Generation in Two Dimensions for CFD. Proceedings of the 5th International Conference on Numerical Grid in Computational Field Simulations, 1996, Mississippi State University, USA.

[DF94] F. Devernay and O.Faugeras: Computing Differential Properties of 3-D Shapes from Stereoscopic Images without 3-D Models. Proceedings of the Conference on Computer Vision and Pattern Recognition (CVPR), 1994, Seattle, USA.

[DoCar76] M. P. do Carmo: Differential Geometry of Curves and Surfaces, Prentice-Hall, Englewood Cliffs, 1976.

[Fua93] P. Fua: A Parallel Stereo Algorithm that Produces Dense Depth Maps and Preserves Image Features. Machine Vision Applications, 1993, 6(1).

[FB96] P. Fua and C. Brechbuhler: Imposing Hard Constraints on Soft Snakes. Proceedings of the European Conference on Computer Vision (ECCV), 1996, Cambridge, U.K., II, p. 495-506.

[FL95] P. Fua and Y.G. Leclerc: Object-Centered Surface Reconstruction: Combining Multi-image Stereo and Shading. International Journal on Computer Vision, 1995, 16(1), p. 35-56.

[KWT88] M. Kass, A. Witkin and D. Terzopoulos: Snakes: Active Contour Models. International Journal on Computer Vision, 1988, 1(4) p. 321-331.

[LFM96] R. Lengagne, P. Fua and O. Monga: Using Crest Lines to Guide Surface Reconstruction From Stereo. Proceedings of the 13th International Conference on Pattern Recognition (ICPR), 1996, Vienna, Austria.

[LMF97] R. Lengagne, O. Monga and P. Fua: Using Differential Constraints to Reconstruct Complex Surfaces From Stereo. Proceedings of the Conference on Computer Vision and Pattern Recognition (CVPR), 1997, San Juan, Puerto Rico, USA.

[LTM96] R. Lengagne, J.-P. Tarel, and O. Monga: From 2D Images to 3D Face Geometry. Proceedings of the 2nd International Conference on Automated Face and Gesture Recognition, 1996, Killington, Vermont, U.S.A.

[LZT96] C. Lawrence, J. L. Zhou and A. L. Tits: User's Guide for CFSQP Version 2.4: A C Code for Solving (Large Scale) Constrained Nonlinear (Minimax) Optimization Problems, Generating Iterates Satisfying All Inequality Constraints. Electrical Engineering Department and Institute for Systems Research, University of Maryland, College Park, MD 20742.

[MB95] O. Monga and S. Benayoun: Using Partial Derivatives of 3D Images to Extract Typical Surface Features. Computer Vision and Image Understanding, 1995, vol 61-2, p. 171-189.

[MLD94] O. Monga, R. Lengagne and R. Deriche: Extraction of the Zero-Crossings of the Curvature Derivative in Volumic 3D Medical Images: a Multi-scale Approach. Proceedings of the Conference on Computer Vision and Pattern Recognition (CVPR), 1994, Seattle, USA.

[Neuen95] W. Neuenschwander: Elastic Deformable Contour and Surface Models for 2D and 3D Image segmentation. PhD Thesis of the Swiss Federal Institute of Technology (ETH), Zürich, Switzerland, 1995.

[TG92] J.-P. Thirion and A. Gourdon: Computing the Differential Properties of Isointensity Surfaces. Computer Vision and Image Understanding, 1995, 61-2, p. 190-202.

[ZT88] O.C. Zienkiewicz and R.L Taylor: The finite element method, Mc Graw-Hill, 1988.

Fast Face Location in Complex Backgrounds

Dario Maio[1] and Davide Maltoni[2]

[1] DEIS - CSITE-CNR - Università di Bologna, viale Risorgimento 2, 40136 Bologna - ITALY.
E-mail: dmaio@deis.unibo.it

[2] Corso di Laurea in Scienze dell'Informazione, Università di Bologna, via Sacchi 3, 47023 Cesena
ITALY. E-mail: maltoni@csr.unibo.it

Abstract. This work presents a new approach to automatic face location on gray-scale images with complex backgrounds. The basic idea is to search on a directional image for all the elliptical objects within a certain range of variation. This is effected through the implementation of a generalized Hough transform, which uses an elliptical annulus as a template. The experimentation carried out on 50 images taken in our laboratories show that the algorithm is robust and very efficient: a gray-level 384×288 image can be processed in a time slightly longer than 0.1 sec. on a Pentium 133 Mhz PC.

Keywords. Face location, generalized Hough transform, elliptical fitting, directional image.

1. Introduction

Automatic face location is a very important task which constitutes the first step of a large area of applications: face recognition, face tracking, surveillance, etc. Several solutions have been proposed in the literature, depending on the type of images (gray-scale images, color images or image sequences) and on the constraints considered (simple or complex background, scale and rotation changes, different illuminations, etc.).

Giving a brief summary of the conspicuous number of approaches proposed requires a pre-classification; unfortunately, due to the large amount of different techniques used by researchers this task is not so easy. While we are aware of the unavoidable inaccuracies, we have tried to make a tentative classification:

- Methods based on template matching and heuristic algorithms which use images taken at different resolutions (multiresolution approaches). [Craw 87] [Yang 94].
- Computational approaches based on deformable templates which characterize the human face [Craw 92] or internal features: eyes, nose, mouth [Yuille 88] [Huang 92] [Chow 93] [Lam 96].

- Face and facial parts detection using dynamic contours or snakes [Huang 92] [Lanitis 95] [Funuyama 96] [Gunn 96].
- Methods based on elliptical approximation and on face searching via least square minimization [Sirohey 93], incremental ellipse fitting [Jacquin 95] and elliptic region growing [Herpers 95].
- Approaches based on the Hough transform [Chow 93] and the adaptive Hough transform [Li 95].
- Methods based on the search of a significant group of features (triplets, constellations, etc.) in the context considered: for example a couple of eyes and a mouth suitably located constitute a significant group in the context of a face. [Govindaraju 90] [Chow 93] [Graf 95] [Burl 95] [Jeng 96].
- Face search on the eigenspace determined via PCA [Moghaddam 95] and face location approaches based on information theory [Lew 96].
- Neural Network approaches [Burel 94] [Sung 94] [Rowley 95] [Schiele 95] [Intrator 95].
- Face location on color images through segmentation in a color-space: YIQ, YES, HSI, HSV, Farnsworth, etc. [Wu 95] [Schiele 95] [Dai 96] [Lee 96] [Sobotka 96] [Sako 96] [Saber 96].
- Face detection on image sequences using motion information: optical flow, spatio-temporal gradient, etc. [Schiele 95] [Lee 96] [Leroy 96].

Some applications work only on static gray-scale images, for example the search by similarity on mug shot databases; hence we believe it is important to develop a method which does not exploit additional information like color and motion. Unfortunately, if we discard color and motion-based approaches, the most robust methods are generally time-consuming and cannot be used in real-time applications.

Our aim is the development of a robust method which is capable of processing images very quickly. The algorithm must operate with structured backgrounds and must tolerate illumination changes, scale variations and small rotations. This work presents a three-stage based approach for automatic face location on static gray-scale images.

The first stage approximately localizes all the elliptical objects present in the image; the second stage refines the localization and the third stage checks whether the objects found are faces or not (fig. 1).

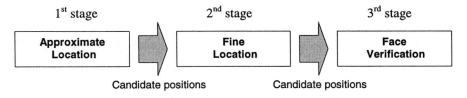

Fig 1. Functional schema of our approach.

We believe the first stage to be the most important, since the efficiency and the robustness of the whole approach are strongly influenced by it; furthermore, several good solutions can be found in the literature for the tasks dealt with in the second and the third stages. In this work we describe in detail the approximate location (section 2), and briefly discuss the fine localization and the face verification (section 3) which are still under development. Section 4 presents some experimental results and section 5 reports our conclusions.

2 Approximate location

Our approach searches for the face on a *directional image* computed over a discrete grid. Each element of the directional image is a non-oriented vector lying on the x, y plane. The vector direction represents the tangent to the edges of the image and the length, named *significance*, is determined as a weighted sum of the *contrast* (edge strength) and the *consistency* (direction reliability) (fig. 2). The directional image is computed by means of the method proposed by Donahue and Roklin [Donahue 93], which uses a gradient-type operator to extract a directional estimate from each 2×2 pixel neighborhood, which is then averaged over a local window by least-squares minimization to control noise. This technique is more robust than the standard operators used for computing the gradient phase angle and enables the contrast and the consistency to be calculated with a very small overhead.

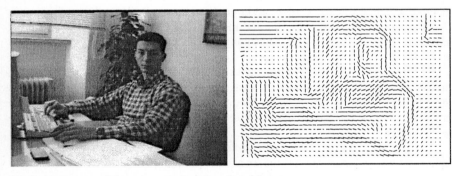

Fig 2. An image and the corresponding directional image.

The analysis of a certain number of directional images (see figure 2) suggested the formulation of a simple method for detecting faces based on the search of ellipses on directional images. Several techniques could be used to this purpose, for example multiresolution template matching [Seitz 91] and least square ellipse fitting [Sirohey 93]. We introduce a new approach based on the generalized Hough transform [Ballard 81] which performs very well in terms of efficiency. Our algorithm estimates the approximate position of elliptical objects within a certain range of variation, since small perturbations induced by scale and rotation changes must be allowed. We have implemented the generalized Hough transform by using as a template an elliptical annulus **C**, calculated according to a prefixed variation range. Actually, the directional information allows the transform to be implemented very efficiently, since for each vector **d** the corresponding template can be reduced to only two sectors of the elliptical annulus. Formally:

Let a and b be the lengths of the semi-axes of an ellipse used as reference, and let ρ_r and ρ_e be respectively the reduction and expansion coefficients which allow the variation range (and hence the elliptical annulus **C**) to be determined: $a_{min} = \rho_r \cdot a$, $b_{min} = \rho_r \cdot b$, $a_{max} = \rho_e \cdot a$, $b_{max} = \rho_e \cdot b$ (fig. 3.a). Let **D** be the directional image and let **A** be the accumulator array, then the algorithm can be sketched as:

Reset **A** ;
$\forall$ vector **d** $\in$ **D**
    { $(x_0, y_0) = origin(\mathbf{d})$;
        $\varphi = direction(\mathbf{d})$;
        $\sigma = significance(\mathbf{d})$;
        $\mathbf{T} = compute\_template((x_0, y_0), \varphi)$;
        $\forall$ pixel $(x, y) \in \mathbf{T}$
            { $A[x, y] = A[x, y] + \sigma \cdot weight_T(x, y)$; }
    }
The high-score **A** cells are good candidates for ellipse centers.

Compute_template$((x_0, y_0), \varphi)$ determines the current template **T** as a function of the direction φ of the vector centered in (x_0, y_0). The points (x_1, y_1) and (x_2, y_2) in fig. 3.a are the only two points where an ellipse tangent to **d** in (x_0, y_0) with semi-axes a, b could be centered. Since we are interested in all the ellipses within the range $(a_{min}...a_{max}$, $b_{min}...b_{max})$, we must take into account all the points lying on the two segments determined by the intersection between the straight line defined by (x_1, y_1), (x_2, y_2) and the elliptical annulus **C**. Finally, by assuming a maximum angular error θ on the directional information, the geometric locus **T** of the possible centers becomes:

$$\mathbf{T} = \left\{ (x, y) \middle| \rho_r^2 \le \left(\frac{x - x_0}{a}\right)^2 + \left(\frac{y - y_0}{b}\right)^2 \le \rho_e^2, \Delta angle\left(arctg\left(\frac{y - y_0}{x - x_0}\right), \phi\right) \le \frac{\theta}{2} \right\}$$

where $\Delta angle(\alpha, \beta)$ returns the absolute value of the smaller angle determined by the directions α, β; ϕ can be computed as a function of φ by deriving the tangent vector expression by the parametric equation of the ellipse:

$$\phi = arctg\left(-\frac{b}{a \cdot tg(\varphi)}\right)$$

The function $weight_T: \mathbf{T} \rightarrow [0, 1]$ associates, to each point (x, y) of **T**, a weight which linearly decreases with the angular distance between the straight line defined by (x, y), (x_0, y_0) and the direction ϕ:

$$weight_T(x,y) = 1 - \frac{2 \cdot \Delta angle \left(arctg \left(\frac{y - y_0}{x - x_0} \right), \phi \right)}{\theta}$$

Figure 3.b shows a representation of a template **T** whose elements are associated to gray-levels proportional to their weights.

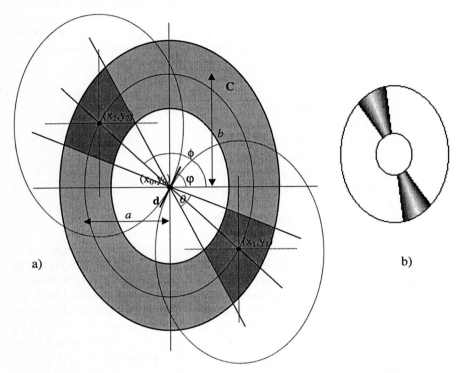

a)   b)

Fig 3. The template **T** (dark gray in fig 3.a) is constituted by those points which are possible centers of ellipses capable of originating in (x_0, y_0) a vector **d** with direction φ. Fig. 3.b shows a graphic representation of a weighted template **T**.

An efficient implementation of the algorithm described can be obtained by adopting the following tricks:

- Discretization of the directions of the elements in **D** (in our simulation we used 256 values).
- Pre-computing of the templates **T**; by using relative coordinates with respect to the ellipse center, the number of different templates corresponds to the number of different directions.
- Discretization of the accumulator array **A** (in our simulation the grid which defines **A** corresponds to that defining **D**).

3 Fine location and face verification

Several approaches have been proposed for the fine location of face and facial parts. Remembering once again that our primary requirement is efficiency, we give some ideas which could be used:

- Refining the ellipse center position (c_x, c_y) through AHT (Adaptive Hough Transform) [Davis 82] [Illingworth 87] which requires the resolution of the "hot" accumulator cells to be gradually increased.
- Local optimization of the center (c_x, c_y), of the semi-axes a and b and of the ellipse tilt angle ξ through a local optimization algorithm (Steepest descent, Downhill Simplex method [Press 92], etc.) which searches for the best-fitting ellipse in the parameter space (c_x, c_y, a, b, ξ).
- Position optimization and face verification through the detection of a symmetry axis [Reisfeld 90]. The symmetry can be measured both on the original and the directional image.
- Projection of the image portion delimited by the ellipse on the symmetry axis and on its orthogonal one. Several authors [Brunelli 93] [Sako 96] [Sobotka 96] [Wu 96] demonstrate that these projections are characterized by local intensity minima in the regions corresponding to the eyes and the mouth. The projection method can also be applied to the directional images: in this case local maxima and minima are present in the eye, nose and mouth regions due to the presence of horizontal and vertical vectors (fig. 4).

We trust that, starting from the approximate location method described in section 2, a complete approach could be assembled by exploiting the above ideas.

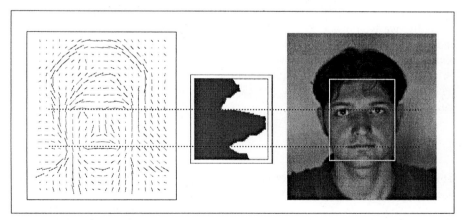

Fig 4. The figure shows the projection on the vertical axis of the vectors belonging to the region delimited by the white rectangle. The local minima, generated by the presence of horizontal vectors in the eye and mouth regions can be used for the registration according to the internal feature positions.

4 Experimentation

We verified the accuracy and the robustness of our approach by using a database of 50 images acquired in our laboratories. All the images are 384×288 pixel - 256 gray-level and were acquired under different illumination, with the subject positioned at different distances from the camera. The parameter values used in the simulation are:

- directional image granularity = accumulator array granularity = 7 pixel
- elliptical annulus: $a = 34$, $b = 45$, $\rho_r = 0.6$, $\rho_e = 1.2$
- maximum angular error : $\theta = 30°$

A straightforward "winner take all" criterion was used to determine the face position on the transform. For 90% of the images a correct location was achieved, that is the global maximum of the transform corresponds to the face position. For the remaining 10% the face position can still be determined by using a threshold, which accepts as candidate centers the high-score transform cells, and by removing the non-face objects during the verification stage. A threshold criterion must be used even when more than one face are present in the same image. Figure 5 reports some examples where the elliptical annulus is superimposed on the image position corresponding to the global maximum of the transform.

Our simulations were conducted on a Pentium 133 Mhz PC; the first stage was carried out in 0.13 sec. (0.09 sec. for the directional image computation and 0.04 sec. for the generalized Hough transform; the templates computation was performed off-line in 0.34 sec.). Most of the computation time was spent on the directional image determination. The granularity of the directional image can be increased if the faces which have to be located are large enough. By operating with faces similar to the second image in figure 5 a granularity of 10 pixels or more can be successfully used, requiring less than 0.05 sec. for the whole process.

Finally, we would like to remark that our code was not particularly optimized and the operating system used (Windows 95) cannot be defined a "real-time" operating system. For these reasons we believe that even better performance can be achieved with an ad hoc implementation and the requirements of certain real-time applications, which must process images at 20-30 frame/sec., could be satisfied.

5 Conclusions

This work proposes a three-stage based approach to fast face location in complex backgrounds. In particular, we presented in detail the stage of approximate location which is, in our opinion, the most important. The experimentation shows that the algorithm is robust with respect to the background and to some type of perturbations: illumination changes, scale changes, small rotations, etc. Very good results have been achieved in terms of efficiency. In section 3 we sketched the basic ideas for developing the fine location and face verification stages.

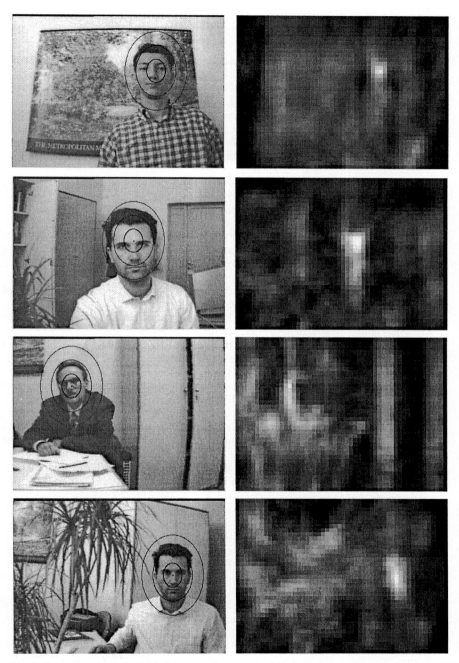

Fig 5. Some images extracted from our database and their corresponding transforms. All the transforms exhibit a light area corresponding to the face position.

576

References

[Ballard 81] D. H. Ballard, "Generalizing the Hough transform to detect arbitrary shapes", *Pattern Recognition*, v. 3, n. 2, pp. 110-122, (1981).

[Brunelli 93] R. Brunelli and T. Poggio, "Face Recognition: Features versus Templates", *IEEE tPAMI*, v. 15, no. 10, pp. 1042-1052, (1993).

[Burel 94] G. Burel and D. Carel, "Detection and localization of faces on digital images", *Pattern Recognition Letters*, v. 15, no. 10, pp. 963-967, (1994).

[Burl 95] M. C. Burl, T. K. Leung and P. Perona, "Face localization via shape statistics", *proc Int. Work. on Automatic Face and Gesture Recognition*, Zurich, pp. 154-159, (1995).

[Chow 93] G. Chow, X. Li, "Towards a system for automatic facial feature detection", *Pattern Recognition*, v. 26, no. 12, pp. 1739-1755, (1993).

[Craw 87] I. Craw, H. Ellis and J.R. Lishman, "Automatic extraction of face-features", *Pattern Recognition Letters*, v. 5, no. 2, pp. 183-187, (1987).

[Craw 92] I. Craw, D. Tock and A. Bennet, "Finding face features", *proc. ECCV*, (1992).

[Dai 96] Y. Dai and Y. Nakano, "Face-texture model based on SGLD and its application in face detection in a color scene", *Pattern Recognition*, v. 29, no. 6, pp. 1007-1017, (1996).

[Davis 82] L.S. Davis, "Hierarchical generalized Hough transform and line segment based generalized Hough transforms", *Pattern Recognition*, v. 15, pp. 277-285, (1982).

[Donahue 93] M. J. Donahue and S. I. Rokhlin, "On the use of Level Curves in Image Analysis", *Image Understanding*, v. 57, pp. 185-203, (1993).

[Funuyama 96] R. Funayama, N. Yokoya, H. Iwasa and H. Takemura, "Facial component extraction by cooperative active nets with global constraints", *proc. 13th ICPR*, v. B, pp. 300-304, Vienna (1996).

[Govindaraju 90] V. Govindaraju, S. N. Srihari and D. B. Sher, "A computational model for face location" *proc. 3rd ICCV*, pp. 718-721, (1990).

[Graf 95] H. P. Graf, T. Chen, E. Petajan and E. Cosatto, "Locating faces and facial parts", *proc Int. Work. on Automatic Face and Gesture Recognition*, Zurich, pp. 41-46, (1995).

[Gunn 96] S. R. Gunn and M. S. Nixon, "Snake head boundary extraction using global and local energy minimisation", *proc. 13th ICPR*, v. B, pp. 581-585, Vienna (1996).

[Herpers 95] R. Herpers, H. Kattner, H. Rodax and G. Sommer, "GAZE: an attentive processing strategy to detect and analyze the prominent facial regions", *proc Int. Work. on Automatic Face and Gesture Recognition*, Zurich, pp. 214-220, (1995).

[Huang 92] C. Huang and C. Chen, "Human facial feature extraction for face interpretation and recognition", *Pattern Recognition*, v. 25, no. 12, pp. 1435-1444, (1992).

[Illingworth 87] J. Illingworth and J. Kittler, "The adaptive Hough transform", *IEEE tPAMI*, v. 9, n. 5, pp. 690-697, (1987).

[Intrator 95] N. Intrator, D. Reisfeld and Y. Yeshurun, "Extraction of facial features for recognition using neural networks", *proc Int. Work. on Automatic Face and Gesture Recognition*, Zurich, pp. 260-265, (1995).

[Jacquin 95] A. Jacquin and A. Eleftheriadis, "Automatic location tracking of faces and facial features in video sequences", *proc Int. Work. on Automatic Face and Gesture Recognition*, Zurich, pp. 142-147, (1995).

[Jeng 96] S. Jeng, H. M. Liao, Y. Liu and M. Chern, "An efficient approach for facial feature detection using geometrical face model", *proc. 13th ICPR*, v. C, pp. 426-430, Vienna (1996).

[Lam 96] K. Lam and H. Yan, "Locating and extracting the eye in human face images", *Pattern Recognition*, v. 29, no. 5, pp. 771-779, (1996).

[Lanitis 95] A. Lanitis, C. J. Taylor, T. F. Cootes and T. Ahmed, "Automatic interpretation of human faces and hand gesture using flexible models", *proc Int. Work. on Automatic Face and Gesture Recognition*, Zurich, pp. 98-103, (1995).

[Lee 96] C. H. Lee, J. S. Kim and K. H. Park, "Automatic face location in a complex background using motion and color information", *Pattern Recognition*, v. 29, no. 11, pp. 1877-1889, (1996).

[Leroy 96] B. Leroy, I. L. Herlin and L. D. Cohen, "Face identification by deformation measure", *proc. 13th ICPR*, v. C, pp. 633-637, Vienna (1996).

[Lew 96] M. S. Lew and N. Huijsmans, "Information theory and face detection", *proc. 13th ICPR*, v. C, pp. 601-605, Vienna (1996).

[Li 95] X. Li and N. Roeder, "Face contour extraction from front-view images", *Pattern Recognition*, v. 28, no. 8, pp. 1167-1179, (1995).

[Moghaddam 95] B. Moghaddam and A. Pentland, "Maximum likelihood detection of faces and hands", *proc Int. Work. on Automatic Face and Gesture Recognition*, Zurich, pp. 122-128, (1995).

[Press 92] W. H. Press, S. A. Teukolsky, W. T. Vetterling and B. P. Flannery, *Numerical Recipes in C*, Cambridge University Press, (1992).

[Reisfeld 90] D. Reisfeld, H. Wolfson and Y. Yeshurun, "Detection of interest points using symmetry", *proc. 3rd ICCV*, pp. 62-65, (1990).

[Rowley 95] H. A. Rowley, S. Baluja and T. Kanade, "Human face detection in visual scenes", *tech. report CMU-CS-95-158R, Carnegie Mellon University*, (1995).

[Saber 96] E. Saber and A. Murat Tekalp, "Face detection and facial feature extraction using color, shape and symmetry-based cost functions", *proc. 13th ICPR*, v. C, pp. 654-657, Vienna (1996).

[Sako 96] H. Sako and A. V. W. Smith, "Real-time expression recognition based on features' position and dimension", *proc. 13th ICPR*, v. C, pp. 643-648, Vienna (1996).

[Schiele 95] B. Schiele and A. Waibel, "Gaze tracking based on face color", *proc Int. Work. on Automatic Face and Gesture Recognition*, Zurich, pp. 344-349, (1995).

[Seitz 91] P. Seitz and M. Bichsel, "The Digital Doorkeeper - Automatic Face Recognition with the Computer", *Proc. of 25th IEEE Carnahan Conference on Security Technology*, (1991).

[Sirohey 93] S. A. Sirohey, "Human face segmentation and identification" *tech. report CAR-TR-695, Center for Automation Research, University of Mariland*, (1993).

[Sobotka 96] K. Sobottka and Ioannis Pitas, "Extraction of facial regions and features using color and shape information", *proc. 13th ICPR*, v. C, pp. 421-425, Vienna (1996).

[Sung 94] K. Sung and T. Poggio, "Example-based learning for view-based human face detection", *A.I. Memo 1521, CBCL Paper 112, MIT*, (1994).

[Yang 94] G. Yang and T.S. Huang, "Human face detection in a complex background", *Pattern Recognition*, v. 27, no. 1, pp. 53-63, (1994).

[Yuille 88] A. Yuille, D. Cohen and P. Hallinan, "Facial features extraction by deformable templates" *tech. report 88-2, Harward Robotics Laboratory*, (1988).

[Wu 95] H. Wu, Q. Chen and M. Yachida, "An application of fuzzy theory: face detection", *proc Int. Work. on Automatic Face and Gesture Recognition*, Zurich, pp. 314-319, (1995).

[Wu 96] H. Wu, Q. Chen and M. Yachida, "Facial Features Extraction and Face Verification", *proc. 13th ICPR*, v. C, pp. 484-488, Vienna (1996).

Recognising Moving Faces

Stephen J. McKenna[1] and Shaogang Gong[2]

[1] Department of Applied Computing, University of Dundee,
   Dundee DD1 4HN, Scotland. `stephen@dcs.qmw.ac.uk`
[2] Department of Computer Science, Queen Mary and Westfield College,
   London E1 4NS, England. `sgg@dcs.qmw.ac.uk`

Abstract. An approach to engineering real-time computer vision systems for face recognition is described. The tasks considered involve recognition of multiple people in poorly constrained dynamic scenes. Modules for focus of attention, face detection, tracking and recognition are described. The need for integration of different processes using prediction and feedback is emphasised. Some examples from working systems are given.

1 Introduction

Many of the face recognition systems developed to date have been applied to a rather artificial problem, namely the identification of people from a single 'snapshot' frontal facial image. Furthermore, identification is usually performed using a model which has been learned from one or a few other similar snapshot images. This paper discusses the more general problem of recognition of multiple moving people in dynamic scenes. An approach to engineering continuously operating real-time computer vision systems for such a task is described. Real-time performance can be achieved by taking an integrated systems approach in which computationally efficient processes cooperate [1]. Robustness is achieved by combining multiple visual cues and by utilising prediction and feedback.

A process for locating and tracking probable face regions for focus of attention is needed in order to keep computation manageable. This incorporates colour and motion information with grouping and prediction and is described in Section 2. Models of facial appearance are utilised to perform face detection and tracking (Sections 3 and 4). Section 5 discusses a process for real-time face identification from image sequences. Section 6 gives examples of operational systems and some conclusions are drawn in Section 7. The need for real-time performance and cooperation between processes is emphasised throughout.

---

[1] Note that "real-time" does not necessarily imply processing at frame rate. In many applications a face tracking and recognition system need only be 'soft' real-time, i.e. video-rate frames can be skipped provided that tracking is robust and that recognition results are produced with acceptably small delays.

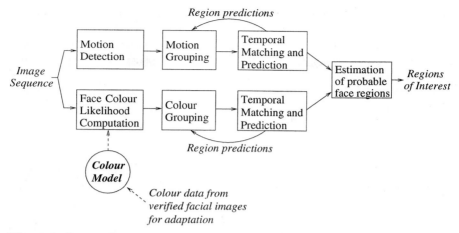

Fig. 2.1. Focus of attention: probable face regions are estimated using motion and colour-based tracking

2 Focus of Attention

In order to detect and track people and their faces sufficiently quickly, efficient methods for focusing attention are necessary. Two visual cues that can be computed with the required efficiency are based upon motion and colour. Furthermore, these fail as attentional cues under different circumstances and can therefore be usefully combined. Colour fails due to other similarly coloured objects and due to changes in the spectral composition of illumination whilst motion can continue to provide an effective cue. Conversely, motion provides a poor cue in the presence of other moving objects, shadows and reflections whilst colour cues remain largely unaffected. Additionally, certain motion algorithms will fail with camera motion whereas colour cues remain effective. A focus of attention process based on motion and colour is illustrated in Fig. 2.1.

2.1 Motion

People are continually in motion. Most of the visual motion in scenes which contain people typically corresponds to the people, at least while the observer remains static. This is especially true of most indoor scenes. Given a static camera, moving contours can be detected by applying a temporal filter to each pixel, $I(x, y, t)$, in an image sequence [7]:

$$S(x, y, t) = \frac{\partial^2 G(t)}{\partial t^2} * I(x, y, t)$$

This temporal convolution with a second-order derivative of a Gaussian, $G(t)$, yields a sequence of images with zero-crossings corresponding to motion contours [2]. This method was found to reliably detect human motion whilst being robust to noise and global illumination changes [13, 16]. Moving people will give rise to areas of motion contours with a certain range of possible sizes and shapes. Such a scheme will of course detect other visibly moving objects in the scene as well as moving shadows and reflections. In the presence of camera motion, more computationally expensive algorithms are needed. However, qualitative motion detection is still possible in real-time [19].

2.2 Colour

Under stable illumination conditions, the apparent colour of human skin forms a relatively compact distribution in the space of observable colours, irrespective of race [10]. This distribution can be modelled as a Gaussian or a mixture of Gaussians in 2D hue-saturation space [17]. The intensity of the observed colour is ignored to give some invariance to the brightness of the illumination. Such a skin colour model is subsequently used to label pixels in an image with log-likelihood values. Skin coloured objects, including faces, will give rise to regions of high likelihood under the model.

Colour models are not robust under significant changes in illumination conditions. Robust colour-based face tracking might therefore seem to require a solution to colour constancy. However, when considered as one module within an integrated system that utilises other visual cues such as motion and facial appearance, this problem is alleviated. In particular, once a face is being reliably tracked and verified using a face model, its apparent colour can be used to update a scene-specific, adaptive colour model. In this way, a system can learn about variations in apparent face colour and can even correlate these changes with different times of day and regions of the scene. The details of an adaptive colour model and its use for object tracking under variations in illumination and camera parameters are reported elsewhere [18].

2.3 Grouping and Tracking

The above processes give rise to (1) clusters of motion contours which often correspond to entire people and (2) regions of high likelihood pixels under the skin colour model which typically correspond to faces, arms and hands. For the purpose of tracking, these motion and colour regions of interest are modelled as Gaussian distributions in the image plane. Each region, therefore, has a mean $\mu = (x_c, y_c)$ and a covariance matrix Σ. In the case of motion, a region is parameterised by the mean and covariance of the coordinates of its temporal zero-crossings. In the case of colour, the mean and covariance are computed using the likelihood values, $p(\mathbf{x})$:

---

[2] Normal components of visual motion can be estimated from the partial derivatives of $S(x, y, t)$ [4, 7] but this is only reliable given small motion magnitude.

$$\mu = \frac{\sum \mathbf{x} p(\mathbf{x})}{\sum p(\mathbf{x})}, \qquad \Sigma = \frac{\sum p(\mathbf{x})(\mathbf{x} - \mu)^T (\mathbf{x} - \mu)}{\sum p(\mathbf{x})}$$

where $\mathbf{x}$ ranges over those image coordinates that have a colour likelihood, $p(\mathbf{x})$, above a threshold.

In many scenarios, the orientation of the regions remains approximately aligned with the image axes. This is the case for motion when people are standing upright and for colour face tracking when the head is upright. In this case, a region's covariance matrix can be modelled as diagonal and each region has just four parameters: $(x_c, y_c, \sigma_x^2, \sigma_y^2)$.

This low-order region parameterisation facilitates efficient and stable tracking. Recall that the aim here is not to obtain any 3D reconstruction of the scene but rather to focus attention for face tracking and recognition. This purpose is well served by the second-order region model described above.

The number of people in a scene is not usually known *a priori*. In general, people can enter (or leave) the scene or become fully occluded (or unoccluded) at any time. Therefore, it is often desirable to dynamically initialise, maintain and terminate tracking of multiple regions of interest. Separate non-overlapping regions of interest are located using grouping processes. In the case of motion, temporal zero-crossings are grouped using a method similar to a minimum spanning tree [13]. Colour regions are grouped by connectivity analysis. Computational efficiency is obtained by performing grouping on sub-sampled motion and colour probability images. Once a region is being tracked, prediction is used to constrain the grouping process. In particular, a region cannot extend outside a bounding window determined from its predicted mean and covariance matrix [21].

Grouping can also be constrained by utilising information from a higher-level face tracking process (see Section 4). In particular, if regions merge while each has an associated face being tracked, the grouping process can be forced to keep them separate [14].

A tracked region is only used as a focus of attention for higher-level processing once confidence can be accumulated that the region is both persistent and consistent. A simple measure of such confidence is the ability to reliably track the region for k consecutive frames.

Tracking is performed using time-symmetric matching and Kalman filtering [13, 16]. A region is tracked for up to p frames in the absence of suitable cluster evidence before it is terminated.

2.4 Estimating probable face regions

The tracked motion and colour regions are used to determine the areas in each image most likely to contain faces. This is the last step shown in Fig. 2.1. In many cases, heuristic rules based upon some simple operating assumptions are sufficient to determine good search areas for face detection. These assumptions include the minimum and maximum possible scale of people, their orientation (heads uppermost) and approximate aspect ratio. Fig. 2.2 shows some example frames from a sequence in which a probable face region is tracked.

Fig. 2.2. Example frames from a sequence in which a probable face region is tracked. The use of a simple, low-order model facilitates stable tracking even under large rotations in depth and partial occlusions.

In summary, colour and motion-based tracking using low-order models and prediction can provide stable, real-time focus of attention. This process can benefit by using information from a higher-level face tracking process to constrain grouping and adapt colour models.

3 Face Detection

A search for a face is initialised in probable face regions where no face is currently being tracked. The face detection process is illustrated in Fig. 3.1. It is performed using a neural network to classify low-resolution images as face or non-face. The network was trained using face images of 1000 different people along with iteratively selected non-face patterns and learned an appropriate discriminant function [13]. Currently, only frontal and near-frontal face views are used. This is mainly due to the current lack of sufficient training data for non-frontal views. This restriction does, however, lead to computational efficiency.

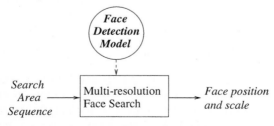

Fig. 3.1. Face detection

Face search is performed by applying the network at several scales to the search area. This is an expensive process so computation is controlled to maintain real-time performance. Firstly, the network is trained with slightly rotated, scaled and shifted images so that it has a small amount of tolerance to such transformations. This reduces the number of times the network must be applied in a search area at the expense of precision in face localisation. Secondly, an MLP with as few as eight sigmoidal hidden units provides sufficient performance. This internal representation is far more compact than that of networks previously developed for face detection in static scenes [22, 23]. Thirdly, search regions are prioritised using the following heuristics: new regions are given high priority and priority decreases the longer that no face is detected.

4 Face Tracking

Once a face is detected it can be efficiently tracked using a template matching approach based on minimising a sum-of-squared difference or maximising a correlation measure [12]. Matching is performed within a small search area centred on the predicted face position. Affine transformations provide improved robustness and the accompanying increase in computational expense is compensated by having to perform fewer face detections since tracking fails less frequently.

Tracking based upon matching a template extracted from the previous image is prone to accumulation of error and can eventually drift away from the face. This can be avoided by using a face appearance model to verify that the best match is indeed a face. Since verification is performed on only a single (or at most a few) matches per frame, the face model used can be relatively expensive to apply. The face detection neural network can successfully verify frontal and near-frontal views and its output can be used as a confidence measure [14]. Alternatively, a multiple view-based face model can be used to perform verification and pose estimation under rotation in depth. In this case, pose prediction is used to constrain model matching [15]. The face model used can be further constrained if information regarding the person's identity is available. This information could be provided by high confidence recognition. Alternatively, in an application such as identity verification for access control, the user must claim an identity and failure to track can be interpreted as a decision to refuse access. In these cases, user-specific face models can be used to track the face.

The tracking process is illustrated in Fig. 4.1. In summary, the face tracking process can provide estimates of face position, scale and pose. These estimates are obtained using fast, low resolution images. Prediction of affine and pose parameters as well as knowledge regarding identity can all be used to improve efficiency and robustness. The tracking process also provides a measure of confidence in each resulting face image. Several low confidence

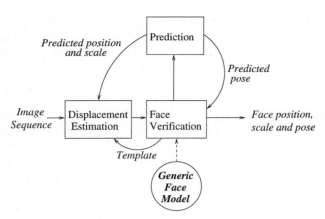

Fig. 4.1. Face tracking

frames indicate that the tracking process has probably failed and if a probable face region still exists, face detection is performed again to re-initialise tracking.

5 Face Recognition

The tracking process yields sequences of face images which have been approximately aligned at low resolution. Recognition of identity typically proceeds using a representation based on more accurately aligned, higher resolution imagery [3]. In general, the greater the precision with which correspondence can be established between facial images, the lower the resulting recognition error. At one extreme, dense correspondence fields have been used [27] and enable shape and texture to be accurately modelled as separate linear vector spaces [3]. Correspondence between large sets of facial features yields similar benefits [5, 11, 26]. Such correspondences are however problematic and expensive to compute. Therefore, recognition based on dense correspondence is typically applied to static 'snapshot' images rather than real-time sequences. At the other extreme is alignment using only affine [9] or even lower-order transformations [25] based on non-deformable template matching. This dichotomy broadly suggests two approaches to recognising identity from real-time sequences:

1. A few frames believed with high confidence to be good quality facial images are selected. Recognition is based solely upon these frames and can employ relatively expensive matching methods with dense correspondence.

---

[3] The resolution required is not necessarily very high. Humans can perform effective recognition of facial identity using images of low spatial resolution (18×24 pixels) [1].

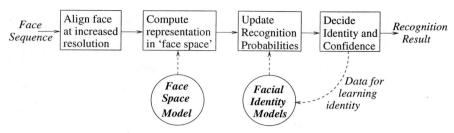

Fig. 5.1. Face recognition

2. A computationally efficient method is applied to all those frames tracked with reasonable confidence. Recognition is a continuous process of adjusting identity probabilities over time.

The first of these approaches has the some major drawbacks: it discards most of the potentially useful information in the sequence, it can make no use of temporal information and it is critically reliant upon the method used to select high confidence frames. Although the second approach does not suffer from these limitations, dense correspondence maps and computationally expensive matching algorithms are prohibitive. However, the possibility of basing recognition upon entire sequences can compensate this limitation. For example, consider a verification task requiring a binary decision: either the person is who he/she claims to be or otherwise. Any method which has an error rate $e < 0.5$ when applied to single images can be usefully applied to an image sequence simply by taking a majority vote over the decisions made using each image in the sequence [4]. Alternatively, probabilities produced from each image can be combined.

Feasible face recognition tasks are (i) verification of a subject's claimed identity, (ii) classification of a subject known to be in a database of known people and (iii) verification of a subject against a *small* database of known people. Verification against large databases requires alternative biometric methods such as iris recognition [6].

The recognition process is illustrated in Fig. 5.1. Once alignment has been performed, the face images are represented as vectors in a space which approximates the space spanned by all reasonable face images. 'Face spaces' have been computed using principal components analysis [5, 20, 25] or linear discriminant analysis [2, 8, 24]. Identification is typically performed by a nearest neighbour or nearest mean match in the face space. However, the use of real-time image sequences means that many hundreds of images of a face can be easily obtained. The distribution in face space of the images of a person can be estimated as a probability density function (pdf). These pdf's can then be used to perform recognition. Gaussian mixture models were used to estimate pdf's of facial identity [17]. Mixture models of appropriate

---

[4] Images in a sequence are highly correlated so this is only true on average.

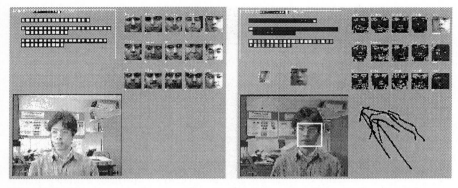

Fig. 6.1. Two screen-dumps of a continuous recognition system running on a PC. The task is to classify the subject as one of the 15 people shown. Hinton diagrams are shown at the top-left of each screen-dump. A plot of the trajectory of the tracked face in a 2D principal component subspace is shown bottom-right. Left screen-dump: initialisation with all faces equally likely. Right screen-dump: The face has been recognised and highlighted.

Fig. 6.2. Three screen-dumps of a continuous recognition system running on a Themis 10MP workstation hosting a Datacube MaxVideo250. The task was to classify the subject as one of 8 people. The histogram shows the current probability for each person with the correct identity shown in white. In this case, recognition clearly improves over time.

order achieved greater accuracy in a classification task than nearest mean classification. They were computationally more efficient than nearest neighbour matching and more accurate when recognition decisions were taken by accumulating probabilities over entire tracked face sequences.

6 Integrated Systems

Fig. 6.1 shows screen-dumps from a real-time system running on a PC and performing continuous recognition. The task here is classification of the subject as one of a database of fifteen people. Recognition confidence is accumulated over time.

Fig. 6.2 shows screen-dumps from a similar system running on a worksta-tion without the use of colour. The recognition performance can be seen to improve over time.

7 Conclusions

An approach to engineering real-time systems for face recognition was de-scribed. These systems utilise cooperative processes for focus of attention, face detection, tracking and recognition. Robustness and efficiency were achieved through the use of multiple attentional cues, prediction and feed-back from high-level processes. Recognition was performed using statistical models of images from continuous video sequences. The work illustrates an integrated systems approach to face recognition which not only addresses the recognition tasks but also presents computationally feasible solutions for real-time face detection and robust data acquisition.

Acknowledgement. S. J. McKenna was supported by the EPSRC Integrated Ma-chine Vision initiative IMV GR/K44657. Thanks are due to Yogesh Raja and Ong Eng-Jon for their part in the work described here.

References

1. T. Bachmann. Identification of spatially quantised tachistoscopic images of faces: how many pixels does it take to carry identity ? *European Journal of Cognitive Psychology*, 3:87–103, 1991.
2. P. N. Belhumeur, J. P. Hespanha, and D. J. Kriegman. Eigenfaces vs. fisherfaces: recognition using class specific linear projection. *PAMI*, 19(7):711–720, July 1997.
3. D. Beymer and T. Poggio. Image representations for visual learning. *Science*, 272:1905–1909, 28 June 1996.
4. B. F. Buxton and H. Buxton. Monocular depth perception from optic flow by space time signal processing. *Proc. Royal Society of London*, B-218, 1983.
5. N. Costen, I. Craw, G. Robertson, and S. Akamatsu. Automatic face recog-nition: what representation ? In *ECCV*, pages 504–513, Cambridge, England, April 1996.
6. J. G. Daugman. High confidence visual recognition of persons by a test of statistical independence. *IEEE PAMI*, 15(11):1148–1161, November 1993.
7. J. H. Duncan and T.-C. Chou. On the detection of motion and the computation of optical flow. *IEEE PAMI*, 14(3), 1992.
8. K. Etemad and R. Chellappa. Discriminant analysis for recognition of human face images. In *AVBPA*, pages 127–142, 1997.
9. S. Fischer and B. Duc. Shape normalisation for face recognition. In J. Bigün, G. Chollet, and G. Borgefors, editors, *AVBPA*, LNCS 1206, pages 21–26, Crans-Montana, Switzerland, 1997. Springer.

588

10. M. Hunke and A. Waibel. Face locating and tracking for human-computer interaction. In *28th Asilomar Conference on Signals, Systems and Computers*, California, 1994.
11. A. Lanitis, C. J. Taylor, and T. F. Cootes. Automatic interpretation and coding of face images using flexible models. *PAMI*, 19(7):743–756, July 1997.
12. J. Martin and J. L. Crowley. Comparison of correlation techniques. In *Conference on Intelligent Autonomous Systems*, Karlsruhe, March 1995.
13. S. J. McKenna and S. Gong. Tracking faces. In *Proc. 2nd Int. Conf. on Automatic Face and Gesture Recognition*, Killington, Vermont, US, October 1996.
14. S. J. McKenna and S. Gong. Non-intrusive person authentication for access control by visual tracking and face recognition. In *Int. Conf. on Audio- and Video-Based Biometric Person Authentication, Lecture Notes in Computer Science 1206*, pages 177–184. Springer, March 1997.
15. S. J. McKenna and S. Gong. Real time face pose estimation. *Real-Time Imaging, Special Issue on Visual Monitoring and Inspection*, 1998. In Press.
16. S. J. McKenna, S. Gong, and J. J. Collins. Face tracking and pose representation. In *BMVC*, Edinburgh, Scotland, September 1996.
17. S. J. McKenna, S. Gong, and Y. Raja. Face recognition in dynamic scenes. In *BMVC*, 1997.
18. S. J. McKenna, Y. Raja, and S. Gong. Tracking colour objects using adaptive mixture models. *Image and Vision Computing*, 1998. In Press.
19. R. C. Nelson. Qualitative detection of motion by a moving observer. *Int. J. Computer Vision*, 7(1):33–46, 1991.
20. A. Pentland, B. Moghaddam, and T. Starner. View-based and modular eigenspaces for face recognition. In *CVPR*, 1994.
21. Y. Raja, S. J. McKenna, and S. Gong. Segmentation and tracking using colour mixture models. In *ACCV*, 1998.
22. H. A. Rowley, S. Baluja, and T. Kanade. Human face detection in visual scenes. Technical Report CMU-CS-95-158R, Carnegie Mellon University, July 1995.
23. K. Sung and T. Poggio. Example-based learning for view-based human face detection. Technical Report AI Memo 1512, CBCL 103, MIT, 1995.
24. D. L. Swets and J. Weng. Discriminant analysis and eigenspace partition tree for face and object recognition from views. In *Proc. 2nd Int. Conf. on Automatic Face and Gesture Recognition*, pages 192–197, 1996.
25. M. Turk and A. Pentland. Eigenfaces for recognition. *J. of Cognitive Neuroscience*, 3(1), 1991.
26. L. Wiskott, J.-M. Fellous, N. Krüger, and C. vonder Malsburg. Face recognition by elastic bunch graph matching. *PAMI*, 19(7):775–779, July 1997.
27. R. P. Würtz. Object recognition robust under translations, deformations and changes in background. *PAMI*, 19(7):769–775, July 1997.

Some Experiments On Face Recognition With Neural Networks

Enrique Cabello[1], Araceli Sánchez[1] and Luis Pastor[2]

[1] Universidad de Salamanca, Facultad de Ciencias, Dpto de Informática y Automática, Plaza de la Merced s/n, 37008 Salamanca, Spain
[2] Universidad Rey Juan Carlos / Universidad Politécnica de Madrid, Fac. de Informática, Dep. de Tec. Fotónica, 28860 Madrid, Spain

Abstract. This paper presents some results on the possibilities offered by neural networks for human face recognition. In particular, two algorithms have been tested: learning vector quantization (LVQ) and multilayer perceptron (MLP). Two different approaches have been taken for each case, using as input data either preprocessed images (gray level or segmented), or geometrical features derived from a set of manually introduced landmarks. The preprocessing steps included resolution reduction and segmentation. For the geometrical features´ case, a Karhunen-Loeve expansion was used to extract features among the different possibilities offered by 14 landmark points.

For the experiments, a database composed of 300 images was used. The pictures correspond to 10 frontal, inclined o rotated views from thirty male persons of similar age and race. If gray level images are used as input data, the experimental results show higher recognition rates for LVQ than for MLP (96.7% versus 83.3%). Applying a previous segmentation stage strongly decreases the recognition rates. For geometrical features, the situation is reversed: MLP yields better results than LVQ (93.3% versus 84.4%).

Keywords. Neural Networks, Face Recognition, Multilayer Perceptron, Learning Vector Quantization

1   Introduction

Computer face recognition is a topic that has been receiving increasing amounts of attention during the last years. In particular, this last decade has witnessed a renewed interest, resulting in large increases both in the number of research centres and personnel involved in this problem and in the methods and techniques proposed to cope with it [3] [9] [12] [5]. Consequently, commercial systems have started to appear.

There are several reasons that explain the present interest in computer processing of human face images. First, there are strong economical reasons:

reliable face processing and recognition algorithms will find a myriad of commercial applications. Among them, the following can be pointed out [3]:

- Security. Enabling authorised people to access restricted areas. Detecting particular persons in sensitive areas that are specifically forbidden to them.

- Services (access to information or services). Automatic bank teller machines. Credit card owner identification. Access to computers and networks. Verification of user's identity for accessing medical services, etc.

- Law enforcement. Passport control. Person identification against a face database. Portrait sketching from witnesses' descriptions.

There are other somewhat related fields that can be mentioned, such as forensic medicine (face reconstruction or person identification from skeletal remains), video conferencing (compression of human face video sequences), etc.

There are also academic or technical reasons spurring interest in facial image analysis: unrestricted, robust face recognition is an extremely demanding task that has attracted attention from researchers in disciplines as diverse as cognitive psychology, forensic medicine, computer vision, etc. The problem's difficulty stems both from the complexity of facial patterns as well as from the variability found on face images: a face is intrinsically a three-dimension entity, and therefore, two-dimensional pictures are largely affected by illumination and pose variations. Furthermore, the importance that face aspect and facial expressions play in social life makes us devote a lot of attention to our external appearance. Consequently, face images undergo deep transformations due to variations in hair style, length and colour; presence of eye glasses, beard and/or moustache; presence of make-up, etc. Temporal and/or gradual changes in weight and age additionally affect our appearance, making the problem more difficult yet (even our own vision system can easily misrecognize faces, especially when other cues such as voice or context are not available).

In general, face recognition applications require the use of different approaches either because of the problem itself (matching two known pictures or matching a picture against a - perhaps large - face database, etc.), or because of the availability of supplementary information such as a person's age, race and gender, additional pictures, etc. Furthermore, there can be differences in the way data is acquired (static pictures or live video; from controlled or unrestricted setups; with uniform or cluttered backgrounds; within a limited or a long-term time span; from cooperative or non-cooperative subjects, etc.) [3] [9]. This volume can give an updated overview of approaches and application areas.

Our paper presents some results for human face recognition using different neural networks (NN). For each case, the NN was fed with two different kinds of data: preprocessed gray level images, and feature vectors computed from manually extracted landmarks. The most important criterion used for comparing results is recognition accuracy, although other key aspects that have to be taken into consideration are the algorithms' robustness and flexibility, and the computational aspects involved in the classifier design and operation. The. following sections describe briefly other methods for human face recognition, the experiments performed and results achieved in this work, and the main conclusions drawn from our experimental results.

2   State Of The Art

Many different approaches have been suggested for face recognition, especially during the last years. The techniques proposed in the literature can be classified according to the following scheme [3]:

Geometrical features: computing geometrical features such as angles, indexes or distances on human faces permits the straightforward application of statistical pattern recognition techniques [3] [9]. The main weakness of the geometrical features approach lies in the feature computation stage: current algorithms for the automatic location of landmarks are not consistently accurate.

Eigenfaces: Turk and Pentland [11] presented a face recognition scheme in which face images were projected onto the principal components of the original set of training images. A related technique ("Fisherfaces") has recently been proposed by Belhumeur et al [1].

Template Matching: Brunelli and Poggio [2] and Yullie et al. [13] performed direct correlations of image segments. In general, template matching is effective when the test images have the same scale, orientation and illumination as the training set.

Neural networks: Lawrence [7] proposes a system with a local image sampling, a self organization map (SOM) neural network and a convolutional neural network. Also, Lin [8] considered a probabilistic decision-based neural network for face detection and recognition. A review of connectionist approaches to face analysis can be found in Valentin et al [12].

Many other techniques, such as von der Malsburg's jets [14] or Nastar et al's deformable intensity surface models [15], have been developed during the last years. Some of them have been compiled in this volume and in two excellent surveys [3], [9]. Additionally, a recent issue of IEEE Transactions on Pattern Analysus and Machine Intelligence [5] has been devoted to face and gesture recognition.

3   Experiment Description

3.1   Data Set Description

The data base used in this study [4] is composed of 30 subjects, each of which has ten frontal or rotated images (Figure 1). All of the available pictures correspond to men of similar ages. Each person's set of images is composed of two frontal images, two with the face looking up, two looking down, two with the face rotated to the right and two rotated to the left. All of the pictures were taken with a white background and with a controlled lighting. The resolution of each image is 512x342 pixels with 256 gray levels, with the faces covering most of the picture area. In total, 300 images were available.

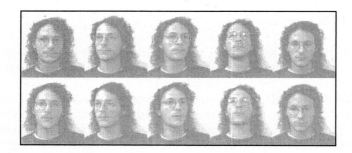

Fig. 1. Set of images for one subject

3.2 Classification Approaches

The results presented here have been obtained using two basic methods: multilayer perceptron (MLP), and learning vector quantization (LVQ). In both cases, two kinds of data have been fed to the classifiers: reduced resolution images (gray level or segmented), and feature vectors.

The first method used was based on a MLP. Some experiments were performed using a topology of two hidden layers with 674, 75, 15 and 30 neurons in the input, two hidden and output layers, respectively. Some other experiments have used a MLP with only one hidden layer, with a topology of 674, 100 and 30 neurons in the input, hidden and output layers. The second method implemented was LVQ (learning vector quantization, [6]). This method works like a 1-NN classifier differing on how the set of labelled patterns is formed: this set is typically obtained by clustering the training data (to reduce the number of labelled patterns), and then using a supervised learning algorithm to move the cluster centres into positions that minimize the classification error. Usually several codebook vectors are assigned to each class, and each test pattern is assigned to the class with the nearest codebook vector. One, two or three codevectors by class have been used here.

For geometrical characteristics, the same two methods (MLP and LVQ) have been tested. Each of them has been fed with different number of features, provided by a Karhunen-Loeve expansion. For MLP, Table I shows the number of neurons in the input layer (equal to the number of selected features) and the number of neurons in the hidden layer. The number of neurons in the output layer is always 30. For LVQ, one, two or three codevectors by class were considered for 5, 10 and 15 features.

Table 1. Number of neurons considered for MLP using geometrical characteristics

Number of neurons (input layer)	5	6	7	8	9	10	11	12	13	14	15
Number of neurons (hidden layer)	18	18	19	19	20	20	21	21	22	22	23

3.3 Data Preprocessing

The use of gray level images permits the consideration of all the information available in each picture, but the amount of data found in raw images advises the use of preprocessing steps to decrease the computational requirements in the analysis task. In our study this was done by creating reduced resolution versions of each image. The process is conceptually similar to computing a Gaussian pyramid, working with levels which are relatively high up in the pyramid. Additionally, the input images were normalized to decrease the influence of the acquisition conditions. Promising results were obtained by using a resolution level of 32x22 pixels. Higher resolutions imply higher computation times, particularly for the NN training.

Once the reduced resolution images were computed, nine of them were selected for each subject as the training set, while the tenth was used for testing the system performance. For some experiments, the test images were frontal views, whereas for others, rotated views were used to check the recognition system's robustness to changes in the viewing angle. In a different experiment, the reduced resolution images were also segmented before being fed to the recognition system (Figure 2). It should be pointed out that, in order to make results comparable, the same data set was used: in both cases, the same nine reduced resolution (gray level or segmented) pictures were used to train the MLP or to form the codebook vectors, using the tenth image for testing the methods' performance.

  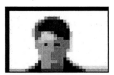

Fig. 2. Original, reduced resolution and segmented images for one subject

Regarding the use of geometrical characteristics for recognition, it is necessary first to define the set of landmarks, and then, to locate their actual position over the face images and to compute the features to be entered to the classification stage. In order to choose the landmarks, a preliminary study was performed over a set of common somatometric points: a group of operators repeatedly introduced the landmarks' positions in different frontal images at different times. The points that showed high placement variability (Figure 3) were discarded, as well as those that were easily occluded by facial hair or small face rotations. Finally, a set of 14 landmarks was selected for the tests. It has to be noted that the manual placement of landmarks permitted the separation of the recognition problem from that of landmark location, a research field in itself.

Fig. 3. The initial landmark set for one of the persons in the database (the circles' radii are estimates of placement variability).

With the 14 selected landmarks, 47 different features were computed, including the most commonly used ratios in human identification through cranial measurements (most of these measurements represented distances which had been normalized by the distance between the eyes). To analyze the information contained in these features, a Karhunen-Loeve expansion was performed in order to obtain feature vectors with lower dimensions; these vectors were introduced afterwards to the classifiers. As expected, decreasing the feature vectors' dimension did not have strong effects until certain limit was reached.

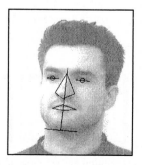

Fig. 4. Selected landmarks for one subject

4 Results And Discussion

The experimental results are summarized in Tables 2 to 4 and in Figures 5 and 6. Table 2 presents the percentages of correct recognition achieved for gray level images and MLP (with 674, 75, 15 and 30 neurons in the input, two hidden and output layers), or LVQ (with one, two or three codevectors per class). The images are reduced resolution versions of the original database pictures, including frontal and rotated views, and they were computed by gaussian averaging and downsampling. In some tests, these coarse images have additionally been normalized or segmented.

Table 2. Percentage of successful recognition for gray level images

Input image	MLP 2 hidden layers	LVQ 1 codevector per class	LVQ 2 codevectors per class	LVQ 3 codevectors per class
Gauss (frontal)	43.3	96.6	96.6	96.6
Gauss (rotated)	26.6	83.3	96.6	96.6
Normalized (frontal)	83.3	93.3	96.6	96.6
Normalized (rotated)	80.0	90.0	93.3	93.3
Gauss & Segment.	None	40.0	40.0	40.0

Figure 5 shows the evolution of the SSE (Sum Square Error) during the training stage of the referred MLP, for normalized and non-normalized input images.

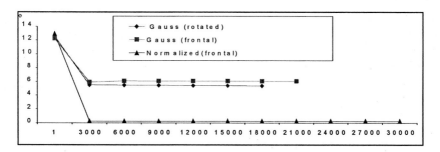

Fig. 5. SSE/o_units for the MLP (with 674, 75, 15 and 30 neurons).

Some tests were also fulfilled to compare the performance of the MLP approach when one or two hidden layers were used. For that purpose, a MLP with 100 neurons in the hidden layer was tested. The results for reduced resolution, non-normalized images are summarized in table 3.

Table 3. Percentage of successful recognition for different MLP topologies

	MLP (one hidden layer)	MLP (two hidden layers)	LVQ (two codevectors per class)
Gauss	73.3%	43.0%	96.0%

Table 4 outlines the main results achieved for the geometrical features case. Like in Table 2, the results have been produced by MLP (with one hidden layer, in this case) and LVQ (with one, two or three codevectors per class). Figure 6 depicts the evolution of success rates when the number of provided features is increased.

Table 4. Percentage of successful recognition for geometrical characteristics

Number of features provided by KL	MLP	LVQ (1 codevector per class)	LVQ (2 codevectors per class)	LVQ (3 codevectors per class)
5	44.4	36.3	45.5	40.0
10	84.8	77.0	78.5	77.7
15	93.3	83.7	81.8	84.4

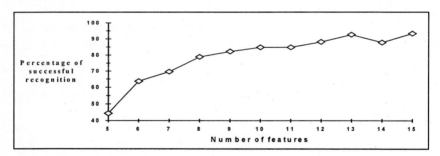

Fig. 6. Percentage of successful recognition versus number of features (number of neurons in the input layer) for MLP

An evaluation of Tables 2 to 4 shows that, for analyzing gray level images, better results were achieved with LVQ than with MLP. This result was consistently obtained for frontal or rotated views, independently of supplementary image preprocessing stages (normalization or segmentation). Additionally, Table 2 indicates that the methods (in particular, LVQ) were quite robust to small or medium head rotations, and that altering the images' gray levels by a segmentation process affected very negatively the methods' results. This can be due to either the gray level information lost in the segmentation process or to the influence that segmentation errors have at such a coarse resolution. For the geometrical features case, the situation was reversed: MLP (with one hidden layer) achieved higher success rates than LVQ. Regarding MLP topology, best results were achieved for only one hidden layer rather than for two (another advantage of using only one hidden layer was reduced training times). In any case, LVQ with gray level images has proven to be the best option tested here, including LVQ with geometrical features. This result is similar to Brunelli's [2], perhaps because gray level images contain more information than geometrical features. It should be noted that automatic or manual introduction of points has lead to similar results (90% in Brunelli [2] and 93.3 and 84.4% in our case).

5   Conclusions

Different NN approaches have been proposed in the literature for dealing with the human face recognition problem. This paper presents some results obtained using LVQ (learning vector quantization) and MLP (multilayer perceptron), fed with gray level images and geometrical features extracted from a set of 14 manually introduced landmarks. When using pictoric face information as input, LVQ behaved better than MLP, showing lower error rates and being more robust against changes introduced during the image preprocessing stage, as can be deducted from the results presented in Table II for segmented or non-normalized images. Furthermore, training times were much shorter for LVQ than for MLP. On the other hand, MLP achieved lower error rates when dealing with geometrical features.

The experimental results also show that, for the approaches considered here, analyzing gray level images produced better results than analyzing geometrical features, either because of the errors introduced during their extraction or because the original images have a richer information content. Increasing the number of geometrical features improved the results, although the process became more time consuming. The poor results achieved for segmented images are also remarkable. In Samaria [10] a similar result was concluded, noting that the process of face segmentation prior to recognition led to unpredictable results. Last, the results presented here indicate that LVQ and MLP are tolerant to small or medium head rotations, such as the ones considered in this work.

6   Acknowledgements

The work presented here was partially supported by the Spanish Commission for Science and Technology (CICYT: TAP94- 0305-C03-02) and Comunidad de Madrid (AE00263/95). Additionally, the help of Juan Alonso on some of the experiments is gratefully acknowledged.

7 References

[1] P.N. Belhumeur, J. P. Hespanha and D. J. Kriegman. Eigenfaces vs Fisherfaces: Recognition Using Class Specific Linear projection. IEEE Transactions on Pattern Analysis and Machine Intelligence. Vol 19, N° 7, p 711-720. Jul. 1997.

[2] R. Brunelli and T. Poggio. Face Recognition: Features versus Templates. IEEE Transactions on Pattern Analysis and Machine Intelligence. Vol 15, N° 10, p.1042-1052. Oct. 1993.

[3] R. Chellappa, C. L. Wilson and S. Sirohey. Human and Machine Recognition of Faces: A Survey. Proceedings of the IEEE. Vol. 83. N° 5. pp 705-740 .May 1995.

[4] Facial Data Base. University of Bern (iamftp.unibe.ch). Switzerland. 1995.

[5] IEEE Transactions on Pattern Analysis and Machine Intelligence: Special issue on face and gesture recognition (July 1997).

[6] T. Kohonen. Self - Organizing Maps. Springer -Verlag. 1995.

[7] S. Lawrence, C. L. Giles, A. C. Tsoi and A. D. Back. Face Recognition: A Convolutional Neural Network Approach. IEEE Transactions on Neural Networks. Vol 8, N° 1, p.98-113. Jan. 1997.

[8] S. Lin, S. Y. Kung and L. J. Lin. Face Recognition/Detection by Probabilistic Decision-Based Neural Network. IEEE Transactions on Neural Networks. Vol 8, N° 1, p.114-132. Jan. 1997.

[9] A. Samal and P. A. Iyengar. Automatic Recognition and Analysis of Human Faces and Facial Expressions: A Survey. Pattern Recognition. Vol 25. N° 1, pp 65-72.1992.

[10] F. S. Samaria. Face Recognition using Hidden Markov Models. PhD. Thesis.Trinity College. University of Cambridge. Cambridge. UK. 1994.

[11] M. Turk and A. Pentland. Face Recognition Using Eigenfaces. Proceedings Computer Vision and Pattern Recognition. pp 586-591. 1991.

[12] D. Valentin, H. Abdi, A. J. O'Toole and Garrison W. Cottrell. Connectionist models of face processing: a survey. Pattern Recognition, Vol. 27 No. 9, pp.1209-1230, 1994.

[13] A. L. Yulie, D. S. Cohen and P. W. Hallinan. Feature Extraction from Faces Using Deformable templates. Proceedings Computer Vision and Pattern Recognition. 1989.

[14] L. Wiskott, J-M Fellous, N. Krüger, C. von der Malsburg. Face Recognition by Elastic Bunch Graph Matching. IEEE Transactions on Pattern Analysis and Machine Intelligence. Vol 19, N° 7. p 775-789. Jul. 1997.

[15] C. Nastar, B. Moghaddam and A. Pentland. Flexible images: matching and recognition using learned deformations. Computer Vision and Image Understanding, Vol. 65, No. 2, Feb. 1997, pp. 179-191

Face Recognition Research at CSIRO

G.T. Poulton

CSIRO Telecommunications and Industrial Physics,
PO Box 76, Epping, NSW 2121, Australia
(Tel.) 61 2 9372 4287   (Fax) 61 2 9372 4411
Geoff.Poulton@tip.csiro.au

Abstract. Face recognition research for the benefit of Australian industry has been carried out over the past four years by CSIRO. A number of demonstrator projects are described which have been developed for access and border control and law enforcement applications. In addition, theoretical developments underpinning the demonstrators are described.

Keywords. pattern recognition/ face recognition/ identity verification/ image databases/ video surveillance/ access control/ passport control/ offender photographs/ identikit images

1 Introduction

The Commonwealth Scientific and Industrial Research Organisation (CSIRO) is Australia's largest civil Government research organisation. With 5000 staff working in 30 Divisions across Australia, research is carried out in a broad spectrum of fields relevant to both primary and secondary industry. As the name implies, CSIRO's main goals are to provide strategic and commercially-oriented research and development for the benefit of Australian Industry.

1.1 Research in face recognition

Research into human face recognition has been carried out over the last four years at CSIRO Telecommunications and Industrial Physics. It is part of a broader research program in Content-based Imaging which covers medical, geophysical and geographic imagery as well as industrial inspection and aspects of robotic vision.

The main application areas for face recognition are border and access control, surveillance and monitoring and the management of large image databases for Police, Government and industry [1].

1.2 Aims

Two factors which categorise a recognition or verification system are:

(a) Subject Cooperation:

COOPERATIVE: - The subject wants to be recognised, or
NON-COOPERATIVE: - The subject is unaware of the recognition process.

(b) Operator Interaction:

INTERACTIVE: - The process is monitored by an operator, or
AUTOMATIC: - The process is carried out automatically by the computer.

The aim at CSIRO is to move from a starting point of Cooperative Interactive recognition to the ultimate goal (grail?) of Non-cooperative Automatic recognition, the recognition and tracking of moving individuals in an unconstrained environment. Figure 1 illustrates this process.

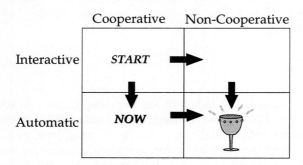

Figure 1. Face recognition goals

The means of achieving this goal is by developing a series of Demonstrator systems, backed up by a program of fundamental research. Since the purpose of the Demonstrators is to provide Australian industry with the basis for products, several constraints have been imposed to ensure industrial relevance. These are:
- All algorithms should run, in software, on a conventional PC platform.
- They should be fast enough for real-time operation.

Image capture is the only exception to the first of these rules, but wherever possible conventional PC cards are used for this purpose.

1.3 Current Status

At the present time we have built Demonstrators for Cooperative Interactive recognition and Cooperative Automatic verification, as described below. By June,

1998 a Non-cooperative Interactive Demonstrator will be completed for people moving in a relatively unconstrained environment.

The main theoretical developments have been in the use of combined global and local features for fast and accurate database search, in sensitivity studies of feature sets and in methods for dealing with images from different measurement modalities.

2 Demonstrators

2.1 Recognition booth

This Cooperative Interactive Demonstrator system comprises a booth with lighting control, in which images of a seated subject may be captured using a conventional video camera. After normalisation and feature extraction the captured image (probe) is compared with a database of images (gallery) which is then ranked according to closeness. This is a fairly conventional recognition booth except that a combined global and local feature comparison is used to achieve the advantages of each - the robustness to pose and relative insensitivity to facial feature location of local, warped-grid, methods whilst retaining the database search speed of global methods such as principal components analysis (PCA). More details are given in Section 3.1.

The performance of this booth is quite good for a live system, and is shown in Figure 2 for gallery and probe sets of 100 and 200 images respectively. Figure 2(a) gives the false positive/false negative performance, whilst Figure 2(b) shows the cumulative ranking for these image sets. The residual 2% error in Figure 2(b) is due entirely to eye-finder failure.

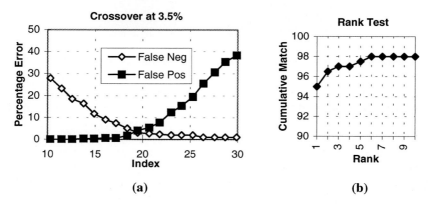

(a)   (b)

Figure 2. CSIRO booth performance. (a) FP/FN score: (b) Cumulative rank

2.2 Passport verification system

In conjunction with CPS Ltd. an automatic passport verification unit has been developed and trialed. Insertion of a passport into a slot allows information to be recorded, including OCR data and a scanned image of the passport photograph. This image is compared against a live video image captured by the unit, allowing automatic identity verification.

This is a relatively difficult verification environment because of the large variation in the scanned passport images. New techniques had to be developed to account for the significant differences in image capture modality for the compared images.

With the cooperation of the Australian Department of Customs and Immigration a trial of this unit has been carried out at Brisbane International Airport. Figure 3 shows the unit under trial. Results are encouraging, with a correct verification rate of 82%. These results are discussed in more detail in Section 3.4.1.

Figure 3. Automatic passport verification unit under trial at Brisbane airport

2.3 Identikit database comparison

"FACE" is a product marketed by the Australian company, Vision Control Pty. Ltd., and provides a facility for the interactive reconstruction of "identikit" facial images for law enforcement applications. It is superior to earlier generations of such systems because portions of actual face images are used to digitally reconstruct a wanted face. This system is currently used by several law enforcement agencies both within Australia and worldwide. As an example, the Victorian Justice Department's database of FACE images currently has about 8000 examples and is growing rapidly.

CSIRO has produced a demonstrator system for database search and comparison of FACE images. This allows cross-referencing of new identikit images with all those previously captured within the State. The next stage of development is to allow comparison of a FACE image with offender photograph databases. As with the comparison of passport photos with live images, this presents difficulties because of the need to compare images deriving from quite different methods of capture.

2.4 Rapid identification of moving objects

Although this does not relate directly to face recognition it is a crucial technology for our ultimate goal of the recognition and tracking of moving individuals in an unconstrained environment.

CSIRO, in conjunction with the Victorian Road Transport Authority, has developed a system for the real-time recognition and identification of trucks moving along a motorway. Using a video camera moving objects are detected, separated from shadows and classified as cars, small trucks or large trucks. For large trucks a second, high-resolution camera captures the number-plate which is then recognised and logged with date, time and place.

The technologies developed for this project of rapid image capture, shadow identification and removal and real-time classification are currently being applied in the next stage of face recognition research.

3 Theoretical Developments

3.1 Global and local features

All face recognition methods depend on the extraction and comparison of a small number of features describing an individual face. There are two main approaches to feature definition:

(a) "Global" features generated from a training set of images. Such features attempt an optimal description of the whole-face region, or of a small number of facial segments. Global methods seek to identify similarities and differences in the population being studied, and may vary from population to population. Principal Components Analysis (PCA) is the best known such method, although clustering and other algorithms have also been used [2][3].

(b) "Local" features describing areas surrounding a deformable grid of points on an image. Such features are normally independent of the population being studied, for example Gabor functions are commonly used in an attempt to emulate characteristics of the human visual system[4].

Global methods are very fast but can suffer from a sensitivity to facial feature location and to variations in pose. Local warped-grid methods are more robust to both these factors but are computationally intensive and usually too slow for database search methods.

We have combined the advantages of both methods to produce a facial database search system which is fast enough for real-time operation and relatively robust to pose and feature location.

3.2 Insensitivity of feature sets

As mentioned above there are several methods of defining "global" feature sets describing an image or part thereof from a training set, including PCA and clustering algorithms. We have examined the sensitivity of recognition performance to the choice of feature set. Several alternative feature sets were derived from the same training set, including "random" features generated by random clustering of the training set images followed by averaging and Gram-Schmidt orthogonalisation. The performance of each feature set was compared with identical sets of gallery and probe images[5].

Figure 4 gives the performance of features derived from random clustering, compared with conventional PCA-derived features. The same training set of 100 images was used in each case. For a gallery of 100 images and a probe set of 200 the false positive/false negative crossover percentage is plotted against the number of features used.

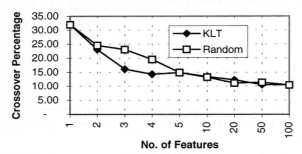

Figure 4. Crossover point as a function of the number of features for PCA (KLT) and "random" features

It can be seen that for more than five features the performance is practically the same for the two methods. It may be concluded that recognition performance is relatively insensitive to how the training set is used to generate features. In particular PCA and sophisticated clustering algorithms perform only marginally better than "random" features.

The practical conclusion is that future effort should concentrate on the other important problems of face recognition rather than searching for better methods of feature generation. Such problems include facial feature location, normalisation and other preprocessing methods aimed at improving robustness to pose and lighting variations.

3.3 Images from different measurement modalities

A particular set of difficulties is associated with the comparison of images taken from significantly different measurement modalities. An example is the comparison of live video images with scanned photographs captured from a passport or identity card. Whilst the capture environment for the former may be relatively well controlled, no control at all exists for passport photographs, which have been taken in a variety of situations with differing lighting conditions, pose and image quality. In addition, passport photos can be up to ten years old, and the scanning process will cause further degradation. Figure 5 gives an example of these difficulties.

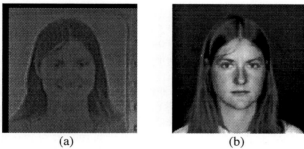

(a)   (b)

Figure 5. Comparison of (a) scanned passport and (b) live video images of the same person.

There are basically two choices for dealing with this situation.
(1)   Development of a model describing the transformation between images of different modalities; and
(2)   The construction of features which automatically take into account such differences.

For methods using local feature sets, for example Gabor functions defined on a deformable grid, only the first method seems feasible. For global feature sets such as PCA or similar both methods may be used to advantage.

In either case, obtaining features which are capable of describing the difference between the two sets of images is important. Such features have other uses, and are described briefly in the next section.

3.4 Optimal difference bases

It is well recognised that conventional global feature sets obtained with PCA are not optimal for discrimination between images in a class, although they may form an optimal basis for representation of the class.

In addition such methods do not differentiate between variations in images caused by different factors. The most important of these factors are:

Type (A):   Fundamental variations between images of different individuals.

Type (B1) Variations in images of a single individual due to change of expression, hairstyle, facial hair, aging etc.; and

Type (B2) Variations in images due to differences in the mode of image capture.

Effective recognition depends on being able to discriminate images on the basis of Type (A) variations whilst ignoring as far as possible variations of Type (B). By concentrating on differences between images rather than the images themselves it is possible to define a feature set which takes these differences into account. Such optimal difference bases require two training sets: P_B, consisting of pairs of images of the same people; and P_{AB}, consisting of pairs of images of different individuals.

Consider the difference sets

D_B: $\{d_{11}, d_{12} ...\}$ - differences between pairs in P_B, and

D_{AB}: $\{d_{21}, d_{22}, ...\}$ - differences between pairs in P_{AB}.

D_B contains information about image differences of Type (B), whilst D_{AB} has information about both Type (A) AND Type (B) differences. This happens because all the factors causing differences from image to image of a single person can also operate to cause part of the difference between images of two people.

Orthonormal bases S_B and S_{AB} may be formed for both D_B and D_{AB} using PCA or a similar method. What must then be done is to produce a basis spanning only Type (A) variations. Such a basis may readily be obtained by finding the orthogonal complement S_{OC} of S_B in S_{AB}. This process of deriving an orthogonal complement (OC) basis is illustrated schematically in Figure 6.

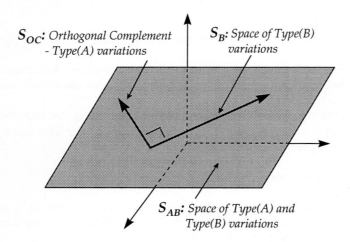

S_{OC}: Orthogonal Complement - Type(A) variations

S_B: Space of Type(B) variations

S_{AB}: Space of Type(A) and Type(B) variations

Figure 6. Schematic diagram illustrating the generation of an orthogonal complement (OC) basis.

This OC basis will account only for differences between individuals, and should be independent of variations between images of a single person and the imaging modality.

3.4.1 Application to Passport Images

The method was tested using images from the passport control trial. This is an ideal application since there are strong characteristic differences between the live video and the scanned passport images.

A training set was selected comprising 100 pairs of images, each pair consisting of a live video and a scanned passport image of an individual. This training set was used to generate features from an OC basis as described above. For comparison purposes conventional PCA features were also derived using the same training set.

Using these feature sets a verification experiment was then carried out with a gallery of 100 passport images and a probe set of 100 live images. The results of this experiment are shown in Figures 7 and 8. Figure 7 illustrates the improvement in false positive/false negative performance achieved by using OC features, whilst Figure 8 shows the relative performance of the two feature sets for a FERET-style cumulative rank measure [6].

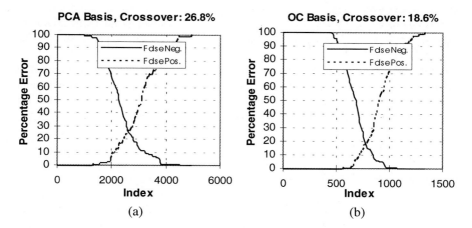

Figure 7   False positive/false negative plots for passport vs. live image verification. (a) PCA features. (b) Orthogonal complement (OC) features.

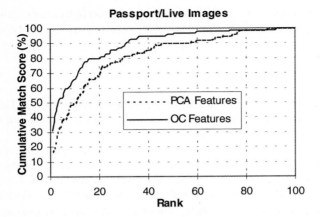

Figure 8 Cumulative rank test for PCA and OC features, with gallery and probe sets of 100 images.

3.4.2 Assessment

Using orthogonal complement features gives a clear improvement in performance over PCA-derived features, reducing the FP/FN crossover point from 26.8% to 18.6%. The cumulative rank test also shows a significant superiority for OC features.

It may be concluded that, at least in cases where there is are real differences in images being compared from two capture mechanisms, an orthogonal complement basis leads to real performance improvements, since it is able to better account for those image differences which are due to the mode of capture.

4 Future Work

Current and future efforts are being focused in the following areas:

(a) Improved performance for our current Demonstrator systems as described above. The prime areas of concentration are improved robustness to lighting and pose, better facial feature location and further work on the comparison of images from different modalities. The accent will be on moving from Cooperative to Non-cooperative recognition.

(b) The study of acceptable failure modes. In practice the way a system fails is often more important than the failure rate. Customer tolerance of a system can be greatly improved if all failures can be seen to be understandable in the context of human recognition.

Unfortunately computer recognition systems often fail in ways which seem inexplicable to a human operator. Future research will investigate why this occurs and will focus on developing, for face recognition, methods of making computer errors more acceptable.

(c) The development of new Demonstrator systems, in particular a real-time system for monitoring and analysing an environment through which a number of people are moving. Using video images, the ultimate aim is to acquire, track and identify all people moving through the environment.

This foray into non-cooperative automatic recognition is an ambitious goal but should be achievable since all the necessary skills exist within CSIRO, including fast video capture and processing technology.

5. References

[1]   D. Rees, G. Poulton and C. Jacka, "The CLICK (CSIRO Laboratory for Imaging by Content and Knowledge) Security Demonstrator", Proceedings, 31st Annual IEEE Carnahan Conference on Security Technology, Canberra, Australia, October, 1997.

[2]   M. Turk and A Pentland, "Eigenfaces for Recognition", Journal of Cognitive Neuroscience, Vol. 3, No. 1, 1991, pp 71-86.

[3]   M. Kirby and L. Sirovich, "Application of the Karhunen-Loeve procedure for the characterisation of human faces", IEEE Trans. Patt. Anal. and Mach. Intell., PAMI-12 (1), 1990, pp 103-108.

[4]   M. Lades, J. Vorbruggen, J. Buhmann, J. Lange, C. v.d. Malsburg, R. Wurtz and W. Konen, "Distortion invariant object recognition in the dynamic link architecture", IEEE Trans. Computers, Vol. 42, No. 3, Mar. 1993, pp300-311.

[5]   G. T. Poulton, "Comparison of Feature Sets for Face Recognition", PCS'96, Melbourne, Vic., March, 1996.

[6]   P. J. Phillips, P. J. Rauss and S. Z. Der, "FERET (Face Recognition Technology) Recognition Algorithm Development and Test Results", US Army Research Lab. Tech. Rep. ARL-TR-995, Oct. 1996.

Face Image Processing Supporting Epileptic Seizure Analysis

Frédéric Ravaut and Georges Stamon

Laboratoire des Systèmes Intelligents de Perception,
U.F.R. Mathématiques et Informatique,
Université René Descartes - Paris 5,
45 rue des Saints-Pères, 75006 Paris.

email: ravaut@math-info.univ-paris5.fr
internet: http://www.univ-paris.fr/sip-lab/

Abstract. Based on the hypothesis of a one-to-one relationship between the external symptoms of epileptic fits and the abnormal cerebral functioning which causes it, the computerized study of epileptic fit video tapes brings new information on abnormal neuron activity. From the analysis of the face movements, we can characterize the seizure.

1. Introduction

The choice of the adequate treatment against epileptic seizure relies upon the determination of the kind of epileptic « syndrome » the patient is suffering. Indeed it is necessary, first, to know the medical foregoing of the patient, second, to analyze the Electroencephalogram (EEG) and third, to observe the outward signs of the seizure.

The improvement of the automatic epileptic seizure analysis essentially concerns the EEG which is now a numerical signal and allows computers to extract different kinds of information.

But the observation of the patient, even if seizures are today recorded on video tapes synchronized with the EEG (see figure 1), is still an heavy and tedious task.

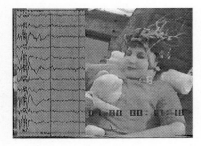

Figure 1: Simultaneous symptom-EEG recording.

For this reason it is useful to improve this part of the epileptic fit analysis, by introducing image processing techniques, and especially those dedicated to face analysis.

2. Background

The term epilepsy comes from the ancient Greek expression meaning "surprise attack".

Today nearly 500,000 adults and children in France are affected by epilepsy.

Epilepsy is a paroxysmal neuron behavior during which an accelerated discharge rate occurs in nerve cells and their elongation. This intense neuron activity is highly synchronic with all affected cells discharging in unison; it begins in a distinct "epileptic center" but then spreads extremely rapidly, and the apparent symptoms are the visible translation of what happened inside brain. [7]
Our research is based on the hypothesis that there is a one-to-one correspondence between the observable epileptic symptoms and this abnormal local neuron behavior; and that the visible conveys the invisible.

Comparing filmed epileptic seizures with EEG interpretation does provide medical experts with insight into the mechanics of a seizure and enables them to trace the development of the condition for a given patient. They can then hypothesize about the patient's cortex disorder and determine the **epileptic syndrome**. However, it is probable that this technique does not detect all pertinent clinical data; nor does it make it possible to assess the variations of this data during different seizures. Computer technology is being applied to video recordings of seizures in the hope of gathering data which doctors would have difficulty in accessing otherwise.

This new technique should make it possible to identify the nature of the very first symptoms of a seizure and then to monitor them. In keeping with our hypothesis concerning the relationship between symptoms and abnormal neuron activity, determining precisely the initial observable manifestation of a seizure may very well enable specialists to pinpoint the elusive epileptic center. This new-found knowledge would represent an important breakthrough in diagnosing and treating epilepsy, for example to reduce the part of the brain to eliminate when surgery is necessary.

3. Methodology

Our research - carried out in collaboration with Dr. Perrine Plouin of the neurological research laboratory (Laboratoire d'Explorations Fonctionnelles Neurologiques) of the Saint-Vincent-de-Paul Hospital in Paris and the Deltamed Numerical EEG equipment corporation - has proven particularly pertinent to children as it is frequently difficult to recognize their symptoms as epileptic.
The highly variable nature of the clinical aspects of epileptic seizures, especially among the newborn and children, significantly complicates their study and renders the process highly time consuming. Given the difficulties involved in filming the entire body of a patient during a seizure, each specific bodily region to be studied

must be filmed separately. We have, therefore, targeted the facial manifestations of epilepsy such as fluttering eyelids, pupil dilatation, loss of eye focus, and discoloration of the lips. [9][10][11]

In order to analyze these symptoms, one have to target specific parts of the face (mouth, nose, eyes, etc.) [2] by segmenting the face as illustrated in the following figure. This is the **segmentation task**.

Later, a set of parameters is defined in order to analyze the motion of each part. This is the **characterization task**.

A - Segmentation

A.1.   Region based approach [1][6]
The images are first binarized to find regions which will be identified by a semantic model of face (figure 2).

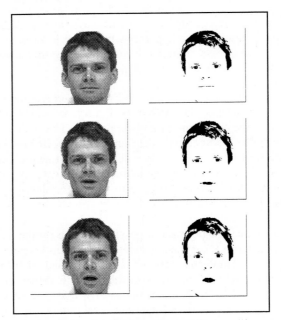

Figure 2: Image thresholding.

The threshold used for the binarization is determined by image histogram (figure 3).

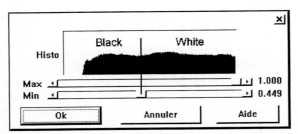

Figure 3: Histogram and threshold determination.

The semantic model is related to constitution of the human face (figure 4) and allows to localize features even if head orientation hides some.

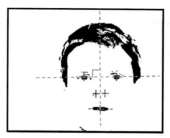

Figure 4: Feature localization.

Segmentation technique depends on the features to be characterized. It is sometimes necessary to proceed with the segmentation after the localization step. Lips for example, need as a second step of processing. Snakes are then used as an « edge based approach ».

A.2.   edge based approach [3][4][5]

Here the results of the previous step are exploited to initialize the snake.

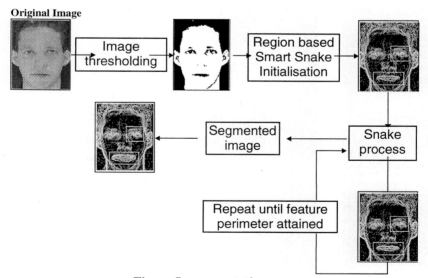

Figure 5: segmentation

We obtain: a) edges of lips providing information about shape and position.
b) centre of eyes for following eye movement.

B - Characterization

Once the different features of the face have been segmented, a set of descriptive parameters applied to the image is defined. [8]

Related to the parameter, we applied the « region based approach », sometimes followed by the « edge based approach ». For example, the first approach provides color information, the second provides information such as mouth deformation in the sequence.

Lip parameters include size, color, and position relative to the middle of the upper lip, the less movable part of the mouth. Eye parameters can be size and position within the image as well as relative position of the iris and pupil diameter in close-ups.

Variations in these parameters are then monitored during seizure in order to identify movement, deformation, lip discoloration, pupil dilatation, fluttering eyelids, etc. This way, a detailed synopsis of the clinical symptoms observable in the video is obtained.

4. Results

Results of the segmentation of the lips are presented in figure 6.

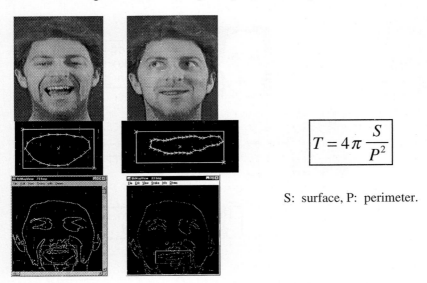

$$T = 4\pi \frac{S}{P^2}$$

S: surface, P: perimeter.

Figure 6: Segmentation result.

One of the parameters that can be defined on these images in order to follow mouth motion in the sequence is the « **Thinness** ».

Figures 7 shows the meaning of this parameter.

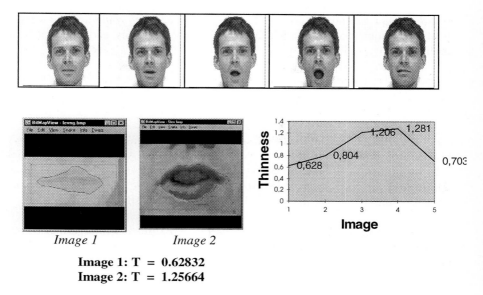

Image 1   Image 2

Image 1: T = 0.62832
Image 2: T = 1.25664

Figure 7: Mouth deformation.

This parameter resists homothetical transformation, as a back-and-forth move of the head, and also side move. This parameter is the opposite of « Circularity ».

5. Trends

The methods presented here are quite time consuming and expensive to apply to a non-interesting part of the face in a medical point of view. That's why we need to know where motion is before to characterise it. We are therefore interested in the **Optical Flow** techniques or other motion detection techniques, to detect motion in the sequence of images before to work on that particular part of the image with tools presented above, in order to choose an adapted method.

In some cases, eye blinking for example, combining image subtraction and morphological mathematics operation seems to give interesting results.

6. Conclusion

The original point of this work is to automatically characterize some observable epileptic symptoms to understand the corresponding abnormal brain activity whose study is very difficult. Automatic treatment leads to finer analysis (in scale) and provides in-depth data which are not previously available. Understanding the sequence of epileptic symptoms and being able to quantify them will surely enable doctors to better prescribe health care for this disorder which still remains extremely difficult to treat effectively.

So, we would like to select from the area of « Face Recognition » and « Face Analysis », some techniques which can be adapted to this particular medical application.

7. References

[1] COCQUEREZ, J.P., PHILIPP, S., *Analyse d'images : filtrage et segmentation*, ed. Masson, 1995.

[2] CRAW, I., ELLIS, H., LISHMAN, J.R., *Automatic Extraction of Face-Features*, Pattern Recognition Letters 1987, p 183-187, North-Holland.

[3] ESSA, Iarfan A., PENTLAND, Alex P., *Facial Expression Recognition Using a Dynamic Model and Motion Energy*, M.I.T. Media Laboratory Computing Section, Tec.Rep. 307, International Conference on Computer Vision 20-23 juin 1995, Cambridge.

[4] HEAP, Tony, SAMARIA, Fernandino, *Real-Time Hand Tracking and Gesture Recognition Using Smart Snakes*, Olivetti Research Limited, Old Addenbrookes Site, Cambridge, UK.

[5] LEROY, Bertrand, HERLIN, Isabelle L., *Un modèle déformable paramétrique pour la reconnaissance de visage et le suivi du mouvement des lèvres*, 15ème colloque GRETSI, Juan-les-Pins, 18-21 Sept. 1995.

[6] SIROHEY, Saad Ahmed, *Human Face Segmentation and Identification*, Computer Vision Lab., Center for Automation Research, University of Maryland, Nov. 1993.

[7] P. THOMAS, P. GENTON, *Epilepsies*, ed. Masson.

[8] TOCK, David, CRAW, Ian, LISHMAN, Roly, *A Knowledge Based System for Measuring Faces*, Dept. of Mathematical Sciences and Computing Sciences, University of Aberdeen, Scotland, 1990.

[9] TURK, Matthew Alan, *Interactive-Time Vision : Face Recognition as a Visual Behavior*, Ph.D. Thesis, Massachusetts Institute of Technology, Sept. 1991.

[10] TURK, Matthew A., PENTLAND, Alex P., *Recognition in Face Space*, SPIE vol. 1381, Intelligent Robots and Computer Vision IX, 1990.

[11] VIAUD, Marie-Luce, *Animation Faciale avec Rides d'Expression, Vieillissement et Parole*, Thèse de l'Université Paris 11 Orsay, 9 Nov. 1992.

Real-time Gaze Observation for Tracking Human Control of Attention

A. Schubert and E.D. Dickmanns
Universitaet der Bundeswehr, Munich
Aero-Space Engineering
D-85577 Neubiberg, Germany

Abstract: A sensible way of determining the subject to which the pilot is paying attention is to see in which direction he is actually looking. Combining this information with knowledge about the arrangement of instruments and windows in a cockpit, the subject of actual interest to the pilot flying can be inferred.

A solution is approached by adapting the well proven 4-D approach to dynamic machine vision to this problem. In order to be able to determine both head and viewing direction simultaneously, a bifocal camera arrangement has been selected as used in other applications before.

Keywords: gaze detection / human control of attention / 4-D approach / spacio-temporal models / recursive state estimation / region-based feature extraction

1 Introduction

Modern knowledge-based pilot assistance systems are developing the capability of supporting the pilot in a wide variety of tasks. [OnS 97], [SzO 96] describe such a system for transport aircraft; because of the wide range of support available, the system should know which partial task the pilot is actually devoting his attention to. It is then able to check, whether this item ranks highest in its own priority schedule too, or whether it should recommend the pilot to look at some other task of higher importance according to its own judgment.

In order to determine the pilot's viewing direction, a set of two miniaturized CCD-video cameras with objectives of different focal lengths is mounted behind the dashboard on a two-axis platform for viewing direction control. The wide angle camera maps the pilot's head on the central third of the image (horizontally) and the platform control keeps the face centered in the image. The tele-camera focuses on the eye region; its resolution is three to four times larger than that of the other camera. The distance between the cameras and the pilot's face is about 0.8 meter.

Figure 1 sketches the arrangement of some items of interest in the experimental setup.

The task is to determine first the spatial head position (x, y, z) relative to the camera set in the dashboard as well as the angular orientation of the head in yaw, pitch and roll, and second the viewing direction of the pilot. The result shall be a statement whether the pilot is looking out of the window (with a rough indication of the viewing direction) or to which instrument he is paying attention.

This general task of determining the spatial direction (stereo angles) into which a person is paying visual attention may be of interest in a wide field of applications; the case discussed is just one example.

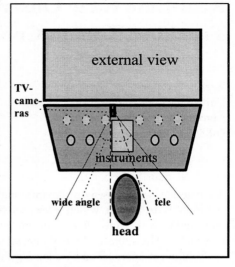

Figure 1: Sketch of experimental setup

The paper is organized as follows: In section 2 the geometrical problem of determining the visual focus is discussed. After a brief description of the hardware used (section 3) the initialization problem is treated in two steps: First the quasi static detection of a face in an image (section 4), and second the determination of face parameters (section 5) needed for the 3-D model used in recursive state estimation (section 6). Some results are discussed in section 7.

2 The geometrical problem of determining the visual focus

The visual focus can be derived from the line of gaze and a model of the environment in which the person is situated. In the case of the cockpit, the relevant environment consists basically of the control panels, screens, the windows to the outside world, and the overhead control switch area, each of which can be represented as planes. In other environments, however, more complex surfaces may appear. Once the line of view is known, the visual focus can be determined by calculating the intersection of the line of view with one of the planes.

The line of view is a fictitious straight line which is identical with the visual axis of the eye. The visual axis and the optical axis both run through the center of the crystalline lens, but whereas the visual axis originates at the fovea centralis, the point of sharpest sight on the retina, the optical axis runs through the center of the eyeball. Even though it is the visual axis which catches most attention in human vision it is assumed here for simplicity that the visual focus can be calculated by the optical axis which is supposed to run through the center of the iris and the center of the eyeball; furthermore this center is supposed to be identical with the point the eyeball revolves around. This simplified model of human gaze is assumed to be sufficient for a start but it is also possible to implement more detailed models.

The center of the iris can be detected directly in the image of the face whereas the point the eyeball revolves around is invisible. Since the pivotal point of the eye has approximately a fixed position in the head, the problem is solved if the relative position of a coordinate system fixed to the head and the coordinates of the pivotal point in this coordinate system are known. Thus, a face coordinate system has been defined relative to which the positions of the facial features have to be determined in the initialization phase. The relative position of the scull-based coordinate system can then be calculated by tracking of facial features. The coordinates of the pivotal point of the eye in the scull-based coordinate system have to be measured during the last part of the initialization phase in which the person observed is asked to look at some predefined spots in the cockpit for calibration.

3 Hardware used for gaze detection

In order to be able to determine both head and viewing direction simultaneously, a bifocal arrangement has been selected as used in other applications before [Dic 94]. In a wide angle camera the pilot's head fills about one third of the image in row direction, which allows for the tracking of head motion. In the tele-camera both eyes will be visible in the standard case with about 40 to 50 pixels on the iris diameter. The cameras are mounted fixed relative to each other on a two axis pan and tilt platform so that the eyes can be tracked during head motion.

The images are sampled at a rate of 25 Hz (video cycle) by means of a PCI framegrabber. The digitized images are processed on a 200 MHz Dual Pentium Pro PC with Windows NT as operating system.

4 Initialization: finding the 2D projection of a face in an image

In our approach the first task in the initialization procedure is to find out whether a 2D projection of a face is visible in the image and to locate the position of typical facial features. From these data the parameters of the generic face model can be adapted and the initial values of the state variables for recursive state estimation of the head can be set. It is assumed that knowledge about typical face projections (e.g. seen from front or from the left or right side) will make the first part of the initialization feasible. To establish whether or not there is a face in the image typical facial features which have to be in a certain arrangement are searched for. Since single facial features have the appearance of characteristically shaped areas in the image plane, area-based feature extraction is employed for this task. The 'triangle- algorithm' [Dea 97] developed for tasks like this one will be described in the following subsection. The second subsection will discuss the generation and verification of hypotheses for a face.

4.1 The triangle algorithm

By means of the triangle algorithm, an arbitrarily oriented (essentially one-dimensional) stripe of a certain width in the image is segmented into regions of relatively homogeneous intensity properties [Dic 97]. First, all pixel values across the stripe width (which are supposed to belong to a homogeneous area) are summed up for the purpose of averaging (transversal low pass filtering) such that a single vector of dimension 'stripe length' results. Depending on the problem at hand a certain number of higher triangle levels are determined by generating more coarse representations. Median filtering has proven to be an efficient method so far, but averaging is also possible. Thus, the 'triangle algorithm' may be considered as a reduced (one-dimensional) version of the well-known 'pyramid'-technique [BHR 81]. Figure 2 demonstrates the construction of a triangle.

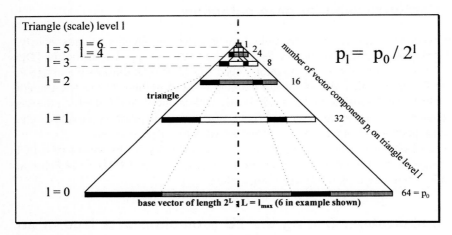

Figure 2: Construction of a triangle for more coarse representations

While using median filtering the reduction window comprises three pixels and since the selected subsampling rate is 1:2 the reduction windows overlap by one. If calculation of the mean value is used, the size of the reduction windows is two and thus no overlapping occurs.

Homogeneous segments are searched for on the highest level built; all areas yielding a below-threshold correlation value with a (-1,0,1)-correlation mask are grouped together. The number of levels of the triangle is determined by the size of the areas to be segmented. By taking into consideration that on level l a single value represents 2^l (in the case of mean filtering) or ($2^{l+1}-1$) pixels (in case of median filtering because of the larger reduction window and the occurrence of overlapping) on the lowest level, the total number of levels required can be calculated approximately. The boundaries of these segments are determined more precisely in as many of the lower levels as necessary.

For each of the segments, characteristic values like mean intensity or the correlation values at the beginning and the end of a segment are calculated.

Usually several parallel triangle stripes at a distance which depends on the recognition problem are used. The segments of neighboring triangle stripes can be merged into areas by using a method called 'chaining'. The rules for the chaining procedure can be chosen according to the specific feature searched for. For example, if a relatively homogeneous area is to be found, only neighboring segments the mean intensities of which differ by no more than a threshold value are 'chained'. Chaining can also be subject to geometric conditions. In figure 3 (subsection 4.2) the results of applying the algorithm may be seen.

4.2 Hypothesis generation and verification

In accordance with the task of detecting the gaze direction of a pilot it is assumed that at the beginning of the initialization phase there is only one face visible in the image which is at a distance of approximately 80 cm of both cameras because these are the regular conditions of operation. This first part of the initialization aims at deciding whether a face is visible and at locating it in the image. From these data the initial values for the relative position of the scull-based coordinate system can be calculated. The verification of the hypothesis that a face is present is done by finding typical facial features that are grouped in a certain way. For this part it is not necessary to use features that can be measured exactly. For example, hair is typical of many faces and often covers a large area in the image as compared to many other facial features. Nevertheless, for determining the relative position of the scull-based coordinate system other features are more appropriate.

The following facial features can be searched for: hair, forehead, eyebrows, nose, eyeballs, beard (if available) and mouth. Some of these features consist of subcomponents. The iris and the sclera are for example parts of the eyeball. These features have different appearance in the image plane because of two sets of factors. The first set results from the fact, that in 3-dimensional reality faces and facial features have different properties. For example, the hairs of a person may be blond or dark. The second set of factors stems from the aspect conditions under which the projection of the 3-dimensional reality into the image plane takes place. The same face has characteristically different appearance depending on the side from which it is looked at.

As for the first set, the different properties of each facial feature and the possible values of these properties can be systematically listed. Permanent visibility conditions independent of the viewing angle are included in this set of factors. For example the forehead may be covered by hair completely or in part. The aspect conditions describe the angle under which the face is looked at. Of the three possible angles only the yaw angle is used in our implementation so far. For certain ranges of the yaw angle the visibility of each facial features can be determined.

By combination of different properties of facial features and aspect conditions hypotheses for the appearance of a face with certain spatial properties in the image can be generated and systematically tested. It has been found useful to develop a search strategy for hypothesizing. For example under the following conditions:

(properties of facial features) : dark hair, hair on either side of the head and on top, forehead completely visible;
(aspect conditions) : view from front,

the following search strategy can be used:
1. search for forehead (light area of certain dimensions)
2. search for hair (dark area on both sides and on top of the forehead)
3. search for a pair of eyebrows (two similar dark lines below the forehead)
4. search for a pair of irises (two similar round and dark areas of a certain size below forehead)
5. search for nostrils (two dark blobs below the forehead).
Figure 3 demonstrates the procedure of this search strategy.

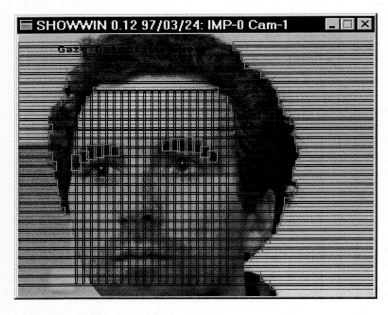

Figure 3: Detecting a face in an image

First, horizontal search stripes are set over the whole width of the image. These search stripes are depicted as pairs of dark horizontal lines. Segmentation by the 'triangle algorithm' is performed for which median filtering is used. The number of levels of the triangle was chosen taking two aspects into account. On one hand the forehead covers about a third of the picture horizontally (about 170 pixels). From this point of view five or six levels would seem appropriate. But since on the other hand also the hair on both sides of the forehead which covers an area of about 30-40 pixels horizontally should be represented, four levels are created. By vertical chaining areas are formed as described in subsection 4.1. Four light areas are detected by the chaining algorithm (One on the forehead, two to the left and one to the right of the head; the segments of them are surrounded by light boxes). One of these areas which is depicted by a dark box on the forehead meets certain geometric requirements (a range for the ratio of width to height) and is labeled internally as hypothesis for a forehead.

Below the forehead a vertical search for eyebrows is started. Usually, at the given distance of the head the eyebrows have a height of about 10 to 20 pixels. Therefore, the highest level of the triangles which are used for the detection of the eyebrows is set to two. Two segments are chained horizontally if they are shorter than a maximum length and the mean intensities differ by no more than a threshold value. If two similar dark chains of a minimum length each are found, these are labeled as a hypothesis for a pair of eyebrows. In figure 3 these areas are marked by vertical boxes in a bright color. The conclusion that a face is visible is established by finding a forehead surrounded by hair and a pair of eyebrows below it; a search for further features then follows guided by knowledge about the structure of faces.

Concerning the number of features to be found, only a majority of facial features and not all that are visible have to be detected in a single image in order to verify the hypothesis that a face is present. Of course, these features have to be grouped in a way that resembles a face. This enhances the robustness of the algorithm. It is also sensible to compare the results of a sequence of pictures. Final verification depends on whether the same hypothesis for a face and facial features has been found in a limited number of images in the same area.

From the position of facial features in the image plain, hypotheses for initial values of the state variables of the head for starting recursive estimation can be derived. The platform has to be turned in such a way that the upper part of the face becomes visible in the tele- camera.

5 Determining the parameters of the 3D internal face model

After the first part of the initialization the state variables of the scull-based coordinate system are known and a recursive state estimation algorithm can be started in both cameras using a standardized face model. Since the exact position of facial features is unknown so far, the parameters of the standardized model have to be adapted to the ones of the person observed. This is achieved by allowing the facial features additional degrees of freedom relative to the scull-based coordinate system in this parameter estimation phase as a second phase in the overall initialization process. In this phase, the parameters in face representation are treated as state variables with derivatives zero; only a noise term drives the parameter adaptation.

6 Recursive estimation of head state and viewing direction

A complete internal representation of the spatial movement of the head relative to the cameras is to be reconstructed from an evaluation of the image sequence of the wide angle camera. For this purpose the origin of a scull-based coordinate system is positioned at the atlas, that is the swiveling point for the head at the upper end of the spine. For this point the x, y, z coordinates are determined. Around this point the rotational motion components in yaw (vertical axis), pitch (horizontal axis, approximately through the ears) and bank or roll (horizontal, approx. through nose) are determined.

Each component is considered to be dynamically independent from the others and is modeled by a second order dynamical system. Of course, feature positions measured contain contributions from all of these states. This is taken care of by proper 3-D modeling of the parts generating the features relative to the atlas point, and by computing the corresponding entries into the Jacobian matrix for each feature/sensor pair. These are the driving factors for spatio-temporal interpretation using conventional recursive estimation algorithms [Wue 88; DiG 88, Dic 97].

Essential parts of the head modeled in 3-D are: The eye brows, the eyes with sclera, iris and pupil, the eye lids, the ears, the lower nose section and the mouth; the skin regions to the side of the face linking the forehead to the ears and the chin are also (coarsely) modeled in 3-D since they have a strong influence on visual appearance of the face in the image even for small changes in heading direction (around the vertical axis).

7 Experimental results

The initialization processes for face detection and for determination of the individual face parameters have been tested separately from the recursive estimation algorithm. Searching with area-based methods for the forehead in horizontal image stripes and then for the eyebrows with vertical stripes beneath the forehead yields good results and robust recognition. The computing power of a Dual Pentium Pro is sufficient for evaluating about two dozen horizontal search stripes over the entire image horizontally, and about the same number vertically in the skin region previously discovered, all at video rate of 25 Hz.

Tracking and spatio-temporal interpretation has been developed separately and partially tested after manual initialization on old transputer hardware exploiting edge features only. The results were promising taking the marginal computing power and feature base into account.

The overall software system is just being integrated on more powerful processor hardware allowing to process edge- and region-based features simultaneously. This will considerably improve robustness and dynamic performance which have been marginal with the transputer based system. The prediction seems to be safe that the task can be solved with a single PC-type computer in the near future.

8 Conclusions

The algorithms developed and tested will allow to determine dynamically the attitude of the head and the viewing direction of the eyes with a bifocal camera arrangement; a PC-type computer of the later 90ies in combination with the 4-D approach to dynamic vision will be sufficient for performing the data evaluation required in real time. The accuracy achievable in the overall system under dynamic motion is still an open question; however, it seems to be safe to state that it will be good enough for solving a wide range of problems.

9 References

[BHR 81] P.J. Burt, T. Hong, A. Rosenfeld: Segmentation and Estimation of Image Region Properties Through Cooperative Hierachical Computation. IEEE transactions on Systems, Man, and Cybernetics, Vol. smc-11, no. 12, December 1981.

[Dea 97] E.D.Dickmanns, S.Fürst, A.Schubert, D.Dickmanns: Intelligently controlled feature extraction in dynamic scenes. Report UniBwM/LRT/WE13/FB 1-97, 1997.

[Dic 97] E.D.Dickmanns: Vehicles Capable of Dynamic Vision. Proc. IJCAI ' 97, Nagoya, Japan, Aug. 1997.

[Dic 94] E.D. Dickmanns: Active Bifocal Vision. In: S. Impedovo (ed.). Progress in Image Analysis and Processing III, World Scientific Publ. Co. Singapore, 1994, pp 481-496.

[DiG 88] E.D.Dickmanns, V.Graefe: Dynamic Monocular machine Vision. J. Machine Vision & Applications. Springer Int., Nov. 1988, pp. 223-261.

[OnS 97] R. Onken, M. Strohal: The Crew Assistant for Military Aircraft. Submitted for the 7th Int. Conf. on Human-Computer Interaction, SanFrancisco CA, Aug. 24-29, 1997.

[SzO 96] P. Stütz, R. Onken: Adaptive Modeling within Cockpit Crew Assistance. Proc. Cogn. Syst. Eng. in Process Control (CSEPC), Kyoto, 1996.

[Wue 88] H.-J.Wünsche: Bewegungssteuerung durch Rechnersehen. Fachberichte Messen, Steuern, Regeln Bd. 10, Springer-Verlag, Berlin, 1988.

A Saccadic Vision System for Landmark Detection and Face Recognition

Barnabás Takács[1] and Harry Wechsler[2]

[1] WaveBand Corporation
375 Van Ness Ave., Suite 1105
Torrance, CA 90501, U.S.A.
http://chagall.gmu.edu/FORENSIC/barna.html

[2] Department of Computer Science
George Mason University
Fairfax, VA 22030-4444, U.S.A.
wechsler@cs.gmu.edu

Abstract. We present a new approach to the problem of face (non-rigid object) recognition. We introduce a novel methodology that exploits the advantages offered by active vision architectures, and utilizes highly compressed feature representations for person identification. Specifically, we describe a unified model of low-level visual attention that combines purely data-driven processes with primitive object recognition mechanisms and model-based reasoning, and show that such process can form the foundations of a high performance face recognition system. The described architecture employs a number of independent, parallel visual routines responsible for object localization, identification, and scene interpretation, corresponding to the "where" and "what" channels of visual perception. The model is biologically plausible and is motivated by processing strategies in the human visual system (HVS).

To test the validity of the described face recognition architecture, a number of experiments were carried out on a large and varied face database (FERET). The active vision components were used to detect faces by locating their individual facial landmarks, and to derive a compact face code invariant to changes in viewing geometry and imaging conditions. Simulation results on 100 subjects (216 images) demonstrated that both the "where" and "what" channels perform with high accuracy and their combined performance reached 100% in detecting all relevant facial landmarks. The identification experiments achieved 89.6% accuracy for the match task and reached 100% for surveillance. These results indicate that the proposed mechanisms are capable of efficiently locating and encoding information relevant for all aspects of face recognition.

1 Introduction

A face is the most distinctive and widely used key to a person's identity. Face recognition is a remarkable example of the ability of humans to perform a complex visual task with great reliability under extreme circumstances. A person is able to recognize thousands of faces encountered during his/her lifetime. This ability is quite robust against a variety of imaging factors, such as changes in head posture or size, background effects, facial expressions, aging, make-up, partial occlusions, or even disguise.

This paper describes a *dynamic attentive vision* architecture to address the problem of object recognition in general, and its application to face identification, in particular. Modeled after characteristic properties of the human visual system the problem of face recognition is addressed as an attention task. Attention, in computer vision, allows for intelligent control to deal with the allocation of computational resources in terms of *where, what* and *how* to sense and process. For example, in the context of face recognition, quickly finding regions of interest (such as the eyes, nose, mouth, etc.), prior to the application of more complex and computationally expensive recognition stages, enhances both performance and accuracy.

We have developed a three-stage *hierarchical attention model* to interpret the whole face image by the analysis of several spatially limited image regions, cued by an interactive cooperative process. The model uses facial landmarks, both as anchor points for geometric normalization (shift, scale, rotation, pose) and as feature descriptors for face identification. It implements the *"where"*, *"what"*, and *"how"* channels of visual processing and operates in a hierarchical manner iteratively screening the input for specific facial features. We combine purely data-driven "bottom-up" *sensory* processing with locally adaptive *reactive* mechanisms and a "top-down" *model-driven* component. The former two stages are dedicated to coarse localization of potential landmark candidates, and primitive pattern detection, respectively. The latter one implements global constraints and arrives at a best set of facial landmarks used to identify the subject. The proposed model expands on earlier active vision paradigms by
- incorporating bottom-up and top-down attentional processing in a unified framework of cooperative "where" , "what", and "how" processing channels,
- introducing biologically motivated new measures of local *conspicuity* along with an integration mechanism across saccadic movements to derive *saliency* on demand,
- using (these) low-level feature representations to drive purely data-driven processes that locate and cue image regions of potential interest (reflexive saccades),
- developing space-variant, *iconic object representations* that encode local image features in an illumination independent manner,

629

- designing neural network based *visual filters* for object and feature detection, and an iterative training strategy capable of constructing an optimal/minimal set of learning samples for two-class decision tasks,
- advancing a pattern completion mechanism (conditional saccades) based on a *geometric object model* of statistically valid landmark constellations, to address recognition tasks in low-image quality environments, and
- suggesting an *incremental object recognition* model that combines locally derived invariant (translation, rotation, scale, illumination) image features and global geometric descriptors for (face) identification.

The following sections discuss the basic building blocks and characteristics of various model components in detail. Despite its biological motivation, the architecture is introduced herein as a computational vision model. Potential biological links, including plausibility and the mapping of specific functionality to those in the primate visual system is detailed in reference [Takács,1996(a)].

2 Methodology

We developed a *three-stage attention scheme* [Takács,1996(b)] that hierarchically integrates potential face- and facial landmark candidates and eventually arrives at a consistent, best configuration of those features (Figure 1). The model is based on a feature extraction scheme using oriented, Gaussian filter banks arranged in non-uniform sampling lattices, and geometric models of valid facial configurations. We suggest that attentional movements are the result of interacting visual processes labeled as *reflex-, conditional-,* and *attentive saccades*, implemented at the *sensory-, reactive-,* and *model-based levels*, respectively. For a given moment in time, the next center of gaze is determined by the competition of these three visual processes and the history of the system.

Specifically, the sensory level "where" channel performs data collection and creates low-level feature descriptions by means of *oscillatory movements* of the non-linear sampling lattice. In particular, it implements a dynamic and multiresolution attention (DMA) model corresponding to early ("low-level") attention, which iteratively shifts the high resolution center of the fovea over "interesting" regions of the input. The generated *reflex saccades* draw the system's attention on highly variant regions of the visual field. At the reactive level, local features are assembled as more complex object properties and further (conditional) fixation points are generated to verify the coherence/coexistence of iconic object primitives. These *conditional saccades* associate local visual stimuli with saccadic movements – much like production rules in AI systems – but without the explicit access to global object models. The new generated fixation points are then used as anchor points for "refined" processing of cued regions. The top-down, task-specific component of the scheme, corresponds to the model-based level, which generates *attentive saccades*. This third level, having access to global constraints, primes both the reactive- and reflex levels as well as it performs eventual face identification.

Sensory Level: At the stage of early vision (data collection), the input is processed in parallel by several banks of oriented Gaussian filters to encode local image characteristics and to form feature representations. The *conspicuity* of locations is integrated across movements of a non-uniform sampling grid forming a *saliency* surface in the *short term visual memory*. Local extrema of this surface correspond to highly variant regions in the image and are used to compute a set of potential candidate fixation points. These *reflex saccades* are thus generated by a purely data-driven, bottom-up process, i.e. without the use of any task specific information.

In the context of face recognition, this *coarse priming* stage implements rough localization of the face bounding box using the saliency map [Takács,1995] and generates saccadic motion to guide/prime the evidence collection process of the reactive stage [Takács,1998].

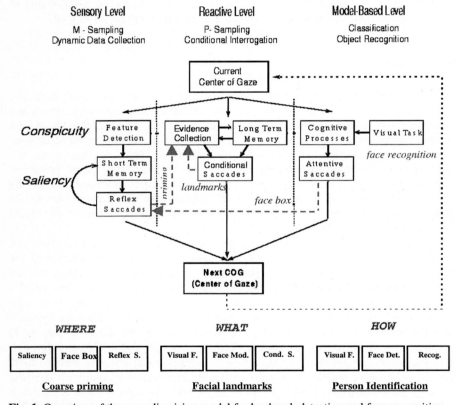

Fig. 1. Overview of the saccadic vision model for landmark detection and face recognition.

Reactive Level: Due to the non-linear sampling strategy employed and the movements of the sampling lattice, information about a specific portion of the image is available at varying degrees of resolution. Thus, for detailed analysis and recognition, the high resolution center (fovea) must be shifted over the regions of interest in a sequential manner. *Conditional saccades* attempt to verify the presence of a face from its locally identified landmark primitives such as the eyes, the nose, or the mouth[1]. Specifically, saccadic movements are the result of interaction with the *long term memory* which associates object "icons" appearing in the fovea with shifts of the sampling grid, according to the *geometric model* of the stored facial landmark configurations. Throughout this *evidence collection* process, the likelihood of the presence of particular facial landmarks, and in turn the existence of a face, is gradually built up and passed to the model-based level for post processing and recognition. From an implementation point of view, this stage is responsible for recognizing facial primitives using (i) visual filters [Takács,1994,1996(c),1997], and (ii) statistically derived geometric face models [Takács,1996(d)] implemented in the form of conditional saccades.

Model-Based Level: Knowledge-driven (top-down) processes optimize the system's performance by implementing *global constraints* specific to the visual problem (*face recognition*). This global mechanism, responsible for generating *attentive saccades* focuses the system's resources by supervising the reflexive and reactive stages. It is also at this level that post processing and final *recognition/identification* takes place using the information (visual filter responses, geometry) delivered by the other two stages.

3 Experimental Results

To evaluate the statistical performance of the proposed active vision-based face recognition model, 216 frontal images of 100 subjects were selected from the FERET database (8,525 images of 1,109 subjects), which is collected and maintained at George Mason University (under contract with the U.S. Army Laboratories) to provide a standard test bed for face recognition applications [DePersia,1995].

3.1 Face and Facial Landmark Detection

Figure 2 shows the output of the sensory (where) channel, for three subjects. The thresholded saliency images are shown on the top (red indicating the most salient region) and the corresponding reflex saccades are displayed at the bottom. The generated saccades are interesting from a computational perspective because they prioritize the order in which parts of the image are assessed and further processed at the reactive stage. As shown in the figure, the saccades visit most of the facial areas (eyes, nose, mouth, and the face outline) within the first few iterations. In fact, based on using the first 20 fixation points only, in 98% of the images (212 cases) at least two of these landmarks were correctly found and only in 1 case no correct fixation points were generated. This corresponds to eliminating 92% of the

---

[1] A face is defined as constellations of its primitives arranged in certain geometric configurations.

total image area from further processing at a very early stage. Examining the distributions by facial features we found that the algorithm correctly located 81.5%, and 81% of the eyes, and noses respectively. However, it missed, the mouth 49% of the time [Takács,1998]. These results are consistent with psychological findings [Groner et al, 1984].

All primed fixation points were subsequently processed by the reactive (what) channel in order to recognize facial primitives by the conditional saccade mechanism driven by the geometric face model supplied by the model-based level. Specifically, the reactive channel employed six banks of ten multi-resolution visual filters [Takács, 1994,1996(c),1997] (responsive to eyes, eye pairs, tip of nose, mouths, and full faces) and achieved *93%* accuracy in finding all six landmarks based on the locations cued by the reflexive saccades.

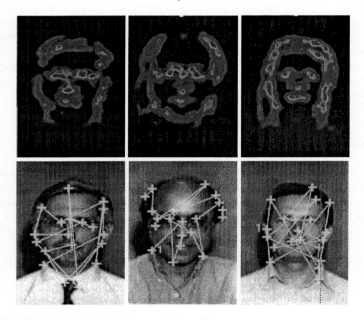

Fig. 2. Facial landmark priming using reflex saccades.

Specifically, the reactive channel employed six banks of ten multi-resolution visual filters [Takács, 1994,1996(c),1997] (responsive to eyes, eye pairs, tip of nose, mouths, and full faces) and achieved *93%* accuracy in finding all six landmarks based on the locations cued by the reflexive saccades. Conditional saccades successfully generated new candidates for missing facial landmarks and improved the overall detection rate significantly reaching *99%* accuracy in marking all six landmark regions.

Figure 3 summarizes this process showing the output of various stages of our algorithm. First, data-driven reflex saccades are generated to find a set of cue locations (Figure 3/a). Those regions marked at this sensory stage are then processed by the reactive "what" channel to find the best matching candidates for each of the facial features stored in the visual filter bank (Figure 3/b). The generated conditional saccades (Figure 3/c) correspond to the geometric facial configuration derived statistically by the system aimed to (i) recover missing facial landmarks and/or (ii) precise the location of those already found. The best final configuration is shown on Figure 3/d.

Figure 4 demonstrates the application of the described facial landmark detection process to criminal identification. Photographs of inmates stored in a large facial database are compared against a drawing prepared by a police artist depicting a wanted criminal. The matching process requires accurate identification of key facial areas. The feature detection algorithm accepts input both from photographs and drawings (*INPUT*). After coarse localization of the regions of interest, such as the face oval and the base-triangle of the eyes and the mouth (*PREPROCESSING*), the system proceeds by locating facial landmarks as described above (*FACIAL LANDMARK DETECTION*).

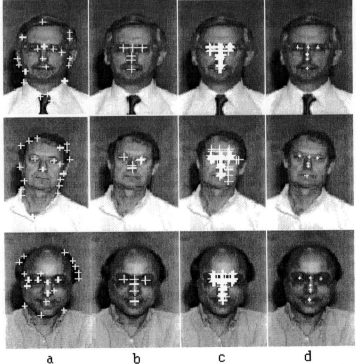

a　　　　b　　　　c　　　　d

Fig. 3. Facial landmark detection process summary (see text).

3.2 Person Identification

After detecting the facial configuration, the system proceeds to identify/match the person in the image against the data base. In the recognition experiments, we used a *face code* derived from the activation responses of four visual filters [Takács,1996(c)]. The combined face code was assembled from vectors corresponding to full face, eye pair, eye, and mouth detectors, respectively. The final 600 bytes code vectors were then used to train a *nearest neighbor* classifier to perform eventual recognition. During recognition, 116 images were encoded in a fully automated manner, using the facial landmarks detected by the process described above. The constructed face code was then matched against the database in two steps as follows:

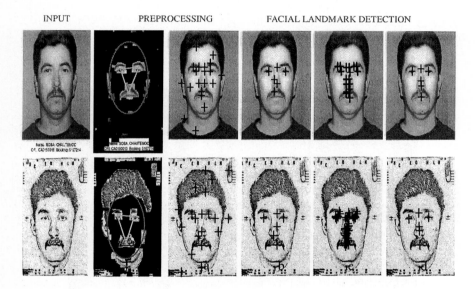

Fig. 4. Application to criminal identification (see text).

- Based on the scale estimate (Se) computed by the facial feature detection algorithm, the ten (10) closest neighbors were selected for subsequent comparisons.
- For all selected candidates, the closest matches at scales (Se+/-1) were computed, and the combined score served as the basis for final output assignment.

The classification algorithm correctly identified *89.6%* of the subjects tested. Among the 12 images missed, 3 belonged to duplicates. When more than one hits (Step 2) were allowed the performance increased to *100%* within the n = 3 best ranking candidates. Note that even using the simplest available final classifier (nearest neighbor) high recognition accuracy was achieved on a large and varied facial database. These results implicate that optimally designed visual filters provide a powerful mechanism to recognize individuals from frontal images.

4 Conclusions

In this paper, a new approach to the problem of face (object) recognition was proposed which exploits the advantages offered by active vision architectures, and utilizes highly compressed iconic feature representations for person identification. We have shown, that a unified model of low-level visual attention that combines purely data-driven processes with primitive object recognition mechanisms and model-based reasoning, can form the core of a face recognition system. The proposed architecture allows the integration of a number of independent visual routines such as object localization, object identification leading to saccadic targeting.

To test the validity of the proposed attention architecture, we applied this model to face recognition tasks. The active vision components were used to detect faces by locating individual facial landmarks and to derive a compact face code invariant to changes in viewing geometry and imaging conditions. Simulation results on 100 subjects (216 images) showed that both the sensory (*where*) and reactive (*what*) channels perform reliably when tested independently. The combined performance of all three stages reached *100%* accuracy in terms of detecting all relevant facial landmarks important for the face identification stage. The recognition experiments achieved 89.6% accuracy for exact match and reached 100% when using the top ranking 3 candidates. These results indicate that the proposed active vision architecture is suitable to address face recognition tasks, and it performs with high accuracy on large and varied data set.

Acknowledgments: this work was supported, in part, by the U.S. Army Research Laboratories under contracts DAAL01-93-K-0099 and DAAL01-94-R-9094. Additional support was provided by WaveBand Corporation Dr. Takács wishes to thank to the Los Angeles County Sheriff's Department for providing face images from their criminal database.

References

DePersia, A.T, Phillips, P.J. (1995) The FERET Program: Overview and Accomplishments, *Proc. of International Workshop on Automatic Face- and Gesture-Recognition*, Zürich, Switzerland.

Groner, R., Waldner, F., Groner, M. *et.al* (1984) Looking at Faces: Local and Global Aspects of Scanpaths, *Theoretical and Applied Aspects of Eye Movement Research,* Elsevier.

Takács, B., Wechsler, H. (1994) Locating Facial Features Using SOFM, *Proc. 12th International Conference On Pattern Recognition (ICPR)*, Jerusalem, Israel.

Takács, B., Wechsler, H. (1995) Face Location Using A Dynamic Model of Retinal Feature Extraction, *Proc. of International Workshop on Automatic Face- and Gesture-Recognition*, Zürich, Switzerland.

Takács, B (1996) Perception and Recognition of Human Faces, *Ph.D. Thesis,* George Mason University.

Takács, B., Wechsler, H. (1996) Attention and Pattern Detection Using Sensory and Reactive Control Mechanisms, *Proc. 13th International Conference On Pattern Recognition (ICPR)*, Vienna, Austria.

Takács, B., Wechsler, H. (1996) Visual Filters for Face Recognition, *Proc. International Conf. on Automatic Face- and Gesture Recognition,* Killington, Vermont, USA.

Takács, B., Wechsler, H., Wegman, E.J. (1996) Geometric Modeling Methods for Facial Landmark Detection and Recognition, *Proc. Interface Graph-Image-Vision*, Sydney, Australia.

Takács, B., Wechsler, H. (1997) Detection of Faces and Facial Landmarks Using Retinal Filter Banks, *Pattern Recognition,* 30, (10).

Takács, B., Wechsler, H. (1998) A Dynamic, Multiresolution Model of Visual Attention and its Application to Facial Landmark Detection, *CVGIP Image Understanding*, (in press).

NATO ASI Series F

Including Special Programmes on Sensory Systems for Robotic Control (ROB) and on Advanced Educational Technology (AET)

Vol. 120: Reliability and Safety Assessment of Dynamic Process Systems. Edited by T. Aldemir, N. O. Siu, A. Mosleh, P. C. Cacciabue and B. G. Göktepe. X, 242 pages. 1994.

Vol. 121: Learning from Computers: Mathematics Education and Technology. Edited by C. Keitel and K. Ruthven. XIII, 332 pages. 1993. *(AET)*

Vol. 122: Simulation-Based Experiential Learning. Edited by D. M. Towne, T. de Jong and H. Spada. XIV, 274 pages. 1993. *(AET)*

Vol. 123: User-Centred Requirements for Software Engineering Environments. Edited by D. J. Gilmore, R. L. Winder and F. Détienne. VII, 377 pages. 1994.

Vol. 124: Fundamentals in Handwriting Recognition. Edited by S. Impedovo. IX, 496 pages. 1994.

Vol. 125: Student Modelling: The Key to Individualized Knowledge-Based Instruction. Edited by J. E. Greer and G. I. McCalla. X, 383 pages. 1994. *(AET)*

Vol. 126: Shape in Picture. Mathematical Description of Shape in Grey-level Images. Edited by Y.-L. O, A. Toet, D. Foster, H. J. A. M. Heijmans and P. Meer. XI, 676 pages. 1994.

Vol. 127: Real Time Computing. Edited by W. A. Halang and A. D. Stoyenko. XXII, 762 pages. 1994.

Vol. 128: Computer Supported Collaborative Learning. Edited by C. O'Malley. X, 303 pages. 1994. *(AET)*

Vol. 129: Human-Machine Communication for Educational Systems Design. Edited by M. D. Brouwer-Janse and T. L. Harrington. X, 342 pages. 1994. *(AET)*

Vol. 130: Advances in Object-Oriented Database Systems. Edited by A. Dogac, M. T. Özsu, A. Biliris and T. Sellis. XI, 515 pages. 1994.

Vol. 131: Constraint Programming. Edited by B. Mayoh, E. Tyugu and J. Penjam. VII, 452 pages. 1994.

Vol. 132: Mathematical Modelling Courses for Engineering Education. Edited by Y. Ersoy and A. O. Moscardini. X, 246 pages. 1994. *(AET)*

Vol. 133: Collaborative Dialogue Technologies in Distance Learning. Edited by M. F. Verdejo and S. A. Cerri. XIV, 296 pages. 1994. *(AET)*

Vol. 134: Computer Integrated Production Systems and Organizations. The Human-Centred Approach. Edited by F. Schmid, S. Evans, A. W. S. Ainger and R. J. Grieve. X, 347 pages. 1994.

Vol. 135: Technology Education in School and Industry. Emerging Didactics for Human Resource Development. Edited by D. Blandow and M. J. Dyrenfurth. XI, 367 pages. 1994. *(AET)*

Vol. 136: From Statistics to Neural Networks. Theory and Pattern Recognition Applications. Edited by V. Cherkassky, J. H. Friedman and H. Wechsler. XII, 394 pages. 1994.

Vol. 137: Technology-Based Learning Environments. Psychological and Educational Foundations. Edited by S. Vosniadou, E. De Corte and H. Mandl. X, 302 pages. 1994. *(AET)*

Vol. 138: Exploiting Mental Imagery with Computers in Mathematics Education. Edited by R. Sutherland and J. Mason. VIII, 326 pages. 1995. *(AET)*

Vol. 139: Proof and Computation. Edited by H. Schwichtenberg. VII, 470 pages. 1995.

Vol. 140: Automating Instructional Design: Computer-Based Development and Delivery Tools. Edited by R. D. Tennyson and A. E. Barron. IX, 618 pages. 1995. *(AET)*

Vol. 141: Organizational Learning and Technological Change. Edited by C. Zucchermaglio, S. Bagnara and S. U. Stucky. X, 368 pages. 1995. *(AET)*

NATO ASI Series F